Desert Christians

D1571791

Desert Christians

*An Introduction to the Literature
of Early Monasticism*

WILLIAM HARMLESS, S.J.

OXFORD

UNIVERSITY PRESS

2004

OXFORD
UNIVERSITY PRESS

Oxford   New York
Auckland   Bangkok   Buenos Aires   Cape Town   Chennai
Dar es Salaam   Delhi   Hong Kong   Istanbul   Karachi   Kolkata
Kuala Lumpur   Madrid   Melbourne   Mexico City   Mumbai   Nairobi
São Paulo   Shanghai   Taipei   Tokyo   Toronto

Published by Oxford University Press, Inc.
198 Madison Avenue, New York, New York 10016

www.oup.com

Oxford is a registered trademark of Oxford University Press

Library of Congress Cataloging-in-Publication Data
Harmless, William, 1953–
Desert Christians : an introduction to the literature of early monasticism / William Harmless.
p.   cm.
Includes bibliographical references and index.
ISBN 0-19-516222-6; 0-19-516223-4 (pbk.)
1. Desert Fathers.   2. Christian literature, Early—History and criticism.   3. Monastic and
religious life—History—Early church, ca. 30–600.   I. Title.
BR190.H37 2004
271'.009'015—dc22   2004000097

9 8 7 6 5 4 3 2 1
Printed in the United States of America
on acid-free paper

For my parents,
Roy and Mary Harmless,
for a lifetime spent in a love
that does not count the cost.

Preface

The desert fathers were gifted storytellers. One story that circulated among them tells of three friends who had a reputation for hard work. Each of the three had staked out for himself a way of life he believed faithful to the Christian Gospel. The first one took to heart Jesus' beatitude "Blessed are the peacemakers" and chose to spend his life reconciling those who fought one another. The second adopted as his life's work the care of the sick. The third went out to the desert to live a life of prayer and stillness. The first, for his all efforts, found himself unable to make peace in a world bent on hatred and vengeance and war. Disheartened, he sought out his friend, the healer, to see if he had fared any better. But the second was equally dispirited. So the two went to the third. They told him of their own lives, how they had pursued the noble ventures of peace-making and healing but had somehow, along the way, lost heart. They begged him to guide them, to tell them somewhere to go, something to do. The three sat in silence a while. Then the third, the desert dweller, poured water into a bowl and told them to look at the water. It lapped up against the sides, agitated, swirling and bobbing up and down. They sat a while. Then he said to them, "Look how still the water is now." When they looked down again, they saw their own faces. The water had become a mirror. And so the desert dweller said to his friends: "It's that way for someone who lives among human beings. The agitations, the shake-ups, block one from seeing one's faults; but once one becomes quiet, still, especially in the desert, then one sees one's failings."[1]

This book is about those early Christian desert dwellers who, like the third man in the story, chose to explore the art of stillness and prayer. These first monks who, in Athanasius's famous phrase, "made the desert a city," ignored or even fled from other noble Christian paths, the hard work of peacemaking or healing or any of the thousand other ways of being a Christian that were possible in their time. And the message they offered their world—and perhaps, ours—was that to learn about stillness and prayer meant seeing harder and humbler things first, like one's true face, and one's failings.

The aim of this book is modest: to introduce readers to the literature by and about the desert Christians of the fourth and fifth centuries. I do not presuppose that readers have already read this literature or that they are familiar with the history and theology of early Christianity. So I will need to tell the story to some extent, tracing out key figures and events and explaining theological issues and terminology. Chapters 1 and 2 provide the background, offering basics on the geography, history, politics, and religious milieu of fourth- and fifth-century Egypt. The chapters that follow concentrate on the classic figures and texts: Athanasius's *Life of Antony* (chapters 3–4), the *Lives of Pachomius* (chapter 5), the *Apophthegmata Patrum* (chapters 6–8), the *History of the Monks in Egypt* and Palladius's *Lausiac History* (chapter 9), Evagrius Ponticus's works, especially his *Praktikos* and *Chapters on Prayer* (chapters 10–11), and John Cassian's works, both his *Institutes* and *Conferences* (chapter 12). Over the last twenty years or so, this literature has finally been translated into English. But much of it is not known, even to graduate students.

I would also like to give readers a taste of current developments in the scholarship. A number of remarkable books on the desert fathers have appeared over the last fifteen years: Peter Brown's *The Body and Society*, Elizabeth Clark's *The Origenist Controversy*, Douglas Burton-Christie's *The Word in the Desert*, Graham Gould's *The Desert Fathers on Monastic Community*, David Brakke's *Athanasius and the Politics of Asceticism*, Susanna Elm's *The Virgins of God*, Columba Stewart's *Cassian the Monk*, and James Goehring's *Ascetics, Society, and the Desert*—to name only a few of the larger works in English. And behind this lie a number of scholars, mostly French—Antoine Guillaumont, Irénée Hausherr, Adalbert de Vogüé, Jean-Claude Guy, and Lucien Regnault—who have spent much of their careers uncovering little-known texts or publishing long-needed critical editions and translations.

That scholarship has steadily undermined old verities, such as Antony as the "father of monasticism" or Egypt as its "cradle." It is clear, for instance, that other regions, such as Syria, Palestine, and Cappadocia, had their own native traditions, as old as Egypt's, if less well documented and perhaps less influential in the long run. New explorations of asceticism in the ancient world have set Egyptian monasticism against a much more variegated horizon. There were groups such as the Manichees and the Melitians, whose orthodoxy or church order proved suspect in the long run but that at the time may have influenced styles or simply provided good competition. Scholars have also shown that while the desert variety of monasticism got all the press, there were other Christian experiments in renunciation, such as households of ascetic women or holy men who lived on the fringes of villages or gyratory monks who wandered as perpetual exiles. These less publicized forms of ascetical living were sometimes either consciously ignored or unfairly written off by influential writers, leaving the historical record biased. We also realize that the orthodoxy of the orthodox, whether Pachomius's monastery in Pbow, the compilers of the *Apophthegmata*, or even Antony himself, may have been more ambiguous than most have imagined, and that significant contributions came from people such as the Origenist Evagrius Ponticus—figures whose orthodoxy was perhaps suspect and whose names history has tended to forget or dismiss. But all this is to get ahead of the story.

I decided to put the chapter on the origins of monasticism at the end rather than the beginning. That may seem counterintuitive, and it certainly defies proper chronology. But the decision is based, I believe, on good pedagogy. I have found from experience that people need to know the basics, the key figures and key texts, to appreciate recent scholarly discussions about origins. And so while the story of Antony may not be the historical beginning of monasticism, it is still best to begin there.

Along the way, I will deal here and there with works little known outside of scholarly circles, such as the *Letters* of Antony and Ammonas, the Ethiopic *Collectio Monastica*, and the Coptic *Life of John the Little*. I will put a number of these into an excursus here and there within chapters to give readers a taste of their exotic flavor. A few of these have not yet been translated, others only very recently. Most are simply intriguing documents that I stumbled across in preparing this book. But several are quite important and have helped shape current scholarly assessment of certain larger issues. In fact, it has been scholarly rummaging through a whole host of lesser works, whether sermons by lesser lights, pseudonymous treatises, or pious fabrications, that has opened fresh perspectives on the classic figures and texts.

I have had to put limits on the scope of the book. I have stuck to Egypt, roughly from 300 to 451—in other words, from the public career of Antony to the Council of Chalcedon. Not all figures covered are Egyptians, of course. Evagrius came from Pontus but made Egypt his home, while John Cassian, who came (perhaps) from Romania, stayed in Egypt long enough for it to shape him indelibly and then took Egypt with him, so to speak, to southern France. Admittedly, only some of the literature was actually written by Egyptians, such as Athanasius or the composers of the *Lives of Pachomius*. Much of it comes from outsiders, such as Palladius or the writer of the *History of the Monks in Egypt*; for that matter, the compilers of the most famous desert text, the *Apophthegmata Patrum*, may well have been monks working not in Egypt, but in Palestine.

These limits in time and locale come from a decision to stick with the monks of Egypt, the so-called desert fathers, and not make this an introduction to early Christian asceticism and monasticism. Such a broadening would have at least doubled the size of this already sprawling survey. This has meant not giving rightful attention to much that an introduction should introduce: Symeon Stylites and other Syrian ascetics, the lauras in Palestine, the enterprises of Basil of Caesarea, and the experiments of women such as Melania the Elder, to say nothing of the later history of Egyptian monasticism when, with its rejection of Chalcedon, Egypt pursued its own increasingly isolated path. I have tried to compromise a bit: in the closing chapter, I point out a few landmarks of what happened elsewhere and later, so that readers might be tantalized to pursue such areas on another occasion.

I must add that I have written this book with some trepidation, for it follows in the wake of a work of genius, Derwas Chitty's *The Desert a City* (Oxford: Basil Blackwell, 1966). Chitty's book, completed a few years before his death, was the fruit of a lifetime's labor. Chitty not only possessed an astounding command of the texts, the languages, and the historical and geographical minutiae, but had, through the course of his career, pioneered the debate on any number of fronts. He subtitled his work *An Introduction to the Study of Egyptian and Palestinian Monasticism*. And it is, in some ways. But it is also a dense network of names and places and events—too dense, I believe, for the real beginner. It is also full of brilliant passing insights and wonderful throwaway lines whose cogency is lost on most. And so I find Chitty's work not so much an introduction, but rather a wise road map for those who are already knee-deep in the literature. I should also add that Chitty's focus (and first love) was the monasticism of Palestine, and he gives Egypt only 70 pages. We also differ markedly in emphasis. His concern was to chart out the historical movement of early monasticism; mine is to probe its literature, including the theology and spirituality it contains.

While my work here is, I hope, the fruit of good scholarship, I write it, in part, for some un-scholarly reasons. I was first exposed to the works of the desert fathers in 1975. I was serving in the Peace Corps at the time and was stationed in the Sahara, or, more precisely, on its arid outskirts, working on a cattle-feeding project in the Republic of Mali. My living conditions were austere: a mud-brick house, with a stone floor, a tin roof, no running water or electricity. It was there I came to appreciate the desert fathers, when at night, by a kerosene lamp, I read Thomas Merton's little anthology *The Wisdom of the Desert*. I was impressed then, as I am now, by the desert fathers' unflinching vision of things, their knack for cutting through our intricate self-deceptions, and their willingness to help us humbly face our fragile dignity. I am convinced that their wisdom has something to say to contemporary spirituality. The translation from a fourth-century desert to a twenty-first-century city is not easy, but I think that we ignore the desert fathers at our peril.

Doing scholarship because of spiritual commitments is out of fashion, I realize. But anyone who presumes that scholarship must be divorced from faith ignores the history of scholarship itself. For it was scholars such as the early seventeenth-century Jesuit Heribert Rosweyde who, put off by the superstitious clutter of legends that disfigured the lives of saints, were led to study the desert fathers. Rosweyde ended up publishing a first-class edition of the Latin text of the *Apophthegmata*, and the quality of his work sparked a movement known as the Bollandists that has, for the last four centuries, brought a rigorous historical scholarship to the concerns of faith.

I mentioned Derwas Chitty. At the time he died, he left incomplete an interesting essay on these desert Christians, entitled "The Books of the Old

Men." There he remarked in passing that the *Apophthegmata* is "a collection in which one can hardly open a page without finding something pungent for our own lives: how human those monks were!"[2] That describes well why I have written this book and what I hope others will find.

A book like this owes many debts. First, I am grateful to the community of Spring Hill College, which has been home for me for many years and which has supported my research sabbaticals. I must also thank Thomas E. Caestecker, who generously established a chair in the liberal arts at Spring Hill and whose donations have made possible several research opportunities. In the spring and summer of 1998, the Center for the Advanced Study of Christianity and Culture at Loyola University Chicago generously gave me a research fellowship and good hospitality; in particular, I need to acknowledge James Brennan, Lawrence Reuter, John McCarthy, and Adriaan Peperzak. And in the fall of 2001, the Jesuit School of Theology at Berkeley supported my efforts at bringing this work to a close. I must thank my many Jesuit brothers without whose friendship and encouragement I could not have written this book, especially William Rewak, Christopher Viscardi, Raymond Fitzgerald, Jesús Rodriguez, John Endres, Thomas Buckley, Ron Anderson, Charles Moutenot, Mark Ciccone, and Stephen Campbell. Many other friends have been a great support through it all. I need to mention especially Phillip Madonia, Deborah Madonia, Dori Berahya, Augustine Martinez, Hugh Muller, Betsy Pautler, Bret Heim, and Pat MacNamara.

This project, which ranges about so widely, allowed me to tap the extraordinary expertise of a number of scholars. They have not only sheltered me from many errors, but also have enriched me by their insights and wisdom. Some have read drafts of chapters, and others have sent me advance copies of articles they are writing. I need especially to acknowledge David Brakke, Jeremy Driscoll, Susanna Elm, Georgia Frank, James Goehring, Graham Gould, Rebecca Lyman, John O'Keefe, Lauren Pristas, Norman Russell, Paul Russell, Tim Vivian, and Columba Stewart. Finally, the editors at Oxford were of great help at every step in the process. A special thanks to Cynthia Read.

NOTES

    1. *AP* Sys 2.29 (SC 387:140; trans. my own) = *AP* N 134 (ROC 13:47).
    2. Derwas J. Chitty, "The Books of the Old Men," *Eastern Churches Review* 6 (1974): 17.

Acknowledgments

Some material in chapters 7 and 8 appeared originally in my essay "Remembering Poemen Remembering: The Desert Fathers and the Spirituality of Memory," *Church History* 69 (2000): 483–518. Sections of chapters 10 and 11 appeared originally in my essay (with Raymond R. Fitzgerald) "The Sapphire Light of the Mind: The *Skemmata* of Evagrius Ponticus," *Theological Studies* 62 (2001): 498–529. I would like to thank editors of both journals for permission to reprint this material. Credits for art and photos are given under individual figures. I need to acknowledge the following publishers and authors for their kind permission to use copyrighted material:

Cistercian Publications for:
John Eudes Bamberger, trans. *Evagrius Ponticus: Praktikos and Chapters on Prayer*. Cistercian Studies Series 4. Kalamazoo, Mich.: Cistercian Publications, 1972, 2002.
Norman Russell, trans. *The Lives of the Desert Fathers*. Cistercian Studies Series 34. Kalamazoo, Mich.: Cistercian Publications, 1981.
Armand Veilleux, trans. *Pachomian Koinonia I–III*. Cistercian Studies Series 45–47. Kalamazoo, Mich.: Cistercian Publications, 1980–82).
Benedicta Ward, trans. *The Sayings of the Desert Fathers: The Alphabetical Collection*. Cistercian Studies Series 59. Kalamazoo, Mich.: Cistercian Publications, 1984.
R. M. Price, *A History of the Monks of Syria*. Cistercian Studies Series 88. Kalamazoo, Mich.: Cistercian Publications, 1985.
Tim Vivian, Kim Vivian, and Jeffrey Burton Russell, trans. *The Lives of the Jura Fathers*. Cistercian Studies Series 178 Kalamazoo, Mich.: Cistercian Publications, 1999.

Paulist Press for:
Robert C. Gregg, trans. *Athanasius: The Life of Antony*. Classics of West-
ern Spirituality. New York: Paulist Press, 1980.
Robert T. Meyer. *Palladius: The Lausiac History*. Ancient Christian Writ-
ers 34. New York: Newman Press, 1965; reprint: Paulist Press, 1991.
Colm Luibhéid, trans. *John Cassian: The Conferences*. Classics of Western
Spirituality. New York: Paulist Press, 1985.
Boniface Ramsey, trans. *John Cassian: The Institutes*. Ancient Christian
Writers 58. New York: Paulist Press, 2000.
Boniface Ramsey, trans. *John Cassian: The Conferences*, Ancient Christian
Writers 57. New York: Paulist Press, 1997.

SLG Press for:
Derwas J. Chitty, trans. *The Letters of Ammonas, Successor of Saint Antony*,
rev. and with an introduction by Sebastian Brock. Fairacres, Oxford:
SLG Press, 1979.

Trinity Press International, Harrisburg, Pa., for:
Samuel Rubenson, *The Letters of St. Antony: Monasticism and the Making
of a Saint*. Studies in Antiquity and Christianity. © 1990, 1995, Samuel Rubenson.

Penguin Books for:
Carolinne White, trans. *Early Christian Lives*. London: Penguin Books,
1998.

Orbis Books for plates 1 and 23 from:
Yushi Nomura, *Desert Wisdom: Sayings from the Desert Fathers*. Maryknoll, N.Y.: Orbis Books, 2001.

Johns Hopkins University Press for the map of Alexandria:
Christopher Haas. *Alexandria in Late Antiquity: Topography and Social
Conflict*. Baltimore: Johns Hopkins University Press, 1997. P. 2.

Martin Parmentier for quotations from the translation in:
"Evagrius of Pontus and the 'Letter to Melania.' " *Bijdragen, tijdschrift
voor filosofie en theologie* 46 (1985): 2–38.

Susanna Elm for quotations of her translation of Evagrius Ponticus's *Ad
virginem*.

Tim Vivian for quotations from translations in the following:
"The Good God, the Holy Power, and the Paraclete: 'To the Sons of God'

(*Ad filios Dei*) by Saint Macarius the Great." *Anglican Theological Review* 80 (1998): 338–365.

"Zacharias of Sakhâ: An Encomium on the Life of John the Little." *Coptic Church Review* 18, nos. 1–2 (1997): 1–64.

"Paul of Tamma: On the Monastic Cell (*De Cella*)." *Hallel* 23, no. 2 (1998): 86–107.

"Paul of Tamma: Four Works Concerning Monastic Spirituality." *Coptic Church Review* 17, no. 3 (1996): 110–112.

"Words to Live By: A Conversation that the Elders Had with One Another Concerning Thoughts (*Peri Logismon*)." *St. Vladimir's Theological Quarterly* 39 (1995): 127–141.

"Coptic Palladiana I–IV." *Coptic Church Review* 20, no. 3 (1999): 66–95; 21, no. 1 (2000): 8–23; 21, no. 3 (2000): 82–109; and 22, no. 1 (2001): 2–22.

Columba Stewart and *Sobornost* for quotations from "Radical Honesty about the Self." *Sobornost* 12 (1990): 25–30.

Contents

Part II.   Antony and Pachomius

Part III.   The Desert Fathers

Abbreviations

Texts

AP   *Apophthegmata Patrum* [*Sayings of the Fathers*]: The Alphabetical Collection (ed. J.-B. Cotelier).

AP N   *Apophthegmata Patrum*: The Greek Anonymous Collection (ed. F. Nau).

AP Supp   *Apophthegmata Patrum*: Supplement (ed. J.-C. Guy).

AP Sys   *Apophthegmata Patrum*: The Greek Systematic Collection (ed. J.-C. Guy)

HE   *Historia Ecclesiastica*: of Eusebius of Caesarea, Rufinus, Socrates, or Sozomen

SBo   *Sahidic-Bohairic Life of Pachomius*, reconstructed by Armand Veilleux

VA   Athanasius, *Vita Antonii* [*The Life of Antony*]

Series, Translations, and Reference Works

ACW   Ancient Christian Writers (New York: Newman Press and Paulist Press)

ANF   Ante-Nicene Fathers (reprint: Peabody, Mass.: Hendrickson, 1995)

BA   Bibliothéque augustinienne (Paris: Desclée de Brouwer)

CCC   J. Stevenson, *Creeds, Councils, and Controversies*, rev. ed. W. H. C. Frend (London: S.P.C.K., 1989)

CCL   Corpus Christianorum, Series Latina (Turnholt)

CS   Cistercian Studies Series (Kalamazoo, Mich.: Cistercian Publications)

CSCO   Corpus Scriptorum Christianorum Orientalium (Louvain)

CSEL   Corpus Scriptorum Ecclesiasticorum Latinorum (Vienna)

CWS   Classics of Western Spirituality (New York: Paulist Press)

FC   Fathers of the Church (Washington, D.C.: Catholic University of America Press)

LCC   Library of Christian Classics (Philadelphia: Westminster Press)

LCL   Loeb Classical Library (Cambridge, Mass.: Harvard University Press)

NE   J. Stevenson, *A New Eusebius*, rev. ed. W. H. C. Frend (London: SPCK, 1987)

NPNF   Nicene and Post-Nicene Fathers (reprint: Peabody, Mass.: Hendrickson, 1995)

OECT   Oxford Early Christian Texts (New York: Oxford University Press).

PL   Patrologia Latina, ed. J. Migne (Paris)

PG   Patrologia Graeca, ed. J. Migne (Paris)

PO   Patrologia Orientalis (Paris)

ROC   Revue d'orient chrétien

SC   Sources chrétiennes (Paris: Éditions du Cerf)

SH   Subsidia Hagiographica (Bruxelles: Société des Bollandistes)

SO   Spiritualité orientale (Bégrolles-en-Mauges: Abbaye de Bellefontaine)

TU   Texte und Untersuchungen zur Geschichte der altchristlichen Literatur (Leipzig and Berlin)

A Note on the Notes and Bibliographies

I have tried to keep notes brief yet precise. Most simply give the reference to quoted texts. I try to avoid using them as mini-bibliographies. Instead, at the end of each chapter, there are annotated bibliographies, and these list the full information for the sources quoted in the text. The endnotes at the end of each chapter use a method of citation commonly used by scholars of early Christianity. When citing an ancient text, one cites not by page number, but by section number or book and paragraph number—much as when citing scripture, one obviously does not put *"The Holy Bible, p. 1235"*; instead, one cites chapter and verse. This makes it possible for scholars to track down a reference, no matter what edition or translation they happen to be using. After this one cites where the ancient text (Greek, Latin, Coptic, etc.) can be found. Most ancient texts are published in large series, such as the Patrologia Graeca (PG), the Sources chrétiennes (SC), or the Corpus Scriptorum Christianorum Orientalium (CSCO). Whenever possible I have also listed where to find the English translation (even if I do not quote it directly). For example:

> 23. Cassian, *De institutis* 5.14 (SC 109:214; ACW 58: 125).

In other words:

> 23. Cassian, *The Institutes*, book 5, paragraph 14 (Sources chrétiennes, vol. 109, p. 214; Ancient Christian Writers, vol. 58, p. 125).

A few series, such as the Loeb Classical Library (LCL) or the Oxford Early Christian Texts (OECT), have both the ancient text and an English translation. Whenever I directly quote a translation, I have added a "trans." and then give the translator's name. For example:

> 23. Cassian, *De institutis* 5.14 (SC 109:214; trans. Ramsey, ACW 58:125).

PART I

The World of Early Monasticism

I

Roman Egypt

For most Romans, Egypt's deserts were the edge of the world, a vast and remote frontier land. Almost overnight, those deserts seized hold of the fourth-century imagination and turned the Roman world to strange new courses. Take the case of Melania the Elder (d. 411). At age twenty-two, she was one of the wealthiest women in the Roman Empire—and a widow. She had been born in Spain of an aristocratic family and inherited vast estates throughout Gaul. Her short life had seen its share of tragedies. Married young, she had lost two sons and had endured a string of miscarriages. When her husband, the prefect of Rome, died, she refused to marry again. Instead, in 374, she quietly gathered every portable piece of wealth she had, boarded a ship, and set off for Alexandria. There she enjoyed a warm welcome. Accompanied by a venerable guide, Isidore the Hosteller, she set out southeast into the desert. She wanted to see monks.

She would have first heard of the monks of Egypt as a young girl. The controversial bishop of Alexandria, Athanasius, had been accompanied by these strange black-robed figures when he spent his exile in Rome in the early 340s. Their example reportedly sparked early enthusiastic experiments in asceticism among Rome's aristocracy. Then, in the late 350s, Athanasius's *Life of Antony*, the brilliant biography of one of monasticism's pioneers, was translated into Latin and circulated in sophisticated circles in Rome.

Melania wanted to see monks at close range, in their native habitat. She and her guide went to Nitria, a city of monks perched on the edge of the sprawling Libyan Desert. There she met one of its leaders, Abba Pambo. Melania decided to give the residents of Nitria a taste of her munificence, donating a large coffer loaded with silver.

When she announced her donation, Pambo was sitting weaving rope out of palm leaves. He hardly looked up from his work but gave her a brief, perfunctory blessing and directed his assistant to distribute the silver throughout the monasteries of Egypt. Melania was miffed. In a world where patrons enjoyed effusive praise, she deserved more. At the very least, he could have gotten up and seen how much she was giving. So she spoke up: "You should know, sir, how much it is: there are three hundred pounds." He did not even lift his head, but simply said, "My child, the One who measures mountains knows the amount of silver. If you were giving it to me, you spoke well. But if you were giving it to God . . . , then be quiet." This was not the way one spoke to an aristocratic benefactor. But it was typical of one of the desert fathers. As Melania told her biographer many years later, "Thus did the Lord show his power when I went to the mountain [of Nitria]."[1]

The world of the desert fathers would have seemed remote, foreign, even to a sophisticated and highly educated woman like Melania. To us it appears even more foreign, more remote. To begin to grasp it, we first need to see it against the broader landscape of fourth- and fifth-century Egypt. So this chapter will survey some background basics on its geography, history, politics, and religious milieu. This will require sketching with broad strokes on a broad canvas; nuance will have to come later, as we move into the texts themselves. And we need to begin not in the silences of Egypt's deserts, but in the bustle of its greatest city, Alexandria. For it was from Alexandria that the literature of the desert was first disseminated, and it was through Alexandria that pilgrims like Melania would pass.

Alexandria

Alexandria was the gateway to Egypt and was one of the largest, most prosperous, and most sophisticated cities of the Roman Empire (for a map, see figure 1.1).[2] It had been named after Alexander the Great, who founded it in 331 BCE. It stood at the western edge of the Nile Delta and served in Roman times as the capital of the province of Egypt. It was second only to Rome in population, having, by recent estimates, at least 200,000 inhabitants. City planners had laid it out on a grid. It was bisected east and west by a spacious colonnaded avenue known as the Via Canopica. Even its secondary streets were wide—wide enough, according to the ancient geographer Strabo, to make them "practicable for horse-riding and chariot-driving."[3] Scattered about the city were great landmarks, such as the Serapeum, a massive temple dedicated to the god Serapis, and the Sema, a pyramidal tomb that supposedly held Alexander's body.

In the bay just north of the city was the island of Pharos, famous for its great lighthouse, taller than New York's Statue of Liberty and numbered as one of the seven wonders of the ancient world. When visitors sailed to Alexandria, as Melania had, they could see its light some thirty miles away. A Frankish pilgrim, Arculf, once described his experience:

FIGURE I.I. Alexandria in late antiquity. From Christopher Haas, *Alexandria in Late Antiquity: Topography and Social Conflict* (Baltimore, Md.: Johns Hopkins University Press, 1997), 2. Reproduced with permission.

At the right-hand side of the port is a small island, on which there is a great tower which both Greeks and Latins called Pharus because of its function [as a light]. Voyagers can see it at a distance, so that before they approach the port, particularly at night-time, the burning flame lets them know that the mainland adjoins them, lest they be deceived by the darkness and hit upon the rocks, or lest they should be unable to recognize the limits of the entrance. Accordingly, there are keepers there who put in torches and other fuel to tend the fire that acts a presage of landfall and a mark for the harbor mouth.[4]

The channel between the city and the harbor island had been bridged by a large earthen causeway, known as the Heptastadion. This, in turn, formed two harbors on the Mediterranean, the eastern or Great Harbor and the western or Eunostos Harbor. Overlooking the Great Harbor was a massive temple complex known as the Caesarion, with two large obelisks out front. (The two obelisks still survive, one located now in London, the other in Central Park in New York.) The Jewish philosopher Philo once described the grandeur of the Caesarion:

[It is] situated on an eminence facing the harbors famed for their excellent moorage, huge and conspicuous, fitted on a scale not found elsewhere; . . . around it a belt of pictures and statues in silver and gold, forming a precinct of vast breadth, embellished with porticoes, libraries, chambers, groves, gateways and wide open courts and everything which lavish expenditure could produce to beautify it.[5]

On the south side of the city was Lake Mareotis, a large freshwater body fed by one of the branches of the Nile River. A network of canals linked the city with the lake. Through these passed Egypt's bounty—vast stores of grain, produce, and luxury items—shipped in from the Nile Valley.

Strabo called Alexandria the "greatest emporium in the habited world."[6] Its markets offered all sorts of exotica: porphyry and alabaster from Aswan, ivory from Ethiopia, frankincense from Yemen, pepper and muslin from India. Local Alexandrian artisans were world renowned for their own specialties: for linen and glassblowing, for gem cutting and drug manufacture, and especially for papyrus, the much-valued writing material of the ancient world. The key to Alexandria's commercial success was its location. It stood, as the orator Dio Chrysostom once remarked, "at the crossroads of the whole world," serving the world "as a citymarket serves a single city," linking the Mediterranean with the rich Nile Valley and beyond to what Chrysostom calls the "outer waters": the Red Sea and the Indian Ocean.[7]

Alexandria was not only a commercial crossroads, but an ethnic one as well. The language of business and of culture was Greek. Alexandria was a Greek "island," so to speak, in the larger Coptic-speaking world of Egypt. Ancient documents speak of it as "Alexandria ad Aegyptum," that is, Alexandria "next to" Egypt, not "of" it or "in" it. Alexandrians thought of themselves as a world apart from Egypt, somewhat like the way New Yorkers see themselves as not really part of New York State. And like New York City, Alexandria was a cosmopolitan melting pot. It had visitors not only from around the Roman Empire, but from far beyond its borders: Arabia, Persia, even India and China.

Alexandria could be a violent place, and its history is checkered with accounts of riots and lynch mobs, as well as bloody street battles between rival political and religious factions. The ancient historian Ammianus Marcellinus spoke of it as "a city which on its own impulse, and without ground, is frequently roused to rebellion and rioting"[8]; and the author of the fourth-century *Expositio totius mundi* remarked that "politicians enter this city with fear and trembling, fearing the people's justice."[9]

Alexandria had an enormously sophisticated and variegated intellectual milieu, again not unlike that of modern New York. One famous landmark had been the Museon, with its research center and its Great Library, which held 500,000 volumes at its peak. Unfortunately, the library was damaged during Caesar's war against Pompey and then tragically destroyed during civil strife in the late third century. The city, throughout its history, was the home of leading intellectuals: the geometer Euclid, the astronomer Ptolemy, the geographer Eratosthenes, poets such as Apollonius of Rhodes and Claudian, and philosophers such as Ammonius Saccas, Plotinus, and Hypatia. Philo, the great Jewish philosopher and contemporary of Jesus, had lived in Alexandria and had boldly applied Greek literary techniques to the interpretation of the

Bible, seeking to uncover symbolic and mystical meanings beneath the literal text. Given this milieu, it is no surprise that Alexandria emerged as the center of Christian intellectualism. The second and third centuries saw a remarkable string of Christian teachers: Pantaenus (d. c. 200), Clement (d. 215), and especially the brilliant, prolific, and controversial Origen. The Alexandrian theological tradition they established would become one of the most significant in the history of Christianity. Its distinctive contours would profoundly shape and, in turn, be shaped by developments in the nearby desert.

The Gift of the Nile

Abba Macarius, an early monastic leader, once happened upon two hermits living in the remote reaches of the desert. Their first questions to him were deeply Egyptian: "Is the water rising in due time? Is the world enjoying prosperity?"[10] The "rising water" was, of course, the yearly flooding of the Nile, and Egypt's prosperity—indeed, its very life—depended upon its "rising in due time."

The Nile River is a long, narrow lifeline in a virtually rainless country (for a map of Roman Egypt, see figure 1.2).[11] The river's yearly flood, which used to begin in June and peak in September, brought not only water but also rich silt down from the highlands of Ethiopia and transformed the Nile Valley into an immensely rich agricultural basin.[12] The valley, as broad as fourteen miles and as narrow as two, is a fertile green belt in an otherwise desolate land. At ground level, the line between the life of the valley and the death zone of the desert is unbelievably stark—visible in the contrast between the valley's black soil and the red-yellow rock of the desert escarpments that line it. The Nile wanders down some 600 miles from the southern frontier of Roman Egypt at ancient Syene (modern-day Aswan) and then splits into three large branches just south of the ancient city of Babylon (modern-day Cairo). There it forms a vast flood plain known as the delta, triangular in shape, 100 miles south to north, some 150 miles at its widest place.

The Nile flows from south to north. This means that Upper Egypt is south and Lower Egypt, north—an odd terminology for those of us who know Egypt's geography more from wall maps than from lived experience. When Macarius's hermits asked about the "world," what they imagined were the Nile and its verdant valley and delta. While some desert fathers were Alexandrians or even foreigners, most came from villages along the river. This world had, of course, been one of the cradles of human civilization and boasted a rich and proud 3000-year-old history and culture. And the prosperity of that world revolved around the regular rise and fall of the Nile; as the ancient historian Herodotus put it, Egypt itself is "a gift of the river."[13]

Egypt was also known as "the granary of Rome." Agricultural production in the region was, by ancient standards, extraordinary. Farmers grew grains, especially wheat and barley; vegetables such as lentils, beans, chickpeas, cucumbers, garlic, artichokes, and onions; and fruits such as figs, grapes, pome-

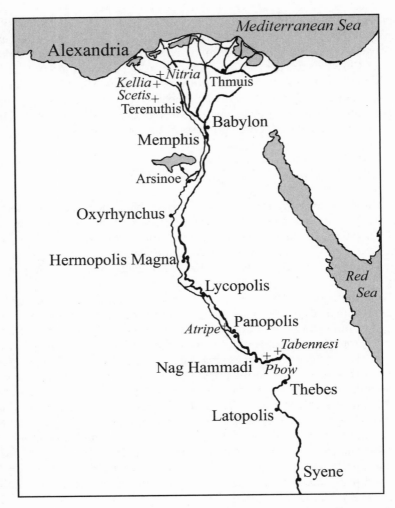

FIGURE I.2. Roman Egypt.

granates, peaches, olives, and dates. High yields were made possible not only by the rich silt left by the flooding, but also by an extensive irrigation system, the use of dikes and canals, and technologies such as the water wheel. Farmers also raised a variety of livestock—cattle, chickens, pigs, oxen, sheep, and goats—and these enabled production not only of meat, but also of eggs, milk, cheese, wool, and leather. Other villagers fished perch and silurus out of the river, produced flax for linen, tended beehives for honey, and harvested reeds for papyrus. Wine of every shade and quality was available. Beer had, for centuries, been the favorite drink of ordinary Egyptians, but mention of it disappears in the fourth century. Egypt was renowned for its gold mines, and its great limestone and granite quarries made possible its monumental temples and massive statuary, even the great columns of the Pantheon in Rome.

Up and down the Nile, there were prosperous cities and towns: Memphis, Arsinoë, Oxyrhynchus, Antinoopolis, Hermopolis, Ptolemais, Tentyra. Some of these may have had populations as large as 30,000. Many were walled cities, built around ancient temple complexes and a central marketplace. At city center were other public buildings: the city council chamber, government offices, public baths, granaries, theaters. These buildings could be quite large. The theater in Oxyrhynchus, for example, seated 11,000 people. The Greek-speaking elite of the towns enrolled their youth in the local gymnasium, which was much more than an athletic facility; it was a well-funded Greek cultural and educational center, with classrooms and lecture halls. Some towns also served as military outposts and housed Roman garrisons.

From ancient documents, we get glimpses of the urban milieu. For example, a papyrus from Oxyrhynchus, dated 270 CE, lists eighteen properties on a single city block; its residents included two fisherman, one vegetable seller, and a man who worked in the cloakroom of the baths; a builder, a carpenter, and a baker; a linen weaver, a dyer, and an embroiderer.[14] As one scans the mass of surviving papyri, a rich commercial landscape emerges. One finds millers, butchers, and fishmongers; masons, carpenters, plasterers, and painters; potters and basket weavers; goldsmiths and silversmiths; sailors and ship builders; barbers, hairdressers, and undertakers; schoolteachers, lawyers, and stenographers; donkey drivers and mouse catchers; prostitutes, athletes, and entertainers.[15] Guilds of artisans often clustered in certain sectors of a city. Oxyrhynchus, for instance, had a Cobbler's Quarter, a Shepherd's Quarter, and a Gooseherds' Quarter. The complex economy was built not only on barter, but also on coinage and currency. There are surviving banking records, accounts of loans and mortgages, and, not surprisingly, records of all the problems that go with finance: complaints about high interest rates, litigation over debts, and bankruptcy proceedings.

Egypt had suffered foreign domination for centuries. Greek domination began in 332 BCE after the conquest by Alexander the Great and continued for the next 300 years under the reign of the Ptolemies. Direct Roman control began in 30 BCE with the victory of Octavian over Marc Antony and Cleopatra VII, the last Ptolemaic ruler of Egypt. Unlike other Roman provinces, Egypt was treated as the personal domain of the emperor and was governed not by senators (as other provinces were) but by a viceroy of equestrian rank, whose title was "prefect of Egypt" (or, later, "Augustal prefect"). In the late third century, the empire underwent great administrative reforms, initiated by Emperor Diocletian, who broke provinces into more manageable units. Over the next century, Egypt found itself divided, initially into two provinces (Aegyptus in the north, Thebaid in the south), then three (when Aegyptus was divided in half), then back to two, then three, and finally four (Aegyptus becoming the three provinces of Aegyptus, Augustamnica, and Arcadia). Diocletian also divided government authority into two spheres: civil and military. This meant that while the prefect remained, he was usually paired with a military counterpart, a "duke" (*dux*). Under them were other high-ranking Roman officials: military commanders, finance officers, temple administrators, and legal advisors.

At the local level, Egypt was organized, as it had been for centuries, into "nomes," roughly the size of large counties, each with its nome capital or metropolis, some twenty-five to forty miles from one another. An official, known as a *strategos*, drawn from the Greco-Egyptian aristocratic elite, led the individual nome. Within each nome, elders headed individual villages, while town councilors (who were members for life) and magistrates (who were elected for short terms) governed the larger towns and cities. In Egypt, as throughout the Roman world, leading citizens were forcibly drafted to supervise "liturgies," that is, public works projects. Typical liturgies in Egypt included maintaining dikes, overseeing irrigation projects, collecting taxes, upgrading public buildings, and financing festivals. These could be onerous tasks, since citizens often had to finance them using their own assets. We have a papyrus from Oxyrhynchus, dated 147 CE, reporting that 120 liturgists fled their responsibilities and that their properties were seized by the government to make up for the shortfall.[16]

The bounty of Egypt—especially its wheat harvest—was sent as taxes to Rome. Once a year great grain ships sailed from Alexandria, and their arrival was an event of singular political importance in the city of Rome, and later in Constantinople, for it assured that the imperial capital would have food. Roman taxation, contrary to the popular view, was surprisingly modest.[17] There was no income tax, nor any tax on urban property. The Emperor Constantine instituted a much-despised tax on businesses and trades, and there was some sort of "head tax." The agricultural sector bore the brunt of the tax burden, but even there the demand seems modest, about 10 percent of the agricultural yield. Taxes were often paid in grain, either wheat or barley, and there was an elaborate administrative apparatus for its collection and transportation, from the village level on up the ladder. There were also periodic additional taxes and one-time levies. A region might have to pay for hosting visiting Roman dignitaries and their entourages, and ordinary citizens could be forced to house or feed soldiers or transport military supplies. A real burden came from the liturgies, those obligatory public works projects. Every adult male was liable to be required to work a certain number of days each year, perhaps, on the dikes or the irrigation system; landowners might be required to send key employees off to work for months at granaries in Alexandria or quarries in Alabastrine. Sometimes, fiscal burdens—whether from debts or taxes or the liturgies—became too much, and a man might run away. To fend off liability, his family would officially have him registered as a missing person, as one of the *anakechorekotes* ("those who had fled"). Note the term: *anachōresis*, "fleeing," would come to mean "fleeing the world to become a monk." Scholars suspect that, at least in some cases, financial burdens prompted some to flee to monastic settlements.

Egypt was a trilingual country. Latin, the least widespread of its languages was the language of the upper echelon of the government and appears mostly in legal and military documents. The native Egyptian language was Coptic. Scholars have detected six dialects of Coptic in this period. The two used in monastic literature were Bohairic, the language of the western Delta, and Sahidic, the language of Upper Egypt. Coptic emerged as a written language relatively late, in the middle of the third century. Writing in the old hieroglyphic script had become a forgotten skill, except for occasional temple inscriptions. The other traditional way of writing the native Egyptian language, a script known as demotic, seems to have largely disappeared after the Roman takeover. Written Coptic is basically the Egyptian language written with Greek letters, and its emergence seems closely tied to the rise of Christianity. The earliest forms of Coptic literature were translations of the Bible and other religious documents. But through this period the dominant language of culture and even of business was Greek. It was spoken throughout Egypt, certainly by local elites, but by many others as well. Most, but not all, of the literature of early monasticism in Egypt was composed in Greek.

Egypt's papyrus production, combined with its dry climate, has meant that great caches of ancient documents have survived. Archeologists have uncovered treasure troves in ancient trash dumps, scraps of papyrus on which we find business receipts, government memoranda, tax rolls, even brief personal letters. The evidence is so abundant that one leading scholar has written a complete social history of late antique Egypt based almost entirely on information gleaned from thousands of papyri. Our concern here is with monasticism, and these papyri offer fascinating glimpses of monastic life. One example: we have a rental contract from the city of Oxyrhynchus, dating from about 400 and written in Greek. It explains that a Jewish man named Aurelius Jose, of Judas, agreed to rent a ground-floor apartment and a basement storage area from two sisters who also happened to be nuns (called *monachai apotaktikai*, "female-monk renouncers"; for the text, see appendix 1.1). This quite mundane document undercuts our usual preconceptions. Whereas most monastic literature focuses on men, the monks here are women; and although much monastic literature dramatizes life in the desert, this shows monks living in the bustling town of Oxyrhynchus, owning property and doing business across religious boundaries. Such papyri can offer vivid images, like long-lost photographs. But as with pieces of a giant jigsaw, it is often hard to know where they fit, whether they give us glimpses of the normal or merely local aberrations. They at least serve as a counterbalance to biases of better-known literary texts and give us a taste of the complex messiness of the ordinary scene.

Early Egyptian Christianity

Egyptian Christians have traditionally claimed Saint Mark as the founder of their church. Eusebius of Caesarea, the fourth-century church historian, says Mark "was the first to be sent to preach in Egypt the Gospel which he had also put into writing, and was the first to establish churches in Alexandria itself."[18] Later texts would cast this claim into narrative. According to the *Acts of Mark* (early fifth-century?), a vision prompted the apostle to sail from his native Cyrene to Alexandria. He landed at the Pharos, then made his way into the city, but just as he passed through the city gate, a strap on his sandal broke.

FIGURE 1.3. The *Pharos* of Alexandria. One of the most famous landmarks of Alexandria was the great lighthouse, known as the *Pharos*. Built sometime around 280 BCE, it survived until the fourteenth century. The illustration above is from a mosaic in Basilica San Marco in Venice, c. 1300. It portrays Saint Mark sailing into the harbor of Alexandria to begin his work of evangelizing the city. (Alinari/Art Resource, NY)

So he headed to the market to find someone to fix it. There he met a cobbler named Ananias. As Ananias set to work repairing the broken sandal, his awl slipped, badly wounding his hand. In his pain he cried out, "God is one!" Mark took the exclamation as a providential sign and miraculously healed Ananias's hand, invoking the name of Jesus. The cobbler, in gratitude, invited Mark to his home. There the apostle preached to him about Jesus and converted him and his entire household. Eventually Mark ordained Ananias the first bishop of Alexandria and appointed other clergy, including three presbyters and seven deacons. According to the story, Mark's very presence aroused the opposition of pagans, who feared that a Galilean had come to rid the city of idols. When he returned two years later, pagans seized him and dragged him through the streets until he died. They then tried to burn his body, but a sudden storm came up and frightened them away. The faithful were able to rescue Mark's body and place it in a tomb east of the city.[19] This account from the *Acts of Mark* tells us less about first-century history and more about the fifth-century Christian imagination (see figure 1.3).

In fact, we know very little about Egyptian Christianity before the year 200. Scholars suspect that Christianity took root at a very early date among the large Greek-speaking Jewish community in Alexandria. But during the

Jewish revolt of 115–117 CE, that community was virtually decimated—and presumably the earliest Christian community along with it. There have been key discoveries of second-century Christian manuscripts in Egypt, including the earliest known New Testament text, a papyrus fragment from Oxyrhynchus, which dates from the 120s and contains a few verses of the Gospel of John.[20] We have a few other scraps of information about second-century Egyptian Christianity. We know, for example, that Egypt was a vibrant center of heterodox theology and that two leading Gnostic teachers, Basilides (active 130s) and Valentinus (active 130s–160s), worked in Alexandria.[21]

Origen and the Alexandrian Theological Tradition

Alexandria had long been one of the great intellectual centers of the Roman world. In the third century, it emerged as the intellectual center of Christianity. No one embodied its scholarly rigor more than Origen (c. 185–254), one of the great theologians in the history of Christianity.[22] Although his career predates the period we are studying, his thought profoundly affected both desert monks and desert literature.

Origen was born into a Christian family in Alexandria. His father died as a martyr during the persecution of 201, leaving the family bankrupt. So the young Origen began work as a *grammateus*, or teacher of Greek literature. He acted fearlessly during the persecutions of 206–211, daring to teach catechumens after church authorities had fled the city. When the persecutions ended, he received official standing as a catechist and came to lead an institution unique to the Alexandrian church: the Catechetical School. Through the course of his career Origen traveled widely—to Rome, Greece, Syria, and Arabia— earning an international reputation for his wisdom and learning. In the 230s, he clashed with Demetrius, the bishop of Alexandria, and ended up settling in Caesarea in Palestine, where he was ordained a presbyter. In 250, during the persecution of Decius, he was arrested and severely tortured. He died a few years later from his wounds.

Origen was, by training and temperament, a scholar. He brought formidable philological and literary-critical skills to the study of the Bible. He was one of the very few gentile Christians of the early church to have some mastery of Hebrew. He put together a remarkable reference work called the *Hexpla*, a six-column edition of the Old Testament that enabled him to compare and contrast different Greek translations with the original Hebrew text. He was incredibly prolific and dictated commentaries on virtually every book of the Bible. Only a fraction of this output survives, but that which does is remarkable. Origen recognized the hazards of literalism, noting the Bible's anthropomorphisms, historical inaccuracies, and internal contradictions. He insisted that the Bible must always be interpreted in a way "worthy of God." This led him to interpret problematic texts allegorically, seeing beneath the literal surface a many-layered density and rich symbolism. Origen's fondness for allegory would influence later monastic writers, who repeated his interpretations and drew inspiration from his methods.

Origen was also a pioneer of systematic theology. He authored a remarkable treatise, *On First Principles* (Greek: *Peri Archon;* Latin: *De principiis*). It is a sort of Christian "physics" that looks at the origin, structure, and destiny of the universe and explores its underlying principles. It is at the same time a systematic reflection on the creed and on the Bible, its story and its interpretation. Throughout his career, and especially in *On First Principles*, Origen proposed bold hypotheses. Some of his most original would earn him fierce opposition during his life and damage his long-term reputation. For example, he recognized that the creation stories found in Genesis 1 and 2 do not match. So he read these not as two different creation stories (the way modern scholars do), but as two creations. Origen suggested that before the creation of the present physical universe, God had originally created souls, all equal to one another, bonded in unity to him. The original fall was not the fall of Adam and Eve, but the fall of these original souls whose love of God had cooled and whose neglect had caused them to fall out of that primordial unity. This hypothesis of a preexistence of souls is one that later monastic theologians, such as Evagrius Ponticus, would explore in their attempt to map the soul's mystical journey to God. Origen proposed other controversial hypotheses on the nature of the Godhead, on the soul of Christ, and on the Resurrection.

Origen powerfully influenced leading church fathers, such as Basil of Caesarea, Gregory of Nazianzus, and Ambrose. He certainly influenced Athanasius, whose *Life of Antony* we will study in chapters 3 and 4. He may have influenced Antony himself, if the *Letters* ascribed to Antony are authentic; and intellectual circles in the desert led by Evagrius Ponticus and the Tall Brothers (so called because of their unusual height) drew heavily on Origen's writings. Their efforts made them the focus of attack in the Origenist Controversy of 400 (see chapter 11). Three centuries after his death, Origen was condemned as a heretic by the Council of Constantinople II in 553. Despite the condemnation and the loss of many of his works, he remained influential. The seventeenth-century biblical scholar Richard Simon once remarked: "Most of the Fathers who lived after Origen scarcely did anything but copy his commentaries and other treatises on Scripture. . . . Even those who were most opposed to his sentiments could not keep from reading them and profiting from them."[23]

The Great Persecution and the Melitian Schism

Egyptian Christians suffered persecution in 201, when Origen's father was martyred, and again in 250, when the Emperor Decius unleashed an empire-wide persecution. Beginning in 303, under the auspices of the Emperor Diocletian, they faced an especially brutal persecution. It was such a watershed event that later the Coptic Church dated "year 1" of its calendar from the beginning of the reign of Diocletian, naming it the Era of the Martyrs. Although the monastic movement largely postdates this era of martyrdom, martyrs and monks became linked in the Christian imagination, with monks proclaimed as successors of the martyrs and monasticism described as a sort of daily martyrdom.

The persecution of Diocletian not only produced martyrs; it also produced a bitter schism.[24] The bishop of Alexandria at the time was Peter I (bp. 300–311). When the persecution began in Alexandria in 304, he and his clergy fled the city. Upriver, Melitius, the newly elected bishop of Lycopolis, viewed Peter's flight as an act of cowardice. And so he stepped into the vacuum, ordaining new clergy for Alexandria. Peter, when he got word of Melitius's action, denounced it as a gross infringement of his jurisdiction. Around 307, when the persecution abated, Peter returned to the city, called a regional council, and had Melitius excommunicated.[25] There is a colorful story that at some point Peter and Melitius were both arrested and held in the same prison cell. While there, they disagreed violently over Peter's supposedly lax policy of reconciling those who had apostatized during persecution. Things got so stormy that a curtain was hung down the middle of the cell.[26] When or whether this happened is disputed.

Peter was eventually martyred in 311, while Melitius was deported to the mines in Palestine. When the last wave of persecutions ended, Melitius returned and set up a network of churches in Palestine and Egypt, a "church of the martyrs." By the time Peter's successor, Alexander (bp. 311–328), came to power, the churches of Alexandria and of Egypt found themselves bitterly divided. According to a list dating from 327, there was a Melitian bishop for every six episcopal cities in the Nile Delta, and one in every other city or so in the Coptic-speaking Thebaid.[27] In other words, nearly half of the churches in Egypt owed allegiance to Melitius. This fracture between Melitians and churches aligned to Peter's successors was a serious one and would haunt Egyptian Christianity, especially over the next generation. It would affect monks throughout the countryside who had to decide which side they recognized. While the classics of desert literature give little indication of Melitians, we know from certain papyri that there were a number of Melitian monks and monasteries.

The Patriarchate of Alexandria.

Egypt rapidly Christianized in the fourth century. One rough indication is the shift in names, from traditional Egyptian ones such as Serapion or Ammon to obviously Christian ones such as Paul or Johannes. Studies of papyri indicate that in the early fourth century, a slight majority of Egyptians had Christian names, but by the beginning of the fifth century, almost 90 percent did.[28] Christianity in Egypt was a paradox of extraordinary unity and extraordinary diversity. Its unity centered on the bishops of Alexandria, who oversaw this growing, complex, and sometimes fractious church. And the history of Egyptian monasticism is deeply interwoven with the history of the bishops of Alexandria.

Bishops of Alexandria claimed apostolic succession from Saint Mark, and a list of names dating back to the apostle is given in Eusebius of Caesarea's

Church History. The first individual who is more than a name to us is Origen's contemporary, Demetrius (bp. 190–232). But the most prominent third-century bishop of Alexandria was Dionysius (bp. 247–264), a former student of Origen and onetime head of the Catechetical School. He led his church through the trauma of Decian persecution and carried on an international correspondence with his namesake, Dionysius, bishop of Rome.

In the fourth century, with the legalization of Christianity and with privileges granted by successive emperors, the bishops of Alexandria gradually assumed both national and international prominence. The title "archbishop" was not applied to them until the fifth century; and only in the sixth century was the title "patriarch" used. But in practical terms, they were already exercising patriarchal authority by the early fourth-century. They directly controlled the selection and consecration of bishops over the entirety of Egypt as well as Libya. By 325, that meant they had authority over almost a hundred bishoprics: forty-four in the Delta, twenty-nine in the Nile Valley, and the rest in Libya and the Pentapolis.[29] These Egyptian and Libyan bishops looked on the bishop of Alexandria as their immediate superior, the one to whom they owed their position and authority, and their tenacious allegiance became visible when they voted as a bloc at councils.

Bishops of Alexandria could also marshal grass-roots support. One prominent organization there was the *parabalani*. Officially, its members exercised a valuable ministry, serving as hospital attendants and as a sort of Christian ambulance service. But in times of crisis or unrest, they could act as the bishops' footsoldiers, and there are rumblings that they were involved in brutal acts, such as the murder of the pagan philosopher Hypatia in 415. In 416, the Roman government decreed that membership was to be limited to 500—which implies their numbers had once exceeded that. The bishops of Alexandria also enlisted monks for their campaigns. In 391, monks helped in the demolition of pagan temples; and in 431, they accompanied Cyril to the Council of Ephesus and led demonstrations on his behalf. In less dramatic but no less significant ways, they served as evangelists to the countryside, winning people to Christianity and, indirectly, to an allegiance to the bishop of Alexandria.

Such internal ecclesiastical power was just the beginning. The ancient historian Socrates once noted that by the early fifth-century "the bishopric of Alexandria went beyond the limits of sacerdotal functions, and assumed the administration of secular matters."[30] What Socrates says about fifth-century bishops could arguably be pushed back to an even earlier date. One measure of their rapid growth in power is the way they helped alter the urban landscape of Alexandria by establishing church buildings in strategic locales. One early center was the Church of Saint Theonas, located just inside the city walls at the Gate of the Sun on the western end of the Via Canopica, the city's prestigious east-west artery. In the early fourth century, under Bishop Alexander, Christians took over the old temple of Kronos and converted it into the Church of Saint Michael. This gave them property close to the heart of the city. Later, in the 340s, the Emperor Constantius bequeathed to the Christian community the Caesarion, the massive temple that had for centuries been the center of the emperor cult. This now became the Great Church, the official seat of the bishop. Christians thus came to occupy the city's prime real estate, overlooking the harbor. When people sailed into the city, their first sight would have been the Great Church. The final coup came in 391, when a violent clash between Christians and pagans led to the seizure and destruction of the greatest pagan shrine in the city, the Serapeum, and the eventual conversion of the site into a Christian church, the Basilica of Saint John the Baptist.

Less visible but no less important was the bishops' patronage power. Under Christian emperors, they received grain from the government, which they, in turn, distributed to the poor. This grain dole allowed them to reward friends, exclude rivals, and generally keep hold of grass-roots support. The church also received major bequests of money and land from the wills of pious donors. We get a glimpse of the extraordinary wealth of the fifth-century Alexandrian church from the chance preservation of a list of "blessings" that Cyril of Alexandria asked his agent to distribute to officials in Constantinople. These "blessings"—we would call them bribes—included 1080 pounds of gold (equal to the annual stipends of thirty-eight bishops), along with twenty-four carpets, twenty-five tapestries, twenty-four silk veils, eighteen curtains, twenty-two tablecloths, fourteen high-backed ivory thrones, and thirty-six throne covers.[31] It is not without reason that bishops around the world chided the bishop of Alexandria, calling him "the new Pharaoh."[32]

Christianity in Egypt thus emerged with unique local contours. The three threads touched on here—its erudite theology, its fierce local divisions, and its potent patriarchate—would weave their way through the drama played out in the fourth and fifth centuries. In the next chapter, we will need to survey both the politics and the theology of that drama, since it forms the wider historical backdrop against which monasticism would rise.

Monasticism in Egypt: Leaders, Writers, and Texts

Christian Egypt has long been regarded as the birthplace of monasticism. That view, as we will see, is only partially true. Still, its desert monasteries and its sage monks would imbue Egyptian Christianity with a distinctive flavor, and by the mid-fourth century would earn it international fame. The writings and example of these desert Christians would influence monastic life for centuries, both in the Greek East and in the Latin West. Even today, texts by and about them remain popular and touch the spirituality of ordinary Christians. Their story is the focus of this book, and the chapters that follow will detail their history, theology, and literature. First, it will be useful to introduce the protagonists. Nowadays, at Broadway theaters, one is usually handed a one-page program listing characters, actors, and scenes. Below is a similar sort of cast list. It is a quick reference, something to come back to when things get confusing.

Founders and Pioneers

Among the founders of Egyptian monasticism, five names appear again and again in the ancient sources. These five were widely admired for the depth of their wisdom and the rigor of their lives.

ANTONY (C. 254–356). Antony is routinely described as "the first monk" and the "father of monasticism." That stock description is imprecise, as we will see. But Antony was certainly a pioneer who won worldwide acclaim because of Athanasius's influential biography, the *Life of Antony* (published c. 357). Athanasius portrays Antony as an "anchorite," that is, a hermit. There is a set of seven letters ascribed to Antony, and virtually every early text passes on sayings of his or stories about him. (See chapters 3, 4, and 6.)

PACHOMIUS (C. 292–346). Pachomius is often singled out as the "founder of cenobitic monasticism"—that is, of monks living in organized communities. This claim, like that of Antony as the "first monk," oversimplifies what we now know of early monasticism. Nonetheless, Pachomius was an early and gifted organizer who established a remarkable confederation of monasteries in Upper Egypt and composed the first known monastic rule. His life was celebrated in a series of biographies, composed in the 390s and preserved in Greek and Coptic. We also have various rules, letters, and addresses attributed to Pachomius and to his successors, Theodore and Horsiesius. (See chapter 5.)

MACARIUS THE EGYPTIAN (C. 300–390). Macarius the Egyptian was the founder of one of the leading monastic settlements of Lower Egypt, Scetis. Sayings from him and stories about him appear in many sources, especially the *Apophthegmata Patrum*. (See chapters 6 and 7.)

AMOUN (C. 290–C.347). Amoun was the founder of two famous monastic settlements of Lower Egypt: Nitria and Kellia. The account of his career appears in Palladius's *Lausiac History*. (See chapter 9.)

MACARIUS THE ALEXANDRIAN (C. 300–393). Macarius the Alexandrian, often confused with his namesake, Macarius the Egyptian, was the priest-superior of Kellia. While not a founder per se, he earned a widespread reputation for his fierce asceticism and his miracle-working. Stories about him appear in Palladius's *Lausiac History* and the *History of the Monks in Egypt*. (See chapter 9.)

Writers and Texts

What we know of these and many other figures comes to us from a core group of writers and anonymous texts. Most were a generation or more younger than the figures they celebrated.

ATHANASIUS (C. 295–373). Athanasius was bishop of Alexandria, off and on, from 328 to 373. He was also a gifted theologian who helped formulate the classic defense of the divinity of Christ. He authored the *Life of Antony*, which popularized desert monasticism throughout the Empire. (See chapters 2, 3, and 4.)

APOPHTHEGMATA PATRUM. The *Apophthegmata Patrum*, or *Sayings of the Fathers*, is an anthology of anecdotes about and pithy sayings from the desert fathers. Its Zen-like stories and sayings focus on monastic leaders active from the 330s to the 460s. The text itself comes from a later date, probably the late fifth or early sixth century. Different versions of it have come down to us in various ancient languages (Greek, Latin, Syriac, Coptic, Armenian, and Ethiopic). (See chapters 6, 7, and 8.)

THE HISTORY OF THE MONKS IN EGYPT. This anonymous work, composed in Greek around 400, is a sort of travelogue. It describes a journey through Egypt taken by seven Palestinian monks in 394. It strings together anecdotes about their meetings with remarkable hermits, healers, and holy men. (See chapter 9.)

EVAGRIUS PONTICUS (C. 345–399). Evagrius grew up in Pontus, near the Black Sea, and eventually settled in Kellia in Lower Egypt. He was a pioneer of monastic theology and is best known for two works, the *Praktikos* and the *Chapters on Prayer*. These and most of his other writings are strings of terse and somewhat cryptic proverbs. After he died, his friends and disciples were persecuted as Origenists and run out of Egypt. Evagrius himself was condemned 150 years later, and his works circulated mostly under the names of others. (See chapters 10 and 11.)

JOHN CASSIAN (D. AFTER 435). John Cassian, probably a native of what today is Romania, helped translate desert spirituality for the Latin West. He was a disciple of Evagrius and, after leaving Egypt, settled in southern France where he composed two major works in Latin, the *Institutes* and the *Conferences*. Saint Benedict, in his *Rule*, made Cassian's memoirs required reading. (See chapter 12.)

PALLADIUS (C. 363–C 431). Palladius, a native of Galatia, traveled to Egypt, settling in Nitria and Kellia, where he became a disciple of Evagrius Ponticus. He left there around 400 and was ordained a bishop by John Chrysostom. He is best known for his *Lausiac History*, a set of brief biographies and vignettes of the desert fathers (and mothers), written in Greek in the 420s. (See chapter 9.)

THE CHURCH HISTORIANS. The earliest and best-known ancient church historian was Eusebius of Caesarea (c. 260–c. 339). His *Church History* went through several editions, the last published around 324. Several authors sought to supplement and update his work. Two were Socrates (c. 380–c. 450) and Sozomen (fifth cent.). Both were laymen who lived in Constantinople, and their works, both entitled *Church History*, offer valuable information on the desert monks that is not found elsewhere.

RUFINUS (C. 345–C. 410). Rufinus grew up near Aquileia and, together with Melania the Elder, established an influential Latin-speaking monastery in Jerusalem. He was bilingual and is best known for his Latin translations of Greek theological and monastic works, including the works of Origen as well as the *History of the Monks in Egypt*. Rufinus also translated Eusebius's *Church History* and supplemented it with two books, which include valuable information on Egyptian monasticism.

JEROME (C. 347–C. 420). Jerome was a native of Dalmatia. He is best known for his translation of the Bible into Latin, the so-called *Vulgate*. After leaving Rome in 385, he and a wealthy widow named Paula established a double monastery in Bethlehem. While best known for his biblical scholarship, he also exerted great influence on Western asceticism via his letters, his biographies of monks (especially his *Life of Paul*), and his translation of the *Rules* of Pachomius. He and his onetime friend Rufinus battled ferociously against one another during the Origenist controversy.

NOTES

1. Palladius, *Historia Lausiaca* 10.1–4 (Butler, 29–30; trans. Meyer, ACW 34:44–45).

2. For studies on Alexandria, see the bibliography for chapter 1.

3. Strabo, *Geography* 17.1.8 (LCL 8:32–33).

4. Adamnanus, *De locis sanctis* 2.30.8–9; quoted in Christopher Haas, *Alexandria in Late Antiquity: Topography and Social Conflict* (Baltimore: Johns Hopkins University Press, 1997), 350–351.

5. Philo, *De legatione ad Gaium* 22 (LCL 10:76, trans. LCL 10:77, modified).

6. Strabo, *Geography* 17.1.13 (LCL 8:52–53).

7. Dio Chrysostom, *Oratio* 32.36 (LCL, 206; trans. my own).

8. Ammianus Marcellinus, *Res gestae* 22.11.4 (LCL 258–259).

9. *Expositio totius mundi* 37.1 (SC 124:174; trans. my own).

10. *AP* Macarius 2 (PG 65:260; trans. Ward, CS 59:126).

11. On Egypt in late antiquity, see the bibliography for chapter 1.

12. The ancient pattern was dramatically altered only in the twentieth century, with the building of the great dam at Aswan.

13. Herodotus, *The Persian Wars* 2.5 (LCL, 1:280).

14. *P. Oxy.* XLVI 3300. For a discussion, see Roger S. Bagnall, *Egypt in Late Antiquity* (Princeton: Princeton University Press, 1993), 51.

15. See Bagnall, *Egypt in Late Antiquity*, 78–92.

16. A. K. Bowman, *Egypt after the Pharaohs, 332 B.C.–A.D. 642: From Alexander to the Arab Conquest* (Berkeley: University of California Press, 1986), 69.

17. For a survey of the papyri, see Bagnall, *Egypt in Late Antiquity*, 153–172.

18. Eusebius of Caesarea, *HE* 2.16 (SC 31:71; FC 19:110–111). For studies on the history of Christianity in Egypt, see the bibliography for chapter 1.

19. *Martyrium Sancti Marci apostoli* 1–3 (PG 115:164–165); see also Getatchew Haile, "A New Ethiopic Version of the *Acts of St. Mark*," *Analecta Bollandiana* 99 (1981): 117–134. For a discussion of the Mark legend, see Birger A. Pearson, "Earliest Christianity in Egypt: Some Observations," in *The Roots of Egyptian Christianity*, ed. Birger A. Pearson and James E. Goehring, Studies in Antiquity and Christianity (Philadelphia: Fortress Press, 1986), 137–145.

20. The fragment, know as P^{52}, is discussed in Bruce Metzger, *The Text of the New Testament*, 2nd ed. (New York: Oxford University Press, 1968), 38–39.

21. On Gnosticism and the Nag Hammadi library, see chapter 5.

22. On the life and thought of Origen, see the bibliography for chapter 1.

23. Richard Simon, *Histoire critique du Vieux Testament* 1.3.1; quoted in Joseph Trigg, *Origen*, Early Church Fathers Series (New York: Routledge, 1998), 62.

24. On the Melitian schism, see the bibliography for chapter 1.

25. Athanasius, *Apologia contra Arianos* 59 (PG 25:356; NPNF 4:131).

26. Epiphanius, *Panarion* 5.68.3. For the account, see Frank Williams, ed., *The Panarion of Epiphanius of Salamis*, Nag Hammadi and Manichaean Studies 36 (Leiden: Brill, 1994), 317.

27. Athanasius, *Apologia contra Arianos* 71 (PG 25:376; NPNF 2.4:137).

28. Roger S. Bagnall, "Religious Conversion and Onomastic Change in Early Byzantine Egypt," *Bulletin of the American Society of Papyrologists* 19 (1982): 105–124.

29. Bagnall, *Egypt in Late Antiquity*, 285.

30. Socrates, *HE* 7.7 (PG 67:749–752), quoted in Haas, *Alexandria in Late Antiquity*, 297.

31. Cyril, *Ep.* 96 (ACO 1.4:224–225; FC 77:151–153). See Peter Brown, *Power and Persuasion in Late Antiquity* (Madison, Wis.: University of Wisconsin Press, 1992), 16–17.

32. Isidore of Pelusium, *Ep.* 1.152. Cf. Leo the Great, *Ep.* 120.2; Socrates, *HE* 7.7.

BIBLIOGRAPHY

Alexandria

The best starting point is the work of Christopher Haas, *Alexandria in Late Antiquity: Topography and Social Conflict* (Baltimore: Johns Hopkins University Press, 1997). The massive study of P. M. Fraser, *Ptolemaic Alexandria*, 3 vols. (Oxford: Clarendon Press, 1972), focuses on an earlier period in the city's history, but has much about landmarks and geographical features that would influence the city in late antiquity. See also:

Fraser, P. M. "Alexandria, Christian and Medieval." In *The Coptic Encyclopedia*, ed. Aziz S. Atiya (New York: Macmillan, 1991), 1:88–92.
Heinen, Heinz. "Alexandria in Late Antiquity." In *The Coptic Encyclopedia*, ed. Aziz S. Atiya (New York: Macmillan, 1991), 1:95–103.
Martin, Annik. "Les premiers siècles du christianisme à Alexandrie: essai de topographie religieuse, 3e–4e siècles." *Revue des études augustiniennes* 30 (1984): 211–225.

Egypt in Late Antiquity

For a survey of the history and the social world of Roman Egypt, see A. K. Bowman, *Egypt after the Pharaohs, 332 B.C.–A.D. 642: From Alexander to the Arab Conquest* (Berkeley:

University of California Press, 1986), and Roger S. Bagnall, *Egypt in Late Antiquity* (Princeton: Princeton University Press, 1993). The latter draws especially on recent discoveries of papyri. On the pre-Christian religious legacy, see David Frankfurter, *Religion in Roman Egypt: Assimilation and Resistance* (Princeton: Princeton University Press, 1998). Other important studies are:

Bell, H. I. *Egypt from Alexander the Great to the Arab Conquest: A Study in the Diffusion and Decay of Hellenism.* Oxford: Clarendon Press, 1948.
Jones, A. H. M. *The Later Roman Empire, 284–602.* 2 vols. Reprint: Baltimore: Johns Hopkins University Press, 1978.
Lewis, Naphtali. *Life in Egypt under Roman Rule.* Oxford: Clarendon Press, 1983.

History of Christianity in Egypt

The most exhaustive study is by Annik Martin, *Athanase d'Alexandrie et l'église d'Égypte au IVᵉ siècle (328–373),* Collection de l'École française de Rome 216 (Rome: École française de Rome, 1996). The standard histories of early Christianity contain a great deal about Egypt; they also help fit the Egyptian experience into the larger history. See especially Henry Chadwick, *The Church in Ancient Society: From Galilee to Gregory the Great,* Oxford History of the Christian Church (New York: Oxford University Press, 2002), and W. H. C. Frend, *The Rise of Christianity* (Philadelphia: Fortress Press, 1984). See also the many valuable articles in *The Coptic Encyclopedia,* 8 vols., ed. Aziz S. Atiya (New York: Macmillan, 1991). Other studies include:

Martin, Annik. "Aux origines de l'église copte: l'implantation et le développement du christianisme en Égypte (Iᵉ–IVᵉ siècles)." *Revue des études anciennes* 83 (1981): 35–56.
———. "L'église et la khôra égyptienne au IVe siècle." *Revue des études augustiennes* 25 (1979): 3–26.
Pearson, Birger A., and James E. Goehring, eds. *The Roots of Egyptian Christianity.* Studies in Antiquity and Christianity. Philadelphia: Fortress Press, 1986.
Roberts, Colin. *Manuscript, Society, and Belief in Early Christian Egypt.* New York: Oxford University Press, 1979.
Wipszycka, E. "La christianisation de l'Égypte aux IVᵉ–VIᵉ siècles: aspects sociaux et ethniques," *Aegyptus* 68 (1988): 117–165. Reprinted in E. Wipszycka, *Études sur le christianisme dans l'Égypte de l'antiquité tardive* (Rome: Institutum Patristicum Augustinianum, 1996), 63–106.

Origen

For an overview, see Joseph W. Trigg, *Origen: Bible and Philosophy in the Third Century* (Atlanta: John Knox, 1983), and Henri Crouzel, *Origen,* trans. A. S. Worrall (reprint: Edinburgh: T. & T. Clark, 1998). For a valuable selection of his writings, see Joseph W. Trigg, ed., *Origen,* Early Church Fathers Series (New York: Routledge, 1998). See also:

Daley, Brian E. "Origen's '*De principiis*': A Guide to the 'Principles' of Christian Scriptural Interpretation." In *Nova et Vetera: Patristic Studies in Honor of Thomas Patrick Halton,* ed. John F. Petruccione. Washington, D.C.: Catholic University of America Press, 1998.
Hanson, R. P. C. *Allegory and Event: A Study of the Sources and Significance of Origen's Interpretation of Scripture.* Richmond, Va.: John Knox Press, 1959.

Kannengiesser, Charles, and William L. Petersen, eds. *Origen of Alexandria: His World and Legacy.* Notre Dame: University of Notre Dame Press, 1988.

Lyman, J. Rebecca. *Christology and Cosmology: Models of Divine Activity in Origen, Eusebius, and Athanasius.* Oxford Theological Monographs. New York: Oxford University Press, 1993.

Nautin, Pierre. *Origen: sa vie et son oeuvre.* Paris: Beauchesne, 1977.

Widdicombe, Peter. *The Fatherhood of God from Origen to Athanasius.* Rev. ed. Oxford Theological Monographs. New York: Oxford University Press, 2000.

Persecution and Martyrdom

The classic studies are those of W. H. C. Frend, *Martyrdom and Persecution in the Early Church: A Study of a Conflict from the Maccabees to Donatus* (New York: Oxford University Press, 1965), and G. E. M. de Ste. Croix, "Why Were the Early Christians Persecuted?" *Past and Present* 26 (1963): 6–38. Also valuable is Robin Lane Fox, *Pagan and Christians* (New York: Alfred A. Knopf, 1987). The most complete collection of texts is that of H. A. Murusillo, *The Acts of the Christian Martyrs* (Oxford: Clarendon Press, 1972), which contains the original Greek or Latin together with a facing English translation.

The Melitian Schism

Barnard, L. W. "Athanasius and the Meletian Schism in Egypt." *Journal of Egyptian Archeology* 59 (1975): 183–189.

Bell, H. Idris, ed. *Jews and Christians in Egypt: The Jewish Troubles in Alexandria and the Athanasian Controversy, Illustrated by Texts from Greek Papyri in the British Museum.* London: British Museum, 1924.

Kramer, Bärbel, and John C. Shelton. *Das Archiv des Nepheros und verwandte Texte.* Mainz: Philipp von Zabern, 1987.

Martin, Annik. "Athanase et les Mélitiens (325–335)." In *Politique et théologie chez Athanase d'Alexandrie: actes du colloque de Chantilly, 23–25 septembre 1973,* ed. Charles Kannengiesser, 33–61. Théologie historique 27. Paris: Beauchesne, 1974.

Telfer, W. R. "Meletius of Lycopolis and Episcopal Succession in Egypt." *Harvard Theological Review* 48 (1955): 227–237.

Vivian, Tim. *St. Peter of Alexandria: Bishop and Martyr.* Studies in Antiquity and Christianity. Philadelphia: Fortress Press, 1988.

Williams, Rowan. "Arius and the Melitian Schism." *Journal of Theological Studies* n.s. 37 (1986): 35–52.

APPENDIX I.I

Papyrus: Women and Monasticism

Discoveries of papyri have profoundly enriched our understanding of the social world of Roman Egypt and of ancient monasticism. The following is an example. The papyrus quoted below is a rental contract between a Jewish man and two sisters, named Theodora and Tauris. What makes this interesting is that the sisters are described as "female-monk renouncers"(*monachais apotaktikais*). This indicates that ascetics—including women—might live in town, remain members of the local community, own property, and carry on business.

> After the consulship of Flavius Theodorus the most illustrious, Epieph. To Aurelia Theodora and Aurelia Tauris, daughters of Silvanus, apotactic nuns [*monachais apotaktikais*] from the illustrious and most illustrious city of Oxyrhynchos, from Aurelius Jose, son of Judas, Jew from the same city. Of my free will I accept to lease from the new moon of the next month Mesore of the present 76 = 45th year at the beginning of the fourteenth indiction, from the property owned by you in the selfsame city of Oxyrhynchos in the Cavalry Camp quarter, one ground-floor room—and a hall—and the single cellar in the basement, with all their fittings. And for the rent of them I shall pay twelve hundred myriads of silver annually, total: 1200 myriads of denarii. And I shall be required to pay the rent, half the amount forthwith each six months. And whenever it is wished, I shall hand back the same rooms clean as I received them. The lease [and] two copies are valid: and in answer to the question I have agreed. [second hand] I, Aurelius Jose, son of Jose, named above, have leased the dining room; and I will give the rent as specified above. I Aurelius Elias, son of Opebaios, wrote for him since he is illiterate. (*P. Oxy.* 3203)

For the text, translation, and commentary, see G. H. R. Horsley, *New Documents Illustrating Early Christianity* (North Ryde, N.S.W: Macquarrie University, 1976), 1:126–130.

2

Patriarchs, Councils, and Controversies: 300–451

The last chapter surveyed the social world of Roman Egypt, its geography, politics, and economics. We also took a brief look at the emergence of Egyptian Christianity, highlighting a few elements that would come to affect monasticism. Now we need to focus on the careers of five patriarchs of Alexandria: Alexander, Athanasius, Theophilus, Cyril, and Dioscorus (for a chronology, see table 2.1). Each cast long shadows over the history and literature of early Egyptian monasticism. While I will touch on their monastic ties, the accent here will be on their international politics and theology, for it is precisely this international role that would help draw the world's attention to Egypt and its monks. This may feel, at times, like a mini-course in early Christian theology. It may also seem a little daunting to newcomers, but the key names and key concepts will soon become familiar when they reappear later in the monastic texts.

Alexander, Arius, and the Council of Nicaea

The great theological debate of the fourth century was the Arian Controversy.[1] It was a debate in which the monks of Egypt played vital roles, and references to it abound in early monastic literature. It has real complexities, but one cannot really grasp the religious milieu without some exposure to its intricate arguments and its equally intricate politics. The controversy began in 318 as a local struggle between Arius (d. 336), an Alexandrian presbyter, and Alexander (d. 328), the bishop of Alexandria. The point of contention touched—and continues to touch—the very heart of Christianity: is Jesus God or not? The problem, logically and theologically, is this: if Jesus is

TABLE 2.1. The Patriarchs of
Alexandria

Theonas	282–300
Peter I	300–311
Achillas	311–312
Alexander	312–328
Athanasius	328–373
(Gregory of Cappadocia)*	339–345
(George of Cappadocia)	357–361
Peter II	373–380
(Lucius)	373–378
Timothy I	380–385
Theophilus	385–412
Cyril	412–444
Dioscorus	444–451
(Proterius)	452–457

*Those whose names are given in parentheses have traditionally been seen as government-imposed intruders rather than legitimate successors of Saint Mark.

God and the Father is God, then how can Christians claim that they believe in only one God? To thoughtful pagans, Christians sounded like ditheists, because of the way they called both Father and Son "God." (Serious reflection on the status of the Holy Spirit arose only later, in the 360s.) Christians had to decide whether they believed Christ is indeed God, and if so, how to speak of his divinity in a way that did not imperil Christian monotheism.

Two approaches had been discarded in the third century. One was associated with the bishop of Antioch, Paul of Samosata (active 260s). He was branded by his opponents as an "adoptionist"—one who claimed that Jesus was not God in any real sense, but was a "mere man" adopted by God as Son. The other extreme was associated with Sabellius (active 220s), a Libyan teacher who had settled in Rome. He reportedly claimed that the Father and Son were not just united, but were identical—that God was a "Son-Father." His orthodox opponents branded this "patripassianism" ("Father-suffering"), since Sabellius's view logically implied that God the Father had suffered and died on the cross. These two extremes were judged heretical, dead ends to be avoided at all costs. At the turn of the fourth century, many thoughtful Christians found Origen's view the best answer: that the Son was truly God, but in some subordinate derivative sense, eternally begotten from the Father.

What we know of Arius, his life and theological views, is limited. It is especially hard to cut through the polemic of later generations and figure out what the terms of the original debate were. In 318, when the conflict broke out, Arius was a presbyter, a respected member of Alexandria's clergy, and served as pastor of a church in the Baucalis district, near the Great Harbor, just outside the walls of the city. He may have been a native of Libya and seems to have studied with the biblical scholar and martyr Lucian of Antioch. Arius had a knack for putting his theology into verse. Opponents claimed that he composed theological ditties that could be sung by the simple people in his congregation.[2] His surviving verse is more erudite. Scholars have been able to reconstruct fragments of his philosophical poem *Thalia* (*Banquet*). From this and from several surviving letters, scholars have been able to piece together an outline of his theology. His position can be summarized in four basic propositions:

1. THE FATHER ALONE IS GOD. Arius was a passionate monotheist, insisting in his *Letter to Alexander of Alexandria*: "We acknowledge One God, alone unbegotten, alone eternal, alone unbegun, alone true, alone having immortality, alone wise, alone good, alone sovereign."[3] Note the way the word "alone" sounds as a drumbeat. Arius's monotheism excluded attributing divinity to Christ, even the derived divinity that Origen held. Arius refused to predicate divine qualities of Christ: if the Father *alone* is eternal, then the Son is *not* eternal; if the Father *alone* is without beginning, then the Son had a beginning; and so on. Arius knew that certain passages in the New Testament call Christ "God." He therefore argued in the *Thalia* that Christ "the Word is not true God (even if he is called God) but he is not true God; by sharing in grace (just as others do), he is God in name only."[4]

2. THE SON WAS MADE. Arius insisted that Christ was (in some sense) a creature. As he states in the *Thalia*: "Since everything that exists has come into being as created, he too is something created."[5] Arius's logic was this: if the Father *alone* is God, then the Son is not God; if the Son is not God, then he must be something created, something made. This meant that the relationship between God and Christ was not really father-son, but artist-artwork.

3. THE SON WAS FROM NOTHINGNESS. Arius took his logic the next step, arguing in the *Thalia*: "Since all things have come into being out of nothingness, the Son of God has also come from nothingness."[6] Arius believed that God had created the universe not from preexistent matter (as Platonists held) but from nothingness. If Christ was a creature, then Christ too had been created from nothingness. Arius's contemporaries found this especially shocking, and even supporters seemed to have distanced themselves from this view.

4. "THERE WAS A 'WHEN' WHEN THE SON WAS NOT." This was to become the best-known Arian slogan. Arius's logic seems to have been that while God is without beginning, the Son had a beginning. But according to John's Gospel, all things were made *through* the Son (John 1:3). That meant the Son played some role in creating the universe. If he helped in its creation, he must have existed before it. So his beginning was before the beginning of the universe. If the Son's beginning was before the beginning of the universe, then his beginning was before the beginning of time. Thus there was a "when"—rather than a "time"—when the Son did not exist.[7]

These four theses are the part of Arius's theology officially branded as heresy. Note that his focus here was not on the Jesus of the Synoptic Gospels, but on the preexistent Christ.[8] Scholars suspect that this touches only one side of Arius's theology—that beneath his speculations on cosmology and the cosmic Christ, he may have held some kind of incarnational theology. Arius clearly saw Christ the Word as a mediator of creation bridging the cosmic gap between a changeable material world and an unchangeable immaterial God. But Arius may have seen this as the basis for Christ the Word as a mediator of salvation, entering into the messy changes and sufferings of humanity in a way that the unchangeable immaterial God cannot.[9] The bottom line was that Arius denied the divinity of Christ. That, at least, is how opponents, both ancient and modern, have read him. In fairness, Arius seems to have thought that Christ, while created, was divine in some sense; and that although created, he was "not as one of the creatures."[10]

Arius's views sparked fierce controversy. He and his bishop Alexander clashed publicly, and Arius ended up accusing Alexander of heresy, claiming that Alexander believed in "two eternals" (i.e., two Gods). Alexander, in turn, excommunicated Arius and a large group of his supporters, including seven presbyters and twelve deacons. Alexander soon called together a council of Egyptian bishops who added their voice to the condemnation of Arius and his views. Arius meanwhile fled to Palestine, where he won the support of Eusebius (c. 264–339), bishop of Caesarea, best known today for his *Church History*. Arius also won the support of another leading bishop, Eusebius of Nicomedia (d. 341). This Eusebius had formidable political skills and contacts, including contacts in the imperial household. A well-run petition drive on Arius's behalf was marshaled. Delegations were sent from church to church, carrying with them a formal statement of Arius's views. Bishops were asked to sign the petition, noting whether they supported Arius's views or not. This meant that what began as a local squabble became an international debate, dividing the Greek East.[11]

Theology and politics soon intersected. In 312, Constantine had defeated his rival Maxentius at the Milvian Bridge and became emperor of the western half of the Empire. What made this event extraordinary was that Constantine was a Christian, the first Christian emperor. In 313, he and his eastern co-emperor, Licinius, agreed on a formal end to the persecution of Christians. Eventually, the partnership disintegrated, and Constantine defeated Licinius on the Bosphorus in September 324, becoming thereby sole emperor (for a chronology of the Roman emperors, see table 2.2). It is not without irony that at this great turning point in the history of Christianity, Christians in the Greek East (where the majority of Christians lived) were seriously divided over Arius. Constantine had faced the bitter Donatist schism in North Africa and had failed, despite repeated efforts, to heal it. So he tried to head off a similar turn of events in the East.

In 325, Constantine (see figure 2.1) called the Council of Nicaea, now considered the first ecumenical (or "worldwide") council. Some 300 bishops from

TABLE 2.2. Roman
Emperors Who Ruled the
Greek East (and thus Roman
Egypt).

Diocletian	284–305
Galerius	305–311
Licinius	308–324
Constantine	324–337
Constantius II	337–361
Julian	361–363
Jovian	363–364
Valens	364–378
Theodosius	379–395
Arcadius	395–408
Theodosius II	408–450
Marcian	450–457

around the empire—and even a few beyond its borders—attended. Most were from the Greek East, but there were a few Latins, such as Ossius of Cordoba and Caecilianus of Carthage. We do not have any official minutes, or *acta*, from Nicaea as we do from later ecumenical councils. But there are reports from eyewitnesses, notably Eusebius of Caesarea and Athanasius, who at the time was Alexander's deacon. Eusebius recounts the fanfare and grand ceremonial. It was certainly a new world for the assembled bishops, who just a few years before had been ruthlessly pursued and persecuted by imperial authorities. Some bishops seemed like living martyrs. The Egyptian bishop Paphnutius, for instance, bore the marks of torture—blinded in one eye and lame from a severed Achilles' tendon. Throughout the council, the emperor made his presence felt: he let the bishops travel via the imperial post (the rapid transit system of the empire, normally reserved for the highest officials), hosted them at an extravagant banquet, and sat in on their deliberations. Eusebius records Constantine's inaugural address, a no-nonsense call to unity. And Constantine made a dramatic gesture of what that unity involved. A number of the bishops, seeing the council as a once-in-a-lifetime opportunity to get the upper hand against rivals, had come armed with their lawsuits against one another. Constantine ordered a charcoal fire to be brought in and ceremonially burned these legal petitions. He wanted unity, not squabbling.

The lasting achievement of the council was its creed (for the full text, see appendix 2.1). Its wording drew on early baptismal formulas, which catechumens used to swear before their baptism, professing faith in Father, Son, and Holy Spirit. The key phrases appear in the article on the Son: "We believe in . . . one Lord Jesus Christ, the Son of God, begotten from the Father, only-begotten, that is, from the being [*ousia*] of the Father, God from God, light from light, true God from true God, begotten not made, one-in-being [*homoousios*] with the Father." Note how the key phrases contradict Arius's four key positions cited above:

FIGURE 2.1. This is from what was a massive statue of the Emperor Constantine. The first Christian emperor, Constantine was responsible for calling the Council of Nicaea in 325. On the other hand, he ended up sending Athanasius, the leading Nicene, into exile in Trier. (Alinari/Art Resource, NY)

1. Whereas Arius had said that the Father *alone* was God, Nicaea insisted that Christ is "true God" from the Father who is "true God."
2. Whereas Arius had said that Christ was "made," Nicaea insisted that Christ was "begotten, not made," that the relationship was Father-Son, not artist-artwork.
3. Whereas Arius had said that Christ was made from nothingness, Nicaea insisted that Christ was begotten "from the being [*ousia*] of the Father." A second phrase was added to emphasize this: the Son was "one-in-being [*homoousios*] with the Father." This phrase provoked intense discussion during the council itself and would prove, decades later, the most controversial phrase in the creed.

4. Whereas Arius and his followers had embraced the slogan "There was a 'when' when the Son was not," the authors of the creed tacked on anathemas, declaring this and several other slogans heretical.

All but two bishops signed, and Arius was excommunicated and sent into exile. That should have ended things. In fact, it was only the beginning. The debate would continue for decades and be resolved only at the Council of Constantinople in 381. This fifty-five-year debate is usually referred to as the Arian Controversy and is portrayed in older studies as a clash between two camps, the Arians and the Nicenes. That is not really accurate. Even to call it the Arian Controversy is something of a misnomer, because it gives Arius a theological importance he probably does not deserve. After the council, he spent his final years either in official exile or at least barred from returning to Alexandria (despite efforts to have him reconciled and reestablished). Arius does not seem to have been a prolific theological writer, and later thinkers labeled as Arian show no real dependence on his views. He is better seen as a catalyst, as the spark that lit the conflagration. The next fifty-five years would not be a clear-cut battle between orthodoxy and heresy, but rather a halting, contentious, and often muddled "search for the Christian doctrine of God," to use R. P. C. Hanson's apt phrase.

The council took up two other issues vital to the Egyptian church. At some point, the council passed a set of canons. One canon formally ratified what had been the effective reality before the council. It officially granted three bishoprics jurisdictional spheres of influence: the bishop of Rome over Italy, the bishop of Antioch over Syria, and the bishop of Alexandria over Egypt and Libya. The council also tried to find some way to heal the Melitian schism. It sent a letter to the Egyptian Church decreeing its solution: Melitius was allowed to retain his title as bishop of Lycopolis but was denied the right to ordain new bishops; his previous ordinations were accepted, but Melitian clergy had to serve as subordinates in towns where one of Alexander's clergy held sway.[12] This compromise gained initial acceptance, but over time, Alexander may not have honored his side of the bargain; nor, apparently, did Melitius honor his, since he appointed a successor, John Archaph. By the time Alexander died, serious divisions had reappeared, and his successor, Athanasius, faced and even provoked fierce Melitian opposition.

Nicaea's creed became the touchstone of Christian orthodoxy only decades later. But it was not apparently seen as such at the time. There was surprisingly little mention of it at first, though the fifth-century church historian Socrates reports that "the term 'one-in-being' (homoousios) was troubling to some people—as we have learned from various letters which the bishops were writing to each other after the Council."[13] The term was troubling for several reasons. First, it had materialist overtones, as though the Father and Son were two things made up of the same material stuff (like two pots made from the same clay). Second, it sounded something like the old heresy of Sabellius, as though the Son and the Father were numerically identical, one person. Third, the word itself was unbiblical; that is, unlike other key phrases in the creed, it did not appear in the scriptures—as was obvious to bishops who read the Bible in their native language.

Not long after the council, leading Nicenes passed from the scene. Alexander of Alexandria died in 328; Eustathius of Antioch was removed in 327, apparently for disciplinary reasons; and Marcellus of Ancyra was deposed in 336 for heresy. The tide began to shift in Constantine's later days. Arius's old supporter, Eusebius of Nicomedia, recovered his see and forged a well-organized ecclesiastical party (called "Eusebians" in the sources). He eventually became bishop of the new imperial capital, Constantinople, and baptized the dying Emperor Constantine.

The reign of Constantine's sons (337–362) saw an extraordinary number of councils. The fourth-century pagan historian Ammianus Marcellinus complained that so many councils were being called that traveling bishops were clogging the rapid transit system of the empire.[14] The ebb and flow of these councils, of their politics and the theology of the creeds they issued is enormously complex. Most of this is beyond the scope of this brief survey, but we do need to be aware of new research on the theological parties active at this period, for they were opposed by the monks of Egypt and their views were attacked in monastic texts. The 350s saw the emergence of three ecclesiastical coalitions: the Anomians, the Homoiousians, and the Homoians. Older textbooks—and some early monastic texts—lump these together as though they were a single group, the "Arians." While they shared hostility to Nicaea, they owed little or nothing to Arius and would have disavowed some of his views (e.g., that the Son was made from nothing). They are more accurately seen not as Arians, but as anti-Nicenes. They differed, sometimes sharply, from one another.

THE ANOMIANS. The Anomians held that the Son was "unlike" (*anomios*) or "different-in-being" (*heteroousios*) from the Father. They were led by Aetius (d. 367) and Eunomius of Cyzicus (d. 394). They applied a sophisticated Aristotelian philosophical analysis to the question and stressed that God was "ungenerated," and since the Son was "generated," he could not really be God.

THE HOMOIOUSIANS. The Homoiousians held that the Son was "like-in-being" (*homoiousios*) with the Father. This party, led by Basil of Ancyra, accepted the divinity of Christ but was uncomfortable with Nicaea's formula, which seemed to blur any distinction between Father and Son. Instead they appealed to the formula of baptism and stressed that Father, Son, and Spirit were distinct, though unequal, "persons."

THE HOMOIANS. The Homoians spoke of Christ as "like" (*homoios*) the Father. They strongly disliked applying the language of "being" (*ousia*) to relationships within the Godhead and were wary of using Greek philosophical language or of going beyond the language of the Bible. They accented the inequality of Father and Son and spoke of Christ as "our God" or as "a second God" and of the Father "the God of our God." They were led by Acacius of Caesarea (d. 364) and included bishops such as Ulfilas (d. 383), the great missionary to the Goths, as well as Valens of Mursa and Ursacius of Singidunum, both with close ties to the imperial court.

The Homoians achieved a short-lived victory at the Council of Rimini-Seleucia in 359, formally ratified at Constantinople in 360. According to Saint Jerome's famous outburst, "The term *ousia* was abolished and 'Down with the faith of Nicaea!' was the cry. The whole world groaned and wondered to find itself Arian."[15] For most of the next twenty years, at least in the Greek East, the Homoians held sway. There were interruptions, such as 362–363, when the Emperor Julian embraced paganism and delighted in Christian disunity. The turn finally came when Theodosius, a Spanish general and a Nicene, became emperor in 379 and called the Council of Constantinople, which met in 381. This council, eventually numbered as the Second Ecumenical Council, would be led by two Cappadocians, Gregory of Nazianzus and his friend Gregory of Nyssa, who, together with the recently deceased Basil of Caesarea, had forged the classic defense of the divinity of the Holy Spirit and had put together the classic formulation of the doctrine of the Trinity. The creed most Christians recite today is often called the Nicene Creed but is actually the creed passed at Constantinople. Through most of this era, from the 320s to the early 370s, the leader of the Nicene opposition was the controversial and combative bishop of Alexandria, Athanasius.

Athanasius

Athanasius (c. 296–373) is one of the most important figures in the history of early Christianity. He served as Alexandria's bishop, off and on, between 328 and 373 and was one of the architects of Christian orthodoxy, forging the classic defense of the divinity of Christ. E. R. Hardy, in a well-known study of Egyptian Christianity, remarked that Athanasius "so completely dominates the history of Egypt for fifty years in the fourth century that its story is primarily the story of his career."[16] Athanasius also plays a central role in the development of monasticism. First, he forged a remarkable alliance between the monks of Egypt and the patriarchate of Alexandria, one that would last for generations. Equally important, he authored the first great work of desert literature, the *Life of Antony*. Here we need to sketch out Athanasius's life and politics; his writings and theology will be treated in the coming chapters (for a chronology of Athanasius' life, see table 2.3).

Born of an Alexandrian family, Athanasius was ordained deacon while in his twenties. In 325 he accompanied his bishop, Alexander, to the Council of Nicaea and looked back on the experience as one that defined his career. Three years later, in 328, Alexander died, and in a controversial election Athanasius was made bishop of Alexandria. Accounts of its circumstances are so contradictory and so biased that sorting out what happened is difficult. It seems that

TABLE 2.3. The Life of Athanasius

c. 295	Birth of Athanasius
318	Beginning of the Arian Controversy
325	Attends the Council of Nicaea as Alexander's deacon
328	Elected Bishop of Alexandria
329 or 330	Tours Upper Egypt
335	Deposed by the Synod of Tyre
335–337	First exile (Trier)
337	Returns to Alexandria
339–346	Second exile (Rome)
346–356	"The Golden Decade"
355	Condemned and deposed by Council of Milan
356–362	Third exile (Desert)
362	Presides over the Council of Alexandria
362–363	Fourth exile
365	Fifth exile
367	*Festal Letter* 39 on canon of scripture
373	Death

Athanasius was young, thirty-three at most, possibly even under the canonical age of thirty. The electoral process may have excluded recently reconciled Melitians, and Athanasius may have been consecrated by a small contingent of bishops. While many Egyptian bishops accepted the result, some Melitians elected and consecrated their own bishop of Alexandria, and the Melitian schism reemerged. Athanasius thus inherited a divided church. He governed this complex, urbane, and sometimes violent church with great political skill. As bishop of Alexandria, he not only had charge of the churches within the city itself, but enjoyed powers of appointment and jurisdiction over churches throughout Egypt and Libya—an authority given official sanction in the canon recently passed at Nicaea.

In his early years as bishop, Athanasius traveled extensively. In 330, he journeyed up the Nile far to the south, to the Thebaid; in 332, he went west to visit the Pentapolis and the Oasis of Ammon, some 600 miles to the deep Sahara and to the western border of modern Libya; in 334, he surveyed sites in the Nile Delta. These pastoral sojourns helped him to forge links with monastic communities just then springing up both in the desert and along the bend of the Nile. This alliance of Alexandrian bishop and Coptic monk was fortunate, and later, in 356, it likely saved Athanasius's life.

Athanasius faced a strategic alliance of Melitian enemies within Egypt and Arian opponents outside. Charges by Melitians in 331 and again in 334 forced Athanasius to defend himself in court. In the latter case, he was charged with the murder of an old bishop, Arsenius; he was even accused of cutting off the dead man's hand and using it for sorcery. The charges were false. The old bishop was very much alive, and Athanasius knew it. He had his agents scour the countryside high and low. They just missed nabbing Arsenius in a monastery in the Thebaid but found him eventually in Beirut, hidden away by Athanasius's enemies. The embarrassment rebounded on his accusers. The synod summoned to meet in Caesarea in 334 was called off, and Athanasius was exonerated.

In 335, Athanasius was summoned to appear before the Synod of Tyre. His enemies accused him of various misdeeds: that he used shady financial dealings (an illegitimate tax on linen and use of bribery), and that he employed thugs to intimidate, beat, jail, and otherwise harass those who opposed him. The truth of these charges—and if true, what that means about one acknowledged as a saint and a leading church father—is much disputed by modern scholars.[17] The chance discovery in the early twentieth century of a papyrus seems to confirm Melitian charges. The papyrus contains a private letter written by a Melitian to two monks and describes how, on the eve of the Synod of Tyre, followers of Athanasius happened upon two Melitian bishops having dinner together in Alexandria. The bishops escaped being roughed up only because some soldiers hid them in an army barracks. Later four Melitian monks were accosted and nearly killed. Athanasius's supporters then raided a hotel where the out-of-town Melitians had been staying and, for a time, kidnapped them. The author mentions how one bishop had been jailed and brutalized, adding in one poignant line, "I thank God our Master that the scourgings which he endured have ceased."[18]

To what degree Athanasius had a hand in all this is not clear. Athanasius proclaimed himself innocent of the charges and claimed to be a victim of an Arian conspiracy. When the Synod of Tyre in 335 formally deposed him, he skipped town before the verdict, claiming (with justice) that the synod was stacked with his enemies, and appealed his case directly to the Emperor Constantine. But his enemies submitted a new charge: that Athanasius had interfered with the sailing of the grain shipment from Alexandria to the imperial capital of Constantinople—technically, a charge of treason. Constantine had had enough. Athanasius was exiled to the opposite end of the empire, to Trier, in Germany.

There he began the first of five exiles that punctuate his career. He stayed in Trier from 335 to 337. During this time (or perhaps even before this), he composed a two-volume theological masterpiece—*Against the Nations / On the Incarnation*—that sketches out his basic defense of the divinity of Christ. On the death of Constantine, Athanasius was granted a reprieve, and he returned home, where he reasserted his leadership over the Alexandrian church. In 339, he was again forced out, and from 339 to 345, he lived in exile in Rome, where he won over Pope Julius I to the justice of his cause. Monks accompanied him to Rome, giving the West its first glimpse of the new asceticism sweeping through Egypt and sparking interest and imitators among aristocratic circles in Rome. During this exile Athanasius probably began writing another of his theological works, the three *Orations against the Arians* (though establishing precise dates for this and many of his works is difficult). Gregory of Cappadocia (reportedly an "Arian") served as bishop of Alexandria through these years.

At the time, the empire was jointly ruled by Constantine's sons, Constans in the Latin West and Constantius in the Greek East. When Gregory died in 345, Constans pressured his brother to allow Athanasius to be reinstated as bishop. In 346, Athanasius returned to a triumphant welcome, greeted by officials and citizens of Alexandria at the 100th milestone. "His triumphant progress into Alexandria," according to one recent biographer, "resembled less the return of an exiled bishop than the *adventus* of a Roman emperor."[19] For the next ten years, sometimes called "the Golden Decade," Athanasius enjoyed enormous popularity and support at home. In 350, Constans was murdered, and his murderer, the usurper Magnentius, posed a serious threat to the Emperor Constantius. So Constantius sent Athanasius a warm letter of support, while Magnentius sent a diplomatic embassy to try and court Athanasius's favor—something Athanasius officially refused, though nasty rumors later surfaced that he had entered into some kind of negotiation. This currying of Athanasius's favor by both sides is one indication of his considerable political power.

The years 356 to 362 marked his third exile. We will look at them in some detail in the next chapter. Suffice to say, these years would be the most dangerous and decisive of his career. He spent them hiding among the desert monks or with allies within Alexandria itself, keeping one step ahead of imperial authorities, who launched a full-scale manhunt. During this time he composed his masterful *Life of Antony* as well as influential theological and polemical works.

Upon the death of Constantius in November 361, the Emperor Julian came to power. Julian was a born-again pagan who fiercely rejected his Christian upbringing (earning him the nickname "the Apostate"). Julian welcomed back all exiled bishops, hoping they would incite division and rancor among Christians. Violence broke out in Alexandria, and Athanasius's "Arian" replacement, George of Cappadocia, was arrested and thrown in jail. George was hated as much by pagans as by Athanasians and was eventually lynched by a pagan mob in December 361. Athanasius returned soon after and took control of affairs in Alexandria. Athanasius, who made a living out of irritating emperors, undercut Julian's program by hosting a peace conference. In 362, this Council of Alexandria struck a compromise among pro-Nicene factions and paved the way for the eventual consensus. Athanasius also had the audacity to baptize some prominent upper-class pagan women. This evangelical campaign against paganism earned Athanasius Julian's wrath and a fourth exile. One example of Athanasius's bravado is a story told about this exile. To escape pursuing imperial detectives, he boarded a ship and began to sail south, perhaps to hide again among the monks. But suddenly, he told his oarsman to turn the boat back around and return to Alexandria. At that moment, they passed a boat full of soldiers who, not recognizing him, called out, "Have you seen Athanasius?" Athanasius stood up in the stern and coyly replied, "He's not far away." After Julian's death in 363, Athanasius again returned to power. For the next ten years, he was generally left alone—except for a final brief exile in the winter of 365–366. Through these final years, he played elder statesman as a new generation of Nicenes took the theological and ecclesiastical lead. He died on May 2, 373. Of his forty-five years in office, he spent more than fifteen in exile.

Theophilus

When Athanasius died, Peter II (bp. 373–380) was elected his successor. However, at the time, government policy favored the "Arians" (or, more accurately, Homoians), and a man named Lucius was imposed on the city as bishop—as had happened earlier when Gregory of Cappadocia and George of Cappadocia served as government-backed bishops while Athanasius was in exile. Peter was forced to flee to Rome. During these years, the monks of Egypt faced harsh persecution for their refusal to support the Arian establishment. Two leading monastic figures, Macarius the Egyptian and Macarius the Alexandrian, were exiled from their desert monasteries and held under arrest on an island in the delta. The tide turned back to the Nicenes in 379, and when Peter died, his brother Timothy became bishop and served from 380 to 385. The alliance Athanasius established between patriarch and monks would continue under the next three patriarchs: Theophilus (d. 412), Cyril (d. 444), and Dioscorus (d. 454).[20] All three are complex and controversial figures.

Theophilus served as Alexandria's bishop from 385 to 412. He came from a family in Memphis, the old capital of pharaonic Egypt, but was orphaned as a teenager. He moved to Alexandria, where he entered the catechumenate and was baptized. There he came to the attention of Athanasius, who took him into his household and eventually made him his personal secretary from 370 to 373. Theophilus moved up the ecclesiastical ladder, eventually becoming archdeacon. In 385, he was chosen as bishop.

His career was marred by controversy and violence. In 391, he embarked on a fierce anti-pagan campaign. At a construction site, workers discovered an underground shrine to Mithra, and to the horror of leading pagans, its occult ritual objects were put on public display in the Agora, the city's central market. This sparked street battles, with pagans killing a number of Christians and taking many others hostage. They barricaded themselves in the great pagan temple complex, the Serapeum. A bloodbath seemed imminent. But then the emperor stepped in and offered amnesty to the pagans if they released their hostages; he also insisted that the pagan cults responsible for the violence would be suppressed. This ended the standoff. During the military occupation of the site, a Christian soldier began to destroy its world-famous statue of the god Serapis. Theophilus then called in monks to help in the takeover and demolition of the temple precincts.

Theophilus played a central role in a turning point in the history of monasticism, the Origenist Controversy (see chapter 11). Put briefly, the controversy began in Egypt in 399 when Theophilus, in his annual letter announcing the date of Easter, denounced the heresy of anthropomorphism. Following Origen, he argued that one cannot take literally biblical passages that speak of God's hand or eye or mouth. These are metaphors that need symbolic interpretation; the true God is incorporeal. This attack deeply offended many monks, who marched en masse to Alexandria and began holding demonstrations. Theophilus abruptly reversed course and, when confronted, anathematized Origen and his writings.

Monasteries in Lower Egypt had circles of intellectual monks who studied Origen's writings and were sympathetic to his boldest speculations. Theophilus then turned his energies against these monastic circles. Things reached a violent climax in 400, when Theophilus enlisted support from the prefect, who sent a military detachment to arrest the Origenists. The leaders, the so-called Tall Brothers, were renowned for their learning and holiness and had once been close associates of Theophilus. They and some 300 monks fled initially to Palestine, while their cells were ransacked and burned. Some continued on to Constantinople. There they appealed to the city's eloquent and ascetic bishop, Saint John Chrysostom. Theophilus, outraged by threats of interference in matters under his own jurisdiction, turned the tables against John. He and a group of Egyptian bishops sailed to Chalcedon, just across from Constantinople, and held a small council, the so-called Synod of the Oak. There he summoned local bishops who held grievances against John and had John formally deposed. This marked the beginning of the end of John's tenure and led ultimately to his death in his exile.

Cyril and the Council of Ephesus

Theophilus's successor was his nephew, Cyril, who served as Alexandria's bishop from 412 to 444. Cyril was an extraordinarily gifted theologian, and is numbered as one of the doctors of the church. However, his early tenure as bishop was marred by violence. The arrest of a Christian provocateur sparked a bitter confrontation with the local Jewish community. After a church was burned and some Christians were killed in the street clashes, Cyril headed a large mob, which seized synagogues and drove Jews out of their houses. This led to a confrontation with Orestes, the prefect of Egypt. Orestes was a Christian, but after these incidents, he distanced himself from Cyril and began to rely on advice and support from the local pagan community. Cyril called in some 500 monks from monastic settlements in Lower Egypt. One day they waylaid the prefect's entourage, pelting his carriage with stones. At some point, Orestes was hit in the face and bloodied, and the culprit, a monk named Ammonius, was arrested and died in custody. Cyril promptly proclaimed the monk a martyr and saint.

A leading figure in Alexandria's pagan community at the time was the philosopher Hypatia. She was deeply respected even by Christian intellectuals, such as Synesius, bishop of Cyrene. In March 415, a Christian mob led by a church lector named Peter ambushed her carriage. They dragged her to the Caesarion, where she was stripped and stoned to death. Her body was then ripped apart and burnt. This savage crime marked a serious failure of Cyril's leadership, and he has been blamed for it from his day to our own. Even if not directly responsible for the mob behavior, he had done much to provoke antagonism with both the Jewish and pagan communities that set the conditions for such bloodshed. The next year, the imperial government stepped in and insisted on regulating the membership of the *parabalani*, limiting its number to 500 and insisting that all those enrolled in its ranks be formally approved by the prefect's office. After these episodes early in his career, Cyril seems to have made an effort to keep things calmer.

Beginning in 428, Cyril was at the center of the great theological debate of the fifth century, the Christological Controversy. The fourth-century Arian Controversy had focused on Christ's divinity; this fifth-century controversy shifted the focus to Christ's humanity. The question was this: if Christ is God, then *how* is he human? Notice that I did not say, "*if* he is human." Both sides would acknowledge that Christ is human, but they conceived of his humanity in different ways and conceived of the unity of Christ's humanity and divinity in different ways. This debate is often described as a clash between partisans of two cities, Alexandria and Antioch. As before, the monks of Egypt would get involved in various ways. But unlike that of the Arian Controversy, the theology of the Christological Controversy plays a minor role in the monastic texts that we will be studying. So I will treat its complex theology and politics very briefly.

The controversy began in 428, after the election of Nestorius as bishop of Constantinople. Nestorius was an Antiochene and a rash and violent orator. Soon after his installation, he began anathematizing any who dared call Mary "mother of God" (*Theotokos*). Simple pious laity applied the title to Mary. But it appeared even in the writings of venerable church fathers, including Athanasius, Cyril of Jerusalem, and Gregory of Nazianzus. The real issue was not Mary, but Christ. Nestorius (rather woodenly) drew on the theology of his Antiochene mentor, Theodore of Mopsuestia, who had carefully distinguished Jesus' actions in the Gospels, noting those that applied to "the Man" and those that applied to "the God." Nestorius applied this distinction to argue that Mary was "mother of the Man" (*anthropotokos*), not the "mother of God" (*Theotokos*). He added that Christians must "divide the natures" of Christ, even as they "unite the worship." To many ears, it sounded as though Nestorius was chopping Christ into two persons, two Sons—a Son of God and a Son of Man.

Cyril got wind of Nestorius's polemic through agents in the capital. Cyril decided to act when the news of the controversy in Constantinople made its way from the capital to the monasteries of Egypt. He first denounced Nestorius's theology in his annual letter to churches of Egypt. He also began diplomatic efforts, writing letters and sending dossiers to Pope Celestine and to members of the imperial family. He even confronted Nestorius directly by letter. In his *Second Letter to Nestorius*, Cyril enunciated his classic view. The letter presents itself as a commentary on the Nicene Creed and focuses on the creedal phrase that Jesus "became flesh and became human." Cyril argued that while one can distinguish theoretically between the divine and the human, Christ remains one undivided person (*hypostasis*). Jesus was not, as Nestorius had said, a mere "conjunction" of two natures. Cyril insisted that Jesus was the "union" of divine and human and that union took place at the level of Jesus's person (thus the famous term "hypostatic union"). Jesus was not a stage mask behind which his human nature and his divine nature played out their various chemistries. Jesus was God-made-human, a seamless union, a single subject. Cyril was well aware of the philosophical complexities and conundrums of this, this joining of an infinite divinity with a finite humanity. He insisted this was an utter and incomprehensible mystery that could not be smoothed over with philosophical niceties.

In the meantime, Pope Celestine and a council of Italian bishops weighed in on Cyril's side, declaring Nestorius's view heretical, and authorizing Cyril to act on Rome's behalf in demanding a formal recantation from Nestorius. Cyril took advantage of this endorsement and composed his *Third Letter to Nestorius*. To this he attached a controversial set of twelve anathemas and demanded that Nestorius subscribe to them. These so-called *Twelve Chapters* were extreme statements that would have forced Nestorius to renounce and condemn his Antiochene tradition. When Antiochene theologians got hold of this document, they closed ranks and began a fierce opposition against Cyril. It sparked a pamphlet war, with each side branding the other as heretical.

This led to the Third Ecumenical Council, the Council of Ephesus, which was to open in June 431 (for excerpts of key texts, see appendix 2.2). Cyril arrived with fifty Egyptian bishops, as well as a troupe of monks, led by Shenoute of Atripe, abbot of the White Monastery (d. c.464). Shenoute was one of the pioneers of Coptic literature; he was also a ferocious iconoclast known for his violent dismantling of paganism. Nestorius arrived with sixteen bishops, but his principal allies, John of Antioch and the Syrian bishops, were delayed. Cyril suspected that John's delay was intentional—that he did not want to condemn a friend. Cyril was the senior cleric and, by custom, had the right to preside over the meeting. So he called the council to order, over the protests of a minority who supported Nestorius. Nestorius was then summoned, but he refused to attend the proceedings. So debate went on without him. First the Creed of Nicaea was read out, then Cyril's *Second Letter to Nestorius*, which was greeted by formal acclamations and approval. After this, Nestorius's reply to Cyril was read out, then denounced and declared blasphemous. The council of 200 bishops then voted to depose Nestorius. When John of Antioch and the Syrians arrived a week later, they were appalled by the fait accompli. They formed a counter-council of forty-three bishops and gathered at John's lodgings (since the churches of Ephesus were closed to them). There they denounced Cyril's *Twelve Chapters* and declared Cyril deposed. Both sides then appealed to the emperor, who initially put the bishops under house arrest while he considered the matter. To everyone's surprise, he upheld the decision of both meetings, declaring both Nestorius and Cyril deposed, and ordering their arrest and exile. He then ordered the council disbanded. But the 200 who supported Cyril refused to leave, and when the pope's delegates finally arrived, they threw their support to Cyril. A summit meeting of seven bishops from each side was convened before the emperor. Nestorius, in frustration, agreed to resign his see and return to his monastery in Antioch. He was allowed to go and was replaced by Maximian as bishop of Constantinople. Meanwhile, the tide turned in Cyril's favor. The bribes, mentioned earlier, helped, but the emperor seems to have been impressed by the stalwart majority who backed Cyril. In the end, he was released from arrest and was allowed to keep his post and return to Alexandria.

The Greek East remained divided in the wake of Ephesus. John of Antioch broke the stalemate in 433, drawing up a compromise entitled the *Formula of Reunion*. It accepted some of Cyril's concerns (Mary as *Theotokos*, unity of the person of Christ); but it also spoke of Christ as the "union of two natures" and in masterful fashion insisted that just as Christ was "one-in-being with the Father" (as Nicaea had said), so Christ was "one-in-being with us." Cyril, to the shock of hard-liners in his own camp, embraced the compromise and later defended it eloquently. Cyril had typically spoken of Christ's "one nature" (*mia physis*), but he could hear in John's *Formula* a way of speaking of Christ's "two natures" that did not chop Christ in two the way Nestorius's language had. Hard feelings on the Antiochene side remained. We have a sharply satirical letter from Theodoret, bishop of Cyrrhus, writing to the new bishop of Antioch, Domnus, announcing news of Cyril's death: "At last the villain has passed away. . . . His departure delights the survivors, but may bother the dead; there is some reason to fear . . . that the dead may send him back again to us. . . . Therefore great care must be taken to order the guild of the undertakers to place a very big and heavy stone on his grave to stop him from coming back here."[21]

Dioscorus and the Council of Chalcedon

Cyril's successor was Dioscorus (bp. 444–451). He had served as Cyril's archdeacon and won election over rivals from Cyril's family. Hard-liners in Cyril's camp bitterly resented his compromise and the *Formula of Reunion*. They sought to reverse things and resurrect Cyril's radical *Twelve Chapters*. Eutyches (d. 454), an elderly abbot in Constantinople, began advocating Cyril's "one nature" formula. He was summoned to a tribunal held by Flavian, bishop of Constantinople, on charges of heresy. Eutyches, while no theologian, had powerful political connections. His godson was Chrysaphius, one of the emperor's key advisors, and when Eutyches finally appeared before the tribunal, he was accompanied by Chrysaphius and armed soldiers. Flavian, despite the show of force, condemned Eutyches, judging him unorthodox. Eutyches appealed his case to bishops around the world, including Dioscorus in Alexandria and Pope Leo in Rome. In 449, a council was called to meet in Ephesus. Dioscorus ruthlessly manipulated the course of events: Eutyches was declared innocent, the *Formula of Reunion* was thrown out, and Flavian was arrested on a technicality and later died from the brutality of his arrest. When Pope Leo got word of the affair, he angrily drew on Jesus's denunciation in the temple: that what should have been a "house of prayer," Dioscorus had made a "den of thieves." Ever since, this Synod of Ephesus has been known as the Robber Council. Leo had composed a masterful response to the Christological question, his so-called *Tome*. He was convinced that it held the solution to the debate, and he was

TABLE 2.4. The Early Ecumenical Councils

Ecumenical council	Date	Theological issue	Victor(s)	The losing side	Conciliar texts	Key formulae
Nicaea	325	Divinity of Christ	Alexander of Alexandria	Arius	The *Creed* of Nicaea; *Letter to the Egyptian Church*	"True God from True God, one-in-being with the Father"
Constantinople	381	Divinity of the Holy Spirit	The Cappadocian Fathers	Pneumatomachians	The *Creed* of Constantinople	"Together with Father and Son, the Spirit is worshipped"
Ephesus	431	Humanity of Christ (unity)	Cyril of Alexandria	Nestorius	Cyril's *Second Letter to Nestorius*; John's *Formula of Reunion*	Mary as *Theotokos*; Christ as "one Son, one Lord"
Chalcedon	451	Humanity of Christ (natures)	Pope Leo I	Dioscorus of Alexandria, Eutyches	The *Definition*	Christ as "one person . . . in two natures"

angry when he learned that Dioscorus had made sure that the *Tome* was never read out.

In 450, Emperor Theodosius II died in a hunting accident, and the new Emperor Marcian called the Fourth Ecumenical Council, the Council of Chalcedon, in 451. This would prove to be the largest council of the early church. There Rome and Antioch joined forces, and Dioscorus found himself deposed. The council affirmed key documents: the Creed of Nicaea, the Creed of Constantinople, Cyril's *Second Letter to Nestorius*, John of Antioch's *Formula of Reunion*, and Leo's *Tome*. The council also drew on these documents, especially Leo's *Tome*, for its *Definition*, a terse formula that sought to balance the Christological insights of Alexandria, Antioch, and Rome. It insisted that Christ is "one person in two natures," "one-in-being with Father as to his divinity" and "one-in-being with us as to his humanity" (for the full text, see appendix 2.3; for an overview of this and the other early councils, see table 2.4).

The Council of Chalcedon proved a watershed event in the history of Christianity. To this day, Catholics, Protestants, and Greek Orthodox look back to Chalcedon's *Definition* as the official summary of the mystery of the person of Christ. But the Coptic Orthodox Church ultimately rejected it, leading it to break communion with both the Latin West and much of the Greek East. The Coptic Orthodox Church is sometimes called "monophysite" (for *monophysis*, "one nature")—as opposed to the "duophysite" ("two-nature") Christology of Chalcedon. The council marked a defeat for Egypt and its theology. Dioscorus died in exile in Gangra in 454. The new bishop of Alexandria, Proterius, had strong local ties and had served as archpriest, governing the church during Dioscorus's absence. But Proterius's support of the council proved his undoing. In 457, with the death of the Emperor Marcian, a mob captured Proterius and lynched him in the baptistery of the Caesarion. From this time until the Arab conquest in 639, the Egyptian Church remained divided between a Chalcedonian minority and a Monophysite majority, with ebbs and flows of power between them.

These divisions affected Egyptian monasteries and Egypt's place in international monasticism. Some monasteries had two churches, a Chalcedonian and a Monophysite. Some monasteries were Chalcedonian strongholds, such as Canopus, just east of Alexandria, while others were Monophysite, such as Enaton, nine miles west of Alexandria. In the aftermath of Chalcedon, Egyptian monasticism, while remaining vibrant locally, lost much of its international appeal. For much of the Christian world, memories of Egyptian monasticism remained locked away in the classic texts of the fourth and fifth centuries.

NOTES

1. For what follows, I have drawn mainly from the landmark study of R. P. C. Hanson, *The Search for the Christian Doctrine of God: the Arian Controversy, 318–381 AD* (Edinburgh: T & T Clark, 1988); and Thomas A. Kopecek, *A History of Neo-Arianism*, Patristic Monograph Series 8 (Cambridge, MA: Philadelphia Patristic Foundation, 1979). For additional studies, see the bibliography for chapter 2.

2. Mentioned by the Arian historian Philostorgius (quoted in Photius's *Epitome* 2.2). Cf. Athanasius, *Contra Arianos* 1.2 (PG 26:16; NPNF 2.4:307); *De Synodis* 15 (PG 26:705; NPNF 2.4:457).

3. Arius, *Letter to Alexander of Alexandria*, quoted in Athanasius, *De synodis* 16 (PG 26:709; trans. Stevenson, NE, 326).

4. Arius, *Thalia*, quoted in Athanasius, *Contra Arianos* 1.6 (PG 26:24; trans. Hanson, *Search*, 13).

5. Arius, *Thalia*, quoted in Athanasius, *Contra Arianos* 1.5 (PG 26:21; trans. Kopecek, *History of Neo-Arianism*, 22).

6. Arius, *Thalia*, quoted in Athanasius, *Contra Arianos* 1.5 (PG 26:21; trans. my own). Cf. Arius, *Letter to Eusebius of Nicomedia* (trans. Stevenson, NE, 325): "We are persecuted because we say, 'the Son had a beginning, but God is without beginning.' This is really the cause of our persecution; and, likewise, because we say that he is from nothing."

7. Arius, *Letter to Alexander of Alexandria* (trans. Stevenson, NE, 326): "God, being the cause of all things, is unbegun and altogether sole but the Son being begotten apart from time by the Father, and being created and found before ages, was not before his generation."

8. The favorite Arian prooftext was Proverb 8:22–31. See Hanson, *Search*, 560.

9. This thesis was first advanced by Robert C. Gregg and Dennis E. Groh, *Early Arianism: a View of Salvation* (Philadelphia: Fortress Press, 1981). While not accepted in its entirety, it has opened important perspectives on neglected elements of Arius' views and those (often incorrectly) associated with his views. For a discussion, see Hanson, *Search*, 96–121.

10. See Hanson, *Search*, 20.

11. Sozomen, *HE* 1.15 (PG 67:908; NPNF 2.2:252). See Kopecek, *Neo-Arianism*, 6–7.

12. Quoted in Socrates, *HE* 1.9 (PG 67:77–84; NPNF 2.2:12–13).

13. Socrates, *HE* 1.23 (PG 67:141–144; trans. NPNF 2.2:27).

14. Ammianus Marcellinus, *Res Gestae* 21.16.18 (LCL, 2:184).

15. Jerome, *Dial. contra Lucif.* 19 (trans. Stevenson, CCC, 46).

16. Edward R. Hardy, *Christian Egypt: Church and People. Christianity and Nationalism in the Patriarch of Alexandria* (New York: Oxford University Press, 1952), 47. For studies on Athanasius' life and thought, see the bibliography for chapter 2.

17. For the case against Athanasius, see Hanson, *Search*, 239–262. The most outspoken modern critic of Athanasius is Timothy D. Barnes, especially in his *Constantine and Eusebius* (Cambridge, MA: Harvard University Press, 1981), 230, in which he charges Athanasius with creating an "ecclesiastical Mafia" and claims that "like a modern gangster, he evoked widespread mistrust, proclaimed total innocence—and usually succeeded in evading conviction on specific charges." A spirited defense of Athanasius has been put forward by Duane W. H. Arnold, *The Early Episcopal Career of Athanasius of Alexandria* (Notre Dame: Notre Dame University Press, 1991). His study usefully traces the gamut of modern assessments and looks with care at each of the charges against Athanasius.

18. The *Papyrus 1914* was first published by H. I. Bell, *Jews and Christians in Egypt: The Jewish Troubles in Alexandria and the Athanasian Controversy* (London: The British Museum, 1924). The text and translation are found in Bell, 58–63. This papyrus seems to confirm reports of Athanasius' enemies found in Socrates, *HE* 2.22 and in Hilary, *De synodis* 4.53.

19. Timothy D. Barnes, *Athanasius and Constantius* (Cambridge, MA: Harvard University Press, 1993), 92. See Gregory of Nazianzus, *Oratio* 21.27–29 (SC 270:166–172); *Chronicon Athanasianum* 18 (SC 317:247; NPNF 4:504).

20. For studies of these three, see the bibliography for chapter 2.

21. Theodoret of Cyrrhus, *Ep.* 180 (PG 83:1489; trans. my own).

BIBLIOGRAPHY

The Council of Nicaea and the Arian Controversy

Remarkable recent studies have considerably revised older perspectives on the Arian controversy. The most thorough is R. P. C. Hanson, *The Search for the Christian Doctrine of God: The Arian Controversy, 318–381* (Edinburgh: T. & T. Clark, 1988). For a quick overview, see Manlio Simonetti, "Arius—Arians—Arianism," in *Encyclopedia of Early Christianity* 2nd ed., eds. Everett Ferguson, Michael P. McHugh, and Frederick W. Norris (New York: Garland, 1997) 1:76–78. See also:

Barnes, Michel R., and Daniel H. Williams, eds. *Arianism after Arius: Essays on the Development of the Fourth-Century Trinitarian Conflicts.* Edinburgh: T. & T. Clark, 1993.

Gregg, Robert C., ed. *Arianism: Historical and Theological Reassessments.* Patristic Monograph Series 11. Cambridge, Mass.: Philadelphia Patristic Foundation, 1985.

Kelly, J. N. D. *Early Christian Creeds.* 3rd ed. London: Longman, 1972.

Kopecek, Thomas A. *A History of Neo-Arianism.* Patristic Monograph Series 8. Cambridge, Mass.: Philadelphia Patristic Foundation, 1979.

Simonetti, Manlio. *La crisi ariana nel iv secolo.* Studia Ephemerides. Rome: Augustianum, 1975.

Studer, Basil. *Trinity and Incarnation: The Faith of the Early Church*, ed. Andrew Louth. Collegeville, Minn.: Liturgical Press, 1993.

Vaggione, Richard Paul. *Eunomius of Cyzicus and the Nicene Revolution*. Oxford Early Christian Studies. New York: Oxford University Press, 2001.

Williams, Daniel H. *Ambrose of Milan and the End of the Nicene-Arian Conflicts*. Oxford Early Christian Studies. New York: Oxford University Press, 1995.

Williams, Rowan. *Arius: Heresy and Tradition*. Rev. ed. Grand Rapids, Mich.: Wm. B. Eerdmans, 2002.

Athanasius: Career

The literature on Athanasius is vast and varied. A good starting point is the overview by David Brakke, "Athanasius," in *The Early Christian World*, ed. Philip F. Esler (New York: Routledge, 2000), 2:1102–1127. It is important to note that recent studies of Athanasius disagree with one another, sometimes sharply, about overall interpretation of Athanasius's character and many details of his career. Other valuable studies of Athanasius's career include:

Arnold, Duane Wade-Hampton. *The Early Episcopal Career of Athanasius of Alexandria*. Christianity and Judaism in Antiquity 6. Notre Dame: University of Notre Dame Press, 1991.

Barnes, Timothy D. *Athanasius and Constantius: Theology and Politics in the Constantinian Empire*. Cambridge, Mass.: Harvard University Press, 1993.

Brakke, David. *Athanasius and Asceticism*. Baltimore: Johns Hopkins University Press, 1998. [Note that the 1995 Oxford edition was published under the title *Athanasius and the Politics of Asceticism*.]

Elliott, T. G. *The Christianity of Constantine the Great*, esp. 271–320. Scranton, Pa.: University of Scranton Press, 1996.

Frend, W. H. C. "Athanasius as an Egyptian Christian Leader in the Fourth Century." In *Religion Popular and Unpopular in the Early Christian Centuries*, XVI:20–37. London: Variorum Reprints, 1976.

Hanson, R. P. C. *The Search for the Christian Doctrine of God: The Arian Controversy, 318–381 AD*, 239–273. Edinburgh: T. & T. Clark, 1988.

Kannengiesser, Charles. "Athanasius of Alexandria and the Ascetic Movement of His Time." In *Asceticism*, ed. Vincent Wimbush and Richard Valantasis, 479–492. New York: Oxford University Press, 1995.

Kannengiesser, Charles, ed. *Politique et théologie chez Athanase d'Alexandrie: actes du colloque de Chantilly, 23–25 septembre 1973*. Théologie historique 27. Paris: Beauchesne, 1974.

Martin, Annik. *Athanase d'Alexandrie et l'église d'Égypte au IVᵉ siècle (328–373)*. Collection de l'École française de Rome 216. Rome: École française de Rome, 1996.

Athanasius: Writings and Theology

The bulk of Athanasius's writings are found in PG 25–26; also Athanasius, *Werke*, 3 vols., ed. Hans-Georg Opitz (Berlin, 1935–1941). Many of his writings are available in English in a mid-nineteenth-century translation: Archibald Robertson, ed., *Select Writings and Letters of Athanasius, Bishop of Alexandria*, NPNF, 2nd ser. (reprint: Peabody, Mass.: Hendrickson, 1994). For an excellent edition of the Greek text and English translation of two of Athanasius's early works, see Athanasius, *"Contra Gentes" and "De*

Incarnatione," ed. R. W. Thomson, OECT (Oxford: Clarendon Press, 1971). For an over-view of his theology, see Khaled Anatolios, *Athanasius: The Coherence of His Thought* (New York: Routledge, 1998). An often-cited older account is that of Alois Grillmeier, *Christ in Christian Tradition*, rev. ed., trans. John Bowden, vol. 1, *From the Apostolic Age to Chalcedon, 451* (Atlanta: John Knox Press, 1975), 308–328. See also:

Hanson, R. P. C. *The Search for the Christian Doctrine of God: The Arian Controversy, 318–381 AD*, 417–458. Edinburgh: T. & T. Clark, 1988.

Louth, Andrew. "Athanasius' Understanding of the Humanity of Christ." *Studia Patristica* 16 (1985): 309–323.

Kannengiesser, Charles. *Athanase d'Alexandrie, évêque et écrivain: une lecture des traités Contre les ariens*. Theologie historique 70. Paris: Beauchesne, 1983.

―――. "Athanasius of Alexandria and the Foundation of Traditional Christology." *Theological Studies* 34 (1973): 103–113.

―――. *Le verbe de Dieu selon Athanase d'Alexandrie*. Paris: Desclée, 1990.

Lyman, J. Rebecca. *Christology and Cosmology: Models of Divine Activity in Origen, Eusebius, and Athanasius*. Oxford Theological Monographs. New York: Oxford University Press, 1993.

Meijering, E. P. "Athanasius on the Father as the Origin of the Son." In *God Being History: Studies in Patristic Philosophy*. Amsterdam: North-Holland, 1975.

Pettersen, Alvyn. *Athanasius*. Harrisburg, Pa.: Morehouse, 1995.

Roldanus, Johannes. *Le Christ et l'homme dans la théologie d'Athanase d'Alexandrie*. Studies in the History of Christian Thought 4. Leiden: E. J. Brill, 1977.

Widdicombe, Peter. *The Fatherhood of God from Origen to Athanasius*. Rev. ed. Oxford Theological Monographs. New York: Oxford University Press, 2000.

Theophilus, Cyril, and Dioscorus

For an introduction to the life and thought of Cyril, together with a selection of his writings, see Norman Russell, *Cyril of Alexandria*, Early Church Fathers (New York: Routledge, 2000). For a valuable study of Cyril's clash with Nestorius and of the Council of Ephesus, see John A. McGuckin, *St. Cyril of Alexandria: The Christological Controversy; Its History, Theology and Texts*, Supplements to Vigiliae Christianae 23 (Leiden: E. J. Brill, 1994). See also McGuckin's translation of one of Cyril's important Christological treatises: Saint Cyril of Alexandria, *On the Unity of Christ* (Crestwood, N.Y.: St. Vladimir's Seminary Press, 1995); this includes an excellent introduction. See also Lionel R. Wickham, ed., *Cyril of Alexandria: Selected Letters*, OECT (Oxford: Clarendon Press, 1983), which includes an edition of the Greek text with a facing English translation. Theophilus and Dioscorus have received much less attention, but discussion of their tumultuous careers appears in studies of Alexandria and Egyptian Christianity cited earlier. See also:

Davis, Leo Donald. *The First Seven Ecumenical Councils (325–787): Their History and Theology*. Collegeville, Minn.: Liturgical Press, 1983.

Frend, W. H. C. *The Rise of the Monophysite Movement: Chapters in the History of the Church in the Fifth and Sixth Centuries*. Cambridge: Cambridge University Press, 1972.

Grillmeier, Alois. *Christ in Christian Tradition.* Rev. ed. Trans. John Bowden. Vol. 1, *From the Apostolic Age to Chalcedon, 451.* Atlanta: John Knox Press, 1975.

McKinion, Steven A. *Words, Imagery, and the Mystery of Christ: A Reconstruction of Cyril of Alexandria's Christology.* Leiden: Brill, 2000.

Meyendorff, John. *Christ in Eastern Christian Thought.* Crestwood, N.Y.: St. Vladimir's Seminary Press, 1987.

APPENDIX 2.1

The Creed of the Council of Nicaea (325)

The Council of Nicaea was called to address the clash between Arius and his bishop, Alexander of Alexandria, over the divinity of Christ. The council met in 325 and was presided over by the first Christian emperor, Constantine (d. 338). We do not have any official minutes, or *acta*, from Nicaea as we do from later ecumenical councils. But we have reports from eyewitnesses, notably from Eusebius of Caesarea, the church historian, and from Athanasius, who at the time was Alexander's secretary. The wording of the famous and controversial creed is found in a number of ancient sources, notably in Athanasius's *Decrees of the Council of Nicaea* (*De decretis*), Socrates' *Church History*, Basil of Caesarea's *Letter* 125, and Rufinus's *Church History* 10.6. Here is the text; phrases in bold were intended to counter the views of Arius:

> We believe in one God, the Father almighty, maker of all things, visible and invisible, And in one Lord Jesus Christ, the Son of God, begotten from the Father, only-begotten, **that is, from the substance [*ousia*] of the Father,** God from God, light from light, **true God from true God, begotten not made, one-in-being [*homoousios*] with the Father,** through whom all things came into being, things in heaven and things on earth, who because of us human beings and because of our salvation came down and became incarnate, becoming human, suffered and rose again on the third day, ascended to the heavens, and will come to judge the living and the dead.
> And in the Holy Spirit.
> **But as for those who say, "There was 'when' he was not," and, "Before being born he was not,' and that "he came into existence out of nothing," or who assert that the Son of God is of a different hypostasis or substance [*ousia*], or is subject to alteration or change— these the catholic and apostolic Church anathematizes.**"

The Creed of Nicaea remains a standard of Christian orthodoxy to this day. The creed recited in many churches today, while often referred to as "the Nicene Creed," is actually that of the Council of Constantinople (381). There are two major differences between these two creeds: the Creed of Constantinople does not have the Creed of Nicaea's concluding anathemas of Arian slogans; and Nicaea has a bare affirmation of the Holy Spirit, while Constantinople adds phrases affirming that the Holy Spirit is "the Lord and giver of life, who proceeds from the Father, who together with the Father and Son is worshipped and glorified." For the Greek text and a thorough analysis, see J. N. D. Kelly, *Early Christian Creeds*, 3rd ed. (London: Longman, 1972), and R. P. C. Hanson, *The Search for the Christian Doctrine of God* (Edinburgh: T. & T. Clark, 1988).

APPENDIX 2.2

Texts from the Council of Ephesus (431)

The Council of Ephesus, numbered as the third ecumenical council, met in 431 to address the clash between Nestorius, bishop of Constantinople, and Cyril, bishop of Alexandria. The clash was sparked by Nestorius's campaign against calling Mary "Mother of God." The real issue was not Mary, but Christ. Nestorius had claimed that it was necessary to "divide the natures," insisting on the stark difference between Christ's divine nature and his human nature. Nestorius, therefore, insisted that Mary is best described as the "mother of the Man," not the "Mother of God." Cyril answered this in his *Second Letter to Nestorius*, which poses as a commentary on the Nicene Creed's phrase "became flesh, became man." This letter was accepted by the Council of Ephesus as its official statement, and this endorsement was repeated by the Council of Chalcedon (451). Here are a few excerpts:

WHAT CYRIL OPPOSED

Here Cyril lists what he sees as wrong-headed positions, such as adoptionism—positions that, while they are a caricature of what Nestorius actually held, were ones that Cyril believed that Nestorius's views led toward:

> We do not say that the Word (*Logos*) became flesh by changing his nature, nor that he was transformed into a complete human being composed out of soul and body. . . . He did not become a human being simply by an act of will or "good pleasure," any more than he did so by assuming [= taking on] a person. . . . It is not the case that an ordinary human being was first born of the holy Virgin and that the Word descended upon him later. . . . We do not worship a human being in conjunction with the Word, lest a division appear to slip in because of the phrase "in conjunction with". . . . Again it is not the case that there are two Sons enthroned together; rather there is one (Son), on account of the [Word's] union with the flesh. If we set aside this union [of Word and flesh] . . . , we fall into the assertion of two Sons. . . . (Cyril of Alexandria, *Second Letter to Nestorius* 3–6)

CHRIST AS THE HYPOSTATIC UNION

Here Cyril gives his classic articulation that the union of human and divine are united at the level of the person of Christ—the "hypostatic union":

On the contrary, we say that in an unspeakable and incomprehensible way, the Word (*Logos*) united to himself, in his person (*hypostasis*), flesh enlivened by a rational soul, and in this way became a human being and has been designated "Son of man." . . . Since the union took place in the womb, he is said to have undergone a fleshly birth by making his own the birth of the flesh which belonged to him. (Cyril of Alexandria, *Second Letter to Nestorius* 3–4).

MARY AS *THEOTOKOS*

And for the Word to become flesh is nothing other than for him to "share in flesh and blood as we do" (Heb. 2:14), to make his own a body from among us, and to be born of woman as a human being. He did not depart from his divine status nor did he cease to be born of the Father. He continued to be what he was, even in taking on flesh. This is what the teaching of the correct faith everywhere proclaims. And this is how we shall find the holy fathers conceived things. Accordingly, they boldly called the holy Virgin "the mother of God" (*Theotokos*), not because the nature of the Word or the divinity took the start of its existence in the holy Virgin but because the holy body born of her, possessed as it was of a rational soul, and to which the Word was hypostatically united, is said to have had a fleshly birth. (Cyril of Alexandria, *Second Letter to Nestorius* 7)

After receiving support from Pope Innocent, Cyril sent his radical *Third Letter to Nestorius*. To this he attached a series of twelve anathemas. These so-called *Twelve Chapters* would rouse Antiochene theologians against Cyril. These were read at the council, but not accepted in any official level. Perhaps the most controversial was the fourth, which disallowed a traditional way of interpreting the Gospels.

MARY AS *THEOTOKOS*

If anyone does not confess that Emmanuel is God in truth, and because of this does not confess that the Holy Virgin is the Mother of God (for she bore according to the flesh the Word-of-God-made-flesh), let him be anathema. (Cyril of Alexandria, *Twelve Chapters* 1)

BIBLICAL INTERPRETATION

If anyone attributes the sayings in the Gospels and the apostolic writings to two persons, that is, to two *hypostases*, . . . and ascribes some to a human being considered separately from the Word of God, and ascribes others, as proper to God, . . . let him be anathema. (Cyril of Alexandria, *Twelve Chapters* 4)

AGAINST NESTORIUS'S "ADOPTIONISM"

> If anyone dares to say that Christ is a God-bearing human being,
> and not God in truth, the one Son by nature, in so far as the Word
> was made flesh and has flesh and blood just as we do, let him be
> anathema. . . . If anyone says that Jesus as a human being was acti-
> vated by the Word of God and that the glory of the only-begotten
> was attributed as if the only-begotten was separate from him, let
> him be anathema. (Cyril of Alexandria, *Twelve Chapters* 5, 7)

A CRUCIFIED GOD

> If anyone does not confess that the Word of God suffered in the
> flesh, and was crucified in the flesh, and tasted death in the flesh,
> and became the firstborn from the dead, since he is life and life-
> giving as God, let him be anathema. (Cyril of Alexandria, *Twelve
> Chapters* 12)

The Council left bitter divisions between Alexandrians and Antiochenes.
The formal resolution came with a sort of theological peace treaty, John of
Antioch's *Formula of Reunion*. It granted the legitimacy of calling Mary "Mother
of God" and acknowledged Cyril's concern over the unity of Christ. But John
insisted that Christ's "two natures" be acknowledged. He even applied to Nicaea's watchword "one-in-being" (*homoousios*) to Christ's humanity, insisting
that Christ is "one-in-being with us according to his humanity." Cyril, to the
surprise of his extremist followers, accepted John's statement. Here is the text:

THE ANTIOCHENE RESPONSE

> We confess that our Lord Jesus Christ, the only begotten Son of
> God, is perfect God and perfect man, of a rational soul and body,
> begotten before ages from the Father according to his divinity, and
> that, in recent days, he was born for us and for our salvation from
> the Virgin Mary according to his humanity, one-in-being with the
> Father himself according to divinity and one-in-being with us ac-
> cording to his humanity, for a union was made of his two natures.
> We confess one Christ, one Son, one Lord. With this understanding
> of a union without fusion we confess that the Holy Virgin is the
> Mother of God (*Theotokos*), because God the Word was made flesh
> and made human, and from his very conception he united to him-
> self a temple taken from her. And we know that theologians regard
> some of the gospel and apostolic sayings regarding the Lord as com-
> mon, that is, they pertain to the "one person," and that theologians
> divide other sayings as they pertain to the "two natures," and they
> apply those belonging to God to Christ's divinity, but [apply] the
> lowly ones to his humanity. (John of Antioch, *Formula of Reunion*
> (433)):

APPENDIX 2.3

The *Definition* of the Council of Chalcedon (451)

The Council of Chalcedon, numbered as the Fourth Ecumenical Council, marked the climax of years of debate over the relationship of the divine and human in Christ. The *Definition* is now seen by Orthodox, Catholics, and most Protestants as the landmark statement about the Person of Christ. The Coptic Church would ultimately reject it, seeing it as divisive of the unity of the Person of Christ and as unfaithful to the theological tradition of Cyril of Alexandria. The Coptic alternative is often described as "monophysite" (or "one nature") as opposed to Chalcedon's "two-nature" formula.

CHRIST AS ONE PERSON IN TWO NATURES

Following, therefore, the holy fathers, we confess one and the same Son, our Lord Jesus Christ, and we all agree in teaching that this very same Son is complete in his divinity and the very same one [is] complete in his humanity, truly God and truly a human being, this very same one, composed of a rational soul and a body, one-in-being [*homoousios*] with the Father as to his divinity and one-in-being [*homoousios*] with us—the very same one—as to his humanity, like us in all things but sin. As for his divinity, he was born from the Father before the ages, but as for his humanity, the very same one was born in the last days from the Virgin Mary, the Mother of God, for our sake and for our salvation: one and the same Christ, Son, Lord, Only-Begotten, acknowledged to be without confusion, without change, without division, without separation in two natures, since the difference of the natures is not destroyed because of the union but, on the contrary, the character of each nature is preserved and comes together in one person [*prosopon*] and one hypostasis, not divided or torn into two persons but one and the same Son and only-begotten God, Logos, Lord Jesus Christ. (Council of Chalcedon, *Definition*)

PART II

Antony and Pachomius

3

The *Life of Antony*: Text and Context

The "Wrath" of 356

In January 356, on a remote mountain in the vast stretch of desert between the Nile River and the Red Sea, an old hermit died and was buried in an unknown spot by two disciples. It should have been an anonymous end to an anonymous life. But the hermit Antony had an international reputation. Word of his death spread rapidly. Serapion, a former disciple and bishop of the delta town of Thmuis, writing to two friends, spoke not as though Antony's mountain were some distant outpost in a no-man's land. Rather, it had been the epicenter of Egypt's life. And so with Antony's death came the expected aftershocks:

> As soon as this earth's great elder, the blessed Antony, who prayed for the whole world, departed, everything has been torn apart and is in anguish, and the Wrath devastates Egypt. . . . While he was truly on earth, he extended his hands and prayed and spoke with God all day long. He did not let the Wrath descend on us. Lifting up his thoughts, he kept it from coming down. But now that those hands are closed, no one else can be found who might halt the violence of the Wrath . . . that may devastate the whole region. . . . I write to you therefore because the churches are filled with desolation, and the city streets are filled with blasphemies. Many crimes, fornication, all sorts of filth fill our city. . . . The source of the corruption: the mad minds of the Arians. . . . The Church of God has no ministers, . . . the sanctuaries stand deserted. . . . People have left the churches deserted, empty.[1]

The "Wrath" Serapion speaks of here began a month after Antony's death, in February 356. It began when imperial troops, by order of the Emperor Constantius, tried to arrest the wily and popular bishop of Alexandria, Athanasius.

By 356, Athanasius had already had a long and controversial career. But the latest round of troubles began when his imperial patron, Constans, was assassinated in 350. In May 353, Serapion headed an Egyptian delegation to Milan to defend Athanasius. A few weeks later, an imperial summons reached Athanasius, "inviting" him to appear personally before the Emperor Constantius. Athanasius seized on an ambiguity in the text, that the invitation was granting a request that Athanasius himself had made. He demurred, noting that he had made no such request, and while he greatly appreciated the invitation, it would be wrong for him to leave his pressing duties in Alexandria. As one scholar has noted, "Constantius had met his match in diplomatic evasion."[2] A council at Arles later that year declared Athanasius deposed and recognized George of Cappadocia as the new bishop of Alexandria. But Athanasius held his ground. Eventually, a council was held in Milan in 355. It was a stormy affair. Leading supporters of Athanasius and of the Nicene Creed—Eusebius of Vercelli, Dionysius of Milan, and Lucifer of Cagliari—were exiled. After Pope Liberius (d. 366) wrote a letter supporting them, he was kidnapped and jailed. Another outspoken Nicene, Hilary of Poitiers (c. 315–364), was exiled the next year. Constantius regarded Athanasius's refusal of his summons as high treason and ordered his arrest.

On the night of February 8, 356, Athanasius was presiding over a vigil service being held at one of the main churches of the city, the Church of Saint Theonas.[3] The military commander, Duke Syrianus, surrounded the church with soldiers—more than 5000, according to Athanasius's account. The congregation was understandably frightened. To prevent panic, Athanasius remained in his chair and had the deacon chant a psalm, and the congregation answered with the steady refrain: "For his mercy will endure forever." All at once, the soldiers broke in, swords drawn and arrows flying. Athanasius claims he stayed in the sanctuary until the last possible moment, until most had fled. Then in the chaos, he was whisked away by his clergy and by "the monks who were there with us."[4]

For nearly six years, he was an outlaw, pursued by imperial police. Rufinus of Aquileia, who visited Alexandria around 370, reports the vigor that authorities used:

> Athanasius was now a fugitive at large in the whole world, and there
> remained for him no safe place to hide. Tribunes, governors, counts,
> and even armies were deployed by imperial order to hunt him
> down. Rewards were offered to informers to bring him in alive if
> possible, or at least his head. Thus the whole power of the empire
> was directed in vain against the man with whom God was.[5]

The search went far and wide. Far to the south, in the Thebaid, the Pachomian monastery of Pbow found itself suddenly surrounded one night by a military detachment. The commanding officer, a duke named Artemios, treated the matter as a military operation, ordering that no monk be allowed to leave the monastery grounds under penalty of death. He then entered the monastery, battle-ax in hand and surrounded by bodyguards and archers, announcing: "Athanasius, the archbishop, is the enemy of the emperor. . . . We have heard that he is hiding among you."[6] The cells were searched, but Athanasius was not to be found. This time on the run became the stuff of legends. Later literature would tell picaresque stories of near misses and spectacular escapes.[7] Most of the time, it seems, he moved among the desert monks. They hid him and became his eyes and ears, a sort of intelligence network, enabling him to keep abreast of affairs and to administer the church from underground.

Back in Alexandria, there was the "Wrath" that Serapion's letter referred to. Athanasius and the anonymous *Historia Acephala* describe a reign of terror. There were violent searches and seizures. Houses of wealthy supporters were confiscated or simply torn down. As Athanasius complained: "Where is there a house which they did not ravage? Where is there a family they did not plunder on pretence of searching for their opponents? . . . What tomb did they not open, pretending they were seeking for Athanasius, though their sole object was to plunder and spoil all that came in their way?"[8] Pagans took advantage of the power vacuum and ransacked the recently completed Great Church, seizing its furniture and curtains for a great bonfire. Bishops and consecrated virgins loyal to Athanasius were roughed up, jailed, even tortured. And the government-subsidized bread supply, once distributed by the churches, was denied to the city's destitute. Through it all, despite threats and brutality, he escaped betrayal. As R. P. C. Hanson notes, "The fact that all attempts to arrest Athanasius failed is a tribute to the remarkable and widespread popularity which he had attained among the ordinary people not only of Alexandria, but of Egypt."[9]

This time on the run proved to be a period of great literary productivity. He defended his career and chronicled his battles in both the *Apology for Flight* and *Apology to Constantius* as well as in his scurrilous "secret" *History of the Arians*. Two other treatises, the *Letter to the Bishops of Egypt and Libya* and *On the Councils of Ariminum and Seleucia*, warned ominously of new "Arian" creeds that bishops would be required to sign on pain of banishment. Against this, he argued—as he had throughout the 350s—that the Creed of the Council of Nicaea represented the best statement of the divinity of Christ. During this same exile, Athanasius got a letter from his old friend Serapion asking for advice on how to answer arguments posed by some who denied the divinity of the Holy Spirit. Athanasius took on this new theological question in his *Letters Concerning the Holy Spirit* and in so doing pioneered a theology that came to fruition a few years later in the writings of a new generation of Nicenes, the Cappadocian fathers (Basil of Caesarea, Gregory of Nazianzus, and Gregory of Nyssa).

During this same desert exile, sometime between 356 and 358, Athanasius composed the first biography of a monk, the remarkable *Life of Antony*. This work, usually known by its Latin title, *Vita Antonii*, would become a classic almost overnight. It created a new genre of Christian literature: the life of a saint. Although Christians had composed accounts of their heroes before this, none would prove so popular or influential. And its popularity drew international attention not simply to Antony, but also to Egypt, its monks, and its emerging monastic institutions. Its publication marked the beginning of the literature of the desert fathers.

A Physician for Egypt

The *Life of Antony* is no modern biography.[10] Closer in spirit to *Beowulf* or, for that matter, *Raiders of the Lost Ark*, it is a tale of high adventure, of pitched battles against nefarious supernatural forces, set within an exotic landscape (for an outline, see table 3.1; for a chronology, see table 3.2).

The Call

According to the *Life*, Antony was an uneducated Copt. He was raised Christian and grew up in a village along the Nile River.[11] His parents had died when he was only eighteen or twenty, leaving him with weighty responsibilities: a younger sister to care for and a large family farm—some 200 acres, according to one modern estimate.[12] By local standards, he was a wealthy man. One day, while walking to church, he found himself mulling over the way the earliest Christians had laid all they possessed at the apostles' feet, that it might be distributed to each according to need. Then, in church, he heard the Gospel reading in which Jesus said to the rich young man: "If you would be perfect, go, and sell what you have and give it to the poor, and you will have treasure in heaven" (Matt. 19:21). It touched Antony deeply. He saw himself in the reading—*he* was the rich young man to whom Jesus was speaking. So, unlike the rich young man of the Gospels, Antony acted "immediately": he gave away his lands, sold off his goods, and gave most proceeds to the poor. He set aside a bit for his sister and sent her to "respected and faithful virgins" to be raised "in virginity."[13]

Having renounced all, Antony then apprenticed himself to an old man from a nearby village in order to practice the "solitary life." Athanasius makes an interesting remark at this point: "There were not yet many monasteries in Egypt, and no monk knew at all the great desert, but each of those wishing to give attention to his life disciplined himself in isolation, not far from his own village."[14] This is one of many easily overlooked but telling passages that dot the text. Although Antony eventually earned the epithet "father of monks," Athanasius does *not* portray him as the first. Egypt already had its monasteries (*monastēria*), at least in the sense of hermitages.[15] What made Antony unusual, according to Athanasius, was not his ascetic lifestyle, but where he practiced it: no longer at the fringe of one's home village, but in "the great desert." The fact that on the fringe of Egyptian villages there existed a recognizable class of ascetics—Athanasius calls them "men of zeal"—seems a tantalizing indicator of more ancient modes of ascetical Christian living.

TABLE 3.1. Outline of the *Life of Antony*

Preface	Letter to foreign monks
Part 1	Chapters 1–7: Beginnings of Ascetical Life
	#1: Youth of Antony
	#2: Call of the Gospel
	#3–4: Apprenticeship in the ascetical life
	#5–6: Sexual temptations
	#7: Antony's ascetical routine
	Chapters 8–14: *Anachōresis*
	#8–10: Antony in the tomb
	#11: Antony moves to the desert
	#12–13: Antony in the desert fort
	#14: Antony emerges; the desert becomes a city
	Chapters 15–48: Antony as Father of Monks
	#15: Antony and disciples cross crocodile-infested canal at Arsinoë
	#16–43: Antony's speech to the monks on demons and discernment of spirits
	#44: Monastic settlement as heavenly city
	#45: Monastic life & the care of the body
	#46: Persecution of Maximin; Antony in Alexandria supporting martyrs
	#47: Daily martyrdom of asceticism
	#48: Cure of military officer's daughter
Part 2	Chapters 49–55: From Alexandria to Inner Mountain
	#49–53: Antony establishes himself at Inner Mountain
	#54–55: Vision of monks in distress; instructs visitors
	Chapters 56–66: Miraculous Healings and Visions
	Chapters 67–88: Virtues of Antony
	#67: Humility: respect for clergy; cheerful face, calm of soul
	#68–71: Orthodoxy: denounces Melitians and Arians
	#72–80: Wisdom of illiterate: discussion with pagan philosophers
	#81: Letters to and from emperors
	#82: Vision of mules kicking altar
	#84: Words to judges
	#85–86: Words to military: the persecution and death of Balacius
	#87–88: Antony as physician given to Egypt
	Chapters 89–93: Death of Antony
	#89–90: Final address to monks at Outer Mountain
	#91–92: Final address to two disciples at Inner Mountain
	#93: Body undiminished; international reputation
Conclusion	Chapter 94: Encouraging reading of *Life of Antony* to monks and pagans

Asceticism

Antony's apprenticeship included rigorous training. The term Athanasius uses for this, *ascēsis*, is better translated "exercise regimen" than "asceticism," for it was really a sports term before it became a monastic one.[16] The routine Antony adopted was as physically demanding as any athlete's. First, he spent the day doing manual labor (such as weaving baskets) to support himself.[17] Second, he practiced "watchfulness," spending whole nights without sleeping, in vigilant prayer. And when he did sleep, his bed was a rush mat, or even the bare ground. Third, he maintained an austere diet: bread, salt, water, no meat, no wine. He ate at most once a day, and sometimes fasted so that he ate only

TABLE 3.2. The Life of Antony

c. 251	Birth of Antony
271	Antony embarks on ascetic life
285	Antony enters the desert fort
304	Beginnings of the Melitian Schism
306	Antony leaves the fort to train disciples
311	Persecution of Maximin Daia; Antony comes to Alexandria
313	Antony goes to Inner Mountain
325	Council of Nicaea
338	Antony in Alexandria to denounce Arians
345	Death of Balacius during attempt to arrest Antony
356	Death of Antony
356	Athanasius flees to desert for third exile
c.357	Athanasius writes *Life of Antony* (*Vita Antonii*)
360s	First Latin translation of *Life of Antony*
370	Evagrius of Antioch publishes second Latin translation of *Life*
376	Jerome publishes *Life of Paul of Thebes*
386	Conversion of Augustine in Milan after hearing story of Antony

The dating of key events in the life of Antony depends on the admittedly disputable chronology given by Athanasius.

every other day or even less often. Fourth, he practiced the "weighing" of his "thoughts," a technique of introspection that enabled him to attend to, without being seduced by, the flood of feelings and memories that might divert him from his single-minded purpose. Fifth, Antony "prayed unceasingly." This echoes a Pauline text, 1 Thessalonians 5:17, often cited in desert literature, leaving one to wonder if later techniques of unceasing prayer had early roots. Finally, Athanasius adds that Antony, while uneducated (or perhaps illiterate), absorbed what he heard from readings of scripture so that for him "memory took the place of books."[18]

Temptations

During this apprenticeship, he faced his first temptations (see figure 3.1). He was haunted by memories—of his sister, of possessions he had given away. He missed the pleasures of food and of relaxing with friends. And he stared hard at the harsh life he had chosen and was haunted by thoughts of the long years that stretched out before him. In this way, the devil raised in Antony's mind "a great dust cloud of considerations."[19] This marked the beginnings of a "wrestling match" in which, according to Athanasius, the devil "saw his own weakness in the face of Antony's resolve, and saw that he instead was being thrown for a fall by the sturdiness of this contestant."[20] So the devil turned to sex, "his first ambush against the young." Antony found it a struggle. Others apparently could see it: that he was so troubled "in the daytime that even those who watched were aware of the bout." When fantasies lost their power over him, the devil took visible form—first as a beguiling seductive temptress and then in the guise of a black boy, the spirit of fornication embodied. The latter figure—a troubling instance of ancient racist stereotypes—symbolized that the

FIGURE 3.1. The theme of the temptations of Saint Antony would
become a favorite one in Christian art, especially during the late Middle
Ages and early Renaissance. *Saint Anthony Tormented by Demons* is a
famous engraving by the German artist Martin Schongauer, c. 1475.
(Metropolitan Museum of Art, Rogers Fund, 1920. [20.5.2])

devil was "black of mind and powerless like a child."[21] Antony fended off the
assaults and never again faced sexual temptations.

After his apprenticeship, Antony shifted the battleground, from the fringe
of the village to the nearby necropolis. He entered one of the crypts and had
his friend close the door on him. The scene has all the makings of a gothic
tale or a Hollywood horror movie. Athanasius does not disappoint. At night,
the inner chamber of the tomb shook violently, as though by an earthquake.
Demons slithered out of the walls, disguised as beasts—lions, bears, leopards,
snakes, scorpions—and pummeled Antony. His first night battle in the tomb
left him badly beaten. When a friend came to deliver bread, he found Antony

motionless, speechless, as if dead. The friend carried him to the village church and laid him on the floor. Relatives and friends gathered round and kept vigil. When Antony recovered, around midnight, he found all except his friend asleep and returned to the tomb to renew the fight. Once inside, he taunted the devil, like a prizefighter who had revived after a tough first round: "Here I am—Antony! I do not run from your blows, for if you give me more, nothing shall separate me from the love of Christ."[22] Again he was beaten up but somehow managed to keep control of his psyche. Then, according to Athanasius, "the Lord did not forget the wrestling of Antony." A light beam pierced the roof, and at once the demons vanished and the pain ceased. Antony addressed the vision of light: "Where were you? Why didn't you appear in the beginning, so that you could stop my distresses?" The voice answered him: "I was here, Antony, but I waited to watch your struggle. And now, since you persevered and were not defeated, I will be your helper forever, and I will make you famous everywhere."[23]

Anachōresis

At the age of thirty-five, Antony moved out of the necropolis and into the desert. He took up residence in an abandoned military fortress, barricading himself inside. It had water, and he brought enough bread for six months. There he became a hermit, an anchorite. That is the term Athanasius uses: Antony had committed *anachōresis* ("withdrawal").[24] The term in its ordinary secular meaning could imply withdrawing from any of a range of things, whether retiring from politics or retreating from battle. It also meant tax evasion—skipping town before the tax collector arrived. But in time, the term would acquire a religious meaning: that one had "withdrawn from the world." According to Athanasius, Antony's "withdrawal" to the desert fort lasted twenty years. Friends would drop off supplies of bread and stand outside and listen with curiosity to the terrifying barrage of noise inside, that turned out to be the clatter of demons. Eventually, would-be disciples came and tore down the door. The description of Antony's emergence from the desert fortress is famous:

> Antony came forth as though from some sanctuary, a mystic initiate, mystery-taught and God-inspired. This then was the first time he left the fortress and was seen by those who had come out. When they saw him, they were amazed to see that his body had kept its same condition, neither fat from lack of physical exercise, nor emaciated from fasting and battling with demons, but was just as they had known him before his withdrawal.[25]

Not only did he emerge physically unchanged; he now possessed a mysterious inner tranquility, visible in his face. His very presence was enough to work healings in some who were there.

The Desert a City

Athanasius then portrays this "God-inspired" Antony as leader of a budding monastic movement. In one of the most famous sentences of the *Life*, Athanasius says: "And so, from then on, there were monasteries in the mountains, and the desert was made a city by monks, who left their own people and registered themselves for the citizenship in the heavens."[26] We in the twenty-first century may not easily appreciate the novelty of this, for we are used to bustling desert cities such as Phoenix or Las Vegas. But these are recent creations, impossible to sustain without contemporary technology. Certainly, no one in the fourth century thought of the desert as a place to build a city. It had no water and therefore no life. To make a city in a desert was an absurdity. As Peter Brown has noted, the monks "had settled on the social equivalent of an Antarctic continent, reckoned from time immemorial to be a blank space on the map of Mediterranean society—a no man's land that flanked the life of the city, flouted organized culture, and held up a permanent alternative to the crowded and relentlessly disciplined life of the villages."[27]

At this point in the story, Antony delivers a long speech to his monastic disciples. It forms a quarter of the work, from chapter 16 to chapter 43. This often seems odd to modern audiences, not used to ancient literary habits. Ancient culture greatly valued rhetoric. Speech-making was a highly cultivated artform and an important type of entertainment. Ancient readers would have both expected and enjoyed such an oratorical interlude. Antony's oration is in part an exhortation encouraging the monks "not to lose heart" because of the rigors of the solitary life. But mostly it is an instruction on demonology, detailing the origins of demons, the physics of their wispy bodies, the stratagems they use, and the techniques of counterintelligence monks need in order to unmask and repel their attacks (see appendix 3.1 and 3.2 for other accounts of the monastic spirituality of Antony and his early disciples).

Daily Martyrdom

After this speech on demons and demonology, Athanasius returns to the story. He describes how Antony, upon hearing of the brutal persecution of Maximin Daia in 311, decided to go to Alexandria that he might "enter the combat, or look upon those that do."[28] There Antony displayed considerable bravado. He openly served the confessors already jailed or sentenced to the mines; he attended trials and stood prominently in the courtroom galleries, hoping to draw attention to himself (by wearing a clean tunic!); he even accompanied those who were to be martyred to the place of execution. Athanasius portrays him as bold, yet just restrained enough that he could not be accused of seeking voluntary martyrdom.

When the persecution ended, Antony was "grieved" that he had not been martyred. He "withdrew" again to his cell and "was there daily being martyred by his conscience, and doing battle in the contests of the faith."[29] Athanasius claims, in essence, that Antony was inventing a new style of martyrdom, the "daily" martyrdom of asceticism; and the athletic and military metaphors once applied to the martyrs would now be applied to Antony, that he did "battle" in "contests of faith." Here we see the beginnings of a stock motif: that monks were the successors to the martyrs.

Inner Mountain

No sooner had Antony withdrawn to his cell than he again attracted a following. His first impulse was to catch a boat and go up the Nile to the Thebaid. But a voice "from above" told him to go to "the Inner Mountain." So he joined some Bedouin nomads and traveled three days into the Eastern Desert. There he found a high hill that had an oasis, even a few date palms. "Then Antony, as if stirred by God, fell in love with the place. . . . Looking on it as his own home, from that point forward he stayed in that place."[30] This so-called Inner Mountain may have been Mount Qulzum, some thirty kilometers from the Red Sea, where today one finds the Monastery of Saint Antony (Dayr Anba Antuniyus).[31] There he planted a vegetable garden and routinely defeated new attacks from demons who appeared, among other things, as a pack of hyenas or a strange donkey-legged man. No sooner did he seem to settle in his furthest remove than he became, as Athanasius portrays him, intensely active. Antony again busied himself teaching fellow monks. And he continued to travel widely, alternating especially between the Inner Mountain and his cell at the Outer Mountain, probably Mount Pispir, near the Nile. Once he even ventured into Alexandria.

The Thaumaturge

At this juncture, Antony emerges as a *thaumaturge*, a wonder-worker. The *Life*, like the gospels themselves, recounts numerous miracles, great and small: the healing of a girl whose eyes and ears secreted a worm-producing mucus; the cure of a demoniac who ate his own excrement and of another who smelled like rotten fish; even an eyewitness account in which Athanasius describes Antony's healing of a girl near the city gates of Alexandria.[32] Antony did not use the incantations or charms employed by run-of-the-mill magicians. Instead, he healed "without issuing commands, but by praying and calling on the name of Christ, so it was clear to all that it was not he who did this, but the Lord bringing his benevolence to effect through Antony and curing those who were afflicted."[33] The wonders Antony worked included nature miracles. Once, when he and some followers wanted to cross the canal of Arsinoë, they found it teeming with crocodiles. Antony simply prayed, and the crocodiles kindly allowed the monks to cross without incident.[34]

The Sage

Antony, though unlettered, earned an international reputation for wisdom. When some philosophers came out to test him, he dazzled them with his command of Neoplatonic philosophy, lecturing them on the Logos and on the origin of the soul and its natural state.[35] He also gave them an apologia for Christianity, chiding them, as pagans, for worshiping creation rather than the Creator and for confusing verbal dexterity with wisdom. Finally, he challenged them to a duel: to see whose religion could heal some demoniacs. But, as he pointed out, Greek dialectic and syllogisms were not very good at effecting cures. So he then turned to the demoniacs, made the sign of the cross over them, and instantly they were healed. The philosophers left amazed. According to Athanasius, Antony's wisdom stemmed from more than shrewd native intelligence. It came from mysterious illuminations he received while in his mountain solitude. This image of Antony as the wise illiterate, the "God-taught" (*theodidaktos*), was to capture the imagination of the fourth century.[36]

Antony's reputation for wisdom attracted requests from judges for help at evaluating court cases and lawsuits. Athanasius gives this an interesting edge. Antony not only aids the judges, but warns them "to value justice over everything else, and to fear God, and to realize that by the judgment with which they judged, they themselves would be judged."[37]

Antony found himself consulted not just by philosophers and judges. Even emperors—Constantine and his two sons—sent him letters. Antony's disciples encouraged him to respond, but he was reluctant. Antony was not impressed by imperial favor: "Do not consider it marvelous if a ruler writes to us for he is a man. Marvel, instead, that God wrote the law for mankind, and has spoken to us through his own Son."[38] To say, as Antony does here, that the emperor is just "a man" is an extraordinary statement, one that would never have been made by average citizens of the Roman Empire. Scholars have wondered whether this reflects Athanasius's situation as an outlaw pursued by imperial police. But it is a statement that appears in the mouth of more than one holy man and might accurately reflect desert sensibilities, a sort of prophetic detachment ready to debunk any human authority that loses sight of the kingship of God.[39] When Antony's disciples persuaded him to answer the emperors' letters, he did not mince words. The emperors needed to consider the "coming judgment" of Christ, who "alone is true and eternal ruler," and so they had better be "men of human concern, and give attention to justice and to the poor."[40]

The Visionary and Prophet

Antony is also portrayed as the recipient of visions and the possessor of mystical foreknowledge. He routinely knew in advance who was coming to visit him and why; he knew the exact moment that Amoun, the great founder of the monastic settlement of Nitria, died; Antony even predicted his own death.[41] His mystical powers could have political consequences. Once, in 345, the commander of the Roman military in Egypt, a man named Balacius, had lent his support to Athanasius's Arian replacement, Gregory of Cappadocia, using strong-arm tactics against Athanasian loyalists while Athanasius was in exile in the Latin West. Balacius was accused of having virgins beaten and monks flogged. Word of this reached Antony, who sent a letter warning: "I see the Wrath coming upon you. Stop persecuting Christians, then, that the Wrath may not overtake you—for even now it is coming upon you!" Balacius threw the letter on the ground, spat on it, then rounded up a search party to go out and arrest Antony. On the way there, one of his own horses turned against him, bit him, and, when he had fallen to the ground, attacked him. He died three days later, ominously fulfilling Antony's prophecy.[42]

Another instance was reported to Athanasius by Serapion of Thmuis, who was visiting his old teacher. Two years before his death, Antony slipped into an ecstatic trance and had a troubling vision foretelling of the violence that would devastate Alexandria in 356. He saw a Eucharistic table surrounded by a circle of mules, who kicked it furiously, madly. This he interpreted as "the Wrath" that would overtake the church; the mules were the Arians who attacked the church with the violence of "irrational beasts." He then prophesied that "just as the Lord has been angry, so again he will heal" and that the persecuted and exiled would be restored.[43]

Last Days

According to the Life, Antony died at the age of 105. Athanasius presents him giving two farewell speeches before dying, one to his disciples at the Outer Mountain and another to those at the Inner Mountain. Their messages are similar: keep up the discipline, keep vigilant watch over thoughts, and, above all, shun schismatics and heretics. He also insisted that his body not be treated in the traditional Egyptian way, mummified and laid out in a well-furnished chamber. Instead, he wanted to be buried, as had been done with the Old Testament patriarchs and with Jesus. Antony had few belongings but willed that one of his sheepskin garments and his cloak be given to Athanasius and his other sheepskin be given to Serapion.[44] His disciples embraced him, and moments before his death, his face brightened mysteriously.

In Athanasius's hands, Antony appears not as a remote hermit, but a servant to all—to victims of injustice, to the sick and the grieving, to burdened soldiers and discouraged monks. Athanasius looked back on Antony, encapsulating his view in a famous sentence: "It was as if he were a physician given to Egypt by God."[45]

Audience, Sources, and Genre

On the surface, the Life of Antony seems a simple folktale. It has a fearless hero who, with equal ease, can charm crocodiles and learned philosophers, who can unflinchingly live in haunted tombs and waterless wastes, whose wisdom is sought by emperors and peasants alike, whose healing touch can remedy what physicians find impossible to cure, and whose magical powers enable him to peer into the future and to fend off the fiercest of evil spirits. From the beginning, the Life's folktale charm proved attractive. As the first biography of a monk, it would break new ground and inspire countless imitators over the next 1000 years. Elements of the Athanasian narrative—the dramatic initial conversion, the ascetical feats, the battles with demons, the miracles—would become standard props in medieval hagiography, so standard that it is hard for us to appreciate the novelty of what Athanasius created. Its folktale surface should not lead the modern reader to underestimate its literary sophistication. It is, as Robert Gregg has noted, "a work of multiple dimensions and considerable literary ingenuity . . . , artfully simple," yet "sensitive to a range of tastes" and "differently attractive to different readers."[46]

The *Life of Antony* purports to be a biography but is not one in any modern sense. Its fantastical worldview and anecdotal flavor are too far removed from modern biography's concern with sober facts, strict chronology, and critical evaluation of sources. On the other hand, this should not lead one to underestimate the verifiable history that can be gleaned from its pages.[47] The *Life* is much closer to a biography in the ancient sense of the genre. Even then, it has contours and shadings unlike its classical counterparts. One of most astute estimates of the *Life of Antony* is also one of the earliest. It comes from Gregory of Nazianzus, who helped lead the final victory of the Nicenes at the Council of Constantinople in 381. During his brief tenure as patriarch of Constantinople, he delivered a number of brilliant orations, including a panegyric on the life of Athanasius. Gregory remarks that Athanasius, in writing the *Life of Antony*, had "composed a rule for the monastic life in the form of a narrative."[48] What Gregory recognized was that the *Life* was not simply a charming or edifying story; it provided a rule of life, an instruction, an image of how one might go about living the monastic life.

That estimate mirrors what Athanasius himself says. In the preface, he addresses those who had requested the biography, some unnamed "foreign monks."[49] It is hard to say exactly who they were, but it seems likely they were Westerners, given both Athanasius's close contacts there and the speed with which the work was translated into Latin. Athanasius says that they had requested certain specifics: who Antony was before his monastic career, how he began his life as an ascetic, and how he died. Each of these is given ample treatment in the text. But the real reason Athanasius tells the story is for exhortation: "Along with marveling at the man, you will want to imitate his purpose, for Antony's way of life provides monks with a sufficient picture for ascetic practice."[50] In other words, Athanasius's concern is a rhetorical one: he wants to spur his hearers to action, to imitation. He has drawn his portrait of Antony as an ideal to be imitated and as the archetype to measure oneself against. Athanasius even plays to his audience's competitive instincts: "You have entered on a fine contest with the monks in Egypt, intending as you do to measure up or even to surpass them in your discipline of virtue."[51]

Biblical Motifs

Athanasius drew on the Bible for literary motifs. His early monastic readers would have noted how the *Life* is permeated by scriptural texts, more than 200 either quoted or paraphrased. There are allusions to the Old Testament. The divine promise to Antony in the tomb—"I will be your helper forever, and I will make you famous everywhere"—echoes covenantal promises that God made to Abraham and to David. When Antony announced his death, he spoke of "going the way of the fathers," just as Joshua and David had.[52] Antony is compared to Old Testament figures. Like the prophet Daniel, he had symbol-laced visions and was "struck dumb" in ecstatic trance.[53] Like Moses, he kept his clear eyes and his teeth to his dying day; also like him, Antony would be buried in an unknown grave.[54]

The most significant biblical type for Antony is Elijah. Athanasius says that Antony "used to tell himself that from the career of the prophet Elijah, as from a mirror, the ascetic must always acquire knowledge of his own life."[55] Like Elijah, Antony is called a "man of God."[56] Like Elijah, he dwells in the desert and is described as "seated in his mountain."[57] Like Elijah, he win duels against those who worship false gods and foretells the death of a military commander who comes out to the desert to seize him.[58] In 2 Kings, Elijah hands down his cloak to his disciple Elisha; in the *Life*, Antony has two Elishas, so to speak, handing down one sheepskin and his cloak to Athanasius and the other sheepskin to Serapion.[59] In the preface, Athanasius says that he learned all that he could of Antony from a longtime disciple who had "poured water over his hands," an allusion to 2 Kings 3:11, in which Elisha is described as pouring water into the hands of Elijah. This Elisha-like informant was, presumably, Serapion.[60]

Athanasius also draws on New Testament texts. Antony fulfills Jesus' call to the rich young man to sell all he has (Matt. 19:21); he fulfills St. Paul's admonitions about praying incessantly and about the necessity of work (1 Thess. 5:17; 2 Thess. 3:10). And in renouncing all for Christ, Antony fulfills Paul's admonition, "forgetting what lies behind and straining forward to what lies ahead" (Philipp. 3:13).[61] In fact, Paul's saying in 1 Corinthians 15:31—"every day I face death"—forms the centerpiece of Antony's spirituality. In his address to the monks, Antony says that by "dying daily" the monk learns to wean himself of cravings, of possessions, of grudges, of sin; he comes to see each day as a gift of God's providence and to "forgive all things to all people."[62] The theme of "dying daily"—living each day as if it were one's last—would become a favorite in the literature of the desert.

Philosophical Models

Monks were not Athanasius' only audience, nor was the Bible his only literary model. In the conclusion, he tells his monastic readers, "If the need arises, read this to pagans as well."[63] The *Life* is punctuated by apologetic episodes and themes. There is the encounter with the pagan philosophers in which the illiterate Antony, using the language of Platonic philosophy, discusses the Logos and the origin of the soul. And in his long speech to the monks, Antony would jab at "the Greeks" who sailed to distant lands to get an education; Christians, by contrast, saw no reason to cross the open sea in search of virtue since they held to what Jesus taught: that "the Kingdom of God is within you"; that "virtue is not distant from us, nor does it stand external to us, but its realization lies in us, and the task is easy if only we shall will it."[64] Here Athanasius presents monasticism in philosophic terms, that it fulfilled better than philosophy itself the ancient philosophic maxim: "Know yourself."

Athanasius drew on literary motifs from the lives of pagan philosophers. Early in the twentieth century, Richard Reitzenstein and other classical scholars found a spate of parallels and borrowings: from Philostratus's *Life of Apollonius of Tyana* and Lucian's *Philopseudes*, from Porphyry's *Life of Plotinus* and various lives of Pythagoras.[65] For example, Lucian's quirky holy man, Pancrates, spent years underground in the tombs of Egypt, studying occult sciences under Isis, and then emerged from his mystic initiation to demonstrate his powers by riding around on crocodiles.[66] Iamblichus's Pythagoras taught his disciples a similar, if less rigorous, asceticism: a rejection of fame and wealth, a spare diet, abstinence from wine, and limited sleep.[67]

The scene in which Antony emerges from the desert fortress provides a remarkable parallel. Porphyry, in his *Life of Pythagoras*, says that the philosopher lived in the Libyan Desert and practiced an occult diet once used by Hercules; because of it, "Pythagoras . . . preserved his body in an unchanging condition, not . . . at one time fat, and at another time lean. Pythagoras' face showed the same constancy that was also in his soul. For he was neither more elated by pleasure nor dejected by grief, and no one ever saw him either rejoicing or mourning."[68] Athanasius's wording bears striking similarity: Antony's body "maintained its former condition, neither fat from lack of exercise nor emaciated from fasting"; and Antony's soul was "not constricted by grief, nor relaxed by pleasure, nor affected by either laughter or dejection"; "he maintained utter equilibrium, like one guided by reason and steadfast in that which accords with nature" (for an image of Antony as a contemplative, see figure 3.2).[69]

Athanasius drew his portrait so that Antony the Christian monk appears in the guise of the classical sage. Yet the contrast is equally important. Antony is not the well-educated urban philosopher of the Neoplatonists, but an unschooled Egyptian peasant. And the reason, or *logos*, that guides Antony is Christ, the Logos of God. In the same passage, Athanasius uses the language of the Greek mystery cults when he speaks of Antony coming out of the desert fort "as though from some sanctuary, a mystic initiate, mystery-taught and God-inspired." Again the contrast is important: the mysteries Antony knows and teaches are the mysteries of the crucified God of the Christians.

Ancient Biographies

Scholars have compared Athanasius's *Life* to earlier Greek literary forms. One precedent seems to be the genre of the encomium. The encomium was a work in which the author praised an individual, setting out his virtues so as to make him an embodiment of a public ideal. Ancient rhetorical textbooks set out a fixed list of topics that an author was expected to cover in praising his chosen

FIGURE 3.2. *The Temptation of Saint Anthony* by Hieronymous Bosch
(1450–1516) portrays a more tranquil image than is usually found in late-
medieval images of Antony. It captures another side of Athanasius's
account: Antony as a contemplative. (Scala/Art Resource, NY)

hero: nationality, parents, education, lifestyle, deeds, death, and burial. Athanasius's *Life* does set Antony out as a figure to be praised and the embodiment
of an ideal, but while Athanasius touches on these set topics, he does so un-
equally. Most are covered in the first 4 chapters, while "deeds" (*praxeis*) take
up the bulk of the work (chapters, 5–89). Also, the traditional encomium, such
as Xenophon's classic *Life of King Agesilaus*, was used to praise figures such as
kings and military men who had spent their careers in public life. Antony the
monk was the exact opposite: he was a hermit whose withdrawal signaled a
rejection of the world of the polis and its politics.

Closer to Athanasius's work is the genre of biography—what ancients simply called "lives" (βίοι, or *vitae*). Ancient biography has been described as a "halfway house between history and oratory"[70]; that is, it was not simply the praise of a person, like an encomium, nor a recitation of deeds and events, like a history. It was somewhere in between. Ancient biographers, such as Plutarch (c. 46–c. 120), distinguished their work from history-writing, insisting their interest was not events but the revelation of character. In a famous passage in his biography of Alexander the Great, Plutarch says, "It is not histories that I am writing, but lives; and in the most illustrious deeds there is not always a manifestation of virtue or vice, nay, a slight thing like a phrase or jest often makes a greater revelation of character than battles where thousands fall."[71] This did not mean that biographers like Plutarch ignored epoch-making events; rather, "the biographer's task was to capture the gesture which laid bare the soul."[72] The ancient biographer explored character not because of an interest in psychology. Plutarch, for instance, was a moralist and hoped to guide his readers to virtue through imitation, through mimesis, of the great figures he wrote about. Athanasius shared this moralist and mimetic purpose. He portrays Antony as both a teacher of virtue and its exemplar.

Scholars distinguish between two main types of ancient biography. One is typified by Plutarch, who used chronological order, an order well suited to his focus on men of politics and action. The other is typified by the Latin biographer Suetonius (d. after 120), who focused not on chronology, but on a sort of geography of character—ordering his account topically to reveal virtues and vice. The *Life of Antony*, follows a largely chronological (and thus Plutarchian) scheme. But there are topical sections, such as chapters 56–66, which focus on Antony's miracles and visions, and chapters 67–72, which focus on Antony's virtues of humility, orthodox faith, and unexpected wisdom.

One subgenre of biography, long cultivated in Alexandria, was the life of a philosopher. The *Life of Antony* resembles this genre not only in specific passages (such as those cited above), but also in its larger purpose. The lives of ancient philosophers, from Plato's *Apology* to Porphyry's *Life of Plotinus*, were not dispassionate accounts written by those wanting to tell a story or praise a venerable person. They come from the pens of committed disciples. These biographies were, in part, propaganda pieces that extolled the superiority of their school of philosophy by extolling its founder. Patricia Cox, in her *Biography in Late Antiquity*, has defined these biographies of philosophers as "creative historical works, promoting models of philosophical divinity and imposing them on historical figures thought to be worthy of such idealization."[73] These lives of philosophers could also be apologies, attempts to answer criticisms. One early example of the genre, Xenophon's *Life of Socrates*, was exactly such a piece. As Cox has noted, "biography was from its inception a genre that found its home in controversy" and had twin aims: polemic and apology, attack and defense.[74] Athanasius's *Life of Antony* shares many of these qualities. In writing the *Life*, he wanted to extol one "school" of philosophical divinity— monasticism—and show its superiority over its pagan rivals. He also idealized Antony, imposing on the historical figure the status of founder and father of this peculiarly Christian brand of philosophy. In addition, he turned Antony into a spokesman for his own polemics; thus one finds Athanasius's Antony shunning schismatics (such as Melitians) and heretics (such as Arians) and repeatedly commanding his disciples to do the same.

Athanasius was a skilled literary artist; he was also a gifted theologian who brought all his theological talents and biases to this work. In the next chapter, we will explore that theological agenda.

NOTES

1. Serapion of Thmuis, *Ep. ad discipulos Antonii* 5, 7–8, 19–20 (trans. my own). For the text of this little-known letter, see René Draguet, "Une lettre de Sérapion de Thmuis aux disciples d'Antoine (A.D. 356) en version syriaque et arménienne," *Le Muséon* 64 (1951): 1–25.

2. Barnes, *Athanasius and Constantius*, 114; cf. Hanson, *Search*, 342.

3. The ancient sources for this incident are the *Chronicon Athanasianum* 28 (SC 317:256); *Historia Acephala* 1.10–11 (SC 317:142–144); and Athanasius, *Apologia ad Constantium* 25 (SC 56:140–142), and *Apologia de fuga* 24 (SC 56:234–236). See Haas, *Alexandria in Late Antiquity*, 278–295.

4. Athanasius, *Apologia de fuga* 24 (SC 56bis:236; trans. NPNF 4:24).

5. Rufinus, *HE* 10.18 (PL 21:491; trans. Amidon, 31).

6. *Bohairic Life* 185 (CSCO 89:164–168; trans. Veilleux, CS 45:220–224); cf. *First Greek Life* 137–138 (CS 45:395–397).

7. Sozomen, *HE* IV.10 (SC 418:224–232; NPNF 2:305–306).

8. Athanasius, *Historia Arianorum* 58 (PG 25:764; trans. NPNF 4:291).

9. Hanson, *Search*, 343.

10. On the *Life of Antony*, see the bibliography for chapter 3. The Greek text used here is the critical edition by G. J. M. Bartelink, ed., *Athanase d'Alexandrie: Vie d'Antoine*, SC 400 (Paris: Éditions du Cerf, 1994); the translation, unless otherwise noted, is that of Robert C. Gregg, *Athanasius: The Life of Antony and the Letter to Marcellinus*, CWS (New York: Paulist Press, 1980).

11. A later tradition, recorded in Sozomen, *HE* 1.13.2 (SC 306:170–171; NPNF 2.2: 249), gives Antony's home village as Koma, the modern village of Qiman al-Arias.

12. Robert T. Meyer, *Athanasius: The Life of Saint Antony*, ACW 10 (Westminster, Md.: Newman Press, 1950), 107n14.

13. *VA* 3 (SC 400:136; trans. my own).

14. *VA* 3 (SC 400:136; trans. Gregg, CWS, 32).

15. One must be alert to the vocabulary of the *VA*, the way it evokes concepts from a later time period. Bartelink, SC 400:137, warns against thinking of as "communities of monks," and translates the word as "hermitages." Among the other terms that will develop special meanings are *ascēsis* and *anachāresis*, which will be discussed later.

16. James E. Goehring, "Asceticism," in *Encyclopedia of Early Christianity*, ed. Everett Ferguson, 2nd ed. (New York: Garland, 1997), 1:127. Also Tomáš Špidlik, *The Spirituality of the Christian East*, CS 79 (Kalamazoo, Mich.: Cistercian Publications, 1986), 179–182.

17. *VA* 3 (SC 400:138; CWS, 32). Athanasius cites Saint Paul's dictum that one who does not work does not deserve to eat (2 Thess. 3:10) as the basis for the practice. On weaving baskets, see *VA* 53.

18. *VA* 3 (SC 400:138; trans. Gregg, CWS, 32); cf. *VA* 1, 72, 73. But was the his-

torical Antony really illiterate? This is an issue if one grants that the *Letters* ascribed to Antony are genuine. For a discussion, see appendix 3.1.

19. *VA* 5 (SC 400:142; trans. Gregg, CWS, 33).

20. *VA* 5 (SC 400:142; trans. Gregg, CWS, 33–34).

21. *VA* 5 (SC 400:142; trans. Gregg, CWS, 34).

22. *VA* 9 (SC 400:158; trans. Gregg, CWS, 38).

23. *VA* 10 (SC 400:164; trans. Gregg, CWS, 39).

24. Antoine Guillaumont, "Anachoresis," in *The Coptic Encyclopedia*, ed. Aziz S. Atiya (New York: Macmillan, 1991), 1:119–120.

25. *VA* 14 (SC 400:172; trans. my own).

26. *VA* 14 (SC 400:174; trans. Gregg, CWS, 42–43). Cf. Athanasius, *Ep. Festal.* 10.6 (A.D.338).

27. Peter Brown, "Late Antiquity," in *The History of Private Life*, vol. 1, *From Pagan Rome to Byzantium*, ed. Paul Veyne (Cambridge, Mass.: Harvard University Press, 1987), 287–289.

28. *VA* 46 (SC 400:258; trans. Gregg, CWS, 65).

29. *VA* 47 (SC 400:262; trans. Gregg, CWS, 66).

30. *VA* 50 (SC 400:268–279; trans. Gregg, CWS, 68).

31. On the Monastery of Saint Antony, see the bibliography for chapter 3.

32. *VA* 58 63, 64, 71. Note the "we" in the final passage. Cf. the *Chronicon Athanasianum*, for the year 338 (SC 317:234–236; NPNF 4:503).

33. *VA* 84 (SC 400:352; trans. Gregg, CWS, 92).

34. *VA* 15 (SC 400:176; CWS, 43).

35. *VA* 73–80 (SC 400:322–340; CWS, 84–89). Cf. Athanasius, *De incarnatione* 50.

36. *VA* 66 (SC 400:308; CWS, 80).

37. *VA* 84 (SC 400:352–354; trans. Gregg, CWS, 92).

38. *VA* 81 (SC 400:342; trans. Gregg, CWS, 89).

39. The same remark appears in the mouth of Macedonius the Barley-Eater, who faced down imperial officials ready to enforce brutal vengeance after the Riot of the Statues in Antioch, 387; see Theodoret of Cyrrhus, *HE* 5.19.

40. *VA* 81 (SC 400:342–344; trans. Gregg, CWS, 90).

41. *VA* 60, 62, and 89 (SC 400:294, 300, 362; CWS, 75–76, 77, 95).

42. *VA* 86 (SC 400:356–358; CWS, 93–94). Cf. *Historia Arianorum* 14.

43. *VA* 82 (SC 400:344–350; CWS, 90–91).

44. *VA* 89–93 (SC 400:362–372; CWS, 95–98).

45. *VA* 87 (SC 400:356; trans. Gregg, CWS, 94).

46. Gregg, *Athanasius: The Life of Antony*, CWS, 2.

47. On this, see Graham E. Gould, "The *Life of Anthony* and the Origins of Christian Monasticism in Fourth-Century Egypt," *Medieval History* 1 (1991): 3–11.

48. Gregory of Nazianzus, *Oratio* 21.5 (SC 270:118), quoted in David Brakke, *Athanasius and the Politics of Asceticism*. Oxford Early Christian Studies (New York: Oxford University Press, 1995), 201.

49. *VA* praef. (SC 400:124; trans. my own). The *First Greek Life of Pachomius* (CS 45:366) refers to it as "the *Life of the Blessed Antony to the Monks and Brothers in Foreign Parts* who had asked the most holy father Athanasius for it."

50. *VA* praef. (SC 400:127; trans. Gregg, CWS, 29).

51. *VA* praef. (SC 400:124–126; trans. Gregg, CWS, 29).

52. *VA* 91 (SC 400:368; CWS, 96); cf. Josh. 23:14 and 1 Kings 2:2.

53. *VA* 82 (SC 400:344; trans. Gregg, CWS, 90); cf. Dan. 4:19.

54. *VA* 92–93 (SC 400:372, 374; CWS, 97, 98); cf. Deut. 34:6–7.

55. *VA* 7 (SC 400:154–156; trans. Gregg, CWS, 37).

56. *VA* 70; cf. 1 Kings 17:18; 2 Kings 1:9–13. Other Old Testament figures called "man of God" include Moses (Deut. 33:1, Josh. 14:6; 2 Chron. 23:14; Ezra 3:2); Samuel (1 Sam. 9:6); and David (2 Chron. 8:14, Neh. 12:24).

57. *VA* 59, 60, 66, 84, 93; cf. 2 Kings 1:9.

58. *VA* 86; cf. 1 Kings 18, 2 Kings 1.

59. *VA* 91 (SC 400:370; CWS, 97); cf. 2 Kings 2:13 ff.

60. *VA* praef. (SC 400:129; trans. my own). The older Montfaucon text (used by Gregg in the CWS translation) implies Athanasius was the Elishalike figure. But Bartelink, the editor of the recent critical edition of the Greek text, argues that the best manuscript tradition indicates a different reading: that Athanasius learned much of what he knew of Antony from this Elishalike disciple (presumably Serapion).

61. *VA* 7 (SC 400:154; trans. Gregg, CWS, 37); cf. Philipp. 3:13.

62. *VA* 19 (SC 400:186; trans. Gregg, CWS, 45).

63. *VA* 94 (SC 400:376; trans. Gregg, CWS, 99).

64. *VA* 20 (SC 400:188; trans. Gregg, CWS, 46).

65. Richard Reitzenstein, *Des Athanasius Werk über das Leben des Antonius: Ein philologischer Beitrag zur Geschichte des Mönchtums*, Sitzungsberichte des Heidelberger Akademie der Wissenschaften, Philosophisch-historische Klasse 5 (Heidelberg: 1914), esp. 12–19. For a critique of Reitzenstein's thesis, see Bartelink, *Athanase d'Alexandrie: Vie d'Antoine*, SC 400:63–64; Samuel Rubenson, *The Letters of St. Antony: Monasticism and the Making of a Saint*, Studies in Antiquity and Christianity (Philadelphia: Fortress Press, 1995), 129–130.

66. Lucian, *Philopseudes* 34 (LCL, 3:370–372).

67. Iamblichus, *De vita Pythagorica* 16.69. For a translation, see Gillian Clark, *Iamblichus: On the Pythagorean Life*, Translated Texts for Historians 8 (Liverpool: Liverpool University Press, 1989).

68. Porphyry, *Vita Pythagorae* 35 (trans. K. Guthrie, *The Pythagorean Sourcebook and Library* [Grand Rapids: Phanes Press, 1991], 130); cf. Iamblichus, *De vita Pythagorica* 31.196.

69. *VA* 14 (SC 400:172–174; trans. Gregg, CWS, 42).

70. Patricia Cox, *Biography in Late Antiquity: A Quest for the Holy Man* (Berkeley: University of California Press, 1983), xiv. For studies on ancient biography, see the bibliography for chapter 3.

71. Plutarch, *Alexander* 1.1–2, quoted in Cox, *Biography*, 12.

72. Cox, *Biography*, xi.

73. Cox, *Biography*, 45.

74. Cox, *Biography*, 135.

BIBLIOGRAPHY

The *Life of Antony* (*Vita Antonii*): Texts and Translations

For a critical edition of the Greek text, together with a French translation and valuable notes, see G. J. M. Bartelink, ed., *Athanase d'Alexandrie: Vie d'Antoine*, SC 400 (Paris: Éditions du Cerf, 1994). This replaces the classic 1698 edition of Bernard de Montfaucon reprinted in PG 26: 837–976. Two good English translations are Robert C. Gregg, trans. and introd., *Athanasius: The Life of Antony and the Letter to Marcellinus*, CWS (New York: Paulist Press, 1980); and Robert T. Meyer, trans. and annot., *Athanasius: The Life of Saint Antony*, ACW 10 (Westminster, Md.: Newman Press, 1950). Both of these are based on the older Montfaucon text.

Biography in the Ancient World

For an introduction to the ancient genre of biography, see Richard A. Burridge, *What Are the Gospels? A Comparison with Graeco-Roman Biography* (Cambridge: Cambridge University Press, 1992), 55–81; David E. Aune, *The New Testament in Its Literary Environment*, Library of Early Christianity (Philadelphia: Westminster Press, 1987), 27–45. The classic study is Friedrich Leo, *Die griechisch-römische Biographie nach ihrer litterarischen Form* (Leipzig: Teubner, 1901); and more recently, Arnaldo Momigliano, *The Development of Greek Biography: Four Lectures* (Cambridge, Mass.: Harvard University Press, 1971). The work of Patricia Cox, *Biography in Late Antiquity: A Quest for the Holy Man* (Berkeley: University of California Press, 1983), presumes familiarity with the key ancient texts.

The *Letters* of Antony

For the text, see Gérard Garitte, *Lettres de Saint Antoine: version géorgienne et fragments coptes*, CSCO 148–149 (Louvain: L. Durbecq, 1955). For an English translation and a detailed analysis, see Samuel Rubenson, *The Letters of St. Antony: Monasticism and the Making of a Saint*, Studies in Antiquity and Christianity (Minneapolis: Fortress Press, 1995). Other scholars are less sure about their authenticity and importance. See also:

Brakke, David. "The Making of Monastic Demonology: Three Ascetic Teachers on Withdrawal and Resistance." *Church History* 70 (2001): 19–48.
Chitty, Derwas J. *The Letters of St. Antony the Great*. Fairacres, Oxford: S.L.G. Press, 1974.
Gould, Graham E. "The Influence of Origen on Fourth-Century Monasticism: Some Further Remarks," in *Origeniana Sexta: Origène et la Bible,* ed. Gilles Dorival and Alain LeBoulluec, 591–598. Leuven: University Press, 1995.
————. "Recent Work on Monastic Origins: A Consideration of the Questions Raised by Samuel Rubenson's *The Letters of St. Antony*." Studia Patristica 25 (1993): 405–416.
Kannengiesser, Charles. "Antony, Athanasius, Evagrius: The Egyptian Fate of Origenism." *Coptic Church Review* 16, no. 1 (1995): 3–8.
Zanetti, Ugo, and Samuel Rubenson. "Les *Lettres* de saint Antoine et la naissance du monachisme." *Nouvelle revue théologique* 113 (1991): 87–93.

The Monastery of Saint Antony

For a valuable account of the monastery and its recently recovered and restored artwork, see Elizabeth S. Bolman, ed., *Monastic Visions: Wall Paintings in the Monastery of St. Antony at the Red Sea* (New Haven: American Research Center in Egypt and Yale University Press, 2002). The work has striking color plates of the cycle of frescoes in the monastery church.

APPENDIX 3.1

The *Letters of Saint Antony*

Antony has traditionally been portrayed as illiterate. But was he? Even Athanasius acknowledged that Antony had sent letters to Constantine and his sons. Other ancient sources knew Antony as a letter-writer. The *First Greek Life of Pachomius* mentions that, after hearing of the death of Pachomius, Antony sent a letter of consolation to Pachomius's community at Tabennesi as well as one to Athanasius. In 392, Jerome published *On Illustrious Men*, listing Christian notables over the centuries. He numbered Antony as one of those "illustrious" and mentions, in passing, that Antony had written seven letters in "the Egyptian language" (i.e., Coptic) and that these had been translated into Greek.

The seven letters Jerome knew seem to have been preserved. We only have fragments of the Coptic, but the first letter is preserved in a Syriac translation. A version of the seven had been known from a not-very-clear fifteenth-century Latin version. But the best text seems to be an ancient version in Georgian preserved at the ancient Monastery of Saint Catherine's in Sinai and published in 1955 by Gérard Garitte.

These letters have been the focus of considerable recent scholarly discussion, for they portray a view of Antony rather different from that found in Athanasius's *Life*. The first letter is a brief treatise on the ascetical life. The others six are brief exhortations and closely resemble one another, repeating over and over the same themes, each with its own interesting variations. Given here is a sampling of important themes and passages.

GNOSIS

Third-century Alexandrian thinkers such as Clement were critical of the Gnostics and their denial of the goodness of the body and of matter; but they were willing to use the term *gnosis* (knowledge) as a way to describe the Christian quest for God. One finds Antony using this same language:

> Truly, my beloved, I write to you "as to wise men" (1 Cor. 10:15), who are able to know themselves. I know that he who knows himself knows God and his dispensations for his creatures. (*Antony, Ep.* 3: 39–40) A wise man has first to know himself, so that he may then know what is of God, and all his grace which he has always bestowed upon us and then to know that every sin and every accusation is alien to the nature of our spiritual essence. (Antony, *Ep.* 7: 58)

Origenist World View

The *Letters* draw on terminology and perspectives associated with Origen. Origen had hypothesized that before the beginning of the material universe, there was an original unity of preexistent minds, and that the original Fall occurred when these preexistent minds "cooled" (*psycho*) in their fervor and fell into "souls" (*psyche*). The *Letters* seem to presume this Origenist terminology and perspective:

> As for those rational beings in whom the law of promise grew cold and whose faculties of the mind thus died, so that they can no longer know themselves after their first formation, they have all become irrational and serve the creatures instead of the Creator. (Antony, *Ep.* 2:4–5)

Christ the Physician

Antony repeatedly refers to Christ as the "physician" who heals the human race of the "great wound" of sin and death. Antony typically sets the image of Christ the physician within what one scholar has called "a vast fresco of the history of salvation which is biblical—and Origenist":

> But the Creator saw that their wound was great and needed care. He who is himself their Creator and healer, Jesus, thus sent forerunners before himself. I do not hesitate to say that Moses, who gave us the law, is one of them and that the same Spirit which was in Moses acted in the assembly of the saints when they all prayed for the Only-begotten Son of God. . . . Those invested with the Spirit [i.e., prophets] saw that no one among the creatures could heal this great wound, but only the goodness of God, his Only-begotten, whom he sent as salvation of the entire world. In his benevolence, and for the salvation of all, the Father of creation did not spare his Only-begotten, but delivered him up for our sins. He was humbled by our iniquities and by his stripes we were healed (cf. Rom. 8:32, Isa. 53:5). Through the word of his power he gathered us from all lands, from one end of the earth to the other, resurrecting our hearts from the earth and teaching us that we are members of one another. (Antony, *Ep.* 3:15–24; see also *Ep.* 2:9–19; 5:18–27; 6:5–13).

Demonology

Athanasius's Antony is the fearless wrestler of demons who spends much time teaching his disciples about demonology. The *Letters* also deal with the wiles of demons and discernment, especially in *Letter* 6. But there are important differences. The demons of the *Life* are visible; they can be seen and heard; they can prophecy, seduce, even beat ascetics. The demons of the *Letters* are invisible and need human beings to make them physical:

We are ignorant of how the secret contrivances and manifold crafts
of the devil work, and how they might be known. . . . I want you to
know, my children, that I do not cease to pray to God for you, day
and night, that he may open the eyes of your hearts that you may
see all the secret evils which they pour upon us every day in this
present time. I ask God to give you a heart of knowledge and a spirit
of discernment, that you may be able to lift your hearts before the
Father as a pure sacrifice in all sanctity, without blemish. Truly, my
children, they are jealous of us at all times with their evil counsel,
their secret persecution, their subtle malice, their spirits of seduc-
tion, their fraudulent thoughts, their faithlessness which they sow in
our hearts every day, their hardness of heart and their numbness.
. . . And if you seek, you will find [the demons'] sins and iniquities
revealed bodily, for they are not visible bodily. But you should know
that we are their bodies, and that our soul receives their wickedness.
(Antony, *Ep.* 6:23, 27–32, 50–51)

RETURN OF BODY AND SOUL TO ORIGINAL NATURE

Athanasius's Antony practiced great feats of asceticism and came to enjoy such
integrity that his body became a perfect instrument of his soul, and this "equilibrium was guided by reason and steadfast in that which accords with nature"
(*VA* 14). The Antony of the *Letters* teaches a similar reintegration of mind, soul,
and body to its original nature; but it is the Holy Spirit rather than Christ the
Logos who instructs the ascetic:

But I believe that those who have entered with all their heart, and
have prepared themselves to endure all the trials of the enemy until
they prevail, are first called by the Spirit, who alleviated everything
for them so that the work of repentance becomes sweet for them.
He sets for them a rule how to repent in their bodies and souls until
he has taught them to return to God, their own Creator. He also
gives them control over their souls and bodies in order that both
may be sanctified and inherit together: First the body through many
fasts and vigils, through the exertion of the exercises of the body,
cutting off all the fruits of the flesh. In this the Spirit of repentance
is his guide, testing him through them, so that the enmity does not
bring him back again. Then the guiding Spirit begins to open the
eyes of the soul, to show it the way of repentance that it, too, may be
purified. . . . The mind is taught by the Spirit and guides us in the
actions of the body and soul, purifying both of them, separating the
fruits of the flesh from what is natural to the body, in which they
were mingled, and through which the transgression came to be, and
leads each member of the body back to its original condition, free
from everything alien that belongs to the spirit of the enemy. (Antony, *Ep.* 1:18–32)

DENUNCIATION OF ARIUS

In the *Life*, Athanasius had portrayed Antony as a vehement opponent of the Arians. That may not be simply a matter of Athanasius putting words in Antony's mouth. In one letter, Antony denounces Arius—and does so in terms different from Athanasius:

> As for Arius, who stood up in Alexandria, he spoke strange words about the Only-begotten: to him who has no beginning, he gave a beginning, to him who is ineffable among men he gave an end, and to the immovable he gave movement. . . . That man has begun a great task, an unhealable wound. If he had known himself, his tongue would not have spoken about what he did not know. It is, however, manifest that he did not know himself. (Antony, *Ep.* 4: 7–18)

If these letters really come from Antony—and that is an important "if"—then we need to adjust our picture of early monasticism and monastic literature. First, they would means that Antony is not the illiterate figure he is often portrayed to be. One might even see him as one of the pioneers of Coptic literature. Second, they show that Antony was not a simple monk with no interest in theological matters. On the contrary, they show a real interest in and knowledge of sometime complex theological issues: for example, the idea of Christ as creator and as Image of the Father, and the debate with Arius.

The scholar who has argued most strongly for the authenticity and importance of these *Letters* is Samuel Rubenson, *The Letters of St. Antony: Monasticism and the Making of a Saint* (Minneapolis: Fortress Press, 1995). This edition offers a very detailed (and technical) analysis. It also includes an English translation of the *Letters*, from which these excerpts have been taken. Rubenson has been criticized for exaggerating the theological sophistication of the *Letters* and overemphasizing the *Letters* at the expense of other sources of early Egyptian monasticism. For other studies of these important documents, see the section of the bibliography dealing with the letters.

APPENDIX 3.2

The *Letters of Ammonas*

Ammonas was reportedly a disciple of Antony who became his successor at the Outer Mountain, Mount Pispir. A set of remarkable and little-studied letters is attributed to him. Fourteen have been preserved in Syriac, and of these, eight are also preserved in the original Greek, though in a somewhat jumbled order. They are early examples of spiritual direction, written by a spiritual father to his monastic sons. They address a variety of issues: discernment, prayer, mystical vision, and endurance. A few excerpts are given here.

THE DESERT AS TRAINING-GROUND FOR HEALERS

You also know, my dear brethren, that ever since the transgression came to pass, the soul cannot know God unless it withdraws itself from men and from every distraction. For then the soul will see the adversary who fights against it. And once it has seen the adversary, and has overcome him every time he engages it in battle, then God dwells in that soul, and all the labour is changed to joy and gladness. . . . This is why the holy fathers also withdrew into the desert alone, men such as Elijah the Tishbite and John the Baptist. For do not suppose that because the righteous were in the midst of men it was among men that they had achieved their righteousness. Rather, having first practiced much quiet, they then received the power of God dwelling in them, and then God sent them into the midst of men, having acquired every virtue, so that they might act as God's provisioners and cure men of their infirmities. For they were physicians of the soul, able to cure men's infirmities. This was the need for which they were dragged away from their quiet and sent to men. But they were only sent when all their own diseases were healed. But those who are sent from God, do not want to go away from their quiet, knowing that through it they have obtained the divine power; but in order not to disobey the Creator, they go from the spiritual edification of men, in imitation of Him. For as the Father sent His very Son from heaven to heal all the infirmities and sicknesses of men (as it is written, "He took our infirmities and bare our sicknesses," Is. 53:4), thus all the saints who come among men to heal them follow the example of the Creator of all, that so they might be made worthy of adoption as sons of God. And as the Father and the Son are, so these should be, unto the ages of ages, Amen. (Ammonas, *Ep.* 12)

ADVICE FROM ANTONY

For Abba Antony used to say to us: "No man will be able to enter into the kingdom of God without trials". . . . And it is said of trees that the more troubled by winds, the more they take root and grow. (Ammonas, *Ep.* 9)

DIVINE SWEETNESS

If any man love the Lord with all his heart and with all his soul and with all his might, he will acquire awe, and awe will beget in him weeping, and weeping joy, and joy will beget strength, and in all this the soul will bear fruit. And when God sees its fruit so fair, He will accept it as a sweet savour, and in all things He will rejoice with that soul, with His angels, and will give it a guardian to keep in all its ways as he prepares it for the place of life, and to prevent Satan from prevailing over it . . . for thus the sweetness of God will provide you with the greatest possible strength. For divine sweetness is "sweeter than honey and the honeycomb" (Ps. 19:10). Not many monks or virgins have known this great and divine sweetness since they have not acquired the divine power, except some few here and there. (Ammonas, *Ep.* 2)

MYSTERIES OF GOD

Night and day I pray that the power of God may increase in you, and reveal to you great mysteries of the Godhead which it is not easy for me to utter with the tongue, because they are great and are not of this world, and are not revealed save only to those who have purified their hearts from every defilement and from all the vanities of this world, and those who have taken up their crosses, and again fortified themselves and been obedient to God in everything. In these the Godhead dwells, feeding the soul. For just as trees do not grow unless the agency of water is available to them, so also the soul cannot mount upwards unless it receives heavenly joy. And if men do receive it, few are they to whom God reveals secrets set in heaven, showing them their places while they are yet in the body, and granting them all their requests. This therefore is my prayer night and day, that you may attain this measure, and know the riches of Christ which are infinite. (Ammonas, *Ep.* 6)

For the Greek text, see F. Nau, *Ammonas, successeur de Saint Antoine,* PO 11.4 (1915); for the Syriac text, see M. Kmosko, *Ammonii eremitae epistulae,* PO 10.6

(1914). The translation here is by Derwas J. Chitty and revised by Sebastian Brock, *The Letters of Ammonas, Successor of Saint Antony* (Fairacres, Oxford: SLG Press, 1979). See the recent analysis of these by David Brakke, "The Making of Monastic Demonology: Three Ascetic Teachers on Withdrawal and Resistance," *Church History* 70 (2001): 32–41.

4

The *Life of Antony*: Themes and Influence

Gregory of Nazianzus had said that the *Life of Antony* is a monastic rule in the form of a narrative. One can also say that it is a theological tract in the form of a narrative. In this chapter, I will highlight three theological themes that wind their way through the text: Christ's victory over the demons, Antony as the image of deified humanity, and Antony as the model of orthodoxy.

Christ's Victory over Demons

The *Life of Antony* seems, at first sight, obsessed with demons and demonology. But a closer look shows that the focus is not on demons, but on Christ's victory over them. The theme is sounded in Antony's long speech to the monks: "Since the Lord made his sojourn with us, the enemy is fallen and his powers have diminished. For this reason, though he is able to do nothing; nevertheless like a tyrant fallen from power he does not remain quiet, but issues threats, even if they are only words."[1] This was a bold claim in the ancient world, for the fear of evil spirits was pervasive. Ancients could point to disease and madness, to drought, plague, and political chaos as sure evidence of the workings of demons. Ordinary people—including Christians—wore amulets and talismans to keep the demons' malevolence at bay. Here Athanasius puts into Antony's mouth his own cosmic optimism: that Christ has decimated Satan's kingdom, and that the devil is powerless, no matter how much noise he makes. Note the political analogy: the devil is a petty ex-tyrant. In the course of his speech, Antony draws on other analogies: the devil is like a beast of burden harnessed in a hard yoke; he is like a runaway slave, tethered with a ring through his nose and an iron clamp on his lips.[2]

Athanasius's Antony did not just speak about Christ's victory; he demonstrated it. During his apprenticeship, he defeated the devil's sexual advances by "thinking about the Christ and considering the excellence won through him"; so the devil was "made a buffoon by a mere youth."[3] When Antony faced down lions and bears and snakes in the tomb, he shook his fist at the devil, so to speak, boasting: "since the Lord has broken your strength, you attempt to terrify me by any means with the mob; it is a mark of weakness that you mimic the shapes of irrational beasts."[4] Again the emphasis: Christ has won the victory. But here Athanasius stresses that what at first sight appears powerful—fearsome creatures—indicates the opposite—weak irrationality. This is important, for it touches on the heart of Athanasius's Christology: that Christ is the Logos, the rationality of God; and the devil cannot mimic what is rational.

Later, in the desert, Antony appears as a sort of spiritual land developer, taming the wilderness and reclaiming it from the demonic. No sooner did he take up residence in the desert fort than the reptiles that had lived there ran away "as if someone were in pursuit," and the demons loudly complained, "Get away from what is ours! What do you have to do with the desert?"[5] In other words, before Antony's arrival, the desert had been the devil's home turf. In fact, making the desert "a city" of monks had cosmological consequences: the devil was losing ground. At one point, Antony tells of a visit from a tall figure who introduced himself as Satan and who had come to Antony to register a complaint. He was tired of monks tormenting him day and night with their prayers and imprecations. Poor Satan had become a homeless vagrant: "I no longer have a place—no weapon, no city. There are Christians everywhere, and even the desert has filled with monks."[6]

Whenever Antony and the monks wished to torment Satan, they used the sign of the cross as their weapon. It was a talisman of extraordinary power. As Antony told the philosophers, "Where the sign of the cross occurs, magic is weakened and sorcery has no effect."[7] Antony used the sign of the cross both to cast demons out of the desert fortress and to exorcise the possessed brought to him for healing.[8] As soon as the sign is invoked, the demons "melt like wax, . . . vanish like smoke."[9] Antony once remarked to his disciples that "the truth is, [the demons] are cowards, and they are utterly terrified by the sign of the cross, because in it the Savior, stripping their armor, made an example of them."[10]

Athanasius was tinkering with a theme from ancient demonology: that demons are creatures of the air. In one episode, Antony had a vision of ascending upward with angelic beings. Suddenly he encountered "some foul and terrible figures standing in the air, intent on holding him back so he could not pass by."[11] The demons demanded an accounting of his life. The angels intervened, blocking the accusations, saying that "the Lord has wiped clean" everything from his birth to his becoming a monk. The upward passage then "opened before him free and unobstructed," and the vision ended. Here Athanasius draws on a cosmology in which demons, as creatures of the air, stand

guard over the region between earth and heaven. They function, as Jean Daniélou once put it, like "celestial customs officers" barring passage through their
airy domain.[12] Antony says as much to his disciples: the demons, "falling from
the heavenly wisdom and thereafter wandering around the earth, . . . meddle
with all things in their desire to frustrate our journey into heaven, so that we
might not ascend to the place from which they themselves fell."[13] The sudden
"unobstructed" passage upward that Antony saw in his vision is explained in
Athanasius's treatise *On the Incarnation*. There he says that the cross of Christ
was raised up, suspended in the air, so that it quite literally cleared the air of
these airborne pests, removing the celestial roadblocks that barred our heavenly
ascent.[14]

While the Antony of the *Life* downplays demonic power, he admits that
the demons are a nuisance. At one point, someone asked Antony if, as a solitary, he found the crowds in the city bothersome. He replied that, no, he was
used to crowds—crowds of demons.[15] Not only were these demons numerous;
they were quick-moving. As creatures of the air, they used "bodies thinner in
substance that those of humans" and thus covered vast distances quickly.[16] This
explained, according to Antony, how demons could sometimes accurately report certain information—such as how much rain Ethiopia had gotten and
thus how high the Nile would rise, facts vital for Egypt's irrigation-dependent
farming. As Antony pointed out, this was not supernatural any more than a
man on horseback bringing news of some distant event was supernatural.[17]

The "airy" nature of the demons not only made them quick-moving. Their
"thin substance" made them capable of shape-shifting. They appeared in fright-
ening guises, such as lions or snakes, but they also could show up disguised
as monks. They might chant hymns or recite scripture. They might even en-
courage the monk to pursue greater asceticism, to fast more, to spend time
contemplating his past sins. But this was simply part of their deception. They
hoped to draw monks to despair and to get them to abandon the solitary life.

Because demons were capable of reporting true things or of uttering pious-
sounding advice—albeit for deceitful ends—the monk needed to know how to
discern spirits. The monk needed to know if a voice or a vision was from God
or from demons. In his speech, Antony set out principles for making such a
discernment. Evil spirits, he noted, are noisy—crashing, shouting, creating the
"sort of disturbance one might expect from tough youths and robbers."[18] The
best measure was the emotions that a voice or a vision stirred up in a monk's
soul. Demons inspired only negative affects: "terror, confusion and disorder of
thoughts, dejection, enmity towards ascetics, listlessness, grief, memory of
relatives, fear of death."[19] Angelic spirits, by contrast, stirred up very different
emotions: tranquility, joy, delight, courage, peacefulness. And if one felt fear
in the presence of these "holy ones," their immediate counsel would be "Be
not afraid"—just as the angel Gabriel had said to Mary at the annunciation or
the angel had said to the women who came to Jesus' empty tomb.[20] This text
proved influential in the history of Western spirituality, reappearing, for instance, in the "Rules for the Discernment of Spirits" in Ignatius of Loyola's
Spiritual Exercises.[21]

God Enfleshed, Humanity Deified

When the philosophers visited Antony, they reportedly "syllogized" against the cross, ridiculing a religion that believed in a crucified God. Antony counter-attacked: if the cross seemed absurd, how much more absurd was it to follow a religion in which its so-called gods committed lewd sexual acts and in which its believers found themselves worshiping "four-footed beings and reptiles and images of men?" He then defended the Incarnation, asserting,

> The Word of God was not changed, but remaining the same he assumed a human body for the salvation and benefit of mankind—so that sharing in the human birth he might enable mankind to share the divine and spiritual nature.[22]

This is a terse summary of Athanasius's own christology. Let me take this apart phrase-by-phrase, teasing out its rationale.

The Unchanging Logos

Notice the first phrase: "the Word of God was not changed, but remaining the same."[23] Why is this an issue? Quite simply, if one says that Christ is God, then one seems to have a changeable God, for the Christ of the Gospels changed in some very obvious ways: he "shared in human birth," and he died on the cross. The problem with a changeable God is this:

1. God is perfect.
2. If the perfect God were to change, then he would change from being perfect to being imperfect.
3. And if he became imperfect, he would cease to be God.
4. Therefore, God must be unchangeable.
5. How, therefore, can the changeable Christ be the unchangeable God?

This presumably is the sort of syllogism that the philosophers raised with Antony.

Antony granted the starting point: Christ as "the Word of God was not changed." How then did Christ "remain the same" and at the same time go from being the Word to being the Word-enfleshed (i.e., "assuming a human body")? The full argument appears in Athanasius's classic treatise, *On the Incarnation*. There Athanasius begins with creation: that God the Father created the universe through Christ, his Word. This means that Christ as God's Word was creator. This also means that Christ as God's Word is present everywhere. As Athanasius says, "The incorporeal and incorruptible and immaterial Word of God came to our realm; not that he was previously distant, for no part of creation is left deprived of him, but he fills the universe, being in union with his Father."[24] Moreover, just as Christ as God can be present everywhere in a changing material universe without its impairing his own unchangeability, so

Christ as God Incarnate could become present in a human body without its impairing his unchangeability. Yet there is a paradox here: while Christ was present in the body of the Incarnate, he was at the time present everywhere in the "body" of the vast visible universe. Here is how Athanasius puts it:

> Christ . . . was not enclosed in the body, nor was he in the body but nowhere else. Nor did he move the [human body] while the universe was deprived of his action and providence. But what is most wonderful is that, being the Word, he was not contained by anyone, but rather himself contained everything. And as he is in all creation, he is in essence outside the universe but in everything by his power, ordering everything and extending his providence over everything. And giving life to all, separately and together, he contains the universe and is not contained, but in his Father only he is complete in everything. So also being in a human body and giving it life himself, he accordingly gives life to everything, and was both in all and outside all. . . . For he was not bound to the body, but rather he controlled it, and was only at rest in the Father. And the most amazing thing is this, that he both lived as a man, and as the Word gave life to everything, and as the Son was with the Father.[25]

Athanasius pointed out that if, as pagans argued, it was "unfitting" for God to become human, then one would have to hold that it was equally "unfitting" that God should even be present in the universe, guiding it, giving it life.[26] In some sense, the Incarnation was simply a special instance of God's presence.

The Incarnate Word

Now look at the second part of Antony's reply to the philosophers: "the Word of God . . . assumed a human body . . . so that . . . he might enable mankind to share the divine and spiritual nature." The wording here echoes one of Athanasius's most famous formulas, first found in *On the Incarnation*. There he says that "the Word of God . . . became human so that we might become God."[27] Western ears can find this a bit disconcerting, to speak of being "made God," of being "deified" or "divinized" (Athanasius's term is *theosis*).

To appreciate what he means, it is important to ask what it is that we do that God doesn't. There are two obvious answers: we sin, and we die. What, then, does Christ do—or rather undo? He makes us sinless and deathless. He undoes sin and death. And in so doing, he deifies us, makes us Godlike. Embedded in this is a powerful argument for the divinity of Christ:

1. Only God can make us Godlike.
2. Christ makes us Godlike.
3. Therefore, Christ has to be God.

And that, simply put, is Athanasius's core view: nothing less than God can save; if Christ saves us, then he must be God.[28]

This formula—that God became human that humans might become God—appears again and again, with subtle changes of wording or emphasis, in works Athanasius wrote over the course of his long career.[29] Here in Antony's statement to the philosophers, the accent is on the physical: that "the Word of God . . . assumed a human body." Athanasius is playing on John 1:14: "the Word of God became flesh." When Athanasius says the Word assumed a human body, he means that God climbed into human skin, so to speak, and renewed it from the inside, restoring it to immortal life. This was like a new creation, as dramatic as the creation that created the human race in the first place. Only this time, Christ as God recreated us from inside, renewing that which is vulnerable to death—the body—and recharging it with divine life, that it not corrupt, die, and drift back into the nothingness from which it was made.[30]

Antony as Humanity Deified

Not only does Antony articulate Athanasius's theology of deification; he becomes an icon for it. Antony is Athanasius's portrait of what a human being renewed in the image and likeness of God should look like (on this theme, see figure 4.1).

First, Antony's body is renewed by Christ, who, as Athanasius reminds his audience, "bore flesh for us and gave to the body victory over the devil."[31] During his stint in the tomb, Antony at first suffered a bad beating from the devil, but by the time he left, after the vision of light, "he was so strengthened that he felt that his body contained more might than before."[32] Even more striking is the robust physique Antony displays when he emerges from the desert fortress, "neither fat from lack of exercise, nor emaciated from fasting and combat with demons." Miraculously, despite twenty years of asceticism, "his body had maintained his former condition."[33] Athanasius claims Antony's exuberant health continued till his dying day. He "possessed eyes undimmed and sound." And in an age before dentists, he lost no teeth; they simply got worn down to the gums.[34] And he died at the unbelievable age of 105.[35]

Equally striking is Antony's renewal of soul. The scene at the desert fortress is again the pivotal episode. When Antony emerged, not only did he display amazing physical fitness, but also "the state of his soul was one of purity, not constricted by grief, nor relaxed by pleasure, nor affected by either laughter or dejection."[36] Earlier, I noted Athanasius's debt to the *Life of Pythagoras* for this description. Yet Athanasius's Christology is also at work here. Athanasius goes on to say that despite the crowds who came out to the fortress, Antony "maintained utter equilibrium, like one guided by reason and steadfast in that which accords with nature."[37] Athanasius chooses his words carefully here: Antony's "equilibrium" comes from "reason." Here the "reason," the *logos*, that guides Antony is not the philosopher's *logos*. For Athanasius, the Logos is a person, Christ, the Logos (or Word) who was in the beginning with God and was God, as the Bible says in John 1:1. It is the same Christ the Logos

FIGURE 4.1. Athanasius's *Life* is not just the story of Antony; it is also the story of the power of Christ. This theology is dramatized in the one of the most famous images of Coptic art, the icon of *Christ and Apa Menas* (sixth century, Bawit). (Giraudon/Art Resource, NY)

who infuses the universe with its good order, its balance and harmony, and who deifies human beings, making them like himself. For Athanasius, becoming like Christ the Logos included taking on the calm unchanging passionlessness of God. In his third *Oration against the Arians*, Athanasius says:

> The Logos is by nature free of passion [*apatheia*]. But because of the flesh which Christ put on, certain things [like being born, hungering, thirsting, weeping, and sleeping] are ascribed to him, since they are proper to the flesh, and the body itself is proper to the Savior. And he himself, being passionless by nature, remains as he is, not harmed by these affections. . . . But human beings themselves—because their passions are changed into passionlessness and done away with in the Impassible [Christ]—become passionless and free of these experiences for eternity.[38]

In other words, if Christ as God is passionless, then humans deified by Christ come to share by grace what Christ is by nature.

This accounts for Athanasius's portrait of Antony. In enumerating Antony's virtues, Athanasius notes:

> It was not his physical dimensions that distinguished him from the
> rest, but the stability of character and the purity of the soul. His soul
> being free of confusion, he held his outer senses also undisturbed,
> so that from the soul's joy his face was cheerful as well, and from
> the movements of the body it was possible to sense and perceive the
> stable condition of the soul. . . . He was never troubled, his soul be-
> ing calm, and he never looked gloomy, his mind being joyous.[39]

Again Athanasius has chosen his words carefully: Antony's soul is "calm"; his
character is "stable"; his senses are "undisturbed"; his face has an imperturbability that radiates joy. This is divine passionlessness rendered visible. This is
the way Athanasius imagines the deification made possible by Christ. Note
also how Antony's deification brings about a reintegration of body and soul,
such that Antony's body becomes a perfect instrument of his soul. Athanasius
repeatedly stresses that Antony's "face had a great and marvelous grace" and
that one could pick him out of a crowd, even if one had never met him before,
drawn by his eyes.[40]

Remember what Athanasius says about Antony's purity of soul when he
left the fortress. Not only does Antony display an "equilibrium . . . guided by
reason"; he is also "steadfast in that which accords with nature." Note the
emphasis: Antony's steadfast calm of soul was "natural." It was human nature
as it was made to be. Later, in his long address to the monks, Antony says that
pursuing virtue is "not difficult if we remain as we were made."[41] He also
remarks, "Let us preserve the soul for the Lord—which we received from him
as a trust—so that he may recognize his work as being just the same as he
made it."[42]

Behind these statements about naturalness of virtue is another side of
Athanasius's Christology from *On the Incarnation*. There he insists that human
beings were made, as the Bible says in Genesis 1:26, in the image and likeness
of God. For Athanasius, this means that human beings were made in the image
of Christ, who is the image of the Father. Because of sin, human beings began
to lose their rootedness in that eternal image. They began to corrupt, die, and
dissolve back into the nothingness from which they were created. To be rescued, the image needed to be redone. In a famous analogy, Athanasius compares the Incarnation to the restoring of a valuable painting:

> For as when a figure which has been painted on wood is spoilt by
> dirt, it is necessary for him whose portrait it is to come again so that
> the picture can be renewed in the same material—for because of his
> portrait the material on which it is painted is not thrown away, but
> the portrait is redone on it—even so the all-holy Son of the Father,
> who is the image of the Father, came to our realms to renew man
> who had been made in his likeness.[43]

Athanasius summarizes his view this way: "The Word of God came in his own
person, in order that, as he is the image of the Father, he might be able to
restore man who is in the image."[44] These theological views undergird Antony's

that Arius denied qualities of Christ's divinity ("no beginning," "ineffable" "immovable"). Even more intriguing, he does not use Athanasius's type of argument, but a more mystical, philosophical one: that Arius "did not know himself." We also know from several sources that in 338 Antony came to Alexandria to lodge his support of Athanasius and is reported to have worked miracles at this time. (This seems to be the visit described in the *Life of Antony*.)[71] Also several ancient historians—among them Sozomen and Rufinus—give independent accounts of Antony sending letters to Constantine in support of Athanasius.[72]

While we cannot independently confirm that the historical Antony spurned all dealings with Arians, we have several reports that other desert monks did, and did so explicitly because of Athanasius's policy. We know that Athanasius wrote a letter during these same years warning monks not to welcome into their monasteries either Arians or even anyone associated with the Arian regime in Alexandria, even if they personally denied the views of Arius. (Given what we saw in chapter 2, it should be no surprise that an anti-Nicene, like a Homoian, would deny Arius's views—that Christ was a creature, was made from nothing, etc.) Archeologists have discovered a monastery in Thebes that had the letter painted on its walls—one indication that Athanasius's policy was widely known and respected.[73] I mentioned earlier that a military detachment, in the search to arrest Athanasius, had surrounded one of Pachomius's monasteries. Its commander happened to be accompanied by Arian clergy. When he asked the monks there to pray for him, they refused, citing the admonition of Athanasius.[74] Sometimes, the policy Antony voiced in the *Life* could be more subtly carried out. One day, some Arians visited Abba Sisoes, a monk who eventually took up residence on Mount Pispir. When they set out their views, Sisoes made no reply. Instead, he called over his disciple and told him: "Abraham, bring me the book of Saint Athanasius and read it." The visitors suddenly realized where their host stood and fell silent. Still Sisoes was said to have "sent them away in peace."[75]

Antony in the Latin West

Athanasius delighted in paradox, and he saw Antony as paradox embodied, for Antony had become "famous everywhere and is marveled at by everyone, and dearly missed by people who never saw him"; people knew of him "in Spain and Gaul, in Rome and Africa," yet he had spent his long years "concealed and sitting in a mountain." Only God could do this, Athanasius insisted. Only God could take one who acted "in secret" and make his virtue a great "light" to shine over the seas.[76]

With the publication of Athanasius's biography, Antony's fame spread to the ends of the Roman world. It was one of the first Christian bestsellers. Gregory of Nazianzus, as we have seen, mentioned it in his panegyric on Athanasius in 380. And Jerome, when he wrote a Christian counterpart to Suetonius's *On Illustrious Men* in 392, listed Antony among the "illustrious" procession of Christian notables and noted that Athanasius had composed "a remarkable book" of Antony's life.[77] Very soon after its appearance in Greek, an anonymous Latin translation appeared. By 370, a second, more elegant translation into Latin was made, by Jerome's friend, Evagrius of Antioch.

Perhaps the highest compliment is imitation, and Athanasius's work spawned a host of imitators. Around 376, Jerome wrote—some would say, fabricated—the *Life of Paul*. In it, Jerome claimed Antony had had a predecessor, one Paul of Thebes, whose exploits had matched and anticipated the extremes of Antony's desert solitude (see appendix 4.1). Sometime before 400, Sulpicius Severus would draw on Athanasian themes for his *Life of Martin of Tours* to give the Latin West a hero to match Antony's exploits (see appendix 12.1). When Paulinus of Milan wrote his *Life of Ambrose*, he admitted in the preface that Athanasius's work was one of his models.[78] Palladius makes a similar admission in the 420s when composing his account of the lives of the desert fathers, the so-called *Lausiac History*.[79] Lives of the saints poured out from Christian pens. And nearly all show signs of using the *Life of Antony* as their literary prototype, mining it for episodes, motifs, even turns of phrase— from the First Greek *Life of Pachomius* (around 400) to Cyril of Scythopolis's *History of the Monks of Palestine* (in the 440s) to Gregory the Great's *Dialogues* (in the 590s).[80] Athanasius's work would profoundly shape hagiography in the medieval West, and Evagrius's Latin translation of the *Life of Antony* could be found on the shelves of nearly all medieval monastic libraries.

But Athanasius's *Life* did not just affect Christian literature: it affected Christian lives. A barometer of its power is an incident that took place in Milan in the mid-380s. A thirty-year-old African had recently arrived in the city, having just won appointment for the municipal chair of rhetoric—a position of considerable prestige, especially given Milan's status as an imperial residence. At the time of his appointment, the man had been a Manichee, that is, a member of an exotic (and illegal) Persian Gnostic sect. He had brought with him his concubine and teenage son. Once there, the young orator began to undergo a dramatic conversion to Christianity. We know him now as Augustine of Hippo (354–430), and the account of his conversion is recorded in his classic work, the *Confessions*.[81] Soon after arriving, Augustine began to come under the sway of the Christian bishop of the Milan, Ambrose (d. 397). Ambrose was a gifted speaker who delighted his congregation with his erudite borrowings from cutting-edge Greek theologians. Augustine came initially not for religious reasons—he thought Christianity was a crude religion. He came to check out his local competition, to see if Ambrose's rhetoric was worthy of its reputation. He was mesmerized, at first not by Ambrose's message, but by his eloquence. In time, however, he came to be impressed by Ambrose's erudition, by the way he interpreted scripture as Origen had—drawing out the symbolic meaning of passages that on their surface had appeared absurd. Augustine decided to abandon the Manichees and once more declared himself a Christian. But he remained what he had been made as a child, back in North Africa: a catechumen, in other words, a Christian, but unbaptized. This was not uncommon in the

LIFE OF ANTONY: THEMES AND INFLUENCE 99

fourth century. Many Christians remained catechumens for years, fearing the all-or-nothing commitment of baptism.

At the same time, Augustine was busy trying to advance his career. In the morning he taught; in the afternoon he made the rounds, visiting potential patrons in hopes of winning an even loftier position, perhaps a governor's post. Meanwhile, Augustine's mother had arrived. She got him to dismiss his mistress of fifteen years and succeeded in arranging a marriage with a proper Catholic girl from a rich Milanese family. But the girl was very young—perhaps only twelve, in any case two years under the age of marriage. Such disparities of age were not uncommon in those days. But that meant Augustine would have to wait. So he had found himself a new mistress. At the same time, he fretted over many matters: he was nervous about delivering a panegyric before the emperor; he had all sorts of questions he wanted to pose to Ambrose, but Ambrose, one of the most powerful figures in the empire, was a busy man. Augustine had also been reading books by Neoplatonist philosophers, certainly Plotinus and perhaps Porphyry, and seems to have been part of an elite Christian circle who saw the way this form of Platonism seemed to dovetail with Christianity, and at the same time offered perspectives and concepts that gave Christianity unexpected depths and greater intellectual coherence.

It was at this moment in his career that Augustine heard the story of Antony. During the summer break, in August 386, Augustine and some friends were staying at a house on the outskirts of Milan. Ponticianus, a fellow African and a government official, was surprised to find Augustine reading the letters of St. Paul. He then told Augustine and his friends the story of Antony. It shook Augustine to his roots. He cried out to a friend of his, named Alypius: "What is wrong with us? What is that that you have heard? Uneducated people are rising up and capturing heaven [Matt. 11:12], and we with our high culture without any heart—see where we roll in the mud of flesh and blood. Is it because they are ahead of us that we are ashamed to follow? Do we feel no shame at making not even an attempt to follow?"[82] Note what of Antony struck Augustine: that Antony was uneducated and yet capable of taking heaven by storm. Ponticianus also told Augustine and his friends of two Roman officials, working in Trier as *agentes in rebus* (the secret police). The two had one day read the *Life of Antony* and were so moved that they resigned their positions. They recognized how precarious it was to be "friends of the emperor" in the topsy-turvy military dictatorship of the late Roman Empire. They saw that Antony had followed a more secure path: that he become a "friend," not of emperors, but "of God." And so they abandoned their job and became monks.

These stories haunted Augustine. Distraught, he wandered into the garden of the house where they were staying and threw himself on the ground and began weeping. Suddenly, he heard the voice of a child calling out: *Tolle, lege, tolle, lege* ("take and read, take and read"). He ceased weeping and stood up and thought again of Antony: "For I had heard how Antony happened to be present at the gospel reading, and took it as an admonition to himself when the words were read: 'Go, sell all you have, give to the poor, and you shall have treasure in heaven, and come, follow me.' By such an inspired utterance, he was immediately converted."[83] This image of Antony's conversion, inspired by a scripture text, inspired Augustine. He rushed back and picked up his copy of Paul's letters. There he read the first passage he came upon, which happened to be Romans 13:13–14: "Not in riots and drunken parties, not in eroticism and indecencies, not in strife and rivalry, but put on the Lord Jesus and make no provision for the flesh in its lusts." He was transformed, "as if a light of relief from all anxiety flooded into my heart."[84]

Augustine soon wrote Ambrose and applied for baptism. The following Easter, during the all-night vigil of April 24–25, 387, he was baptized together with his friend Alypius and his teenage son Adeodatus. He had already re-signed from his prestigious job. But his imitation of Antony would continue. He would return to North Africa and set up a small, tight-knit community of *servi Dei*, "servants of God," on his family farm in Thagaste. It was a monastic community of sorts—very different from Antony's. Augustine, for one, could never have imagined a monastic retreat without books and without the joys of conversation with friends. Once he became a presbyter in Hippo in 391, he was allowed to bring his monastic experiment to the city. After he became bishop in 396, this community came to play an important role not only in Hippo, but throughout the North African province of Numidia. It became a seminary of sorts, a "seed-bed" that produced a number of the leading bishops of North Africa.

We will see much more about Antony. He makes an appearance, even if only a cameo, in virtually every work about the desert fathers (for a sampling, see appendix 4.2). But let me return to where we began this study of Antony: the fact that he was buried in an unknown tomb. The significance of this should not be underestimated. The late fourth century witnessed the rapid rise of the cult of the saints. Shrines and *martyria* were springing up around the empire—in Jerusalem, Rome, and North Africa. Pilgrims such as the Spanish woman Egeria would travel hundreds of miles to visit such sacred sites. Yet no such cult was possible for Antony. He had died in a remote spot in an unknown grave. The international cult of Antony came not from relics, but from a text. In other words, Athanasius's *Life* made possible a new type of cultic devotion, a *cultus* of text (for recent debate on the text and its authorship, see appendix 4.3).

NOTES

1. *VA* 28 (SC 400:212; trans. Gregg, CWS, 52).
2. *VA* 24 (SC 400:202; CWS, 49). Cf. *De incarnatione* 27–32.
3. *VA* 5 (SC 400:144; trans. Gregg, CWS, 34).
4. *VA* 9 (SC 400:162; trans. Gregg, CWS, 39).
5. *VA* 12, 13 (SC 400:168-170; trans. Gregg, CWS, 40–41).
6. *VA* 41 (SC 400:246; trans. Gregg, CWS, 62).
7. *VA* 78 (SC 400:334; trans. Gregg, CWS, 88). Cf. *De incarnatione* 31 and 48.
8. *VA* 13 and 80.

9. *VA* 13 (SC 400:172; trans. my own).

10. *VA* 35 (SC 400:230; trans. Gregg, CWS, 57).

11. *VA* 65 (SC 400:304; trans. Gregg, CWS, 79).

12. Jean Daniélou, "Les démons de l'air la *Vie d'Antoine*," in *Antonius Magnus Eremita, 356–1956: Studia ad Antiquum Monachismum Spectantia*, Studia Anselmiana 38, ed. Basilius Steidle (Rome: Herder, 1956), 142.

13. *VA* 22 (SC 400:196; trans. Gregg, CWS, 47). The same idea appears in *De incarnatione* 25 (OECT, 194–195). The biblical basis is Eph 2:2, in which Paul speaks of Satan as "the ruler of the power of the air."

14. Athanasius, *De incarnatione* 25 (OECT, 194–197). Cf. Athanasius, *Epistula ad Adelphium* 7 (PG 26:108; trans. NPNF 4:577): "stretching out His hands upon the Cross, He overthrew the prince of the power of the air . . . and made the way clear for us into the heavens."

15. *VA* 70 (SC 400:318; CWS, 83).

16. *VA* 31 (SC 400:220; trans. Gregg, CWS, 55).

17. *VA* 32-33 (SC 400:222–228; CWS 55–56).

18. *VA* 36 (SC 400:232; trans. Gregg, CWS, 58).

19. *VA* 36 (SC 400:232–234; trans. Gregg, CWS, 58).

20. *VA* 35, 37 (SC 400:230, 234; CWS, 58, 59).

21. Ignatius of Loyola, *Spiritual Exercises* #315–318. For the text and a commentary, see George E. Ganss, *The Spiritual Exercises of Saint Ignatius* (St. Louis: The Institute of Jesuit Sources, 1992), 121–122.

22. *VA* 74 (SC 400:324; trans. Gregg, CWS, 85).

23. See Athanasius, *Orationes contra Arianos* 1.35–36, 2.8 (PG 26:84–88, 164; NPNF 4:326–327, 352).

24. Athanasius, *De incarnatione* 8 (OECT, 151).

25. Athanasius, *De incarnatione* 17 (OECT, 175).

26. Athanasius, *De incarnatione* 41 (OECT, 237).

27. Athanasius, *De incarnatione* 54 (SC 199:458; trans. my own).

28. Athanasius, *Orationes contra Arianos* 2.70 (PG 26:296; NPNF 4:386).

29. For example: *Orationes contra Arianos* 1.38–39; *De decretis* 14; *Epistula ad Adelphium* 4.

30. Athanasius, *De incarnatione* 44 (OECT, 244–45).

31. *VA* 5 (SC 400:144–146; trans. Gregg, CWS, 34).

32. *VA* 10 (SC 400:164; trans. Gregg, CWS, 39).

33. *VA* 14 (SC 400:172; trans. Gregg, CWS, 42).

34. *VA* 93 (SC 400:374; CWS, 98).

35. *VA* 89 (SC 400:362; CWS, 95).

36. *VA* 14 (SC 400:172–174; trans. Gregg, CWS, 42).

37. *VA* 14 (SC 400:174; trans. Gregg, CWS, 42).

38. Athanasius, *Orationes contra Arianos* 3.34 (PG 26:396–397; trans. my own).

39. *VA* 67 (SC 400:312–314; trans. Gregg, CWS, 81).

40. *VA* 67 (SC 400:312–314; trans. Gregg, CWS, 81).

41. *VA* 20 (SC 400:190; trans. Gregg, CWS, 46).

42. *VA* 20 (SC 400:190–192; trans. Gregg, CWS, 46–47).

43. Athanasius, *De incarnatione* 14 (OECT, 166; trans. Thomson, OECT, 167).

44. Athanasius, *De incarnatione* 13 (OECT, 166; trans, Thomson, OECT, 167).

45. *VA* 50 (SC 400:270–272; CWS, 68–69).

46. *VA* 44 (SC 400:252–254; trans. Gregg, CWS, 64).

47. *VA* 67 (SC 400:310; trans. Gregg, CWS, 81).

48. *VA* 92 (SC 400:372; trans. Gregg, CWS, 98).
49. *VA* 68 (SC 400:314, trans. Gregg, CWS, 81).
50. *VA* 68 (SC 400:314; trans. Gregg, CWS, 82).
51. Athanasius, *Apologia contra Arianos* 59 (PG 25:357; trans. NPNF 2.4:131).
52. Athanasius, *Historia Arianorum* 79 (PG 25:789; trans. NPNF 2.4:300).
53. Athanasius, *Historia Arianorum* 78 (PG 25:788–789; trans. NPNF 2.4:300); *Ad Episcopos Aegypti* 22 (PG 25:589; NPNF 2.4:234–235).
54. *VA* 68 (SC 400:314; trans. Gregg, CWS, 81–82).
55. *VA* 89 (SC 400:364; trans. Gregg, CWS, 95).
56. *VA* 91 (SC 400:386; trans. Gregg, CWS, 97).
57. On Melitian monasticism, see Chapter 13.
58. *VA* 69 (SC 400:316; trans. Gregg, CWS, 82). Cf. *Orationes contra Arianos* 1.1 (PG 26:13; NPNF 2.4:306); *De synodis* 5 (PG 26:688; NPNF 2.4:453); *Ad Episcopos Aegypti* 9 (PG 25:557; NPNF 2.4:227).
59. *VA* 69 (SC 400:316; trans. Gregg, CWS, 82).
60. *VA* 69 (SC 400:316; CWS, 82). Cf. Athanasius, *Epistula ad Adelphium* 3 (PG 26:1073–1076; NPNF 4:575); *Orationes contra Arianos* 2.14, 3.15.
61. *VA* 68–69 (SC 400:314–316; trans. Gregg, CWS, 82). Cf. *Orationes contra Arianos* 1.9; *Ad Episcopos Aegypti* 12–15.
62. *VA* 68 (SC 400:314; CWS, 82). Cf. *Orationes contra Arianos* 1.4, 2.70, 3.1; *De synodis* 13.
63. *VA* 68 (SC 400:314; trans. Gregg, CWS, 82). Cf. *Orationes contra Arianos* 1.30, 2.43, 3.1; *Ad Episcopos Aegypti* 9; *Historia Arianorum* 66.
64. Athanasius, *Orationes contra Arianos* 2.32 (PG 26:216; NPNF 4:365). Cf. *De decretis* 1.
65. *VA* 82 (SC 400:350; trans. Gregg, CWS, 91).
66. *VA* 68 (SC 400:314; trans. Gregg, CWS, 82).
67. *VA* 68, 89, and 91.
68. *VA* 70 (SC 400:318; trans. Gregg, CWS, 83).
69. *VA* 86 (SC 400:356–358; trans. Gregg, CWS, 93–94).
70. Antony, *Ep.* 4.17 (Rubenson, 211).
71. The *Chronicon Athanasianum* (SC 316:234–236; trans. NPNF 2.4:503), the Syriac index of Athanasius' festal letters, says of 337: "in this year, Constantine having died on 27 Pachon [=May 22, 337], Athanasius, now liberated, returned from Gaul triumphantly on 27 Athyr [=Nov. 23, 337]. In this year, too, . . . Antony, the great leader, came to Alexandria, and though he remained only two days, showed himself wonderful in many things, and healed many. He went away on the third of Messori [=July 27]."
72. Sozomen, *HE* 2.31 (SC 306:368; NPNF 2.2:280); Rufinus, *HE* 10.8 (PL 21: 477; Amidon, 18). The timing of these letters of support is somewhat confusing. See Bartelink, SC 400:340–341, note #2.
73. On the inscription, see Hugh Evelyn-White and W. E. Crum, *The Monastery of Epiphanius at Thebes* (New York: Metropolitan Museum of Art, 1927), 2:124, no. 585.
74. *Bohairic Life* 185 (CSCO 89:167; CS 45:223); cf. *First Greek Life* 137–138.
75. *AP* Sisoes 25 (PG 65:400; trans. Ward, CS 59:217).
76. *VA* 93 (SC 400:374; trans. Gregg, CWS, 98–99).
77. Jerome, *De uiris illustribus* 88 (TU 14.1:45; FC 100:122).
78. Paulinus of Milan, *Vita Ambrosii*, praef.
79. Palladius, *Historia Lausiaca* 8, 6; 26, 5.15 and 28, 18.

80. Bartelink, *Athanase d'Alexandre: Vie d'Antoine,* SC 400:68–70.
81. On Augustine and the *Confessions,* see the bibliography for chapter 4.
82. Augustine, *Confessions* VIII.viii.19 (BA 14:36; Henry Chadwick, 146).
83. Augustine, *Confessions* VIII.xii.29 (BA 14:66; Chadwick, 153).
84. Augustine, *Confessions* VIII.xii.29 (BA 14:66–68; Chadwick, 153).

BIBLIOGRAPHY

The *Life of Antony:* Studies

For basic overview, see Columba Stewart, "Anthony of the Desert," in *The Early Christian World,* ed. Philip F. Esler (New York: Routledge, 2000), 2:1088–1101. See also G. J. M. Bartelink, introduction to *Athanase d'Alexandrie: Vie d'Antoine,* SC 400 (Paris: Éditions du Cerf, 1994), 42–108, for a good survey of the issues. Some important studies include:

Baynes, Norman H. "St. Antony and the Demons." *Journal of Egyptian Archeology* 40 (1954): 7–10.

Bouyer, Louis. *La vie de S. Antoine: essai sur la spiritualité du monachisme primitif.* Rev. and corr. ed. SO 22. Bégrolles-en-Mauges: Abbaye de Bellefontaine, 1978.

Brakke, David. *Athanasius and Asceticism.* Baltimore: Johns Hopkins University Press, 1998.

Brennan, Brian R. "Athanasius' *Vita Antonii*: A Sociological Interpretation." *Vigiliae Christianae* 39 (1985): 209–227.

Desprez, Vincent. "Saint Anthony and the Beginnings of Anchoritism." *American Benedictine Review* 43 (1992): 61–81, 141–172.

Francis, J. A. "Pagan and Christian Philosophy in Athanasius' *Vita Antonii.*" *American Benedictine Review* 32 (1981): 100–113.

Gould, Graham E. "The *Life of Anthony* and the Origins of Christian Monasticism in Fourth-Century Egypt." *Medieval History* 1 (1991): 3–11.

Gregg, Robert C., and Dennis E. Groh. "Claims on the Life of St. Antony." In *Early Arianism: A View of Salvation,* 131–159. Philadelphia: Fortress Press, 1981.

Luibhéid, Colm. "Antony and the Renunciation of Society." *Irish Theological Quarterly* 52 (1986): 304–314.

Nugent, Andrew. "Black Demons in the Desert." *American Benedictine Review* 49 (1998): 209–221.

Petterson, Alvyn. "Athanasius' Presentation of Antony of the Desert's Admiration for His Body." *Studia Patristica* 21 (1987): 438–447.

Roldanus, J. "Die *Vita Antonii* als Spiegel der Theologie des Athanasius und ihr Weiterwirken bis ins 5. Jht." *Theologie und Philosophie* 58 (1983): 194–216.

Steidle, Basilius, ed. *Antonius Magnus Eremita, 356–1956: Studia ad Antiquum Monachismum Spectantia.* Studia Anselmiana 38. Rome: Herder, 1956. See especially: Christine Mohrmann, "Note sur la version latine la plus ancienne de la *Vie de saint Antoine* par saint Athanase," 35–44; Michael J. Marx, "Incessant Prayer in the *Vita Antonii,*" 108–135; Jean Daniélou, "Les démons de l'air dans la *Vie d'Antoine,*" 136–147. Jean Leclerq, "Saint Antoine dans la tradition monastique médiévale," 229–247.

Vogüé, Adalbert de. *Histoire littéraire du mouvement monastique dans l'antiquité.* Vol. 1, pt. 1, *Le monachisme latin: de la mort d'Antoine à la fin du séjour de Jérôme à Rome, 356–385,* 17–80. Paris: Éditions du Cerf, 1991.

The *Life of Antony*: Disputes on Authorship

For an overview, see G. J. M. Bartelink, introduction to *Athanase d'Alexandrie: Vie d'Antoine*, 27–35, SC 400 (Paris: Éditions du Cerf, 1994). On the current debate, see:

Barnes, Timothy D. "Angel of Light or Mystic Initiate: The Problem of the *Life of Antony*." *Journal of Theological Studies* n.s. 37 (1986): 353–368.

Brakke, David. "The Greek and Syriac Versions of the *Life of Antony*." *Le Muséon* 107 (1994): 29–53.

Draguet, René, ed. *Athanase d'Alexandrie: la vie primitive de saint Antoine; conservée en syriaque*, CSC. 417–418. Louvain: Secrétariat du Corpus SCO, 1980.

Lorenz, R. "Die griechische *Vita Antonii* des Athanasius und ihre syrische Fassung. Bemerkungen zu einer These von R. Draguet." *Zeitschrift für Kirchen geschichte* 100 (1989): 77–84.

Louth, Andrew. "St. Athanasius and the Greek *Life of Antony*." *Journal of Theological Studies*, n. s. 39 (1988): 504–509.

Tetz, Martin. "Athanasius und die *Vita Antonii*. Literarische und theologische Relationen." *Zeitschrift für die neutestamentliche Wissenschaft* 73 (1983): 1–30.

Augustine of Hippo

On the conversion of Augustine, an excellent starting point is Peter Brown, *Augustine of Hippo: a Biography*, rev. ed. (Berkeley: University of California Press, 2000). For the Latin text of the *Confessions*, together with a commentary, see James J. O'Donnell, *Augustine: The Confessions*, 3 vols. (New York: Oxford University Press, 1992). The best recent translation is that of Henry Chadwick, *Augustine: The Confessions*, Oxford World Classics (New York: Oxford University Press, 1992). Other studies include:

Bonner, Gerald, ed. *St. Augustine of Hippo: Life and Controversies*. 3rd ed. Norwich: Canterbury Press, 2002.

Courcelle, Pierre P. *Recherches sur les "Confessions" de saint Augustin*. Paris: E. de Boccard, 1950.

Dodaro, Robert, and George Lawless, eds. *Augustine and His Critics: Essays in Honour of Gerald Bonner*. New York: Routledge, 2000.

Fitzgerald, Allan D., and John Cavadini, eds. *Augustine through the Ages: An Encyclopedia*. Grand Rapids, Mich.: Wm. B. Eerdmans, 1999.

Harmless, William. *Augustine and the Catechumenate*. Collegeville, Minn.: Liturgical Press, 1995.

Harrison, Carol. *Augustine: Christian Truth and Fractured Humanity*. Christian Theology in Context. New York: Oxford University Press, 2000.

Lancel, Serge. *Saint Augustin*. Paris: Fayard, 1999.

O'Donnell, James J. "Augustine: His Time and Lives." In *The Cambridge Companion to Augustine*, ed. Eleonore Stump and Norman Kretzmann, 8–15. New York: Cambridge University Press, 2001.

O'Meara, John J. *The Young Augustine: The Growth of Augustine's Mind up to His Conversion*. 2nd ed. New York: Alba House, 2001.

Wills, Garry. *Saint Augustine*. Penguin Lives. New York: Viking Press, 1999.

Jerome, *The Life of Paul of Thebes*

Jerome composed the *Life of Paul of Thebes* (*Vita S. Pauli*) in the 370s, probably not long after he himself had abandoned living in the desert of Chalcis in Syria. A friend of his, Evagrius of Antioch, had recently translated Athanasius's *Life of Antony* from Greek into Latin. Jerome claims that ascetics debated who the first monk was. Some claimed Antony, but Jerome asserts that he had learned from two of Antony's disciples that Paul of Thebes had embarked on desert living even earlier. Jerome claims that Paul fled to the desert because of the persecution of Decius. Only many years later is he discovered at the age of 113 by Antony (who was at the time a mere 90 years old). Jerome's tale is full of beasts, both wild (lions and wolves) and mythical (centaurs and satyrs). As Owen Chadwick has noted, "Jerome was criticized in his own day for writing about someone who never existed. There appears to be no good reason for doubting that an early hermit named Paul existed. There appears to be every reason for believing that Jerome knew nothing about him. The *Life* is a piece of literature, a historical novel" (*John Cassian*, 5). The work proved popular and influential. Medieval artists such as Hieronymous Bosch loved to portray the dramatic first meeting of Paul and Antony. Here are a few excerpts from Jerome's account:

ANTONY NOT THE EARLIEST MONK

It has often been a matter of discussion among many people as to which monk was the first to inhabit the desert. Some, going back further into the past, have ascribed the beginning to the blessed Elijah and to John; of these, Elijah seems to us to have been more than a monk, while John seems to have started to prophesy before he was born. Others, whose opinion is commonly accepted, claim that Antony was the first to undertake this way of life, which is partly true, for it is not so much that he came before all the others but rather he inspired everyone with a commitment to this way of life. Amathas and Macarius, Antony's disciples (of whom the former buried his master's body), affirm to this day that a certain Paul of Thebes was the originator of the practice, though not of the name, of the solitary life, and this is the view I also take. (Jerome, *Vita S. Pauli*, prologue)

MEETING OF ANTONY AND PAUL

Antony continued on his journey, seeing nothing but the tracks of wild animals and the immense vastness of the desert. . . . He saw a she-wolf near by. . . . He followed it with his eyes and when the wild beast disappeared into a cave he went up close and tried to look inside. . . . At last, through the terrifying darkness of the night which made it impossible to see anything he discerned a light in the distance. As he quickened his pace in his eagerness, he bumped his foot against a stone, making a noise. When the blessed Paul heard this noise he closed and bolted a door that had been open. Then Antony fell down in front of this door and continued to beg to be allowed in until it was the sixth hour of the day or even later, saying, "You know who I am, where I come from and why I have come. I know that I do not deserve to see you but I will not go away unless I do. Why do you, who welcome animals, drive a person away? I have sought you and I have found you: I knock that it may be opened to me. If I do not get what I want, I shall die here in front of your door— and I trust you will bury my body when I am dead." . . . Then Paul smiled and unbolted the door. When it was open, they embraced each other, and greeting each other by name, they joined in giving thanks to the Lord. (Jerome, *Vita S. Pauli* 9)

ANTONY DISCOVERS PAUL'S CORPSE

Paul sent Antony to get Athanasius's cloak to use as a burial cloth. While Antony returned back to his hermitage to retrieve the cloak, Paul died:

When [Antony] entered the cave he saw the lifeless corpse in a kneeling position, its head erect and its hands stretched out toward heaven. At first he thought that Paul was still alive and so he knelt down beside him to pray, but when he heard no sighs from the praying man, as he usually did, he fell upon him in a tearful embrace, realizing that even as a corpse the holy man, by means of his reverent posture, was praying to God for whom all things live. (Jerome, *Vita S. Pauli* 14–15)

WILD LIONS BURY PAUL

Antony therefore wrapped Paul's body up and brought it outside, singing hymns and psalms according to Christian tradition, but he was upset that he did not have a spade with which to dig the earth. . . . Behold two lions came running from the inner desert, their manes flowing over their necks. At first Antony was terrified at the sight of them but when he focused his mind on God he was able to stand still without fear as if what he saw was a pair of doves. They came straight towards the corpse of the blessed old man and stopped there; wagging their tails in devotion they lay down at his feet, roaring loudly as if to show that in their own way they were lamenting as best they could. They then began to dig the ground near by with their paws: vying with each other to remove the sand, they dug out a space large enough for one man. They then went straight up to Antony, their necks bent and their ears laid back, and licked his hands and feet as if demanding a reward for their hard work. He realized that they were asking him for a blessing. Immediately he burst out in praise of Christ because dumb animals, too, were able to understand that there was a God. . . . Making a sign to them with his hand, he ordered them to depart. (Jerome, *Vita S. Pauli* 16)

The Latin text is found in PL 23:17–60. The translation is by Carolinne White, *Early Christian Lives* (New York: Penguin Books, 1998), 75–84.

APPENDIX 4.2

The Many Faces of Antony

Athanasius presents Antony as a many-sided ideal: as a fearless wrestler of demons, as a healer and philosopher, as a "daily" martyr and a model of orthodoxy. In other literature of the desert, Antony appears in other guises. Here are a few snapshots:

THE MAN OF PRAYER (SERAPION OF THMUIS, 356)

In 356, soon after Antony's death, Serapion, bishop of Thmuis, wrote two of Antony's disciples. The letter, first published in the 1950s, exists only in Syriac and Armenian:

> As soon as this earth's great elder, the blessed Antony, who prayed for the whole world, departed, everything has been torn apart and is in anguish, and the Wrath devastates Egypt. . . . While he was truly on earth, he extended his hands and prayed and spoke with God all day long. He did not let the Wrath descend on us. Lifting up his thoughts, he kept it from coming down. But now that those hands are closed, no one else can be found who might halt the violence. (*Ep. ad discipulos Antonii* 5, 7–8, 19–20; trans. my own)

THE TEACHER OF *GNOSIS* (*LETTERS OF ANTONY*)

Jerome reports that he knew of seven letters that Antony wrote in Coptic to monks. It is possible that a text of the letters in a Georgian translation found at the Monastery of Saint Catherine's are authentic. They show an Antony at home with the ideas of the third-century teacher Origen (e.g., the preexistence of souls). Antony appears in these letters as a teacher of *gnosis*, of "knowledge."

> But you, my beloved in the Lord, know yourselves, so that you may know this time, and "be prepared to offer yourselves to God as a pleasing sacrifice" [cf. Rom. 12: 1]. Truly, my beloved, I write to you "as to wise men" [1 Cor. 10: 15], who are able to know themselves. I know that he who knows himself knows God and his dispensations for his creatures. (*Ep.* 3:39–40; trans. Samuel Rubenson, 208).

THE STRUGGLING DESERT MONK (*APOPHTHEGMATA PATRUM*, FIFTH CENTURY)

The *Apophthegmata Patrum*, a collection of sayings of the desert fathers, opens with thirty-eight sayings attributed to Antony. They portray a more human and vulnerable elder who passes on a pithy wisdom. For example:

> When the holy Abba Antony lived in the desert he was afflicted with boredom, and attacked by many sinful thoughts. He said to God: "Lord, I want to be saved but these thoughts don't leave me any peace. What shall I do? How can I be saved?" A little later, when he got up to go out, Antony saw a man like himself sitting and working, getting up now and then from his work to pray. It was an angel of the Lord sent to correct and reassure him. He heard the angel saying to him, "Do this and you will be saved." At these words, Antony was filled with joy and courage. He did this, and he was saved. (*AP* Antony 1 [PG 65:75; trans. Benedicta Ward, CS 59:1–2])

THE UNLETTERED SAGE (EVAGRIUS PONTICUS, 390S)

Evagrius Ponticus was a well-educated theologian who once fought in the great doctrinal struggles in Constantinople. He settled in Egypt and was fascinated by the native Coptic wisdom he found. This is a story in his *Praktikos*:

> A certain member of what was then considered the circle of the wise once approached the just Antony and asked him: "How do you every manage to carry on, Father, deprived as you are of the consolation of books?" His reply: "My book, sir philosopher, is the nature of created things, and it is always at hand when I wish to read the words of God." (*Praktikos* 92 [SC 171:694; trans. John Eudes Bamberger, CS 4:39])

THE GOOD HOST (PALLADIUS, 420S)

Palladius, in his *Lausiac History*, speaks of the way Antony, "the Great One," handled tourists who visited him:

> Whenever the Great One came to their monastery, he would call out and ask: "Brother Macarius, have any brothers come?" He would answer that they had. "Are they from Egypt or from Jerusalem?" For he had given him the code for identification. "If they are easy-going, say that they are Egyptians; if reverend and erudite, say that they are from Jerusalem". . . . Whenever Macarius said they were Egyptians, Antony would say: "Prepare the lentils and give them to eat." Then he would say a prayer for them and bid them farewell. But when he said that they were from Jerusalem, then he would sit up all night

talking to them about salvation. (*Historia Lausiaca* 21.8–9 [Butler, 66; trans. Robert Meyer, ACW 34:73–74])

THE TEACHER OF VIRTUE (JOHN CASSIAN, 420S)

John Cassian, living in southern France, wrote to his Latin-speaking audience, extolling the wondrous achievements of the monks of Egypt. Here, in *The Institutes*, he describes Antony as the teacher and model of virtue:

> For it is an ancient and admirable saying of the blessed Antony to the effect that when a monk, after having opted for the cenobium, is striving to attain to the heights of a still loftier perfection, has seized upon the consideration of the discretion and is already able to rely upon his own judgment and to come to the pinnacle of the anchoritic life, he must not seek all the kinds of virtue from one person, however outstanding he may be. For there is one who is adorned with the flowers of knowledge, another who is more solidly founded in patience, one who excels in the virtue of humility and another in that of abstinence, while still another is decked with the grace of simplicity, this one surpasses the others by his zeal for magnanimity, that one by mercy, another one by vigils, yet another by silence, and still another by toil. Therefore the monk who, like a most prudent bee, is desirous of storing up spiritual honey must suck the flower of a particular virtue from those who possess it more intimately, and he must lay it up carefully in the vessel of his heart. (*De institutis* 5.4.1–2 [SC 109:194–195; trans. Boniface Ramsey, ACW 58: 118–119])

Did Athanasius Really Write the *Life of Antony*?

The *Life of Antony* was translated not only into Latin, but into the languages of the Christian East—Syriac, Coptic, Arabic, and Armenian. Discussion has focused recently on the Syriac version. In 1980, René Draguet published a critical edition, and he and other scholars have been intrigued by some of its striking differences from the Greek text.[1] One is the scene in which Antony emerges from the desert fortress. The Greek *Life* says: "Antony came forth as though from some sanctuary, a mystic initiate, mystery-taught and God-inspired." But the Syriac *Life* says: "When he came out like a man who rises from the depths of the earth, they saw his face as that of an angel of light."[2] Note the contrast in the Syriac, he is an "angel of light." In the Greek, Antony is called a "mystic initiate." In other words, the Greek uses the language of pagan mystery cults— apparently as part of its apologetic appeal to pagan readers—while the Syriac uses biblical imagery. Second, there is the passage in which Antony is portrayed as the leader of the burgeoning monastic movement. The Greek *Life* says: "And so, from then on, there were monasteries in the mountains, and the desert was made a city by monks who left their own people and registered themselves for the citizenship in the heavens." The Syriac *Life* says: "And from that time the life of the solitaries in the desert and the mountains began to multiply and increase in the manner of a tabernacle of the new world."[3] Note again the stark contrast. The Greek uses the image of a "city," no doubt an attractive (and paradoxical) image to a city-dweller like Athanasius. The Syriac, on the other hand, uses "tabernacle," an image drawn from cultic worship.

What accounts for these and many other interesting differences in wording and detail? Draguet claimed that the Syriac translation shows signs of having come not from the Greek text attributed to Athanasius, but from some other cruder Greek text, full of Coptic phraseology and vocabulary. In other words, Draguet claimed that Athanasius was not the true author of the original *Life of Antony*, and that the original was not by someone fluent in Greek, as Athanasius was, but by a Hellenized Copt. Draguet's hypothesis met with little initial response.

Soon after, Timothy Barnes proposed a modification, (1) that the original *Life of Antony* was composed not in a coptizing Greek, but directly in Coptic; (2) that the Syriac version was a faithful and early translation made directly from the Coptic original; (3) that the Greek *Life* not only translates the Coptic original, but reworks it, altering emphases and passages in ways more attractive to the urban culture of the Roman world; and (4) that the one responsible for the Greek *Life* was *not* Athanasius.[4] To justify the final part of his view, Barnes notes that certain vocabulary in the Greek version is un-Athanasian; more decisively, he claims that it is hard to believe that Athanasius would put himself on equal footing with Serapion as inheritor of Antony's mantle. Barnes is willing to admit that the Greek *Life* may well have come from someone in Athanasius's entourage, but he argues that "nothing in the text" of the Greek version "need point to Athanasius himself as the redactor."[5] Barnes concludes with the claim that "it is not the historical Coptic hermit of the Egyptian *chora* [countryside] who exerted a formative influence on western monasticism and Byzantine asceticism, but an Alexandrian refurbishment more attuned to the spiritual yearnings of an urban Mediterranean culture."[6]

The theses of Draguet and Barnes have not convinced many. But they have provoked valuable discussion, forcing scholars to reassess the case for Athanasius's authorship. First, we need to remember that the contemporaries of Athanasius—Gregory of Nazianzus, Jerome, and the author of the First Greek *Life of Pachomius*, among others—unanimously attributed the *Life* to Athanasius. Besides these external attributions, there is much internal evidence. For example, Andrew Louth, while he was willing to grant (provisionally) part of Barnes's thesis—that the original *Life of Antony* may have been composed in Coptic—insists that the Greek version was definitely the work of Athanasius. Louth points to many of the features we have examined: the way that the *Life*, at least in its Greek form, draws heavily and pervasively on Athanasius's theology of the Incarnation and of deification; and the way it uses Athanasius's characteristic anti-Arian vocabulary (such as calling Arians "Ario-maniacs," or referring to them as "mindless" [*alogoi*]).[7] Another scholar, R. Lorenz, has rejected Draguet's claim that the Syriac text witnesses to an independent literary tradition.[8] He has taken the differences in detail between the Greek and the Syriac and shown the way that it says more about the Syriac context, about its spirituality and its audience.

A different challenge to Athanasius's authorship has come from Martin Tetz.[9] Tetz has suggested that Athanasius was not the author of the *Life of Antony*, but rather its editor, and that the author of the original was Serapion of Thmuis. He points out that in the preface, the author says that he learned all he could from one who "poured water in the hands" of Antony—a reference, as we saw, to 2 Kings, in which Elisha is said to have poured water in the hands of Elijah. This Elisha-like informant may well have been Serapion, for he appears in two other spots in the *Life*: he reported the vision of the mules kicking the altar table, and he received one of Antony's sheepskins. Tetz also has contrasted Serapion's theology with that of Athanasius. As we saw, Serapion wrote a letter to Antony's disciples soon after he heard the news of Antony's death. There he describes Antony as a man of prayer whose interventions in the heavenly court had spared Egypt the Wrath of God. That is not the portrait that appears in the version of the *Life* we have. Instead, the version from Athanasius portrays Antony as the exemplar of the incarnation and grace of Christ. This portrait squares well with a theology one finds not only in Athanasius's theological treatises, such as *On the Incarnation* or *Orations against the Arians*, but also in various letters he wrote to monks. G. J. M. Bartelink, who has spent much of his career working on the *Life of Antony* and has produced the critical edition of both the Latin and Greek versions, is unconvinced by Tetz's arguments. He admits that Serapion may well be Athanasius's key informant, but there is no evidence that Serapion wrote a prior version. On the contrary, the Greek text shows "a great unity of style" that would preclude the existence of some prior version not written by Athanasius.[10]

NOTES

1. René Draguet, *La vie primitive de saint Antoine conservée en syriaque*, CSCO 417–418 (Louvain, 1980).

2. *VA* 14 (SC 400:172; trans; my own); *VA* Syriac 14 (CSCO 417:34); trans. Timothy D. Barnes, "Angel of Light or Mystic Initiate: The Problem of the *Life of Antony*," *Journal of Theological Studies* n.s. 37 (1986): 360.

3. *VA* 14 (SC 400:174; Gregg, CWS, 42–43); *VA* Syriac 14 (CSCO 417:35; trans. Barnes, 362).

4. Barnes, "Angel of Light," 353–368.

5. Barnes, "Angel of Light," 367.

6. Barnes, "Angel of Light," 368.

7. Andrew Louth, "St. Athanasius and the Greek *Life of Antony*," *Journal of Theological Studies* n.s. 39 (1988): 504–509.

8. R. Lorenz, "Die griechische *Vita Antonii* des Athanasius und ihre syrische Fassung: Bemerkungen zu einer These von R. Draguet," *Zeitschrift für Kirchen geschichte* 100 (1989): 77–84.

9. Martin Tetz, "Athanasius und die *Vita Antonii*: Literarische und theologische Relationen," *Zeitschrift für die neutestamentliche Wissenschaft* 73 (1983): 1–30.

10. Bartelink, *Athanase d'Alexandrie: Vie d'Antoine*, SC 400:35.

5

Pachomius

A monastery, strictly speaking, is a contradiction in terms. After all, the word "monk" (*monachos*) literally means "one who lives alone." Thus, a monastery is where those who live alone live together.

How did monasteries arise? How did monks—those who choose to live alone—choose to live together? The person traditionally credited with this innovation is Pachomius (c. 292–346). Textbooks typically speak of him as the "founder of cenobitic monasticism" (from *coenobium*, "community") and contrast him with Antony, the "founder" of anchoritic monasticism.[1] The contrast makes a nice diptych—too nice actually, for the historical record is more complex and more ambiguous. Pachomius may not have invented the monastery as such, but he was certainly a pioneer. He was also an organizational genius. By the time of his death, he headed a confederation of nine monasteries for men and two for women. These housed hundreds, perhaps thousands, of monks. His achievement earned him an international reputation, and the rules he composed provided a model for later monastic legislators, notably Basil of Caesarea in the Greek East and Benedict of Nursia in the Latin West.

Early sources claim that Pachomius himself recognized the scale of his achievement. He reportedly told Theodore, his eventual successor:

> In our generation in Egypt I see three important things that increase God's grace for the benefit of all who have understanding: the bishop Athanasius, the athlete of Christ contending for the faith unto death; the holy Abba Antony, the perfect model of the anchoritic life; and this *koinonia*, which

is a model for all those who wish to assemble souls in God, to suc-
cor them until they be made perfect.[2]

These words—whether uttered by Pachomius himself or, more likely, placed
in his mouth by later biographers—are striking in perspective and terminology.
Note how he sets his life's work on a par with the heroics of his famous
contemporaries Athanasius and Antony. His work is equally a sign and vehicle
of God's grace. Note also the terminology: he speaks not of monasteries, but
of the *koinonia*, the "fellowship," a term drawn from the New Testament. Pachomius and his successors made this New Testament term their own, investing
it with rich resonances. They saw themselves not simply as pioneers of monasticism, but as pioneers in the art of Christian living, called to resurrect the
New Testament's most radical vision of human community.

The Sources

A host of ancient biographers—almost all, anonymous—traced out Pachomius's career. The array of documents is formidable.

The Coptic Lives

Twenty-two recensions survive in Coptic, most in very fragmentary form. Of
these, twenty-one were written in Sahidic Coptic, the dialect of Upper Egypt
(where Pachomius was from). Most are brief, some merely a page or two,
others, twenty-five to thirty pages. The remaining version is in Bohairic Coptic,
the dialect of Lower Egypt and the Nile Delta. This *Bohairic Life of Pachomius*
gives the best-preserved account in Coptic, over 200 pages in a modern edition.
It has some lacunae, but scholars have been able to fill these in using Sahidic
fragments. (This reconstruction is, therefore, abbreviated SBo.) Also important
is the *First Sahidic Life*, which, while fragmentary, offers fascinating—and
somewhat embarrassing—glimpses into Pachomius's early career.

The Greek Lives

Eight recensions survive in Greek. Of these, the earliest and most important
is the *First Greek Life of Pachomius* (or *Vita Prima*, usually abbreviated G[1]).
Scholars believe that it was composed in the 390s by a Pachomian monk living
near Alexandria in the monastery of Metanoia. The author, while a native
speaker of Greek, was conversant in Coptic. He admits that he did not know
Pachomius personally, but claims to have spoken with those who did.[3] The
First Greek Life parallels the *Bohairic Life* not only in the incidents it recounts,
but even in the very wording it uses. It is more sober than the Coptic versions,
dwelling less on the fantastical, and seems, in spots, to be an abridgement.
There are two other key documents in Greek. One is the *Paralipomena*, a miscellany of anecdotes about Pachomius. The other is the *Letter of Ammon*, written

by an Egyptian bishop who, as a young man, had spent three years in the Pachomian monastery of Pbow. He talks of meeting Pachomius's successor, Theodore, and passes on stories he heard about Pachomius.

Other Accounts

A Latin version of the life of Pachomius, based largely on the *Second Greek Life*, was translated in the early sixth century by Dionysius Exiguus (that is, Denis the Little). In addition, there are several Arabic versions. These Arabic versions drew on Coptic originals and have been used by scholars to help piece together the order of the surviving Sahidic fragments and to fill in gaps and correct mistakes in the surviving *Bohairic Life*. In addition to these biographical materials, there are collections of Pachomius's *Rules*—preserved especially in Latin—and a miscellany of his letters and catecheses.

Even seasoned scholars find this welter of biographies dizzying. The search for the historical Pachomius is a task every bit as complex as the search for the historical Jesus. And the methods that New Testament scholars use to study the Gospels—setting texts in parallel columns, looking for oral units behind the written text, probing the bias of the redactor—have been applied to the study of the Pachomian documents. For nearly a century, from the 1880s to the 1970s, scholars waged erudite battles over which sources were the oldest and most trustworthy. Fervor peaked in the 1950s in the brilliant, though acrimonious, debate between Louis-Théophile Lefort, who argued for the priority of the Coptic, and Derwas Chitty, who argued for the priority of the Greek.[4] The consensus seems to be this:

1. The oldest versions in all traditions—Coptic, Greek, Latin, and Arabic— preserve authentic material (for a chart of the major sources and their interconnection, see appendix 5.1).
2. These different versions draw on a pool of memories that was originally Coptic and oral.
3. The two great compilations, the *Bohairic Life* and the *First Greek Life*, share a common written source, now lost, which accounts for their similar order and phraseology.
4. None of these *Lives* can be taken at face value as "historical." We saw earlier that Athanasius brought a formidable agenda—both political and theological—to his *Life of Antony*. An agenda—both political and theological—colors the *Lives of Pachomius*, though the concerns are rather different.

Whatever their biases, the *Lives* of Pachomius do allow us to sketch out the main lines of his career. For what follows, I draw mostly on episodes preserved both in the *Bohairic Life* and the *First Greek Life* and will note whenever an episode is preserved in only one source or in the fragmentary *Sahidic Lives* or other sources. The sheer volume and complexity of Pachomian sources means that I have had to simplify and gloss over much. What follows is no more than a first glimpse.

Early Career

Pachomius was born in 292 in Upper Egypt, south of Thebes, in the town of Šne (Latopolis). (For a chronology of the life of Pachomius, see table 5.1.) His Coptic name, "Pachom," means "king's falcon." His parents were apparently pagans, of peasant stock but reasonably well off. In 312, at the age of twenty, he was drafted into the Roman army. Initially, he and other new recruits were locked up in a prison and "sunk in deep affliction"—tired, hungry, and frightened. That evening, some locals visited the prison and gave the young conscripts something to eat and drink. Pachomius was genuinely touched: "Why are these people so good to us when they do not know us?" His companions answered, "They are Christians," and (the *First Greek Life* adds) Christians are "merciful to everyone, including strangers."⁵ This experience of charity would come to define Pachomius's view of Christianity in general and of monasticism in particular.

Pachomius served in the army about a year but was discharged after the defeat of the Emperor Maximin Daia. He returned to Upper Egypt and settled in the village of Šeneset (Chenoboskion), where he was baptized around 313. On the night of his baptism, he had a mysterious dream-vision: dew from heaven descended onto his head, then condensed in his hand as a honeycomb and spread its sweetness over the whole earth.⁶ He spent the next three years serving the needs of the villagers—at least according to Coptic sources—but then decided to become a monk.

The *Letter of Ammon* claims that both Melitians and Marcionites heard of Pachomius's monastic aspirations and tried to recruit him. But he had a dream: Christ instructed him to choose the true church, the one represented by Alexander of Alexandria. This story reflects Ammon's own pro-Athanasius, pro-Alexandrian leanings, but it also highlights that sectarians had monks and monasteries, and that rival Christian groups competed for recruits.⁷

Pachomius decided to apprentice himself under a local anchorite named Palamon who headed a small group of anchorites and who taught a fierce asceticism: sleepless prayer vigils half of every night, and if possible, all night; unceasing manual labor, weaving rope and baskets; a diet limited to bread and salt, no wine, no meat, no oil, eating but once a day in summer, once every other day in winter.⁸ This regime was not for the faint-hearted. Pachomius remained with Palamon some seven years. Pachomius's apprenticeship reminds one of Antony's. Both sought out local holy men who resided not far from their villages. This is one of the faint clues that hint at traditions of monasticism that predate our sources, traditions in which holy men lived on the fringe of villages and practiced a complex of ascetical disciplines and methods of prayer (on this, see chapter 13).

Two mysterious revelations sparked—or at least signaled—Pachomius's shift from an anchoritic to a cenobitic life. Once, while gathering wood near the abandoned village of Tabennesi, he heard a voice calling him: "Pachomius, Pachomius, struggle, dwell in this place and build a monastery; for many will

TABLE 5.1. Pachomius and the *Koinonia*

c. 292	Birth of Pachomius
c. 312	Pachomius drafted into the Roman army
c. 313	Pachomius baptized
c. 316	Pachomius becomes a monk; apprentices under Palamon
c. 323	Pachomius settles in Tabennesi
c. 328	Arrival of Theodore
c. 329	Athanasius visits the *Koinonia*
	Foundation of Pbow and other monasteries
c. 336	Theodore made steward of Tabennesi;
	Pachomius settles in Pbow
c. 340	Second set of foundations
345	Synod of Latopolis
346 (May 9)	Death of Pachomius
346 (July 21)	Petronius dies; Horsiesius becomes superior of the *Koinonia*
350	Horsiesius resigns; Theodore becomes superior of the *Koinonia*
351	Ammon arrives at Pbow
360	Duke Artemios searches for Athanasius at Pbow
367	Theodore brings Horsiesius back to Pbow
368 (April 27)	Death of Theodore; Horsiesius again superior of the *Koinonia*
387 (or after)	Death of Horsiesius
391	Foundation of the Monastery of Metanoia (near Alexandria)
404	Jerome translates Pachomian *Rules* and *Letters* into Latin

come to you to become monks with you, and they will profit their souls."⁹ He convinced Palamon of the authenticity of the call and moved his cell to Tabennesi, probably around 323. The two kept in close contact until Palamon's death not long after. Pachomius's older brother, John, soon joined him and embraced the monastic life. (The sources never say how John became a Christian or how he discovered his brother's whereabouts.)

Pachomius then experienced a second great revelation. One day, he and his brother were out on a small island, harvesting reeds. As night fell, Pachomius went off alone to pray as usual. Here he encountered an angel who told him three times: "Pachomius, Pachomius, the Lord's will is [for you] to minister to the race of men and to unite them to himself" (or, as the *First Greek Life* puts it, "to reconcile them to himself").¹⁰ This captures Pachomius's vocation in a nutshell. There was nothing modest in its scope: his vocation was to reach out to the whole of humanity, to unite—and unite by reconciling—the human race to God, and to do so by humble service. It was a vision of the monastic life quite different from Antony's.

At some point, the two brothers squabbled about the size of the monastery. John wanted things small, in keeping with the poverty and solitude of the anchoritic life, while Pachomius had a larger vision of things and began extending the walls "because of the crowds that would come to him." But his brother chided him as only an older brother can: "Stop being conceited." To the writers of the *Lives*, John seemed shortsighted and short on faith. But they had the advantage of hindsight. At the time, Pachomius's vision must have sounded like delusions of grandeur, and early monastic literature is littered with tales of self-aggrandizing and deluded monks. Pachomius was both angry at his brother's chiding and shocked by the depths of his own anger. He spent the whole night praying and sweating out the anger. The *First Sahidic Life* says that his sweat literally disintegrated the earthen brick he was standing on and turned it to mud. Not long after this, John died.[11]

According to both the *Bohairic Life* and the *First Greek Life*, things began to expand rapidly after the angel's call. First, three neophytes came. Soon after, five anchorites joined, then fifty more. Before long, the community numbered 100. But things may not have gone so smoothly at the beginning. The *First Sahidic Life* describes a first experiment in community-building that ended in failure. According to this version, anchorites attracted by Pachomius's reputation began to build their cells near him. So he proposed that they adopt the rudiments of a common life. Each would remain self-supporting, but they would establish a common fund to pay for food and hospitality. Pachomius acted as servant for the others, serving as both treasurer and cook, and the small community came together daily to share a common meal. But all did not go well. The Coptic biographer says that "they treated him with contempt and great irreverence because of the lack of integrity of their hearts." A few specifics are cited. When Pachomius's circle hired themselves out as farm workers to help bring in the harvest, Pachomius would, at day's end, load food and his cooking gear on a donkey and come serve the men in the fields. After dinner, the monks clowned around, riding the donkey and ordering Pachomius around as though he were their slave, telling him to hurry up and pack up his utensils. He put up with their abuse and pranks a long while, some four or five years. But then they began to neglect the *synaxis*, that is, a liturgy of scripture reading and prayer (held daily? weekly?). This proved the last straw, and he drove them away. When they appealed to the local bishop, the bishop sided with Pachomius.[12]

The *First Sahidic Life* breaks off there—with what sounds like a false start. Was it? The *Bohairic Life* and the *First Greek Life* may have suppressed this unpleasant episode, though both note that amid the early success, there was an expulsion of some judged unworthy.[13] The *First Greek Life* gives a different impression of early arrangements. Here Pachomius acted not as a facilitator of a community of equals, but as an elder of a circle of young neophytes. Whenever newcomers arrived, Pachomius tested them to see whether they could renounce "the world" and family and follow Christ and his cross. He then formally clothed them in the *schema*, the monastic habit. Pachomius acted as servant, handling the cooking, answering the door, caring for the sick, and reportedly would send the neophytes off to pray, telling them: "Strive, brothers, to attain to that to which you have been called: to recite psalms and teaching from other parts of the Scriptures, especially the Gospel. As for me, it is by serving God and you according to God's commandment that I find rest."[14] It was Pachomius's silent, selfless service that moved the monks to shift things. They adopted a cenobitic life—monasticism lived in community—and drew their rules from scripture.

The community began to expand rapidly. The monks built a church for the village of Tabennesi and covered all the expenses. Then, as their numbers grew, they built a church for themselves within the monastery grounds. One unexpected arrival was Pachomius's sister, Mary. He had the brothers build a monastery for her, and soon other women joined her community and she served as superior, while an elder monk served as spiritual adviser. This, like Antony's sister who was "raised in virginity," raises vital questions about women's roles in the monastic movement (on this, see chapter 13).

Around 328, a young man named Theodore arrived. He was from a prominent Christian family in Šne and had sought Pachomius out after reading a transcript of one of his catecheses. According to the *Bohairic Life*, Theodore arrived at the age of twenty, after a six-year stint in a monastery in his hometown, while the *First Greek Life* and other sources list his age as fourteen or younger.[15] He soon emerged as a charismatic figure, a born leader, and, eventually would become Pachomius's successor. This later prominence guides the perspective of the *Lives*. The *First Greek Life* proclaims, for instance, that from the day of his arrival Theodore "became for Pachomius a true child after his likeness"; soon after, "our father Pachomius, seeing Theodore's remarkable progress, realized in his heart that God would entrust him with souls after himself."[16] The *Lives* take great pains to document each step in Theodore's spiritual development and career, with the result that Theodore receives nearly as much narrative space as Pachomius. The two men's highly charged and sometimes rocky relationship gives the *Lives* much of their drama.

One such moment occurred early. Theodore's mother came to visit her son about six months after his arrival. She had heard that Pachomius's disciples were not allowed to see their relatives again. So she came armed with a letter from the bishop of Šne addressed to Pachomius. She also brought Theodore's younger brother, Paphnutius, along with her. When they arrived at Tabennesi, they were made to wait outside the monastery walls while the gatekeeper took the bishop's letter to Pachomius. Pachomius read it and called Theodore in and asked him if he would go out and see his mother and brother. Theodore refused to see her, claiming that if he did so, he would transgress the "commandment which is written in the Gospel"; presumably, he is referring to Luke 14:26: "If anyone come to me and does not hate his own father and mother and wife and children and brothers and sisters, yes, and even his own life, he cannot be my disciple."[17] Pachomius did not push: "If you wish to obey the Gospel's commandment, am I going to make you transgress it? It would never occur to me to urge you to do that; but when it was announced to me that she was weeping at the door, I was afraid that you might hear of it and that your heart might be wrung over it. As for me, my whole wish is for you be firm in all the commandments of life."[18] Pachomius ordered that Theodore's mother be given special hospitality and lodging. She waited three days and was finally informed he would not see her. The only consolation she was offered was the chance to stand on the roof of a building and see her son go out with the other monks for work. In the *Bohairic Life*, her anguish is doubled when the younger brother decides to join the monastery as well: "As for their mother, she left to return south to deep affliction and weeping very bitter tears for her sons."[19] The *First Greek Life* mollifies the anguish of the scene: the mother decides to stay and join the convent of virgins run by Pachomius's sister Mary.[20]

Not much later, in 329 or 330, Athanasius paid his first visit. He had been chosen a few years before in a controversial election and spent his early years in office making the rounds of Egypt and Libya to shore up support. The local bishop pressed Athanasius to ordain Pachomius as a presbyter, but Pachomius, informed of the plan, hid and escaped ordination. The lives stress that Pachomius thought that ordination would be divisive, a cause of jealousy and pursuit of honors.[21] That is certainly a plausible concern. But the sources do not mention what may have been an underlying issue: namely, was Pachomius fleeing ordination to prevent interference from the local bishop? There is no indication of any immediate conflict between Pachomius and the local hierarchy, nor of any sectarian feeling. Nonetheless, Pachomius's monastic system enjoyed considerable autonomy. The sources indicate a strong, heartfelt allegiance to Athanasius and his successors. And from all indications, Athanasius and his successors made every effort to cultivate a close alliance with the Pachomians. While this story has been colored by later events—both Athanasius's later heroic struggles and later Pachomian successes—it is clear that the two sides struck up a relationship early on.

The *Koinonia*

By 329, numbers in Tabennesi had reached the point where Pachomius decided to expand things. So he established a major new foundation, Pbow. This, in the long run, would become the central monastery and Pachomius's own residence. Soon after, two other monasteries were added: Šeneset and Tmoušons. Both reportedly existed from "of old," but their leaders requested formal affiliation and agreed to come under Pachomius's rule.[22] In 340, a second expansion occurred, once again a combination of new foundations and alliances with existing monasteries. By 345, the year before Pachomius died, there were nine monasteries for men and two for women[23] (for a map of the Pachomian monasteries, see figure 5.1).

So began the *Koinonia*, the "fellowship." Pachomius, a Coptic speaker, adopted this Greek word, drawn from the New Testament, to describe his federation of monasteries. Pachomius's originality comes not from inventing the monastery as such. It is clear that there were monasteries contemporary with (if not before) his, such as Šeneset and Tmoušons. Pachomius's achievement comes from the way he brought together a collection of monasteries into a tightly regulated whole, with a single head, a carefully ordered hierarchy of offices, and an intricate rhythm of work and prayer and spiritual formation. Not until the Middle Ages, with the rise of Cluny and the Cistercians, would a monastic order match Pachomius's in size and sophistication of organization.

Estimates of numbers vary. Ammon says that the monastery of Pbow alone

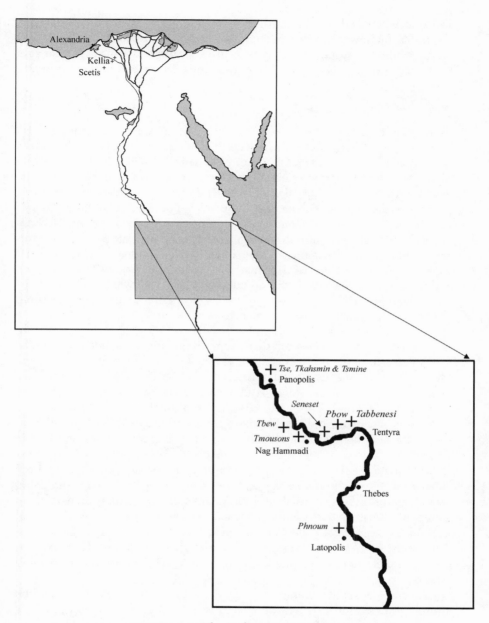

FIGURE 5.1. The Pachomian *Koinonia*.

had 600 when he lived there in the year 352. Jerome makes the outrageous claim that there were 50,000 Pachomian monks; but closer to the mark may be the estimates of John Cassian, who gives 5,000, and Palladius, who says there were 3,000 in Pachomius's day and 7,000 by the end of the century.[24]

The *Pachomian* Rules

Pachomius composed the first known monastic rule. The very concept of a monastery without a monastic rule seems odd to us, so much has Pachomius's achievement became part and parcel of Christian experience. Pachomius's reputation as a legislator rests partly on a later legend, first told by Palladius. His widely read *Lausiac History* describes Pachomius as one "deemed worthy of prophecies and angelic visions" and "a great lover of men and of his brothers." He goes on to say that Pachomius was sitting in his cave when an angel appeared to him and told him to assemble monks and legislate for them according to the rules written on a bronze tablet.[25] His story does not square what we know from other sources (for instance, Pachomius did not live in a cave), and the rules that Palladius cites do not match very well what we know of key Pachomian practices. Yet the story of the angel and the bronze tablet captured the ancient imagination and was repeated again and again.[26]

The *Rules* of Pachomius do not seem like a book dropped from heaven. Like most rulebooks, they are rather dry reading, long lists of dos and don'ts. But if one can get beneath this surface, they offer fascinating clues into the life of the *Koinonia*, its everyday rhythms and its all-too-human problems. Scholars suspect that the *Rules*, as they have come down to us, evolved over time, and that some of the legislation dates from the time of Pachomius's successors, Theodore and Horsiesius. Technically speaking, the *Rules* of Pachomius are not one book, but four: the *Precepts*, the *Precepts and Institutes*, the *Precepts and Judgments*, and the *Precepts and Laws*. One of these is a handbook for those who lead individual houses within the monastery; another is for the superior of the whole monastery. Some contain rules about work and living arrangements, others, rules about liturgy, and still others, rules on what to do about rule breakers and troublemakers. They have neither the eloquence of Basil of Caesarea's *Long Rules* nor the orderly moderation of Benedict's *Rule*. They seem more ad hoc, framed to counter specific abuses. They take for granted a daily routine, so one has to reconstruct some things from passing remarks.

A complete version comes to us via the Latin translation done by Jerome around 404. Jerome says that he made the translation from Greek originals sent to him from the Pachomian Monastery of Metanoia, near Alexandria, which needed the translation for Latin-speaking monks who had entered there. About a third of the *Rule* survives in Coptic, and about half survives in Greek.[27] The *Rules*, together with comments in the *Lives* and early eyewitness accounts, have enabled scholars to reconstruct the main lines of the life and organization of the *Koinonia*—though some matters may date from the time of Pachomius's immediate successors rather than from that of Pachomius himself.[28]

The Physical Layout

High walls were the most distinctive feature of a Pachomian monastery. These served as the very visible boundary separating monastery from the outside world. They obviously limited access, whether from neighboring farmers or from families trying to contact sons or brothers. This barrier proved especially valuable later, as a defense against barbarian raiders.

One entered a Pachomian monastery through the gatehouse, typically manned by a brother who carefully screened those coming and going. Near the gatehouse was a guesthouse, used to house postulants or to offer hospitality to passing dignitaries, or clergy, or non-Pachomian monks. Further in was a complex of other buildings: a kitchen, a bakery, a dining hall, an infirmary for the sick, an assembly hall (called a *synaxis*), and a church. In 1989, archaeologists discovered the remains of Pachomius's original church in Pbow (buried under two later and larger ones). It was a sizable building, some forty-one meters long and twenty-four meters wide, with five aisles and an apse, probably built to accommodate the great twice-a-year meetings of monks from all the affiliated monasteries.[29]

In addition to these larger communal buildings, there were the houses where the monks themselves lived. According to Jerome, there were forty monks per house, and thirty to forty houses per monastery.[30] Each monk had his own cell where he prayed and slept.[31] Each house also had some sort of common area where the members of the house met for prayer and instruction. There is frequent mention of storerooms where clothing or food was kept.[32]

Later observers say that if one strolled through a Pachomian monastery, one saw an amazing variety of skilled craftsmen. There were, of course, basket makers and mat weavers, but also carpenters, tailors, tanners, shoemakers, blacksmiths, bakers, camel drivers, metalworkers, and calligraphers. The monks also owned a fleet of boats that enabled them to travel up- and downriver between monasteries or to deliver their goods to market. The Pachomian monasteries, in other words, had all the trades and activities one expected to find in a prosperous and thriving Egyptian village. Jerome claims that those who worked the same craft lived in the same house, forming a sort of monastic guild. But such specialization may have been a later development.[33]

Leadership and Organization

The sources portray a clear chain of command. At the top was the "father" of the *Koinonia*, Pachomius himself, later succeeded by Petronius (very briefly), Horsiesius, and Theodore. The word "father" here is *apa*, the Coptic equivalent of the New Testament term *abba*. In the literature of early monasticism, calling someone *apa* (or *abba*) did not mean he was a priest. After all, neither Pachomius nor his successors were ordained; rather, *apa* (or *abba*) was a term of respect for a venerable and charismatic elder. Pachomian sources speak with great affection for "our father Pachomius" and bestow the title *apa* rather rarely on others. Pachomius lived at Pbow but routinely traveled up and down the

Nile visiting other foundations, giving instructions, and meeting with superiors and ordinary monks. He exercised authority in appointing and deposing superiors, setting rules and policies, and judging difficult cases or disputes.

Under the "father" of the *Koinonia* was the superior of the individual monastery, referred to as the "steward" (*oikonomos*).[34] He had a personal assistant, referred to as a "second" (*deuteros*). Each monastery, in turn, was divided into "houses." Each house was headed by a "housemaster" (*oikiakos*), who likewise had an assistant or "second" (*deuteros*).[35] Modern commentators have noted that the housemaster was the linchpin that held together the whole Pachomian system.[36] For the average monk, the housemaster was at once supervisor and superior, teacher and spiritual father.[37] The housemaster assigned work duties, gave permissions, judged conflicts, even pulled thorns from his men's feet.[38] He walked at their lead, was the first to eat, and was held accountable for everything under his purview, whether a missing tool or a runaway monk.[39] Pachomius himself lived in one of the ordinary houses and remained subject to a housemaster's authority for his everyday needs.[40] Certain liturgical and work duties rotated from house to house on a week-by-week basis. Jerome claims that a cluster of three or four houses was grouped together as a "tribe."[41]

Not only were officeholders structured in a hierarchy.[42] Everyone had an assigned position, one that determined where one sat during meals or during worship. Seating order was fixed by date of entrance into the monastery. One's worldly rank was irrelevant in the monastery. It did not matter whether one came from a rich or poor family, from the nobility or peasant classes. What mattered was date of entrance. This practice—which proved to be a great social leveler—was retained by later monastic legislators such as Benedict.

Entering the Community

Pachomius outlined specific steps for welcoming newcomers into the community. When someone presented himself at the door of the monastery "wishing to renounce the world," he was not welcomed in immediately. The father of the monastery was informed of a candidate's arrival, but the porter took charge of his initial training.[43] Pachomius knew that first impressions matter, and he insisted that the porter be hospitable and that, as the *Bohairic Life* puts it, "his speech [be] seasoned with salt."[44] The candidate was taught basics: the Lord's Prayer and as many psalms as he could memorize. He was also discreetly interviewed. What brought him to the monastery? Had he done something wrong? Was he fleeing someone's authority? (This is ambiguous—the "authority" may have been a father, the military, a patron, even a slavemaster.)[45] Could he renounce parents and possessions? If accepted, he would then enter into the monastery's life as such, the round of prayer and work.

Once he had mastered the monastic routine and proven himself adequate, he would be formally accepted as a monk. There is no clear mention of taking vows. That, it seems, belonged to a later age. The only ritual mentioned is a formal vesting: the candidate was stripped of his secular clothes and clothed in the monastic habit (to be discussed in the next section).[46]

Candidates were expected to learn scripture—lots of scripture. Initially they memorized twenty psalms or two letters of Paul. Pachomius expected his monks eventually to know both the Psalter and the New Testament by heart.[47] Not surprisingly, some who entered were illiterate. Such candidates were taught to read. It was a high priority, for the *Rules* specify that the illiterate candidate go to a monk-teacher three times per day and practice "very studiously with all gratitude" the fundamentals—syllables, nouns, verbs. Pachomius was adamant: "even if he does not want to, he shall be compelled to read."[48]

It may seem surprising, but a number who entered were still unbaptized. Of these, most (presumably) were catechumens, but some may even have been pagans. In these cases, the catechumenate and monastic formation became one and the same. In the fourth century, the catechumenate was a vigorous institution, and adult baptism was still the norm. The catechumenate bore little resemblance to what one sees in parishes today. Surviving Egyptian church orders describe a rigorous three-year process. It was a journey punctuated by a panoply of rites—formal interrogations, blessings, exorcisms. In ordinary parishes, instruction took place not in a classroom, but in daily Liturgies of the Word. The Eucharist was still a secret rite, and only the baptized were permitted to witness it; so catechumens were dismissed after the sermon. Admission to baptism was not a foregone conclusion. At the beginning of Lent, the catechumen's morals were scrutinized: did he really live as a Christian? It is hard to be sure how monastic life altered the rhythms, rites, and timetables of the catechumenate. We do know that each year at Easter, catechumens from the various Pachomian monasteries gathered at Pbow and were baptized.[49] In one of Theodore's surviving letters, he instructs the leaders of the individual monasteries to exhort the catechumens "expecting the awesome remission of sins and the grace of spiritual mystery" to repent and to prepare for the "awesome" Eucharist.[50]

Monastic Garb

From an early date, Egyptian monks wore distinctive garb that marked them out from laypeople. In the *Precepts*, Pachomius specifies quite precisely what his monks were to wear. They had a sleeveless linen tunic (called a *lebiton*), belted around the waist. Thrown over their shoulders was a goatskin (called a *melote*). They also wore a hood, which bore the symbol of their particular monastery and house. They wore sandals or simple boots, for the area where they lived had lots of thornbushes. When traveling, they carried a staff. They also had a mantle, worn at night and during the morning *synaxis* but not when going to work.[51] From the earliest days, Pachomius insisted that the Gospel required neither extravagance nor penury, but "proper measure in clothing."[52]

The Daily Order

How did a Pachomian monk spend his day? The sources, while somewhat sketchy, do allow us to plot out the key moments. The day began at dawn, when the monks were wakened by the sound of a gong. They promptly got up and left their individual cells, reciting scripture privately to themselves as they went.[53]

The entire monastic community gathered for morning prayer, which they called the *synaxis* (or "assembly"). The terminology can get confusing here, because the word *synaxis* is used both for the worship service itself and for the building where it was held. During the liturgy, each monk sat by rank in an assigned spot. Piled in front of him were reeds, for, as Pachomius decreed, "you shall not sit idle in the *synaxis*, but with a quick hand you shall prepare ropes for the warps of mats."[54] This is an odd image for us, but working during a prayer service was the Egyptian norm. During the weekday *synaxis*, a monk-lector stood at the ambo and recited, apparently from memory, passages from scripture. At the end of each passage, he clapped his hand and invited those plaiting reeds to stand. The monks rose, signed themselves with the sign of the cross on the forehead, and then recited the Lord's Prayer with arms extended in the form of a cross. Another clap signaled that they were to sign themselves again, to kneel and then prostrate themselves on the ground, and to weep inwardly for their sins. They then rose, signed themselves a third time, and prayed in silence. At a third clap, they returned to their seats and resumed their reed-plaiting, and the lector began his recitation again.[55] How many times this ritual sequence was repeated is not known. For those accustomed to Benedictine services of chanted psalms, such a rite seems quite unusual. Yet it is striking in the way it modulates between scripture, gesture, and silent prayer.

After the *synaxis*, the monks returned to the cells to await word about the day's work assignment. Once word came, they lined up, house by house, in an arrangement reminiscent of a military regiment on a parade ground. Then, led by the housemaster, each house went out to do the assigned task for the day, whether working the fields or orchards, preparing food, or doing one's specific craft. We saw earlier how wide-ranging the trades and crafts of a Pachomian monastery could be. Pachomius stressed that "the brothers shall not be forced to work excessively, but a moderate labor shall incite everyone to work."[56] Apparently the monks worked in silence.

Two meals were served daily, a larger one at noon and a lighter one late in the day—though a fast of some sort was practiced on Wednesdays and Fridays. At noon, the monks were called to the refectory house by house. As at liturgy, the monks sat by rank in assigned places and began eating only after the housemaster had begun. Meals consisted of bread and cooked vegetables, perhaps even luxurious fare such as fruit, cheese, and olives.[57] Contemporary observers were struck by Pachomian table manners: each monk ate in silence, with his eyes lowered and his head bowed and covered with his hood, never looking up at those around him. If someone needed something, he rapped on the table rather than speaking. As the monks left the refectory, they were given some sort of sweets or fruit called *tragematia*.[58] While this diet sounds austere, it was really quite moderate by Egyptian monastic standards. Most anchorites ate only once a day and limited their intake to bread and salt; vegetables (especially cooked ones) were considered a luxury, reserved for guests and for the sick.

After dinner, the monks returned to their houses and there celebrated evening prayer, what the sources refer to as "the Six Prayers." How this was performed is not very clear, though it likely resembled the pattern of the morning *synaxis*.[59] There is no reason to presume that the prayers were six psalms. On Wednesdays and Fridays, the schedule differed slightly since, because of the fast, no meals were served. On those days, the housemasters delivered a catechesis. Pachomius considered this vital: "when the housemaster teaches the brothers about the holy way of life, no one shall be absent without very serious necessity."[60] Pachomius was equally insistent that "everything that is taught them in the assembly of the brothers they must absolutely talk over among themselves, especially on the days of fast, when they receive instruction from their masters."[61] In other words, silence was put aside, and the monks were to ponder, probe, even disagree with what they heard.

After the Six Prayers (and any discussion), the monks retired to their cells to pray and keep vigil. Ancient commentators express admiration for a distinctive Pachomian practice: the monks did not lie down to sleep; rather, they kept vigil and, if they slept, they did so sitting up in "reclining seats" (*kathismatia*).[62] In these seats, one could doze, but probably not sleep deeply. The practice is a remnant of the harsh asceticism of Pachomius's early days.[63]

This was the weekday rhythm. One feature of this schedule immediately strikes Western Christians: what about daily Eucharist? Daily Eucharist was not the Egyptian norm, neither in parishes nor in monasteries. Monks in Egypt celebrated Eucharist twice a week, on Saturdays and Sundays, and that was true in Pachomius's monasteries. Whereas the housemasters gave the catecheses on Wednesdays and Fridays to members of their house, the superiors gave catecheses to the whole monastery on the weekends, one on Saturday and two on Sunday.[64]

Easter & the Day of Remission

Twice a year, all the Pachomian monks gathered at the central monastery at Pbow. In Pachomius's later years, these would have been huge affairs, with perhaps thousands of monks gathered together. One gathering took place each year at Easter when, among other things, the catechumens were baptized. One of Pachomius's surviving letters was written to announce the Easter meeting, and it exhorts the monks to prepare themselves.[65]

The other great assembly took place on the twentieth of Mesore, roughly our month of August. This assembly, referred to as the "Day of Remission," had a twofold function.[66] The first was financial. This date marked the end of the fiscal year, and the superiors of the individual monasteries offered a detailed financial report to the Great Steward, as he was called; he seems to have been some sort of chief financial officer for the *Koinonia* as a whole.[67] These reports must have been astonishingly detailed. We know, for instance, that each housemaster was required by the *Precepts* to give an exact count of the number of ropes woven at the daily *synaxis* for the last year![68] This yearly settling of financial accounts was not unique to Pachomian monasteries; old Egyptian temples had done the same, also in the month of Mesore.

The second purpose of this Day of Remission was spiritual. It was used as a time for mutual forgiveness. This spirituality is beautifully articulated in one of Pachomius's surviving letters, written to the heads of the monasteries:

> The time is coming near for us to assemble together, according to the custom of remission, following the early prescriptions to convene together in order to carry out the remission and pardon. Let then everyone pardon his brother according to the commandment of God and in conformity with the laws which were written for us by God. Let everyone totally open his heart to his brother. Let the brothers share their judgments with one another. Let their souls be cleansed in sanctification and fear of God. Let there not be any enmity in their hearts. Let them rather know how to act in truth with one another, for it is a commandment of the law of God to seek peace and to walk in it before God and men.[69]

These words were put into practice. Jerome remarks that "those who have had any quarrel are reconciled to each other" and "sins are forgiven everyone." He compared them, with some justice, to the Old Testament practice of the Jubilee.[70] Under Theodore's administration, Easter and the Day of Remission also served an administrative function. He used the occasions to rotate superiors or housemasters or to appoint new ones.[71]

The Catecheses

As we saw earlier, monks in Pachomian monasteries received formal instructions from both the superiors and the housemasters. The *Lives* report that the "father" of the *Koinonia*—initially Pachomius, later Theodore and Horsiesius— also gave addresses when they made their rounds of the monasteries. Two of Pachomius's catecheses have been preserved. (We also have three fragmentary ones attributed to Theodore and seven to Horsiesius.) These talks are saturated with biblical quotations and presume that their hearers possessed an extraordinary mastery of both Old and New Testaments.[72] In the catechesis entitled *Instruction Concerning a Spiteful Monk*, Pachomius takes a few jabs at those who presumed the anchoritic life superior to the cenobitic: "It is better for you to live with a thousand in all humility than alone with pride in an hyena's den." He also stresses obedience and links a life of obedience in the *Koinonia* with the Spirit-charged lives of the Old Testament prophets: "If you cannot get along alone, join another who is living according to the Gospel of Christ, and you will make progress with him. Either listen, or submit to one who listens; either be strong and be called Elijah, or obey the strong and be called Elisha. For obeying Elijah, Elisha received a double share of Elijah's spirit."[73]

The Coded Letters

The *First Greek Life* notes that Pachomius not only dictated "ordinances" and "talks" but also sent cryptic letters to the heads of the various monasteries, using "in them the names of the character from Alpha to Omega expressing to those fathers of the monasteries in a secret spiritual language things for the governance of souls, when he had no leisure to come to them."[74] Some of these have survived. In 404, Jerome translated eleven of them into Latin. Recently, scholars discovered versions of several of these both in Coptic and in Greek. They are, for the most part, quite mysterious documents, many sprinkled with Greek letters, whose meaning no cryptographer has yet decoded (see appendix 5.2 for a sample). Yet the Greek letters are not the only code. *Letter* 3, for instance, is a dense, almost unintelligible network of biblical quotes and allusions. This biblical code may refer to specific issues and figures that we simply have no knowledge of. But, as Pachomius admits in one letter, he could be purposely oracular: "I have written to you with images and parables so that you would search them with wisdom, following the footsteps of the saints."[75] Not all the letters were so obscure. Several, such as those summoning the monks to the great assemblies at Easter and the August Day of Remission, contain more straightforward exhortations.

Koinonia *as Spirituality*

As one reads the *Rules* of Pachomius, one is impressed by the care for good order in everything, down to the smallest details: fruits that fell from trees in the orchard were to be neatly stacked in small piles; every rope woven in the morning *synaxis* was duly counted. Often enough, the legislation is cast in negative phraseology: "No one shall have such-and-such," "no one shall do such-and-such." And the negatives focused unduly on minutiae. For example:

> *Precept* 71: No one shall take vegetables from the garden unless he is given them by the gardener.
> *Precept* 72: No one on his own authority shall take palm leaves for basket-plaiting, except the one in charge of the palms.[76]

Behind negative rules of this sort is a deeper issue: respect—respecting each person and the work he does, not taking upon oneself the authority to interfere in another's expertise. Other negative legislation strikes at other issues. For instance:

> *Precept* 74: The cook shall not take any of the food before the brothers eat.
> *Precept* 75: The one in charge of the palm trees shall not eat any of their fruits before the brothers have some first.[77]

Behind these negatives is the issue of power. This sort of legislation undercuts those who used their job for perks, either for themselves personally, for their friends, or for those whose favor they sought. Pachomius knew that people could use house jobs to create tiny fiefdoms and manipulate their positions either for personal pleasure or for dispensing (or withholding) favors. He recognized that nothing so damages the equality of a community as this sort of behavior, and that it was precisely little perks—food from the kitchen or fresh fruit from the orchards—that threatened that equality.

At the heart of Pachomius's legislation was the desire to create, down to the most nitty-gritty details of everyday life, a community of equals. The New Testament vision, enunciated in the Acts of the Apostles, was central: "Now the company of those who believe were of one heart and soul, and no one said that any of the things which he possessed was his own, but they had everything in common" (Acts 4:32). This text and its parallel in Acts 2:42–45 appear again and again in Pachomian literature. In one of his surviving *Catecheses*, Theodore calls on his hearers to reflect on the meaning of Pachomius and his vocation: "May he cause each of us to go back to the beginnings of his vocation, that is, to the expectation of the promises God made to our father Apa, to him whose commandments we have promised [to observe], walking in fulfillment of the law, that is to say, 'being of one heart,' toiling for one another, practicing brotherly love, compassion and humility."[78] Similarly, in his later *Regulations*, Horsiesius describes what he saw as the deeper purpose of the Pachomian *Rules*:

> And every other duty which we must perform in conformity with
> the law of the holy *Koinonia*, let us all perform with the prudence of
> piety, as one man, as it is written: "All who believed formed but one
> heart and one soul"; so that God may bless our bread, that we may
> eat it with joy and pleasure in the Holy Spirit, and that a blessing
> may rest upon it, remain there, and not vanish rapidly.[79]

As Philip Rousseau has noted, "The *Rules* . . . were rooted in something more general than the piecemeal demands of the various *Praecepta*"; they flowed from "Pachomius's desire to gain humanity, soul by soul, for God."[80]

Later Career

The *Lives* interweave the story of Pachomius's later career with Theodore's rise. According to the *Bohairic Life*, Theodore "strove to acquire great graciousness, with the result that, despite his age, he became the comforter of many, raising up by his soothing words whoever had fallen."[81] From an early date, Pachomius missioned Theodore to deal with various thorny problems, especially personnel problems: he was sent to handle inquiries from visiting philosophers, to comfort a monk downcast by Pachomius' reprimands, to accompany a wavering brother on a home visit.[82] Theodore came into public prominence when Pachomius invited him to give a catechesis to the whole monastery, a privilege normally enjoyed only by Pachomius himself or the superior of the monastery. The *Lives* report grumbling, no doubt back in the discussion groups held in the houses, by older brothers who complained about favors bestowed on one so young.[83] Finally in 336 or 337, Theodore was made superior (*oikonomos*) of Tabennesi, even though he was still quite young—in his early thirties according to the *Lives*.[84]

The *Lives* stress Theodore's deep loyalty to Pachomius. He reportedly walked a couple of miles each day over to Pbow to listen to Pachomius's regular catechesis, and then returned to Tabennesi and repeated to his monastery what he heard Pachomius say. Eventually, Pachomius moved Theodore permanently to Pbow, made him his chief lieutenant, and routinely sent him to make the rounds of the monasteries as his personal delegate.[85] But the sources do not show Pachomius to have been uncritical of his gifted disciple. Pachomius reprimanded Theodore, for example, for the way he mistrustfully interrogated those he governed; another time Pachomius gave him a three-week penance because he had let his bakers chatter away in violation of the rules.[86]

The relationship between Pachomius and Theodore soured quite suddenly. At some point, Pachomius took sick. This apparently prompted an emergency meeting of the heads of the monasteries. The other superiors pressed Theodore to agree to become "father" of the *Koinonia* should Pachomius die. Theodore reluctantly agreed. This should have been a moot point, since Pachomius soon recovered. But not long after, he invited the leaders to share the temptations they faced. After sharing his own, Pachomius had Theodore speak. So Theodore admitted that he felt tempted by ambition, tempted to desire to lead the *Koinonia*. Pachomius reacted harshly. He immediately deposed Theodore as superior of Tabennesi and ordered him to do penance. For the next two years, Theodore, stripped of all office, did penance. Apparently various monks came to him and consoled him, and eventually, Pachomius began to assign him responsibilities. For instance, Theodore was allowed to join the boat that made the once-a-year delivery of goods to Alexandria.[87] Finally, around 345, Theodore was formally restored, again invited to speak to the brothers and used by Pachomius as a visitor to the various monasteries. The *Bohairic Life* portrays the whole episode as Pachomius's effort to train Theodore in humility and has him proclaim, "He has grown in his progress far beyond what he formerly was, because of the humility with which he patiently endured" his public demotion. It should be no surprise that scholars are skeptical here, for it appears that the *Lives* are struggling to cope with the embarrassment of their hero's very public removal from authority and tendentiously interpret it as spiritual pedagogy.

Pachomius was more than a legislator, and his community, more than a law-abiding enterprise. Pachomius was a charismatic, Spirit-charged, and participating in his community meant participating in a Spirit-governed community. When modern readers encounter the *Lives*, they notice the heavy dose of the miraculous. On closer inspection, one finds only a few healing miracles. The accent, rather, is on the miracle of discernment—on Pachomius's ability to sort through the complexities of human dynamics and the human psyche by his ability to read hearts.

While the *Lives* play up his visionary gifts, the Pachomius of the *Lives* tends to play them down. Once, when a group of monks approached Pachomius and asked him to share one of his visions, he replied: "A sinner like me does not ask God to see visions. It is against God's will, and a mistake. But all the same, listen to this great vision." Perhaps his hearers expected to hear about an ecstatic episode. Instead, Pachomius described a more down-to-earth mysticism: "What can be a greater vision than this: to see the invisible God in a visible person?"[88] He noted that Old Testament visionaries such as Elisha had only enjoyed clairvoyance in a hit-or-miss fashion, whenever God happened to dwell in them. But, he added, if one just looks around and sees one's fellow human beings, then one can enjoy an uninterrupted clairvoyance; and, besides, God judges us not by our intermittent visions, but by the way we treat the images of God that are before us all our lives. This terminology, speaking of human beings as "images of God" or simply as "images," seems to have been a regular habit of speech of his, if his surviving *Catecheses* are any indication.[89] For Pachomius, seeing the invisible God in the visible human being was vision enough.

The visions Pachomius routinely enjoyed were not of God, but of his disciples' hearts. The *Lives* portray Pachomius as a clairvoyant. This must not be thought of some later hagiographic imposition onto the historical figure. That the historical Pachomius was thought of a clairvoyant—and thought of himself as one—becomes clear in a serious and embarrassing event that took place quite late in his career. In 345, a synod of bishops and monks meeting at Latopolis formally summoned Pachomius to appear. The charge concerned his gift of clairvoyance. The incident appears both in the *First Greek Life* and in the *Arabic Lives*, but not in the *Bohairic*, which may have suppressed it.[90] Among the bishops at the synod were two former Pachomian monks, and one senses that they viewed their former abbot with some ambivalence. In the *First Greek Life*, the bishops reportedly say, "We confess that you are a man of God and we know that you saw the demons, making war against them to ward them off souls. But since clairvoyance is a great things, give some answer again about that, and we will persuade the murmurers." Pachomius answered in dramatic fashion, retracing his own spiritual journey: he was born a pagan, "not knowing what God is"; the "man-loving God" had graced him and enabled him to become a Christian; and when he began his monastic career, "there were few monks, one could scarcely find groups of two or five, or ten at the most, living on their own," but now "we are this great multitude—nine monasteries—striving night and day by God's mercy to keep our souls blameless." As for the issue of clairvoyance, he noted that there was nothing unnatural about psychological insight: "When those who are wise and sensible according to the world spend a few days in the midst of men, do they not distinguish and recognize each one's disposition?" He then defended his gift as a graced extension of that natural ability. It enabled him to distinguish who was a monk in his heart and who was one only in appearance. He then linked his grace of reading hearts with the cross of Christ and God's will to save the human race:

And if the one who shed his own blood for us, the wisdom of the
Father, sees someone trembling with all his heart for the loss of his

neighbor—especially of many—will he not give him the means to save them blamelessly, either by the discernment of the Holy Spirit, or by an apparition when the Lord wills? For I do not see the realities of our salvation when I wish, but when He who governs everything shows us his confidence.[91]

The story ends on a mysterious note. At the end of this speech, a spectator—"possessed by the enemy," according to the *First Greek Life*—came at Pachomius wielding a sword. The brothers stepped in and prevented an assassination. Even the *First Greek Life* had to admit that controversy remained, that "some spoke this way and some that," and the brothers had to escape to their nearby monastery of Phnoum. One senses that the *Lives* are giving here only a glimmer of the ecclesiastical complexities—and potential perils—of the case.

Not long after this, in 346, a plague came sweeping through Upper Egypt. It devastated the Pachomian monasteries, killing nearly 100 monks, including three of the major superiors—Sourous, Cornelius, and Theodore's brother Paphnutius. Pachomius himself soon fell victim. The *Lives* portray Theodore keeping watch at Pachomius's deathbed. Reportedly Pachomius grabbed Theodore by the beard and whispered to him not to leave his body where they were to bury it—he feared "some people would steal his body and build a *martyrion* for it as they do for the holy martyrs. For many times [Theodore] had heard him criticize those who did such things . . . because everyone who does this is commercializing the bodies of the saints."[92] Pachomius soon fell unconscious and died on May 9, 346. His death left the *Koinonia* facing a terrible crisis of leadership.

Not long after Pachomius's death, Theodore and another brother named Zaccheus were en route to Alexandria, about the time of Athanasius's return from his third exile. The monks heard that Antony happened to be at his cell on Outer Mountain, near the Nile. So they moored their boat and paid him a visit. After giving the two monks his blessing, Antony inquired, "How is Abba Pachomius?" They broke down in tears and told him of Pachomius's death. Antony, to console them, then replied, "Do not weep. All of you have become Abba Pachomius. I tell you, it was a great ministry he received, this gathering of so many brothers; and he walks the way of the apostles." Zacchaeus protested, "It is you, Abba, who are light of the world." Then Antony offered a tribute:

I will persuade you by my answer, Zacchaeus. In the beginning, when I became a monk, there was no community to nurture other souls; each one of the ancient monks after the persecutions practiced his *ascesis* alone. And then your father did that beautiful thing from the Lord. Another before him, called Aotas, wanted to obtain this ministry, but since he did not do it with wholehearted zeal, he did not succeed. Concerning your father, I often heard how well he walked according to the Scriptures. And truly, I too often desired to see him in the body. Perhaps I was not worthy of it. In the kingdom of heaven, however, by God's grace, we shall see each other and all

the holy fathers, and especially our Master and God, Jesus Christ.
Therefore take courage, and be strengthened and perfect.[93]

This speech is a masterful literary touch. The author of the *First Greek Life* has
put his own elegy for Pachomius into Antony's mouth. It reminds one of the
way that Dante, in the *Paradiso*, has Saint Dominic sing the praises of the
Franciscans and Saint Francis sing the praises of the Dominicans. Here
the author has Antony, the paradigm of anchoritic monasticism, praise Pachomius for making this "beautiful thing from God," namely, the *Koinonia*. The
author goes further by having Antony say that he was probably not "worthy"
of ever seeing Pachomius—at once a statement of Antony's humility and a
proclamation of Pachomius's superiority. The *Bohairic Life* draws out the episode even more. There, Antony proclaims that when he became an anchorite,
"the path of the apostles" had not yet been revealed to the world; that was "the
work of our able Apa Pachomius." Antony goes on to say, in this version, that
he lacked the skill to create a *koinonia* even if he wanted to, nor could he at
this point join the Pachomians, since he was too set in his ways. In this story,
we see the way Pachomian community understood itself—its intense sense of
its historic destiny, and its unwavering conviction about the superiority of its
mission and its way of life.

Theodore and Horsiesius

Theodore, after his demotion, no longer seemed the heir apparent. In his final
days, Pachomius appointed a relative newcomer as successor, a man named
Petronius. Petronius had come from a wealthy Christian family in Diospolis
Parva (Coc) and, after a conversion to the ascetic life, had turned his family
estate into a monastery.[94] (This is another of those clues that monastery founding per se was not where Pachomius's originality lay.) Petronius heard of Pachomius's *Koinonia* and asked that his family-estate-turned-monastery might join
the federation. Much of his family joined as well: his father, one brother, some
sisters, and other relatives. Petronius's monastery, called Tbew, received the
typical Pachomian arrangement of housemasters and seconds, while Petronius
became part of Pachomius's inner circle, serving as superior of Tsmine and
overseer of two nearby monasteries. So the designation of Petronius as Pachomius's successor did not come as a complete surprise. But the appointment
proved ill fated, for Petronius himself lay sick with the same plague that felled
Pachomius. A mere three months later, in July 346, Petronius died.

Before his death, Petronius appointed Horsiesius, then superior of Šeneset, as "father" of the *Koinonia*. The sources portray Horsiesius as protesting
that the demands of the position were beyond him.[95] They may well have been,
at least at that moment. He initially held office for four years, from 346 to 350,
but in his first administration, the monasteries soon grew restive, proclaiming,
"We will have nothing to do with Horsiesius nor will we have anything to do
with the rules which he lays down."[96] The crisis came to a head when Apol-

lonios, the abbot of the monastery of Tmoušons, pressed Horsiesius to widen the agricultural scope of the *Koinonia*.[97] When Horsiesius opposed the expansionist policy, Apollonius and his monastery broke off from the *Koinonia*. So Horsiesius, after an agonizing night of prayer and a consoling vision, abruptly resigned. The next day, at a meeting of local elders, he nominated Theodore as his replacement and retired to his old monastery of Šeneset.[98]

Under Horsiesius, Theodore had held modest positions, first as housemaster of the carpenters at Pbow, then as manager of the bakery at Phnoum. The sudden appointment caught him by surprise, and he was reportedly wary of assuming office.[99] After meeting with Horsiesius, Theodore finally agreed to take control, and though he headed the *Koinonia* for the next eighteen years, from 350 to 368, he continued to describe himself simply as Horsiesius's "deputy" or "assistant."[100] It is hard to know what politics lay behind this legal fiction. The sources report that Theodore did consult Horsiesius on certain major decisions (such as new foundations), but Theodore certainly wielded full authority over the monasteries, and Horsiesius maintained what was clearly a self-imposed and probably bitter exile.

Theodore's first order of business was restoring the *Koinonia*'s unity. He met with Apollonius, who had led the revolt, and brought him and his monastery back into the fold only "after much struggle and spiritual understanding."[101] The *Sixth Sahidic Life* reports that, prompted by a vision, Theodore decided to rotate superiors from monastery to monastery every six months.[102] This probably lessened opportunities for future revolts. Theodore continued expanding the *Koinonia*, setting up two new monasteries further downriver.[103] The collective strength of the federation proved a mixed blessing. The *Lives* report that, near the end of his life, Theodore became deeply anguished that economic success of the *Koinonia* imperiled its spiritual purpose. He used to go out at night and pray with tears over the tomb of Pachomius. It did no good. The good order and efficient work habits of the *Koinonia* proved too successful—a pattern that would be repeated many times in the history of medieval monasticism.[104]

Three important features of his leadership emerge. First was his care for souls. The *First Greek Life* speaks of him "encouraging each one privately and tending them as a doctor." The *Bohairic Life* notes how he adapted his medicine to the man: some he comforted, others he reprimanded, some he moved to another house or monastery, others he simply prayed for.[105] Second, and more importantly, he called on and idealized the memory of Pachomius and invoked it as a force for a spiritual revival. In his inaugural address he eloquently proclaimed:

> Now it is not yet five years since he passed away and we have forgotten that very great joy and peace which we then had with each other. For in the days of our father we did not have either in heart or in mouth anything but the word of God, which is sweeter than honey and the honeycomb. We were not conscious of living on earth but of feasting in heaven. A man who finds himself in the cold and deep

frost runs somehow until he reaches the heat of the fire; then he is delighted and revives. So also was it with us then; the more we sought God, the more his goodness manifested itself, bringing sweetness to our souls. But how are we now? Let us, however, all return. We do believe that God will renew us in his mercy.[106]

The *Bohairic Life* notes that Theodore told stories from the life of Pachomius stressing that "it is through our contact with such a righteous man that we have learned the will of God even in such details as the manner of stretching our hands upward to the Lord and how one should pray to God."[107] One senses that such exhortations stand behind and led eventually to the writing of all those biographies, first of Pachomius, then of Theodore himself. Third, Theodore, like Pachomius before him, is portrayed as a clairvoyant, one able to read hearts. And like Pachomius, he used this gift both to guide individuals and to govern the *Koinonia* as a whole. While this theme appears prominently in the *Lives*, it is perhaps clearest in the *Letter of Ammon*, which gives an eyewitness account of Theodore's spiritual guidance (for excerpts, see appendix 5.3).

The *Koinonia* under Theodore strengthened its ties to Athanasius. During his third exile (356–361), Athanasius was hotly pursued by imperial authorities after his dramatic escape from Alexandria. In 360 the authorities heard rumors that he was hiding with the Pachomians. So they dispatched a sizable contingent led by the region's senior military officer, Duke Artemios, to capture him. One night, the army suddenly laid siege to the great monastery of Pbow, surrounding it and threatening to kill any monk who dared to leave. Artemios then entered the monastery grounds, battle-ax in hand, surrounded by a bodyguard of archers. Theodore was absent at the time, visiting the monasteries. So Artemios confronted Apa Psahref, who as Great Steward was second in command, and announced, "Athanasius the archbishop is the enemy of the emperor. . . . We have heard that he is hiding among you." Psahref answered, "Athanasius the archbishop is our father after God but we testify to you before God that not only is he not hiding among us, but I have never seen his face."[108] The soldiers rummaged through all the cells but found nothing.

Athanasius did visit the Pachomian monasteries in the 360s. We have two divergent accounts. The *Letter of Ammon* reports that during his fourth exile in 363—this time it was the Emperor Julian who had put out the arrest warrant—Athanasius fled to the Thebaid and planned to hide among the Pachomians. He was reportedly to sail with Theodore and another Pachomian, but the boat got stuck. Theodore, as he was out towing the boat, suddenly had a moment of clairvoyance and announced that there was no longer anything to fear, for at that moment, the Emperor Julian had just been killed by the Persians in his ill-fated military campaign.[109]

The *Lives* describe a (second?) visit of Athanasius that makes no mention of exile or flight. Athanasius was reportedly making a triumphal tour of the Thebaid just before Easter. When Theodore got word of it, he hurried north with "all the brothers" from the northernmost monasteries to offer a formal greeting. Athanasius came ashore near Hermopolis, gave his blessing, and then came to town riding on a donkey, allowing Theodore to lead it by the bridle. The brothers formed a long torchlight procession and, singing psalms, led him up to the monasteries for a tour. (The political symbolism of this ceremonial was certainly intentional; in political terms, it was an ideal "photo op.") Athanasius was reportedly impressed by their lives, by their good order and asceticism. The *Lives* also report that Athanasius sent a letter to Horsiesius to be carried by the hand of Theodore. The political symbolism here is important: Theodore acted as letter carrier and thus was inferior.[110] The letter effected a reconciliation between the two men, and Horsiesius agreed to move back to Pbow and began to assume leadership functions, such as giving catecheses. Theodore died not long after this, in 368. The *First Greek Life* poignantly ends its narrative with a letter from Athanasius to Horsiesius. In it, Athanasius praises "blessed Theodore" and prays that "everyone sailing" be like Theodore and "moor his own boat in that distant haven free of storms."[111]

The late rapprochement with Horsiesius made possible a smooth transition. The *First Greek Life* says that "Abba Horsiesios was again in possession of his own rank and he governed the brothers according to his capacity."[112] This understated sentence is poignant: it shows that if Horsiesius "again" had "his own rank," then Theodore's pose as "deputy" was a fiction. One can also hear an understated criticism of Horsiesius: that he governed "according to his capacity"—which may have been a limited one. He led the *Koinonia* until his death sometime after 387. Quite a few documents attributed to Horsiesius have come down to us. These include seven *Catecheses*, four *Letters*, a set of *Regulations*, and a treatise called *The Testament of Horsiesius*. The latter is one of the most eloquent expressions of Pachomian spirituality (for excerpts, see appendix 5.4).

In 391, Theophilus, archbishop of Alexandria, had the great Temple of Serapis in Canopus torn down. Its destruction signaled, more than that of any other, the demise of paganism—at least, that is how people like Augustine, halfway across the empire, interpreted it. Theophilus then invited Pachomian monks to come and establish a monastery there. It became known as the Metanoia, "the Conversion," and became the Pachomian outpost that connected the *Koinonia* to Alexandria and beyond. From here the fame of Pachomius, Theodore, and the *Koinonia* spread abroad to the wider Roman world. It is likely that the *First Greek Life* was composed there, or at least composed for use by monks who lived there. It was from his contacts at the Metanoia that Jerome came across the Pachomian *Rules* and *Letters* and was pressed into translating them into Latin. Jerome's translations did much to spread the fame of Pachomius to the West. Meanwhile, Evagrius Ponticus, in his treatise *On Prayer*, written sometime in the late 390s, reports that he has in hand a book entitled *Lives of the Monks of Tabennesi* and describes an episode from the life of Theodore.[113] Scholars wonder what all this might have included, but it seems that he had some version of the *Life of Pachomius*.

Given that the Monastery of the Metanoia was built, quite literally, on the ruins of paganism, it was no accident that the author of the *First Greek Life* situates the work of Pachomius against the horizon of Christianity's worldwide mission. In the prologue, he explicitly quotes Matthew 28:19, in which the risen Jesus sends forth his apostles to go to all nations and baptize them in the name of the Father, Son, and Holy Spirit. He goes on to cite the divine promise made to Abraham, that his descendants will be as numerous as the stars (Gen. 22:17). He then links the demise of paganism with the rise of monasticism in general and Pachomius in particular. The life of Pachomius is thus set on the world stage, a world "made drunk" by the coming of Christ, flooded by the "grace" which "has poured forth from the lips of the blessed one who blesses all."[114]

The author of the *First Greek Life* meditates from time to time on his task as a writer, and these reflections provide a glimpse into the agenda that shapes his account. One item I have already mentioned several times: the defense and praise of Theodore.[115] Given the tumultuous succession, Theodore needed some defense. But there are other issues at work. The author says that his work is not a panegyric for Pachomius: "Our purpose was not to praise him, for he does not want human praise." Pachomius counted himself only as a sinner. But the author insists: "Yet he walked in the ways of the saints, according to what Scripture says, 'Be my imitators.' For the way is open for everyone. This is why we have put together these things in writing, that we may gather without any loss the fruit of the things we say. . . . This text we have just written, we have not written for the sake of writing but as a memorial."[116] Like Athanasius, the author of the *First Greek Life* had mimetic concerns. Pachomius is a figure worthy of imitation, for "he walked in the way of the saints." The author, in fact, refers explicitly to the *Life of Antony* composed by "the most holy father Athanasius" and notes that it too was written for "edification."[117] But the author had other concerns. He writes because he fears a loss of memory, amnesia. The author twice admits that he had not seen Pachomius "in the flesh" but got his stories from "those who were with him and of the same age." He felt obliged to answer critics who chide him: why did the intimates of Pachomius not write it all down? The author was hard pressed to answer: "perhaps it was not yet the time." But, he believed, the time had come: "we wrote a few out of many things that we might not forget altogether what we had heard about this perfect monk who is our father after all the saints."[118] The time for writing had come because people were forgetting. The issue was continuity: "we have been writing as children eagerly desire to recall the memory of the fathers who brought us up."[119] In this sense, the *Lives of Pachomius* were a "memorial."

But the author of the *First Greek Life* wrote not merely as a "son" about his "holy father Pachomius." He wrote as a father who had a new generation in view. He aptly quotes Psalms 78:3: "what we have heard and known and our fathers have told us should not be hidden from the next generation." He then adds:

> For, as we have been taught, we know that these words of the psalm
> are about the signs and portents accomplished by God for Moses
> and those after him. And after the model of the benefit given by
> them, we have also recognized in the fathers of our time their chil-

dren and imitators, so that to us and to the rising generation, until
the end of the world, it might be made known that "Jesus Christ is
the same yesterday, today and forever" (Heb. 13:8).[120]

The author's plea to imitate the heroics of the fathers, Pachomius and Theodore and the many figures who cross the pages, sprang from a concern not
with the past, but with the future. The author, as Henry Chadwick has noted,
"is acutely conscious that things are not now as they used to be; in his time
there is moral and spiritual decline, and the readers need warnings of the perils
of allegiance. . . . The portrayals of the intense severity of Pachomius and of
the self-extinguishing humility of Theodore are sermons addressed to a generation where discipline has fallen off."[121]

The later history of the Pachomian *Koinonia* is difficult to trace. Quite
simply, we lack the documents.[122] For whatever reason, the impulse to compose
biographies and histories seems to have ebbed. The later Pachomians did leave
behind one very significant monument: the massive basilica at Pbow constructed in the mid-fifth century and completed in 459. Recent archaeological
excavations have uncovered just how massive it was: thirty-six meters wide by
seventy-two meters long, making it the largest church in Roman Egypt. It was
a five-aisled basilica, with enormous rose granite columns. Even after its destruction centuries later, those massive pillars marked the site where thousands
of Pachomian monks routinely gathered for worship and for their great assemblies. Those pillars are, in a way, a striking memorial of and testimony to the
grandeur of the Pachomian experiment in Christian community.[123] (See appendix 5.5 on the discovery of a Gnostic library near the Pachomian *Koinonia*.)

Usually Pachomius is spoken of in the same breath with Antony and numbered among the desert fathers. This ignores the obvious: Pachomius and his
disciples did not live in the desert; they lived near the Nile. They did not make
the desert a city; they turned deserted villages into thriving communities. They
cultivated fields and orchards, trained craftsmen, produced handiwork, and
sold their wares. With their fleet of boats, they carried on far-reaching and
thriving commercial dealings. As James Goehring has noted, whereas Antony
the anchorite withdrew from the world, Pachomius and his followers withdrew
from the desert.[124] But the Pachomians withdrew from the desert not for economic reasons, but for religious ones. They sought to fulfill what they remembered of Pachomius's original vocation: "to minister to the human race" and
"unite it" with God.

NOTES

1. See, for example, the *Oxford Dictionary of the Christian Church*, 3rd ed., ed.
Elizabeth Livingstone (New York: Oxford University Press, 1997), 1207 and *The Coptic
Encyclopedia*, ed. Aziz S. Atiya (New York: Macmillan, 1991), 6:1859.
2. *First Greek Life of Pachomius* 136 (SH 19:86; trans. Veilleux, CS 45:395).
3. *First Greek Life* 98 (SH 19:65; CS 45:364–365).
4. For a survey of the debate, see James E. Goehring, *The Letter of Ammon and*

Pachomian Monasticism, Patristische Texte unde Studien 27 (Berlin: Walter de Gruyter, 1986), 3–33. For a taste of the debate, see Derwas J. Chitty, "Pachomian Sources Reconsidered," *Journal of Ecclesiastical History* 5 (1954): 38–77, and Louis-Théophile Lefort, "Les sources coptes pachômiennes," *Le Muséon* 67 (1954): 217–229.

    5. *Bohairic Life* 7 (CSCO 89:4–5; trans. Veilleux, CS 45:26–27) = *First Greek Life* 4 (SH 19:3; CS 45:300).

    6. *Bohairic Life* 8 (CSCO 89:6; CS 45:28–29) = *First Greek Life* 5 (SH 19:4; CS 45:301).

    7. *Ep. Ammonis* 12 (SH 19:103; CS 46:79–80).

    8. *Bohairic Life* 10 (CSCO 89:8–10; CS 45:30–31) = *First Greek Life* 6 (SH 19:4–5; CS 45:301–302).

    9. *Bohairic Life* 17 (CSCO 89:18; trans. Veilleux, CS 45:39) = *First Greek Life* 12 (SH 19:8; CS 45:305).

    10. *Bohairic Life* 22 (CSCO 89:22; trans. Veilleux, CS 45:45) = *First Greek Life* 23 (SH 19:14; trans. Veilleux, CS 45:311–312).

    11. Versions of this story appear in the *First Greek Life* 15–16 (SH 19:10; CS 45:307–308); *Bohairic Life* 19—actually the pages are missing here, and the story is reconstructed from the *Third Sahidic Life* (CSCO 99:104, 109; CS 45:42–43); and the *First Sahidic Life*, frag. III, nos. 7–10 (CSCO 99:2–3; CS 45:428–430). This incident is a classic example of confusion among the different sources. The *First Greek Life* and the (reconstructed) *Bohairic Life* portray the fraternal wrangle as occurring *before* the second revelation; the *First Sahidic Life* says the wrangle occurred *after* it—and in fact, *because of* it. The *First Sahidic Life* portrays a second clash that is missing from the other two accounts; the (reconstructed) *Bohairic* makes no mention of sweating of the brick into mud.

    12. *First Sahidic Life*, Fragment III, 10–14, and Fragment IV, 17–19 (CSCO 99:4–7, 116–117; CS 45:430–438).

    13. *First Greek Life* 38 (SH 19:23–24; CS 45:324); cf. *Bohairic Life* 24 (CSCO 89:23–24; CS 45:47).

    14. *First Greek Life* 24 (SH 19:15; trans. Veilleux, CS 45:312).

    15. This discrepancy in this and other points in the chronology of Theodore's career is complex, to say the least. On this, see Veilleux, *Pachomian Koinonia I*, CS 45: 272–273, note on SBo 31, and Goehring, *Ascetic Behavior in Greco-Roman Antiquity*, 353n10.

    16. *First Greek Life* 36 (SH 19:22; trans. Veilleux, CS 45:323) = *Bohairic Life* 32 (CSCO 89:35; CS 45:57).

    17. *Bohairic Life* 37 (CSCO 89:39; trans. Veilleux, CS 45:60) = *First Greek Life* 37 (SH 19:22–23; CS 45:323). In both accounts, Theodore goes on to cite the appalling account in Ex. 32:27–28, noting: "The sons of Levi killed their own parents and brothers to please the Lord and escape the dangers of his wrath. I too, I have no mother, nor anything of the world, for it passes." In the *First Greek Life*, Pachomius explicitly cites the Matthean parallel (Matt. 10:37).

    18. *Bohairic Life* 37 (CSCO 89:39–40; trans. Veilleux, CS 45:61); cf. *First Greek Life* 37 (SH 19:23; CS 45:323).

    19. *Bohairic Life* 38 (CSCO 89:41; trans. Veilleux, CS 45:62).

    20. *First Greek Life* 37 (SH 19:23; CS 45:324).

    21. *Bohairic Life* 28 (CSCO 89:29; CS 45:52) has Athanasius give a highly tendentious speech about the evils of ordination; this reflects Pachomian ideology, not Athanasius's. Compare the parallel account in the *First Greek Life* 30. For a valuable analysis, see Brakke, *Athanasius and the Politics of Asceticism*, 111–120.

22. *First Greek Life* 54 (SH 19:36–37; CS 45:334–335) = *Bohairic Life* 49–51 (CSCO 89:51–52; CS 45:71–72).

23. *First Greek Life* 81, 83 (SH 19:54, 56; CS 45:352, 354) = *Bohairic Life* 56–58 (CSCO 89:55–57; CS 45:73–74, 77–78). The "monastery" built for Pachomius's sister was an affiliated house and not numbered in the list of the nine.

24. Jerome, *Praef. in Regulam s. Pachomii* 7 (Boon, 8; CS 46:143); Cassian, *De institutis* IV.1 (SC 109:122; ACW 58:79); Palladius, *Historia Lausica* 32.8 and 7.6 (Butler, 93 and 26; ACW 34:94 and 34:41).

25. Palladius, *Historia Lausiaca* 32.1 (Butler, 88; ACW 34:92).

26. For instance, it appears in the *Second Greek Life*, in the *Latin Life* of Dionysius Exiguus, and in the *Church History* of Socrates.

27. Vincent Desprez, "Pachomian Cenobitism II," *American Benedictine Review* 43 (1992): 359, notes that comparison of the three versions leads scholars to conclude that Jerome "was more concerned with elegance and clarity than with material exactitude; he translates rather freely, often adding precisions of his own."

28. The most extensive analysis of life in the *Koinonia* has been done by Armand Veilleux, *La liturgie dans le cénobitisme pachômien au quatrième siècle*, Studia Anselmiana 57 (Rome: Herder, 1968); Philip Rousseau, *Pachomius: The Making of a Community in Fourth-Century Egypt*, rev. ed., Transformation of the Classical Heritage 6 (Berkeley: University of California Press, 1999).

29. James E. Goehring, "New Frontiers in Pachomian Studies," in *Ascetics, Society, and the Desert: Studies in Early Egyptian Monasticism* (Harrisburg, Pa.: Trinity Press International, 1999); see the addendum, 184–186, which updates the original essay.

30. Jerome, *Praef. in Regulam s. Pachomii* 2 (Boon, 5; CS 46:142). Scholars think the numbers per house is probably too high, twenty being a better estimate. The *Ep. Ammonis* 7 (SH 19:100; CS 46:76) reports that there were twenty in the Greek-speaking house in Pbow, but that house may have been more an exception.

31. Implied in certain legislation: Pachomius, *Praecepta* 89, 126, etc. Palladius, *Historia Lausiaca* 32.2 (CS 46:126 / ACW 34:92), allows no more than three per cell, which implies that the surge in numbers made keeping one per cell difficult.

32. Chitty, *The Desert a City*, 22, noted that "the general plan of the monastery may be reminiscent of the military camps Pachomius would have known as a soldier." However, the sources hardly speak of him as a soldier. Bagnall, *Egypt in Late Antiquity*, 296, notes that cenobitic monasteries "seem to have draw inspiration from the regularized order of army camps, partly from the rambling assemblages of Egyptian villages. . . . The similarities [of monasteries] to army camps are extensive enough that it can be difficult to be certain whether a particular archaeological site is one or the other."

33. Jerome, *Praef. ad Regulam s. Pachomii* 6 (Boon, 7–8; CS 46:143).

34. The Coptic term was *rome ntsoouhs*, literally "man of the monastery," i.e., superior. See Fidelis Ruppert, *Das pachomianische Mönchtum und die Anfänge klösterlichen Gehorsams*, Münster-schwarzacher Studien 20 (Münster: Vien-Türme, 1971), 282–296; Desprez, "Pachomian Cenobitism II," 372.

35. The Coptic term was *rmn hei*, literally "man of the house," i.e., the presider. See Ruppert, *Das pachomianische Mönchtum*, 250–251, 296–315; Desprez, "Pachomian Cenobitism II," 373.

36. Rousseau, *Pachomius*, 79; Desprez, "Pachomian Cenobitism II," 373.

37. For example, Pachomius, *Praecepta ac Leges* 12 (Boon, 73; CS 46:182); *Praecepta* 19, 20 (Boon, 17–18; CS 46:148).

38. Pachomius, *Praecepta et Instituta* 16 (Boon, 57; CS 46:171); *Praecepta* 1, 15, 17,

52–54, 84 (Boon, 13, 16–7, 27–30, 38; CS 46:145, 147–148, 154–155, 160); on removing thorns, see *Praecepta* 82, 96 (Boon, 37, 40; CS 46:160, 161).

39. Pachomius, *Praecepta et Instituta* 11–12 (Boon, 56–57; CS 46:171).

40. *First Greek Life* 110 (SH 19:71; CS 45:372).

41. On the rotation of duties, see Jerome, *Praef. in Regulam s. Pachomii* 2 (Boon, 5–6; CS 46:142); also Pachomius, *Praecepta* 15, 23–27 (Boon, 16–20; CS 46:147–150); *Praecepta et Instituta* 1–2 (Boon, 54; CS 46:169–170). "Tribes" are mentioned only in passing in the *Rule*: Pachomius, *Praecepta* 15 (Boon, 16–17; CS 46:147). The clearest mention is in Jerome, *Praef. in Regulam s. Pachomii* 2 (Boon, 5–6; CS 46:142). Pallad- ius, *Historia Lausiaca* 32.4 (CS 46:126 / ACW 34:93), says that there were twenty-four "classes," each known by a Greek letter, so that a superior of a monastery might ask, "How is the Zeta class doing?"

42. The *Testament of Horsiesius* (Boon, 116–121; CS 47:179–183) follows the orga- nization discussed here: superiors of monasteries (no. 13), "seconds" of monasteries (no. 14), housemasters (no. 15–17), "seconds" of houses (no. 18), "brothers . . . each ac- cording to his rank" (no. 19).

43. The *Second Greek Life* 58 (SH 19:228), somewhat fancifully, portrays Pachom- ius coming to the porter every morning to ask whether, in the last twenty-four hours, someone has decided to leave the world.

44. *Bohairic Life* 26 (CSCO 89:25; trans. Veilleux, CS 45:48–49) = *First Greek Life* 28 (SH 19:18; CS 45:315).

45. Rousseau, *Pachomius*, 70, notes that this "was a legal question, perhaps as much as a psychological one."

46. Pachomius, *Praecepta* 49 (Boon, 26; CS 46:153).

47. Pachomius, *Praecepta* 140 (Boon, 50; CS 46:166).

48. Pachomius, *Praecepta* 139 (Boon, 49–50; trans. Veilleux, CS 46:166).

49. *Bohairic Life* 81 and 193 (CSCO 89:86 and 183; CS 46:105 and 236–237).

50. Theodore, *Ep.* 1.6 (Boon, 106; trans. Veilleux, CS 47:124).

51. The basic description is found in *Praecepta* 81 (Boon, 37; CS 46:159–160) and in Jerome, *Praef. in Regulam s. Pachomii* 4 (Boon, 6; CS 46:142). Mention is also made in *Praecepta* 2, 61, and 67 (Boon, 13, 32, 33; CS 46:142, 156–157).

52. *First Greek Life* 25 (SH 19:16; trans. Veilleux, CS 45:313).

53. Pachomius, *Praecepta* 3 (Boon, 14; CS 46:145). Jerome calls it a "trumpet blast."

54. Pachomius, *Praecepta* 5 (Boon, 14; trans. Veilleux, CS 46:146).

55. The clearest account of the rite is found in the somewhat later *Regulations of Horsiesius* 7–10 (CSCO 159: 84–85; CS 46:199–200). Other aspects are touched on in *Praecepta* 6, 7, 11, 12, etc. (Boon, 14–16; CS 46:146–147). See Veilleux, *La liturgie dans le cénobitisme pachômien* For an overview of both Egyptian practice and practices found elsewhere in the early church, see Robert Taft, *The Liturgy of the Hours in East and West: The Origins of the Divine Office and Its Meaning for Today* (Collegeville, Minn.: Liturgical Press, 1986), esp. 57–73.

56. Pachomius, *Praecepta ac leges* 3 (Boon, 71; trans. Veilleux, CS 46:181).

57. Pachomius orders a brother to eat bread and vegetables: *First Greek Life* 69 (SH 19:46–47; CS 45:344–345). Mention of fruit appears in *Praecepta* 75–76 (Boon, 35; CS 46:158–159). The *Bohairic Life* 59 (CSCO 89:57; CS 45:78–79) speaks of a "frugal meal" of cheese, olives, and vegetables, though this may reflect food for travelers and not normal fare. The sick were given a good diet: fish soup, even meat and wine; see Pachomius, *Praecepta* 45–46 (Boon, 24–25; CS 46:152); *First Greek Life* 53 (SH 19:34–36; CS 45:333–334).

58. On the *tragematia*, see Rousseau, *Pachomius*, 84–85.

59. Pachomius, *Praecepta ac leges* 10 (Boon, 73; CS 46:182); *Praecepta et Instituta* 14 (Boon, 57; CS 46:171).

60. Pachomius, *Praecepta ac leges* 12 (Boon, 73; trans. Veilleux, CS 46:182). See also *Praecepta et Instituta* 15 (Boon, 57; CS 46:171); *Bohairic Life* 26 (CSCO 89:26; CS 45:49) = *First Greek Life* 28 (SH 19:18–19; CS 45:315–316). In his translation of *Praecepta* 20 (Boon, 18; CS 46:148), Jerome incorrectly says that an instruction is given by the housemasters three times per week; it is the superiors of the monastery who give such a catechesis three times per week. This will be discussed later.

61. Pachomius, *Praecepta* 138 (Boon, 49; trans. Veilleux, CS 46:166). The time of day is not clear; cf. *Praecepta* 19 (CS 45:148), which refers to a discussion in the morning in the individual houses after the prayers.

62. Pachomius, *Praecepta* 87 and 88 (Boon, 38–39; CS 46:160–161). While this requirement was not imposed upon the sick and dying, many maintained the discipline till their dying day (*First Greek Life* 79). The *First Greek Life* 144 claims that the "reclining seats" received Athanasius's admiration when he visited. Palladius, *Historia Lausiaca* 32.3, notes them.

63. *First Greek Life* 14 (SH 19:9; trans. Veilleux, CS 45:306–307): "And for a long time whenever he wanted to refresh his body with sleep after growing weary in keeping awake for prayer, he would simply sit on something in the middle of the place without leaning his back against the wall. This he did for about fifteen years. Many of the ancient fathers, hearing or rather seeing this, tried also to humble the flesh by this and similar practices to enhance the salvation of their souls. . . . Later on they made reclining seats for themselves. For each of them practiced ascesis with faith according to his capacity."

64. *Bohairic Life* 26 (CSCO 89:26; CS 45:49) = *First Greek Life* 28 (SH 19:19; CS 45:316). Note, for instance, that Pachomius has Theodore give one of the Sunday catecheses (*First Greek Life* 77), though he was not yet the head of one of the monasteries. Cf. *Praecepta* 20 (Boon, 18; CS 46:148), where in Jerome's translation, it says (mistakenly) that the housemaster gives instructions three times per week. The first three *Catecheses* of Horsiesius give time indications: *Catecheses* 1 and 2 were delivered on a Saturday morning; *Catecheses* 3 an 4 were delivered on Sunday morning; and *Catechesis* 5 was delivered on Sunday evening.

65. Pachomius, *Ep.* 5 (Boon, 89–90; CS 47:63–67).

66. Mention of this appears repeatedly in the sources: *First Greek Life* 83 (SH 19:56; CS 45:354) = *Bohairic Life* 71 (CSCO 89:73; CS 45:93); Pachomius, *Praecepta* 27 (Boon, 19–20; CS 46:150); Jerome, *Praef. in Regulam s. Pachomii* 8 (Boon, 8; CS 46:143–144). Cf. *SBo* 144 (CS 45:205), which Veilleux reconstructs from the Sahidic.

67. The "Great Steward" (*megalos oikonomos*) is mentioned in *First Greek Life* 83 (SH 19:56; CS 45:354) in regard to this account. He may have also functioned as a sort of second-in-command whenever the "father" of the *koinonia* was absent—e.g. when Duke Artemios searched the monastery of Pbow while Theodore was away (*First Greek Life* 138).

68. Pachomius, *Praecepta* 27 (Boon, 20; CS 46:150).

69. Pachomius, *Ep* 7 (Boon, 95; trans. Veilleux, CS 47:69). See also the remarks on the Day of Remission given by Theodore, *Ep.* 2.3 (CS 47:128).

70. Jerome, *Praef. in Regulam s. Pachomii* 8 (Boon, 8; trans. Veilleux, CS 46:143–144).

71. *SBo* 144 (CS 45:205), which Veilleux reconstructs from the Sahidic; cf. *First*

Greek Life 83 (SH 19:56; CS 45:354), which is ambiguous and seems to involve house masters, but not the superiors of the individual monasteries.

72. Heinrich Bacht, "Pakhôme et ses disciples," in *Théologie de la vie monastique: études sur la tradition patristique*, ed. G. Lemaître, Collection Théologie 49 (Paris: Aubier, 1961), 44; he notes that in Pachomius's first *Catechesis*, he quotes or alludes to fifty-two books of the Bible.

73. Pachomius, *Instruction* 1.17 (CSCO 159:6; trans. Veilleux, CS 47:19).

74. *First Greek Life* 99 (SH 19:66; trans. Veilleux, CS 45:366).

75. Pachomius, *Ep.* 4.6 (Boon, 89; trans. Veilleux, CS 47:62).

76. Pachomius, *Praecepta* 71–72 (Boon, 34; trans. Veilleux, CS 46:158).

77. Pachomius, *Praecepta* 74–75 (Boon, 35; trans. Veilleux, CS 46:158).

78. *Instruction of Theodore* 3.23 (CSCO 159:51; trans. Veilleux, CS 47:107); cf. *Testament of Horsiesius* 50 (Boon, 142; CS 47:208–209). For a survey of Pachomian spirituality, see Bacht, "Pakhôme et ses disciples," 39–72.

79. *Regulations of Horsiesius* 51 (CSCO 159:96; trans. Veilleux, CS 46:216). Other instances: the *First Sahidic Life* 11 (CSCO 99:4; CS 45:431), which cites it as a description of "a perfect *koinonia*" and notes that Pachomius's first community was not ready for such standards; *Bohairic Life* 194 (CSCO 89:184; CS 45:237), in which Theodore alludes to it as a description of Pachomius's life work.

80. Rousseau, *Pachomius*, 90.

81. *Bohairic Life* 32 (CSCO 89:35; trans. Veilleux, CS 45:57); cf. *First Greek Life* 36 (SH 19:22; CS 45:323).

82. *Bohairic Life* 55, 62, 63 (CSCO 89:52–55, 60–64; CS 45:74–76, 80–84).

83. *Bohairic Life* 69 (CSCO 89:71–72; CS 45:91–92) = *First Greek Life* 77 (SH 19: 51–52; CS 45:350–351).

84. *Bohairic Life* 69 (CSCO 89:72; CS 45:91) says that Theodore was thirty-three when he gave his first public instruction (i.e., just before becoming superior), while the *First Greek Life* 78 (SH 19:52–53; CS 45:351) says he was thirty when he was made superior.

85. *Bohairic Life* 78 (CSCO 89:83–84; CS 45:102).

86. *Bohairic Life* 77, 80 (CSCO 89:82–86; CS 45:100–104).

87. *Bohairic Life* 96 (CSCO 89:120–121; CS 45:133–134) = *First Greek Life* 109 (SH 19:71; CS 45:374).

88. *First Greek Life* 48 (SH 19:31; trans. my own).

89. Pachomius, *Catechesis* 1.22 and 1.36 (CS 47:21, 29); a similar coinage appears in *Bohairic Life* 106 (CSCO 89:139; CS 45:150).

90. Veilleux, *Pachomian Koinonia I*, CS 45:282, notes that "the account of this Synod is not found in SBo, but is in Ag. It must have been in the source common to SBo-G¹ but left aside by the SBo group. It is the only story from Ag absent from SBo which we find in G¹."

91. *First Greek Life* 112 (SH 19:72–73; trans. Veilleux, CS 45:375–376).

92. *SBo* 122 (trans. Veilleux, CS 45:177), restored from the *Arabic Life* (Av); cf. *First Greek Life* 116 (SH 19:75; CS 45:379), which seems abbreviated and is bit more cryptic.

93. *First Greek Life* 120 (SH 19:77–78; trans. Veilleux, CS 45:382–383). Cf. the longer and more polemical account in the *SBo* 126–127, 128–129 (CS 45:182–187), in which Antony is made to rail against his own monks; this section is missing from the surviving *Bohairic Life*, and has been reconstructed by Veilleux from the Sahidic.

94. *Bohairic Life* 56 (CSCO 89:55–56; CS 45:77) = *First Greek Life* 80 (SH 19:54; CS 45:352).

95. *First Greek Life* 117 (SH 19:76; CS 45:380).

96. *SBo* 139 (trans. Veilleux, CS 45:195), reconstructed from the Sahidic.

97. *First Greek Life* 127 (SH 19:80–81; CS 45:387).

98. *First Greek Life* 130 (SH 19:82; CS 45:389).

99. *First Greek Life* 129 (SH 19:82; CS 45:389).

100. *First Greek Life* 130 (SH 19:82; CS 45:390), which uses the term *diadochon . . . kai hupēretēn* (literally "successor and servant"). See Veilleux, *Pachomian Koinonia I*, CS 45:421.

101. *First Greek Life* 131 (SH 19:83; trans. Veilleux, CS 45:391).

102. *Sixth Sahidic Life*, *SBo* 144 (CSCO 89:278–280; CS 45:205); the story is in the *Bohairic*, but the manuscript is defective at this point.

103. *First Greek Life* 134 (SH 19:84; CS 45:392–393).

104. *First Greek Life* 146 (SH 19:92–93; CS 45:403–404); cf. *Bohairic Life* 197–198 (CSCO 89:191–194; CS 45:243–246).

105. *First Greek Life* 132 (SH 19:83; trans. Veilleux, CS 45:391); see the extended discussion in the *Bohairic Life* 191 and 195 (CSCO 89:179–180, 189–190; CS 45:233–234, 242–243).

106. *First Greek Life* 131 (SH 19:82–83; trans. Veilleux, CS 45:390–391); cf. *Bohairic Life* 141–143.

107. *Bohairic Life* 194 (CSCO 89:185–186; trans. Veilleux, CS 45:238–239).

108. *Bohairic Life* 185 (CSCO 89:167; trans. Veilleux, CS 45:223); cf. *First Greek Life* 137–138 (SH 19:86–87; CS 45:395–397).

109. *Ep. Ammonis* 33–34 (SH 19:119–120; CS 46:102–104). The Syriac index to Athanasius's festal letters reports that he sent the letter for 363 while being "pursued from Memphis to the Thebaid" (*Chron. Ath.* 35). The *Historia acephala* 4.3.11–16 confirms this, saying that he "went up to the upper parts of Egypt as far as Upper Hemopolis in the Thebaid and as far as Antinoë."

110. For a valuable analysis of the texts and the intricate political symbolism of this ceremonial, see Brakke, *Athanasius and the Politics of Asceticism*, 120–126.

111. *First Greek Life* 150 (SH 19:95–96; trans. Veilleux, CS 45:406–407).

112. *First Greek Life* 149 (SH 19:95; trans. Veilleux, CS 45:406).

113. Evagrius, *De oratione* 108 (PG 79:1192).

114. *First Greek Life* 2 (SH 19:2; trans. Veilleux, CS 45:298).

115. Veilleux, *Pachomian Koinonia I*, CS 45:293, refers to it as an *apologia pro Theodoro*. The same perspective is noted by Chadwick, "Pachomios," 16, and Rousseau, *Pachomius*, 178 ff.

116. *First Greek Life* 98–99 (SH 19:65–67; trans. Veilleux, CS 45:365).

117. *First Greek Life* 99 (SH 19:66; trans. Veilleux, CS 45:366).

118. *First Greek Life* 98 (SH 19:65; trans. Veilleux, CS 45:364–365).

119. *First Greek Life* 99 (SH 19:66; trans. Veilleux, CS 45:366).

120. *First Greek Life* 17 (SH 19:11; trans. Veilleux, CS 45:308).

121. Chadwick, "Pachomios," 16.

122. On this later history, see Goehring, "Chalcedonian Power Politics and the Demise of Pachomian Monasticism," in *Ascetics, Society, and the Desert*, 241–261.

123. For a basic account, see Goehring, "New Frontiers in Pachomian Studies," reprinted in *Ascetics, Society, and the Desert*, 179–186; this version includes an update since this essay's original publication in the mid-1980s.

124. James Goehring, "Withdrawing from the Desert: Pachomius and the Development of Village Monasticism in Upper Egypt," *Harvard Theological Review* 89 (1996): 267–285; reprinted in *Ascetics, Society, and the Desert*, 89–109.

BIBLIOGRAPHY

Pachomius: Texts and Translations

The Coptic *Lives of Pachomius*

For a critical edition of the Sahidic *Lives of Pachomius*, see Louis-Théophile Lefort, ed., *Sancti Pachomii vitae Sahidice scripta*, CSCO 99–100 (Louvain: L. Durbecq, 1933–1934. For a critical edition of the Bohairic *Life of Pachomius*, see Louis-Théophile Lefort, ed., *Sancti Pachomii vitae Bohairice scripta*, CSCO 89 (Louvain: L. Durbecq, 1953). Lefort translated the entire corpus into French: *Les vies coptes de s. Pachôme et de ses premiers successeurs*, Bibliothèque du Muséon 16 (Louvain: Bureaux du Muséon, 1943). For an English translation of the *Bohairic Life*, the *First Sahidic Life*, and several fragments, see Armand Veilleux, *Pachomian Koinonia I: The Life of Saint Pachomius*, CS 45 (Kalamazoo, Mich.: Cistercian Publications, 1980), 23–295 and 425–457. Another translation of the *First Sahidic Life* has been done by James Goehring and appears in *Religions of Late Antiquity in Practice*, ed. Richard Valantasis (Princeton: Princeton University Press, 2000), 19–33.

The Greek *Lives of Pachomius*

For a critical edition of the Greek *Lives of Pachomius*, see François Halkin, ed., *Sancti Pachomii Vitae Graecae*, SH 19 (Brussels: Société des Bollandistes, 1932). For an English translation of the *First Greek Life*, see Armand Veilleux, *Pachomian Koinonia I: The Life of Saint Pachomius*, CS 45 (Kalamazoo, Mich.: Cistercian Publications, 1980), 297–423. Another good English translation, with the Greek text on facing pages, is Apostolos A. Athanassakis, *The Life of Pachomius (Vita Prima Graeca)* (Missoula, Mont.: Scholar's Press, 1975). See also the French edition by A. J. Festugière, *Les moines d'orient*, vol. 4, pt. 2, *La première vie grecque de saint Pachôme* (Paris: Éditions du Cerf, 1965), which includes a careful 150-page preface comparing the Greek and Coptic lives. An eighth Greek *Life of Pachomius* was published some fifty years after the original critical edition; see François Halkin, ed., *Le Corpus Athénien de saint Pachôme* (Geneva: Patrick Cramer, 1982).

The *Rules of Pachomius*

For the Latin text of Jerome's version of Pachomius's *Rules* with a French translation, see A. Boon, *Pachomiana latina: règle et épîtres de s. Pachôme, épître de s. Théodore et "Liber" de s. Orsiesius; texte latin de s. Jerôme*, Bibliothèque de la Revue d'histoire ecclésiastique 7 (Louvain, 1932). Some Coptic fragments have been discovered; see Louis-Théophile Lefort, ed., *Oeuvres de s. Pachôme et de ses disciples*, CSCO 159–160 (Louvain: L. Durbecq, 1956). For an English translation, see Armand Veilleux, *Pachomian Koinonia II: Pachomian Chronicles and Rules*, CS 46 (Kalamazoo, Mich.: Cistercian Publications, 1981), 139–195.

The *Letter of Ammon*

For a critical edition of the Greek text of Ammon's *Letter*, with an English translation and commentary, see James E. Goehring, *The Letter of Ammon and Pachomian Monasticism*, Patristische Texte unde Studien 27 (Berlin: Walter de Gruyter, 1986). An earlier edition is available in François Halkin, ed., *Sancti Pachomii Vitae Graecae*, SH 19 (Brussels: Société des Bollandistes, 1932), 97–121. For another English translation, see Armand Veilleux, *Pachomian Koinonia II: Pachomian Chronicles and Rules*, CS 46 (Kalamazoo, Mich.: Cistercian Publications, 1981), 71–109.

The *Paralipomena*

For the Greek text, see François Halkin, ed., *Sancti Pachomii Vitae Graecae*, SH 19 (Brussels: Société des Bollandistes, 1932), 122–165. For an English translation, see Armand Veilleux, *Pachomian Koinonia II: Pachomian Chronicles and Rules*, CS 46 (Kalamazoo, Mich.: Cistercian Publications, 1981), 19–70.

The *Letters* and *Instructions* of Pachomius, Theodore, and Horsiesius

For the Coptic texts with a French translation, see Louis-Théophile Lefort, ed., *Oeuvres de s. Pachôme et de ses disciples*, CSCO 159–160 (Louvain: L. Durbecq, 1956). For an English translation, see Armand Veilleux, trans., *Pachomian Koinonia III: Instructions, Letters and Other Writings of Saint Pachomius and His Disciples*, CS 47 (Kalamazoo, Mich: Cistercian Publications, 1982).

Pachomius: Studies

For brief introductory studies, see the pair of articles by Vincent Desprez, "Pachomian Cenobitism" (I and II), *American Benedictine Review* 43 (1992): 233–249, 358–394. An important book-length survey, geared to a more advanced audience, is Philip Rousseau, *Pachomius: The Making of a Community in Fourth-Century Egypt*, rev. ed., Transformation of the Classical Heritage 6 (Berkeley: University of California Press, 1999). Over the last fifteen years, James Goehring has published a number of important articles that deal with Pachomius and the Pachomians. Representative of his perspective is the essay "New Frontiers in Pachomian Studies," in *The Roots of Egyptian Christianity*, ed. Birger A. Pearson and James E. Goehring, Studies in Antiquity and Christianity (Philadelphia: Fortress Press, 1986), 236–257. Goehring has collected this and other valuable articles in *Ascetics, Society, and the Desert: Studies in Early Egyptian Monasticism* (Harrisburg, Pa.: Trinity Press International, 1999). See also:

Bacht, Heinrich. "Pakhôme et ses disciples." In *Théologie de la vie monastique: études sur la tradition patristique*, ed. G. Lemaître, 39–72. Collection Théologie 49. Paris: Aubier, 1961.

Brakke, David. *Athanasius and the Politics of Asceticism*. New York: Oxford University Press, 1995. [See especially 111–129, "Athanasius and the Pachomians."]

Burrows, Mark S. "On the Visibility of God in the Holy Man: A Reconsideration of the Role of the Apa in the Pachomian *Vitae*." *Vigiliae Christianae* 41 (1987): 11–33.

Chadwick, Henry. "Pachomios and the Idea of Sanctity." In *The Byzantine Saint*, ed. Sergei Hackel, 11–24. London: Fellowship of St. Alban and St. Sergius. Reprinted in *History and Thought of the Early Church*. London: Variorum Reprints, 1982.

Chitty, Derwas J. "A Note on the Chronology of the Pachomian Foundations." *Studia Patristica* 2 (1957): 379–385.

———. "Pachomian Sources Once More." *Studia Patristica* 10 (1970): 54–64.

———. "Pachomian Sources Reconsidered." *Journal of Ecclesiastical History* 5 (1954): 38–77.

Gould, Graham E. "Pachomian Sources Revisited." *Studia Patristica* 30 (1997): 202–217.

———. "Pachomios of Tabennesi and the Foundation of an Independent Monastic

Community." In *Voluntary Religion*, ed. W. J. Shields and D. Wood, 15–24. Studies in Church History 23. Oxford: Blackwell, 1986.

Kardong, T. G. "The Monastic Practices of Pachomius and the Pachomians." *Studia Monastica* 32 (1990): 59–77.

Ruppert, Fidelis. *Das pachomianische Mönchtum und die Anfänge klösterlichen Gehorsams*. Münster-schwarzacher Studien 20. Münster: Vien-Türme, 1971.

Veilleux, Armand. *La liturgie dans le cénobitisme pachômien au quatrième siècle*. Studia Anselmiana 57. Rome: Herder, 1968.

Vogüé, Adalbert de. *De saint Pachôme à Jean Cassien: études littéraires et doctrinales sur la monachisme égyptien à ses débuts*. Studia Anselmiana 120. Rome: 1996.

The Nag Hammadi Library

For an account of the discovery as well as a translation of the texts, see James M. Robinson, ed., *The Nag Hammadi Library*, 3rd ed. (San Francisco: HarperCollins, 1988). On the history of the debate about possible links between the Pachomians and the Nag Hammadi library, see especially James E. Goehring, "The Provenance of the Nag Hammadi Codices once more," *Studia Patristica* 35 (2001): 234–256. For a sampling of the debate, see:

Barns, John W. B. "Greek and Coptic Papyri from the Covers of the Nag Hammadi Codices." In *Essays on the Nag Hammadi Texts: In Honour of Pahor Labib*, ed. Martin Krause, 9–18. Nag Hammadi Studies 6. Leiden: Brill, 1975.

Veilleux, Armand. "Monasticism and Gnosis in Egypt." In *The Roots of Egyptian Monasticism*, ed. Birger A. Pearson and James E. Goehring, 271–306. Studies in Antiquity and Christianity. Philadelphia: Fortress Press, 1986.

APPENDIX 5.1

The Versions of the *Life of Pachomius*

The *Lives of Pachomius* clearly have a complex genealogy. The stemma given on the following page is based on the one first proposed by Armand Veilleux; see his *Pachomian Koinonia I*, CS 45:1–17. I have simplified it somewhat and have written out the full titles of the individual works.

SBo

The original SBo was a Sahidic Coptic work, now lost. However, it has been well preserved in two quite complete translations: the *Bohairic Life* and the *Arabic Life* found in the Vatican. Fragments of it have been preserved in a family of Sahidic fragments: the third, fourth, fifth, sixth, seventh, and fourteenth *Sahidic Lives*. This whole group of documents transmits basically the same *Life*.

GREEK

The most important of the Greek sources is the *First Greek Life*. From this one, all the other Greek sources derive. The other Greek sources combine in various ways other documents, such as the *Rules*, the *Paralipomena*, Palladius's *Lausiac History*, and the *Ascetica* (that is, the *Letters, Instructions*, etc.).

LOST SOURCES

Veilleux speculates that behind the SBo document there were originally two separate documents, a brief life of Pachomius and a life of Theodore—both lost. Veilleux's hypothesis on this has met with a mixed reception.

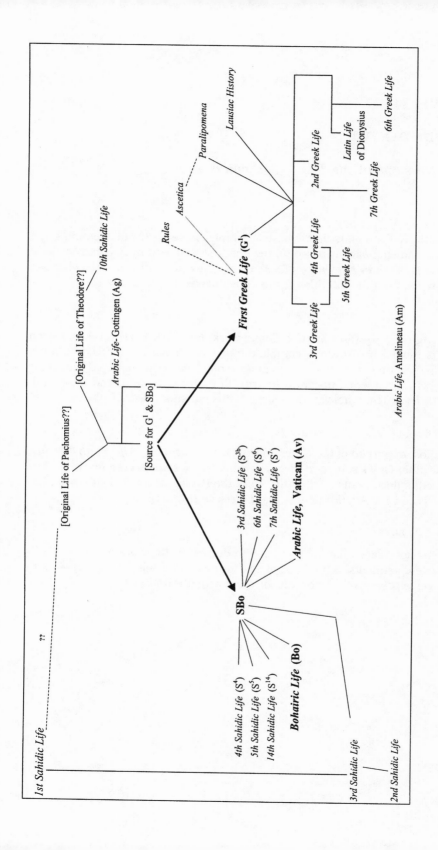

APPENDIX 5.2

The *Letters of Pachomius*

In the preface to his translation of the *Rule of Pachomius*, Jerome says that "to Pachomius, Cornelios and Sourous . . . an angel gave knowledge of a secret language, so that they might write to each other and speak through a spiritual alphabet, wrapping hidden meanings in certain signs and symbols." The *Letters* of Pachomius are dotted with coded language. Here is an excerpt from *Letter* 6 of Pachomius, as preserved by Jerome:

Letter of our Father Pachomius to Sourous, the Father of the monastery called Phnoum, and John, one of the housemasters of the same monastery.

I want you to understand the characters that you wrote to me and that I wrote to you in answer, and how important it is to know all the elements of the spiritual alphabet. Write ν and η; write ζ above χ, μ, λ, and ι, when you have finished reading these characters. I wrote to you so that you might understand the mysteries of the characters. Do not write ν above χ, θ, and ηι; but rather write ζ above χ, and ν above η and θ. As soon as I received the characters you wrote, I wrote back and to mysterious (words) I also answered with sacred (words). I notice indeed that the characters of your letters were η and θ; therefore I also understood the meaning and the words in the same manner, so I could be even with your understanding, lest you suffer some loss from us. Therefore I wrote to you ϛφθμ, lest perhaps some one might say that my name is not written ϛφθμ. And do not say: we can write χη, for you said indeed that it is written this way.

Now, therefore, ϛφθμλουυουυλιλ. Behold, I wrote to you also χ, complete and perfect all around. You write χ and φ, so that you can write ϛ and μ. Behold θ is written before them. Let it be enough for you to take care of κ and τ, in case you are to go forth. We have written to you ηι because of your labor, so that you might show every-solicitude before you depart.

The following is *Letter* 9 of Pachomius, as preserved in Coptic:

Words of our Father Pachomius through characters, in a hidden language, about what is going to happen:

αω: The generations have effervesced with evil, which is δ;

βψ: The fruit has been accomplished on the lips, which is τ;

ιχ: God caused me to forget the poverty in my house, from the begin-
       ning of the mountains to their summit, which is ρ.

δψ: The repose of the widow and the glory of the poor, which is ο.

ευ: The mountains have heard the joy of the earth, which is ξ;

ζτ: The earth has been hidden without price, which is ν;

ης: They cried on account of my eyes till evening, which is ι;

θρ: Do you think they will look on the earth? which is η;

ιπ: They drank hidden in joy, which is ι;

κο: The spoils of the earth were taken without blood, which is η;

λξ: Unfathomed depths were made in the sorrow of the heart, which is
       ξ;

μν: Those who were hidden fled without fear, which is ο.

The Latin text of the Letters of Pachomius is found in A. Boon, *Pachomiana latina*, Bibliothèque de la Revue d'histoire ecclésiastique (Louvain, 1932); the Coptic text is found in Hans Quecke, *Die Briefe Pachoms*, Textus Patristici et Liturgici 11 (Regensburg, 1975), 111–118. The translations here are by Armand Veilleux, *Pachomian Koinonia III*, CS 47 (Kalamazoo, Mich.: Cistercian Publications, 1982), 67–68, 72–73.

APPENDIX 5.3

The *Letter of Ammon*

The *Letter of Ammon* excerpted here offers a fascinating glimpse of the Koinonia under Theodore's leadership. The document, more a memoir than a letter, was composed in the 390s by a pro-Athanasian bishop who had spent three years of his youth in the Pachomian monastery of Pbow. The *Letter* is addressed to "a certain Theophilus," presumably the Theophilus who was then patriarch of Alexandria. Ammon—not to be confused with Ammonas, the disciple of Antony—was a native of Alexandria. In the letter, he traces his religious development. Born a pagan, he converted to Christianity at age seventeen. After hearing Athanasius's praise of monasticism, he decided to become a monk, and was encouraged by a local priest to meet some Pachomian monks who had sailed down from Tabennesi. With some reluctance, the Pachomians took the young man back with them. He was met at the gatehouse by Theodore himself and formally welcomed into the community. The author dates the events quite precisely: he entered the monastery in 352 and ended up staying only three years. When he later got word of his parents' grief at his sudden departure, he requested a visit home. Theodore advised him not to return to Pbow, but to settle closer to home, in the monastic settlement of Nitria. The *Letter of Ammon* has a remarkable eyewitness account of seeing Pachomius's successor, Theodore, preaching, prophesying, and reading hearts.

In the early twentieth century, Louis-Théophile Lefort attacked the work as a late forgery, pointing to various inaccuracies in its account of Pachomian liturgies and its terminology for various leadership positions. Since then, it has been ably defended by Derwas Chitty and others. The inaccuracies can be explained by the fact that Ammon was describing events forty years after the fact. Moreover, his long years at the monastic settlement of Nitria had confused him on certain Pachomian liturgical practices.

CONVERSION TO MONASTICISM

Here Ammon describes how his conversion to Christianity became a conversion to monasticism (a not-uncommon occurrence in the early church). He also explains how he was steered to join a Pachomian monastery:

> At the age of seventeen, having become a Christian, I heard the blessed pope Athanasius relating in church the way of life of the monks and ever-virgins and, marvelling at "the hope stored up for them in the heavens" (Coloss. 1:5). Loving what I had heard from

him. After I had received "the cleansing water of rebirth" (Tit. 3:5), I
met with a certain theban monk in the city and I proposed to follow
him. Then I offered [God] what I had and I took the advice of Paul
of blessed memory, the priest of the Church called Pereou. As he
detected the monk to be a heretic, he sent me to holy Theodore in
the Thebaid, with Theophilus and Copres, men devoted to God, who
happened to have been sent by Theodore to the blessed pope Athanasius with letters. (*Epistula Ammonis* 2)

EYEWITNESS ACCOUNT OF THEODORE AND THE MONASTERY OF PBOW

Ammon describes his initiation at Pbow and his first meeting with Theodore:

> And when we came to the monastery where the servant of God
> Theodore was—which is called Phbow and is in the nome of Upper
> Diospolis—the man of God Theodore deigned to meet me at the
> gate. After he had told me what was necessary, he made me change
> my clothing and introduced me into the monastery. There I found
> about six hundred monks assembled and waiting in the middle of
> the monastery. Theodore sat down under a palm tree and they all
> sat down with him. Then, seeing that I was surprised at their order
> and was blushing, he made me sit down near him. (*Epistula Am-
> monis* 2)

THEODORE PREDICTS THAT AMMON WILL BECOME A BISHOP

Theodore assigned Ammon to a Greek-speaking house within the monastery
and prophesied that Ammon would eventually be made a bishop. Ammon's
housemaster was also named Theodore—so Ammon refers to the housemaster
as "Theodore the Alexandrian" to distinguish him from Pachomius' successor:

> While all were staring at me, the holy Theodore rose up and ordered
> everyone to go to prayer. Then he took me by the hand and en-
> trusted me to teachers and guides, namely Theodore the Alexan-
> drian and to his second, Ausonius. He said to Ausonius, "Urge him
> to learn the divine Scriptures, for he will not remain in the monas-
> tery, but will be a minister of the Church of God." (*Epistula Am-
> monis* 7)

LIFE IN A PACHOMIAN HOUSE

In the *Rules*, Pachomius had insisted that the monks discuss in their individual
houses what they remembered and learned from the address given by the head
of the monastery. Here Ammon describes this practice as he saw it in action:

They received me and brought me to the house where lived the twenty greek monks who were under them. [The monks] sat down and required each one to say what he remembered from the questions addressed to the holy Theodore and from his answers. And so I heard each one of the twenty, and after them Ausonius and Theodore the Alexandrian, saying what they had remembered. "I pondered it in my heart" (Luke 2:19), and was able to remember what I have written. For, when I asked him, Theodore the Alexandrian immediately interpreted to me the meaning of what Theodore had said to each of those who had questioned him. (*Epistula Ammonis* 7)

MEMORIES OF PACHOMIUS

Soon after Ammon's arrival, Theodore the Alexandrian recounted stories of Pachomius. Here is his initial description:

"There was a certain Pachomius, leader of these monasteries, who was well pleasing to God. God made known many things to him by revelations, still more by "speaking to his heart" (Hos. 2:16), and other things through angels; and he honored him with divers gifts. Six years ago, "he absented himself from the body and made his home with the Lord" (2 Cor. 5: 8)." (*Epistula Ammonis* 9)

For the Greek text, as well as an English translation and commentary, see James E. Goehring, *The Letter of Ammon and Pachomian Monasticism*, Patristische Texte und Studien 27 (Berlin: Walter de Gruyter, 1986). The translation used here is by Armand Veilleux, *Pachomian Koinonia II*, CS 46 (Kalamazoo, Mich.: Cistercian Publications, 1981), 71–77.

APPENDIX 5.4

The *Testament of Horsiesius*

Horsiesius (d. after 387) had a tumultuous career as the "father" of the Pachomian *Koinonia*. He was appointed by Petronius, Pachomius's short-lived successor. After four years in office, Horsiesius was forced to step down and went
into a self-imposed exile at the monastery of Šeneset (Chenoboskion). Around
366, Theodore and Horsiesius were finally reconciled, thanks in part to an
intervention by Athanasius. About a year later, Theodore died, and Horsiesius
resumed authority for the *Koinonia*. He led it for twenty more years. Seven
catecheses and four letters attributed to him have been preserved in Coptic,
and there has been no serious challenge to their authenticity. Perhaps the most
intriguing of these is his so-called *Testament*, translated into Latin in 404 by
Jerome. Best known by its Latin title, *Liber Horsiesii*, it stands as an eloquent
statement of Pachomian spirituality. Like other Pachomian documents, it is
saturated with quotes and allusions to biblical texts. This appendix gives a few
excerpts.

RENUNCIATION AS FREEDOM

> Let us be even more vigilant, in the knowledge that God has granted
> us, through our father Pachomius, the great grace to renounce the
> world and consider as nothing all the worries of the world and the
> cares of worldly affairs. What opportunity has been left to us to have
> anything as our own, "from a thread to a shoe strap" (Gen. 14:23),
> since we have masters who "with fear and trembling" (1 Cor. 2:3) are
> so solicitous on our behalf both for food and clothing and during ill
> health, if it should occur, that we need not worry about anything
> and thereby lose the soul's benefits for the sake of the flesh? We are
> free; we have cast from our necks the yoke of enslavement to the
> world. . . . And let us think of the traditions of our father as a ladder
> which leads to the kingdom of heaven. (*Liber Horsiesii* 21)

EQUALITY WITHIN THE *KOINONIA*

> Therefore, brothers, let us be equal, from the least to the greatest,
> whether rich or poor, perfect in harmony and humility. . . . Let no
> one look after his own pleasure when he sees a brother living in
> poverty and hardship; let this saying of the prophet be told of you,

"Did one God not create [all of] you? Have you not all one father? Why has each of you abandoned his brother, thus profaning the covenant of your fathers? Judah has been forsaken, and abomination has been committed in Israel' (Mal. 2:10–11). Our Lord and Savior gave his apostles this precept, "I gave you a new commandment: Love one another, as I have loved you. By this you shall truly be known as my disciples" (John 13:34–35). We should, therefore, love one another and show that we are truly the servants of our Lord Jesus Christ and sons of Pachomius and disciples of the *Koinonia*. (*Liber Horsiesii* 23)

PACHOMIUS AS A LAMP FOR THE SPIRITUAL JOURNEY

Therefore, let us be imitators of the saints and not forget the formation that our Father gave us while he was still alive. Let us not extinguish the burning lamp he placed above our heads. Walking [in] this world by the light of this lamp, let us remember that it is through his zeal that God has received us into his household. He gave a hospice to wayfarers, he showed a harbor of peace to those on a storm-tossed sea. [He provided] bread in hunger, shade in heat, clothing in nakedness. He instructed the ignorant by spiritual precepts. He encircled with chastity those enslaved by vices and joined to himself those from afar. (*Liber Horsiesii* 47)

THE *KOINONIA* AND ACTS OF THE APOSTLES 4

The Apostle taught us that our community, the community by which we are joined to one another, springs from God, when he said, "Do not forget good works and communion, for God takes pleasure in such sacrifices" (Heb. 13:16). We read the same thing in the Acts of the Apostles: "For the multitude of believers had one heart and soul, and no one called anything his own. They held everything in common. And the apostles gave witness to the resurrection of the Lord Jesus with great power" (Acts 4:32–33). The psalmist is in agreement with these words when he says, "Behold, how good and how delightful it is for brothers to live together" (Ps. 133:1). And let us who live together in the *Koinonia*, and who are united to one another in mutual charity, so apply ourselves that, just as we deserved fellowship with the holy fathers in this life, we may also be their companions in the life to come. (*Liber Horsiesii* 50)

For the Latin text, see Heinrich Bacht, ed., *Das Vermächtnis des Ursprungs*, Studien zum frühen Mönchtum 1 (Würzburg: Echter, 1972), 58–188. The English translation here is from Armand Veilleux, *Pachomian Koinonia III*, CS 47 (Kalamazoo, Mich.: Cistercian Publications, 1982), 171–224.

APPENDIX 5.5

Did the Nag Hammadi Library Belong
to the Pachomians?

In 1945, a tremendous discovery of early Christian manuscripts was made near the village of Nag Hammadi, at the great bend of the Nile in Upper Egypt. The Nag Hammadi Library, as it is called, contained a large cache of hitherto unknown documents, some fifty-three texts in thirteen codices. The titles are striking: *The Gospel of Truth, The Apocryphon of John, The Gospel of Thomas, The Gospel of Philip, The Hypostasis of the Archons, The Book of Thomas the Contender, The Gospel of the Egyptians, The Sophia of Jesus Christ, The Apocalypse of Adam.* Scholars quickly realized that they had stumbled upon an ancient Gnostic library.

The Gnostics were scattered groups of second-century Christians who claimed to possess and teach a secret and saving "knowledge" (*gnosis* is the Greek word for "knowledge"). The "knowledge," the *gnosis*, that they taught centered on elaborate myths about the origin of the universe and the origin of evil. Gnostics claimed that we human beings suffer from a sort of cosmic ignorance: we have forgotten who we are, where we have come from, and where we are going; we are really spirits from an upper world trapped in material bodies; and we have become drunk and drugged on the material world and have lost all memory of our ancient divine origins and the vast upper world to which we are destined to return. In the Gnostic view, salvation comes from enlightenment, an enlightening knowledge about our present condition and about how to escape it.

Christ figures prominently in many Gnostic texts. But the Gnostic Christ is very different from the Christ of the New Testament. The Gnostic Christ does not really take flesh, but only *appears* human; he does not work miracles, nor does he really die on the cross. Instead, he is the revealer of secret knowledge, of the upper world and of how the liberated soul can discover its divine twin and divine destiny. By the turn of the third century, the Gnostics came to be branded as heretics, and their views were gradually rejected as contrary to the emerging canon of scripture and the emerging creed.

For centuries, we have known of Gnosticism only through the eyes of its bitterest opponents: from the writings of early church fathers such as Irenaeus of Lyons, Tertullian, Hippolytus, and Epiphanius of Salamis. All that changed with the discovery of the documents at Nag Hammadi. These newly discovered texts made it possible for scholars to hear the Gnostics speak in their own voices. We can now better sort out fact from exaggeration and accusation. The discovery of the Nag Hammadi codices lets us appreciate the rich diversity of

Gnostic schools and teachers, their views, their rituals, and their spirituality. In fact, the diversity of this literature is so great that one leading scholar has argued that "Gnosticism" itself is simply a "dubious category" that needs to be "dismantled."

Gnosticism—and the battle against it—were defining issues for second-century Christianity. But the Nag Hammadi manuscripts themselves date from the fourth century, not the second. And they come to us in the form of Coptic translations of Greek originals. While these texts give us tremendous new insights into and raise important questions about second-century Christianity, they also raise profound questions about fourth-century Egyptian Christianity. Who were the fourth-century owners of these documents? Whose library was this? Why would fourth-century Egyptian Christians be reading such obviously heterodox literature? Why were the codices so carefully buried? The question is all the more intriguing because they were discovered only five miles from the central Pachomian monastery of Pbow and only three and a half miles from Šeneset. Could they have belonged to Pachomians?

One of the earliest Nag Hammadi experts, Jean Doresse, ruled out the possibility of the Nag Hammadi documents' being Pachomian almost from the start. Writing in his 1958 study *The Secret Books of the Egyptian Gnostics*, Doresse pointed out that in the surviving *Lives*, Pachomius and the whole Pachomian movement are shown to be fiercely committed to orthodoxy. Doresse noted that Theodore had ordered that Athanasius's *Festal Letter* 39 (367 A.D.)—which set out the canon of biblical books and condemned the reading of apocryphal books—be translated into Coptic and "placed it in the monastery as a law for them."[1] According to Doresse, all this meant that "the contents of these Gnostic collections had led us to suppose that, whoever may have possessed them, they cannot have been monks."[2]

This hard-and-fast view began to be questioned. Scholars recognized that the surviving Pachomian lives sometimes retrojected later views and practices onto the earlier stages of the movement. Was this deep concern with orthodoxy Pachomius's own, or was it a feature of a later period, say, under Theodore or even later? The question became acute when John Barns reported new evidence. The Nag Hammadi codices had been bound within fine-tooled leather covers, and these covers had been padded and stuffed with scraps of papyrus. In this cartonnage, as it is called, Barns had discovered certain telltale fragments of letters and other documents that pointed to a monastic source. One document in particular caught his eye: a letter from a man named Papnoute "to my beloved father Pachome," who on the papyrus's reverse side is called "my prophet and father." Barns suggested that this letter may well be one written to Pachomius from Paphnutius, Theodore's brother, who served as chief steward at the Monastery of Pbow. It seemed sure evidence according to Barns: "We should be justified in concluding, even without further evidence, that the Nag Hammadi material came from a Pachomian monastery."[3]

This forced scholars to reevaluate things. Had later Pachomians suppressed earlier ambiguities in the movement? Scholars noted the odd code found in Pachomius's surviving letters and reports of ecclesiastical opposition, most notably at the Synod of Latopolis in 345. Even such a careful and conservative scholar as Henry Chadwick was willing to give some credence to the idea that the Nag Hammadi library had once belonged to the Pachomians. He noted Barns's "suggestion has not yet been either vindicated or disproved, but in principle it has obviously inherent probability. . . . That the codices were read in the nearby monastery is surely as good as certain."[4] Chadwick also noted the sometimes ambiguous line between orthodoxy and heresy and the need to appreciate the evolution of the Pachomian movement:

> It is not inherently probable that Pachomios was interested in the niceties of orthodox doctrine as a theological system. . . . Pachomios's links to the ordinary life of the church may have gradually grown as local bishops either came to assert jurisdiction over his houses or, as at Panopolis, saw how useful monks could be in a missionary situation and encouraged them to build a monastery as an assertion of a Christian presence in a predominantly pagan city. But initially such links will have been few and weak. . . . This is not a matter of naively setting out to "discover" Pachomios to have been a heretical ascetic subsequently covered in orthodox plasterwork, but rather of asking to what extent it is reasonable to think the early Pachomian tradition largely indifferent where dogma is concerned, content to make use of a diversity of gifts so long as they all encourage renunciation of the world.[5]

James Goehring, in a similar vein, argued that while the clear-cut orthodoxy of the Pachomian movement portrayed in the sources does not fit the facts, the "alternative to this 'orthodox' movement is not a heretical movement but a movement that did not yet define its being in these either/or terms. As difficult as it may be for us to fathom in this modern age of reason, it was not impossible for one to support Athanasius and read the Nag Hammadi texts."[6]

Meanwhile, the papyrologists continued their work on the cartonnage. When the critical edition was published, the editor J. C. Shelton was critical of Barns, arguing that he had overstated the case. He pointed out that some scraps Barns had read as monastic were not; and that the names Barns found both in the cartonnage and in the Pachomian literature were simply common Egyptian names, too common to guarantee a link; and that even the letter from "Paphnoute" to "Pachome" was not necessarily Pachomian. A vast hodgepodge of documents showed up in the cartonnage: tax lists, imperial laws, tidbits of scripture, private letters, monastic letters, and business contracts. Shelton has suggested one likely source for this material: "the town rubbish heap."[7] In other words, the cartonnage says nothing sure about who owned and who read the Nag Hammadi codices.

Other scholars, while acknowledging that Pachomian self-understanding evolved and that the later *Lives* cleaned up ambiguities, denied any clear link. Armand Veilleux, the translator of the Pachomian material, has argued that "we have the impression of being in the presence of two universes of thought that have evolved in parallel courses." He noted especially that the vast Pachomian sources quote scripture frequently and in an orthodox manner and never quote heterodox sources. He admitted that "it seems very unlikely that at a period without concordances or computers, an editor could have succeeded so well in expurgating the whole of Pachomian literature of any trace of a heterodox or gnosticizing use of the Scripture."[8]

Scholars skeptical about the Pachomian origins of the Nag Hammadi library have offered their own views of its owners. One possibility remains monks. There were a host of anchorites and other monastic communities in the Thebaid—including Melitian monks. Other scholars argue that the codices come not from anchorites, but from urban Christians, who operated outside the oversight of church authorities and who shared with their contemporaries a not-uncommon taste for religious syncretism. James Goehring, who has wrestled with this issue for years, has moved gradually to a more neutral position: "The basic arguments in favor of a Pachomian origin for the codices have been made, and in the end, the evidence simply is not in hand to establish a certain link."[9] He does not rule out the possibility of Pachomian origins but argues that one must simply acknowledge the limits of the current evidence.

NOTES

1. Bohairic *Life of Pachomius* 189 (CSCO 89:175–178; Veilleux, CS 45:230–232).

2. Jean Doresse, *Secret Books of the Egyptian Gnostics: An Introduction to the Gnostic Coptic Manuscripts Discovered at Chenoboskion* (New York: Viking Press, 1960), 135.

3. John W. B. Barns, "Greek and Coptic Papyri from the Covers of the Nag Hammadi Codices," in Martin Krause, ed., *Essays on the Nag Hammadi Texts. In Honour of Pahor Labib*, Nag Hammadi Studies 6 (Leiden: Brill, 1975), 13–15.

4. Henry Chadwick, "Pachomios and the Idea of Sanctity," *History and Thought of the Early Church* (London: Variorum Reprints, 1982), 17–18.

5. Chadwick, "Pachomios and the Idea of Sanctity," 18.

6. Goehring, "New Frontiers in Pachomian Studies," 247.

7. J. C. Shelton, introduction, to J. W. B. Barns, G. M. Browne, and J. C. Shelton, eds., *Nag Hammadi Codices: Greek and Coptic Papyri from the Cartonnage of the Covers*, Nag Hammadi Studies 16 (Leiden: Brill, 1981), 11.

8. Armand Veilleux, "Monasticism and Gnosis in Egypt," in *Roots of Egyptian Christianity*, 291–292.

9. James E. Goehring, "The Provenance of the Nag Hammadi Codices Once More," *Studia Patristica* 35 (2001): 241. This article offers the best survey to date of the debate. The most thorough review of the evidence is the hard-to-find study by Alexandr Khosroyev, *Die Bibliotheque von Nag Hammadi: Einige Probleme des Christentums in Ägypten während der ersten Jahrhunderte*, Arbeiten zum spataniken und koptischen Ägypten 7 (Altenberge, 1995).

PART III

The Desert Fathers

6

The *Apophthegmata Patrum*: Text and Context

Abba Antony

Athanasius's portrait of Antony was not the only one.[1] There were
other traditions about him that circulated among desert Christians.
Some were recorded in a remarkable collection known as the
Apophthegmata Patrum, or *Sayings of the Fathers*. Antony appears
here not as a mythic hero unflinchingly battling the forces of evil.
Instead, he speaks as a venerable *abba* ("father"), one of the "old
men" consulted by younger monks for advice on monastic living.

In the *Life*, Antony dramatically renounced his family holdings
after hearing the story of Jesus's call to the rich young man. The
Apophthegmata, likewise, portrays Antony as an advocate of radical
renunciation. One day, he was approached by a monk who had supposedly renounced the world but had actually kept back a little
money for safekeeping, something to fall back on. The monk
wanted Antony's advice on the matter. Antony told him that if he
really wanted to be a monk, he needed to go buy some meat and
cover his naked body with it. An odd demand—but the monk did as
he was told. He found himself nipped at by local dogs and pecked at
by birds. It left him wounded all over. When he returned, Antony
told him, "Those who renounce the world but want to keep something for themselves are torn in this way by the demons who make
war on them."[2]

Athanasius's *Life* portrays Antony as a teacher of asceticism.
The *Apophthegmata* stresses this as well. But here he delivers his ascetical message not in long orations, but in terse epigrams:

> Abba Antony said: . . . Always have the fear of God before
> your eyes. Remember him who gives death and life. Hate

the world and all that is in it. Hate all peace that comes from the flesh. Renounce this life, so that you may be alive to God. Remember what you have promised God, for it will be required of you on the Day of Judgment. Suffer hunger, thirst, nakedness, be watchful and sorrowful; weep and groan in your heart; test yourselves, to see if you are worthy of God; despise the flesh, so that you may preserve your souls.[3]

Here the accent is stern, austere. But other sayings offer balance. In one, he warns against excesses: monks who fast too much lack discernment and are "far from God."[4] According to the *Apophthegmata*, Antony sometimes practiced a measured laxity. Once a hunter was scandalized when he happened upon Antony enjoying himself with some of the brothers. To explain his behavior, Antony had the hunter shoot one arrow after another. After a while, the hunter grumbled that such overuse would break the bow. Antony then replied that it is the same with the brothers—that stretched too taut too often, they risk snapping.[5]

The *Life* emphasizes Antony's majestic calm and integrity. The *Apophthegmata* too mentions the power of his presence. One story recounts how three monks used to go out to visit him every year. Two used to pour out their inner thoughts and ply him with questions. But the third remained silent. One time, Antony asked the silent one: "You come to see me, but ask nothing." The monk replied: "Abba, it is enough just to see you."[6]

The *Life* portrays Antony as heroic, larger than life. The *Apophthegmata* too accords him great respect. When Abba Hilarion, a Palestinian monk, visited Antony, he called him a "pillar of light, giving light to the world."[7] And when Abba Sisoes, who took up residence on the Inner Mountain after Antony's death, was asked when he would reach his predecessor's stature, he replied, "If I had one of the Abba Antony's thoughts, I would become all flame."[8] But such veneration is balanced by other statements. One saying notes, for instance, that Antony received a revelation that there was in Egypt a man of equal sanctity—and that man achieved his sanctity not in the desert, but amid the temptations of the city. The man, it turns out, was a doctor who gave the bulk of his earnings to the poor and each day sang the *Trisagion* ("Holy, Holy, Holy") with the angels.[9]

While there are kindred themes between the *Life* and the *Apophthegmata*, even a few direct parallels, the differences are striking.[10] The *Apophthegmata* makes no mention of the theological issues so central to the *Life*. The Antony of the *Apophthegmata* denounces neither Melitians nor Arians. He shows no knowledge of a theology of deification, nor does he make pronouncements on the generation of the Son from the Father. In the *Apophthegmata*, Anthony teaches a simpler, blunter faith. When asked by a monk what he ought to do, Antony tells him, "Whoever you may be, always have God before your eyes; whatever you do, do it according to the testimony of the holy Scriptures; in whatever place you live, do not easily leave it. Keep these three precepts and you will be saved."[11]

There are other contrasts. When the Antony of the *Life* received a letter from Constantine, he was reluctant to respond, saying the emperor was a mere man; when the Antony of the *Apophthegmata* received a letter from Constantius summoning him to the imperial capital, he was tempted to go and asked the advice of his disciple, Abba Paul. Paul offered a shrewd warning: "If you go, you will be called Antony; but if you stay here, you will be called Abba Antony."[12] In the *Life*, Athanasius claims that after his fierce early battle, Antony was ever after free from sexual temptation. The Antony of the *Apophthegmata* offers a very different perspective. He is remembered as saying that while most people face three sources of conflict—from what they hear, what they say, and what they see—the desert solitary is left with only one: fornication.[13]

But the contrast goes deeper. Whereas the Antony of the *Life* is fearless and unwavering in the face of ascetic hardships and demonic onslaughts, the Antony of the *Apophthegmata* is more human—and vulnerable. He anguishes about the justice of God—that some die young, that the wicked prosper, that human society is rent by fissures between rich and poor.[14] He gets depressed, afflicted by the tedium of desert living. And when he is rescued from it by a vision, the vision itself is hardly spectacular. He sees a man—actually an angel in the appearance of a man—braiding rope, occasionally rising to pray, and then returning to his work. "And the angel said to him, 'Do this and you will be saved.' At these words, Antony was filled with joy and courage. He did this, and he was saved."[15]

The Collections: Alphabetical and Systematic

The *Apophthegmata Patrum* is an extraordinary anthology. In its pages, one finds "a motley band of colorful characters, wild adventures, and stinging, memorable 'one-liners.' "[16] Its publication marked an important milestone in the literature of late antiquity. As Peter Brown has noted, "The *Sayings* provided a remarkable new literary genre, close to the world of parable and folk-wisdom . . . In these *Sayings*, the peasantry of Egypt spoke for the first time to the civilized world."[17] And Philip Rousseau has remarked, "Each entry . . . in this fascinating series captures the attention of the reader like a flash of a signaling lamp—brief, arresting, and intense."[18]

The *Apophthegmata* was sometimes known by other titles, such as *Gerontikon* ("Book of the Old Men") or *Paterikon* ("Book of the Fathers"). The sixth-century Palestinian monks Barsanuphius and John of Gaza, as well as their disciple Dorotheos, used these terms. Another common title, the *Paradise of the Fathers*, was used by Ânân Îshô for his seventh-century Syriac collection.

The *Apophthegmata* has come down to us in two basic forms: the Alphabetical Collection and the Systematic Collection. The Alphabetical gathers some 1,000 sayings and brief narratives under the names of 130 prominent monks and arranges these according to the Greek alphabet.[19] Thus *Alpha* begins with thirty-eight sayings from Antony and follows with those from other notables, such as Arsenius, Agathon, Ammonas, and so on; *Beta* includes Basil of Caesarea and Bessarion; *Gamma*, Gregory of Nazianzus, Gelasius, and so on. Attached to certain manuscripts of the Alphabetical Collection is an additional set of sayings and stories that had come down to the ancient editors without names. This series, referred to as the Anonymous Collection, had as its original core some 240 sayings, but eventually 400 more came to be attached to this core.

The Systematic Collection contains many of the same sayings and stories but gathers them under twenty-one different headings or themes, such as "discernment," "unceasing prayer," "hospitality," and "humility." The Greek version contains some 1200 sayings. In the mid-sixth century, an early version of this Systematic Collection was translated from Greek into Latin by two Roman clerics, the deacon Pelagius and the subdeacon John (who perhaps became the later Popes Pelagius and John). This version, called the *Verba Seniorum* ("Sayings of the Old Men"), was apparently known to Saint Benedict and powerfully influenced the spirituality of medieval monasticism.

In time, vast collections of *Apophthegmata* appeared not only in Greek and Latin, but also in Syriac, Coptic, Armenian, Georgian, Arabic, Ethiopic, and Old Slavonic (see appendix 6.1). The linguistic complexity of all this can be daunting. But things are made even more difficult if one seeks to answer the sort of questions scholars raise. For example:

- Does a saying ascribed to Antony really go back to the historical Antony?
- Who gathered these sayings together? When? And why?
- What sources—oral or written—did they draw on?
- Has the wording of individual sayings been altered over time? If so, how? And why?

A number of twentieth-century scholars—Wilhelm Bousset, Jean-Claude Guy, Derwas Chitty, Antoine Guillaumont, and Lucien Regnault, to name a few of the most prominent—have carefully sifted through this huge mass of material and tried to trace out the origins, transmission, and assembling of these collections. Many features of their pathbreaking studies presume a mastery of the texts, languages, and history that lie beyond the scope of this introduction. But I would like to trace a few of their remarkable discoveries in following chapters. For the moment, let me simply note a couple of their conclusions.

LANGUAGE. The *Apophthegmata*, though written first in Greek, drew on an oral tradition that was originally Coptic and that stretched back well over 100 years.

ORIGIN. The *Apophthegmata* focuses primarily (but not exclusively) on the wisdom of monastic leaders from Lower Egypt, active from the 330s to 460s, especially those from the monastic settlement of Scetis.

DATE AND PLACE OF PUBLICATION. Although the *Apophthegmata* preserves memories of Egyptian monasticism—and does so with what seems to be remarkable accuracy—the final recording of those memories was not done in Egypt, but in Palestine, probably in the late fifth century. It was from the Holy Land, with its traffic in pilgrims to and from the sacred sites, that these stories of the Egyptian monks spread throughout the ancient Christian world.

"Abba, Give Me a Word"

Stories in the *Apophthegmata* open simply: "One day a brother went to Abba So-and-so and asked him such-and-such . . ." or "Abba So-and-so used to say this about Abba So-and-so . . ." Most are brief, from a few lines to half a page, and on rare occasions a bit more. Many describe encounters between two monks, usually one elder, one younger. They speak simply, and directly. There is no theorizing, no trains of logical argument, no intricate analysis of biblical texts. Their exchanges focus on the specifics of desert living and the spiritual quest. Each word seems measured, spare, chosen after long silence. Even the most everyday encounters take on an almost oracular quality.

Let us begin with one famous genre of apophthegms: those that portray a young monk coming to an elder to ask for a "word of salvation." These stories open with a standard formula: "Abba, give me a word [*rhema*]." Here's an example: One day a brother came to Abba Macarius the Egyptian with the classic request, "Abba, give me a word that I might be saved." Macarius demanded action: "Go to the cemetery and abuse the dead." And so the monk went to the cemetery and hurled insults at those buried there. The account gives no hint of what the monk felt during this odd display of wrath. Nor is there any hint what colorful insults he used. Only that he "threw rocks." The monk then returned to Macarius, who questioned him: "Didn't they say anything to you?" "No," the monk replied. Macarius then told him to go back the next day, and this time he was to praise the dead. The monk did as he was told. He poured out compliments: "Apostles, saints, righteous ones." Again the monk returned to Macarius, who again asked him: "Did they answer you back?" "No," the monk again replied. Macarius then gave him a *rhema*: "You know how you insulted them and they did not reply, and how you praised them and they did not speak; so you too, if you wish to be saved, must do the same and become a dead man. Like the dead, take no account of either the scorn of men or their praises, and you can be saved."[20]

This story is remarkable—for its humor and its unexpected poignancy. Beneath its spare narrative is a wisdom, an intensity of insight, that leaps out and touches something deep in us. It touches on something universal: the way we all can let our lives be determined by praise and blame, by honors and curses. We all know how easy it is to let those voices of praise and blame so distort the course of our lives that we never become the person that we sense in our depths we were made to be. The secret of this apophthegm, its power, comes from the way it effortlessly crosses the centuries—to say nothing of other barriers, such as geography, language, and culture—and speaks to us with uncanny immediacy. Macarius's word to the monk is somehow able to become a word for us too. This story gives a good first glimpse of the *Apophthegmata* as a whole, and why its wisdom has been compared to a "flash of a signaling lamp—brief, arresting, and intense."

This type of saying is common in the *Apophthegmata*. Scholars have highlighted several of its features. First, this "word of salvation" was not meant, in the first instance, for everyone. It was a "word" for *this* monk on *this* occasion, a key specially fitted to unlock a particular heart.[21] Certainly this advice had wider application—which is precisely why it was remembered and written down. Not all "words" were this dramatic. Often the advice can seem, detached from its original moment and reduced to written form, almost pedestrian. For instance, a "word" Macarius once gave to Abba Paphnutius was: "Do no evil to anyone, and do not judge anyone; observe this and you will be saved."[22] But even if a "word" looks like a commonplace to us now, that does not mean the original hearer found it so. In one case, Abba Eupreprius went to an old man and asked for a "word." The old man replied, "If you wish to be saved, when you go to see someone, do not begin to speak before you are spoken to." This "word" hit home. Eupreprius was filled with compunction and prostrated himself. Later he proclaimed it better advice than any he had found in all his years of reading.[23]

Second, if a "word of salvation" was a key specially fitted to open a particular monk's heart, then the abba's ability to speak that word implied astute discernment. At one level, such psychological insight is natural, and the desert fathers would not have disputed this. The insight of the "old men" came from their long experience in the desert, their own apprenticeship under a venerable teacher, and, of course, their own prayerful reflection. But the fathers also saw it—at least sometimes—as a prophetic charism, a "living word" from God. Abba Poemen, for instance, was known to have "the charism of word" (*tou logou to charisma*)[24]; and Abba Paul the Simple, a disciple of Antony, was described as having the "grace from the Lord of seeing the state of each one's soul, just as we see their faces."[25]

One gets a glimmer of this "charism of word" in a story about Abba Pambo. Two monks approached him for advice, one inquiring about fasting habits, another about earnings from manual labor. They asked if by their practices they would be saved or lost. Pambo made no reply—nothing for four days. Just as the monks were ready to leave, some of Pambo's disciples approached and assured them not to be discouraged: "It is the old man's custom not to speak readily till God inspires him."[26] Pambo eventually received an inspiration and spoke. But this was not always the case. One day a brother came to Abba Theodore of Pherme and spent three days begging him to say a word. Theodore gave no reply, and the monk went away disheartened. Theodore's disciple inquired: "Abba, why did you not say a word to him? See, he has gone away grieved." The old man replied: "I did not speak to him, for he is a trafficker who seeks to glorify himself through the words of others."[27] In this case, discernment led Theodore to judge that a word given to this monk would remain an empty word, a word unfulfilled, or worse, a borrowed wisdom pawned off proudly as one's own.

Third, this "word of salvation" depended ultimately on the obedience of the monk. In the case first cited, the monk had to obey Abba Macarius and actually go to the cemetery and hurl insults at the dead, and then turn around and praise them, and without being given any reason beforehand for doing so. But the monk's real task of obedience would come later, from a lifetime of making the "word" his own. In this case, he had to become as one dead, immune to insult and praise. Such obedience stood at the heart of the relationship of a young monk and his abba. One of the anonymous sayings puts it vividly: "An old man said: 'Be like a camel, bearing your sins and following, bridled, someone who knows the way of God.' "[28]

The intimate link between the charismatic word of the *abba* and the obedience of the disciple plays itself out in another story in which a "word" is refused. Some brothers once approached Abba Felix and begged him to say a "word." After some silence, he asked: "You wish to hear a word?" "Yes, abba," they said. Then Felix replied: "There are no more words nowadays. When the brothers used to consult the old men and when they did what was said, God showed them how to speak. But now, since they ask without doing that which they hear, God has withdrawn the grace of the word from the old men and they do not find anything to say, because there are no longer any who carry their words out."[29] This seems to be a late saying. It describes a time in which some believed that the fervor of the good old days had declined. It highlights how the monks saw the elder's word not only as God's good gift to the community, but also as a gift contingent on obedient response. The failure of obedience could lead, or had led, to the loss of the charism itself.

This genre, the "word of salvation," is simply one of many found in the *Apophthegmata*. But it does give a hint about the collection as a whole: it is a precious archive from communities that made spiritual direction the centerpiece of their spirituality and turned it into finely honed art.

Scetis

In the next two chapters, we will look at the *Apophthegmata*'s leading figures and key themes. But first we need to examine the context in which it arose. This is not usually done. Too often people quote the work as though its memorable sayings and stories belonged in some vague way to "early monks." Most of the figures described in the *Apophthegmata* come one definite locale: the monastic settlement of Scetis (for a map of the monasteries of Lower Egypt, see figure 6.1).

Scetis was founded around 330 by Macarius the Egyptian, the wily spiritual advisor mentioned earlier (for more on Macarius, see appendix 6.2; see also chapter 7). The *Apophthegmata* refers to this region as "the great desert" (*en tē panerēmō*).[30] The name Scetis is said to come from the Coptic *shi hēt*, meaning "to weigh the heart"—an apt name for a place where men, in the quest for God, spent their lives probing the depths and vagaries of the human heart.[31] The site was located some forty miles south of the other great monastic settle-

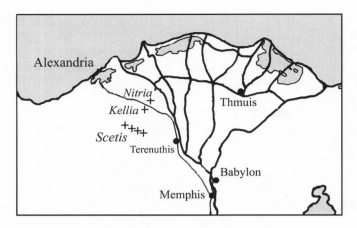

FIGURE 6.1. The monastic settlements of Lower Egypt.

ment of Lower Egypt, Nitria, which in turn was located forty miles southeast of Alexandria.³² Rufinus of Aquileia, who helped popularize Egyptian monasticism in the Latin West, has left a description of the hazards of traveling to Scetis from the north:

> The place where Saint Macarius lived is called Scetis. It is in a vast wilderness, a day and a night's journey from the monasteries of Nitria, and the way to it is not found or shown by any track or landmarks on the ground, but one journeys by the signs and courses of the stars. Water is hard to find, and when it is found it has a bad smell, bituminous, yet inoffensive to the taste. Here men are made perfect in holiness, but none but those of austere resolution and supreme constancy can endure such a terrible spot.³³

Rufinus's description here is accurate. Scetis is in a twenty-two-mile-long valley, west of the Nile, in the Libyan or Great Western Desert. The area, now known as Wādī al-Natrūn, is partly below sea level and is dotted with marshes and oases. Niter was mined in the region—which is likely how Macarius, an ex–camel driver and ex–niter smuggler, knew its location. Notice that Rufinus says that one had to use the stars to navigate the passage. Another ancient author who knew of Scetis, but had not seen it, remarked, "It is a very perilous journey for travelers. For if one makes even a small error, one can get lost in the desert and find one's life in danger."³⁴ The dangers were quite real. We have reports of even experienced desert travelers getting lost and dying.³⁵ The safer route in antiquity was to come to Scetis not across the desert from the north, but from the east from settlements along the Nile. Ancient descriptions stress its stark isolation. But such inaccessibility is a thing of the past. Today, it is a one-and-a-half-hour drive from Cairo, just off the main road between there and Alexandria. And irrigation has turned verdant what was once lifeless desert.

It is more accurate to speak of Scetis as a monastic settlement rather than a monastery. Too often the word "monastery" evokes images of the medieval European variety: serene cloisters, massive stone churches, communal chanting at fixed hours, cowled figures tilling the land or copying manuscripts, and a written rule. All this is quite removed from the monasticism of this early period—though, as we saw, Pachomius was already experimenting with a communal and highly organized style far to the south. Scetis was more like a colony of hermits, with monks living in individual cells widely scattered about a vast area. Scholars sometimes refer to this as "semi-anchoritic" to distinguish it from the anchoritic lifestyle of Antony, on the one hand, and the cenobitic lifestyle of Pachomius and, later, of Benedict. These labels, while a common shorthand, can mask the wide spectrum and intricate variations of ascetical lifestyles experimented with in Egypt, to say nothing of elsewhere in the Roman Empire.

The *Apophthegmata* and other ancient sources do not offer a thorough portrait of the life in Scetis, but enough tidbits can be gleaned to put together a rough sketch.

Housing

If one visits Scetis today, one sees monasteries that look like great desert fortresses. High walls enclose the monastic buildings. But in the fourth century, Scetis was a constellation of small cells scattered along the wadi. Elsewhere in Lower Egypt monks lived in small mud-brick huts. An *abba* might gather his disciples and in a single day build a cell for a newcomer.[36] Scetis may have had huts like this. But at least some cells were in caves or were small bungalows built up against the rock face of the valley. The rock face would form the back wall of a cell, while the front was filled in with mud brick or stones. These may have looked a bit like the cliff dwellings of the Pueblo Indians in Arizona. One report says that Macarius dug a long tunnel that linked his cell to a deep cavern so that "whenever too many people crowded in on him, he would secretly leave his cell and go to the cave, and no would find him."[37] Most cells had two rooms, one as a place to work, eat, and receive visitors, the other as a place for prayer. But they could be more elaborate. Abba Isaac complained to John Cassian about monks who, "moved by worldly ambition," built cells with four or five rooms, "exquisitely furnished" and larger than their needs required.[38] Cells had windows, doors with locks, cupboards for storage, and niches for books or other valuables. The monks might sit on mats during the day and sleep on them at night. They also had small stools, known as *embrimia*, woven from papyrus stalks. The monks sat on these when they prayed the office and, at night, used them as a kind of a pillow or headrest.[39]

Work

The monks of Scetis spent much time in their cells doing manual labor. The usual enterprises were rope making and basket weaving. One story records how Macarius trained two young novices, teaching them "the rudiments of weaving and how to handle the reeds."[40] Reeds and palm leaves were harvested from the nearby marshes and brought back to the monks' cells. The monks themselves sometimes took the finished handiwork to market, or they could sell them to camel drivers who might pass by.[41]

During harvest time, the monks often went down to the Nile Valley and hired themselves out as farm laborers. Even leaders—such as Macarius, Sisoes, and John the Little—did so.[42] There is mention of other types of labor, such as manufacturing sieves or weaving linen.[43] The *Apophthegmata* even reports that some monks were skilled copyists. Much later, in Europe during the Middle Ages, monks often worked in a scriptorium, creating manuscripts still renowned for the beauty of their calligraphy and marginalia. While such work was not the norm in Egypt, at least some monks at Scetis, such as Mark, the disciple of Abba Silvanus, and Paphnutius, worked as *kalligraphoi*, as scribes.[44]

Manual labor was not an end itself. As Cassian remarks, "They practice their incessant manual labor for the sake of spiritual meditation."[45] But in practice, things did not always work out that way. Abba Theodore of Pherme once complained: "When I was in Scetis, the work of the soul was our real job (*ergon*), and our handiwork we thought of as a sideline (*parergon*). But now the work of the soul has become the sideline and the handiwork has become the real job."[46]

Food, Fasting, and Hospitality

Many sayings in the *Apophthegmata* touch on food and fasting. It was a hot topic. There are reports of monks eating only once every two, four, even seven days. One has the impression that they were trying to test the limits of human endurance. Abba Poemen, one of the great moderates of Scetis, was critical of such extremes. He admitted past experiments, saying, "The Fathers tried all this out as they were able and they found it preferable to eat every day, but just a small amount. They have left us this royal way, which is light."[47]

Poemen may have thought it easy by desert standards, but the normal diet of the monks was austere, to say the least. They ate two small loaves of bread per day—the two loaves together weighing about one pound.[48] This bread, called *paxamatia*, could be kept for months, but it became rock-hard (remember Antony had a six-month supply of it stored in the desert fort). If necessary, the monks soaked it in water to soften it and make it edible.[49] They also seasoned their bread with salt—an absolute necessity in the desert. Monks at Scetis sometimes used olive oil, but sparingly.[50] During the week, monks drank no wine, only water, and that in limited quantities. There is mention of vegetables, especially lentils and beans, and of fruits such as figs, but these seemed to have been reserved for visitors or for the sick.[51] This diet, however austere it seems to us, did not differ much from that of a poor Egyptian peasant.[52]

The monks relaxed all rigor when travelers arrived. Once a visitor apologized to his host for causing him to break his "rule" of fasting. But the *abba* replied, "My rule is to refresh you and send you away in peace."[53] Visitors were greeted with a prostration. According to Abba Apollo, one bows before visitors "because it is not before them, but before God we prostrate ourselves."[54] If they had come from some distance, they were given water, bread, even a cooked meal. To have a cooked meal for oneself during the week would be a scandalous breach of monastic custom, but the charity of hospitality always took precedence.[55] Visits could be frequent. Cassian visited one elder who told him that he was the sixth visitor the elder had provided a meal for that day.[56]

The Weekday Schedule

Monks at Scetis spent Monday through Friday in their cells. It is difficult to generalize about how they spent their day, partly because the sources do not provide a consistent picture and partly because as hermits they enjoyed some freedom in shaping their personal rule. Still, there were some regular rhythms. Typically, the monks rose in the middle of the night (midnight? two o'clock in the morning?), and each prayed the night office privately in his cell. In Egypt at this time, the night office included the recitation or chanting of twelve psalms.[57] The monk was not to return to sleep but to continue meditating until dawn.[58] During the daylight hours—and perhaps even during these predawn hours—they did manual labor. They did not punctuate the hours of the day with the five other offices of psalms (prime, terce, sext, none, and compline) found in the Latin West. Rather, as Cassian notes, "they spend the whole day in those offices which we celebrate at fixed times," for "manual labor is incessantly practiced by them in their cells in such a way that meditation on the psalms and the rest of the Scriptures is never entirely omitted."[59] At the "ninth hour" (around three o'clock in the afternoon), the monks enjoyed their one meal. Some delayed eating until sunset, but this was considered a sign of special austerity.[60] At sunset, vespers was celebrated, and it, like the night office, included the recitation of twelve psalms. Soon after dark, the monks would go to sleep.

Abbas and Disciples

Unlike Pachomius's Tabennesi, Scetis had no written rule. Aelred Cody has noted that "the norms of life were those of the gospels, supplemented by custom and by the wisdom of any experienced monastic father to whom a newly arrived monk apprenticed himself."[61] Small clusters of elders and their disciples formed the basic organization of Scetis. As we have seen, an elder would be called *abba*, or "father." This was a term of respect, not of office. It did not mean that the elder was a priest. In fact, only a few figures in the *Apophthegmata* were clerics, and when they were, the text often added this to their name. For instance, one of Macarius's early companions was Abba Isidore the Priest. The title *abba* might, on rare occasions, be bestowed upon a young man if he showed wisdom beyond his age, but it seems to have been more freely used of any older monk.⁶² The term "old man" (*gerōn*) is also common. Younger monks often spoke in a kindly or playful way about how "the old man" had said this or "the old man" had done that.

As we saw, young monks would approach an *abba* and ask for a "word" from him. Some would go on to attach themselves permanently as disciples. For instance, Abba Silvanus, a native of Palestine, led a group of twelve monks at Scetis. There is no mention of vows, though the expectation was of a lifelong commitment to monastic life. The elder would train his disciples in the basics of desert living, such as how to build a cell, how to weave baskets, and how to pray the psalms. But the deeper and more serious guidance came from the young monk's regular visits to the *abba*. On these occasions, he manifested his "thoughts" (*logismoi*), all those inner stirrings—memories, ideas, feelings— that had welled up during his time alone in the cell. Many of the stories in the *Apophthegmata* flow from these exchanges between a young monk and his *abba* about the underlying meaning of his "thoughts." Other sayings report that elders might deliberately test their disciples with harsh remarks or bizarre acts. We saw earlier how Macarius ordered a monk to yell insults at the dead in a cemetery. As Abba Isaiah once remarked, "Nothing is so useful to the beginner as insults. The beginner who bears insults is like a tree that is watered every day."⁶³ It is hard to be sure, but it seems that monks did not move out on their own without permission, and at least some remained with their *abba* until his death.⁶⁴

The Four Congregations

By the time Macarius died in 390 or soon after, four "congregations" or "churches" had merged.⁶⁵ In time, these four would become distinct monas- teries in the medieval sense, both architecturally and organizationally. In fact, three still exist today: the Monastery of Saint Macarius (Dayr Anbā Maqār), of Saint Bishoi (Dayr Anbā Bishoi; see figure 6.2), and of the Romans (Dayr Al Baramūs). The fourth, the Monastery of John the Little, lies abandoned, buried under the sands. (Another monastery, the Monastery of the Syrians [Dayr Al- Suryān], dating from the eighth century, still exists.)

At this early date, however, neither the fortress walls nor the communal lifestyle one now finds existed. Nor did they seem to have the names now associated with them. However, each did have its own church building, and perhaps other structures such as a kitchen or bakery. These buildings formed an architectural nucleus for the far-flung clusters of cells. Each also seems to have had its own priest, who presided at the weekly Eucharist and who exer- cised some functions of a monastic superior. There is also mention of a mo- nastic council that exercised judicial functions. It judged breaches of discipline and could decree excommunication or other disciplines for violations.

One of the four priest-monks also seems to have served as "Father of Scetis" (later called "*hegumenos* of Scetis"). As Scetis developed in prominence, this person came to serve as the settlement's representative to the larger civil

FIGURE 6.2. An early image of Abba Bishoi, the late fourth-century founder of one of the four monastic settlements in Scetis. While no sayings of his are preserved in the *Apophthegmata*, early hagiographic reports say that he was a friend of Abba John the Little and that he left Scetis after it was sacked in 407 by barbarian raiders. (From Hugh Evelyn White, *The Monasteries of Wadi 'n Natrûn, part 2, The History of the Monasteries of Nitria and of Scetis* (New York: The Metropolitan Museum of Art, 1932), plate IVB. Reproduced with permission.

and ecclesial world. It eventually became customary for him to make an annual report to the patriarch of Alexandria.

Saturday and Sunday

On Saturday and Sunday, the monks came together for worship and for meals. Each congregation gathered at its respective church and celebrated publicly what during the week they did privately: vespers and the night office. Both liturgies had the same structure. A soloist would chant a psalm, while the rest remained seated. When he finished, all would rise and stand in silent prayer with arms extended. They would then prostrate themselves on the ground, remaining silent and continuing in prayer. Finally, the presider would rise and everyone would stand up as he prayed out loud a "collect," gathering the community's silent prayers into one. This pattern would be repeated eleven times. The last psalm included an alleluia. Only then did they recite the doxology, "Glory to the Father and to the Son and to the Holy Spirit . . ." Two readings from the New Testament followed, one from the Epistles or Acts and one from the Gospels. Cassian, who witnessed these liturgies, stressed their silent dignity, apparently in contrast to the less-than-dignified behavior he saw in southern France: "There is no spitting, no clearing of the throat, or noise of coughing, no sleepy yawning with open mouths, and gasping, and no groans or sighs are uttered, likely to distract those standing near. No voice is heard save that of the priest concluding the prayer."[66] The *Apophthegmata* refers to this liturgy as a *synaxis*, or assembly. The same name is used when a monk prayed the psalms privately in his cell.

In Scetis, the monks celebrated the Eucharist only on both Saturday and Sunday. In Egypt, as throughout the Greek East, daily Eucharist was not the norm. The time of the Saturday eucharist is not clear, but the one on Sunday was held at the third hour (about nine o'clock in the morning). Also on Sunday, they celebrated an *agape*, or common meal. Because of its religious overtones, it was likely held inside the church building. The brothers received not only bread, but also wine and cooked food. These weekend gatherings were times of celebration. But they had their perils, for it was at such times that gossip or hurtful remarks might come out. After the meal, the monks picked up supplies for the next week—bread, water, raw materials for work—and returned to their cells.

We have had a first glimpse at both the text and the context. These will provide the essential background for the next two chapters. Chapter 7 will focus on the Alphabetical Collection, while chapter 8 will focus on the Systematic Collection.

NOTES

1. The opening section of this chapter was published without my permission and without clear acknowledgement of my authorship in the essay by Tim Vivian, "St. Antony the Great and the Monastery of St. Antony at the Red Sea," in *Monastic Visions: Wall Paintings in the Monastery of St. Antony at the Red Sea*, ed. Elizabeth S. Bolman (New Haven: American Research Center in Egypt and Yale University Press, 2002), 6–8. Both Dr. Vivian and Yale University Press have acknowledged the mistake.

2. *AP* Antony 20 (PG 65:81). Translations from the Alphabetical Collection, unless otherwise marked, are from Benedicta Ward, *The Sayings of the Desert Fathers: The Alphabetical Collection*, CS 59 (Kalamazoo, Mich.: Cistercian Publications, 1984).

3. *AP* Antony 32, 33 (PG 65:85; trans. Ward, CS 59:8).

4. *AP* Antony 8 (PG 65:77; trans. Ward, CS 59:3).

5. *AP* Antony 13 (PG 65:77–80; CS 59:3).

6. *AP* Antony 27 (PG 65:83; trans. my own); cf. *VA* 67, 70, 88.

7. *AP* Hilarion (PG 65:241; trans. Ward, CS 59:111).

8. *AP* Sisoes 9 (PG 65:393; trans. Ward, CS 59:214).

9. *AP* Antony 24 (PG 65:84; CS 59:6).

10. Two sayings seem to be drawn directly from the *Vita Antonii*: (i) *AP* Antony 10 = *VA* 49; (ii) *AP* Antony 30 = *VA* 59. Two other sayings attributed to Antony in the *Apophthegmata* come from the *Letters*: (i) *AP* Antony 22 = *Ep. Antonii* 1:35–41; (ii) *AP* Poemen 87 = *Ep. Antonii* 7:60.

11. *AP* Antony 3 (PG 65:76; trans. Ward, CS 59:2).

12. *AP* Antony 31 (PG 65:85; trans. Ward, CS 59:8).

13. *AP* Antony 11 (PG 65:77; CS 59:3).

14. *AP* Antony 2 (PG 65:75; CS 59:2).

15. *AP* Antony 1 (PG 65:75; trans. Ward, CS 59:1–2).

16. Douglas Burton-Christie, *The Word in the Desert: Scripture and the Quest for Holiness in Early Christian Monasticism* (New York: Oxford University Press, 1993), vii-viii.

17. Peter Brown, *The World of Late Antiquity: AD 150–750* (New York: W. W. Norton, 1971), 100.

18. Philip Rousseau, *Ascetics, Authority, and the Church in the Age of Jerome and Cassian* (New York: Oxford University Press, 1978), 12.

19. See the bibliography for chapter 6 for a listing of the texts and translations of the *Apophthegmata Patrum*.

20. *AP* Macarius 23 (PG 65:272; trans. Ward, CS 59:132).

21. This insight is drawn out forcefully by Jean-Claude Guy, in a classic article, "Remarques sur le texte des *Apophthegmata Patrum*," *Recherches de science religieuse* 43 (1955): 252–258. Guy tends to portray these "words of salvation" as the most original and authentic. Against this overvaluation, see the useful corrective of Graham E. Gould, "A Note on the *Apophthegmata Patrum*," *Journal of Theological Studies* 37 (1986): 133–138.

22. *AP* Macarius 28 (PG 65:273; trans. Ward, CS 59:133).

23. *AP* Eupreprius 7 (PG 65:172; trans. Ward, CS 59:62). Other examples of this genre include *AP* Antony 19, Moses 6, Macarius 41, Poemen 69, N 91, and N 387.

24. *AP* Poemen 108 (PG 65:348; trans. my own).

25. *AP* Paul the Simple 1 (PG 65:381; trans. Ward, CS 59:205).

26. *AP* Pambo 2 (PG 65:368; trans. Ward, CS 59:196).

27. *AP* Theodore of Pherme 3 (PG 65:188; trans. Ward, CS 59:74).

28. *AP* N 436, quoted in Graham Gould, *The Desert Fathers on Monastic Community*, Oxford Early Christian Studies (New York: Oxford University Press, 1993), 29.

29. *AP* Felix 1 (PG 65:433; trans. Ward, CS 59:242). Similar reports about a decline in the charism of the word appears, strangely enough, in an exchange between Abba Macarius and Abba Poemen: *AP* Macarius 25 (PG 65:272; CS 59:133). Two sayings from the Ethiopic Collection bring out the relationship between the loss of the "word" and the diminished fervor: *Collectio Monastica* 13.16 and 13.26 (CSCO 238:87, 89).

30. *AP* Macarius 3 (PG 65:261; trans. Ward, CS 59:126).

31. This popular etymology is played on in the eighth-century work of Zacharias of Sakhâ, *Encomium on the Life of John the Little*, where he speaks of "Shiêt, the place where they weigh hearts and thoughts with judgment." On Scetis, see the bibliography for chapter 6.

32. Hugh Evelyn-White, *The Monasteries of the Wadi 'n Natrūn*, part 2, *The History of the Monasteries of Nitria and of Scetis* (New York: Metropolitan Museum of Art Egyptian Expedition, 1932; reprint: New York, Arno Press, 1973), esp. 17–43.

33. Rufinus, *Historia monachorum* XXIX (PL 21:453; trans. Russell, CS 34:152–

153). I have slightly altered this because Russell mistakenly translated *in eremo vastis-sima* as "in a great valley." While it is true that Scetis is in a great valley, *eremus* means "desert," not "valley." The word Rufinus uses is not a normal Latin term, but simply transliterates the Greek word ἔρημος ("wilderness," "desert").

34. *Historia monachorum in Aegypto* 23.1 (SH 53:130–131; trans. Russell, CS 34: 113).

35. Palladius, *Historia Lausiaca* 47 (Butler, 137; ACW 34:126), tells of a monk who got lost and died on the journey. See also *AP* John Colobos 17.

36. *Historia monachorum* 20.10 (SH 53:121; CS 34:106), describing the practice of Kellia. *AP* Or 1 (PG 65:437; CS 59:246) speaks of Or building a "cell out of clay." Some could be more elaborate: *AP* Agathon 6 (PG 65:109; CS 59:21) reports that Agathon and his disciples spent a long time building a cell.

37. Palladius, *Historia Lausiaca* 17 (Butler, 47; trans. Meyer, ACW 34:57). *AP* Macarius 33 (PG 65:276; CS 59:134) shows Macarius instructing two novices how to build a cell. Evagrius, *De oratione* 107 (PG 79:1192; trans. Bamberger, CS 4:73), says that John the Little "lived his solitary life in a ditch."

38. Cassian, *Collationes* 9.5.5 (SC 54:49; trans. Ramsey, ACW 57:333).

39. Cassian, *Collationes* 1.23.4 (SC 42:108; ACW 57:64).

40. *AP* Macarius 33 (PG 65:276; trans. Ward, CS 59:134); cf. *AP* Theodore of Pherme 21 (PG 65:192; CS 59:76).

41. *AP* John Colobos 31, Macarius 33.

42. *AP* Macarius 7, John Colobos 6 and 35; cf. *AP* N 291 and 375.

43. *AP* N 375 (ROC 18:141) lists five common professions: making rope, weaving mats, making sieves, copying books, and weaving linen.

44. *AP* Mark 1. Cf. *AP* Abraham 3; *AP* N 375. The Ethiopic *Collectio Monastica* 13.36–38 refers to Paphnutius, the copyist of Scetis. Evagrius Ponticus, who lived at Kellia, also worked as a scribe (*HL* 38.10).

45. Cassian, *De institutis* 2.14 (SC 109:84; trans. NPNF 2.11:211).

46. *AP* Theodore of Pherme 10 (PG 65:189; trans. my own).

47. *AP* Poemen 31 (PG 65:329; trans. Ward, CS 59:171).

48. *AP* Agathon 20 (PG 65:113; CS 59:23). Cf. *AP* Serinus 1 (PG 65:417; CS 59: 228); Cassian, *Collationes* 2.19 (SC 42:133; ACW 57:100–101).

49. Palladius, *Historia Lausiaca* 20 (Butler, 72; ACW 34:78). Since Scetis had its own bakery, this may not have been necessary. See *AP* Achillas 3 (PG 65:124; CS 59: 29), in which Abba Isaiah is jokingly admonished for luxuriously eating his bread with "sauce"—though the sauce was only water and salt.

50. *AP* Benjamin 1 and 2 (PG 65:144; CS 59:43); cf. Palladius, *Historia Lausiaca* 38.

51. *AP* Moses 13 (PG 65:288; CS 59:141); Arsenius 16 (PG 65:92; CS 59:11); Achilles 2 (PG 65:124; CS 59:29).

52. *AP* Abba of Rome 1 (PG 65:388; CS 59:209), where a poor herdsman who became a monk and visited Scetis says that his previous diet had been dry bread, and, on occasion, green herbs and water.

53. *AP* N 283 (ROC 14:373; trans. Ward, *Wisdom*, 42).

54. *AP* Apollo 3 (PG 65:136; trans. Ward, CS 59:37). Cf. Cassian, *De institutis* 5.24 (SC 109:232–234; trans. my own): "Fasting is always possible for me. But I can-not always keep you—whom I'm going to be sending off soon—here with me. And a fast, while it is useful and necessary, is still a free-will offering. But the work of char-ity is a commandment; its dictates require fulfillment. And so I receive Christ in you and ought to refresh him. But after you have taken your leave, I shall be able to bal-

ance hospitality offered for his sake by a stricter fast on my own account. For the children of the bridegroom cannot fast while the bridegroom is with them, but when he has departed, then it is right for them to fast."

55. AP Moses 5 (PG 65:284; CS 59:139).

56. AP Cassian 3 (PG 65:244; CS 59:113) = Cassian, De institutis 5.25 (SC 109: 234; ACW 58:133).

57. Cassian, De institutis 2.4–12 (SC 109:64–80; NPNF 2.11:206–210).

58. Cassian, De institutis 2.13–14 (SC 109:82–84; NPNF 2.11:210–211).

59. Cassian, De institutis 3.2 (SC 109:92; trans. NPNF 2.11:213).

60. AP Macarius 3 (PG 65:264; CS 59:127); Agathon 20 (PG 65:113–116; CS 59: 23); Ares (PG 65:132; CS 59:34).

61. Aelred Cody, "Scetis," in The Coptic Encyclopedia, ed. Aziz S. Atiya (New York: Macmillan, 1991), 7:2103.

62. AP Poemen 61 (PG 65:336; CS 59:175).

63. AP Isaiah 1 (PG 65:180–181; trans. CS 59:69).

64. See the case of John the Little in chapter 7. Cf. AP Heraclides 1.

65. Cassian, Collationes 10.2 (SC 54:75–76; ACW 57:372).

66. Cassian, De institutis 2.5–11 (SC 109:64–78; trans. NPNF 2.11:207–208). For an analysis, see Robert Taft, "Praise in the Desert: The Coptic Monastic Office Yesterday and Today," Worship 56 (1982): 515–520.

BIBLIOGRAPHY

Apophthegmata Patrum: Texts and Translations

The range and variety of collections can be overwhelming to the newcomer. The best place to start is with the Alphabetical Collection.

Alphabetical Collection

The Greek text of the Alphabetical Collection was published by Jean-Baptiste Cotelier in 1647 from a twelfth-century manuscript and is reprinted in PG 65:71-440. The Cotelier edition has 948 sayings. Jean-Claude Guy has supplemented this with 53 more sayings from other Greek manuscripts; see *Recherches sur la tradition grecque des Apophthegmata Patrum*, SH 36 (Brussels: Société des Bollandistes, 1962), 236–238. For an English translation, see Benedicta Ward, trans., *The Sayings of the Desert Fathers: The Alphabetical Collection*, CS 59 (Kalamazoo, Mich.: Cistercian Publications, 1984). See also the French edition by Lucien Regnault, trans., *Les Sentences des Pères du Désert: collection alphabétique* (Sablé-sur-Sarthe: Solesmes, 1981).

Anonymous Collection

F. Nau published only the first 396 sayings from the Anonymous Collection in "Histoires des solitaires égyptiens," *Revue d'orient chrétien* 12–14 (1907–1909) and 17–18 (1912–1913). For a translation of N 1–132, see Columba Stewart, trans., *The World of the Desert Fathers: Stories and Sayings from the Anonymous Series of the "Apophthegmata Patrum*," Fairacres Publication 95 (Oxford: SLG Press, 1986); for a translation of N 133–396, see Benedicta Ward, trans., *The Wisdom of the Desert Fathers: The "Apophthegmata Patrum" (the Anonymous Series)*, Fairacres Publication 48 (Oxford: SLG Press, 1986). The additional 370 or so sayings are listed in Jean-Claude Guy, *Recherches sur la tradition grecque des Apophthegmata Patrum*, SH 36 (Brussels: Société des Bollandistes, 1962),

63–74; these have not yet been translated into English. For a complete translation in French, see Lucien Regnault, *Les Sentences des Pères du Désert: série des anonymes* (Sablé-sur-Sarthe: Solesmes, 1985).

Greek Systematic Collection

For the Greek text of the Systematic Collection, with a French translation, see Jean-Claude Guy, *Les Apophtegmes des Pères: collection systématique*, books 1–9, SC 387 (Paris: Éditions du Cerf, 1993). This volume includes only the first half; the remainder, books 10–21, has not yet been published. There is as yet no translation of it in English, but a complete translation is available in French: Lucien Regnault, *Les chemins de Dieu au désert: collection systematique des Apophtegmes des Pères* (Solesmes: Éditions de Solesmes, 1992).

Latin Systematic Collection (*Verba Seniorum* of Pelagius and John)

The Latin text of Pelagius and John was edited by Heribert Rosweyde at Antwerp in 1615 and is reprinted in Migne, PL 73:855–1022. For a translation, see *The Desert Fathers: Sayings of the Early Christian Monks*, trans. Benedicta Ward, Penguin Classics (London: Penguin Books, 2003). See also Owen Chadwick, ed., *Western Asceticism: Selected Translations with Introductions and Notes*, LCC 12 (Philadelphia: Westminster Press, 1958), 37–189. For a complete translation in French, see J. Dion and G. Oury, *Les Sentences des Pères du Désert: recueil de Pélage et Jean* (Solesmes: Abbaye Saint-Pierre, 1966).

Coptic Collections

There are several versions of the *Apophthegmata Patrum* in Coptic. For sayings in the Sahidic dialect, see M. Chaîne, ed., *Le manuscrit de la version copte en dialect sahidique des "Apophthegmata Patrum,"* Bibliothèque d'études coptes 6 (Cairo: Institut Français d'Archéologie Orientale, 1960). There is no English translation; for a partial French translation, see Lucien Regnault, comp., *Les Sentences des Pères du Désert, nouveau recueil: apophtegmes inédits ou inconnus* (Sablé-sur-Sarthe: Solesmes, 1970), 277–285. There is a Bohairic version of sayings attributed to Antony and Macarius; see Emile Amélineau, *Histoire de monastères de la Basse Egypte*, Annales du Musée Guimet 25 (Paris: E. Leroux, 1894) 15–45. Again, there is no English translation. For a French translation, see Lucien Regnault, *Les Sentences des Pères du Désert: troisième recueil et tables* (Sablé-sur-Sarthe: Solesmes, 1976), 139–194.

Syriac Collection

The seventh-century Syriac collection by 'Ânân Îshô' of Bêth 'Âbhê has been translated into English by E. A. Wallis Budge, *The Sayings and Stories of the Christian Fathers of Egypt: The Syrian Version of the "Apophthegmata Patrum,"* 2 vol., reprint of 1934 ed. (London: Kegan Paul Limited, 2002).

Armenian Collection

For the Armenian version, see Louis Leloir, ed., *Paterica armeniaca a P. P. Mechitaristis edita (1855) nunc latine reddita*, CSCO 353, 361, 371, 379 (Louvain: Secrétariat du Corpus SCO, 1974–1976). There is no English translation; a partial French translation is available in Lucien Regnault, *Les Sentences des Pères du Désert, nouveau recueil: apophtegmes inédits ou inconnus* (Sablé-sur-Sarthe: Solesmes, 1970), 253–275.

Ethiopic Collections

There are two important collections in Ethiopic. The first is Victor Arras, ed., *Collectio monastica*, CSCO 238 [with the Ethiopic text] and CSCO 239 [with a Latin translation] (Louvain: Secrétariat du Corpus SCO, 1963). A French translation is found in Lucien Regnault, *Les Sentences des Pères du Désert, nouveau recueil: apophtegmes inédits ou inconnus* (Sablé-sur-Sarthe: Solesmes, 1970), 287–331. The second is Victor Arras, ed., *Patericon aethiopice*, CSCO 277 [Ethiopic text] and CSCO 278 [Latin translation] (Louvain: Secrétariat du Corpus SCO, 1967). A partial French translation is available in Lucien Regnault, *Les Sentences des Pères du Désert, nouveau recueil: apophtegmes inédits ou inconnus* (Sablé-sur-Sarthe: Solesmes, 1970), 332–338.

Greek Collection of Paul Evergetinos

The eleventh-century Byzantine scholar Paul Evergetinos put together a vast anthology: *Synagōgē tōn theophtoggōn rēmatōn kai didaskaliōn tōn theophorōn kai hagiōn paterōn*, 4 vols. (Athens: 1957–1966). A partial French translation is found in Lucien Regnault, *Les Sentences des Pères du Désert, nouveau recueil: apophtegmes inédits ou inconnus* (Sablé-sur-Sarthe: Solesmes, 1970), 163–198.

Apophthegmata Patrum: Introductions and Surveys

There are two fine studies which, while focused on particular topics, can serve as both an introduction and a survey to the *Apophthegmata Patrum*: Douglas Burton-Christie, *The Word in the Desert: Scripture and the Quest for Holiness in Early Christian Monasticism* (New York: Oxford University Press, 1993), and Graham Gould, *The Desert Fathers on Monastic Community*, Oxford Early Christian Studies (New York: Oxford University Press, 1993). The bibliography for chapter 8 lists studies of specific themes; the following are studies that deal with the *Apophthegmata* as a whole:

Gould, Graham E. "A Note on the *Apophthegmata Patrum*." *Journal of Theological Studies* 37 (1986): 133–138.

Guillaumont, Antoine. "L'enseignement spirituel des moines d'Égypte: la formation d'une tradition." In *Études sur la spiritualité de l'Orient chrétien*, 81–92. SO 66. Bégrolles-en-Mauges: Abbaye de Bellefontaine, 1996.

Guy, Jean-Claude. "Les *Apophthegmata Patrum*." In *Théologie de la vie monastique: études sur la tradition patristique*, ed. G. Lemaître, 73–83. Collection Théologie 49. Paris: Aubier, 1961.

———. "Educational Innovation in the Desert Fathers." *Eastern Churches Review* 6: (1974): 44–51.

———. "Remarques sur le texte des *Apophthegmata Patrum*." *Recherches de science religieuse* 43 (1955): 252–258.

Harmless, William. "Remembering Poemen Remembering: The Desert Fathers and the Spirituality of Memory." *Church History* 69 (2000): 483–518.

Hausherr, Irénée. *Spiritual Direction in the Early Christian East*, CS 116. Trans. Anthony P. Gythiel. Kalamazoo, Mich.: Cistercian Publications, 1990.

Regnault, Lucien. *Les pères du désert à travers leur apophtegmes*. Sablé-sur-Sarthe: Abboye Saint-Pierre de Solesmes, 1987.

Rousseau, Philip. "The Desert Fathers, Antony and Pachomius." In *The Study of Spirituality*, ed. Cheslyn Jones, Geoffrey Wainwright, and Edward Yarnold, 119–130. New York: Oxford University Press, 1986.

Ward, Benedicta. "Traditions of Spiritual Guidance: Spiritual Direction in the Desert
Fathers." *The Way* 24 (1984): 61–70. Reprinted in *Signs and Wonders: Saints, Miracles, and Prayers from the Fourth Century to the Fourteenth*. London: Variorum Reprints, 1992.

Scetis

The starting point remains the classic study of Hugh Evelyn-White, *The Monasteries of
Wadi'n Natrūn*, part 2, *The History of the Monasteries of Nitria and of Scetis* (New York:
Metropolitan Museum of Art Egyptian Expedition, 1932; reprint: New York, Arno Press,
1973). It masterfully assembles a vast array of texts. On daily life at Scetis and the other
desert sites, see Lucien Regnault, *The Day-to-Day Life of the Desert Fathers in Fourth-
Century Egypt*, trans. Étienne Poirer, Jr. (Petersham, Mass.: St. Bede's, 1998). See also:

Cody, Aelred. "Scetis." In *The Coptic Encyclopedia,* ed. Aziz S. Atiya, 7:2102–2106.
New York: Macmillan, 1991.
Donahue, Cecil. "The Agape of the Hermits of Scete." *Studia Monastica* 1 (1959): 94–
114.
Guy, Jean-Claude. "Le centre monastique de Scété dans la littérature du Vᵉ siècle." *Orientalia Christiana Periodica* 30 (1964): 129–147.
Taft, Robert. "Praise in the Desert: The Coptic Monastic Office Yesterday and Today."
Worship 56 (1982): 513–536.

APPENDIX 6.1

The Many Languages of Desert Literature

The literature of the desert fathers appeared in many ancient languages: Greek and Latin, of course, but also Syriac, Coptic (both the Sahidic and the Bohairic dialects), Ethiopic, Armenian, and Georgian. Here is a sampling of what some of the texts look like in the original.

GREEK

Ἠρώτησέ τις τὸν ἀββᾶ Ἀντώνιον λέγων· Τί φυλάξας τῷ Θεῷ εὐαρεστήσω; Καὶ ἀποκριθεὶς ὁ γέρων εἶπεν· Ἃ ἐντέλλομαί σοι φύλαξον· Ὅπου δ' ἂν ἀπέρχῃ, τὸν Θεὸν ἔχε πρὸ ὀφθαλμῶν σου πάντοτε· καὶ ὅπερ ἂν πράττεις, ἔχε ἐκ τῶν θείων γραφῶν τὴν μαρτυρίαν· καὶ ἐν οἵῳ δ' ἂν καθέζῃ τόπῳ, μὴ ταχέως κινοῦ. Τὰ τρία ταῦτα φύλαξον καὶ σώζῃ.

The text above is from the Greek Systematic Collection of the *Apophthegmata Patrum*. Here Antony offers a "word of salvation" to an inquirer (*AP* Sys 1.1, from Jean-Claude Guy, ed., *Les Apophtegmes des pères: collection systématique*, SC 387:102).

SYRIAC

The text above is from a Syriac collection of the *Apophthegmata Patrum*. It is a saying in which a monk asks Abba Ammonas, the disciple of Antony, what he must do to be saved. Its parallel in the Alphabetical Collection is Ammonas 1 (from F. Nau, ed., *Ammonas, successeur de saint Antoine*, PO 11 [1911]: 410).

SAHIDIC COPTIC

    Ⲁϥϣⲱⲛ ⲇⲉ ⲉⲝⲉⲕⲝⲟⲩⲱⲧⲉ ⲛⲣⲟⲙⲡⲉ ⲉⲃⲟⲗ ⲉϥⲁⲥ-
ⲕⲉⲓ ⲛⲧⲉⲓϩⲉ ϩⲁⲣⲓϩⲁⲣⲟϥ ⲉⲛϥⲛⲏⲩ ⲉⲃⲟⲗ ⲁⲛ ⲟⲩⲇⲉ ⲛⲥⲉⲛⲁⲩ
ⲉⲣⲟϥ ⲁⲛ ⲛϩⲁϩ ⲛⲥⲟⲡ ϩⲓⲧⲛⲗⲁⲁⲩ ⲛⲣⲱⲙⲉ. ⲙⲛⲛⲥⲁⲛⲁⲓ
ⲇⲉ ⲉⲣⲉϩⲁϩ ⲙⲟⲕϩ ⲛϩⲏⲧ ⲉⲩⲟⲩⲱϣ ⲉⲧⲛⲧⲱⲛⲟⲩ ⲉⲣⲟϥ
ⲁⲩⲱ   ⲛⲉϣⲁⲩⲧⲁⲩⲟ ⲉⲡⲉⲥⲏⲧ ⲙⲡⲣⲟ ⲛⲁⲛⲁϩ· ⲁϥⲉⲓ
ⲇⲉ ⲉⲃⲟⲗ ⲛϭⲓⲁⲛⲧⲱⲛⲓⲟⲥ ⲉⲣⲉⲡⲛⲟⲩⲧⲉ ⲧⲟ ϩⲓⲱⲱϥ·
ⲛϣⲟⲣⲡ ⲇⲉ ⲛⲧⲁϥⲉⲓ ⲉⲃⲟⲗ ϩⲛⲧⲡⲁⲣⲉⲙⲃⲟⲗⲏ ⲁϥⲟⲩⲱⲛϩ
ⲉⲃⲟⲗ ⲛⲛⲉⲛⲧⲁⲩⲉⲓ ϣⲁⲣⲟϥ. ⲛⲧⲉⲣⲟⲩⲛⲁⲩ ⲇⲉ ⲉⲡⲉϥ-
ⲥⲱⲙⲁ ⲁⲩⲣϣⲡⲏⲣⲉ ⲉϫⲙⲡⲉϥⲕⲛⲛⲉ ⲁⲩⲱ   ⲝⲉⲛϥⲕⲩ-
ⲛⲁϫⲉ ⲁⲛ ⲁⲩⲱ ⲙⲡⲉϥⲃⲃⲉ ϩⲱⲥ ⲉⲁϥⲉⲓ ⲉⲃⲟⲗ ϩⲛⲛⲉⲛⲏⲥⲧⲁ
ⲙⲛⲛⲙⲙⲓϣⲉ ⲛⲛⲇⲁⲓⲙⲱⲛ, ⲉϥϣⲟⲟⲡ ⲇⲉ ⲛⲧⲉϥϩⲉ ⲛⲑⲉ
ⲉⲧⲟⲩⲥⲟⲟⲩⲛ ⲙⲙⲟϥ ⲙⲡⲁⲧⲉϥⲁⲛⲁⲭⲱⲣⲉⲓ· ⲉⲩⲛⲁⲩ   ⲇⲉ
ⲟⲛ ⲉⲡⲙⲉⲉⲩⲉ ⲛⲧⲉϥⲯⲩⲭⲏ ⲉⲥⲧⲃⲃⲏⲩ ⲁⲩⲱ ⲉⲛϥⲁⲩⲡⲉⲓ ⲁⲛ
ϩⲛⲟⲩⲕⲁϩ ⲛϩⲏⲧ ⲟⲩⲇⲉ ⲛϥϣⲧⲣⲧⲱⲣ ⲁⲛ ϩⲓⲧⲛⲛⲛⲟⲩ-
ⲇⲟⲛⲏ ⲟⲩⲇⲉ ⲛⲉⲩⲁⲙⲁϩⲧⲉ ⲙⲙⲟϥ ⲁⲛ ϩⲓⲧⲛⲟⲩⲥⲱⲃⲉ
ⲏ ⲟⲩⲱⲕⲙ· ⲟⲩⲇⲉ ⲟⲛ ⲛⲧⲉⲣⲉϥⲛⲁⲩ ⲉⲡⲙⲏⲏϣⲉ ⲙⲡⲉϥ-
ϣⲧⲟⲣⲧⲣ ⲟⲩⲇⲉ ⲙⲡⲉϥⲣⲁϣⲉ ⲉⲩⲁⲥⲡⲁⲍⲉ ⲙⲙⲟϥ, ⲁⲗⲗⲁ
ⲛⲧⲟϥ ⲧⲏⲣϥ ⲉⲛⲉϥϣⲏϣ ϩⲱⲥ ⲉⲣⲉⲡⲗⲟⲅⲟⲥ ⲣϩⲙⲙⲉ ⲙⲙⲟϥ .

The text above is an excerpt from the Sahidic Coptic *Life of Antony* 14. It describes Antony's emergence from the desert fort (from Gérard Garitte, *S. Antonii Vitae: Versio Sahidica*, CSCO 117:20).

BOHAIRIC COPTIC

    [Ⲁⲥ]ϣⲱⲡⲓ ⲇⲉ ⲉⲧⲁⲩⲑⲱϣ ⲛⲁⲁⲃⲃⲁ ⲁⲑⲁⲛⲁⲥⲓⲟⲥ
ⲉⲛⲁⲣⲭⲏⲉⲡⲓⲥⲕⲟⲡⲟⲥ ⲉⲣⲁⲕⲟϯ ⲛⲉⲁϥⲓ ⲉⲣⲏⲥ ⲉⲑⲃⲁⲓⲥ ⲉϥⲟⲩ-
ⲱϣ ⲉϣⲉ ⲉⲣⲏⲥ ⲉⲥⲟⲩⲁⲛ ⲉϥⲧⲁϫⲣⲟ ⲛⲛⲓⲉⲕⲕⲗⲏⲥⲓⲁ
ⲉⲑ[ⲟ]ⲩⲁⲃ   [ⲉⲧ]ⲁⲡⲉⲛⲓⲱⲧ ⲡⲁϩⲱⲙ ⲇⲉ ⲛⲁⲩ ⲉⲣⲟϥ
ⲉⲣⲉ[ⲟ]ⲩⲧⲏⲛϣ ⲛⲉⲡⲓⲥⲕⲟⲡⲟⲥ ⲥⲱⲕ ϩⲁϫⲱϥ   [ⲛ]ⲑⲟϥ ϩⲱϥ
ⲟⲛ ⲁϥⲱⲗⲓ ⲛⲛⲓⲥⲛⲏⲟⲩ ⲁϥⲙⲟ[ϣ]ⲓ ⲉⲃⲟⲗ ϩⲁϫⲱϥ ⲛⲟⲩ-
ⲛⲓϣϯ ⲛⲟⲩⲉⲓ   [ⲟ]ⲩⲟϩ ⲛⲁⲩⲉⲣⲯⲁⲗⲓⲛ ϩⲁϫⲱϥ ϣⲁⲛⲧⲟⲩ-
[ⲉⲛ]ϥ ⲉϧⲟⲩⲛ ⲉⲧⲙⲟⲛⲏ ⲛⲧⲉϥϣⲗⲏⲗ ϧⲉⲛ[ⲛ]ⲟⲩⲙⲁⲛ-
ⲑⲱⲟⲩϯ ⲛⲉⲙⲛⲟⲩⲙⲁⲛϣⲱⲡⲓ ⲧⲏⲣⲟⲩ   Ⲁⲃⲃⲁ ⲥⲁⲣⲁⲡⲓⲱⲛ
ⲇⲉ ⲡⲓⲉⲡⲓⲥⲕⲟⲡⲟⲥ ⲛⲧⲉⲛⲓⲕⲉⲛⲧⲱⲣⲓ ⲁϥⲁⲙⲟⲛⲓ ⲛⲧϫⲓϫ ⲙⲡⲓ-

The text above is from the Bohairic Coptic *Life of Pachomius* 28. It describes the visit of Athanasius to Pachomius's community in Tabennesi (from Louis-Théophile Lefort, *S. Pachomii Vita: Bohairice Scripta*, CSCO 89:28).

GEORGIAN

განნა მხოლოდშობილი, რომელ არს გონებაი ჭეშმარიტი
მამისაი და ზატი მისი, რომლისა ზატად თუსისა ზატისა
შექმნა ყოველი მეტყუელი დაბადებული ; რაამეთუ იგოდეს
ამათ ვითარმეე მაცხოვარი არს დიდი იგი მკურნალი ; შეკრძეს
ყოველნი ერთბამად და შეწირეს ლოცვაი თუსითა ასოთა თოს,
რომელ ესე ჩუენ ვართ ; დადადებდეს და იტყუდეს :
« ნუკეთჯ მკურისკევი არა არსა გალადს, ანუ მკურნალნი
არა არიან მუნ? რაისა არა აღვიდა განკურნებად ასული
ერისა ჩემისაი ? ჭკურნებდით მას ჩუენ და არა განიკურნა;

The text above is from the Georgian version of the *Letters of Antony*. It is an
excerpt from *Letter* 2:14–17, describing Christ the Physician coming to heal
humanity's "great wound" (from Gérard Garitte, *Lettres de S. Antoine: version
géorgienne et fragments coptes*, CSCO 148:3).

ETHIOPIC

፲፻፰ ፡ ነገሪት ፡ ለእሩግ ። ተስእሉ ፡ ፩ ፡ ለአበ ፡ አንጦነስ ፡ አ
ንh ፡ ይብሉ ፡ ምንት ፡ ዐቲብቲ ፡ አዐር ፤ ፡ ለአምላh ። ዋአውሥአ ፡ ወይቤሉ ፡
አረጋዊ ፡ ዘአwC ፡ ለh ፡ ዐቀብ ። ንበ ፡ ሐርh ፡ አምላh ፡ የUሉ ፡ ቀድመ ፡
አዐይንቲh ፡ ወተረ ፡ ወበሉ ፡ ዘተገብC ፡ ለየUሉ ፡ ንበh ፡ አምቀ ዱሳት ፡ ወ
ጸሕፍት ፡ ለስምዐ ፡ ወበዙሉ ፡ መhን ፡ ንበ ፡ ነበርh ፡ ፍቱነ ፡ ኢተፍልስ ። ዘ
ንተ ፡ ፪ ፡ ዐቀብ ፡ ወተይነን ።

The text above is from the Ethiopic *Collectio Monastica*. It is a "word of salvation" given by Antony to an inquiring monk, and parallels the Greek text given
earlier (from Victor Arras, ed., *Collectio Monastica* 16.1, CSCO 238:132).

ARMENIAN

[Armenian text in cursive script]

The text above is the opening of the Armenian version of Serapion of Thmuis's *Letter to the Disciples of Antony*. Here Serapion speaks of "the Wrath" that swept through Egypt after Antony's death in 356 (from René Draguet, "Une lettre de Sérapion de Thmuis aux disciples d'Antoine (A.D.) en version syriaque et arménienne," *Le Muséon* 64 [1951]: 7).

LATIN

> 4. Frater aliquando in Scythi inventus est culpa-
> bilis, et fecerunt seniores conventum, et miserunt
> ad abbatem Moysem, dicentes ut veniret; ille autem
> venire noluit. Misit autem ad eum presbyter, dicens:
> Veni, quia plebs fratrum te exspectat. Et ille surgens
> venit. Tollens autem secum sportam vetustissimam,
> implevit eam arena, et post se portavit. Illi vero
> exierunt ei obviam, dicentes: Quid hoc est, Pater?
> Dixit autem eis senex: Peccata mea sunt post me
> currentia, et non video ea, et veni ego hodie judicare
> aliena peccata? Illi autem audientes, nihil locuti
> sunt fratri, sed ignoverunt ei.

This is from the sixth-century *Verba Seniorum* of Pelagius and John 9.4. It is the story of Abba Moses defending a brother accused of wrongdoing; the parallel in the Alphabetical Collection is Moses 2 (PL 73:910B).

APPENDIX 6.2

Macarius the Egyptian, *Letter to the Sons of God*

In the late 470s, Gennadius of Marseilles composed a sequel to Jerome's *On Illustrious Men*. Among Gennadius's "illustrious" was Macarius the Egyptian, "famous for his miracles and his spiritual powers." Gennadius reports also that he knew of a letter that Macarius had written to "younger people of his monastic profession." He then summarized Macarius's letter: a person can serve God "by understanding that he is contingent on his creation . . . by struggling and entreating God's help against everything that is comfortable in life"; and if the monk does this, he will come "to a natural purity" and "obtain a reward due his nature" (*De viris illustribus* 10). The letter Gennadius knew seems to be the one that has come down to us under the Latin title, *Ad filios Dei* ("To the Sons of God"). Versions of it are found in Greek, Latin, Coptic, and Syriac. Antoine Guillaumont, a leading scholar of early monasticism, has noted that among the many writings ascribed to Macarius, this is the one document that has "some chance of being authentic" ("Macaire l'Egyptien," *Dictionnaire de Spiritualité* 10:12).

Macarius's *Letter*, excerpted here, bears a kinship with the *Letters* of Antony and of Ammonas, both in terms of general style and of themes. As in the *Letters of Antony*, emphasis is placed on *gnosis* (knowledge). And as in the *Letters of Ammonas*, there is the theme of a "divine power"—presumably the Holy Spirit—that comes to indwell in the ascetic. This "power" comes in two stages: first as the spirit of repentance, then as the Paraclete. It is important to realize that Macarius's *Letter* dates from the very period in which theologians in the larger church—notably Athanasius and Basil of Caesarea—were working out the classic doctrine of the divinity of the Holy Spirit. Note the way Macarius speaks of the ebb and flow of this "power" of God. Note also the image of the rudderless ship—an interesting image for a desert-dweller.

CONVERSION TO SELF-KNOWLEDGE

> When a person turns to what is good and abstains from evil and devotes himself to learning about himself and regrets the things he has done in times of careless indifference and seeks God with his whole soul, then the good God makes him sorrowful for what he has done. (*Ep. ad filios Dei* 1)

TEMPTATION

> Then come our enemies, sowing wickedly contrived thoughts, plac-
> ing weakness in him; as a result, he is not strong enough to keep
> even a short fast but instead counts the minutes while the enemies
> say to him, "How long will you be able to endure this suffering?"
> And "Your body is weak," and "It is great suffering for God to in-
> dwell [in] a human being, especially you, who have committed so
> many sins," and "How many of the sins you've committed will God
> forgive you?" (*Ep. ad filios Dei* 4)

THE INDWELLING POWER

> But if the heart grows weary and faint-hearted in these matters so
> that it becomes enfeebled on account of what it has suffered in
> these wars, then the good and compassionate God sends to him
> holy power and strengthens his heart and gives him weeping and
> gladness and rest in his heart. As a result, he becomes stronger than
> his enemies; they fear the power indwelling him, and do not wish
> [to contend with it]. As Paul proclaims "Strive, and you will receive
> power" (Acts 1:8; Luke 13:24). . . . When the good God sees that the
> heart has been strengthened against its enemies, then he removes
> the power hour by hour and, once the power has become like a rud-
> derless ship, listing aimlessly, he allows the enemies to wage war
> through licentiousness and with the pleasures that come from see-
> ing and the pleasures of spiritual pride and haughtiness. When the
> heart grows weary beneath the assaults of the enemies, then the
> good God, taking thought of his creature, once again sends the holy
> power to him and strengthens his heart and soul and body and all
> the rest of his members by means of the [yoke] of the Paraclete. As
> he says, "Take my yoke upon you and learn from me, for I am gen-
> tle and humble in heart" (Matt. 11:29). Then the good God begins to
> open "the eyes of the heart" (Eph. 1:18) so that the person might
> know that God is the one who strengthens him. . . . Then the power
> begins to reveal heavenly things before the heart and how to pray
> and recite the psalms and the honors that will come to those who
> persevere. (Ep. ad filios Dei 9–13)

For the complete text and an analysis, see Tim Vivian, "The Good God, the
Holy Power, and the Paraclete: 'To the Sons of God' (*Ad filios Dei*) by Saint
Macarius the Great," *Anglican Theological Review* 80 (1998): 338–365.

7

The *Apophthegmata Patrum*: Portraits

The *Apophthegmata* was not meant to narrate the lives of the desert fathers in the way the *Life of Antony* does. Its purpose, according to its ancient editor, was to "commit to writing a few fragments of their best words and actions."[1] Often the figures mentioned in its pages are no more than names to us. But sometimes, as one reads the Alphabetical Collection, the poignant anecdotes about a figure come together, like a set of snapshots in a photo album, and offer glimpses of the person and his teachings. In this chapter, I would like to explore four key figures as they appear in its pages. Before I do, I must add an important proviso. We cannot presume that the *Apophthegmata* is giving us an unvarnished portrait. It gives not the historical figure per se, but the figure as he was remembered in the desert tradition. Memory can do all sorts of things. It can record, but it also selects and edits; it can forget and make mistakes; it can even distort or suppress things. So we need to be alert to how desert memory works. Earlier we saw the way Athanasius's theology and politics powerfully colored his portrait of Antony. While the editorial agenda of the *Apophthegmata* is not as apparent, it does have one, and its stories and sayings went through a long oral tradition before they were written down. Still, the portraiture of the *Apophthegmata* is remarkable, and we need to be familiar with its leading dramatis personae (see appendix 7.1 for a listing of the famous and not-so-famous in the Alphabetical Collection).

Abba Macarius the Egyptian

One of the most engaging characters found in the pages of the *Apophthegmata Patrum* is Abba Macarius the Egyptian (c. 300–390). We caught a glimpse of Macarius earlier. That he would require a disciple to shout insults and praises in a cemetery says something about his colorful personality. In the sources, he is called Macarius the Egyptian or Macarius the Great to distinguish him from his namesake and contemporary, Macarius the Alexandrian—though even ancient sources sometimes confused the two.[2] The name Macarius (Μακάριος in Greek) means "blessed."

Macarius was born in the village of Jijber (present-day Shabshîr), in the southwest part of the Nile Delta. Before becoming a monk, he had been a camel driver and, on the side, a smuggler, stealing niter out of the remote desert. Niter (sodium carbonate) was used both as a preservative in mummification and as a reagent in manufacturing glass. It was a valuable commodity, and the government had a monopoly on it and strictly regulated its mining. This touches on an interesting story told of Macarius. Much later, after he came to be venerated as a spiritual leader, whenever one of the brothers approached with fear and respect "like someone coming to see a great and holy old man," Macarius maintained a gruff silence. But when a brother came "as though to humiliate him" and reminded him of his days as a camel driver and as a thief who was sometimes pursued by government authorities and when caught, was beaten, then Macarius opened up and talked joyfully about whatever the brother wanted.[3]

At some point, Macarius abandoned camel-driving and became an ascetic living on the fringe of his village, much as the young Antony once had. When villagers went to force him to become a cleric, he fled to another village. Sometime after he had settled there, a young girl accused him of getting her pregnant. The villagers were incensed. They barged into his hermitage, beat him, dragged him around the village, and, in a gesture meant to signal his disgrace, hung soot-blackened pots around his neck. The girl's parents demanded Macarius pay support for their daughter and for the future baby. Strangely, he did not deny the charge, even though it was false. Instead he said to himself, "Macarius, you have found yourself a wife; you must work a little more in order to keep her." So he wove baskets and sent the earnings to his "wife." When it came time for the girl to have the baby, she went into labor, but it went on and on for days. She was unable to give birth. Finally, in desperation, she admitted that it was not Macarius who had gotten her pregnant, but a young man from the area. So the villagers who had slandered and beaten Macarius decided to come and do penance before him. On learning of this he fled.[4]

Around 330, Macarius founded the monastic settlement of Scetis. He soon attracted a large circle of disciples and acquired a reputation for the ability to read hearts, a charism normally possessed only by elders. This earned him a paradoxical nickname: the "young old man" (παιδαριογέρον).[5] Another epithet given him was "the Spirit-bearer" (πνευματοφόρος), again indicative of prophetic gifts.[6] He had resisted ordination earlier in his career, but by about 340, he consented, concerned that his disciples at Scetis have access to the Eucharist.[7]

The *Apophthegmata* records that Macarius made the long journey to see Antony at least once, perhaps to get advice about ordination. When he knocked on the door and introduced himself, Antony closed the door in his face— supposedly a test. Eventually, Antony opened up, received him, and rendered the traditional duties of hospitality. Antony even admitted that he had heard of Macarius and had wanted to meet him for a long time. That evening, when Antony went to soak some palm leaves for making rope, Macarius asked to join him. The two spent the evening braiding strands of rope and talking of the soul and its salvation.[8]

Earlier we saw the nightmarish stories told of Antony's encounters with demons. A humorous story is told about one of Macarius's. Once he traveled from Scetis to Terenuthis, a settlement in the Nile Valley. He needed a place to sleep and decided to camp out in one of the old abandoned temples there. Most people, pagan or Christian, would have thought of such places as haunted. But Macarius was fearless—so fearless, in fact, that he used an old mummy case as a pillow. And as the story goes, "The devils, seeing his audacity, were filled with jealousy" and tried to scare him off. One of them, as though addressing a woman in the mummy case, called from outside, "So-and-so, come on out and go swimming with us." Macarius was unmoved. He banged on the coffin: "Wake up. Go on, get out there into the darkness, if you can." The demons fled.[9]

Macarius used to travel widely. Early in his career, he would journey some forty miles across the trackless desert to attend the Eucharist of Abba Pambo at the monastic settlement of Nitria.[10] When Macarius returned from one such desert journey, he found a thief robbing his cell, loading everything he owned onto a beast of burden. Macarius did not get angry or even try to chase the thief off. Instead, he helped the man load the animal. The text even says that he saw the thief off "in great peace of soul, saying, 'We have brought nothing into the world, and we cannot take anything out of the world' (1 Tim. 6:7) and 'The Lord gave and the Lord has taken away; blessed be the name of the Lord' (Job 1:21)."[11]

Macarius taught an austere road to virtue. He was remembered for saying: "If slander has become to you the same as praise, poverty as riches, deprivation as abundance, you will not die."[12] He knew that in the stillness of the desert, memories well up and one can spend long hours nursing old wounds. And so he warned, "If we keep remembering the wrongs which men have done us, we destroy the power of the remembrance of God."[13] Macarius also passed on to his disciples how to pray: "There is no need at all to make long discourses; it is enough to stretch out one's hands and say, 'Lord, as you will, and as you know, have mercy.' And if the conflict grows fiercer say, 'Lord, help!' He knows very well what we need and he shows us his mercy."[14]

Several sayings stress Macarius's humility. Once, when asked to speak to a group of monks, he began with the self-effacing remark "I have not yet become a monk myself, but I have seen monks."[15] Another time, according to one fanciful story, he had gone to the nearby marsh to harvest palm leaves for his basket-weaving. On the way back, he ran into the devil who complained: "All you do, I do too; you fast, so do I; you keep vigil, and I do not sleep at all; in one thing only do you beat me. . . . Your humility. Because of that I can do nothing against you."[16]

In 374 Macarius and his namesake, Macarius the Alexandrian, were reportedly exiled to an island in the Nile Delta. This was part of the violent persecution conducted by Lucius, the Arian bishop of Alexandria installed by the government after Athanasius died.[17] The exile seems to have lasted a while, but at some point, Macarius made his way back to Scetis, where he died about 390.

Like Antony, Macarius acquired an international reputation and became one of the revered figures in the Coptic tradition (for an early image of him, see figure 7.1). Legends accumulated about him. A fanciful *Life of Macarius* was written in Coptic and attributed to Athanasius's friend, Serapion of Thmuis; the attribution is odd given that the real Serapion died about twenty-five years before Macarius. Another Coptic work, the *Virtues of Macarius*, portrayed him as a great visionary who kept company with angels and taught his disciples the Jesus prayer (see appendix 7.2). Various writings came to be attributed to Macarius himself. The most famous is a remarkable collection of fifty homilies, which would become classics of the Byzantine tradition and would deeply shape its spirituality. Only in the twentieth century were these shown to be Syrian, not Egyptian, and to have originated from circles associated with the Messalians. There is one work that might have some claim to authenticity, a letter called *To the Sons of God* (see appendix 6.2).

We do have a handful of other authentic sayings from Macarius that appear in the writings of Evagrius Ponticus. Evagrius knew Macarius personally, calling him "our holy and most ascetic master" and "the vessel of election."[18] In the *Praktikos*, Evagrius recounts advice Macarius once gave him about a balanced asceticism: he said "that the monk should always live as if he were to die on the morrow but at the same time that he should treat his body as if he were to live on with it for many years to come."[19]

A touching—and telling—tribute about Macarius is found in the *Apophthegmata* itself: "They said of Abba Macarius the Great that he became, as it is written, a god upon earth, because as God protects the world, so Abba Macarius would cover the faults which he saw, as though he did not see them; and those which he heard, as though he did not hear them."[20]

Abba John the Little

Abba John (c. 339–409) became one of the leading figures of Scetis in the late fourth and early fifth centuries. In the sources, he is called either John the Little (Greek: *kolobos;* Latin: *brevis staturae*) or John the Dwarf (*nanus*) (see figure 7.2).[21] Some fifty sayings and stories are listed under his name, though one

FIGURE 7.1. This is a wall painting of Macarius the Egyptian from the Monastery of Apa Jeremias at Saqqarah. The lettering to the right of the head (φορος) is from the word πνευματοφόρος ("Spirit-bearer"), one of the common epithets given Macarius. From Hugh Evelyn-White, *The Monasteries of Wadi 'n Natrûn, part 2: The History of the Monasteries of Nitria and of Scetis* (New York: Metropolitan Museum of Art, 1932), plate IVA. Reproduced with permission.

famous story attributed to him really belongs to his namesake, John of Lyco-polis (on this, see appendix 7.3).

John the Little grew up in the village of Tsê near the city of Oxyrhynchus (modern al-Bahnasa). In 357—soon after Antony's death, while Athanasius was on the run—John went to Scetis to become a monk. A humorous anecdote describes his early idealism. One day, he announced to one of the brothers that he wanted to become like the angels who do not work, but worship God without ceasing. He wrapped himself in his cloak and wandered off into the desert. A week later he was back, exhausted, suffering from hunger and thirst. He knocked on his friend's cell, but the monk did not unlock the door. Instead, he called out, "Who's there?" "John, your brother." The monk refused to open the door: "No, no, John has become an angel. He no longer lives with human beings." John begged: "But it *is* me." But the monk again refused and left John

FIGURE 7.2. This painting from the Monastery of Saint Antony in Egypt portrays three leading figures: Pishoi the Great, John the Little, and Sisoes. From Elizabeth Bolman, ed., *Monastic Visions: Wall Paintings in the Monastery of St. Antony at the Red Sea* (New Haven, Conn.: American Research Center in Egypt and Yale University Press, 2002), plate 3. Reproduced with permission.

outside all night. In the morning, he opened the door: "You are a human being. To eat, you have to work." John prostrated himself, begging the monk's forgiveness.[22]

After arriving at Scetis, John became a disciple of Abba Ammoes. Ammoes was a stern, distant figure. When he walked to church, he refused to let his disciples walk beside him. He made them keep their distance, fearing that "irrelevant conversation would creep in."[23] Once Ammoes asked one of his disciples what he thought of him. The monk said, "You are an angel, Father." When Ammoes asked the same disciple the same question some time later, the monk changed his tune: "You are like Satan. Even when you say a good word to me, it is like steel."[24] John was kind to the harsh old man. For the last twelve years of his life, Ammoes was sick and, much of the time, bedridden. John cared for him faithfully, though the old man did not give him much credit and never blessed him. But on his deathbed, when the other elders came and kept vigil, Ammoes finally commended John publicly, saying, "He is an angel, not a man."[25]

Sometime after Ammoes' death, around 375, John went out on his own. He soon attracted a circle of disciples. One of the fathers complained: "Who is this John, who by his humility has all Scetis hanging from his little finger?"[26] John had a gift for discernment. On weekends, he used to sit in front of the church at Scetis so that monks could approach him to discuss their "thoughts," all those inner stirrings—feelings, memories, temptations—that had risen in their solitary time during the week.[27] One story tells of a simple-minded monk who went to John again and again for advice. He became worried that he was pestering John. John told him, "Go, light a lamp." The monk did so. Then John ordered him, "Bring in some more lamps, and light them from the first one." Then John asked him whether the first lamp had lost anything from lighting the others. "No," the monk replied. Then John explained: "So it is with John. Even if all of Scetis came to see me, they would not separate me from the love of Christ. So come to me whenever you want, without hesitating."[28]

Contrary to the anecdote about his angelic aspirations, John valued hard work. Once he was asked, "What is a monk?" His answer: "He is work. The monk works at everything he does. That's what a monk is."[29] For John, manual labor was not an end in itself. Rather, it was a vehicle for contemplation. Several stories describe John hard at work weaving rope and baskets. One day, one of the brothers knocked on his door and asked him to bring out any baskets he had finished—presumably so the brother could take them to market and sell them. John went in, but instead of grabbing the baskets, he sat down and returned to his weaving. Again the monk knocked, again John answered the door, and again he returned to his work without giving the brother the baskets. The brother knocked a third time. Finally, John got a bit testy and led him inside: "If you want the baskets, take them and go away, because really, I have no time for such things."[30] John's absent-mindedness was really single-mindedness. One saying reports that he became so absorbed in his contemplation that he accidentally wove two baskets together into one.[31]

John struggled with anger. Once someone came in and praised his craftsmanship. John said nothing. The visitor spoke a second time, and John again kept silence. When the man spoke a third time, John erupted: "Since you came here, you have driven God from me."[32] John worried that even others' anger could become his own. Once, he witnessed an argument during the weekend gathering of the monks. Later, some saw him walk around the outside of his cell, round and round three times. Only then did he go in. When asked about it, he told the brothers: "My ears were full of that argument. So I circled around in order to purify them. And so I went in to my cell with my mind at peace."[33]

The *Apophthegmata* portrays John as a teacher of virtue. One remarkable saying offers a compendium of the virtues expected of the monk:

> I think it best that a man should have a little bit of all the virtues. Therefore, get up early every day and acquire the beginning of every virtue and every commandment of God. Use great patience, with

fear and long-suffering, in the love of God, with all the fervor of
your soul and body. Exercise great humility, bear with interior dis-
tress; be vigilant and pray often with reverence and groaning, with
purity of speech and control of your eyes. When you are despised do
not get angry; be at peace, and do not render evil for evil. Do not
pay attention to the faults of others, and do not try to compare yourself with others, knowing you are less than every created thing. Renounce everything material and that which is of the flesh. Live by
the cross, in warfare, in poverty of spirit, in voluntary spiritual asceticism, in fasting, penitence and tears, in discernment, in purity of
soul, taking hold of that which is good. Do your work in peace. Persevere in keeping vigil, in hunger and thirst, in cold and nakedness,
and in sufferings. Shut yourself in a tomb as though you were already dead, so that at all times you will think death is near.[34]

This passage is interesting in several respects. First, its length: normally,
in the *Apophthegmata*, one would expect that the eleven sentences here would
be made into eleven entries, not one. The editors who put together this anthology of monastic wisdom treasured one-liners and wanted their readers to
savor the density of wisdom in every word. Yet they recognized John's central
point here: that monastic living demands not one virtue in its perfection, but
a "little bit of all the virtues"—if not lived perfectly, at least competently.

Second, this highlights the wide scope of the monastic disciplines. Being
a monk involves the whole person, with "all the fervor of your soul and body."
John lists physical aspects (fasting; vigils; controlling one's gaze; praying with
tears and groans; enduring cold, nakedness, hunger, and thirst). He also highlights inner attitudes (patience, long-suffering, poverty of spirit, discernment,
and humble recognition that one is "less than every created thing"). Some
concern social matters, the tensions of living in the monastic community (not
getting angry, not rendering evil for evil, not paying attention to the faults of
others, not comparing oneself to others). Notice the final admonition: "Shut
yourself in a tomb as though you were already dead." We saw how Athanasius
described Antony doing that in quite literal terms; we also saw how Macarius
advised one monk to become as one dead. There is a scriptural key to it: it
echoes the spirituality of Saint Paul, who called on Christians to be crucified
and buried with Christ that they might be raised with him (Rom. 6). John—
and many other desert fathers—seemed to have had a three-days-in-the-tomb
spirituality. They sought to "live *by* the cross" and live *in* the empty tomb, so
to speak, anticipating the Last Judgment and resurrection.

In this passage, John does not prioritize virtues. But in another saying, he
stresses one as foundational: love. He notes that houses are built not from the
top down, but from the ground up. And for John, "the foundation is our neighbor, whom we must win, and that is the place to begin. For all the commandments of Christ depend on this one."[35] This sounds almost like a cliché. But,
in the *Apophthegmata*, the language of love of neighbor is not spoken of frequently. It is demonstrated in practical terms: hospitality, acute sensitivity to

other's needs, humble deference to others, and forgiveness of enemy. But John articulates that even for those committed to the solitary life, love of neighbor remains central.

John often used little parables or allegories to communicate his message. Once he spoke of a king who laid siege to his enemy's city. The king cut off the water and blockaded all the entrances to starve his enemies into submission. Then John noted, "It is the same with the passions of the flesh: if a man goes about fasting and hungry the enemies of the soul grow weak."[36] In another parable, he spoke of a courtesan who had the good fortune to marry the governor of a city. Her old lovers, afraid of the governor, sneaked around the back of the great house and whistled. She heard her old lovers' whistles but plugged up her ears, fled to the innermost rooms of the mansion, and closed the doors. John decoded the story this way: the courtesan is the soul, the ex-lovers are the passions, the governor is Christ, the whistling is the evil demons, and the inner chamber is the dwelling-place where the soul takes refuge in the Lord.[37] In the Western mystical tradition, the image of Christ as the bridegroom and the soul as the bride is a favorite one. It would be evocatively explored in the writings of Bernard of Clairvaux, Teresa of Avila, and John of the Cross. But it appears in the *Apophthegmata* only among the sayings of John the Little. Origen had used it in his commentary on the Song of Songs. This leads one to suspect that John, like so many, was familiar with currents of Origenist theology—whether or not he had actually read Origen.

Prostitutes were not simply characters in John's parables. One famous story concerns John's dealings with a prostitute named Paësia (or Thaësia). She had been orphaned while still young and, to make ends meet, had turned her house into a small hotel. She was well known at Scetis for the generous hospitality she offered monks whenever they came to town. As time went on, her finances took a bad turn, and she became a prostitute. Some elders of Scetis were alarmed and begged John to intervene: "While she could, she gave us charity. So now it is our turn to offer charity and to go to her assistance. Go to see her then, and according to the wisdom which God has given you, put things right for her." So John went to town and knocked on the woman's door. He was apparently a familiar figure, because he told the doorkeeper, "Tell your mistress I am here." The doorkeeper took the opportunity to give him a piece of her mind: "From the beginning you have eaten her goods, and see how poor she is now." But John insisted that he needed to see Paësia, for he had something "very helpful" for her. This piqued the doorkeeper's interest. She went to her mistress and said, "These monks are always going about in the region of the Red Sea and finding pearls." Meanwhile, the doorkeeper's children—who seemed to have a knowledge of things beyond their years—teased the old monk: "What have you got that makes you want to meet her?" John was led to Paësia's bedroom. She was ready for him and lay seductively on the bed. John came in and sat down on the bed next to her. He looked into her eyes and said, "What have you got against Jesus that you behave like this?" She stiffened, and John began to weep. She asked why he was crying. "I see Satan playing in your face," he answered. She then asked, "Abba, is it possible to repent?" "Yes," replied John. Paësia then said, "Take me wherever you wish." And so the two left town and by evening reached the desert. When it came time to sleep, John made a pillow in the sand for the woman, carving a small cross in it. He then went off a ways and did the same for himself. In the middle of the night, he awoke to see a light beam that stretched from the heavens to the earth and saw angels carry her soul away. He went back to where she lay and touched her feet. She was dead. He then prayed and heard a voice: "One single hour of repentance has brought her more than the repentance of many who persevere without showing much fervor in repentance."[38]

Thérèse of Lisieux was deeply touched by this story and discusses it her autobiography.[39] But scholars have raised questions about its antiquity and its attribution to John. It is not well attested in the manuscript tradition. The story is not found in the sixth-century Latin Collection of Pelagius and John, nor in the seventh-century Syriac Collection of Ânân Îshô. A nearly identical story appears in the Anonymous Collection. There the monk is left unnamed, but he is from Kellia, not Scetis, and the woman is his sister, not a benefactor.[40] A similar legend circulated about Abba Paphnutius and a woman named Täisis. In defense of its antiquity, Lucien Regnault has pointed out how embarrassing the whole story is—for instance, that a benefactor of Scetis was a prostitute or that John dared to sit on a bed with a prostitute. But as Regnault notes, "The most shocking is its climax, the entrance into heaven of this sinner so soon after her conversion, without her having done the slightest work of penitence."[41] He is not surprised that the story was sometimes suppressed or changed in its details.

John is known in several sources outside the *Apophthegmata*. Evagrius Ponticus knew him, if not personally, at least by reputation. In one passage, he plays on John's nickname, saying that though called John the Short (*Micros*), he was actually "John the Greatest of monks." Evagrius knew of John's reputation for singleminded concentration in contemplation. He says that John "would remain unmoved in his communion with God even though the demon wrapped himself around him in the form of a great serpent that squeezed his flesh and vomited in his face."[42]

Like Macarius the Egyptian, John became one of the heroes of the Coptic tradition. In the eighth century, Zacharias, bishop of Sakhâ, composed an *Encomium on the Life of John the Little* (for excerpts, see appendix 7.4). It relies heavily on sayings and stories from the *Apophthegmata*, but Zacharias had access to other traditions about John. He speaks of John as "our holy father the priest and *hegumen* of Scetis." The term *hegumen*, or "monastic superior," is of a later date, but may have some accuracy here. It is quite possible that John headed one of the four congregations of Scetis, though the *Apophthegmata* makes no mention of it. If he did, it is quite possible he was ordained. Again, the *Apophthegmata* makes no mention of John as a priest, and it usually (but not always) mentions clerical status. In time, one congregation even came to be named after John. However, he left Scetis in 407, after a barbarian raid sacked it, and lived his final years in the area of Clysma, where he died in 409 at the age of seventy.

Abba Moses the Ethiopian

Another leader of Scetis was Abba Moses (c. 332–407). Ancient sources sometimes refer to him as Moses the Ethiopian or Moses the Black to distinguish him from other monks with the same name (see figure 7.3).[43] Palladius, who had apparently met him, says that Moses was an "Ethiopian by birth," but this seems to be simply an ancient way of referring to anyone of sub-Saharan ancestry. Before becoming a monk, Moses had had quite a career. He had been a house slave of a government official but was dismissed, according to Palladius, "because of his great recalcitrance and penchant for robbery." Later he led a band of highwaymen and was rumored to have committed murder. One picaresque tale describes Moses swimming, sword in mouth, across the mile-wide Nile River to plunder the sheep herd of a man he hated. When he came ashore, he caught and slaughtered the herd's only four rams, thereby crippling the herd's future. He then tied the slaughtered rams together and swam back across the river. Once in his own camp, he skinned them, ate the best parts, and sold the sheepskins for some good Italian wine. It is not known what

FIGURE 7.3. This image of Abba Moses the Ethiopian is from the Monastery of Saint Antony in Egypt. From Elizabeth Bolman, ed., *Monastic Visions: Wall Paintings in the Monastery of St. Antony at the Red Sea* (New Haven, Conn.: American Research Center in Egypt and Yale University Press, 2002), plate 1.9. Reproduced with permission.

brought Moses to monastic life. One would half expect that if no conversion story had been known, then some pious author would have made one up. But Palladius, with admirable restraint, reports only that "he was brought to his senses by some circumstance and he took himself to a monastery."[44]

His apprenticeship at Scetis was not easy. He had to endure racial prejudice. One story describes a council of monks in which some treated Moses "with contempt" and grumbled, "Why does this black man come among us?" The *Apophthegmata* reports that this was ostensibly said "to test him"—but one wonders. In any case, Moses held his tongue. Afterwards friends approached him: "Abba, did that not grieve you at all?" Moses was honest: "I was grieved, but I kept silence."[45] Moses even faced crude prejudice from the archbishop who ordained him priest. During the ceremony, he was clothed in a white ephod, and the archbishop remarked, "See, Abba Moses, now you have become *all* white." Moses turned the jibe into moral self-accusation: "That's so on the outside—would that it were also so on the inside."[46]

Abba Moses was sensitive to those society excluded. One story tells how a council was called at Scetis to judge a monk who had committed some unnamed crime. Moses was invited but refused to come. A messenger was sent: "Come, everyone is waiting for you." So he came, but he took an old leaky jug along with him. When he arrived, he had the jug on his back, and from it water leaked onto the sand. He then walked into the council saying: "My sins run out behind me, and I do not see them, and today I am coming to judge the errors of another." Moses's acted parable silenced the council, which granted forgiveness to the accused brother.[47]

Abba Moses earned fame beyond the borders of Scetis. One story describes how a provincial judge wanted to meet him, much as judges had once sought out Antony. Word of this reached Moses, who went into hiding. Meanwhile, somewhere along the way the judge, ran into an old monk and asked him where the cell of Abba Moses was. The old monk said to the judge: "Why do you want to see him? He is a fool and a heretic." When the judge reached Scetis, he told the clergy there about his encounter with the old monk. When asked to describe the one who insulted "the holy man," the judge answered that he had been an old man, wearing the oldest of old clothes, a tall man, black. And so the clergy had to explain that it was Abba Moses himself who had called Abba Moses "a fool and a heretic." The judge, as the story goes, "went away greatly edified."[48]

This story implies that Moses was skittish about visitors. In fact, it was just the opposite. He was well known for his hospitality, welcoming brothers "joyfully" and "with open arms," as one saying puts it.[49] His friendliness became a problem for him. One story records that he sought out Abba Macarius for advice, saying, "I should like to live in quiet prayer and the brethren do not let me." Macarius read Moses well: "I see that you are a sensitive man and incapable of sending a brother away. Well, if you want to live in peace, go to the interior desert, to Petra, and there you will be at peace."[50] Even in this more remote and arid locale he had visitors. One story tells how he ran out of the last of his water while cooking lentils for some guests. The guests became puzzled by his odd behavior, his going back and forth, into his cell and then back out again to his cooking. Finally a raincloud came overhead and poured down rain, enough to fill the cisterns. When asked, he explained: "I was arguing with God, saying, 'You brought me here and now I have no water for your servants.' This is why I was going in and out; I was going on at God till he sent us some water."[51]

When the compilers of the *Apophthegmata* began gathering sayings and stories, they had at hand several small collections that may have served as models. Abba Moses had put together one of the earliest of these, a document entitled *Seven Headings of Ascetic Conduct*. He sent it to Abba Poemen, with the preface that "he who puts them into practice will escape all punishment and will live in peace, whether he dwells in the desert or in the midst of the brethren."[52] Several of the dicta are striking. In one, a brother asks Moses what it means to think in his heart that he is a sinner. Moses replies, "When someone is occupied with his own faults, he does not see those of his neighbor."[53] Moses knew well that abstaining from judgment was no small task in a tight-knit community dedicated to high standards. In another dictum, he stressed the necessary integrity between prayer and action—that "if a man's deeds are not in harmony with his prayer, he labors in vain."[54] Moses's spiritual leadership must have impressed John Cassian, for he chose the figure of Abba Moses to serve as the opening speaker in his account of life among the desert fathers, the *Conferences*. In the first two *Conferences*, Cassian portrays Moses setting out an eloquent exposition of the goal and purpose of monastic life.

Moses died a martyr. In 407, a tribe of barbarian raiders known as Mazices came sweeping off the Libyan desert and attacked Scetis. Many of the monks fled, but Moses stayed put. When some encouraged him to run, he said, "As for me, I have been waiting for this day for many years, that the word of the Lord Jesus Christ may be fulfilled which says, 'All who take the sword will perish by the sword' (Matt. 26:52)." It sounds as if he saw this as God's judgment on his past life of crime, but it is also an indication of his fearlessness. Seven monks stayed on with him. One of the seven hid under a pile of rope and witnessed the slaughter of Moses and the six other monks. He also claimed to have had a vision, seeing "seven crowns descending and crowning them."[55] Palladius did not seem to know how Moses died; he reports that Moses died at age seventy-five as a presbyter, leaving behind seventy disciples. This implies that Moses had headed one of the four congregations at Scetis.

Those who survived the destruction of Scetis looked back on it as the judgment of God. Scattered through the *Apophthegmata* one finds ominous statements noting a decline in fervor and forewarnings of disaster. Abba Poemen remarked that "since Abba Moses and the third generation in Scetis, the brothers do not make progress any more."[56] Moses himself was remembered to have prophesized the catastrophe: "If we keep the commandments of our Fathers, I will answer for it on God's behalf that the barbarians will not come here. But if we do not keep the commandments of God, this place will be devastated."[57] Word of the attack spread even to the Latin West. Augustine knew of it and counted it among the great disasters of the time.[58] And when the sack of Rome took place a couple of years later, in 410, one of the survivors of Scetis, Abba Arsenius, linked the two events: "The world has lost Rome and the monks have lost Scetis."[59]

Abba Poemen

The destruction of Scetis marked a turning point. The site was resettled a few years later and in fact suffered other barbarian raids, notably in 434, 444, and 570. But after this first one, many of its leading figures never returned.[60]

This diaspora proved providential. A group of seven brothers led by Abba Poemen and Abba Anoub fled from Scetis to Terenuthis on the Nile. They first took refuge in an old abandoned pagan temple. Soon after arriving, Anoub asked the group to spend a week in silent retreat. Each morning he would throw rocks at one of the temple's stone statues, and each evening he would kneel down and ask it to forgive him. He did the same all week. At week's end, Poemen asked Anoub to explain his behavior. He answered: "I did this for you. When you saw me throwing stones at the face of the statue, did it speak? Or did it get angry?" "No," Poemen replied. "Now there are seven of us. If all of you want to live together, let us be like this statue—unmoved whether one beats on it or flatters it. If you do not wish to live like this, there are four doors here in the temple. Let each one go out the one he wishes." The seven accepted Anoub's proposal and bound themselves to one another.[61]

The decision would prove momentous, for it is from Abba Poemen and his circle that the core of the *Apophthegmata* would come. It was they who kept alive the memory of the wisdom of the "old men," especially those of Scetis. Abba Poemen is the single most prominent figure in the *Apophthegmata*. In the best-known version of the Alphabetical Collection, 187 sayings are listed under Poemen's name; another 21 sayings are attributed to him in other Greek recensions. Poemen also appears in 25 sayings listed under the names of other figures. In addition, 16 sayings unique to the Systematic Collection are attributed to him. In other words, nearly a quarter of the *Apophthegmata* is sayings from or stories about Abba Poemen.[62]

The name Poemen (Ποιμήν) means "shepherd." In many ways, it sums up his personality—something Poemen's own spiritual director remarked on at the outset of his career.[63] Poemen was remembered not so much for ascetic feats or visions or miracle working as for his gifts as a spiritual guide. He was deeply tolerant of human weakness. Once some of the old men asked him what to do with monks who, weary from their prayer vigils, fell asleep at the weekend liturgies: "Should we rouse them so that they will be watchful?" Poemen advised compassion: "For my part, when I have seen a brother who is dozing, I put his head on my knees and let him rest."[64] On another occasion, one of his neighbors was a monk who kept a mistress. Poemen cast no judgment on the man. And when the monk's mistress became pregnant and had a child, Poemen sent one of his brothers over with a bottle of wine as a gift.[65]

On several occasions, monks came to Poemen, asking what to do about such overt sinners. Once he responded: "If I have to go out and I see someone committing a sin, I pass on my way without reproving him."[66] But Poemen was no laxist. As he said on another occasion, his tolerance sprang from a spiritual rationale: "At the very moment when we hide our brother's fault, God hides our own and at the moment when we reveal our brother's fault, God reveals ours too."[67]

Compassion could lead Poemen to contradict a venerable colleague. One day, a monk came to Poemen deeply troubled about lust. The monk explained that he had already gone to another *abba* whose admonition—"Don't let it stay in you"—gave him no solace. Poemen diplomatically circumvented this just-say-no advice. He told the monk: "Abba Ibiston's deeds are up with the angels. And he does not realize that you and I remain in fornication. If a monk controls his stomach and holds his tongue, if he lives like a foreigner, he will not die— be confident of that."[68]

Poemen tried to teach others such empathy. Once there were some monks who used to go to town too often and indulged themselves by going to the baths. The local priest heard of this and publicly defrocked the monks at the liturgy. Later he worried about his harshness and sought Poemen's advice. Poemen asked, "Don't you sometimes have a bit of the old Adam in you?" The priest nodded: "I have my share." So Poemen said, "Look, you're like them. If you have even a little share of the old Adam, then you too are subject to sin." The priest called the defrocked brothers back, returned to them their monastic habits, and asked their pardon.[69] Poemen himself mitigated harsh penances. When one who had committed some "great sin" came to him, Poemen reduced the penance from three years to three days.[70]

One story portrays Poemen with a devotion to the Virgin Mary and to the crucified Christ that has an almost late medieval flavor about it. One day, Abba Isaac, one of Poemen's disciples, saw his master have an ecstatic experience. Isaac, who was "on terms of great freedom of speech," prostrated himself before Poemen and asked what had happened. Poemen said: "My thought was with Saint Mary, the *Theotokos*, as she wept by the cross. I wish I could always weep like that."[71] Note the way Poemen refers to Mary as *Theotokos* (Mother of God), the disputed title that Cyril of Alexandria would defend against Nestorius at the Council of Ephesus in 431.

Poemen was remembered by his peers for having the "charism of speech."[72] His remarks about teachers and teaching give us a glimpse of what made him attractive. Once, a brother came to Poemen asking if he should assume authority over some monks who lived with him. Poemen told him, "No, be their example, not their legislator."[73] Poemen insisted that a teacher do what he would teach others; as he put it, "Teach your heart to guard that which your tongue teaches."[74] At the same time, he insisted that the teacher speak with integrity: "Teach your mouth to say what you have in your heart."[75] Poemen is portrayed as an astute judge of the human heart and once remarked that "a man may seem to be silent, but if his heart is condemning others he is babbling ceaselessly."[76]

Poemen sometimes framed his teachings in easy-to-remember threesomes. Once he listed the three necessary virtues of the monk: "fear of God, prayer, and doing good to one's neighbor."[77] Another time he enumerated the three great guides for the soul's journey: vigilance, self-knowledge, and discernment.[78] And in a saying found in the Ethiopic version, Poemen says that he centered his own meditation on "three mysteries": "to pray at every moment before the Lord, without ceasing; to place my death before me at every moment; and to think that, when I die, I will be thrown into the fire because of my sins."[79]

Poemen the pedagogue had a fondness for analogies. In one saying, he compares a man of discernment to a woodsman who can fell a tree with a few quick blows.[80] In another, he speaks of unexamined thoughts as old clothes tossed in a chest, wrinkled and rotting.[81] Another time he compared hard-working monks to bees and warned, "Just as smoke drives the bees away and also takes the sweetness out of their work, so bodily ease drives the fear of God from the soul and dissipates all its activity."[82] Poemen often drew on everyday desert experience for his imagery. The desert dweller has to be alert for snakes and scorpions hiding in dark places in his house—for instance, under pots and pans. Poemen played on this to illustrate a favorite theme:

> See this empty jar. If someone were to fill it with serpents, lizards, and scorpions and then leave the lid sealed and abandon it, all these reptiles—aren't they going to die there? And if you open the jar, won't all the creatures get out and sting people? And so, it's the same for a man: if he watches his tongue and shuts his mouth, all the creatures die inside. But if he works his tongue and speaks, the venomous creatures will come out and sting his brother and the Lord will be angry.[83]

Here Poemen recognizes how words can wound, and that in the silence of the desert old and callous words can well up in the memory and haunt the monk. Thus he felt it essential to "keep a lid" on things, especially during the weekend gatherings. That is why, according to one saying, he spent the hour before the weekend *synaxis* examining his own heart.[84]

While Poemen appears as both a skilled teacher and a spiritual guide, his real gift was his memory. As Jean-Claude Guy has noted, "If there were a term to define his personality, we would willingly say that Poemen appears not so much as a pioneer, but as a wise administrator of a treasure of which he has found himself the inheritor. Understanding perhaps that with the devastation of Scetis a page of history had been turned, he worked hard to harvest all the fruits of the great century of Scetis, gathering up the fragments so that nothing would be lost."[85] Again and again, the *Apophthegmata* shows Poemen passing on wisdom gleaned from earlier generations. A standard formula that opens sayings throughout the Collections is "Abba Poemen said that Abba so-and-so used to say. . . ." One finds him quoting sayings from or telling stories about earlier monastic figures on at least forty-seven occasions; and in these he quotes an extraordinary range of figures—at least twenty-three different abbas, including Antony, Ammonas, Macarius the Egyptian, Pambo, Sisoes, John the Little, and Moses the Black.[86]

Several citations open up a problem of interpretation and chronology. One saying portrays Antony speaking directly to Poemen: "Abba Antony said to Abba Poemen: 'This is the great work of a man: always to take the blame for his own sins before God and to expect temptation to his last breath.' "[87] This implies that Poemen's career overlapped with Antony's, perhaps in the 350s. Another saying states that he was still alive when Abba Arsenius died, that is, shortly before 450.[88] It is virtually impossible that the same man spoke to Antony in the 350s and was alive until the 450s. Derwas Chitty therefore proposed that there must have been two men named Poemen, one of the generation of Antony and another from the first half of the fifth century.[89] The editors of the *Apophthegmata* did sometimes confuse things and put sayings from more than one figure under the same name. As we have seen, sayings by Macarius the Alexandrian are found scattered among those listed under the name of Macarius the Egyptian; and a story about John of Lycopolis is ascribed to John the Little.[90] But Lucien Regnault has argued that such an interpretation is not necessary here. Sayings that show Poemen talking directly to figures of an earlier generation probably reflect confusion in the oral tradition. For instance, this same saying about Antony and Poemen appears a second time in the collection, and the wording of the second differs slightly—but significantly. It reads: "Abba Poemen said that blessed Abba Antony used to say, 'The greatest thing a man can do is to throw his fault before the Lord and expect temptation to his last breath.' "[91] Here Poemen appears not as one speaking directly with Antony, but as one who passes on what he has presumably heard about Antony from others. In light of this, it seems likely that there was just ᴏne Poemen, who was active from the 380s at the earliest and who passed on ᴡʰat his teachers said about Antony's generation.[92]

Remembering the wisdom of the elders—and reusing it in new settings—was a hallmark of Poemen's practice as a spiritual director. This is evident in a remarkable but little-known saying preserved in the Ethiopic collection. In the story, a monk comes to Poemen and opens up his heart about one of his great fears: because he could not accomplish the "word" that Poemen had given him, he no longer feels it right that he seek Poemen's counsel. We saw earlier how young monks came with the request, "Abba, give me a word that I might be saved"; how the "word" of the *abba* was venerated as a prophetic word given by God as a key to unlock the individual's spiritual journey; and how monks were expected to obey wholeheartedly and bring that "word" to fruition in the way they lived. The monk in this case feared his failure. He feared that by not living out the "word" Poemen had given him, God would hold it against him. As he exclaimed to Poemen, "May your word not be my condemnation on Judgment Day!" Poemen was sympathetic and admitted that he had suffered from the same fear. He recounted how one day, when he lived at Scetis, he had approached Abba Macarius about the problem. Macarius ordered him: "Don't stop visiting the old men. There will come a day when, if you wish to serve God, you will conquer by the words of old men. If thoughts erupt in you all over again, remember the words of the old men, and you will find help in them and you will be saved."[93] This incident captures much about Poemen, about the way that the desert tradition remembered his personality and his spirituality. It illustrates his warmhearted sympathy for those in anguish. It also shows the way Poemen passed on and reused wisdom from venerable figures of the past. But what makes it so striking is the way it precisely articulates what might be called Poemen's "spirituality of memory." Poemen embraced remembering the words of the "old men." He was convinced that their words possessed a saving wisdom, that if he could just remember them, especially at moments of crisis, he and his disciples would be saved.

A later Coptic author, Zacharias of Sakhâ, mentions that Poemen was a writer.[94] Was he perhaps one of the first to write down the sayings and stories that would come to make up the *Apophthegmata*? That is not impossible. One saying mentions Poemen sending a letter to an anchorite, though another one mentions that he knew very little Greek.[95] That might mean either that he was literate in Coptic, but not in Greek; or that he may have dictated things to a scribe. But all of this could have happened orally. He could have collected oral stories and sayings and passed them on orally to his disciples. The literary form that those sayings and stories eventually took, the apophthegm, is one rooted in oral storytelling. The impetus for such collecting could well have come from the admonition of Macarius and could have been spurred further by the destruction of Scetis. In 407, Poemen and his circle had fled and had witnessed the anguishing destruction of their whole way of life. On the far side of that destruction, that living circle of *abbas* where a saving wisdom could be found no longer existed. It now dwelt in memory. Back in Scetis, Poemen was known to have deferred to his elders: "It was said of Abba Poemen that he never wished to speak after another old man, but that he preferred to praise him in everything he had said."[96] After the destruction of Scetis, he carried on this deference in a new way: by collecting and passing on the saving words of the "old men" to his disciples.

But Poemen was not just a subject who remembered. He was also an object of memory. Poemen's own sayings and deeds—several hundred of them— were treasured, preserved, passed on, and, in the end, committed to writing. The Greek *Apophthegmata* preserves one set of memories; another set also circulated, and the Ethiopic *Collectio Monastica* seems to preserve these. These stories show that the circle around him valued Poemen's compassion and his knack for teaching. Most of all, that circle valued his memory, his habit of passing on the wisdom of a bygone age. If we are to appreciate this spirituality of memory, we need to note not just Poemen remembering, but also the community remembering Poemen remembering.

We need to understand how memory worked in that community of disciples. The community around Poemen did, from all indications, take great pains to remember accurately. But it was not accuracy for accuracy's sake. It was not the accuracy that might move a modern historian or that might have moved an ancient historian. It was accuracy for the sake of spirituality. This religious community remembered because it was convinced that remembering provided access to the holy, to salvation. It needed Poemen's words and, even more, his memories, because it desired holiness and sought pathways to find holiness. Its concern was not past facts, but past wisdom that might serve the present quest. In the wilderness of the human spirit, as in the wilderness of the desert, landmarks are precious. And the memory of Poemen—his words, his deeds, his memories, his very act of remembering—provided landmarks. Memory of Poemen harkened back to a golden age, when God showered charisms on the "old men," when God allowed them to read their disciples' hearts like an open book and speak a word that would reveal to them a pathway across the demon-ridden landscape of the human heart.

NOTES

1. *AP* Prologue (PG 65:73; trans. Ward, CS 59:xxxvi).
2. For example, the *Historia monachorum in Aegypto* XXIII (CS 34:113) claims incorrectly that Macarius of Alexandria was the founder of Scetis; one finds modern historians, such as Hans Lietzmann, *A History of the Early Church*, vol. 4, *The Era of the Church Fathers*, trans. Bertram Lee Woolf (New York: Scribner's Sons, 1952), 138, passing on the mistake. For an excellent discussion of this issue, see Antoine Guillaumont, "Le problème des deux Macaires dans les *Apophthegmata Patrum*," *Irénikon* 48 (1975): 41–59.
3. *AP* Macarius 31 (PG 65:273: trans. Ward, CS 59:134). Roger S. Bagnall, *Egypt in Late Antiquity* (Princeton: Princeton University Press, 1993), 146n188, cites an interesting papyrus that is reminiscent of the trouble that the young Macarius used to be involved in: in *P.Abinn.* 9, a government official who dealt with the natron monopoly reminds a man named Abinnaeus "that any natron imported is to be impounded, and the persons importing it, together with their beasts (presumably camels) detained." Cf. *AP* Agathon 12 (PG 65:112–113; CS 59:22), which notes that a brother found a piece of natron on the road; Agathon sent his disciple to put it back where he found it.
4. *AP* Macarius 1 (PG 65:257–260; CS 59:124–125).
5. Palladius, *Historia Lausiaca* 17 (Butler, 43; ACW 34:54).
6. *AP* Macarius 38 (PG 65:280; CS 59:136). Palladius, *Historia Lausiaca* 17 (Butler, 43–44; trans. Meyer, ACW 34:54–55), mentions that "by the time he was forty he received the gifts of fighting spirits and of prophecy. The epithet "Spirit-bearer" is repeated in later Coptic sources—e.g., the *Virtues of Abba Macarius the Great* (See appendix 7.2).
7. Palladius, *Historia Lausiaca* 17 (Butler, 44; ACW 34:55). Cf. *AP* Macarius 26.
8. *AP* Macarius 4 (PG 65:263; CS 59:127–128). *AP* Macarius 26 (PG 65:273; CS 59:133) mentions a visit to Antony (presumably a second one) in which the two discussed the fact that the "offering" (the Eucharist) was not celebrated in Scetis. The question may have been whether Macarius needed to get ordained, so that the disciples he had attracted would not have to trek the forty miles to Nitria as he seems to have done. Later Coptic sources make much of these visits and portray Antony formally investing Macarius with monastic robes. All this is an anachronism. While Macarius seems to have visited Antony, he was not, properly speaking, one of Antony's disciples.
9. *AP* Macarius 13 (PG 65:267; trans. my own).

10. *AP* Macarius 2 (PG 65:260; CS 59:125). Cf. *AP* Macarius 39 which also speaks of him going from Scetis to Nitria; Macarius 34 speaks of a delegation being sent to Scetis by the "old men of the mountain" (presumably Mount Nitria) requesting Macarius visit before dying.

11. *AP* Macarius 18 (PG 65:269; trans. Ward, CS 59:131). Guillaumont thinks it possible that this story may in fact not belong to Macarius the Egyptian, but to his namesake, since it seems reminiscent of the jovial personality of the Alexandrian: "Le problème des deux Macaires," 55.

12. *AP* Macarius 20 (PG 65:269; trans. Ward, CS 59:131).

13. *AP* Macarius 36 (PG 65:277; trans. Ward, CS 59:136); Evagrius Ponticus, *Praktikos* 93, has a variant of this.

14. *AP* Macarius 19 (PG 65:269; trans. Ward, CS 59:131).

15. *AP* Macarius 2 (PG 65:260; trans. Ward, CS 59:125).

16. *AP* Macarius 11 (PG 65:277; trans. Ward, CS 59:130). Cf. *AP* Macarius 35.

17. Rufinus, *HE* 11.4 (PL 21:512–513; Amidon, 64–66); Socrates *HE* 4.24 (PG 67: 524; NPNF 2.2:109).

18. Evagrius Ponticus, *Praktikos* 29 and 93 (SC 170:566, 696; trans. Bamberger, CS 4:24, 39).

19. Evagrius Ponticus, *Praktikos* 29 (SC 170:566–568; trans. Bamberger, CS 4: 24). Evagrius also quotes him in *Praktikos* 93. *Praktikos* 94, which speaks of "holy father Macarius," refers to his namesake, Macarius the Alexandrian. On this, see Antoine Guillaumont and Claire Guillaumont, *Évagre le Pontique: Traité pratique, ou le Moine*, SC 171:698–700.

20. *AP* Macarius 32 (PG 65:273; trans. Ward, CS 59:134).

21. "John the Dwarf" (Joannes Nanus) appears in *Verba Seniorum* 1.8, 10.28 (PL 73:855, 917).

22. *AP* John Colobos 2 (PG 65:204–205; trans. my own).

23. *AP* Ammoes 1 (PG 65:125; trans. Ward, CS 59:30).

24. *AP* Ammoes 2 (PG 65:125; trans. Ward, CS 59:30).

25. *AP* John the Theban 1 (PG 65:240; trans. Ward, CS 59:109); "John the Theban" seems to be the same person as "John the Little"; cf. *AP* Ammoes 3 (PG 65:125–128, CS 59:30–31).

26. *AP* John Colobos 36 (PG 65:216; trans. Ward, CS 59:93).

27. *AP* John Colobos 8 (PG 65:205; CS 59:87).

28. *AP* John Colobos 18 (PG 65:209–212; trans. my own).

29. *AP* John Colobos 37 (PG 65:216; trans. my own).

30. *AP* John Colobos 30 (PG 65:213; trans. Ward, CS 59:91).

31. *AP* John Colobos 11 (PG 65:208; CS 59:87).

32. *AP* John Colobos 32 (PG 65:213–216; trans. Ward, CS 59:92). René Draguet discovered a longer narrative which may be the source for this saying; see "À la source de deux apophtegmes (*Jean Colobos 24 et 32*)," *Byzantion* 32 (1962): 53–61. This version sets the story not in John's workshop, but with the two seated together at a community meal. After the confrontation, John abruptly leaves the table and goes out and sits down to his weaving. When confronted by his disciple, John tells him: "It is much preferable, better, fitting, and just not to irritate God and not to displease his holy angels. For it is written: 'I used to speak in the presence of kings and I was not ashamed' (Ps. 118:46). . . . The monk who speaks at table does not differ from a pig or a cat. Doesn't the pig grunt while it eats, and doesn't the cat purr away while it devours its food. I will go the old man's place, I will repent and prostrate, and he will pardon me. He will profit from the lesson and I will find peace. As for you, go back

to your cell without hurt." Cf. *AP* John Colobos 5 (PG 65:205; CS 59:86), in which a talkative camel driver makes him angry.

33. *AP* John Colobos 25 (PG 65:213; trans. my own).

34. *AP* John Colobos 34 (PG 65:216; trans. Ward, CS 59:92).

35. *AP* John Colobos 39 (PG 65:217; trans. Ward, CS 59:39).

36. *AP* John Colobos 3 (PG 65:205; trans. Ward, CS 59:86).

37. *AP* John Colobos 16 (PG 65:209; CS 59:88–89). There are two other allegorical parables listed among his sayings: the parable of the two naked women (*AP* John Colobos 15) and the parable of the philosopher's son (*AP* John Colobos 41 = Supp 1).

38. *AP* John Colobos 40 (PG 65:217–220; trans. Ward, CS 59:94).

39. Thérèse of Lisieux, *Manuscrits autobiographiques*, C f. 141–142 (Lisieux, 1957), 313.

40. *AP* N 43 (ROC 12 [1907]: 174; Columba Stewart, *The World of the Desert Fathers* [Oxford: SLG Press, 1986], 23–24).

41. Lucien Regnault, "Le vrai visage d'un père du désert ou Abba Jean Colobos à travers ses apophtegmes," in *Mémorial André-Jean Festugière: antiquité païenne et chrétienne*, ed. E. Lucchesi and H. D. Saffrey (Geneva: Patrick Cramer, 1984), 232.

42. Evagrius Ponticus, *De oratione* 107 (PG 79:1192; trans. Bamberger, CS 4:73).

43. The account of Moses's background is in Palladius, *Historia Lausiaca* 19 (Butler, 58–59; ACW 34:67–70). Moses is also called "the Robber" in *AP* Arsenius 38 (PG 65:105; CS 59:17). Palladius, *Historia Lausiaca* 39.4 (Butler, 124–125; ACW 34:115–116), speaks of another Moses, Moses the Libyan.

44. Palladius, *Historia Lausiaca* 19 (Butler, 58; trans. Meyer, ACW 34:68).

45. *AP* Moses 3 (PG 65:284; trans. Ward, CS 59:139).

46. *AP* Moses 4 (PG 65:284; trans. my own). Note the term "archbishop" (*archiepiskopos*) found in the saying. Among the clergy of Egypt, only the bishop of Alexandria was spoken of in this way. The bishop of Alexandria at this time would have been Theophilus.

47. *AP* Moses 2 (PG 65:281–284; trans. Ward, CS 59:138–139).

48. *Verba Seniorum* 8.10 (PL 73:907; trans. Chadwick, LCC, 99). *AP* Moses 8 (PG 65:283; CS 59:140), speaks only of Moses calling himself a "fool," not "a fool and a heretic." The Latin version is stronger. It is possible that the editor of the Alphabetical Collection was sensitive about such matters. In *AP* Agathon 5 (PG 65:109; trans. Ward, CS 59:20–21), Agathon allows himself to be called a fornicator and a proud man, and then one who talks nonsense, but he refused to let himself be called a heretic: "The first accusation I take to myself, for that is good for my soul. But heresy is separation from God. Now I have no wish to be separated from God."

49. *AP* Arsenius 38 (PG 65:104–105; trans. Ward, CS 59:17–18).

50. *AP* Macarius 22 (PG 65:272; trans. Ward, CS 59:132).

51. *AP* Moses 13 (PG 65:288; trans. Ward, CS 59:141).

52. *AP* Moses 13 = "Seven Headings," preface (PG 65:287–288n34; trans. Ward, CS 59:141).

53. *AP* Moses 16 = "Seven Headings," no. 3 (PG 65:288; trans. Ward, CS 59:141).

54. *AP* Moses 17 = "Seven Headings," no. 4 (PG 65:288; trans. Ward, CS 59:141).

55. *AP* Moses 10 (PG 65:285; trans. Ward, CS 59:140).

56. *AP* Poemen 166 (PG 65:361; trans. Ward, CS 59:190).

57. *AP* Moses 8 (PG 65:285; trans. Ward, CS 59:140). An anonymous saying, *AP* N 361 (ROC 18 [1913] 137–138; Ward, *Wisdom*, 62), reports an old man having a vision

of cells on fire throughout Scetis. Ominous also is a prophecy associated with Abba Macarius. See *AP* Macarius 5 (PG 65:264; CS 59:128), which, in part, is not very clear, but its reference to "boys" coming to Scetis seems to refer to temptations to pederasty; cf. *AP* Eudemon (PG 65:176; CS 59:64), in which Eudemon says that as a youth he was not allowed to live in Scetis because his "womanish" face would cause "conflict with the enemy."

58. Augustine, *Epistula* 111.1 (CSEL 34:643; FC 18:245). The letter dates from late 409.

59. *AP* Arsenius 21 (PG 65:93; trans. Ward, CS 59:12).

60. *AP* Theodore of Pherme 26 (PG 65:193; CS 59:77).

61. *AP* Anoub 1 (PG 65:129; trans. my own). Cf. *AP* Poemen 198 (=Suppl. 11) (Guy, *Recherches*, 30; CS 59:194). For studies on Poemen, see the bibliography for chapter 7.

62. William Harmless, "Remembering Poemen Remembering: The Desert Fathers and the Spirituality of Memory," *Church History* 69 (2000): 487.

63. *AP* Poemen 1 (PG 65:317).

64. *AP* Poemen 92 (PG 65:344; trans. Ward, CS 59:179–180).

65. This is preserved in the collection of the eleventh-century Byzantine scholar Paul Evergetinos, *Synagôgê tôn theophtoggôn rématôn kai didaskaliôn tôn theophorôn kai hagiôn paterôn* (Athens, 1957–1966), vol. 3, 2B, 22.

66. *AP* Poemen 113 (PG 65:352; trans. Ward, CS 59:183).

67. *AP* Poemen 64 (PG 65:337; trans. Ward, CS 59:175).

68. *AP* Poemen 62 (PG 65:356–357; trans. my own). Cf. *Verba Seniorum* 5.9 (PL 73:876).

69. *AP* Poemen 11 (PG 65:324–325; trans. my own).

70. *AP* Poemen 12 (PG 65:325).

71. *AP* Poemen 144 (PG 65:358; trans. Ward, CS 59:187).

72. *AP* Poemen 108 (PG 65:348; trans. my own).

73. *AP* Poemen 174 (PG 65:364; trans. Ward, CS 59:191).

74. *AP* Poemen 188 (=Suppl. 1) (Guy, *Recherches*, 29; trans. Ward, CS 59:193). Cf. *AP* Poemen 25.

75. *AP* Poemen 63 (PG 65:337; trans. Ward, CS 59:175).

76. *AP* Poemen 27 (PG 65:329; trans. Ward, CS 59:171).

77. *AP* Poemen 160 (PG 65:362; trans. Ward, CS 59:189).

78. *AP* Poemen 35 (PG 65:331; CS 59:172); cf. *AP* Poemen 29, 36, 62, 91, 103, 140, 185.

79. Ethiopic *Collectio Monastica* 13.46 (CSCO 238:95–96; trans. my own).

80. *AP* Poemen 52 (PG 65:333; CS 59:174). This image appears with a different interpretation in Ethiopic *Collectio Monastica* 14.11 (CSCO 238:111).

81. *AP* Poemen 20 (PG 65:328; CS 59:169).

82. *AP* Poemen 57 (PG 65:336; trans. Ward, CS 59:174).

83. *Collectio Monastica* 13.84 (CSCO 238:106; trans. my own). See *AP* Poemen 21 (PG 65:328; CS 59:170), in which similar imagery is used to explain the idea of impure thoughts. Other sayings about watching one's tongue include *AP* Poemen 49, 57, and 84.

84. *AP* Poemen 32 (PG 65:329; CS 59:172).

85. Guy, introduction to *Apophtegmes des Pères*, SC 387:78.

86. A basic list is as follows: Antony (*AP* Poemen 75, 87, 125); Adonias (*AP* Poemen 41); Ammonas (*AP* Poemen 52, 96); Alonois (*AP* Poemen 55); Ammoes (*AP* Ammoes 4); Bessarion (*AP* Poemen 79); Copres (*AP* Copres 1); Dioscorus (*AP* Dios-

corus 2); Isidore the Priest (*AP* Isidore the Priest 5, 6, 10; *AP* Poemen 44); John the Little (*AP* John Kolobos 13, 43, *AP* Poemen 46, 74, 101); Joseph of Panephysis (*AP* Joseph of Panephysis 2, *Verba Seniorum* 10.30); Macarius the Egyptian (*AP* Poemen 25); Moses (*AP* Moses 12; *AP* Poemen 166, *Verba Seniorum* 10.63); Nisterus the Cenobite (*AP* Nisterus 1, 2; *AP* Poemen 131); Paësius (*AP* Poemen 65); Pambo (*AP* Poemen 47, 75, 150); Paphnutius (*AP* Paphnutius 3, *AP* Poemen 190); Pior (*AP* Poemen 85); Simon (*AP* Poemen 137); Sisoes (*AP* Poemen 82, 187); Theonas (*AP* Poemen 151); Timothy (*AP* Poemen 79); and Zacharias (*AP* Zacharias 5).

87. *AP* Antony 4 (PG 65:77; trans. Ward, CS 59:2).

88. *AP* Arsenius 41 (PG 65:105).

89. Chitty, *The Desert a City*, 69–70.

90. Guillaumont, "Le problème des deux Macaires," *Irénikon* 48 (1975): 41–59.

91. *AP* Poemen 125 (PG 65:353; trans. Ward, CS 59:185); cf. *AP* Antony 4 (PG 65: 77).

92. Regnault, "Poemen," in *The Coptic Encyclopedia*, ed. Aziz S. Atiya (New York: Macmillan, 1991), 6:1983–1984.

93. *Collectio Monastica* 13.72 (CSCO 238:101; trans. my own).

94. Zacharias of Sakhâ, *Encomium on the Life of John the Little* 71; for the text, see E. Amélineau, *Histoire des monastères de la Basse-Egypte*, Annales du Musée Guimet 25 (Paris: Leroux, 1894), 379; the translation is by Maged S. Mikail and Tim Vivian, "Zacharias of Sakhâ: An Encomium on the Life of John the Little," *Coptic Church Review* 18, no. 1–2 (1997): 46.

95. *AP* Poemen 90, 183 (PG 65:344, 365–368).

96. *AP* Poemen 105 (PG 65:348; trans. Ward, CS 59:182).

BIBLIOGRAPHY

Macarius the Egyptian

For a valuable discussion of Macarius's place in the *Apophthegmata*, see Antoine Guillaumont, "Macaire L'Égyptien," *Dictionnaire de Spiritualité*, (1980) 10:11–13. On sorting out the confusion in the sources, see Guillaumont's classic article "Le Problème des deux Macaires," *Irénikon* 48 (1975): 41–59.

John the Little

For an introduction, see Jean-Claude Guy, "Jean Colobos ou Le Petit," *Dictionnaire de Spiritualité* 7, pt.2 (1971): 8:390–392. See also:

Draguet, René. "A la source de deux apophtegmes (*Jean Colobos 24 et 32*)." *Byzantion* 32 (1962): 53–61.

Regnault, Lucien. "Le vrai visage d'un père du désert ou Abba Jean Colobos à travers ses apophtegmes." In *Mémorial André-Jean Festugière: Antiquité Païenne et Chrétienne; vingt-cinq études*, ed. E. Lucchesi and H. D. Saffrey, 225–234. Geneva: Patrick Cramer, 1984.

Moses the Ethiopian

For a translation of texts that deal with Moses (except those from Cassian), see Kathleen O'Brien Wicker, "Ethiopian Moses," in *Ascetic Behavior in Greco-Roman Antiquity: A Source book*, ed. Vincent L. Wimbush (Minneapolis: Fortress Press, 1990), 329–348. For an overview, see Vincent L. Wimbush, "Ascetic Behavior and Color-ful Language: Stories about Ethiopian Moses," *Semeia* 58 (= *Discursive Formations, Ascetic Piety, and the Interpretation of Early Christian Literature*) (1992): 81–92. On the role of Moses in the *Conferences* of John Cassian, see Columba Stewart, *Cassian the Monk* (New York: Oxford University Press, 1998), 10, 31–32, and 138–140. On blacks in antiquity, see Peter Frost, "Attitudes towards Blacks in the Early Christian Era," *Second Century* 8 (1991): 1–11; Frank M. Snowden, Jr., *Blacks in Antiquity: Ethiopians in the Greco-Roman Experience* (Cambridge, Mass.: Belknap Press of Harvard University Press, 1970).

Poemen

For a detailed analysis of Poemen, see William Harmless, "Remembering Poemen Remembering: The Desert Fathers and the Spirituality of Memory," *Church History* 69 (2000): 483–518. See also Jeremy Driscoll, "Exegetical Procedures in the Desert Monk Poemen," in *Mysterium Christi: Symbolgegenwort und theologische Bedeutung; Festschrift für Basil Studer*, Studia Anselmiana 116, ed. Magnus Löhrer and Elmar Salmann (Rome: Pontificio Ateneo S. Anselmo, 1995), 155–178.

APPENDIX 7.1

The Famous and Not-So-Famous of the Alphabetical Collection

This chapter focuses on few of the *Apophthegmata*'s figures (Macarius, Moses, John the Little, and Poemen); but there are many others, some 130 in the overall collection. Many are little more than names to us, such as Achilles, Alonius, Pityrion, and Matoes. The editors of the Alphabetical Collection included some figures known from other sources, including famous non-Egyptians who made Egypt their monastic home, such as Evagrius and Cassian. They also included several leading church fathers who had not lived in Egyptian monasteries, such as Basil of Caesarea and Ephrem the Syrian. The inclusion of these "foreigners" is one indication that the final edition of the Alphabetical Collection may have been done not in Egypt, but in Palestine. Here are a few of those who appear in the pages of the collection.

Amoun of Nitria (295–353)

Amoun was the founder of the great monastic settlements of Nitria and Kellia. Together with Antony, Pachomius, and Macarius, he is numbered among the founders of Egyptian monasticism. See chapter 9 (three sayings).

Ammonas (Mid-Fourth Century)

Ammonas was one of Antony's disciples and became a leader at Antony's Outer Mountain (Mount Pispir). He was eventually ordained a bishop. For excerpts of letters attributed to him, see appendix 3.2 (eleven sayings).

Arsenius (354–449)

One of the best educated of the desert fathers; also one of the crustiest. He had served in the imperial palace of Theodosius I, working as tutor to the future emperors Arcadius and Honorius. In 394 he secretly fled Rome and sailed to Alexandria. He eventually settled in Scetis, survived its first destruction in 407, and left after its second in 434 (forty-four sayings).

Basil of Caesarea (330–379)

Basil, one of the great theologians of the early church, was the leader of the Nicenes after Athanasius. He formulated the classic defense of the divinity of Holy Spirit and, together with his friend Gregory of Nazianzus and his brother Gregory of Nyssa, was the architect of the classic doctrine of the Trinity. He created monasteries on his family estates in Pontus and Cappadocia. See chapter 13 for a discussion of his contributions (one saying).

CASSIAN (C. 365–C. 435)

John Cassian settled for some years in Scetis. Around 399, he left Egypt, perhaps because of the Origenist controversy. He eventually settled in southern France, where he authored the *Institutes* and the *Conferences*, works that brought Egyptian monastic spirituality to the Latin West. Cassian is the only Latin-speaking figure in the collection. His works are the focus of chapter 12 (eight sayings).

CRONIUS (D. 386)

Cronius was one of Antony's disciples. He served as Antony's interpreter whenever the latter had Greek-speaking visitors. After Antony's death, he settled in Nitria, was ordained, and had a number of disciples (five sayings).

EPHREM THE SYRIAN (306–373)

Perhaps the greatest poet of the early church, Ephrem composed his works in Syriac. He worked in Nisibis and, after its capture by the Persians in 363, left for Edessa. Many of his works were composed for musical performance during the liturgy. See chapter 13 on Syriac monasticism (three sayings).

EPIPHANIUS OF SALAMIS (C. 315–403)

Epiphanius was a Palestinian but absorbed Egyptian monasticism from his teacher, Abba Hilarion. He became a bishop of Salamis in Cyprus. He was famous as a hunter of heresies, and his most famous work, the *Panarion* (or "Medicine Chest"), is a massive catalog of them. He was a violent opponent of Origenism. It is interesting to find his name alongside men such as Evagrius and Cassian, whose views he would have violently opposed (seventeen sayings).

EVAGRIUS PONTICUS (345–399)

Evagrius was one of the earliest monastic theologians and is best known for formulating the list that would become the Seven Deadly Sins. A native of Pontus, near the Black Sea, he came to Egypt in 383, settling eventually in Kellia where he emerged as a leader of the so-called Origenists. His works are the focus of chapters 10 and 11 (seven sayings).

GREGORY OF NAZIANZUS (329–389)

Gregory was one of the leading theologians of the early church. Together with his friends Basil of Caesarea and Gregory of Nyssa, he was an outspoken defender of Nicaea. He also defended the divinity of the Holy Spirit and became one of the architects of the classic doctrine of the Trinity. He served briefly as bishop of Constantinople and presided over the Council of Constantinople, whose creed is still recited in churches today (two sayings).

LONGINUS (MID-FIFTH CENTURY)

Longinus was abbot of Enaton, a monastery nine miles west of Alexandria, and was one of the most outspoken leaders of the Monophysite resistance to the Council of Chalcedon. His inclusion in the collection has led some scholars to suggest that the *Apophthegmata* itself may have been composed in circles sympathetic to the Monophysite cause (five sayings).

PAMBO (C. 304–375)

Pambo was one of Amoun's early disciples in Nitria. He appears also in Palladius's *Lausiac History*. Prominent Westerners such as Jerome acclaimed him, and he was visited by the aristocratic Melania the Elder at the end of his life (fourteen sayings).

SILVANUS (D. BEFORE 414)

Silvanus was a Palestinian and the leader of a group of monks at Scetis. Around 380, he and his disciples migrated to Sinai. They later moved on to Gaza (twelve sayings).

SISOES (LATE FOURTH CENTURY)

Sisoes was trained at Scetis and claimed to have left there in the 350s because he found it too crowded. After Antony died, he settled on Antony's mountain (fifty-four sayings).

THEODORA (LATE FOURTH–EARLY FIFTH CENTURY)

The Alphabetical Collection lists three desert mothers among its notables: Sarah, Syncletica, and Theodora. Palladius mentions an Amma Theodora who had been the wife of a tribune, was widely consulted by monks, and died at the monastery of Hesychas. See the discussion of her in chapter 13 (ten sayings).

THEOPHILUS OF ALEXANDRIA (D. 412)

Theophilus became bishop of Alexandria in 385. He was famous for leading the violent destruction of pagan temples in Egypt, especially the Serapeum in 391. In 399, he began a fierce persecution of the Origenist party, led by Evagrius and the Four Tall Brothers, and in 403 he engineered the downfall of John Chrysostom as bishop of Constantinople. For a discussion, see chapter 2 (five sayings).

APPENDIX 7.2

The *Virtues of Abba Macarius the Great*

Stories about Macarius the Egyptian abound in later Coptic sources. They probably contain little of value concerning the historical Macarius or his milieu. But they often reflect a remarkable spirituality—though of a much later date. One of the most interesting accounts is the so-called *Virtues of Our Righteous Father, Abba Macarius the Great*, excerpted here. The work portrays Macarius as an advocate of the Jesus Prayer, a prayer in which a monk continually repeats the name of Jesus.

THE JESUS PRAYER AS CHEWING GUM:

Abba Poemen said: "I was seated once with the brothers, near Abba Macarius. I said to him: 'My father, what work can a person do in order that he might acquire life?' The old man said to me: 'I remember that in my childhood, when I was in my father's house, I used to notice that the old women and young girls had something in their mouth, some chewing-gum, that they chewed on in order that it sweeten the saliva in their throat and the bad smell in their mouth, and so moisten and refresh their liver and all their inward parts. If this material thing can produce so much sweetness for those who chew it, how much more can the food of life, the fountain of salvation, the source of living waters, the sweetness of all sweet things, our Lord Jesus Christ, whose precious and blessed name makes demons disappear like smoke when they hear it in our mouth. This blessed name, if we ruminate on it and chew on it constantly, produces a revelation for the intellect, that driver of soul and body. [This prayer] chases all evil thoughts away from the immortal soul and reveals to her the things of the heavens and, above all, reveals him who is on high, our Lord Jesus Christ, King of kings, Lord of Lords, the heavenly reward of those who seek him with all their heart.' " (*Virtues of Abba Macarius the Great* [Amélineau, 133–134])

THE JESUS PRAYER IN STORMY TIMES

Abba Evagrius said: "I went to find Abba Macarius, for I was tormented by thoughts and the passions of the flesh. I said to him: 'My father, say a word, that I might live.' Abba Macarius said to me: 'Bind the rope of the sail to the mast, and by the grace of Our Lord

Jesus Christ, the ship will sail through the devilish winds, the waves of this deceptive sea, and the darkening dusk of this vain world.' I said to him, 'What is the ship? What is the rope? What is the mast?' Abba Macarius said to me: 'The ship—that's your heart. Keep watch over it. The rope—that's your spirit. Tie it to the Our Lord Jesus Christ who is the mast—the mast which has the power over all waves and demonic winds which blow against the saints. But isn't it easy to say with each breath: "My Lord Jesus Christ, have pity on me. I bless you, my Lord Jesus. Help me"? . . . And we, if we are constantly *in* the savior's name, our Lord Jesus Christ, he will grab the devil by the nostrils, because of what he has done to us; and we, who are weak, will know that our help comes from Our Lord Jesus Christ.' " (*Virtues of Abba Macarius the Great* [Amélineau, 160–161])

MACARIUS THE SPIRIT BEARER

At the close of the work, the author puts into the mouth of Abba Poemen an encomium on Macarius. It expresses well the veneration the Coptic tradition has for Macarius:

> Abba Poemen said: "Each time that we would recall Abba Macarius, we could not even say a word except that his thought knew it, because there was a spirit-bearer and a prophetic spirit living in him, as in Elijah and all the other prophets. In effect, he was clothed in humility, as in a double cloak [like the prophet Elisha], by virtue of the Paraclete who was in him. In effect, in the sight [of him] alone filled with the grace of God, the glory of the Lord being on his face, the consolation of the Holy Spirit Paraclete who was in him descended on all those who were seated around him. And when we were filled with happiness, with the joy and with the charm of his talks—invigorating and full of grace—we would go to our dwellings, giving glory to God and to his servant, Abba Macarius, for the glory of the Father, of the Son, and of the Holy Spirit, now and always, until the ages of the ages. Amen." (*Virtues of Abba Macarius the Great* [Amélineau, 204])

The Coptic text is found in E. Amélineau, *Histoire des monastères de la Basse-Égypte*, Annales du Musée Guimet 25 (Paris: E. Leroux, 1894), 118–204. There is a French translation by Antoine Guillaumont in Lucien Regnault, ed., *Les Sentences des Pères du désert: troisième recueil et tables* (Solesmes, 1976), 151–191. The translations here are mine adapted from Guillaumont's version. Much of the work has recently been translated by Tim Vivian, "The Virtues of Saint Macarius (Excerpts)," *Hallel* 24, no. 2 (1999): 116–135, and *Hallel* 25, no. 1 (2000): 1–20.

APPENDIX 7.3

The "Tree of Obedience"

Ancient sources sometimes confused Macarius the Egyptian with Macarius the Alexandrian even though they had quite different personalities and lived in different monastic settlements. A similar confusion surrounds one of the most famous stories in the *Apophthegmata Patrum*: the story of the so-called Tree of Obedience. The Alphabetical Collection lists the story as the first entry under the name of John the Little.

ACCOUNT FOUND IN THE *APOPHTHEGMATA*

It was said of Abba John the Dwarf that he withdrew and lived in the desert at Scetis with an old man of Thebes. His abba, taking a piece of dry wood, planted it and said to him, "Water it every day with a bottle of water, until it bears fruit." Now the water was so far away that he had to leave in the evening and return the following morning. At the end of three years the wood came to life and bore fruit. Then the old man took some of the fruit and carried it to the church saying to the brethren, "Take and eat the fruit of obedience." (*AP* John Colobos 1 [PG 65:204; trans. Ward, CS 59:85–86])

However, we have earlier versions of the story. In the early fifth century, the story circulated in the Latin West. Sulpicius Severus (d. c.420) in his *Dialogue* cited it as a model of the obedience demanded in the monasteries of Egypt. But he gave no names. And in his account, the dead-stick-turned-tree was growing in the courtyard of a monastery just two miles from the Nile. Scetis, of course, was much farther away from the river.

ACCOUNT FOUND IN JOHN CASSIAN'S *INSTITUTES*

John Cassian, who had actually lived at Scetis in the 390s, tells a rather different version of the story.

This book is about the training of one who renounces the world so that—starting out with true humility and perfect obedience—he might be able to move on and reach perfection in all the virtues. Because of this, I believe it necessary to set out, by way of example, certain deeds of the elders who excelled in this virtue [of obedience]. . . . First of all, Abba John, who lived near Lyco[polis], a town in the Thebaid and who, because of his obedience, was lifted up to the

grace of prophecy and shined brilliantly through the whole world.
. . . And so this blessed John—from his youth to the full maturity of
manhood—remained as a servant to an old man as long as the latter
lived, and carried out his commands with such humility that the old
man himself was completely amazed at his obedience. The old man
wanted to make sure whether this virtue came from genuine faith
and profound simplicity of heart, or it was put on. . . . So he fairly
often ordered John to do superfluous or unnecessary things, even
impossible ones. . . . [For example,] the old man took from his wood-
pile a stick that had been cut down a long time before . . . —it was
not just dry, but a bit rotten. And when he had stuck it into the
ground right in front of him, he ordered him to water it twice a day,
so that this moistening might make it take root and, once revived
into the tree it had once been, its outstretched branches would offer
a pleasant sight and some shade for those who might sit under it in
the heat of the day. And accepting this command with his usual respect and without taking into any account its impossibility, the
young man followed through on it every day. He carried the water
the distance of two good miles, and never ceased to water the stick
all year—not even because of physical fatigue or the celebration of
some feast, or any other urgent business which might have legiti-
mately excused him from doing it—not even the rigors of winter
could stop him from following this order. And without saying anything, the old man used to secretly examine John's zeal each day
and used to see the way John observed the command in complete
simplicity of heart—as though coming from God—and did so without any change of expression on his face, and without bringing up
any question about it. Once convinced of John's humble and sincere
obedience, at the same time recognizing how long [had been] the hard-
work which had been carried out through the whole year with great
fervor, he came over to the dry stick and said: "John, has this tree
put down roots or not?" And when the other said that he did not
know, the old man, making it seem like he was checking the truth
of the matter and trying to see if the roots had taken hold, pulled up
the stick. He then threw it away and told him to stop watering it any
more. (*Institutes* IV.23–24 [SC 109:154–157]; trans. my own)

Notice the key differences. The stick was watered one year, not three. And
the charming legendary ending is missing. The abba who demanded the test
of obedience simply pulled it up and threw it away. And the obedient disciple
is not John the Little but another famous monastic figure, John of Lycopolis.
Scholars presume that Cassian was closer in time to the event and may be the
more dependable reporter; some scholars, suspicious of the accuracy of the
Apophthegmata, point to this story as evidence of their skepticism.

APPENDIX 7.4

Zacharias of Sakhâ, *Encomium on the Life of John the Little*

Later Coptic writers looked back on John the Little as one of the founding fathers of desert monasticism. Zacharias, the eighth-century bishop of Sakhâ, had lived for a time at the monastery of John the Little in Scetis and decided to compose an "encomium" to celebrate the memory of John's words and deeds. Zacharias's work draws heavily upon anecdotes and sayings found in the *Apophthegmata*, but he creates a continuous narrative, closer in tone and style to that of the *Life of Antony*. Zacharias says that his major source is a text entitled *Paradise*.

A BOOK CALLED "PARADISE"

> Even more, we will know clearly by rightly seeking after in the book of the holy elders in which they narrated the history of this saint whom we celebrate today. This book they have appropriately called "*Paradise*"; it is very fitting that they have called it by this name because the list of saints enrolled in this spiritual paradise, this great paradise of joy, has been completely filled. Furthermore, up to the present and until the consummation of this age, this unique book will not cease preparing souls as gifts to God, those persons who live rightly and who will receive from it knowledge in true discernment in order to become altars of the Holy Spirit and obtain the inheritance of eternal life through emulating the works and saving labors of the luminaries who are written therein. (Zacharias of Sakhâ, *Encomium on the Life of John the Little* 1)

Was this *Paradise* a Coptic version of the *Apophthegmata*? Possibly. The sixth–seventh-century Syriac version of the *Apophthegmata* is entitled "Paradise of the Fathers." Zacharias goes on to list the figures found in his source, most of whom are also found in the *Apophthegmata*: Antony, Macarius the Egyptian, Moses, Poemen, Arsenius, and others. However, this lost Coptic *Paradise*, unlike the Greek *Apophthegmata*, included the leading figures from the Pachomian literature: not only Pachomius himself, but also Palamon, Theodore, Horsiesius, and Petronius. Twenty-nine of the text's eighty paragraphs have exact parallels in the *Apophthegmata*. However, Zacharias also offers striking anecdotes about John that have no known parallel in the *Apophthegmata*, a few examples of which are given here.

CALL TO SCETIS

With regard to our thrice-blessed father the priest and hegumen Abba John the Little, it is said, my beloved, that his family was from a village in the region of Pemje [= Oxyrhynchus], the famous city of upper Egypt whose name is Tsê; but with regard to noble and exalted virtue, he is a metropolitan of heaven. According to wealth and plenty of this life he was indeed poor, for he was of the poorest. . . . [God] set him apart from the time he was in the womb of his mother and he chose him especially from the time he was eighteen years old. God also spoke with him spiritually through the power of spiritual perception, saying to him, "Leave your land and your family! Come to the Mountain of Natron, that is, Scetis; there, as its name indicates, hearts and thoughts are weighed by true discernment; the place where spiritual salt seasons souls with perfect peace; the place of the wisdom, knowledge, and theological understanding of the orthodox doctrines of the trinitarian and apostolic faith; the place of full instruction in angelic piety. From there rises incense from the pure chosen altars, that is, the souls of the saints, those who are pure in my presence. And once again it will be acceptable to me because of you." (Zacharias of Sakhâ, *Encomium on the Life of John the Little* 2–3)

ALL-NIGHT MYSTICAL ADVISING

[John] had received prior knowledge, and a spirit of prophecy; he saw from afar and spoke with the brothers mystically of what was, what will be, and what is in the present, as his speech richly overflowed with the grace of the Lord. As a result, whenever a brother came to our father Abba John at dusk to ask him about what is profitable for a soul, they spoke about virtue until they noticed the first light of morning. (Zacharias of Sakhâ, *Encomium on the Life of John the Little* 56)

THE BARBARIANS AND HUMAN DIGNITY

Many days after he returned from Alexandria, the barbarians ruled Scetis with tyrannical and despicable deeds, it was said, destroying the peace, tranquility, and way of life of our fathers with their animalistic ways, threatening the monks and destroying the holy places. . . . As our holy father was making haste to leave Scetis, it is said that all the brothers tearfully surrounded him, saying to him, "Will you also leave, our father? Are you afraid of the barbarians?" Our holy father Abba John answered them, "By the name of Christ God, I am not afraid. No, the perfect goodness in God's presence does not allow each of us to pursue his own salvation alone; instead, according to an angelic purpose, each of us, especially the devout person, performs all his deeds while regarding his own good and that of his brother equally. This barbarian, even if he is separated from me by faith, nevertheless is an image and creature of God in the same way that I am. If I resist this barbarian he will kill me and will go to punishment because of me." And with these words he left Scetis. (Zacharias of Sakhâ, *Encomium on the Life of John the Little* 76–77)

For the Coptic text, see E. Amélineau, *Histoire des monastères de la Basse-Égypte,* Annales du Musée Guimet 25 (Paris: Leroux, 1894), 316–413. The translation here is from Maged S. Mikail and Tim Vivian, "Zacharias of Sakhâ: *An Encomium on the Life of John the Little,*" *Coptic Church Review* 18, no.1–2 (1997): 1–64.

8

The *Apophthegmata Patrum*: Themes

Reading the Alphabetical Collection can lead one to focus on colorful personalities, the way we did in the last chapter with Macarius, John the Little, Moses, and Poemen. Reading the Systematic Collection leads one to focus on themes. Here I will survey some key ones that wind their way through the collection: interior stillness (*hesychia*), thoughts (*logismoi*), sexuality, anger, compunction (*penthos*), visions, and scripture. The choice comes in part from the organization of the Systematic Collection itself, and in part from perspectives explored by recent scholarship.

The term "Systematic Collection" is a misnomer, for the *Apophthegmata* really defies system (for an outline, see appendix 8.1). It never systematically examines a topic the way, for instance, theologians of the time analyzed issues in the trinitarian controversy. Rather, the *Apophthegmata* has stock themes to which the different elders return again and again. A musical analogy may be more appropriate: the *Apophthegmata* is a polyphony of solo voices that sometimes combine, sometimes diverge, sometimes even clash around a core of favored motifs. The *Apophthegmata* does not have one theology of the monastic life, but many.[1] Certain issues it touches upon, such as fasting or methods of prayer, received more thorough, even systematic, treatment in other monastic authors, some who predate it (Evagrius Ponticus, John Cassian, and Isaiah of Scetis) and some who post-date it (Dorotheos and John Climacus). It is always a temptation, given the undoubted poignancy of certain stories and sayings, to overgeneralize instead of hearing a given saying as one voice among many. The challenge is to hear the polyphony.

Hesychia

Once a brother came to Scetis and asked Abba Moses for a "word." Moses answered, "Go, stay inside your cell, and your cell will teach you all things."[2] The command was a common one. Again and again, monks were sent by their *abba* back to the solitary center of their solitary lives. Life in the cell could be excruciating, a place of loneliness, temptation, boredom. One of the anonymous sayings expresses it in biblical imagery: "The monk's cell is the furnace of Babylon, in which the three children saw the Son of God, and it is the pillar of cloud from which God spoke to Moses."[3] The temptation was always to leave, to flee the testing and to lose sight that it is precisely in the "furnace" of the cell that one sees the Son of God. That is why the admonition was always to return. One of Antony's best-known sayings puts it this way: "Fish die if they stay a long time out of water. In the same way, monks who hang around outside their cells or who waste time with worldly people lose the intensity of their peace [*hesychia*]. We have to rush back to our cells—like fish to the sea—for fear we will forget our inner vigilance if we stay outside too long."[4]

In the cell the monk became what he was called to be: a solitary. That, after all, is what "monk," *monachos*, means: one who is alone (from *monos*).[5] The cell was the outward architectural expression of an inner solitude of heart (see appendix 8.2). As Abba Alonius put it, "Unless a person says in his heart, 'there are only God and I in the world,' he will not have peace."[6] This solitude meant, in part, a flight even from other monks. Once Abba Macarius dismissed the assembly at Scetis with the words: "Flee, brothers." It seemed an absurd command. One of the elders asked him, "Where should we flee to beyond this desert?" Macarius put his finger to his lips—a sssssh-ing—and said, "Flee that." He then went to his cell, closed the door, and sat down.[7]

The flight from others, the entry into the solitude of the cell, was only a starting point. The real goal was what the desert fathers called *hesychia*, "quiet," a graced depth of inner stillness. It is no accident that *hesychia* serves as the title of one of the opening chapters of the Systematic Collection. A brief exposition is found in a saying attributed to Abba Rufus. When asked about *hesychia*, he responded:

> Interior stillness [*hesychia*] means to remain sitting in one's cell with fear and knowledge of God, holding far off the remembrance of wrongs suffered and pride of spirit. Such interior peace brings forth all the virtues, preserves the monk from the burning darts of the enemy, and does not allow him to be wounded by them. Yes, brother, acquire it. Keep in mind your future death, remembering that you do not know at what hour the thief will come. Likewise be watchful over your soul.[8]

This is a terse compendium of desert spirituality. Note especially the last phrase. The desert fathers, in their meditation, sought to be "watchful" over their "thoughts," that steady stream of memories, desires, and fears that run continually through us. These "thoughts" (*logismoi*) surfaced as the monks went about their solitary routine in the cell, in the back-and-forth rhythm of manual work and prayer. Within that alternating rhythm, the monk tried to stay interiorly watchful. But often "thoughts" surfaced, distracting the monk and derailing his peace of soul. These "thoughts" could even become obsessive. Note the one Rufus cites: ruminating on memories of past wrongs done. These he advises putting "far off"—no easy task given the lack of distraction in the desert. And Rufus echoes the advice Antony gave in the *Life*: to keep one's mortality always before one's eyes; or the counsel Macarius gave to Evagrius: to live each day as though it were one's last.

But the key is Rufus's opening phrase: "the fear and knowledge of God." The search is ultimately for that awe, that depth of reverence, encapsulated in the biblical phrase "fear of God." This "fear" is at the same time a "knowledge," a *gnosis*, that comes from encountering the divine. A couple of sayings from Abba Isaiah touch on this. When a monk asked Abba Isaiah, "How should one practice *hesychia* in the cell?" he responded, "*Hesychia* in the cell: That means to throw oneself down in the presence of God and to do everything possible to resist every thought sown by the enemy; that is what it is to flee the world." In another saying, he remarks that "one living in stillness needs three things: to fear God without ceasing, to pray with constancy, and never to release one's heart from the memory of God."[9]

The Manifestation of Thoughts

Abba Poemen once remarked that "a man may remain for a hundred years in his cell without learning how to live in the cell."[10] The art of learning to live in the cell came from the guidance he gained from the *abba*. The cell was the crucible where the monk did his interior work. But what happened to him there, particularly if he was young or new to the desert, he was expected to discuss with an *abba*. This was the discipline of the "manifestation of thoughts."

The practice sounds very much like private confession. And in a sense, it was. But it was also very different. It differed from later sacramental practice in certain obvious ways. First, the *abba* was not necessarily, or even usually, a priest. Wisdom, not ordination, was what counted. Second, while the *abba* might have prayed before dismissing the monk, it was not a liturgical prayer signaling absolution or formal reconciliation.

Third, and most important, the conversation between monk and *abba* centered not on sins per se, but on *logismoi*, on "thoughts." In the vocabulary of the desert, the term "thoughts" tended to have negative connotations (see appendix 8.3). It might include temptations, but just as often, it might be any preoccupation, something the monk might not be able to get off his mind. A "thought" could simply be a desire or a feeling, innocent enough in itself, such as missing one's family or wanting to go explore the nearby desert, feeling stung by someone's gossip or simply wondering what it really took to be a monk. The *abba* helped the monk discern the "thought," whether it was good, evil, or neutral, whether it should be acted upon, ignored, or fought against. This dynamic was not so much private confession as spiritual direction. Even this terminology is a bit misleading, for the *abba* did not "direct" the monk. As Columba Stewart has noted:

> The whole life was about opening up: of self to another and of the self to God, with no obsessive concentration on the self or on the relationship with one's abba. . . . Perhaps another way to understand this is to remember that it was the commitment to truth, to seeing things as they are, which disposed the monk for contemplation of God. . . . To see fantasy, projections and pious wishes, depends in the first place upon stripping away the mask of fantasies and projections about ourselves. We find that the masks we place on ourselves and the masks we see on the face of God are, in the end, the same, and are of our own making. The goal of the elder was utter transparence to divine light. The elder, far from being a centre of power and a "director," served in his or her transparence to divine light as a lens which focuses the light of truth on the dark places in the disciple's heart.[11]

The monk was expected to manifest his "thoughts" regularly. Abba Paphnutius reports that he went to see elders twice a month, walking some twelve miles; and Abba John the Little used to sit in front of the church on weekends so that monks might approach him about their "thoughts."[12] But emergency consultations could take place anytime. Some stories mention monks coming a couple of times during a single night.[13]

While many stories in the *Apophthegmata* allude to the practice, few describe the actual experience in such vivid detail as the following story about Abba Zeno.

> When I was young, I had this experience. I had a passion in my soul which mastered me. Having heard it said that Abba Zeno had healed many, I wanted to go find him and open myself to him. But the devil prevented me from doing so, saying, "Since you know what you must do, conduct yourself according to what you have read. Why go and scandalize the old man?" Each time that I was ready to go to him, the warfare in me abated to see the old man, and I did not go. And when I had given up the idea of going to see the old man, once more the passion would assail me. I would begin to fight in order to leave, and the enemy would deceive me by the same trick and would not let me open myself to the old man. Often I would actually go to the old man in order to tell him everything, but the enemy would not let me speak by putting shame in my heart and saying to me, "Since you know how to heal yourself, what is the point of speaking about it? You are not giving yourself enough credit: you know what the fathers have taught." Such is what the adversary

suggested to me so that I would not reveal my sickness to the physician and be healed. . . . [Finally] I went and found no other person there. The old man, as was his custom, gave me some teaching about the salvation of the soul and the ways of cleansing oneself of impure thoughts. But once more I was ashamed, and I did not open up. I asked him for his blessing. The old man got up, said a prayer, and led me to the door. He walked ahead of me, and meanwhile I was tormented by my thoughts. Would I speak to the old man, or would I not? I walked a little behind him without his paying me any attention. He put his hand to the door to open it for me, but when he saw me tormented by my thoughts, he turned towards me, tapped me on the chest, and said: "What is the matter with you? Am I not a man, too?" When the old man said this to me, I thought that he had uncovered my heart. I prostrated myself at his feet begging him with tears, saying, "Have pity on me." He said to me, "What is the matter with you?" I told him, "You know what it is, what is the use of saying it?" He said to me, "It is you who must say what is the matter with you." Covered with shame, I made known to him my passion, and he said to me: "Am I not a man too? Do you want me to tell you what I know? That you have been coming here for three years with these thoughts and you have not let them out." I prostrated myself, begged and said, "For the Lord's sake, have pity on me." He said to me, "Go, do not neglect your prayer, and do not speak ill of anyone." I returned to my cell, and did not neglect my prayer; and by the grace of Christ and by the prayers of the man, I was bothered no longer by that passion.[14]

This account has several interesting features. First, the monk noted that Abba Zeno had the custom of giving "some teaching about the salvation of the soul." This confirms what other literature from the desert, such as Abba Isaiah's *Asceticon* or Cassian's *Conferences*, shows: these *abbas* spoke not just in snappy one-liners. The *Apophthegmata* sometimes gives that impression. But they could also expound things at length and in a more formal didactic fashion.

Second, the narrator shows astute self-observation: the "warfare," he says, would abate whenever he was ready to reveal his "passion." He identifies other mechanisms of the unconscious: patterns of rationalization and of denial, and the flight from shame. He had apparently been trained in introspection, for Zeno had taught him how to "cleanse" himself of "impure thoughts."

Third, the *abba* displays remarkable skill in discernment. Zeno waited a long time, three full years, before he acted. And when he did, it was gentle, yet pointed: a tap on the chest and the words "Am I not a man too?" The reaction he evoked was cathartic: "I thought he had uncovered my heart." Yet Zeno's ability to uncover the monk's heart came, in the end, from admitting his own vulnerability: "Am I not a man too?"

Finally, there was Zeno's insistence that healing came from speaking. This sprang from a central desert insight. As Abba Isaiah of Scetis put it, "The man who will not reveal his thoughts finds them marshaled against him; but the man who speaks out with confidence before his fathers puts these thoughts to flight, and wins himself peace."[15]

The exchange between Zeno and his disciple illustrates the high drama of the manifestation of "thoughts." More often, troubling "thoughts" sprang from the ordinary tensions of human community. Once a brother was owed some money by another monk. The matter bothered him, and so he consulted Abba Poemen. Poemen told him to go ahead and ask the monk for the money, but just once. The brother then complained, "What shall I do, for I cannot control my thought?" Abba Poemen's reply was pointed: "Never mind your thought— just do not trouble your brother."[16] Poemen and the desert fathers recognized that the battle with "thoughts" was not an end in itself. And it was not about self-actualization. It was about becoming human and becoming Christian, and that meant charity before all else.

The Demon of Lust

One early term used for monks was *apotaktikoi*, "renouncers." They lived lives in which they renounced career, status, property, marriage, and family. This was not a new gesture. Ascetic renouncers, both male and female, had long held an esteemed place in Christian communities in Alexandria and through-out the empire. Athanasius once proclaimed that such sexual renunciation was made possible by the miracle of the Incarnation: "The Son of God, our Lord and Savior Jesus Christ, having become human on our account, and having destroyed death and delivered our race from the bondage to corruption, in addition to all his other benefits bestowed this also: that we should possess upon earth the state of virginity as an image of the angels' holiness."[17] The new element introduced by the desert fathers was not sexual renunciation as such, but the setting: the desert. No longer was this "image of the angels' holiness" simply a fixture within the urban Christian community. The angels had moved out to the desert, so to speak, and formed frontier colonies in the waterless, lifeless wastes.

Sexuality and its renunciation form a persistent thread within the *Apo-phthegmata*. In its stories and sayings, we hear snippets of how the monks themselves spoke of their renunciation. We find troubling sexual stereotypes, an often unyielding stress on repression, and an unwillingness to affirm the goodness and dignity of sexuality. Still, it is important to try to pitch one's ear to hear the ascetics speaking to their world, not ours.

Peter Brown, in a landmark study, *The Body and Society: Men, Women, and Sexual Renunciation in Early Christianity*, has noted the distinct contours that sexual renunciation took among the monks: "The problems of sexual temp-tation were most often seen in terms of the massive antithesis of 'desert' and 'world.' Sexual temptation was frequently treated in a somewhat offhand man-ner, presented as if it were not more than a drive toward women, toward mat-rimony, and hence toward fateful conscription, through marriage, into the structures of the settled land."[18] Brown's insight is best illustrated by a humorous story told about Abba Olympius. Olympius was haunted by a "thought": "Go, and take a wife." He decided to test out the impulse. He did not return to his home village, but instead got some mud and made a large mud statue of a woman. He said to himself: "Here is your wife. Now you must work hard in order to feed her." So he began working longer and harder. The next day, he got some more mud and shaped it into a baby girl. He said to himself: "Your wife has had a child. You must work harder to feed her and to clothe your child." And so he stepped up his work output. He found himself exhausted. In his inner self, his thoughts finally answered him: "If you cannot bear such weariness, stop wanting a wife." And so at story's end, the *Apophthegmata* records that "God, seeing his efforts, took away the conflict from him and he was at peace."[19] This anecdote is brutally unromantic. But it reveals how marriage might look to a fourth-century Egyptian peasant: a wife meant hard work; children meant even more work.

The *Apophthegmata* makes no attempt to gloss over things. It documents sexual lapses as a not unexpected fact of desert living. One story, for example, tells of two monks who had gone to town to sell their handiwork. Once in town, the two separated, each going his own way. After finishing their business dealings, they got back together. But one was suddenly very reluctant to return to the desert. When the other asked about the sudden change of heart, the first confessed that he had met a woman and slept with her. So the other, to win over his friend, claimed that the same thing had happened to him. In fact, he was innocent, but he told his friend, "Let's go and do penance intensely, and God will forgive us." And so the two returned to the desert and did penance, one for his sin, the other for the sake of his fellow monk.[20]

Sexual escapades took place even in the desert itself. Abba Ammonas, a bishop and onetime disciple of Antony, was once making the rounds of his jurisdiction. A group of monks asked him to intervene because they were convinced that they had caught red-handed a monk suspected of keeping a mistress. In fact, they had. But the monk quickly hid the woman in a large cask just before Ammonas and the other monks entered his cell. Ammonas immediately realized where the woman was hidden and sat himself on the cask. The other monks meanwhile scurried about, searching everywhere, but to no effect. So Ammonas dealt curtly with the monks who had judged their brother so harshly: "May God forgive you!" He then prayed and sent them out. He then turned to the monk with the mistress: "Brother, be on your guard." He then left.[21]

There were also problems with homosexuality and pederasty. Among the monks there were a certain number who were young teenage boys. Zacharias, for instance, had accompanied his father Carion to Scetis. These young men posed a serious temptation to some. Abba Eudemon, who had been quite young when he first applied to be a monk, was sent away in no uncertain terms by Abba Paphnutius. Paphnutius, who at the time was "Father of Scetis," told him: "I do not allow the face of a woman to dwell in Scetis, because of the conflict with the enemy."[22] John the Little warned his disciples of the dangers of pederasty: "One who stuffs himself and talks with a boy has already committed fornication with him in thought."[23] And even the normally compassionate Poemen did not mince words on the severity of this: "A man who lives with a boy, and is incited by him to no matter what passions of the old man, and yet keeps him with him, that man is like someone who has a field which is eaten up with maggots."[24]

The "demon of lust" figures among one of the routine "thoughts" discussed between abba and disciple. As Brown notes, "This did not mean that most ascetic spiritual guides treated sexual temptation as uniquely alarming. Far from it: sexual desire was frequently overshadowed, as a source of spiritual danger, by the dull aches of pride and resentment and by dread onslaughts of immoderate spiritual ambition."[25] The desert fathers often described the struggle in athletic metaphors: "In the world there are those who fight in the arena. . . . Often, a single athlete is struck by two others and, invigorated by the blows, he overcomes those who are hitting him. . . . Act with vigor, therefore, and God will fight for you against the enemy."[26] This macho strategy of "toughing out" the demon even appears in the mouth of Amma Sarah, one of three women listed in the *Apophthegmata*. She supposedly battled with fornication for some thirteen years and yet "she never prayed that the battle should wane, but only used to say: 'O my God, strengthen me.' "[27] There was standard advice: don't hide it, reveal the battle to the elders. One story tells of a monk who one night came back again and again to his *abba*.[28] Another routine bit of advice was to "watch your belly," for failure in fasting was seen as the doorway to unleash other passions. As John the Little put it, "If a man is earnest in fasting and hunger, the enemies which trouble his soul will grow weak."[29]

This stock ascetical advice could backfire. Once a widower was haunted by the memory of his wife. He told the elders of his struggles, and they imposed on him a harsh discipline. It had little effect, but left him so weak that he could not even stand. A venerable foreign monk happened to come to Scetis "by the Providence of God," as the *Apophthegmata* puts it, and knocked on the monk's door. He was surprised to find it open and went in and discovered the monk terribly weakened. When the widower explained his case, the foreigner gently contradicted the elders and advised him to put their harsh "medicine" aside:

> The fathers are powerful men, and did well in laying these burdens
> upon you. But if you will listen to me who am but a child in these
> matters, stop all this discipline, take a little food at the proper times,
> recover your strength, join in the worship of God for a little, and
> turn your mind to the Lord—for this is a thing you cannot conquer
> by your own efforts. The human body is like a coat. If you treat it
> carefully, it will last a long time. If you neglect it, it will fall into tat-
> ters.[30]

Such common sense was the desert tradition at its best. But often this "cloak" of the body was pushed to the limit by the athleticism of the desert.

Some stories record gestures that shock modern sensibilities. A monk at

Scetis had been plagued by seductive memories of the wife he had left behind. When he got word of his wife's death, he slipped back to his home village at night and went to where she was buried. He dug up the gravesite and wiped the blood of her corpse on his cloak. He returned to the desert, and the cloak began to smell horribly. And so when he faced temptation to lust, he put the smelly cloak before himself and told himself, "Look, this is what you desire. You have it now, fill yourself."[31]

An equally disturbing story tells of a prostitute who made a bet with some young men in town that she could seduce an old hermit. That night, she wandered out to the desert and knocked on the hermit's door, pretending to be lost and frightened. So he took her in. While he felt sorry for her, he also burned with desire. So he lit a lamp and said to himself, "People who do things like this go into the torment [of hell]. Test yourself, and see whether you can bear a fire which is everlasting." So he stuck his finger in the fire, but felt no pain, only lust. So through the night, he burned one finger after another. The woman, terrified as she watched, lay rigid in the monk's cell. The next morning, the young men came out from the town to see what had happened. When they asked the monk about the woman, he pointed them to her saying she was asleep. But they found her dead. Then he turned back his cloak and showed them his hands: "Look what that child of the devil had done to me. She has cost me every finger I possess." The desert fathers did not end this morality tale on a negative note. Supposedly the monk admitted that it was wrong to render evil for evil, and so he prayed and raised the woman from the dead. She, of course, was converted and lived chastely ever after.[32]

As Brown notes, "Many of the ugly stories that circulated in monastic circles in the fourth and fifth centuries would have struck contemporaries as banal. They were culled from the extensive rubbish heap of Near Eastern misogyny."[33] Women often appear as little more than irresistible objects of desire or villainous vixens.

What was new was not such tales and the attitudes they encapsulate. Rather, it was the way the desert fathers began to identify the depth and persistence of sexual "thoughts." They did not see sexual fantasy as the most dangerous of the "thoughts." Rather, its pervasiveness and resilience served, as Brown has noted, "as barium-traces, by which the Desert Fathers mapped out the deepest and most private recesses of the will." And Brown adds:

> What mattered . . . was a sharpened awareness of the permanence of sexual fantasy. Because of this observed quality of permanence, sexual desire was now treated as effectively coextensive with human nature. Abiding awareness of the self as a sexual being, forever subject to sexual longings, and troubled—even in dreams—by sexual fantasies highlighted the areas of intractability in the human. But this intractability was not simply physical. It pointed into the very depth of the soul. Sexual desire revealed the knot of unsurrendered privacy

that lay at the very heart of fallen man. Thus, in the new language of the desert, sexuality became, as it were, an ideogram of the unopened heart.[34]

Anger

In their desert "cities," the monks wanted to create a new world. They sought a harmony of human relations free of the greedy grasping that pervaded the towns and villages they had left behind. Some stories gently mock their former world. One tells of two old men who had lived together many years and never fought. One said to the other, "Let's have an argument like other people do." But the other said, "I don't know how to have an argument." So the first told him, "Look, I'll put a brick between us. Then I'll say, 'That's mine.' Then you say, 'No, it's mine.' " So the first monk put the brick between them and started the argument: "That's mine." The second played his part: "No, it's mine." The first immediately relented: "Okay, it's yours. Take it." So the two gave up, unable to argue.[35]

This quaintly expressed the desert ideal. But the reality was otherwise. Modern readers often imagine that for monks, sexuality posed *the* great struggle. But ancient sources indicate otherwise. Anger, not sex, figured more prominently. The challenge was human relations.[36]

The world the desert fathers had left behind had intricate codes of retribution and vengeance. Augustine tells how such codes even crept into the piety of ordinary urban Christians: "Each day people come to church. They bend their knees, touch the earth with their foreheads, sometimes moistening their faces with tears. And in all this great humility and anguish, they pray: 'Lord, avenge me. Kill my enemy.' "[37]

Although the desert fathers had withdrawn from normal town and village life, they could not as easily abandon its fierce ethic. One story tells of a monk who had been the victim of some injustice. He went to Abba Sisoes and told him that he was going to get his revenge. Sisoes did not deny that the monk had been wronged, but begged him to leave vengeance to God. But the brother was adamant: "I cannot rest until I get vengeance." So Sisoes told him, "My brother, let's pray." Raising up his hands, Sisoes prayed, "God, we don't need you. We can avenge ourselves." The brother heard Sisoes's prayer and fell at the old man's feet and begged forgiveness.[38] He recognized in that instant that anger and vengeance presupposes a godless world, a world in which the crude violence of human justice replaces the wisdom of God's.

Prominent figures mention their battles with anger. Abba Isidore the Priest once went to market to sell his goods, but when he felt anger overwhelming him, he fled; John the Little dropped his handiwork on the road, furious with some talkative camel driver.[39] Abba Ammonas admitted the depth of his struggle: "I have spent fourteen years at Scetis asking God night and day that he give me the grace to conquer anger."[40]

Anger sometimes erupted among the monks themselves because of harsh or hurtful remarks. Some monks once saw Abba Achillas spitting blood out of his mouth. When asked about it, Achillas answered, "It was the words of a brother who had hurt me. I fought not to let him know it, and I begged God to take them away from me. And the words became blood in my mouth and I spit it out. Now I am peaceful and have forgotten the hurt."[41]

In the *Apophthegmata*, one finds frequent admonitions against the loose tongue. The desert fathers recognized how easily gossip could rend the fabric of a community. Abba Hyperechius, for instance, compared the whisperings of a gossip to the whisperings of the serpent that drove Eve from Paradise.[42] And he insisted that it was better to eat meat and drink wine than to feast on a brother's flesh with slander.[43] Of course, the desert fathers recognized that one did not always need words to strike out at one's neighbor. As Abba Isaiah once put it, "When someone wants to render evil for evil, he can hurt his brother with a single nod of his head."[44]

One tactic was to flee into greater solitude. There is a story of a monk who was often angry and became convinced that the solution was to leave his desert community: "I will go, and live somewhere by myself. And since I shall be able to talk or listen to no one, I shall be tranquil, and my passionate anger will cease." So he went out further into the desert and took up residence in a cave. One day, he went to fill his terra-cotta jug with water. When he set it down, it fell over and the water spilled out. He refilled it. Again it fell over. A third time he filled it and a third time it spilled. He went into a rage. He picked up the water jug and flung it down. When it shattered, he came to his senses. He recognized that the battle lay not with others, but with himself. So he packed up his things and returned to his old community.[45]

The desert fathers recognized that a nonviolent world began with a nonviolent heart. Once a monk asked Abba Poemen how not to repay for evil for evil. Poemen explained that passion—of which anger was one kind—had four levels. First it welled up from the heart; then it flashed into visibility in the face; it might then come to expression in words; finally it played itself out as evil in deeds. So he advised that one get to the root of the problem, the heart, and seek to purify it. But Poemen was a pragmatist. He knew such interior purification was not always possible. And his concern was to stop the last step: evil acts. So he advised that if anger flashes across one's face, don't speak; if one must speak, then cut short the conversation.[46] Poemen did not hold to what one hears among talk-show psychologists: that it is best to let it all out, to stand one's ground, and if necessary get in someone's face. For him and the desert fathers, the first step toward a less violent world was silence, biting one's tongue. But the real solution was interior, locating the inner fury in the heart.

In the *Apophthegmata*, discussion of anger often appears under the heading of self-mastery. But the desert fathers sometimes located the antidote to anger's fury in the virtue of humility. As Graham Gould has noted, they thought of humility as "the capacity to resolve situations of conflict by renouncing your own right to expect reparation or penitence when you have a grievance against someone."[47] This is best summed up in one of the anonymous sayings.

When an old man was asked what humility was, he answered: "If you forgive a brother who has wronged you *before* he is penitent towards you."[48]

Blessed Are the Sorrowful

Earlier I pointed out how manifesting "thoughts" differed from private confession. I should now add: the roots of private confession do lie in this practice, at least in part. At the end of the sixth century, when Irish monks worked to reevangelize Europe after the barbarian invasions, they handed down a version of the manifestation of "thoughts" as a way to deal with sins. This emerging practice of private confession effectively bypassed and in the long run replaced the older tradition of public penance. In the period we are studying, public penance was still the norm. It had reached its basic ritual form sometime during the third century and was intended for dealing with serious sins— murder, apostasy, adultery—committed on the far side of baptism. The process was harsh, lengthy, and humiliating, and could be used only once in one's life.

The ritual of public penance had several stages. My description necessarily oversimplifies what varied from place to place and time to time and what we know about sometimes only in hard-to-interpret fragments. One first admitted one's sin to the bishop (or his delegate) and then enrolled in the Order of Penitents. One began wearing penitential garb and undertook a strict regimen of fasting, prayer, and almsgiving. Gregory Thaumaturgos, a Cappadocian bishop from the late third century, once described a four-step process of bringing penitents back into full communion. First, one was a "mourner," sitting outside the church begging the faithful to pray on one's behalf. Then one became a "hearer," effectively returning to one's pre-baptismal status as a catechumen. These penitents were dismissed with the catechumens after the sermon and before the liturgy of the Eucharist. Later one became a "faller," permitted to stay for the Eucharist, but not to stand. Instead, one lay prostrate on the floor during the rite. Finally, one became a "stander," permitted to witness the Eucharist, but not to receive communion. One was eventually welcomed back to the Eucharist, usually on Holy Thursday, after the bishop had laid on hands.

I give this excursus on public penance because while the desert fathers are often seen as harsh—and they were in many respects—they were sometimes more tolerant than the larger church. The rigorous public penitential process just outlined lies behind a story about Abba Poemen. One day, a brother admitted that he had committed a grave sin and said that he would impose upon himself a three-year penance. In other words, he gave himself a sentence he would have faced in most churches. But Poemen said: "That's a long time." "One year?" the monk then proposed. Poemen again said: "That's a long time." "Forty days?" "That's a long time," Poemen replied, adding, "I think that if a man repents with his whole heart and resolves not to sin that way again, God accepts a three-day penance."[49] This is startling. As Hermann Dörries has noted, monastic practice consciously and pointedly broke with ecclesiastical tradition: "long periods of penance are rejected. . . . The desert abandons the order obtaining in the church."⁵⁰

The desert fathers were perhaps more lenient because they saw themselves, in a sense, as permanent penitents. Once, a monk asked Abba Macarius for a "word" by which he might be saved. Macarius told him, "Sit in your cell and weep for your sins."⁵¹ It was a common command, and one that brings us to a core element of desert spirituality: the virtue of *penthos* ("sorrow," "compunction").⁵² A twelfth-century Byzantine writer, Nicholas Kataskeperios, has given a definition that reflects the view of the Desert Fathers: "*Penthos* is a godly sorrow, engendered by repentance."⁵³ The term, or rather its derivative, is found in one of Jesus's Beatitudes: "Blessed are the sorrowing [*penthountes*], for they will be comforted" (Matt. 5:4). Monks sought to be *penthountes*, men of sorrow. In fact, the Syriac equivalent of this term—'*abila*—was used by Syriac Christians as the name for "monk," so much were sorrow for sin and monasticism seen as synonymous.⁵⁴

Some of the desert fathers had sins to weep over. The most extreme case was that of Abba Apollos, who had worked as a shepherd up to about the age of forty. Even the understated *Apophthegmata* refers to him as "very uncouth" and describes his brutality in stark terms: "He had seen a pregnant woman in the field one day and being urged by the devil, he had said, 'I should like to see how the child lies in her womb.' So he ripped her up and saw the fetus. Immediately his heart was troubled and, filled with compunction, he went to Scetis and told the Fathers what he had done." Apollos spent the remainder of his life, some forty years, distraught, begging God incessantly for forgiveness. After many years, he felt himself forgiven for the woman's murder, but the death of the unborn child continued to haunt him. Toward the end, an old man finally said to him, "God has forgiven you even the death of the child, but he leaves you in grief because that is good for your soul."⁵⁵

Not all the monks were violent men like Apollos. Some had an almost scrupulous sensitivity. Abba Macarius the Alexandrian, for example, was haunted by a childhood memory of eating a fig that some of his companions had stolen. When the memory welled up, he would sit down and weep.⁵⁶ The story is strangely reminiscent of Augustine, who in the *Confessions* recounts how he and some teenage friends stole pears not for hunger, but for the sheer delight of doing something evil. Perhaps Macarius, like Augustine, was haunted not so much by the severity of the deed as by its symbolic import, echoing as it did the sin of Adam.

Being a man of compunction, of *penthos*, was a central feature of Abba Poemen's spirituality. Earlier, I noted that he wished he could, like Mary the *Theotokos*, weep at the foot of the cross. It was a spirituality he passed on to others. Once when a monk asked what to do about his sins, Poemen answered: "He who wants to pay the ransom for sins pays for them with tears. . . . Weeping is the path the Scriptures and our Fathers handed down to us. They say: 'Weep!' Truly there is no other path than this one."⁵⁷ In another story, Abba Poemen saw a woman in a cemetery weeping bitterly over the loss of her husband, her son, and her brother. He remarked to Abba Anoub that "this woman's whole life and spirit are sorrow"; to be a monk one needed such sorrow.[58]

Weeping was the outward expression of inward sorrow. It was said that Abba Arsenius had hollowed out a channel in his chest from a lifetime of tears.[59] Ultimately, this came from an eschatological sense, of the coming kingdom of God, with its reckoning judgment. When a brother asked for a "word," Abba Ammonas told him:

> Go, let your mindset be like that of criminals who are in prison.
> They ask where the judge is, and when he's going to come, and,
> while waiting for him, weep. The monk should be that way: always
> attentive and reproaching his soul, saying: "How unhappy I am!
> How will I ever stand before the judgment seat of Christ the judge?
> And what will I have to say in my defense?" If you meditate so all
> the time, you can be saved.[60]

And in one of the sayings preserved in Ethiopic, an *abba* remarks that at the day of judgment, "the Lord will not reproach us for not having worked miracles, nor for not having understood the mysteries [of the sacraments], nor for not having possessed the eloquence of the ancients nor theology. But he will judge us for not having lived with tears and lamentations all the days of our lives because of our sins—yes, for this he will reproach us."[61]

All this talk of weeping can sound neurotic and can give the wrong impression. The desert fathers definitely did not cultivate depression or gloom (*lupē*)—a condition they numbered as one of the deadly "thoughts" to be carefully avoided.[62] Nor was it their habit to scour their memory, cataloguing and enumerating their past sins, as later medieval piety would do. In fact, Antony once told Abba Pambo: "Don't worry about what was done in the past."[63] It was not really a matter of recognizing sins, but of recognizing oneself as sinner. In so doing, one saw one's true status before God. And that recognition came not so much from dwelling on past deeds, but on present "thoughts," those haunting *logismoi*, that convicted one again and again of one's status as a sinner. As Antony would put it, "This is a person's *magnum opus*: to place guilt [for sins] upon himself and himself alone before God, and to expect temptation up until the last moment of his life."[64]

From this recognition came a deep sense of solidarity with others. It is the root of those extraordinary gestures of compassion that dot the pages of the *Apophthegmata*. Once, for instance, a brother was refused communion by one of the priests; Abba Bessarion walked out of church with him, saying, "I too am a sinner."[65]

This sense of self as sinner was also, paradoxically, an indicator of one's sense of God's immediacy. As Abba Matoes put it, "The nearer a person comes to God, the more he sees himself as sinner. Thus Isaiah the prophet, upon seeing the Lord, spoke of himself as miserable and unclean."[66] Matoes's insight brings us to the heart of the matter: the sense of sin is the corollary of the sense of divine presence. Intimacy with God and unworthiness before God go hand in hand. No story illustrates the profound link between holiness and *penthos* more clearly than the account of the death of Abba Sisoes:

> It was said of Abba Sisoes that when he was at the point of death, while the Fathers were sitting beside him, his face shone like the sun. He said to them, "Look, Abba Antony is coming." A little while later he said, "Look, the choir of prophets is coming." Again his countenance shone with brightness and he said, "Look, the choir of apostles is coming." Then the old men asked him, "With whom are you speaking, Father?" He said, "Look, the angels are coming to fetch me, and I am begging them to let me do a little penance." The old men said to him, "You have no need to do penance, Father." But the old man said to them, "Truly, I do not think I have even made a beginning yet." Now they all knew that he was perfect.[67]

Visions

One day a pagan priest came to Scetis and visited Abba Olympius. The priest was amazed at the rigor of the monks' lifestyle. So he asked Olympius, "Do you not receive visions from your God?" Olympius said, no, he did not. So the priest then said: "Well, as for us, when we sacrifice to our god, he reveals his mysteries. And you—with all your labors, vigils, your retreat and asceticism—you say that you don't have any visions. If you don't have visions, then you must have evil thoughts in your hearts that separate you from your God. That is why you are denied your mysteries." Abba Olympius went and reported these words to the old men of Scetis; they "were filled with admiration and said: 'Yes, impure thoughts separate us from God.' "[68]

The pagan priest expected what most of us would have expected: that the desert fathers enjoyed visions and mystic experiences. But things were not so straightforward. As the story illustrates, pagan spirituality presumed a certain quid pro quo; the pagan priest had only to perform the requisite sacrifice, and he was rewarded with visions and mystical knowledge. The desert fathers, some of whom were ex-pagans, had opted out of any quid pro quo spirituality. They knew that their asceticism was no guarantee of vision. Not cited but echoing in the background is Jesus's Beatitude: "Blessed are the pure of heart, for they shall see God" (Matt. 5:8). The desert fathers did not expect to see God because they knew they were not pure of heart. "Thoughts" effectively blocked the monk's vision.

Sometimes the desert fathers, conscious of their sins, seem to reject the visionary quest. Once a monk went to one of the old men and reported that certain monks claimed to see visions of angels. But the old man replied, "Blessed is the one who sees his sins always."[69] Part of the concern over such visions was the risk of demonic delusion. Once, an angel appeared to an old man and announced that he was the angel Gabriel and that he had been sent especially to him. The old man was nonplussed: "Check to see if you weren't sent to someone else. I am really not worthy to have an angel sent to me."[70] With these words, the demon-disguised-as-Gabriel vanished. It was incidents such as this that led Abba Poemen to tell his disciples: "If you have visions or hear voices, don't tell your neighbor about it. It's a delusion from the [heat of] battle."[71]

Another saying seems, at first sight, to flow from the same attitude: "Some old men said: 'If you see a young man climbing up to heaven by his own will, catch him by the foot and pull him down to earth: it is not good for him.'"[72] The accent seems to be on rejecting the pursuit of visions. But the key phrase here is "young man." Perhaps the young were thought too inexperienced, too vulnerable to demonic temptation. Whatever the reason, it was clearly inappropriate for a *young* man to embark on the visionary quest.

But what about old men? There are scattered reports of experienced elders who had ecstasies and visions. Zacharias once came to visit Abba Silvanus and found him in prayer with his hands stretched out toward heaven. So Zacharias slipped out, not wanting to disturb the *abba*. Zacharias returned at three in the afternoon and again at six and found Silvanus in the same state. Finally at sunset, Zacharias knocked and found Silvanus sitting peacefully. When Zacharias asked what had happened, Silvanus explained that he had been ill all day. So Zacharias prostrated himself and grabbed Silvanus's feet, saying, "I will not let you go unless you make known what you saw." Silvanus then admitted, "I was taken up to heaven and I saw the glory of God and I stayed there until now and now I have been sent away."[73] Silvanus was not the only one to pretend as though he had not had such an experience; a similar reticence is found in a story about Abba Arsenius.[74] What is striking is Silvanus's admission. According to Antoine Guillaumont, the elders consented to revealing their revelations when they believed it would serve others, increasing their faith in some way.[75]

Visionary experiences figure prominently in other works of desert literature. As we saw earlier, both Antony and Pachomius enjoyed visionary gifts. In the *Apophthegmata*, some abbas have visions not of heaven, but of the invisible world of angels and demons. Abba Paul the Simple was reputed to have the gift of "seeing the state of each man's soul, just as we see their faces." One weekend, he was sitting outside the church watching the monks go in to the *synaxis*. In his vision, he saw the monks entering "with sparkling eyes and shining faces"; he also saw "each one's angel rejoicing over him." But Paul noted one monk who appeared "dark," accompanied by demons, while his guardian angel followed behind at a distance, downcast and grieving. But when the monks emerged from the liturgy, the monk who had previously been accompanied by demons and enveloped in gloom appeared "with a shining face and white body." Paul began jumping up and down and shouting, "O the ineffable loving kindness and goodness of God!" He ran to an elevated spot and announced to the congregation his vision. Then the once gloomy monk confessed that he had undergone a conversion while at the liturgy: he had been guilty of fornication, but the scriptural reading from the prophet Isaiah had

provoked in him a transformation of heart.[76] It is hard to evaluate this somewhat bizarre narrative. The story is quite long by the standards of the *Apophthegmata* (it goes on for several pages); it also has a distinctly folkloric tone, unlike
so much of the text. But it narrates a commonly mentioned phenomenon: that
certain elders had a sort of second sight that enabled them to peer into the
spiritual world that bristled around human beings.

Among the sayings attributed to Macarius the Egyptian is a similar account
of visionary gifts—and of similar length. Once Macarius decided to go visit
two young foreigners whom he had initiated into the monastic life and the
basics of desert living. After their initiation, they had not returned to see him
for some three years. Before going to visit them, he devoted a whole week to
prayer and fasting, praying for the gift of seeing their way of life. When he
arrived at their cell, they paid him quiet respect and hospitality, offering him
a cooked meal and a place to sleep. In the middle of the night, the two young
monks rose to do the night office of psalms while Macarius pretended to sleep.
He was able to observe them praying because he received the gift of a sort of
spiritual "night vision." A mysterious light poured through the roof and "it
became as light as day." There in this spiritual light, he could see the younger
one attacked by demons. They flitted around and landed on his eyes and mouth
like flies. At the same time, he saw an angel with a fiery sword chasing the
demons off. As the two monks prayed the psalms, Macarius witnessed a tongue
of fire coming from the mouth of the younger, while a column of fire came
from the mouth of the elder.[77] Here Macarius's visionary gifts enabled him to
see into the inner life of his disciples, or more precisely, to see the invisible
spirit world that clamored around his disciples.

While the *Apophthegmata* generally downplays ecstasy and visions, here
and there it encourages their pursuit. Abba Lot once went to visit Abba Joseph
of Panephysis and asked his advice: "Abba, I keep to a moderate rule, as best
I can, and do a little fasting and a little meditation and quiet; and as best I can,
I try to purge my heart of evil thoughts. What else should I do?" So Joseph
stood up and stretched out his hands toward heaven, in the traditional posture
of prayer. His fingers became "like ten lamps of fire" and he told his disciple,
"If you want, you can become all flame."[78]

"Becoming flame" refers to the quest for transfiguration. The desert fathers sought to recover the "glory of Adam": "They said of Abba Pambo that
he was like Moses, who received the image of the glory of Adam when his face
shone. His face shone like lightning and he was like a king sitting on his
throne. It was the same with Abba Silvanus and Abba Sisoes."[79]

For the desert fathers, the quest was not for transitory visions; it was for
the permanent transformation of the human person, soul and body. Nothing
less. It was seeking the glory of Adam before the Fall and the glory of heaven
with the resurrected body. To pursue it demanded strength and courage. It
demanded facing evil, both outside and inside oneself. It demanded humility
and forgiveness. And demanded a certain single-mindedness. Once a monk
went to his *abba*, discouraged about those who had given up the quest and
returned to the world. The *abba* answered him: "Watch the dogs that chase

hares. When one of them has seen a hare he pursues it, until he catches it, without being concerned with anything else. . . . So it is with him who seeks Christ as Master; ever mindful of the cross, he cares for none of the scandals that occur, till he reaches the Crucified."[80]

Scripture

The church fathers quoted scripture constantly. Many times their writings seem little more than a vast quilt of quotations. Some, like Origen or Chrysostom or Augustine, so made the Bible's vocabulary and phraseology their own that they could seem to speak "scripturally." By contrast, the desert fathers seem to cite scripture sparingly—that, at least, is a common first impression.[81] There are even passages in which they express an aversion to discussing scripture. Abba Pambo, whenever asked to interpret scripture, used to say that he did not know the text in question. If the inquirer persisted, he retreated into silence.[82] Abba Poemen, in a similar way, said that it was better to discuss the sayings of the desert fathers than those of scripture, for they posed less danger.[83]

Poemen's reservations come out dramatically in another story. Once, a famous hermit, who had heard of Poemen's reputation for holiness, traveled a long distance to see him. When he arrived, he began speaking with Poemen about the scriptures. At this, Poemen turned his face away and remained silent. The visitor left, deeply hurt by Poemen's silence. Poemen's disciple asked him why he had been so unkind to such a famous man who had traveled so far to speak with him. Poemen replied, "He is great and speaks of heavenly things, and I am lowly and speak of earthly things. If he had spoken of the passions of the soul, I should have replied, but he speaks to me of spiritual things and I know nothing about that." The disciple passed on Poemen's comments to the visitor. And so the visitor returned, and admitted that he too was controlled by his passions, and Poemen spoke with him gladly.[84]

Armed with such sayings, the mid-twentieth-century church historian Hans Lietzmann, in a widely read survey, belittled monasticism as unscriptural. He claimed that "the only genuinely Christian element in monasticism" was its sense of human sinfulness; "otherwise it has nothing more than external relations with the Christian religion."[85] This notorious and influential judgment has been soundly refuted by recent studies, notably Douglas Burton-Christie's *The Word in the Desert*. These studies have shown how deeply scriptural desert Christianity was.

The lives of the desert fathers were saturated by scripture. They encountered scripture during weekend liturgies (vespers, the night office, the Eucharist). During the week, they chanted or recited the psalms while they did their manual labor. As one *abba* noted, "Meditation, psalmody, and manual labor—these are the foundations. The beginner must first learn all this."[86] By "meditation," the desert fathers mean something quite specific: the oral recitation of scripture. When Ammoes and a friend visited Abba Achilles, he noted that "we *heard* him meditating on this saying, 'Do not fear, Jacob, to go down to Egypt' (Gen. 46:3). For a long time, he remained making this meditation."[87] Achilles's visitors presumably knew he was meditating because they could hear him repeating the phrase again and again. Monks might do such meditation even when they traveled. Palladius recounts how he accompanied a monk named Heron who, on the forty-mile trip from Nitria to Scetis, recited from memory sixteen psalms (including the lengthy Ps. 119), the Epistle to the Hebrews, Isaiah, part of Jeremiah, the Gospel of Luke, and Proverbs.[88] This practice illustrates one dimension of desert biblicism: scripture was more an oral word than a written text; it was spoken aloud and heard, not read and seen.

While the desert fathers chanted, recited, and chewed on biblical texts, they saw scripture less as something to be talked about than as something to be done. This squared with their general temperament: they were doers, not talkers. Once, when Abba Theodore of Pherme heard a brother speaking about things he had not yet put into practice, he chided him: "You haven't found a ship yet nor put your cargo on board; and [you act as though] you've already entered the city before you've sailed. Do the work first."[89] This stress on doing shaped how they approached the scriptures. Once a monk asked a scribe at Scetis to copy out something from the Bible. When the monk noticed missing words and phrases, he returned it to the scribe and complained. But the scribe told him, "Go, and practice first that which is written, then come back and I will write the rest."[90]

As Burton-Christie has shown, the desert fathers rooted the core themes of their spirituality—repentance, renunciation, vigilance, the combat with evil, humility, forgiveness of enemy, and love of God and neighbor—in biblical admonitions. In the *Apophthegmata*, they most often quote the Psalms, among Old Testament books, and the Gospel of Matthew, among New Testament ones. Quoting the Psalms is no surprise given its role in their daily prayer. Quoting from Matthew is also no surprise since it is the most often cited Gospel not just among the desert fathers, but in early Christian literature in general. But the desert fathers showed a special fondness for Jesus's great discourses, especially the Sermon on the Mount. We saw earlier how they drew the idea of *penthos*, of sorrowing, from the Beatitudes. They rooted other virtues as well, such as purity of heart and humility, in the Beatitudes. Abba John of Thebes, for example, insisted, "The monk ought above all to be humble. For this is the Savior's first commandment: 'Blessed are the poor in spirit, for theirs is the kingdom of heaven' (Matt 5:3)."[91] The *Apophthegmata* gives the impression that the desert fathers were more attuned to biblical aphorisms than to narratives— which explains their fondness not only for the Gospel of Matthew but also for the admonitions that close Paul's letters. For instance, as Abba Benjamin lay dying, his disciples asked for a "word." He quoted them 1 Thess. 5:16–18: "Rejoice always. Pray without ceasing. In all things give thanks." He then told them, "Do this and you can be saved."[92]

The accent on practice led the desert fathers to criticize any who equated knowledge of the scriptural text with knowledge of scripture. Once a monk came to one of the elders of Scetis claiming that he had memorized both the Old and New Testaments. Such feats of memory were not uncommon in the ancient world. Memorizing classics was a standard practice in ancient education, and educated Christians brought such habits to their piety. Still, memorizing the Bible was quite a feat. But the *abba* was unimpressed and chided the monk: "You have filled the air with words."[93] For the desert fathers, words without deeds were just so much hot air.

Once a woman came to Antony and made a similar claim about memorizing the Bible, adding that she had practiced long fasts. So Antony decide to test the woman's knowledge: "For you, is being despised the same as being honored?" "No," she answered. He then went on: "Is loss the same as gain? Are strangers the same as your parents? Is poverty the same as wealth?" Each time she answered, "No." His judgment was curt: "You have neither fasted nor learned the Old and New Testaments. You have deceived yourself."[94] For Antony and the desert fathers, knowledge of texts was not knowledge. Genuine knowledge of scripture was lived knowledge, making one's own the values and way of life that the scriptures called for.

The desert fathers also shared Origen's fondness for allegory and sometimes applied his methods to the biblical text. For example: "Abba Poemen also said, 'If Nabuzardan, the head-cook, had not come, the temple of the Lord would not have been burned: that is to say, if slackness and gluttony did not come into the soul, the spirit would not be overcome in its combat with the enemy.' "[95] This saying alludes to the tragic story in 2 Kings 25 in which Judea was vanquished by the Babylonians, its king bound and blinded, its leaders dragged into exile. Nebuzardan was the Babylonian military commander who allowed both Jerusalem's royal palace and Solomon's temple to be ransacked and burned to the ground. The original Hebrew text refers to him as "captain of the guard"; but the Septuagint (the Greek version of the Old Testament used by the monks) mistranslated it as "head cook." This bizarre, even comical image of a cook burning down the temple and leading Judea into exile seems to have inspired Poemen and led him to interpret the passage allegorically. Here Poemen reads the story with desert eyes: the head-cook symbolizes the soul (*psychē*), while the temple symbolizes the human spirit (*nous*), the inner sanctum of the human person. This plays on a widespread view among the desert fathers that the stomach is the gateway to the soul. Gluttony was numbered as the first of the deadly "thoughts," the one that helped bring down Adam. For this reason, admonitions to control one's stomach are commonplace in the literature of the desert.[96] According to Poemen's interpretation, if the soul fails to be vigilant over the stomach, which is the gateway and outer precincts of the human person, then it leaves one vulnerable to attack at the core, the spirit. Demonic attack diverts the human spirit, that temple of God in the human person, from its natural activity, which is the contemplation of God. Poemen's exegesis here may strike the modern reader as odd. But allegory was not simply a matter of decoding obscure texts. It had profound implications for spirituality, as Jeremy Driscoll has noted:

If Poemen only wished to speak about gluttony and contemplation, he did not need to talk about Nabuzardan to do so. But allegory is a tool that enables him to discover a deeper mystery; namely, that there is a continuity between the history of Israel—in this case, one particular detail about a head-cook burning down a temple—and the struggle of the monk. With such a discovery the monk's life is taken up into a drama far larger than a personal struggle with gluttony, or for that matter, any other of the principal evil thoughts. The monk is living the very story of the Bible.[97]

Another instance is Poemen's allegorical exegesis of Psalm 42:1: "As the deer longs for flowing streams, so my soul longs for you, O God." As he tells an inquirer:

> [Deer] in the desert devour many reptiles and the snake-venom burns them. They try to come to the springs to drink so as to quench the venom's burning. It is the same for monks: sitting in the desert they are burned by the venom of evil demons, and they long for Saturday and Sunday to be able to go to the springs of waters, that is to say, the body and blood of the Lord, so as to be purified from the bitterness of the evil one.[98]

Here Poemen takes the thirsty deer of Psalm 42 and transforms them into snake-devouring desert stags. The legend that deer fed on snakes appears in certain ancient scientific texts and apparently had wide currency.[99] Once again the *Apophthegmata* portrays Poemen bringing monastic experience to his exegesis: during his weekday solitude in the cell, the monk had to grapple with demonic temptation; on weekends, he joined the larger community of anchorites for Eucharist. Here Poemen reads the psalm's thirsty deer as a cipher for monks who are "thirsty" after a week-long battle with demons. Poemen also reads the passage with Christological eyes: the refreshing spring of the Old Testament psalm is a prophetic foreshadowing of Christ, the true life-giving spring. The monk thus finds his identity in the venom-drinking stag refreshed by the divine life of Christ made available in the Eucharist.

One last example from Poemen. Here he speaks not about a particular text, but rather the role of scripture in the life of the monk. Once a brother journeyed to see him in order to get his advice on the quest for purity of heart. Unfortunately, the monk only spoke Greek, and Poemen's command of the language was shaky. Since no interpreter could be found, they had to muddle through the interview. Poemen wanted to find a way to talk about the mystery of the hardness of the human heart. So he noted that if one puts a bottle of water above a rock and lets it drip, it slowly but surely wears down the rock. In the same way, the word of God slowly touches and saturates the heart of the one who listens to it. In time, it wears down and softens our hard hearts, opening them to the fear of God.[100]

From Oral Word to Written Text

How were these stories in the *Apophthegmata* preserved and written down? That question has been the focus of much scholarly study in the last century. We saw earlier the pivotal role of Abba Poemen and his circle, the value they placed on preserving the wisdom of the "old men." Recall the story that marked their coming together: how after the destruction of Scetis, Poemen and the brothers spent a week in retreat at a pagan temple at Terenuthis, how one of the brothers, Anoub, threw rocks at a statue there and then each evening knelt down to ask its forgiveness, and how Anoub then called on the brothers to maintain a similar calm with one another. An earlier version of this very story has been discovered in certain manuscripts of the little-known *Asceticon* of Abba Isaiah (d. c. 491). Isaiah's version begins with a key phrase missing from the *Apophthegmata*'s version: "Abba John said to me. . . ."[101] In other words, it appears that Abba Isaiah moved in the circle of Poemen's disciples and knew the story from an eyewitness. Isaiah's work predates the *Apophthegmata* and is a precious testimony to the shift from oral tradition to written text (for excerpts, see appendix 8.4).

Abba Isaiah saw himself as a faithful inheritor of a venerable wisdom. At the heading of this same chapter, Isaiah writes, "Brothers, what I have understood and seen among the old men, I pass on to you, leaving out nothing nor adding anything to it." [102] And after telling stories of Poemen and others, he adds, "And so, brothers, if we love our life, let us imitate those who pleased God, and let us walk in their footsteps, for they have found the good path."[103] Abba Isaiah's work not only marks the transition from oral tradition to written text; it also marks the transition from Egypt to Palestine. Isaiah was an Egyptian and had been a monk, possibly at Scetis, as late as 431. At some point, he moved to Palestine, first making a pilgrimage to Jerusalem and then settling down in Gaza at Beit Daltha. Eventually, he enclosed himself in a cell and communicated with no one except his disciple, Peter, who was also an Egyptian. A monastic community attached itself to him, and he served as their spiritual guide until his death in 491.

Isaiah's *Asceticon* is not an organized treatise, but a hodgepodge of monastic rules, exhortations, questions and answers, homilies, strings of apophthegms—even a letter to Isaiah's disciple, Peter, on his entering the monastic life. The editor, and in some cases the writer, of all this seems to be Peter, who put it together either late in Isaiah's career or soon after his death, gathering the mass of material into some thirty *Logoi* ("discourses" or "essays"). The chapter that records Isaiah's memories of the masters of Egypt, *Logos* 30, passed almost entirely into the *Apophthegmata*. A few other sayings from Isaiah also came to be included.[104] Isaiah's friends and disciples were staunch anti-Chalcedonians, but there is no hint of Christological polemic in his works. Rather, he passes on and systematizes desert teaching on a host of issues— the search for *hesychia*, the combat with "thoughts," the value of manual labor—but he also had his personal accents, such as the unique theme of "the ascent of the cross," in which the believer identifies himself with the crucified Jesus.

Another work, the Ethiopic *Collectio Monastica*, offers a precious glimpse into the long oral tradition that lies behind the *Apophthegmata* (for excerpts, see appendix 8.5). First published in 1963, its significance has only recently begun to be appreciated.[105] The *Collectio* is a sprawling anthology of monastic literature. A number of its sixty-eight chapters contain mini-collections of sayings. Most of these sayings are found in the Greek and Latin versions of the *Apophthegmata*. But two chapters (13 and 14) are unusual. Of the 166 sayings found there, only 22 have any known parallels. These chapters seem to preserve a primitive collection dating from the mid-fifth century, similar to but independent from the classic collections in Greek and Latin.

Many sayings in the Ethiopic *Collectio* open with a phraseology different from that found in the Greek *Apophthegmata*. In the Greek collections, sayings typically begin with stereotyped formulae, such as "Abba Antony once said such-and-such" or "A brother asked Abba Macarius about such-and-such." In the Ethiopic *Collectio*, sayings often begin not in the third person, but in the first:

> A brother said *to me* . . . (13.6, 13.26, 13.54)
> *I asked* my father, Abba Joseph, [the disciple] of Abba Alonois . . . and he said *to me* . . . (13.70)
> *I heard of* a brother who lived in Scetis and who spoke with Abba Moses the Black . . ." (13.3)

Of the 166 sayings, 57 contain such first-person openings; that is, more than one-third of the sayings. These claim, in other words, to offer personal reminiscences. What is more extraordinary is the way certain ones carefully preserve each link in the chain of transmission. For example:

> A brother said *to me*: "Abba Isaac of Harahu said *to me*: 'I visited Abba Sisoes of Petra, the disciple of Abba Antony, and I asked him saying: "Tell me a word by which I might live." He said *to me*: "Go, guard these three works and you will live: endure insults as glory, misery as riches, love your neighbor as yourself. And the Lord will be with you; he will make you strong against your enemies." ' "[106]

Notice the links:

- A "word of salvation" is spoken by Abba Sisoes of Petra (whose authority is linked to Antony the Great).
- This "word" is then passed on to Abba Isaac, who gives it to "me" (an unnamed brother).
- This unnamed brother in turn gives it to "me," the writer of the text.

For the compiler of the Ethiopic *Collectio*, recording each link in the chain of transmission was crucial. These links served as a touchstone of the authenticity and antiquity of the saying and linked his generation to the precious wisdom of a bygone golden age.

The Greek *Apophthegmata* focuses on Egyptian monks, but those who compiled its sayings and stories seem to have lived not in Egypt, but in the Holy Land. That, at least, is the current consensus of scholars.[107] Lucien Regnault, in a key study, has pointed out that both the Alphabetical and Systematic Collections, while focused on Egyptian monks, also contain stories of Palestinians (such as Abba Silvanus); the Ethiopic *Collectio*, by contrast, contains stories only of Egyptians. Also, one finds sixth-century Palestinian writers—Cyril of Scythopolis, Barsanuphius, John of Gaza, and Dorotheos—speaking of the "words of the old men" and quoting stories from the *Apophthegmata*. Moreover, Palestine was *the* great pilgrimage center to which visitors from throughout the Christian world came. If the early versions of the *Apophthegmata* were composed in Palestine, that would do much to explain their wide and rapid dissemination to all corners of the Christian world, East and West.

Those who compiled the *Apophthegmata* wrote in Greek, but the tradition they preserved was largely oral and Coptic, a reservoir of memories from the 330s to the 450s—from the later days of Antony to the Council of Chalcedon. Only a handful of stories go beyond that time. This has led scholars to surmise that the work of writing down and editing the stories took place in the late fifth century. Some of these late stories indicate that the compilers probably came from monastic circles opposed to the Council of Chalcedon.[108] Chalcedon, with its *Definition* of the person and natures of Christ, left monks in Palestine deeply and bitterly divided. The *Apophthegmata* says nothing about Christology; it neither touches on nor encourages such theological concerns. Is this silence intentional? It is an intriguing possibility. The sayings of the *Apophthegmata* cluster around other matters: the practical stuff of desert living, the tangled passions of the heart and the tangled conflicts that divide monk from monk; the need for a honest sorrow for sin and the need for a honest and self-effacing compassion if monks hope to live together in some measure of peace. The *Apophthegmata* seems to be the work of a peacemaker (or of a circle inspired by one).

Why did the compilers of the *Apophthegmata* use this literary genre? Why an anthology of anecdotes, proverbs, and snappy dialogues? Partly because the form reflects how oral wisdom typically passed from teacher to disciple, from generation to generation: through easy-to-remember narratives and easy-to-remember proverbs. But it also accords well with a spirituality born and bred in a desert climate. The spare narrative, the refined understatement: these seem to flow from a desire to cut through what is superfluous and deceptive in human communication and return us to that bracing simplicity that got lost after Adam's Fall. As Columba Stewart has noted, "The very form of the apophthegmata arose from and leads back into the heart of the desert quest. . . . The desert itself gave [monks] a landscape which mirrored what they sought for their own hearts: an uncluttered view through clear air."[109]

The ancient compilers of the *Apophthegmata* had no illusions that wise words might remain only un-practiced words. An anonymous saying puts it this way: "The prophets wrote books. Our Fathers came after them, and worked much at them, and then their successors memorized them. But this generation has come, and it copies them on papyrus and parchment and leaves them unused on the window-ledge."[110] Even so, this shift from oral wisdom to written text made possible a new spirituality. One no longer had to receive a "word of salvation" from an *abba* who saw and read one's heart. One no longer even had to travel to Egypt. The textuality of the *Apophthegmata* created, in essence, a portable desert wisdom, making it possible for Egypt to be carried around the empire.

NOTES

1. Jean-Claude Guy, "Les *Apophthegmata Patrum*," in *Théologie de la vie monastique: études sur la tradition patristique*, Collection Théologie 49, ed. G. Lemaître (Paris: Aubier, 1961), 73–83.

2. *AP Sys* 2.19 (SC 387:134, trans. my own).

3. *AP Sys* 7.46 (SC 387:376–378; trans. my own).

4. *AP Sys* 2.1 (SC 387:124; trans. my own); cf. *VA* 85 (SC 400:354; CWS, 93).

5. James E. Goehring, "Monasticism," in *Encyclopedia of Early Christianity*, ed. Everett Ferguson, 2nd ed. (New York: Garland, 1997), 2:769.

6. *Verba Seniorum* 11.5 (PL 73:934; trans. my own).

7. *AP Sys* 4.30 (SC 387:201; trans. my own).

8. *AP Rufus* 1 (PG 65:389; trans. Ward, CS 59:210). *AP Sys* 2.35 (SC 387:142–146) gives it as an anonymous saying; there it appears as a lengthy panegyric on *hesychia*.

9. *AP Sys* 2.15 and 2.17 (SC 387:132, 134; trans. my own). The compiler of the Systematic Collection has drawn these sayings from Abba Isaiah, *Asceticon* 21.13 (de Broc, 165) and 26.40 (de Broc, 246).

10. *AP Poemen* 95 (PG 65:345; CS 59:180).

11. Columba Stewart, "Radical Honesty about the Self: The Practice of the Desert Fathers," *Sobornost* 12 (1990): 27.

12. *AP Paphnutius* 3 (PG 65:380; CS 59:202–203); *AP John Colobos* 8 (PG 65:205; CS 59:87).

13. *AP Sys* 5.16 (SC 387:252–254).

14. *AP N* 509, quoted in Stewart, "Radical Honesty," 31–32. A similar story of a reluctance to admit "thoughts" is found in *AP Poemen* 93 (PG 65:344–345; CS 59:180); there the "thought" is blasphemy.

15. Abba Isaiah, *Asceticon* XV.76. While this is not from the *AP* itself, Isaiah is one of the figures in it, and his *Asceticon* is one of the early sources and models for it. Similar remarks appear in *Verba Seniorum* 4.25 (PL 73:868; LCC, 52); *AP Poemen* 101 (PG 65:345; CS 59:181).

16. *AP Poemen* 169 (PG 65:364), quoted in Gould, *The Desert Fathers on Monastic Community*, 115.

17. Athanasius, *Apologia ad Constantium* 33.1–12 (PG 25:640), quoted in Brakke, *Athanasius and the Politics of Asceticism*, 17.

18. Peter Brown, *The Body and Society: Men, Women, and Sexual Renunciation in Early Christianity* (New York: Columbia University Press, 1988), 217.

19. *AP* Olympius 2 (PG 65:313–316; trans. Ward, CS 59:160–161). *AP* Sys 5.50 (SC 387:302–304) contains the same story, but there it is attributed to an unnamed "old man established at Kellia."

20. *AP* Sys 5.31 (SC 387:268–270; trans. my own).

21. *AP* Ammonas 10 (PG 65:121–124; trans. Ward, CS 59:28).

22. *AP* Eudemon (PG 65:176; trans. Ward, CS 59:64).

23. *AP* Sys 5.3 (SC 387:243; trans. my own).

24. *AP* Poemen 176 (PG 65:365; trans. Ward, CS 59:191).

25. Brown, *The Body and Society*, 230.

26. *AP* N 166 (ROC 13:54; Ward, *Wisdom*, 8) = *AP* Sys 5.18 (SC 387:254–256).

27. *AP* Sys 5.13 (SC 387:252; trans. my own).

28. *AP* Sys 5.16 (SC 387:252–254).

29. *Verba Seniorum* 4.19 (PL 73:867; trans. Chadwick, LCC, 51).

30. *Verba Seniorum* 5.40 (PL 73:886; trans. Chadwick, LCC, 74–75).

31. *Verba Seniorum* 5.22 (PL 73:879; trans. Chadwick, LCC, 66) = *AP* Sys 5.26 (SC 387:262).

32. *Verba Seniorum* 5.37 (PL 73:883–884; trans. Chadwick, LCC, 71–72).

33. Brown, *The Body and Society*, 243.

34. Brown, *The Body and Society*, 230.

35. *Verba Seniorum* 17.22 (PL 73:977; trans. my own).

36. Gould, *The Desert Fathers on Monastic Community*, 112.

37. Augustine, *Sermo* 211.6 (PL 38:1057–1058; trans. my own). Cf. *Sermo* 22A.1 on the way his congregation used to sing with tears psalms that stressed God's wrath against the supplicant's enemies.

38. *Verba Seniorum* 16.10 (PL 73:971; trans. my own).

39. *AP* Isidore 7 (PG 65:221; CS 59:97); *AP* Sys 4.21 (SC 387:194).

40. *AP* Sys 7.3 (SC 387:336–338; trans. my own).

41. *AP* Sys 4.9 (SC 387:188; trans. my own).

42. *AP* Sys 4.60 (SC 387:214).

43. *AP* Sys 4.59 (SC 387:214).

44. *AP* Isaiah 8 (PG 65:181; trans. Ward, CS 59:70).

45. *Verba Seniorum* 7.33 (PL 73:901; LCC, 92) = *AP* Sys 7.40 (SC 387:372–374).

46. *Verba Seniorum* 18.18 (PL 73:983–984).

47. Gould, *The Desert Fathers on Monastic Community*, 118.

48. *Verba Seniorum* 15.60 (PL 73:964; trans. Chadwick, LCC, 169).

49. *Verba Seniorum* 10.40 (PL 73:920; trans. my own).

50. Hermann Dörries, "The Place of Confession in Ancient Monasticism," *Studia Patristica* 5 (1962): 291.

51. *AP* Macarius 27 (PG 65:273; trans. Ward, CS 59:133).

52. Technically speaking, *penthos* is "sorrow," while *katanyxis* is "compunction." But early on, *penthos* came to be translated in the Latin tradition as *compunctio*. In recent translations, Lucien Regnault is consistent in translating *penthos* as "sorrow," while Jean-Claude Guy and Benedicta Ward both frequently translate *penthos* as "compunction."

53. Nicholas Kataskerperios, *Life of Saint Cyril of Philea*, cited in Irénée Hausherr, *Penthos: The Doctrine of Compunction in the Christian East*, CS 53 (Kalamazoo, Mich.: Cistercian Publications, 1982), 18.

54. Hausherr, *Penthos*, 15.

55. *AP* Apollos 2 (PG 65:133–136; trans. Ward, CS 59:36).

56. *AP* Macarius the Egyptian 37 (PG 65:277–280; CS 59:136). On attributing

this to Macarius the Alexandrian instead of the Egyptian, see Guillaumont, "Le problème des deux Macaires," 43.

57. *AP* Sys 3.29–30 (SC 387:166; trans. my own).

58. *AP* Sys 3.25 (SC 387:164; trans. my own).

59. *AP* Arsenius 41 (PG 65:105; Ward, 18). The parallel *AP* Sys 3.3 (SC 387:150) = *Verba Seniorum* 3.1 (PL 73:860; LCC, 43) is more plausible: "he kept a handkerchief in his breast" because tears fell so often.

60. *AP* Sys 3.4 (SC 387:151; trans. my own).

61. Ethiopic *Patericon* 169 (CSCO 277:117; trans. my own). On the issue of picturing oneself at the Last Judgment, see *Verba Seniorum* 3.3 (PL 73:860; LCC, 44).

62. Evagrius Ponticus, in his *Antirrhetikos*, would list seventy-seven varieties of this and counter them with appropriate scriptural consolations; see chapter 10.

63. *AP* Sys 1.2 (SC 387:102; trans. my own).

64. *Verba Seniorum* 15.2 (PL 73:953; trans. my own).

65. *AP* Sys 9.2 (SC 387:426; trans. my own).

66. *Verba Seniorum* 15.28 (PL 73:959; trans. my own).

67. *AP* Sisoes 14 (PG 65:396; trans. Ward, CS 59:214–215).

68. *AP* Sys 11.109 (trans. my own) = *AP* Olympius 1 (PG 65:313; CS 59:160).

69. *Verba Seniorum* 15.87 (PL 73:968; trans. my own).

70. *Verba Seniorum* 15.68 (PL 73:965; trans. my own). See also *Verba Seniorum* 15.70, in which the elder turns down having a vision of Christ.

71. *AP* Poemen 139 (PG 65:356–357; trans. my own).

72. *Verba Seniorum* 10.111 (PL 73:932; trans. Chadwick, LCC, 130).

73. *AP* Silvanus 3 (PG 65:409; trans. Ward, CS 59:222–223) = *Verba Seniorum* 18.21 (PL 73:993).

74. *Verba Seniorum* 18.1 (PL 73:978).

75. Antoine Guillaumont, "Les visions mystiques dans le monachisme oriental chretien," in *Aux origines du monachisme chrétien*, SO 30 (Bégrolles-en-Mauges: Abbaye de Bellefontaine, 1979), 139.

76. *Verba Seniorum* 18.20 (PL 73:985–986).

77. *Verba Seniorum* 20.2 (PL 73:1004–1006).

78. *Verba Seniorum* 12.8 (PL 73:942; trans. my own).

79. *AP* Pambo 12 (PG 65:372; trans. Ward, CS 59:197).

80. *AP* N 203 (ROC 13:279; Ward, *Wisdom*, 62) = *AP* Sys 7.42 (SC 387:374–376).

81. Numbers differ from expert to expert. Take, for example, the 1000 sayings in the Alphabetical Collection. Benedicta Ward, who translated it into English, lists 93 citations, 45 from the Old Testament, 48 from the New, while Lucien Regnault, who translated it into French, lists 224 citations, 98 from the Old Testament, 126 from the New. The discrepancy comes from how one counts allusions (as opposed to direct quotations).

82. *AP* Pambo 9 (PG 65:372; CS 59:197).

83. *Verba Seniorum* 11.20 (PL 73:936). In the Alphabetical Collection (*AP* Amoun of Nitria 2 [PG 65:128; CS 59:31–32]), this saying is listed under the name of Amoun, the founder of Nitria (d. 353). But that is clearly a mistake. In *AP* Amoun of Nitria 3, a brother comes to Scetis (!), not Nitria, to visit Amoun. The Amoun of this saying is clearly Poemen's disciple, whereas Amoun of Nitria died probably before Poemen was born. In the Latin version, the name given is Ammon, not Amoun. This story appears also in Abba Isaiah's *Asceticon* Logos VI.4b (Syriac version), where it is part of a set of first-person narratives about Poemen and his disciples.

84. *AP* Poemen 8 (PG 65:321–324; trans. Ward, CS 59:167).

85. Lietzmann, *A History of the Early Church*, vol. 4, *The Era of the Church Fathers*, trans. Bertram Lee Woolf (New York: Scribner's Sons, 1952), 155.

86. *AP* N 168 (ROC 13:54; trans. Ward, *Wisdom*, 8–9); cf. *Verba Seniorum* 5.18 (PL 73:877–878; LCC, 64).

87. *AP* Achilles 5 (PG 65:125; CS 59:29).

88. Palladius, *Historia Lausiaca* 26.3 (Butler, 81–82; ACW 34:86–87).

89. *AP* Sys 8.11 (SC 387:406; trans. my own).

90. *AP* Abraham 3 (PG 65:132; trans. Ward, CS 59:34).

91. *Verba Seniorum* 15.23 (PL 73:958; LCC, 162).

92. *AP* Benjamin 3 (PG 65:145; trans. my own).

93. *Verba Seniorum* 10.94 (PL 73:929–930; LCC, 126).

94. *AP* N 518, quoted in Burton-Christie, *Word in the Desert*, 161.

95. *AP* Poemen 16 (PG 65:325; trans. Ward, 169, altered).

96. On food and fasting, see Brown, *The Body and Society*, 218–222. Cf. *AP* John Kolobos 3; Evagrius Ponticus, *Praktikos* 7.

97. Driscoll, "Exegetical Procedures," 163.

98. *AP* Poemen 30 (PG 65:329; trans. Ward, CS 59:171).

99. Burton-Christie, *The Word in the Desert*, 211, notes that the legend of reptile-devouring deer appears in an Alexandrian scientific text known as the *Physiologus*, dating from about 140 B.C.

100. *Verba Seniorum* 18.16 (PL 73:983).

101. Abba Isaiah, *Asceticon*, Logos 30.2 (= Logos VI.2 of the Syriac recension). For the text, see Réné Draguet, ed., *Les cinq recensions de l'Ascéticon syriaque d'Abba Isaïe*, CSCO 293 (Louvain: 1968). See the bibliography for chapter 8.

102. Abba Isaiah, *Asceticon*, Logos 30.1 (= Syriac Logos VI.1) (trans. my own).

103. Abba Isaiah, *Asceticon*, Logos 30.5G (= Syriac Logos VI.5G) (trans. my own).

104. *AP* Isaiah 9, 10, and 11 are from Logos 28.2, "Branches of Evil."

105. *Collectio Monastica*, ed. Victor Arras, CSCO 238–239 (Louvain: Peeters, 1963). For a study, see William Harmless, "Remembering Poemen Remembering: The Desert Fathers and the Spirituality of Memory," *Church History* 69 (2000): 483–518.

106. *Collectio Monastica* 14.64 (CSCO 238:125).

107. Regnault, "Les Apophtegmes des pères en Palestine aux Ve–VIe siècles," *Irénikon* 54 (1981): 320–330; reprinted in *Les pères du désert à travers leurs Apophtegmes* (Sablé-sur-Sarthe: Abbaye Saint-Pierre de Solesmes, 1987) 73–83. Chitty had made the claim earlier: "Books of the Old Men," 16–17, and *The Desert a City*, 67–68.

108. Chitty, *The Desert a City*, 74. *AP* includes the sayings of Longinus, who was abbot of the monastery of Enaton, outside Alexandria, and an outspoken opponent of the council. Also, *AP* Poemen 183 (PG 65:365; CS 59:192), speaks of Abba John, who was exiled by Emperor Marcian; presumably John was a Monophysite. *AP* Phocas 1 mentions a time after Chalcedon when in the Cells, there are two churches, one for the Chalcedonians, one for the Monophysites, while *AP* Gelasius 4 (PG 65:149; CS 59:48) is supportive of Juvenal of Jerusalem and the council. But it should be noted both Gelasius 4 and Phocas are absent from the Latin and Greek Systematic collections, implying that they may have been late additions.

109. Stewart, "Radical Honesty," 25.

110. *Verba Seniorum* 10.114 (PL 73:933; trans. Chadwick, LCC, 131).

BIBLIOGRAPHY

Themes in the *Apophthegmata Patrum*

Two works cited earlier take up many of the themes covered in this chapter: Douglas Burton-Christie, *The Word in the Desert: Scripture and the Quest for Holiness in Early Christian Monasticism* (New York: Oxford University Press, 1993); and Graham Gould, *The Desert Fathers on Monastic Community*, Oxford Early Christian Studies (New York: Oxford University Press, 1993). Other valuable studies include:

Brown, Peter. *The Body and Society: Men, Women, and Sexual Renunciation in Early Christianity*. New York: Columbia University Press, 1988.

Burton-Christie, Douglas. "Oral Culture and Biblical Interpretation." *Studia Patristica* 30 (1997): 144–150.

———. "Practice Makes Perfect': Interpretation of Scripture in the *Apophthegmata Patrum*." *Studia Patristica* 20 (1989): 213–218.

Chryssavgis, John. "The Sacredness of Creation in the *Sayings of the Desert Fathers*." *Studia Patristica* 25 (1993): 346–351.

Dörries, Hermann. "The Place of Confession in Ancient Monasticism." *Studia Patristica* 5 (1962): 284–311.

Gould, Graham E. "Lay Christians, Bishops, and Clergy in the *Apophthegmata Patrum*." *Studia Patristica* 25 (1993): 397–404.

———. "Moving On and Staying Put in the *Apophthegmata Patrum*." *Studia Patristica* 20 (1989): 231–237.

Guillaumont, Antoine. "La conception du désert chez les moines d'Égyptes." In *Aux origines du monachisme chrétien: Pour une phénoménologie du monachisme*, 69–87. SO 30. Bégrolles-en-Mauges: Abbaye de Bellefontaine, 1979.

———. "The Jesus Prayer among the Monks of Egypt." *Eastern Churches Review* 6 (1974): 66–71.

———. "Le séparation du monde dans l'Orient chrétien." In *Études sur la spiritualité de l'Orient chrétien*, 105–112. SO 66. Bégrolles-en-Mauges: Abbaye de Bellefontaine, 1996.

———. "Les visions mystiques dans le monachisme oriental chrétien." In *Aux origines du monachisme chrétien: pour une phénoménologie du monachisme*, 136–147. SO 30. Bégrolles-en-Mauges: Abbaye de Bellefontaine, 1979.

Hausherr, Irénée. *Penthos: The Doctrine of Compunction in the Christian East*. CS 53. Trans. Anselm Hufstader. Kalamazoo, Mich.: Cistercian Publications, 1982.

———. *Spiritual Direction in the Early Christian East*. CS 116. Trans. Anthony P. Gythiel. Kalamazoo, Mich.: Cistercian Publications, 1990.

Miquel, Pierre. *Lexique du Désert: étude de quelques mots-clés du vocabulaire monastique grec ancien*. SO 44. Bégrolles-en-Mauges: Abbaye de Bellefontaine, 1986.

Miller, Patricia Cox. "Desert Asceticism and 'The Body from Nowhere'." *Journal of Early Christian Studies* 2 (1994): 137–153.

Regnault, Lucien. *The Day-to-Day Life of the Desert Fathers in Fourth-Century Egypt*. Petersham, Mass.: St. Bede's, 1999.

———. "The Beatitudes in the *Apophthegmata Patrum*." *Eastern Churches Review* 6 (1974): 22–43.

———. "La prière continuelle 'monologistos' dans la littérature apophtegmatique." *Irénikon* 47 (1974): 467–493. Reprinted in *Les pères du désert à travers leur apophtegmes*, 113–139. Sablé-sur-Sarthe: Abbaye Saint-Pierre de Solesmes, 1987.

Špidlik, Tomáš. *The Spirituality of the Christian East: A Systematic Handbook.* CS 79. Trans. Anthony P. Gythiel. Kalamazoo, Mich.: Cistercian Publications, 1986.

Stewart, Columba. "Radical Honesty about the Self: The Practice of the Desert Fathers." *Sobornost* 12 (1990): 25–39.

Isaiah of Scetis

For the text of *Asceticon* of Abba Isaiah, see René Draguet, *Les cinq recensions de l'Ascéticon syriaque d'Abba Isaïe*, CSCO 289–290 (Syriac text), 293–294 (Greek and Latin texts and French translation) (Louvain: Secrétariat du Corpus SCO, 1968). For a translation, see *Abba Isaiah of Scetis: Ascetic Discourses*, ed. John Chryssavgis and Pachomios (Robert) Penkett, CS150 (Kalamazoo, Mich.: Cistercian Publications, 2003). For a French translation, see H. de Broc, *Isaïe de Scété: recueil ascétique*, 2nd ed., SO 7bis (Bégrolles-en-Mauges: Abbaye de Bellefontaine, 1985). For an introduction, see John Chryssavgis, "Abba Isaiah of Scetis: Aspects of Spiritual Direction," *Studia Patristica* 35 (2001): 32–40. See also:

Chitty, Derwas J. "Abba Isaiah." *Journal of Theological Studies* n.s. 22 (1971): 47–72.

Regnault, Lucien. "Isaïe de Scété ou de Gaza." In *Dictionnaire de spiritualité ascétique et mystique: doctrine et histoire*, 7:2083–2095. Paris: G. Beauchesne et ses fils, 1932–1995.

———. "Isaïe de Scété ou de Gaza? Note critiques en marge d'une introduction au probleme iasïen." *Revue d'ascétique et mystique* 46 (1970): 33–44.

Apophthegmata Patrum: Studies of the Text and Its History

Remarkable research has been done on the text and its history over the last eighty years. These studies tend to be rather technical but are crucial for the interpretation of the text. A valuable overview to this is in Graham Gould, *The Desert Fathers on Monastic Community*, Oxford Early Christian Studies (New York: Oxford University Press, 1993), 1–25. The two great pioneering studies are Wilhelm Bousset, *Apophthegmata. Studien zur Geschichte des ältesten Mönchtums* (Tübingen: Mohr, 1923), and Jean-Claude Guy, *Recherches sur la tradition grecque des Apophthegmata Patrum*, SH 36 (Brussels: Société des Bollandistes, 1962). Two key studies on the origins and development of the collections are by Lucien Regnault: "Aux origines des collections d'apophtegmes," *Studia Patristica* 18 (1989): 61–74; and "Les apophtegmes des pères en Palestine aux Vᵉ–VIᵉ siècles," *Irenikon* 54 (1981): 320–330; reprinted in *Les pères du désert à travers leurs apophtegmes* (Sablé-sur-Sarthe: Abbaye Saint Pierre de Solesmes, 1987), 73–83. Other valuable studies include:

Chitty, Derwas J. "The Books of the Old Men." *Eastern Churches Review* 6 (1974): 15–21.

Draguet, Réné. "Les apophtegmes des moines d'Égypte: problèmes littéraires." *Academie royalle de Belgique, bulletin de la classe des lettres et des sciences morales et politiques* 5ᵉ ser., t. 47 (1961): 134–149.

Goehring, James E. "The Encroaching Desert: Literary Production and Ascetic Space in Early Christian Egypt." *Journal of Early Christian Studies* 1 (1993): 281–296.

Guillaumont, Antoine. "L'enseignement spirituel des moines d'Égypte: la formation d'une tradition." In *Études sur la spiritualité de l'Orient chrétien*, 81–92. SO 66. Bégrolles-en-Mauges: Abbaye de Bellefontaine, 1996.

Guy, Jean-Claude. "Note sur l'évolution du genre apophtégmatique." *Revue d'ascétique et de mystique* 32 (1956): 63–68.

———. "La tradition manuscrite des *Apophthegmata Patrum*." *Revue d'ascétique et de mystique* 41 (1965): 113–118.

Regnault, Lucien. "La transmission des apophtegmes." In *Les pères du désert à travers leurs apophtegmes*, 65–72. Sablé-sur-Sarthe: Abbaye Saint-Pierre de Solesmes, 1987.

Sauget, J. M. "Une nouvelle collection éthiopienne d'*Apophthegmata Patrum*." *Orientalia Christiana Periodica* 31 (1965): 177–188.

APPENDIX 8.1

The Systematic Collections of the
Apophthegmata Patrum

In this appendix are the chapter titles for the four major versions of the Systematic Collection of the *Apophthegmata Patrum*. These titles give a rough indication of major themes and emphases. Also listed is the number of sayings per chapter (or book).

The Greek Systematic Collection

	Chapter Titles	No. of sayings
Book I	Exhortation of the holy fathers concerning progress toward perfection	37
Book II	Concerning peace (*hesychia*) to be pursued with all eagerness	35
Book III	Concerning compunction	56
Book IV	Concerning temperance in food and concerning the mastery of all	104
Book V	Various stories to keep on guard against assaults of luxury	54
Book VI	Concerning poverty and the necessity of keeping oneself from avarice	28
Book VII	Various stories training us to patience and courage	62
Book VIII	That nothing be done for show	32
Book IX	To be on watch to not judge anyone	26
Book X	Concerning discernment	194
Book XI	Concerning the necessity of constant vigilance	127
Book XII	Concerning unceasing prayer	28
Book XIII	Concerning hospitality and almsgiving done with joy	19
Book XIV	Concerning obedience	32
Book XV	Concerning humility	136
Book XVI	Concerning long-suffering	30
Book XVII	Concerning charity	35
Book XVIII	Concerning great visionaries	53
Book XIX	Concerning those who work miracles	21
Book XX	Concerning virtuous behavior	24
Book XXI	Sayings of those who endure in asceticism, showing their eminent virtue	66
Total		1199

Verba Seniorum of Pelagius and John (Latin)

	Chapter Titles	No. of Sayings
Book I	Concerning the perfecting of the fathers	23
Book II	Concerning quiet	16
Book III	Concerning compunction	27
Book IV	Concerning continence	70
Book V	Concerning fornication	41
Book VI	Concerning [the idea] that a monk should possess nothing	22
Book VII	Concerning patience, or fortitude	47
Book VIII	Concerning [the idea] that nothing should be done for show	24
Book IX	Concerning that we should judge no man	12
Book X	Concerning discernment	113
Book XI	Concerning [the idea] that it is right to live soberly	54
Book XII	Concerning [the idea] that we ought to pray unceasingly and soberly	15
Book XIII	Concerning [the idea] that it is best to be hospitable and show mercy with cheerfulness	14
Book XIV	Concerning obedience	19
Book XV	Concerning humility	89
Book XVI	Concerning patience	19
Book XVII	Concerning charity	25
Book XVIII	Concerning foresight or contemplation	36
Book XIX	Concerning the holy old men who used to work signs	17
Book XX	Concerning the best sayings of various saints	18
Book XXI	The 7 chapters that Abba Moses sent to Abba Poemen [and other miscellaneous sayings]	24
Total		725

The Syriac Paradise of the Fathers by Ânân Îshô

	Chapter Tittles	No. of Sayings
Book I, Chapter 1	Palladius on flight from men and silent contemplation	Sayings 1–62
Book I, Chapter 2	Concerning fasting and abstinence	Saying 63–104
Book I, Chapter 3	Concerning the reading of the scriptures, night vigils, the service of the Psalms, and constant prayer	Saying 105–135
Book I, Chapter 4	Concerning the weeping and mourning for sins	Sayings 136–157
Book I, Chapter 5	Concerning voluntary poverty	Saying 158–182
Book I, Chapter 6	Concerning patient endurance	Saying 183–237
Book I, Chapter 7	Concerning obedience to God and man	Saying 238–247
Book I, Chapter 8	Concerning watchfulness in thought, word, and deed	Sayings 248–392
Book I, Chapter 9	Concerning love, charity, and hospitality	Sayings 393–443
Book I, Chapter 10	Concerning humility	Sayings 444–558
Book I, Chapter 11	Concerning fornication	Sayings 559–597
Book I, Chapter 12	Concerning the acceptance of repentance	Sayings 598–613
Book I, Chapter 13	Concerning the fathers who wrought wonderful works	Saying 614–630
Book I, Chapter 14	Concerning the greatness of the solitary life	Sayings 631–635
Book II, Chapters 1–15	Questions and answers on the ascetic rule	Sayings 1–539
Book II, Chapters 16–17	Questions and answers by the fathers and monks	Sayings 540–576
Book II, Chapter 18	Questions and answers on the vision of the mind	Sayings 577–602
Appendix		Sayings 603–705

The Armenian *Paterica*

	Chapter Titles	No. of Sayings
Book I	Concerning perfect virtue	46 + 116R
Book II	Concerning quiet	28 + 37R
Book III	Concerning compunction and tears	50 + 36R
Book IV	Concerning abstinence	58 + 63R
Book V	Concerning fornication	81 + 47R
Book VI	Concerning destitution	20 + 23R
Book VII	Concerning strength and forbearance	45 + 49R
Book VIII	Concerning doing nothing for show	18 + 15R
Book IX	Concerning discernment	27 + 19R
Book X	Concerning divine and right judgment	79 + 114R
Book XI	Concerning vigilance and sobriety	34 + 51R
Book XII	Concerning prayer	11 + 14R
Book XIII	Concerning being hospitable and merciful	17 + 19R
Book XIV	Concerning obedience	17 + 19R
Book XV	Concerning humility	71 + 100R
Book XVI	Concerning forgetfulness of injuries	9 + 18R
Book XVII	Concerning loving God and neighbor	26 + 35R
Book XVIII	Concerning spirit-seeing and wonder-working of the fathers	93 + 39R
Book XIX	Concerning the conversation of the fathers	28 + 26R
Total		1598

APPENDIX 8.2

Paul of Tamma, *On the Cell*

Numerous sayings in the *Apophthegmata* discuss the rigors and joys of the solitary life in the cell. This theme forms the centerpiece of the writings of Paul of Tamma. Paul was a fourth-century hermit and is celebrated as a saint in the Coptic church. But since he makes no appearance in the classic Greek and Latin texts, such as the *Apophthegmata* or Palladius's *Lausiac History*, he is virtually unknown in the West, even in scholarly circles. A life of Paul attributed to his disciple Ezekiel has been preserved, but it offers little of historical value. Its often fanciful episodes tell us more about the hagiographic imagination than about the fourth-century hermit. It claims, for instance, that Paul practiced such a severe asceticism that he ended up dying six times, including once by burying himself in sand and another time by flinging himself off a cliff; after each deadly instance, Jesus appeared and resuscitated him.

The extant writings of Paul of Tamma are in Sahidic Coptic and have only recently been published and translated. The texts, excerpted here, are all brief: *On the Cell*, *On Humility*, and *On Poverty*, as well as a letter and an untitled work on life in the cell. The texts are, for the most part, short strings of proverbs reminiscent of Old Testament wisdom literature such as Proverbs and Sirach. They celebrate an uncompromising devotion to the solitary life.

The Cell as Meeting Ground of God and Monk

> My son, obey God and keep his commandments, and be wise and
> remain in your dwelling, which is your delight, and your cell will
> remain with you in your heart as you seek its blessing, and the labor
> of your cell will go with you to God. . . . For you will know God in
> your cell. Keep him with you and the Devil will depart from you,
> which will allow you to tame him. . . . Do not forsake God. Do not
> forsake your cell. For the incense of God is a wise man in his cell.
> The altar of God is a wise man in his cell. The glory of God will
> appear to him there. . . . A poor man who remains in his cell is a
> king and lord. Honor him, for God is dwelling in him. (Paul of
> Tamma, *De Cella* 1, 34, 51–55, 119)

The Monk as Desert Lion

In most early Christian literature, the lion is a symbol of the devil—following
1 Peter 5:8, which speaks of the devil as a "lion prowling around looking for

someone to devour." Paul, by contrast, uses the image positively, as a symbol of the monk's hiddenness and endurance:

> Truly the lion leaves the desert and erases his pawprints with his tail. If he prevails over the person who has come out to [hunt] him, he goes up in complete confidence. . . . Now then, you who are poor, you shall look boldly upon your enemies like the roaring lions."
> (Paul of Tamma, *De Cella* 7 and 28)

THE MONK AS SHIP'S PILOT

Paul compares the monk skilled in the discernment of spirits to a ship's pilot. This was perhaps a familiar image to one who grew up near the Nile:

> Be like the master sailors piloting their ships as you watch the wind to see what direction it is taking you, whether it is a good wind or bad that is coming. (Paul of Tamma, *Untitled Work*, 100)

WORDPLAY

Paul, like the prophet Jeremiah, sometimes fashioned oracular sayings that joined poetic imagery with puns. The following proverbs rely on a wordplay between the Coptic terms for "God" (*pnoute*) and "abyss" (*pnoun*):

> Do not be like the thorny acacias that grow on the mountain, which is God. Instead, be like a reed growing in the water, which is the abyss. (Paul of Tamma, *Untitled Work*, 203–204)

For the texts, see Tito Orlandi, *Paolo di Tamma: Opere* (Rome, 1988). For a translation and analysis, see Tim Vivian, "Paul of Tamma: Four Works Concerning Monastic Spirituality," *Coptic Church Review* 17, no. 3 (1996): 110–112, and "Paul of Tamma: On the Monastic Cell (*De Cella*)," *Hallel* 23, no. 2 (1998): 86–107.

APPENDIX 8.3

Concerning Thoughts (*Peri Logismon*)

The editors of the great collections of apophthegms certainly drew on oral traditions about famous *abba*s of Egypt. But they also had at hand smaller collections of written apophthegms, such as the ten that Evagrius Ponticus appended to his work *Praktikos* or the *Seven Headings on Ascetic Conduct* that Abba Moses composed. Some of these small written collections continued to circulate independently. This collection—usually called *Concerning Thoughts* (*Peri logismon*)—is one of those. It is a list of thirty-one questions and answers. We have seen how young monks manifested their "thoughts" to the old men, seeking their wisdom to discern the issues that haunted them in their solitude. This collection seems to contain terse distillations of such encounters.

KNOWLEDGE OF GOD AND THE CELL

Question: How should the monk live in his cell? Answer: He should keep away from human knowledge so that when he is freed from thought the knowledge of God might dwell in him. (*Peri logismon* 1)

MONK AS DOVE

Question: What does the monk try to do? Answer: The monk is a dove: when it's time for a dove to fly it spreads its wings and flies, but if it remains outside its nest too long it's set upon by wild birds and loses its dignity and beauty. It's the same with the monk: there comes a time for him at the public assembly to "give wing" to his thoughts, but if he remains outside his cell too long he's set upon by the demons and his thoughts are darkened. (*Peri logismon* 2)

FURNACE OF ANGER

Question: I want to be a witness for God. Answer: If someone bears with his neighbor during a fit of temper, it is equal to the furnace at the time of the three youths. (*Peri logismon* 13)

DEVIL AS FISHERMAN

Question: How can a person keep away from the plots of the demons? Answer: A fish cannot stop a fisherman from casting his hook into the sea, but if the fish is aware of the hook's evil he can avoid it and be saved, leaving the fisherman empty-handed. It's the same for a person. (*Peri Logismon* 18)

THOUGHTS AS CRASHING WAVES

Question: Can a person sin because of an idea? Answer: Waves never injure [a] rock; in the same way an unsuccessful assault will never harm a person, for it is written that any sin not brought to completion is not a sin. (*Peri logismon* 19)

For the Greek text, see J.-C. Guy, "Un dialogue monastique inédit: ΠΕΡΙ ΛΟΓΙΣΜΟΝ," *Revue d'ascétique et mystique* 33 (1957): 171–188. For a translation and an analysis, see Tim Vivian, "Words to Live By: A Conversation that the Elders Had with One Another Concerning Thoughts (*Peri logismon*)," *St. Vladimir's Theological Quarterly* 39 (1995): 127–141.

APPENDIX 8.4

Isaiah of Scetis, *Asceticon*

A handful of writers were especially important in popularizing and promulgating the spirituality of Egyptian monasticism to the larger Roman world. John Cassian, for instance, played a key role in bringing Egyptian ideals and practices to the Latin West. One might say something similar about Abba Isaiah of Scetis: he helped bring Egyptian spirituality to Palestine. Isaiah—as best as scholars can reconstruct things—seems to have been an Egyptian monk who left Scetis sometime in the 430s. He made a pilgrimage to the Holy Land and settled finally in Beit Daltha, near Gaza. He was accompanied by a disciple named Peter and emerged as the head of a community of monks there in Gaza, where he lived until his death in 491. Isaiah himself was a Monophysite, and some of his disciples were stalwart opponents of the Council of Chalcedon. But Isaiah was, to his disciples' dismay, deeply tolerant of competing views and was consulted by and respected by Monophysites, Chalcedonians, and Nestorians alike. We today would call Isaiah an ecumenist.

A large work known as the *Asceticon* (or "Ascetic Discourses") has come down to us under his name. The work, composed originally in Greek, is a sprawling anthology, over 200 pages in a modern edition. The best-known manuscript contains twenty-nine Logoi ("discourses," "essays"), but an important thirtieth one has been discovered both in certain Greek manuscripts and in an early Syriac translation. Logos 30 contains stories that would make their way into the final edition of the *Apophthegmata Patrum*, and the differences between it and the final edition of the *Apophthegmata* offer clues about how the *Apophthegmata* finally assumed written form. Isaiah and his circle, it seems, was one of those monastic groups responsible for compiling the stories and saying that eventually became the *Apophthegmata*.

But Isaiah's work is fascinating in its own terms. It contains a diverse mix of genres: brief essays, letters, sayings, and sermons. Some Logoi are instructions for beginners:

Logos 3: "Statutes for Novices"
Logos 9: "Precepts for Those Who Have Renounced the World"

Some Logoi are brief anthologies of sayings by and stories about Isaiah recorded by his disciple Peter (e.g., Logoi 8, 10, 18, 23, and 26); in fact, Logos 8 is entitled "Apophthegmata." Much of Isaiah's teaching is practical and apodictic, closely mirroring the brand of teaching that appears in the *Apophthegmata*.

MANUAL LABOR

If you do your manual labor, do not be negligent, but apply yourself with the fear of God, in order not to sin by ignorance. (Isaiah of Scetis, *Asceticon*, Logos 3.29)

HESYCHIA AND LIFE IN THE CELL

Someone also asked [Isaiah]: "What is it to live in peace within the cell?" And he answered: "To live in peace within the cell means to throw oneself before God and do whatever possible to resist every evil thought suggested by the enemy. That is what it means to flee the world." (Isaiah of Scetis, *Asceticon*, Logos 21.13)

MANIFESTATION OF THOUGHTS

If you ask an old man about a "thought," freely disclose the "thought" to him if you know that he is worthy of confidence and that he will keep confidential what you have said to him. (Isaiah of Scetis, *Asceticon*, Logos 4.3)

DON'T CRITICIZE THE COOK

If your brother has prepared a dish that is not good, don't say to him: "You cooked it wrong!" For that is death for your soul. Rather, examine yourself. If it had been you who had heard that from someone else, how you would have been troubled by it! (Isaiah of Scetis, *Asceticon*, Logos 5.5)

SEEKING FORGIVENESS

If you do something wrong in some matter, do not be steered by shame, but be converted and say, "Forgive me," and your fault will pass away. (Isaiah of Scetis, *Asceticon*, Logos 3.24)

HUMILITY

Love humility, and it will protect you from your sins. (Isaiah of Scetis, *Asceticon*, Logos 9.15)

EACH DAY AS LAST

Think each day: "I have only today to live in the world," and you will not sin against God. (Isaiah of Scetis, *Asceticon*, Logos 9.21)

UNCEASING PRAYER

Love to pray without ceasing, so that your heart will be enlightened. (Isaiah of Scetis, *Asceticon*, Logos 16.23)

But these brief sayings and admonitions are only one side of Isaiah's teaching. There are also extended homilies that use Origenist style of biblical interpretation: that is, rich detailed allegories (e.g., Logoi 4, 11, 12, and 21). There is also a long and touching letter that Isaiah wrote to Peter when he first entered monastic life (Logos 25). Some treatises are intended for anchorites and some for cenobites:

> Logos 4: "Concerning the Conscience of Those Who Live Habitually in the Cell"
> Logos 5: "Concerning Sure Precepts and the Edification of Those Who Wish to Live Together in Peace"

There are also brief treatises on individual virtues and the spiritual life:

> Logos 14: "The Practice of Almsgiving"
> Logos 15: "Concerning Renunciation"
> Logos 20: "Humility"
> Logos 21: "On Penitence"
> Logos 23: "Concerning Perfection"
> Logos 24: "Concerning Passionlessness"

Isaiah had some very distinctive theological views, and theories about nature, grace, and Christ's redemptive work. The passage below is an excerpt from Logos 2, a treatise entitled "On the Natural State of the Spirit."

Our Original Nature and the Unnaturalness of Sin

"I do not want you to be ignorant, brothers, that in the beginning, when God created humankind, he placed [Adam] in paradise with his faculties pure and stable in their natural state. But when [Adam] listened to the seducer, all his faculties got turned around into a state of anti-nature, and he fell precipitously from his glory. Our Lord had pity on the human race because of his great love. "The Word became flesh" (John 1:14), that is to say, "but without sin" (Heb. 4:14), in order to bring what was anti-nature back into conformity with nature by means of his holy body; and having pitied humankind, he made fit to return to paradise, revealing to those who walk in his footsteps and according to his commandments which he gave to us such that we can conquer those things that had rejected us from our glory; and he taught us a [way of] holy service and a law such that humankind can hold itself in its natural state, the one God had created it for. (Isaiah of Scetis, Asceticon, Logos 2.1–4)

Climbing onto the Cross of Christ

Abba Isaiah, like John Cassian, would compare the monastic journey to the journey of Christ to the cross. Yet Isaiah gives it some unique accents: the monk needs to "climb onto the cross," and this "climbing onto the cross" signals an entrance not into suffering, but into passionlessness:

> [Abba Isaiah] also said: "If our Lord Jesus Christ had not first healed all the passions of humankind for whom he came [into the flesh], he would not be raised onto the cross. So before the Lord came into the flesh, humankind was blind, mute, paralyzed, deaf, leprous, and lame, taken to death by all that is contrary to nature. When he had pity for us and came among us, he raised up the dead, he made the lame walk, made the blind see, made the mute speak, made the deaf hear, and raised up the new man, free of every infirmity. So that is what he raised onto the cross. (Isaiah of Scetis, *Asceticon*, Logos 8.55)

THE GOOD THIEF'S VIEW FROM THE CROSS

> And two thieves were hung with [Jesus]; the one on the right gave glory to him and implored him, saying: "Remember me, Lord, when you come into your Kingdom" (Luke 22:42); and the one on the left blasphemed against him. This is the meaning: before the spirit is awakened from its negligence, it is with the Enemy; and if our Lord Jesus Christ resurrects it from its negligence and makes it recover its vision and discern all things, it can thus climb up onto the cross. (Isaiah of Scetis, *Asceticon*, Logos 8.55)

CHRIST'S PASSION AS MODEL

> The cross is the sign of immortality. . . . Jesus prayed [in the garden]: "If it is possible, let this cup pass far from me in this hour" (cf. Matt. 26:39). This word is for us: if the spirit wishes to climb onto the cross, it needs a great deal of prayer and abundant tears; it must be submissive at every hour before God in asking the help of his bounty, such that he fortify us and guard us until he resurrects us into a holy and invincible newness. For the peril is great in the hour on the cross. . . . Our teacher himself, our beloved Lord God Jesus, was our model in everything, as the Apostle says of him: "to know Christ and the power of his resurrection and the sharing of his sufferings by becoming like him in his death, if somehow I may attain the resurrection from the dead" (Philipp. 3:10–11). . . . The vinager he tasted for us was in order that we might extinguish every vain agitation. . . . The crown of thorns, braided and placed on his head, is an example to us in order that we might carry the blame which comes to us, in suffering insults at every hour without being troubled by them. . . . That Jesus was delivered up in order to be flogged before being crucified is an example to us that we might mistrust every human affront and every infamy. . . . These are the things a person must do in order to climb up with him onto the cross. (Isaiah of Scetis, *Asceticon*, Logos 13.2–3)

THE CROSS AS ENTRY INTO PASSIONLESSNESS

Who are those who hold tight to Jesus during the temptations if not those who have resisted the counter-natural vices until they at least cut them off? . . . Therefore the one who wishes to eat and drink at his table walks with him toward the cross. The cross of Jesus is thus the abstaining from all the passions. (Isaiah of Scetis, *Asceticon*, Logos 16.125)

For the text of *Asceticon* of Abba Isaiah, see René Draguet, ed., *Les cinq recensions de l'Ascéticon syriaque d'Abba Isaïe*, CSCO 289–290, 293–294. For a French translation, see H. de Broc, *Isaïe de Scété: recueil ascétique*, SO 7bis (Bégrolles-en-Mauges: Abbaye de Bellefontaine, 1985). The translations here are my own. See the bibliography for chapter 8 for suggested studies.

APPENDIX 8.5

The Ethiopic *Collectio Monastica*

In 1963, Victor Arras published a newly discovered Ethiopic text entitled *Collectio Monastica* (or *Monastic Collection*). The work, as it has come down to us, is a hodgepodge divided into sixty-eight chapters of varying length. Some chapters contain only a single story, while others have excerpts from sermons or treatises. Interspersed through the *Collectio* are several mini-collections of sayings of the desert fathers. Chapters 13 and 14 are especially interesting. Of the 166 sayings found there, only 22 have any known parallels in the classic Greek and Latin collections. In other words, these two chapters contain a great deal of previously unknown material. They preserve what seems to be a primitive collection of sayings composed originally in Greek or Coptic. Careful analysis of the text indicates that the monk-compiler lived in the mid-fifth century. Either he himself had lived at Scetis, or he knew monks who had. He also seems to have known Poemen personally and records a number of unique sayings and episodes about him. Here is one example of a saying that appears both in the Ethiopic *Collectio* and the Greek *Apophthegmata*. In it, Abba Poemen plays on a common experience of the desert dweller: one must be alert for snakes and scorpions hiding in dark places in one's house:

Ethiopic *Collectio Monastica* 13.84	Greek *Apophthegmata Patrum* Poemen 21
A brother said to me:	Abba Joseph put the same question
"Abba Poemen said to me,	and Abba Poemen said to him,
'See this empty jar. If someone were to fill it with serpents, lizards, and scorpions	"If someone shuts a snake and a scorpion up in a bottle,
and then leave the jar sealed and abandon it, aren't all these reptiles going to die there? And if you open the jar, won't all the creatures get out and sting people? And so, it's the same for a man:	in time they will be completely destroyed. So it is with evil thoughts:

| if he watches his tongue | they are suggested by
the demons, |
| and shuts his mouth,
all the creatures die under him.
But should he work his tongue and speak,
the venomous creatures will come out
and sting his brothers
and the Lord will be angry.' " | they will disappear
with patience." |

The differences are interesting. The Ethiopic version gives the saying as a first-person narrative and shows it to be at one generation's remove, while the Greek names Abba Joseph as the source. Both versions play on the same analogy: creatures with a deadly sting sealed in a bottle. But their precise morals differ somewhat. In the Greek *Apophthegmata*, the issue is impure thoughts suggested by demons that will, in time, disappear. In the Ethiopic *Collectio*, the issue is hurtful words. Here Poemen echoes a common teaching in desert spirituality: that words can wound, and the monk needs to keep a lid on things. The following are some additional excerpts of sayings unique to the *Collectio Monastica*; all are attributed to Abba Poemen.

HUMILITY OF SPIRIT

A brother also said to me: "I asked Abba Poemen: 'What is humility of spirit?' He said to me: 'Reject your desire, put it behind you; that is, cut out your own desire and put it behind that of your brother. That is perfect humility of spirit of the Lord.' "(*Collectio Monastica* 14.60 [CSCO 238:124])

THREE MYSTERIES

Abba Poemen said: "There are three mysteries that I always try to keep before me: to pray before the Lord, always, without ceasing; to place my death before me at all times; and to consider that, when I die, I will be thrown into the fire because of my sins." (*Collectio Monastica* 14.11 [CSCO 238:111])

OSTRICH HUNTING

I went over to Abba Poemen . . . and he said to me: "It is said that when the ostrich lays eggs in the desert, the hunters come and follow it by its claw tracks; that they find the egg and take it away. That is why you must guard the works which you do for the Lord and keep them lest you waste your efforts. For whatever a man does in secret, that the Lord loves. The pure man's inner toil is this. For it is by that that a man wins the victory. For his soul desires pride—and that [pride] is death. The fear of the Lord and discernment blot out every stain." (*Collectio Monastica* 13.7 [CSCO 238:84–85])

VISITING THE OLD MEN

A brother said to me: "Many days I visited the old man. A brother had harbored jealousy about it and said to me: 'How often you visit that old man! Don't you have any work [to do]?' I said to the old man: 'Don't you see this brother who reproaches me for coming to you?' And the old man said to me: 'I often asked Abba Poemen about that and he responded to me: "Do you see this field? When the produce in it is abundant many guard it. But if you go at the end of the harvest, you will find there only a few pieces of produce. The field's proprietor and his workers arm themselves with clubs and keep vigil so that neither animals nor birds might come and eat the fruit. This field is the end times. You come across a few old men as friends. So today, don't get irritated against those who visit the old men so as to live on account of the Lord." ' " (*Collectio Monastica* 13.6 [CSCO 238:84])

ALLEGORY: THE MONK AS MOSES

Abba Poemen said: "The rocks Moses placed under his two arms until Joshua had conquered Amalek and exterminated them are the fear of the Lord and the humility of the spirit. To flee sin and not be submissive to it: that is the fear of the Lord. And to carry all your sins: that is humility of spirit. When Achan, the son of Carmi, stole the gold ingot and the mantle of Shinear in Jericho, and when Israel went to war against the Philistines and the Philistines conquered Israel, Joshua was in pain and shed tears before the Lord and said: 'Why, Lord, have you delivered us into the hands of our enemies in order that they may exterminate us?' The Lord said to Joshua: 'Why do you weep before me? Go, remove from yourself the objects of anathema and I will deliver your enemies into your hands.' And when the Israelites had removed from their midst the objects of anathema, the Lord delivered their enemies into their hands. We too should push away now from our midst the objects of anathema. But now the bad thought is always with us. And the bad thought—that's the object of anathema. The bad thought—that's to submit ourselves to these objects and do their wills. So the Lord does not live in us and it is why our enemies are victorious against us. But if we remove them from ourselves, we will conquer and we will exterminate them, because God will be with us." (*Collectio Monastica* 13.78 [CSCO 238:102–103])

REMEMBER THE WORDS OF THE OLD MEN

An old brother said to Abba Poemen: "When I remain here at your place, Father, thoughts assault me: that I should no longer come to you." And Abba Poemen said to him, "Why?" The brother said to

Abba Poemen: "Because I come to you and I hear your word, but I cannot do it. May your word not be my condemnation on that [last] day!" And Abba Poemen said to him: "I once talked with Abba Macarius at Scetis and Abba Macarius told me: 'Don't stop visiting the old men. There will come a day when, if you wish to serve [God], you will conquer by the word of old men. If thoughts erupt in you all over again, remember the words of the old men, and you will find help in them and you will be saved.' " (*Collectio Monastica* 13.72 [CSCO 238:101])

For the Ethiopic text, see Victor Arras, ed., *Collectio Monastica*, 238–239, CSCO (Louvain: Peeters, 1963). There is as yet no complete English translation, but Lucien Regnault translated chapters 13 and 14 into French in *Les sentences des pères du désert: nouveau recueil* (Solesmes, 1970), 287–338. The translations here are my own; special thanks to Getatchew Haile, who kindly checked their accuracy. For a study, see William Harmless, "Remembering Poemen Remembering: The Desert Fathers and the Spirituality of Memory," *Church History* 69 (2000): 483–518.

9

The Histories

If, as in Athanasius's words, the desert had become a city, then that city soon had to cope with the bustle and demands of tourists. Pilgrims from around the empire began flocking to the sages of Egypt, upsetting long-standing traditions of desert hospitality. Even the venerable Antony found himself needing to find ways to keep pilgrims at bay. According to one account, whenever visitors arrived, Antony used to ask his disciple: "Are they from Egypt or from Jerusalem?" This was a code. If they were easygoing tourists, the answer was, "They are from Egypt"; if sincere ascetics, the answer was, "They are from Jerusalem." Those "from Egypt" got the bare basics: a simple meal of lentils, a blessing, and a quick adieu. Those "from Jerusalem," on the other hand, received his full attention. He would "sit up all night talking to them about salvation."[1] This image of Antony differs from others we have seen. Here Antony appears not as the demon wrestler (as in Athanasius's *Life*) or the wise *abba* (as in the *Apophthegmata*), but as the paradigm of desert hospitality.

This story is found in the *Lausiac History* (*Historia Lausiaca*). Its author, Palladius (c. 363–c. 431), was a Galatian by birth and, after a stint in monasteries in Palestine, moved to Egypt around 388 (see table 9.1 for a chronological outline of his career). He lived for three years in Alexandria and studied with various teachers, including Didymus the Blind, head of Alexandria's Catechetical School. He then set out for the desert, living for a year at Nitria before moving on to Kellia, where he apprenticed for nine years under Evagrius Ponticus. Palladius left the desert, ostensibly for health reasons, around 399 or 400, just as the Origenist Controversy was heating up, and made his way to Constantinople. There he befriended the imperial capital's provocative and eloquent bishop, John Chrysostom, who, in

TABLE 9.1. Chronology of the *History* Writers

c. 345	Birth of Rufinus
c. 363	Birth of Palladius
374	Rufinus travels to Egypt
c. 375	Rufinus and Melania the Elder establish monastery on Mount of Olives
388	Palladius moves to Alexandria, studies with Didymus the Blind
391	Palladius moves to Nitria
392	Palladius moves to Kellia, apprentices with Evagrius Ponticus
394–395	Writer of the *History of the Monks* and companions travel through Egypt
399 or 400	Palladius leaves Egypt; beginning of the Origenist Controversy in Egypt
400	The *History of the Monks in Egypt* is published
c. 401 or 402	John Chrysostom ordains Palladius bishop of Helenopolis in Bithynia
403	Palladius attends Synod of the Oak, defends John Chrysostom
403	Rufinus leaves the Holy Land and returns to Italy; translates *History of the Monks in Egypt* into Latin
c. 404	Palladius goes to Rome to plead Chrysostom's case to Pope Innocent I
c. 406	Palladius exiled to Syene, writes *Dialogue on Life of John Chrysostom*
c. 410	Death of Rufinus
412	Palladius returns to Galatia
420s	Palladius composes *Lausiac History*
c. 431	Death of Palladius

turn, ordained him bishop of Helenopolis in Bithynia. After John was rail-roaded out of office (through Theophilus's skillful connivings at the Synod of the Oak in 403), Palladius went to Rome to plead the case of "blessed John" before Pope Innocent I. Upon his return, he was arrested and exiled to Upper Egypt by the Emperor Arcadius. It was there, sometime between 406 and 408, that he composed a biography of Chrysostom, defending his friend against detractors. In 412, after Theophilus's death, Palladius was able to return to his native Galatia.

A decade later, sometime in the early 420s, Palladius turned his literary energies to composing the *Lausiac History*, a memoir of his years in Egypt. He dedicated the work to the emperor's chamberlain, Lausus—thus the title. He notes that at the time of its publication, he was fifty-six years old, having been a monk for thirty-three years and a bishop for twenty. In this work, Palladius sketches some seventy portraits—"miniatures" might be the better term—of religious men and women that he had met or heard about. Each figure typically receives one chapter, though here and there he intersperses group portraits. Chapters range in length from a paragraph to a few pages and string together colorful anecdotes and brief morality tales. The larger work seems, at first sight, a hodgepodge without design or structure, but, as scholars have shown, it rests on a loose and rather complex autobiographical framework.[2] And while his work is narrative and not theology, Palladius does have definite theological biases and concerns (drawn, in part, from his teacher Evagrius), and these can shape the moral cast of his stories.[3] The *Lausiac History* became quite popular from an early date and was translated into Latin, Syriac, Armenian, Coptic, Ethiopic, and Arabic. (The Coptic version has been the focus of much recent work; for excerpts, see appendix 9.1.)

Palladius's work is often paired with another "history," the *History of the Monks in Egypt* (usually known by its Latin title, *Historia monachorum in Aegypto*). We do not know who wrote it, but the unnamed author recounts his adventures with six other Palestinian monks who journeyed through Egypt from September 394 to January 395 to visit the great ascetic figures there. The work uses a geographical outline, tracing the troupe's more-than-300-mile journey from south to north, from Lycopolis in the Thebaid to Diolcos in the delta (for a map, see figure 9.1). Like Palladius's work, the *History of the Monks* offers a string of miniatures, thirty-five portraits in twenty-six chapters. It is tourist literature and self-consciously draws on motifs from ancient travelogues. Like the *Odyssey*—or for that matter, *Gulliver's Travels*—it is full of exotic marvels and miraculous tales. The *History of the Monks* overlaps here and there with Palladius's *History*: the two works discuss some of the same figures and, on occasion, recount the same stories.

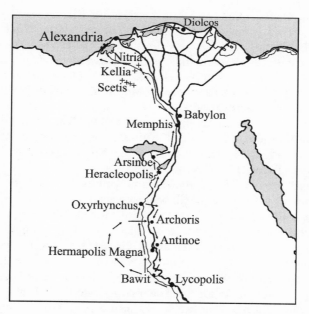

FIGURE 9.1. The author of the *History of the Monks* and his companions toured Egypt for several months, from 394 to 395. Their journey moved, for the most part, downriver, south to north. The narrative begins in Lycopolis with their visit to John of Lycopolis. They sailed downriver to Hermopolis Magna and then to Oxyrhynchus. They then turned back upriver to Archoris and Antinoë. The party then split up, and the author and two friends continued to Bawit. From there, they set off into the desert and, after getting lost, finally found their way back to Archoris. There the author rejoined his party, and the whole group moved south, stopping at Heracleopolis. They passed Memphis and Babylon and continued on to Nitria, visiting the monks there. Finally they traveled down to Alexandria, and then moved along the coast to Diolcos.

Soon after its publication, the *History of the Monks* was translated into Latin by Rufinus. Rufinus (c. 345–c. 410) had come from a wealthy family near Aquileia and received a fine education in Rome. There he became close friends with Saint Jerome, a cantankerous soul best known for his magisterial translation of the Bible into Latin, the so-called *Vulgate*. In 374, Rufinus traveled to Egypt to see firsthand all things monastic. Jerome gushed with envy: "I hear you are probing into the secrets of Egypt, visiting choruses of monks and making the rounds with heaven's family on earth."[4] After his tour, Rufinus moved to the Holy Land, where he collaborated with Melania the Elder in establishing a Latin-speaking monastery in Jerusalem. He would go on to earn lasting fame—and infamy—for his translations of Greek Christian works for the Latin West. These included controversial treatises and sermons by Origen, monastic works by Basil, and the *Church History* by Eusebius of Caesarea (which Rufinus supplemented with a two-volume appendix of his own). Around 403, soon after returning to Italy, Rufinus translated the anonymous *History of the Monks* into Latin.[5] And he translated it the way he translated everything: correcting errors, cleaning up the prose, adding tidbits not found in the original. In this case, he drew on his personal experiences of Egypt to fill in important details about famous monks he had met and famous monastic sites he had visited. The original Greek *History of the Monks* had been dedicated to brother monks in a monastery on the Mount of Olives in Jerusalem—presumably the same monastery where Rufinus had been superior. So Rufinus's translation is not surprising. Palladius and Rufinus had known one another from their days in Jerusalem. In fact, Rufinus makes a cameo appearance in the *Lausiac History*, and Palladius says of him, "Never was a more learned and reasonable man found."[6]

Palladius's *Lausiac History* and the anonymous *History of the Monks* (including Rufinus's Latin edition) will be our focus in this chapter. They deserve attention for several reasons. First, they give valuable glimpses of two of the great monastic settlements, Nitria and Kellia. Second, they highlight the link between the monastic and the miraculous. Finally, they powerfully influenced, both in content and in style, how monks and monasticism would appear in later Christian literature. The church historians Socrates and Sozomen lifted anecdotes from both works for their own large-scale narratives of the fourth- and fifth-century church. The two works also served as paradigms for later monastic writers who wished to publicize the heroics of monks in their own regions: for example, Theodoret of Cyrrhus's *Religious History* (on Syrian ascetics), Cyril of Scythopolis's *Lives* (on Palestinian monks), and Gregory the Great's *Dialogues* (which celebrates great Italian abbots, most famously Benedict).

Both texts have suffered precisely because of their popularity. Cuthbert Butler, the modern editor of the *Lausiac History*, has wryly noted, "So popular was it that no respect whatever was felt for its text: it was re-written, re-arranged, enlarged, shortened, paraphrased, combined with kindred works, without any scruple. Thus every known process of corruption—revision, interpolation, redaction, intermixture of texts—has had free play among the manuscripts, both of the Greek texts and the versions."⁷ A.-J. Festugière, the modern editor of the *History of the Monks,* faced a similar textual muddle. While text criticism lies beyond the scope of this introduction, we do need to be aware how these and other monastic texts took on a life of their own. Only works that touched something profound in the monastic soul could draw out such insistent scribal reworkings.

Nitria

In earlier chapters, we looked at three men usually credited with founding Egyptian monasticism: Antony, Pachomius, and Macarius the Egyptian. Here we meet a fourth, Amoun. According to Palladius, Amoun came from a wealthy family but at an early age was orphaned.⁸ When he was twenty-two, his uncle pressured him into getting married. But on his wedding night, after the guests had left, Amoun turned to his new bride and there in their bridal chamber exhorted her to celibacy, reading passage after passage from the Gospels and from the Letters of Paul. She acquiesced, and for the next eighteen years, they lived together under the same roof as brother and sister. Such celibate marriages were an old-fashioned and venerable tradition of Christian asceticism, attested especially in the Syrian tradition.⁹ Amoun spent these years cultivating his balsam plantation and devoting himself to prayer. Finally, Amoun's wife encouraged him to go public: "It is unspeakable that you hide such virtue as yours living together with me in virginity."¹⁰

And so sometime between 325 and 330, Amoun left and built for himself on the desert's edge two domed cells. There he would live for the next twenty-two years, returning twice a year to visit his wife. He soon attracted disciples, and his settlement would rapidly grow into one of the great centers of Egyptian monasticism: Nitria. In earlier chapters, we saw two others, Pachomius's Tabennesi and Macarius's Scetis. All three centers were founded within a decade of one another. Tabennesi and Scetis were remote and rarely visited by pilgrims from abroad—but not so Nitria. Nitria would achieve worldwide fame, in part because it was relatively accessible to the larger world, and pilgrims from elite circles, such as Rufinus, Melania the Elder, and Jerome, would broadcast what they saw.

For a long time, scholars misconstrued the whereabouts of Nitria, thinking it to be in Wādī al-Natrūn, where ancient Scetis was located. But in the 1920s, Hugh Evelyn White, with his brilliant command of the ancient sources and detailed knowledge of the geography, was able to pinpoint its location.¹¹ It was not, as one would imagine, in the depths of the desert. Rather, it stood on the western edge of the delta, some forty miles southeast of Alexandria, ten miles south of modern Damanhūr, where today one finds the village called (in Arabic) al-Barnūji or (in Coptic) Pernoudj. Palladius says that it took him a day and a half to get there from Alexandria—and that he came by boat!¹²

Nitria got its name from its proximity to lakes where niter was extracted. Niter was a valuable commodity used for (among other things) cleaning linen.

Ancients loved their etymologies, and Rufinus claimed that the monastery earned its name "because the providence of God foresaw that in these parts the sins of men would be washed away and obliterated just as stains are cleansed by niter."[13] Ancient sources routinely speak of it as "the mountain of Nitria." While the spot is slightly elevated, it is no mountain. In Coptic the term "mountain" can also refer to an uninhabited desert region. An odd link perhaps, but it makes sense given the steep clifflike desert escarpments lining the Nile Valley. It was in just such places where monks established themselves; so the term "mountain" commonly came to designate a site—elevated or not— where monks lived.[14]

Palladius has left us a vivid image of Nitria, of its life and organization. His view is especially valuable because he was no passing tourist, but lived there a full year, around 390 C.E. He claims that Nitria had 5000 inhabitants, some living in cells alone, others in pairs, still others in larger houses. Through the week, the monks stayed in their cells working and praying. A favorite and lucrative occupation was the manufacture of linen, the monks importing flax from the nearby delta. The monks also produced wine not only for their own consumption, but also for profit. They cultivated gardens, and there were seven large bakeries that met the needs both of the 5000 at Nitria and the 600 at its outpost settlement, Kellia.

We do not know details of the daily order, but around the ninth hour (three o'clock in the afternoon) "one can stand," Palladius says, "and hear the divine psalmody issuing forth from each cell and imagine one is high above, in paradise."[15] On Saturdays and Sundays, the monks gathered for liturgies. The community had eight priests, but one had seniority and he alone had the authority both to preside at Eucharist and to preach. Discipline was tough. Palladius says that near the church were three date palm trees on which hung whips: one was for backsliding monks; another, for marauders; and the third, for any robber who happened by.

Yet Nitria was renowned for its hospitality. Palladius speaks of a guesthouse near the church, where postulants might stay a week or a few years. Rufinus, who had visited Nitria fifteen years earlier, offers a colorful, if melodramatic, account of the hospitality he enjoyed:

> So as we drew near to that place and they realized that foreign
> brethren were arriving, they poured out of their cells like a swarm of
> bees and ran to meet us with delight and alacrity, many of them
> carrying containers of water and of bread. . . . When they had wel-
> comed us, first of all they led us with psalms into the church and
> washed our feet and one by one dried them with the linen cloth
> which with they were girded, as if to wash away the fatigue of the
> journey, but in fact to purge away the hardships of worldly life with
> this traditional mystery. What can I say that would do justice to their
> humanity, their courtesy, and their love; each of them wanted to take
> us to his own cell, not only to fulfill the duties of hospitality but
> even more out of humility, in which they are indeed masters, and

out of gentleness and similar qualities which are learned among them according to the graces that differ but with the one and the same teaching, as if they had left the world for this one end.[16]

Life at Nitria does not fit later categories well. It was not like the extreme anchoritic life of Antony. Nor was it like the cenobitic model of Pachomius, with its written rules, its nonclerical hierarchy, and its tightly organized communities. Nor was it exactly the semianchoritic lifestyle associated with Scetis. It was more a desert city with clerical leadership and clear links to the larger world. I note this because the diversity of these monastic experiments defies easy labels.

Kellia

Near Nitria was the equally famous monastic settlement of Kellia ("the Cells").[17] The *Apophthegmata* gives an account (perhaps legendary) of its foundation. One day, Antony came to visit Amoun, and the two talked. Amoun noted that some of the brothers wanted to move away "that they may live in peace." Nitria, it seems, had become a little too successful, and some yearned for the solitude of the early days. In response, Antony suggested that the two have their usual three o'clock meal and then go for a walk in the desert. They walked until sunset, then prayed and planted a cross to mark the site of the new foundation. Antony recommended this site to ensure that hermits who moved there could remain in touch with brethren back in Nitria—a simple after-dinner stroll away. The distance is not what we would expect; they would have to walk twelve miles.[18]

The Greek *History of the Monks* makes no distinction between Nitria and Kellia, but Rufinus's Latin version does. Rufinus had personally seen Kellia and adds useful comments about what he experienced. He says that it lay in the "interior desert" (*in deserto interiore*), that it was "a vast wasteland" (*eremus . . . vasta*) where "cells are divided from one another by so great a distance that no one can catch sight of another nor can a voice be heard." Kellia's solitude was reserved for advanced monks, for those who wanted "to live a more remote life, stripped down to bare rudiments." One had to have already mastered the basics of desert living in Nitria before moving to Kellia. The monks of Kellia, like those in Nitria, gathered on Saturdays and Sundays. Rufinus was touched by what he saw at such gatherings: "They meet in church and, glimpsing this way and that, see one another as the heaven-restored." But he was struck even more by what he heard. The silence of Kellia seemed palpable; it was a *silentium ingens et quies magna*, "a prodigious silence and a great stillness." Only for a grave reason did one dare to disturb this tranquility, only "to anoint one another with words of encouragement, as do athletes priming for a game."[19]

Palladius says that in the years he lived in Kellia, that is, in the 390s, some 600 monks called it home. Oversight of the community came from a priest-monk, assisted by a council of elders. For Palladius's first three years, the superior was Macarius the Alexandrian (d. 393 or 394), a figure often confused with but very different from his namesake and contemporary, Macarius the Egyptian. Kellia may have originated as a colony of anchorites, but by Palladius's time, it had become a cluster of congregations or groups centered around a notable *abba*.

In 1964, the French scholar Antoine Guillaumont discovered the buried ruins of Kellia.[20] The site proved to be massive, some forty-nine square miles. It was also seriously imperiled because the Egyptian government, in an effort to increase the nation's arable land, had begun irrigating the region. The situation worsened in 1977 when the government decided to construct a rail line directly across the site. So in a series of forays from the mid-1960s to the mid-1980s, two archeological teams, one French, the other Swiss, worked carefully but rapidly to uncover and salvage what they could. The archeologists have unearthed extraordinary finds that offer intriguing glimpses into the life of the monks who lived there from the fourth to the seventh century.

The hermitages were ringed by walls that formed large compounds. One small one measures 40 × 50 feet, while a very large one measures 145 × 195 feet. Mid-sized hermitages housed not only an elder monk, but also one or more disciples. The main building, often in the northwest corner of the compound, had a number of rooms: an oratory, a kitchen, a vestibule, storage rooms and bins, and bedrooms for each monk. The roof had an intriguing design. Typically they were low domes punctured with holes to create a sort of skylight. The walls, constructed of mud brick, were covered with a whitewash glaze. Walls often had a decorative border painted dark red and were ornamented with geometric designs: braids, scrolls, intertwining vines. Some walls have depictions of lions, camels, stags, and birds. Most striking is the dazzling array of crosses, usually painted bright red and gold. In the center of most courtyards, one finds a well, with irrigation channels, and in the southeast corner, a latrine. Entrance into the compound was controlled by a gatehouse. Most of these large compounds date the mid-sixth century, a few early dwellings dating from the late fourth century have been uncovered and seem to have used a much simpler and rather different design. They are built partially below ground, and one would have entered them by descending down a short flight of steps.

Other Sites

Nitria and Kellia dominate the pages of the *Lausiac History*. They were sites Palladius knew first hand, and he understandably concentrates his narrative on people he met there and on stories he heard there. But he does mention a number of others. He notes that he once made the dangerous cross-desert trek to Scetis.[21] Another time, he traveled eighteen days, partly on foot across the desert and partly by boat down the Nile, to Lycopolis to consult with its famous seer, John of Lycopolis.[22] He mentions other sites as well, such as Pherme, a mountain near Scetis where some 500 monks lived, or "the Solitudes," a set of hermitages only five miles from the city limits of Alexandria.[23] He also knew of but did not visit Pachomius's monastery at Tabennesi; however, he had seen the Pachomian foundation in Panapolis. Palladius's vision was not limited to Egypt. The last third of his narrative surveys holy people he met or knew of from Jerusalem, Bethlehem, Edessa, even Rome and the Latin West. While Egypt remained the narrative center, Palladius was concerned that Lausus understand the pursuit of holiness was a worldwide enterprise.[24]

The *History of the Monks* also helps us scan the wide sweep of early Egyptian monasticism, to glimpse the welter of sites and of experiments in lifestyle. Monks lived in all manner of styles and environments: some lived scattered in the marshes near the Nile, others perched on rugged outposts outside Antinoë, and still others dwelled in smooth-running monasteries such as the Pachomian establishment near Hermopolis Magna.[25] The author gives big numbers: Abba Or directed 1000 monks; so did Abba Isidore; Abba Ammon had 3000, Abba Sarapion had 10,000; and Abba Apollo only had 500, but "almost all of them [had] the power to work miracles."[26] One cannot, of course, take the author's numbers at face value given his fondness for biblical typology and especially for grouping everything into multiples of three, seven, and ten.[27]

Most remarkable is the *History of the Monks'* description of the city of Oxyrhynchus. The author describes it as a city "bursting with monks," a place where monks nearly outnumbered laity. The numbers given are astounding: 10,000 monks and 20,000 nuns. It was a city whose "very walls resound with the voices of monks."[28] He adds that Oxyrhynchus was something almost unimaginable in the ancient world: a completely Christian *polis*, a city without either pagans or pagan temples, a place where the Christian bishop could enter the public square and bless the whole populace. Even more important, Oxyrhynchus bore witness to the gospel demands of charity: the poor were fed and clothed, and pilgrims were lavished with hospitality. For the author, Oxyrhynchus was a glimpse of heaven on earth.

Both texts, however exaggerated or idealized, provide a helpful reminder that while the image of monks charting out cities in the desert captured the imagination, both ancient and modern, the actual course of monasticism was hardly limited to the desert regions. Palladius, in particular, stresses the varied landscape of Christian holiness, noting in his prologue to the *Lausiac History*: "I shall leave unmentioned no one in the cities, or in the villages, or in the desert. For we are concerned not with the place where they settled, but rather it is their way of life that we seek."[29] Some scholars, such as James Goehring, have strongly questioned whether the dominant image of the desert may be more literary than numerical.[30] Many ascetics led their lives more like Antony's unnamed mentor or Pachomius's teacher Palamon, holy men who dwelt within earshot of villages; or they gathered in communities along the Nile, like the Pachomians. Their asceticism was often fierce, but their *anachōresis*—their withdrawal—could be more social than geographical.

Portraits: The *Lausiac History*

Let us turn now from places to people, for people were the real interest of both authors—*and* of both their audiences. The author of the *History of the Monks* says that "the pious community that lives on the holy Mount of Olives has asked me repeatedly to write them an account of the practices of the Egyptian monks which I have witnessed, their fervent love and great ascetic discipline."[31] Palladius too faced demands from Lausus, his patron: "Now you wanted stories." And Palladius would oblige, passing on tales "of both male and female anchorites, those I have seen and others I have heard about."[32] As we survey these two works, we need to keep these story-craving audiences in mind. Both authors are, in a sense, portrait painters who want to make holiness visible to their readers. Neither paints simply for the sake of verisimilitude. Both cast their artist eyes not just on the subject whose holiness they are trying to bring to light, but also back on their readers, whose lives they are trying to mold.

Let me focus first on Palladius's portraiture, drawing on the *History of Monks* only for occasional comparisons and contrasts. In the next section, I will reverse the accent and give the portraiture and purposes of the *History of the Monks* its due.

The Many Faces of Holiness

Palladius does not limit his portrait gallery to Egyptians, as the *History of the Monks* does. He tells Lausus that he will pass on stories "of those I have lived with in the Egyptian desert and Libya, in the Thebaid and Syene . . . , those in Mesopotamia, Palestine, and Syria, and, in the West, those in Rome and Campania."[33] Egyptians do occupy much of the text, but Palladius carefully notes a number, like himself, who were foreigners in Egypt.[34] His vision leads him, in the latter third of the text, to highlight the international scene: Syrians like Ephrem, Latins like Melania the Elder, and Palestinians like Sabas.

Palladius's portraiture is broader in another way: it includes, as he tells Lausus, "male *and female* anchorites." In the texts we have surveyed thus far, men have been the focus. But Palladius consciously balances things: "I must also commemorate in this book the courageous women to whom God granted struggles equal to those of men, so that no one could plead as an excuse that women are too weak to practice virtue successfully. Now I have seen a good many of them and I have associated with refined women among virgins and widows."[35] The role of women in early monastic literature is a complex and important issue, and I will devote special attention to it in the concluding chapter. But here we need to note that Palladius consciously maps women's varied experiments in holiness. These include the martyr Potamiaena, a slave who died in a cauldron of pitch rather than be seduced by her owner; an anchoress named Alexandra, who for ten years was walled up in a tomb and offered sage advice through a window; an unnamed virgin who risked her life hiding Athanasius during his harrowing years of flight from imperial police;

and ascetics such as Magna and Olympias, who poured their wealth out to build hospitals and to care for the poor.[36] And one of Palladius's heroes is Melania the Elder, whom he knew from his time in Palestine and whom he repeatedly quotes as the source for certain of his tales.[37]

Palladius's variety is not limited to gender and national origin. He also draws on figures from varied social strata. Some came from elite circles: Melania, of course, but also Verus, a count from Galatia, and Innocent, an ex-dignitary from the court of the Emperor Constantius. There are figures from the merchant class, such as Paesius and Isaias, sons of a Spanish trader, or Apollonius, who put his business skills to work for the monks of Nitria, procuring whatever medicines and groceries they needed. Some monks were ex-urbanites, such as Macarius the Alexandrian; others were country bumpkins, such as Paul the Simple. There were ex-slaves, such as Sisinnius, and ex-bandits, such as Moses the Ethiopian.[38] This broad social portrait was no accident. Palladius consciously stressed how the counterculture of the Christian gospel could undercut worldly distinctions and reverse secular standards of nobility.[39]

Literary Style

On first reading, Palladius's work seems a rambling anthology of disparate anecdotes and memorabilia. One example: chapter 11 focuses on Ammonius, a disciple of Pambo and one of the four Tall Brothers. Palladius begins by noting that Ammonius and his brothers, as well as two of his sisters, "went down to the desert." Timothy, patriarch of Alexandria, had heard that Ammonius was a "very learned scholar" and decided to ordain him bishop. When a crowd arrived at his doorstep to carry Ammonius off for a forced ordination, he immediately went inside, took out pruning shears and chopped off his left ear. The physical disability should have rendered him unfit for ordination. After hearing of Ammonius's self-mutilation, Timothy brushed aside the action, saying that not even such disfigurement would stop the ordination. At this, Ammonius then threatened to chop out his tongue. So they gave up the effort. Palladius neither prefaces the story nor concludes it with any moralizing comment. He then abruptly shifts his narrative and adds brief remarks about Ammonius's self-discipline: Ammonius "never pampered his flesh"; whenever he found himself struggling with some desire or other, he heated an iron rod in the fire and then seared his flesh with it until "he became ulcerated all over"; and he never ate food cooked over a fire, except for bread. Palladius shifts his narrative again and adds that Ammonius had memorized not only the entire Old and New Testaments but also six million lines from the theological works of Origen and Didymus the Blind. Palladius then gives two concluding remarks: his own judgment ("if anyone was a guide to the brethren in the desert, he was the one") and the judgment of his teacher Evagrius Ponticus ("I have never seen a man more free from passion than he was").[40]

This example typifies Palladius's scattershot literary style (as well as his sometimes gothic taste in spirituality). But beneath this disorderly surface, is a fairly coherent spiritual framework. That framework, charted in detail in a recent study by Nicholas Molinier, would become the classic Christian map of holiness: one begins the journey to holiness through conversion and renunciation (family, marriage, wealth); then one enters, through disciplined asceticism and discipleship, into an ever-deepening purgation of habit and affect and opens oneself to a life of contemplation; and this in turn leads one to a life of selfless charity. However, in the long run, what stays with the reader is not the framework, but the individual tale. It is hard to forget a story like that of Ammonius chopping off his ear. Such stories—and there are dozens in the *Lausiac History*—may be bizarre and repulsive, but they are memorable. Palladius is at heart a moralist, and his anecdotes are miniature morality plays.

Let me highlight here three themes that criss-cross the text and give some sense of the way that Palladius embodied theme into narrative: asceticism, prayer, and virtue.

Tales of Ascetic Feats

Palladius is at pains to detail the ascetical regimen of key figures, what they ate and drank and what they denied themselves. For example, Dorotheos, an ascetic who lived in a cave near Alexandria, ate only six ounces of bread and a small bunch of vegetables[41]; Evagrius, Palladius's teacher, ate only bread and a little oil and claimed that for sixteen years "I did not touch lettuce or any vegetable greens, or fruit, or grapes, nor did I even take a bath, since the time I came to the desert."[42] On one level, Palladius knows that such matters are not the heart of the spiritual life. As he tell Lausus, "To be sure, neither eating nor abstinence is any account, but it is faith which has extended itself to work done in charity that counts."[43] Despite the disclaimer, food and drink do preoccupy him.

In fact, Palladius seems to delight in recounting stories of ascetical feats, as though abstinence was an end in itself. The great exemplar is Macarius the Alexandrian, who served as priest-superior of Kellia during Palladius's first three years there. Palladius portrays Macarius as an ascetic extremist, eager to outlast and outfast all rivals. When Macarius heard that Pachomians ate no cooked food during Lent, he followed the same regimen not for forty days, but for seven years. He met with less success in combating sleep. Once he refused to sleep for twenty days, but finally gave up, admitting that "my brain would have shriveled up for good."[44] His mortification could be both extreme and flamboyant. Once he half-consciously swatted a mosquito that had stung him. He then declared himself guilty of the sin of revenge and wandered out to the marshes of Scetis, where the mosquitoes were known to be so fierce that their stings could pierce a wild pig's tough hide. For the next six months, he let the mosquitoes sting him at will. The result was cartoonish: Macarius had swollen up so much "that some thought he had elephantiasis"; the brothers only recognized this inflated figure by his voice.[45]

Macarius's taste for ascetical competition led him to go south and join Pachomius's monastery in Tabennesi, disguising himself as a laborer. Pachomius tried to discourage him from entering the monastery, warning that as an old man he would not be able to keep pace with either the asceticism or the workload of the other monks. Despite this refusal, Macarius persisted and after seven days was finally admitted. It was Lent, and Macarius observed that different monks followed varied ascetical regimens. So to top them, Macarius embraced the most stringent of each type and did so all at the same time: he stood for forty days; he never spoke, but worked in silence weaving rope; he neither ate bread nor drank water, consuming nothing but a few cabbage leaves, and then only on Sunday. His fellow monks complained to Pachomius: "Where did you get this bodiless man for our condemnation? Either you throw him out or we leave." Pachomius then, in a divine revelation, realized who the disguised ascetic was. At the liturgy, he called Macarius forward, expressed his pleasure at finally getting to meet him, and formally introduced him to the community: "I am grateful to you for having made my children not become haughty about their own ascetic practices."[46]

As literature, these tales are memorable, even entertaining: the image of a mosquito-bloated Macarius is comical, while the story of Macarius among the Pachomians plays to our fondness for stories of disguise and revelation. Whatever their literary skill, one has to wonder about the spirituality they seek to promote—and, of course, promoting spirituality is what Palladius says he is about. They seem to play to a not uncommon prejudice that early monasticism was really a covert Manicheism, a rejection of the body and a denial of the goodness of creation. After all, the Pachomians in the story complain that they are competing against a "bodiless" man. But Palladius's real point is the last line—that Macarius taught them not to be haughty. Similarly with the story of mosquitoes: it seems, on the face of it, an assault on the body. But Palladius's point is that Macarius detected in his killing the mosquito a hidden, half-conscious propensity for revenge; standing in the swamp was not from a hatred of the body, but from a desire to purge himself of "the sin of revenge." Discipline of the body is really a way to discipline the spirit. That said, one cannot deny that the force of the narrative and its imagery can overwhelm that moral message—as though the body, and not the disordered psyche, were the culprit. That implicit message even becomes explicit in one often-quoted tale. Once Palladius asked Dorotheos, an ascetic who lived near Alexandria, why he gathered rocks in the heat of the day: "What are you doing, Father, killing your body in such heat?" Dorotheos answered, "It kills me, I will kill it."[47] Some textbooks cite Dorotheos's one-liner as though it were a typical view of the desert fathers. It is not even the typical view of Palladius, who dismisses Dorotheos's way of life as "squalid and harsh" and says that he broke off his commitment of a three-year apprenticeship under Dorotheos.

Tales of Prayer

One finds in the *Lausiac History* scattered indications of monastic rhythms of prayer. There is discussion of psalm singing, of memorizing and reciting scripture. The term "continual prayer" is used, but it seems to mean not wordless contemplation, but rather the unceasing recitation of verbal prayers. Palladius reports that prayer could provide prophetic knowledge: Didymus the Blind saw in a moment of ecstasy the fatal battle in which the pagan Emperor Julian was killed; Pachomius enjoyed a miraculous revelation which, as we saw, allowed him to recognize the disguised Macarius.[48]

Once Macarius decided he wanted to fix his entire attention on God, without wavering, without distraction, for five full days. So he locked the door of his cell to any would-be visitors and ordered himself, "Do not descend from heaven, for there you have angels, archangels, the powers above, the God of all of us; only do not descend from heaven." For two days, he kept centered. Everything in the cell, even the rush mat he was standing on, burned in fire— the result of a demon. On the third day, he became distracted, and "I came down to view the world lest I be thought arrogant."[49] In this tale, as in so many of Palladius, the moral is in the last line: the great danger to ecstatics is pride.

The competitive spirit that pervaded asceticism could pervade prayer. Palladius tells the story of Paul of Pherme, who did not do manual labor. His sole "work" was "continual prayer": Paul tried to say 300 prayers per day, and to keep count he had pebbles in his lap that he would toss out after each prayer said. He then became dejected when he learned of a virgin who had spent thirty years saying 700 prayers. So he went to Macarius the Alexandrian for advice. Macarius pointed to his own practice (and implied, without saying it directly, that Paul's life was out of kilter): he said fewer prayers, 100 per day; but he added, "I support myself [by manual labor], and I give time for consultations with the brethren, and my reason tells that I am not negligent."[50] This was Palladius's ideal of the contemplative life: not all-consuming prayer, but a balance of prayer, manual labor, and ministry.

Tales of Virtue Gone Awry

Palladius is less sanguine about the monastic life than the author of the *History of the Monks*, whose figures are always hospitable, always ascetical, and always wonder-working. Sprinkled through the *Lausiac History* are a number of cautionary tales. For example, Palladius knew of a monk named Valens, a Palestinian by origin, who lived with him in Kellia. Valens's downfall began when, by a miraculous light (ultimately of demonic origin), he discovered a needle he had dropped in the dark. He then became haughty. First he refused "to partake of the Mysteries" (i.e., the Eucharist). He then rejected a gift of pastry that Macarius the Alexandrian had sent around to all the monks: "Go and tell Macarius: 'I'm not your inferior that you need to send me an offering.' " Finally, he became the victim of demonic hallucinations. He had a vision of a thousand angels, one of whom approached him saying, "Christ has loved you and because of your way of life . . . and He has come to visit you." And so Valens left his cell and bowed before a "fiery disc" he believed was Christ but was actually—as Palladius informs the reader—the Antichrist. The next day he came to the monastic assembly and proclaimed, "I have no use for communion, for I saw Christ this very day." The monks recognized the madness and "put him in irons for a year." Valens was cured "through their prayers and the living of an ordinary, unbusied life."[51]

Palladius follows this with a second tale. He recounts the downfall of one of his monastic neighbors, an Alexandrian named Heron. Palladius remembers him fondly as "a courteous and good-natured young man who led a pure life." Heron was so zealous in his asceticism that except for the Eucharist and a little wild lettuce, he ate only every three months. He could travel long distances in the desert without eating or drinking and lived only on the Word of God, reciting large portions of Scripture by heart. He attacked Palladius's teacher Evagrius, citing Jesus's saying about calling no one on earth "teacher." Yet this same monk's restlessness led him to abandon the desert and wander back to Alexandria, where he not only frequented the theater and horse races, but lost himself in gambling and whoring. He ended up catching some venereal disease and died soon after returning to the desert.[52]

For Palladius, both figures were living morality tales, embodiments of monastic life gone awry. Both were deluded by their ascetic accomplishments and their mystical gifts. Both distorted their Eucharistic devotion—Valens by abandoning it and Heron by eating nothing but the host. And both men's relationship to monastic authority—as seen in Valen's refusal of the generosity of Macarius of Alexandria, and in Heron's declaration that he needed no teacher but Christ—was symptomatic of their pride. Palladius had no doubt that the Eucharist was central to Christian life and that any distortion of Eucharistic piety meant a distortion in the spiritual quest. He also recognized that the greatest hazards of desert living were psychological, and that the teacher played a vital role in the discernment of spirits. As Palladius remarks in his dedicatory letter to Lausus, "Now those who think they need no teacher or those who do not believe those who teach them in the way of love, are afflicted with the disease of ignorance, which is the mother of overweening pride."[53] Palladius consciously included such cautionary tales:

> It is useful to insert in this little volume the lives of such as these (just as among the holy trees of Paradise there was a tree that gives knowledge of good and evil) as a caution for those who come across it, so that if they ever do a good act, they might not become too puffed up in their virtues. Often, indeed, even a virtue, whenever it is not perfected with right intention, may be responsible for a fall.[54]

Note his closing line: even virtue can cause a fall. Palladius knew from hard experience that the virtuous life needs balance, that one needs "right intention." The downfall of these monks and several others upset not just Palladius. His teachers Evagrius and Ammonius (the Earless) were deeply disturbed, so much so that they made a pilgrimage to Abba Paphnutius "to learn why brethren should go astray, or leave, or be frustrated in the proper life."[55]

Windows onto the Holy

Early in the twentieth century, Wilhelm Bousset argued that the *Lausiac History* was fiction, pure and simple, a compilation drawn from earlier accounts and strung together under an autobiographical guise. And he could point, with some force, to inconsistencies in chronology. All acknowledge that Palladius did draw here and here on literary sources—notably for his discussion of the Pachomians at Tabennesi, whom he admits he had not actually visited. But, overall, Bousset's arguments have not convinced many. Most accept that Palladius was, in the main, speaking from experience, and that many of his flamboyant anecdotes are not eyewitness accounts but a record of what he heard from others. As E. D. Hunt has noted, "It was the very fact that Palladius wrote from personal experience of the Egyptian desert, of arduous journeys across the empire in the quest of spiritual improvement, which gave to his work its authority as a piece of edification. The importance lay, not in the chronological details of Palladius' autobiography . . . but in his individual encounters as historical incidents."[56]

Palladius did not see himself as a purveyor of desert tales; rather, he sought to be a physician of the soul. As he tells Lausus:

> May this account, then be a constant reminder for the good of your
> soul and a constant medicine against forgetfulness. May it dispel the
> drowsiness which arises from senseless desire, indecision, and petti-
> ness in necessary affairs. May it free your character of hesitation
> and meanness of spirit. May it rid you of excitability, disorders,
> worldly conceit, and irrational fear . . . and may it be a guide both to
> you and to those who are with you, not only your subordinates but
> your rulers as well.[57]

Palladius agreed with Evagrius and the whole desert tradition that the demonic is all around us: "Your mind is by its nature subject to various evil influences, both seen and unseen."[58] Palladius's book is therefore medicinal in the sense that it offers images both of health and of pathology. But his accent is on the healthy, and he recommends that Lausus gaze on these portraits of the holy. Palladius then switches metaphors, from healing to illumination: "Go to a clear window—as you would with a book with small print—and seek meetings with holy men and women so that you may see clearly your own heart."[59] Reading books to read one's heart, meeting holy people to meet oneself—these are the ends that guide Palladius. His portraits of holy people are, at once, windows and mirrors, windows to gaze out onto the holy, mirrors to see one's true face.

Signs and Wonders: The *History of the Monks in Egypt*

We turn now from the portraits found in the *Lausiac History* to those in the *History of the Monks*. While both works are called "histories," they are not histories in any modern sense. In the nineteenth century, it became fashion-able to attack the historical reliability of early monastic texts. One scholar, de-termined to "lay the axe to the root of the superstitions," wrote off these two *Histories* as mere "fairy tales"; another branded Palladius a "monkish falsifier of history" and claimed that the author of the *Lausiac History* had not even set foot in Egypt—a claim ably refuted by a pioneer of Coptic studies, E. Améli-neau.[60] Fanciful tales play a part, as we have seen, in the *Life of Antony* and the *Lives of Pachomius*. But in the *History of the Monks* (and, to a lesser extent, the *Lausiac History*), miracles and marvels take center stage. Such tales can be off-putting to moderns. While we love the outlandish in our fiction and applaud special effects in our movies, we want sobriety in our spiritual literature. An-cient Christians felt no such inhibitions (nor did their medieval successors). This gap in sensibility means we need to read these texts with special care, sensitizing ourselves to the spiritual concerns of this literature lest quick judg-ments about "history" blind us to what is going on in the texts.

Before embarking, we need to clarify a few presuppositions about history and about miracles. People today—both scholars and nonscholars—tend to work from the Enlightenment's definition of a miracle: namely, an event that violates or overturns the laws of nature. Since many historians presume that *no* event can violate or overturn the laws of nature, they presume that miracles reported in ancient texts could not possibly have happened. One may interpret matters that way, but in doing so, one is staking out not a historical position, but a philosophical one.[61] Our interest here is not the broad philosophical question, can miracles happen? It is not even the question, did the miracles reported in this literature actually happen? To move behind a literary text to the historical fact is difficult even with a well-documented modern event. Con-sider, for example, the task of going from newspaper reports about the assas-sination of John F. Kennedy to the truth of what actually took place. It is vastly more difficult when one is trying to determine the historicity of an event—any event—at a distance of 1500 years. It is extremely difficult to determine even an ordinary event, such as the year when an ancient figure was born or died. It is all the more perilous when dealing with reports of miracles at a distance of 1500 years. Here we will make no attempt to move behind the texts to the historical events. The focus will be much more modest: namely, how did the *author* of the *History of the Monks* understand *the meaning* of the events he reports?

We need to be alert to terminology. "Miracle" (*teras, miraculum*) was not the only or even the usual term the author of the *History of the Monks* used. Look, for example, at his summary of the miracles of Abba Apollo:

> He was renowned in the Thebaid and great works were ascribed to
> him, the Lord performed many deeds of power [*dunameis*] through
> him, and a multitude of signs [*sēmeia*] were accomplished at his
> hands. . . . He dwelt, then, in the desert adjoining the settled region,
> living in the power of the Spirit and performing signs and wonder-
> ful miracles of healing. They were so amazing [*thaumatos*] that they

defy description, according to what we heard from the old men who were with him.[62]

The author does speak of "miracles," but more often, he speaks of "deeds of power" (*dunameis*), "signs" (*sēmeia*), and "wonders" (*thaumata*); and one finds Rufinus's Latin translation using the same vocabulary: *virtutes, signa, prodigia*. The accent in this passage and elsewhere in the text is not on nature or over-turning natural laws; instead, it is on power and its meaning. Abba Apollo achieved renown for his deeds of power, but those deeds pointed not to his own strength, but beyond him, to God. The deeds were "signs" of divine pres-ence, of "the power of the Spirit." Obvious, perhaps, but it illustrates how oblique modern concerns about natural law are to the author's thought world.

The author's terminology is drawn from the New Testament. In the Acts of the Apostles, Peter, at Pentecost, stands before a crowd in Jerusalem and proclaims "Jesus of Nazareth, a man attested to you by God with deeds of power, wonders, and signs that God did through him among you" (Acts 2:22). For the author of the *History of the Monks*, the signs and wonders of the biblical era are alive and well and at work in the lives of the monks, and what was said of Jesus and the prophets and apostles can be said of the monks. The author makes this explicit in a story about Abba Apollo. Once a great famine swept through the Thebaid, and the people approached Apollo for relief. So he or-dered the monastery's last three baskets of bread to be brought forward and then assured everyone that the Lord would multiply these loaves for the fam-ine's duration. For the next four months, these three baskets sufficed. Satan then came to Apollo and chided him for his arrogance: "Are you Elijah, or one of the other prophets or apostles . . . ?" Apollo replied: "Were not the holy prophets and apostles, who have handed on to us the power to do such things, men themselves? Or was God present then, but is now away on a journey? God can always do these things, for with him nothing is impossible."[63] For the author of the *History of the Monks*, the wonder-working God of the Bible is the wonder-working God of the present age; where he once used prophets and apostles, he now uses monks as his chosen instruments.

The events described in the *History of the Monks* as "signs" and "deeds of power" cluster into five basic categories: nature miracles, angelic visitations, gifts of prophecy and clairvoyance; miracles of judgment; and miraculous heal-ings. Let us survey a few examples of each and touch briefly on the theological dynamic underlying the report.

Nature Miracles

The *History of the Monks* routinely reports events that seem, to our eyes, like violations of the natural order. For example, Abba Patermuthius once prevented the sun from setting. It stood fixed on the western horizon "for many hours" until he was able to arrive at a village. This multi-hour sunset is meant as an echo of Gideon's great feat, reported in the book of Judges.[64] Other monks reportedly stopped rivers and crossed the Nile "dry-shod"—much as the Israelites had crossed the Red Sea.[65] Both instances play out what we saw above: the unbroken continuity between biblical miracles and monastic miracles.

Most nature miracles concern the animal world. One day, while Macarius the Egyptian was praying, a hyena came into his cell and began licking his feet and pulling at the hem of his tunic. So he followed the animal out to its den, where he found that its litter of cubs had been born blind. He prayed and the hyena cubs recovered their sight. The mother hyena returned the next day bearing a gift: a large ram's fleece. It laid the gift at Macarius's feet, and "he smiled at her as if at a kind and sensitive person, and taking the skin, spread it under him."[66] The story is touching. It is apt to remind modern readers of a scene from a Disney movie, such as *Fantasia* or *Beauty and the Beast*. For an ancient audience, this was not just a charming tale. It was a story about holiness. Macarius's holiness was such that the fissure between the human and animal world, a fissure wrought by Adam's sin, had been healed. The author makes Macarius an icon of what unfallen humanity should have looked like— or, better, of what humanity now fully restored in Christ should look like.

This same story appears in Palladius, with some interesting variants. First, Palladius associates it not with Macarius the Egyptian, but with Macarius the Alexandrian. In Palladius's version, there is *one* blind cub, not a whole litterful, and the mother hyena comes into Macarius's cell and tosses her cub at Macarius's feet, who then picks it up, puts spittle in its eyes, and prays. The cub is immediately healed and then goes to its mother, who suckles it before leaving Macarius's cell. Palladius too recounts the gift of the fleece and says that Melania the Elder received it from Macarius as a gift.[67] Palladius ends his story there, but we know from another source, Paulinus of Nola, that Melania later brought it back home to Italy and gave it as a gift to Paulinus, who gave it in turn to Sulcipius Severus.[68]

The story of Macarius and the hyena is the most colorful of the nature miracles in the *History of the Monks*. There are others: Abba Bes commanded a hippopotamus to stop ravaging farmlands[69]; Abba Helle used a crocodile as a ferry to cross the Nile[70]; and Abba Amoun hired two large snakes to guard his cell against thieves. These stories, like that of Macarius, offered glimpses of a redeemed cosmos. No longer would deadly animals terrorize human beings; rather, as Amoun told some thieves terrified by his guard snakes, "these, thanks to God, obey our wishes."[71] These are not really nature miracles; they are stories of paradise regained. This is evident in the case of Abba Theon, who used to go out at night and befriend antelopes and gazelles who came to his cell in search of water; as the author notes, "These creatures delighted him always."[72] In this new creation, wild animals cease to be objects of fear and become sources of delight.

Angelic Visitations

The *History of the Monks* says that monks enjoyed not only an easy commerce with the world of animals. They enjoyed an equal intimacy with the world of angels. For instance, early in his career, Abba Apollo lived in a cave in the desert, where he was daily fed food miraculously provided by angels; Abba Anouph, too, claimed an angel fed him with heavenly food.[73] Angels routinely helped monks. Once, when a garrison commander arrested Apollo and his disciples to force them into military service, an angel came at night and opened up their prison cell.[74] In another case, the author notes how Abba Piammonas, during the Eucharist, saw an angel writing down names of those who came to Communion and erasing the names of those who did not. The author adds matter-of-factly that those who missed died soon afterward.[75]

This intimacy with angels made sense because, as the author saw it, the monks were "living the angelic life as they advanced steadily in the imitation of our divine Savior."[76] The author says that, for example, Abba Bes "lived a life of utmost stillness, and his manner was serene, since he had attained the angelic state."[77] Such monks not only lived like angels; they began to resemble them. Abba Or, for example, "looked just like an angel. He was about ninety years old and had a snowy white beard down to his chest. And his face was so radiant that the sight of him alone filled one with awe."[78]

Prophecy and Clairvoyance

In the *History of the Monks*, some figures, such as Abba Theon, were noted for their gifts of prophecy or clairvoyance.[79] On occasion, the author explains what such clairvoyance might entail. Abba Eulogius's gift, for instance, enabled him to read the souls of his disciples as they approached communion, to discern whether they were worthy to receive.[80]

No one embodied the prophetic charism more than John of Lycopolis (d. 394 or 395). John was one of the best-known and most celebrated monks in fourth-century Egypt, and appears not only in the *History of the Monks*, but also in accounts by Palladius, Evagrius, Cassian, Rufinus, and Sozomen, and in the *Apophthegmata*. John had lived some forty-eight years in a three-room cell perched on a desert escarpment five miles from the city of Lycopolis in the Thebaid.[81] Access to him was limited, scrupulously guarded by a community of attendant-monks, who kept the door locked during the weekdays and opened things only on Saturdays and Sundays, when John would greet and converse with pilgrims through a window. John is the subject of the first and longest chapter in the *History of the Monks*, nearly one-fifth of the text. The author summarizes John's prophetic skills this way: "He foreknew and revealed things hidden in the future; he told each man what he had done in secret; and he predicted the rise and fall of the Nile and the annual yield of crops."[82] Note the last: John was not forecasting the weather, but diagnosing the pulse of the nation's life; all knew that any arrhythmia in the Nile's rise and fall meant hardship, even famine.

The *History of the Monks* notes that John had used his prophetic gifts to predict the Emperor Theodosius's victory over a formidable usurper Eugenius in 394; John had also prophesied to a Roman general not to fear an invading Ethiopian army, even though the Romans were badly outnumbered.[83] These were high-stakes prognostications, and his success in both earned him an international reputation. Other writers, both Greek and Latin—Palladius, Cassian, Augustine, Eucherius of Lyons, Sozomen, and Theodoret—report the same stories and proclaim John's renown as a prophet.[84]

In the *History of the Monks*, the author presents a firsthand account of John's clairvoyance. The author says that when he and his six friends met John, he welcomed them with a "bright smiling countenance," even though the rest of his body was "worn out by his ascesis" and "his beard no longer grew on his face." He asked whether any of the seven was a cleric. When they all denied it, John then pointed out that, contrary to their disavowals, one of them was indeed a deacon—something the monk had kept secret even from his companions. So John reached through the window, kissed the deacon's hand, and gently reprimanded him: "Do not spurn the grace of God, my child, and do not lie by denying the gift of Christ. For a lie is something alien regardless of whether its matter is grave or light."[85] The group then prayed, and John offered a long address on the ascetic life—a carefully constructed address, reminiscent of the long address that Athanasius attributes to Antony in the *Life*. Afterward, the author adds, John gave them gifts, sent them off in peace, and prophesied that "today the victory proclamation of the pious Emperor Theodosius has arrived in Alexandria announcing the destruction of the tyrant Eugenius and that 'The emperor will die a natural death.' " The author then adds these things did take place. He also appends a notice of John's death, noting that John foresaw it coming: he ordered that no one visit him for three days, then knelt down in prayer and died.[86]

John of Lycopolis also makes a noteworthy appearance in the *Lausiac History*. Here again he appears as a man with a gift for oracular utterance and for reading hearts, but Palladius's portrait seems less stylized. Palladius says that he had heard about John's reputation from his teacher Evagrius and decided to make the demanding eighteen-day pilgrimage to see John face to face. When he arrived, he was annoyed to find John's cell locked up. It had been a rigorous journey, and he had high hopes. On Saturday, John sat at his window greeting visitors. Seeing Palladius, he asked who he was, but before Palladius had responded, John prophetically surmised that he was part of Evagrius's entourage. Palladius admitted that he was. Their conversation was then interrupted by one of the locals, and Palladius stood by silently grumbling to himself, hurt and ready to walk out. John chided him later for being "petty" and asked, "Why are you angry at me? What do you find so blameworthy that you would think such things which are neither true of me nor proper to you?" This reading of Palladius's heart left him chastened and led him to believe that John was indeed "a spiritual man." Their conversation turned to Palladius, his spiritual state and his future. John zeroed in on Palladius's secret desire to abandon the desert under the noble guise of converting his brother and sister to monasticism and of seeing his elderly father one last time. John told Palladius to stay put, that his "well-sounding excuses" were demon-inspired, that his father would live for many years, and that his brother and sister had already embraced the ascetic life. He playfully struck Palladius on the cheek and warned him of future anguish. He also asked Palladius if he yearned to be made a bishop. Palladius joked that he was already a bishop of sorts, since he was "overseer" (*episkopos*) of the kitchen; he had been ordained by gluttony and had jurisdiction over the diocese of pots and pans and excommunicated all sour wine. John chided him for his puns and warned that he would indeed be ordained, but that it would cause him great tribulation.[87] Palladius's John seems more realistic, less stylized than the man in the *History of the Monks*, but verisimilitude was not Palladius's primary concern. Rather, he saw John as a cogent spokesman for his own theology of God's providence.

Judgment Miracles

There are other remarkable events in the *History of the Monks* that do not fit the aforementioned categories. They are, for want of a better term, miracles of judgment. Perhaps the most dramatic of these is told in Rufinus's version of the *History of the Monks*. Once, a man accused of murder fled to Macarius the Egyptian. When the authorities arrived on the scene, the man protested his innocence under oath. Macarius intervened and asked where the victim was buried. They all went to the tomb, and Macarius called upon the dead man and asked him if the accused was in fact the guilty. The dead man spoke from his grave and pronounced the accused innocent. The frightened authorities fell at Macarius's feet and begged him to ask the dead man who the real murderer was. Macarius refused: "This I will not ask; it is enough for me to have the innocent free; it is not up to me to discover the guilty."[88] Macarius's deed is more than just a display of power; it is a work of justice, dramatic indeed. It is one of those stories that signal the emergence of the holy man in the politics of late antiquity.[89] A holy man like Macarius came to serve a crucial political function: as a mediator, one who stood above the fray, above the tangled and contentious world of vested interests, and could ensure that justice would win out.

A story about Abba Apollo plays out issues of judgment in a different way. Once, a pagan village had a ritual in which the priests carried a statue of a god down to the Nile and the accompanying crowd worked itself up into bacchic frenzy. Ancient Christians had no doubt about the moral import of such a ceremony: it was demon worship, pure and simple. So Abba Apollo, when he saw what was happening, knelt down and began praying. At once, the priests and crowd froze in their tracks, unable to move; "all day they roasted in the hot sun, at a loss to explain what had happened to them." When they discovered that Apollo had paralyzed them, they sent diplomatic envoys who agreed they would renounce their errors if he freed them. When he did, "they all rushed towards him, committing themselves fully to belief in the Savior of the universe and the God who works miracles, and at once set fire to the idol. When he had catechized them all, he handed them over to the Christian congregations."[90] In the end, many became monks, and paganism ceased in the village. The point is clear: miracles vindicate the truth of Christianity. In a world of contentious supernatural powers, Christianity proves its truth by deeds of power. It is a story of judgment against paganism and of Christ's victory over the demonic. This sort of story is a commonplace and hints that Christianity was not so much imposed from above, by imperial favors and edicts, but demolished from below, by the deeds of monks.[91]

Miraculous Healings

Given all these miracles, one would expect reports of spectacular cures. Surprisingly, though, they play only a modest role. A number of the figures are described as healers—Theon, Elias, Apollo, Copres, Patermuthius, and John of Dioclos—but the notices are often vague and global.[92] It is said of Copres, for instance, that "every day he worked many miracles and did not cease healing the sick"; at the same time, the author mentions no specific cases.[93] When specifics are given, the miracles are relatively modest. John of Lycopolis, for instance, once gave oil to a woman blinded by cataracts; after treatment once a day for three days, she regained her sight.[94]

But there are a handful of spectacular, even bizarre cases. In one instance, a sorcerer turned a young virgin into a horse. She was brought to Macarius the Egyptian by her parents. Macarius had her locked up for seven days, while he prayed the whole while. On the seventh day, he went in with the girl's parents and anointed her with oil and said a final prayer. At that moment, the girl-turned-horse turned back into a girl.[95] We have, in fact, another version of the story in Palladius. According to Palladius, the girl was not a virgin, but a married woman, and it was not her parents who brought her to Macarius, but her husband. More striking is the climax of Palladius's version. Macarius reveals that the woman had not in fact been transformed into a mare; the spell the sorcerer cast had affected not the woman, but all those who saw her. It was psychological delusion, not a physical transmutation. He poured holy water over her, and the power of the spell was broken and all saw her as a woman. Palladius adds a brief moral: Macarius reprimands the couple for not going to Eucharist for five weeks, something that made them vulnerable to sorcery.

In the *History of the Monks*, the monks are not only healers; they themselves are immune to disease. The author tells of a monastery, headed by Isidore, that housed 1000 monks. According to its gatekeeper, "When the time came for each [monk] to depart, he announced it beforehand to all the others and then lay down and fell asleep."[96] This medical wonder stands in marked contrast to accounts in Palladius, who notes monks' not infrequent struggles with disease.

Treasures of God in Human Vessels

The *History of the Monks* inextricably links the monastic with the miraculous. Derwas Chitty, an otherwise sympathetic historian of monasticism, has judged its author unduly "gullible."[97] Yes, but that is not really the point. The point, as the author insists in the prologue, is a fundamental theological conviction "that even in these times the Savior performs through [the great fathers] what he performed through the prophets and apostles. For the same Lord now and always works all things in all men."[98] This principle shapes the portraiture: the wonders of the biblical age have not ceased, but continue unabated in the monastic present. In a sense, monks are icons of the incarnate Christ. As the author proclaims in the prologue: "I have truly seen the treasure of God hidden in human vessels."[99] This phrase encapsulates his portraiture. It is not a collection of morality tales, as Palladius's account is. It is an account of divine presence in the human; and if this divine "treasure" is "hidden," the veneer is very thin. This theological perspective leads the author to offer a more stylized portraiture. Individual variety—so much a part of Palladius's accent—matters less in the History of the Monks than the divine presence peeking out beneath the human.

The prologue emphasizes not individual monks, but their collective meaning. The author had no doubt that the monks were the leading edge of the human race:

> For in Egypt I saw many fathers living the angelic life as they advanced steadily in the imitation of our divine Savior. I saw new prophets who have attained a Godlike state of fulfillment by their inspired and wonderful and virtuous way of life. For they are true servants of God. They do not busy themselves with any earthly matter or take account of anything that belongs to this transient world. But while dwelling on earth in this manner they live as true citizens of heaven.[100]

The author sees monasticism as, literally, a sort of avant-garde: "One can see them scattered in the desert waiting for Christ like loyal sons watching for their father, or like an army expecting its emperor."[101] He draws repeatedly on military metaphors: "There are so many of them that an earthly emperor could not assemble so large an army," and their hermitages surround and protect town and villages "as if by walls."[102] Indeed, monks collectively were, according to the author, the very guardians of the universe: "Indeed, it is clear to all who dwell there [in Egypt] that through them the world is kept in being, and that through them too human life is preserved and honored by God."[103] It is hard to imagine a loftier—and less self-critical—theology of monastic life.

In a recent study, Georgia Frank explored the History of the Monks and the Lausiac History as pilgrim tales and showed their debts to and differences from the tourist literature of antiquity. She explores not just literary motifs, such as a fondness for exotica, but also the desires of the readers. She notes that both works were written by pilgrims for people who wanted a taste of pilgrimage without ever leaving home. In other words, text substituted for journey; reading, for walking. The armchair pilgrim is spared the hazards of the journey and via a text gets a glimpse of the face of the holy. Both authors are attuned to their reader's thirst for a holiness made visible. As Frank notes, "Although written in the first person neither work could be called introspective or personal. There are no 'interior castles' to speak of. Both works face outward, to the surfaces of Egyptian monasticism, from the vast, desert landscape to the furrows of a monk's brow."[104]

Both authors are portrait painters, similar in frame but different in accent. Palladius is a miniaturist with a taste for morality plays, while the anonymous author of the *History of the Monks* is an iconographer with a taste for magical realism. In the next chapter, we turn to Palladius's teacher, Evagrius, and so turn from outer to inner, from portrait painters to abstract expressionist. Evagrius shows us not what monks look like, but what they think and feel, what they hope for and fear, how they pray and what they seek in prayer.

NOTES

1. Palladius, *Historia Lausiaca* 21.8–9 (Butler, 66; trans. Meyer, ACW 34:73–74).

2. See D. F. Buck, "The Structure of the *Lausiac History*," *Byzantion* 46 (1976): 292–307. Much, but not all, of the complexity comes from the way Palladius interrupts the autobiographical flow with stories about figures he has heard about rather than met; for example, he first tells the story of Isidore, then passes on a story Isidore told him about the early-fourth-century martyr. Chronologically it is out of order, but it is not out of order in the flow of Palladius's own memory.

3. See the classic study of Réné Draguet, "L'*Histoire Lausiaque*: une oeuvre écrite dans l'esprit d'Évagre," *Revue d'histoire ecclésiastique* 41 (1946): 321–364, and 42 (1947): 5–49.

4. Jerome, *Ep.* 3.1 to Rufinus (Labourt 1.11; trans. my own).

5. On the date of Rufinus's translation, see de Vogüé, *Histoire littéraire du mouvement monastique dans l'antiquité*, 3:317n3.

6. Palladius, *Historia Lausiaca* 46.5 (Butler, 135–136; trans. Meyer, ACW 34:124).

7. Butler, *The Lausiac History of Palladius*, 2:iii.

8. Palladius, *Historia Lausiaca* 8.1–3 (Butler, 26–27; ACW 34:41–42).

9. See Brown, *The Body and Society*, 97–101.

10. Palladius, *Historia Lausiaca* 8.4 (Butler, 28; trans. Meyer, ACW 34:43). Other versions are found in *Historia monachorum* XXII.1–2, in which the couple live together only few days, not eighteen years; and in Socrates, *HE* IV.23, in which the couple retire *together* in Nitria. See Elm, *Virgins of God*, 325–326.

11. Evelyn-White, *Monasteries of Wadi 'n Natrûn*, 2:17–24; Guillaumont, "Nitria," in *The Coptic Encyclopedia*, 6:1794–1795.

12. Palladius, *Historia Lausiaca* 7.1 (Butler, 24–25; ACW 34:40).

13. Rufinus, *Historia monachorum in Aegypto* XXI.1.1 (Schulz-Flügel, 356; trans. Russell, CS 34:148).

14. Evelyn-White, *Monasteries of Wadi 'n Natrûn*, 2:21–22; Guillaumont, "Nitria," in *The Coptic Encyclopedia*, 6:1795.

15. Palladius, *Historia Lausiaca* 7.5 (Butler, 26; trans. Meyer, ACW 34:41).

16. Rufinus, *Historia monachorum in Aegypto* XXI.1,3–1,6 (Schulz-Flügel, 356–357; trans. Russell, CS 34:148).

17. For studies on Kellia, see the bibliography for chapter 9.

18. *AP* Antony 34 (PG 65:85–88; CS 59:8).

19. Rufinus, *Historia monachorum in Aegypto* XXII.2.1–4 (Schulz-Flügel, 358; trans. my own).

20. For a valuable overview of the recent archeological discoveries, together with photos, see P. Miquel, ed., *Déserts chrétiens d'Égypte* (Nice: Culture Sud, 1993).

21. Palladius, *Historia Lausiaca* 23 (Butler, 75; ACW 34:81).

22. Palladius, *Historia Lausiaca* 35 (Butler, 101–102; ACW 34:99–100).

23. On Pherme, see *Historia Lausiaca* 27; the Solitudes, *Historia Lausiaca* 2. Other sites he mentions are along the shores of Lake Maroetis (*HL* 15, 24); Atripe (*HL* 29, 30); and "the Ladder" beyond Scetis (*HL* 27).

24. Palladius, *Historia Lausiaca*, prol. 2 (Butler, 10; ACW 34:23–24).

25. *Historia monachorum in Aegypto* VII.1, III.1 (SH 53:45, 41; CS 34:69, 65).

26. Or (*HM* II.1); Ammon (*HM* III.1); Apollo (*HM* VIII.2); Isidore (*HM* XVII.1); Sarapion (*HM* XVIII.1).

27. See Paul Devos, "Les nombres dans l'*Historia monachorum in Aegypto*," *Analecta Bollandiana* 92 (1974): 97–106.

28. *Historia monachorum in Aegypto* 5.2–6 (SH 53:42–43; trans. Russell, CS 34:67).

29. Palladius, *Historia Lausiaca*, prol. 16 (Butler, 15; trans. Meyer, ACW 34:29).

30. See Goehring, "The Encroaching Desert," in *Ascetics, Society, and the Desert*, 73–88.

31. *Historia monachorum in Aegypto*, prol. 2 (SH 53:6; trans. Russell, CS 34:49).

32. Palladius, *Historia Lausiaca*, prol. 2 (Butler, 10; trans. Meyer, ACW 34:23).

33. Palladius, *Historia Lausiaca*, prol. 2 (Butler, 10; trans. Meyer, ACW 34:23–24).

34. Foreigners include Stephen, a Libyan (*HL* 24); Valens, a Palestinian (*HL* 25); Evagrius, from Pontus (*HL* 38); and Moses, described as an Ethiopian (*HL* 19). Palladius also recounts stories of foreigners he had not met, such as the Spaniards Paesius and Isaias (*HL* 14).

35. Palladius, *Historia Lausiaca* 41 (Butler, 128; ACW 34:117).

36. Palladius, *Historia Lausiaca* 3, 5, 63, 56, 67.

37. For his account of the life of Melania the Elder, see *Historia Lausiaca* 46 and 54. Melania serves as the source for a number of tales: see *Historia Lausiaca* 5.2 (about Alexandra), 9.1 (about Or), 10.2 (about Pambo), 18.28 (about Macarius the Alexandrian).

38. Palladius, *Historia Lausiaca* 44 (on Innocent); 13 (on Apollonius); 14 (on Paesius and Isaias); 17 and 18 (on Macarius the Alexandrian); 22 (on Paul the Simple); 49 (on Sisinnius); 19 (on Moses the Ethiopian).

39. Palladius, *Historia Lausiaca* 49.1 (Butler, 143; ACW 34:132), in speaking of Sisinnius, as an ex-slave becoming a priest, notes that "one should mention these things for the glory of Christ who uplifts us and leads us to true nobility."

40. Palladius, *Historia Lausiaca* 11.1–5 (Butler, 32–34; trans. Meyer, ACW 34: 46–47).

41. Palladius, *Historia Lausiaca* 2.2 (Butler, 17; ACW 34:33).

42. Palladius, *Historia Lausiaca* 38.10, 12 (Butler, 120, 122; trans. Meyer, ACW 34: 113–114).

43. Palladius, *Historia Lausiaca*, prol. 13 (Butler, 13; trans. Meyer, ACW 34:27).

44. Palladius, *Historia Lausiaca* 18.3 (Butler, 48; trans. Meyer, ACW 34:59).

45. Palladius, *Historia Lausiaca* 18.4 (Butler, 49; ACW 34:59).

46. Palladius, *Historia Lausiaca* 18.16 (Butler, 53; trans. Meyer, ACW 34:63).

47. Palladius, *Historia Lausiaca* 2.2 (Butler, 17; trans. Meyer, ACW 34:32–33).

48. Palladius, *Historia Lausiaca* 4.4, 18.15 (Butler, 20, 53; ACW 34:36, 62–63).

49. Palladius, *Historia Lausiaca* 18.17–18 (Butler, 53–54; trans. Meyer, ACW 34:63).

50. Palladius, *Historia Lausiaca* 20.1–3 (Butler, 62–63; trans. Meyer, ACW 34: 70–71).

51. Palladius, *Historia Lausiaca* 25.1–5 (Butler, 79; trans. Meyer, ACW 34:84–85).

52. Palladius, *Historia Lausiaca* 26.1–4 (Butler, 81–82; ACW 34:86–87).

53. Palladius, *Letter to Lausus* 2 (Butler, 7; trans. Meyer, ACW 34:21).

54. Palladius, *Historia Lausiaca* 25.6 (Butler, 80; trans. Meyer, ACW 34:86).

55. Palladius, *Historia Lausiaca* 47.3 (Butler, 137; trans. Meyer, ACW 34:125–126).

56. E. D. Hunt, "Palladius of Helenopolis: A Party and Its Supporters in the Church of the Late Fourth Century," *Journal of Theological Studies* n.s. 24 (1973): 459.

57. Palladius, *Historia Lausiaca*, prol. 3 (Butler, 10; trans. Meyer, ACW 34:24).

58. Palladius, *Historia Lausiaca*, prol. 7 (Butler, 11; trans. Meyer, ACW 34:25).

59. Palladius, *Historia Lausiaca*, prol. 15 (Butler, 14; trans. my own).

60. For a survey, see Butler, *The Lausiac History of Palladius*, 1:3–4.

61. On this complex of issues concerning miracles, ancient minds and modern minds, see especially John Meier, *A Marginal Jew: Rethinking the Historical Jesus*, vol. 2, *Message, Mentor, Miracle* (New York: Doubleday, 1994). For sample texts, see Wendy Cotter, ed., *Miracles in Graeco-Roman Antiquity: A Sourcebook*, Context of Early Christianity 1 (New York: Routledge, 1999).

62. *Historia monachorum in Aegypto* VIII.2, 7 (SH 53:47–49; trans. Russell, CS 34:70–71).

63. *Historia monachorum in Aegypto* VIII.45–47 (SH 53:64–65; trans. Russell, CS 34:76–77).

64. *Historia monachorum in Aegypto* X.12–14 (SH 53:80–81; CS 34:84).

65. *Historia monachorum in Aegypto*, prol. 9 (SH 53:7–8; CS 34:50).

66. *Historia monachorum in Aegypto* XXI.15–16 (SH 53:118–119; trans. Russell, CS 34:110).

67. Palladius, *Historia Lausiaca* 18.28 (Butler, 57–58; ACW 34:66–67).

68. Paulinus of Nola, *Epistula* 29.5 (CSEL 29:251).

69. *Historia monachorum in Aegypto* IV.3 (SH 53:41; CS 34:66).

70. *Historia monachorum in Aegypto* XII.8 (SH 53:95; CS 34:91).

71. *Historia monachorum in Aegypto* IX.5–7 (SH 53:72–73; trans. Russell, CS 34:80).

72. *Historia monachorum in Aegypto* VI.4 (SH 53:45; trans. Russell, CS 34:68).

73. *Historia monachorum in Aegypto* VIII.5–6, XI.5 (SH 53:48–49, 91; CS 34:70–71, 88).

74. *Historia monachorum in Aegypto* VIII.12 (SH 53:50–51; CS 34:71).

75. *Historia monachorum in Aegypto* XXV.2 (SH 53:134; CS 34:116). See also the bizarre account about Macarius and the Eucharist in Rufinus, *Historia monachorum in Aegypto* XXIX.4.1–16 (Schulz-Flügel, 371–373; CS 34:153–154): in his vision, Macarius sees good monks receiving the Eucharist from angels, while impure monks receive pieces of coal from little Ethiopians (presumably symbols of demons).

76. *Historia monachorum in Aegypto*, prol. 4 (SH 53:7; trans. Russell, CS 34:49).

77. *Historia monachorum in Aegypto* IV.1 (SH 53:40; trans. Russell, CS 34:66).

78. *Historia monachorum in Aegypto* II.1 (SH 53:39–40; trans. Russell, CS 34:63).

79. *Historia monachorum in Aegypto* VI.1 (SH 53:43; CS 34:68).

80. *Historia monachorum in Aegypto* XVI.2 (SH 53:112–113; CS 34:100).

81. The chronologies of the various accounts do not match: the *Historia monachorum* says that John was ninety years old and had spent forty years as a recluse; Palladius says that John was seventy-eight years old and had spent forty-eight years as a recluse. Chitty, *The Desert a City*, 51–52, recommends following Palladius on such details, because of the *Historia monarchorum*'s tendency to round off numbers and to exaggerate.

82. *Historia monachorum in Aegypto* I.11 (SH 53:12; trans. Russell, CS 34:53).

83. *Historia monachorum in Aegypto* I.1–2 (SH 53:9–10; CS 34:52). The text does not report a second prediction over a second usurper, named Maximus.

84. See Palladius, *Historia Lausiaca* 35.2 (Butler, 100–101; ACW 34:99); Cassian, *Institutes* 4.23; Augustine, *De civitate Dei* 5.26 and *De cura gerenda pro mortuis* 17.21; Sozomen, *HE* 6.28.1 and 7.22; Theodoret of Cyrrhus, *HE* 5.24.1–2. For an example of the acclaim he was given, note the following from John Cassian, *Conferences* 24.26 (SC 64:205; trans. Ramsey, ACW 56:851–852): "The very lords of things present, who hold the government of this world and of the Empire and who are awesome even to all powers and kings, venerate [John] as their lord, seek out his oracles from far-off regions, and commit the welfare of their Empire, their salvation, and the success of their wars to his prayers and good works."

85. *Historia monachorum in Aegypto* I.13–17 (SH 53:13–15; trans. Russell, CS 34:54).

86. *Historia monachorum in Aegypto* I.64–65 (SH 53:34–35; trans. Russell, CS 34:62).

87. Palladius, *Historia Lausiaca* 35.10–11 (Butler, 103–105: trans. Meyer, ACW 34: 101–102).

88. Rufinus, *Historia monachorum in Aegypto* XXVIII.2,1–6 (Schulz-Flügel, 365–366; trans. Russell, CS 34:151).

89. See Peter Brown, "The Rise and Function of the Holy Man in Late Antiquity," *Journal of Roman Studies* 61 (1971): 80–101; reprinted in *Society and the Holy in Late Antiquity* (Berkeley: University of California Press, 1982).

90. *Historia monachorum in Aegypto* VIII.24–29 (SH 53:56–58; trans. Russell, CS 34:73–74).

91. Peter Brown, *The World of Late Antiquity*, 104.

92. *Historia monachorum in Aegypto* VI.1, VII.2, VIII.7, X.1, X.24, XXVI (SH 53: 43, 45–46, 49, 75, 85, 135; CS 34:69, 71, 82, 108, 117).

93. *Historia monachorum in Aegypto* X.1 (SH 53:75; trans. Russell, CS 34:82).

94. *Historia monachorum in Aegypto* I.12 (SH 53:12–13; CS 34:53–54).

95. *Historia monachorum in Aegypto* XXI.17 (SH 53:119; CS 34:110).

96. *Historia monachorum in Aegypto* XVII.3 (SH 53:103; trans. Russell, CS 34:101).

97. Chitty, *The Desert a City*, 52.

98. *Historia monachorum in Aegypto*, prol. 12 (SH 53:8; trans. Russell, CS 34:51).

99. *Historia monachorum in Aegypto*, prol. 3 (SH 53:6; trans. Russell, CS 34:49).

100. *Historia monachorum in Aegypto*, prol. 5 (SH 53:7; trans. Russell, CS 34: 49–50).

101. *Historia monachorum in Aegypto*, prol. 7 (SH 53:7; trans. Russell, CS 34:50).

102. *Historia monachorum in Aegypto*, prol. 10 (SH 53:8; trans. Russell, CS 34:50).

103. *Historia monachorum in Aegypto*, prol. 9 (SH 53:7–8; trans. Russell, CS 34:50).

104. Georgia Frank, *The Memory of the Eyes: Pilgrims to the Living Saints in Christian Late Antiquity*, Transformation of the Classical Heritage 30 (Berkeley: University of California Press, 2000), 35–36.

BIBLIOGRAPHY

Lausiac History (*Historia Lausiaca*): Text and Translation

For a critical edition of the Greek text, see Cuthbert Butler, *The Lausiac History of Palladius: A Critical Discussion, together with Notes on Early Monachism*, Texts and Studies 6, pts. 1–2 (Cambridge: Cambridge University Press, 1898–1904; reprint, Hildesheim: Olms, 1967). For an English translation, see Robert T. Meyer, *Palladius: The Lausiac History*, ACW 34 (New York: Newman Press, 1965; reprint: Paulist Press). The authenticity of the material contained in longer Coptic version is now generally accepted. This reassessment came from the work of Adalbert de Vogüé and Gabriel Bunge in a series of five articles published initially in *Studia Monastica* 32–34 (1990–1992). Their work, both a study and a French translation of the Coptic fragments, has been collected into a single volume: *Quatre érmites égyptiens: d'après les fragments coptes de l'Histoire Lausiaque*, SO 60 (Bégrolles-en-Mauges: Abbaye de Bellefontaine, 1994). Tim Vivian has translated these Coptic fragments into English; see the following:

Vivian, Tim. "Coptic Palladiana I: The Life of Pambo." *Coptic Church Review* 20, no. 3 (1999): 66–95.
———. "Coptic Palladiana II: The Life of Evagrius." *Coptic Church Review* 21, no. 1 (2000): 8–23.
———. "Coptic Palladiana III: The Life of Macarius of Egypt." *Coptic Church Review* 21, no. 3 (2000): 82–109.
———. "Coptic Palladiana [IV]: St. Macarius of Alexandria." *Coptic Church Review* 22, no. 1 (2001): 2–22.

Lausiac History: Studies

A book-length study of Palladius is that of Nicolas Molinier, *Ascèse, contemplation et ministre: d'après Histoire Lausiaque de Pallade d'Hélénopolis*, SO 64 (Bégrolles-en-Mauges: Abbaye de Bellefontaine, 1995). See also:

Buck, D. F. "The Structure of the Lausiac History." *Byzantion* 46 (1976): 292–307.
Draguet, Réné. "L'*Histoire Lausiaque*: Une oeuvre écrite dans l'esprit d'Evagre." *Revue d'histoire ecclésiastique* 41 (1946): 321–364; 42 (1947): 5–49.
Driscoll, Jeremy. "Evagrius, Paphnutius, and the Reasons for Abandonment by God." *Studia Monastica* 39 (1998): 259–286.
Elm, Susanna. *Virgins of God: The Making of Asceticism in Late Antiquity*. Oxford Theological Monographs. New York: Oxford University Press, 1994.
Fisher, A. L. "Women and Gender in Palladius' *Lausiac History*." *Studia Monastica* 33 (1991): 23–50.
Hunt, E. D. "Palladius of Helenopolis: A Party and Its Supporters in the Church of the Late Fourth Century." *Journal of Theological Studies* n.s. 24 (1973): 456–480.

History of the Monks in Egypt (*Historia monachorum in Aegypto*): Text and Translation

For a critical edition of the Greek text, together with a French translation: André-Jean Festugière, *Historia Monachorum in Aegypto: Édition critique du text grec et traduction annotée*, SH 53 (Bruxelles: Société des Bollandistes, 1971). For a critical edition of Rufinus's Latin version, see Eva Schulz-Flügel, *Tyrannius Rufinus: Historia monachorum, sive, De vita sanctorum patrum,* Patristische Texte und Studien 34 (Berlin and New York: W. De Gruyter, 1990). For an English translation of the Greek text, as well as the Latin and Syriac revisions, see Norman Russell, trans., *The Lives of the Desert Fathers: The "Historia monachorum in aegypto,"* CS 34 (Kalamazoo, Mich.: Cistercian Publications, 1981).

History of the Monks in Egypt: Studies

For a careful analysis of the text, see Adalbert de Vogüé, *Histoire littéraire du mouvement monastique dans l'antiquité* (Paris: Éditions du Cerf, 1994), 3:317–386; this focuses more on Rufinus's Latin version. For a study of the *History of the Monks* (and Palladius) as travel literature, see Georgia Frank, *The Memory of the Eyes: Pilgrims to Living Saints in Christian Late Antiquity,* Transformation of the Classical Heritage 30 (Berkeley: University of California Press, 2000). She gives a useful précis of her view in the essay "Miracles, Monks, and Monuments: The *Historia Monachorum in Aegypto* as Pilgrims' Tales," in *Pilgrimage and Holy Space in Late Antique Egypt,* ed. David Frankfurter (Leiden: Brill, 1998), 483–507. See also:

Devos, Paul. "Les nombres dans l'*Historia monachorum in Aegypto.*" *Analecta Bollandiana* 92 (1972): 97–108.
Ward, Benedicta. "Monks and Miracles." In *Miracles in Jewish and Christian Antiquity: Imagining Truth,* ed. John C. Cavadini, 127–138. Notre Dame: University of Notre Dame Press, 1999.
———. "Signs and Wonders: Miracles in the Desert Tradition." *Studia Patristica* 18 (1982): 539–542. Reprinted in *Signs and Wonders: Saints, Miracles, and Prayers from the Fourth Century to the Fourteenth.* London: Variorum Reprints, 1992.

Rufinus of Aquileia: Studies

See Philip R. Amidon, trans., *The Church History of Rufinus of Aquileia: Books 10 and 11* (New York: Oxford University Press, 1997); this contains a brief but useful introduction to Rufinus's career and a translation of the two books that he appended to his translation of Eusebius's *Church History.*

Nitria and Kellia

Recent archeological discoveries have dated certain aspects of the magisterial study of Hugh B. Evelyn-White, *The Monasteries of Wadi 'n Natrûn,* pt. 2, *The History of the Monasteries of Nitria and of Scetis,* ed. W. Hauser (New York: Metropolitan Museum of Art, 1932). But his treatment of the literary sources is still valuable. In fact, his survey of the ancient sources laid the groundwork for the discovery of the site of Kellia. For a valuable overview of the recent archeological discoveries (together with photos), see P. Miquel, ed., *Déserts chrétiens d'Égypte* (Nice: Culture Sud, 1993). Brief accounts in English are available in the article by Antoine Guillaumont et al., "Kellia," in *The Coptic Encyclopedia,* ed. Aziz S. Atiya (New York: Macmillan, 1991), 5:1396–1410. See also:

Guillaumont, Antoine. "Histoire des moines aux Kellia." In *Aux origines du monachisme chrétien: pour une phenomenology du monachisme,* 151–167. SO 30. Bégrolles-en-Mauges: Abbaye de Bellefontaine, 1979.
———. "Nitria." In *The Coptic Encyclopedia,* ed. Aziz S. Atiya (New York: Macmillan, 1991), 6:1794–1796.

The Coptic Palladiana

The Coptic liturgical tradition has preserved four brief *Lives* of monks who appear in Palladius's *Lausiac History*: Pambo, Evagrius Ponticus, Macarius the Egyptian, and Macarius the Alexandrian. The four *Lives*, seem at first glance, to be translations, reworkings, and expansions of material drawn from Palladius. That, at least, was the judgment of the great early-twentieth-century editor of Palladius, Dom Cuthbert Butler. It is true that later Coptic sources can uncritically expand on earlier Greek material. But in the early 1990s, two leading scholars, Adalbert de Vogüé and Gabriel Bunge, argued against Butler's judgment in this case. They believe that these *Lives* do contain authentic material from Palladius. These *Lives*, they argue, are not translations of material from the *Lausiac History*. Rather, they come from the pen of Palladius himself—from an earlier period in his career. The material seems to have been a sort of first draft for the four chapters in the *Lausiac History* that deal with these four monks. Given here is an example of what led Bunge and de Vogüé to this conclusion. It is an excerpt that now appears in the Coptic *Life of Pambo*.

PAMBO LEARNS A PSALM

> There appeared in the monastic community of Pernouj [= Nitria] a certain person named Apa Pambo. He was second after Abba Antony. Apa Pambo was thus called *alêthênos*, the "true or righteous one," concerning whose virtues the whole brotherhood testified. I myself did not meet him in my time there, but the brothers spoke with me about him, saying that that man never said a lie nor ever committed a sin with his tongue from the time that he became a monk. . . . When he came to the brothers he went and found an old man and said to him, "Teach me a psalm," for he was illiterate, and the old man began to teach him this psalm: "I said, 'I will watch my ways so as to be unable to sin with my tongue' " (Ps. 38:2, LXX). And after the old man had given him the beginning of the text, Pambo stopped him, saying, "My father, since I haven't yet learned the beginning of the text, I will not learn the rest." And when Abba Pambo went to his cell, he spent eight years putting into practice the saying that he had learned, for he came into contact with no one, saying, "Unless I first master my tongue, I will come into contact with no one lest I fall on account of my tongue." After eight years,

he went and paid a visit to the old man who had given him the psalm. The old man said to him, "Pambo, why haven't I seen you until today? Why didn't you come to learn the psalm?" Apa Pambo said to him, "Since I hadn't learned the first verse, I didn't return to you to get the second since God had not given me the grace until now to learn it. In order not to act as if I despised you, I have come to visit you, my father. For if I learn the first verse, I will come to see you again." And when he returned to his cell, he stayed there another ten years and did not come into contact with anyone. (Coptic *Life of Pambo* 1–2)

This same story about Pambo appears not in the Greek version of Palladius's *Lausiac History;* but in a section of the *Church History* by the ancient historian Socrates, who says that he is drawing material from "Palladius the monk." De Vogüé and Bunge have argued that passages such as this indicate that Socrates was drawing not on the later *Lausiac History,* which Palladius wrote in the 420s as a bishop; instead, Socrates was using earlier drafts, material now found in the four Coptic *Lives*—works written when Palladius was still a monk in the 390s.

If Bunge and de Vogüé are right, then the Coptic *Lives* are not an expansion of the *Lausiac History;* rather, the *Lausiac History* is an abbreviation of these earlier and longer *Lives.* One can see this by comparing the opening of chapter 38 on Evagrius in the *Lausiac History* with the opening of the Coptic *Life of Evagrius.*

INTRODUCTION TO EVAGRIUS IN THE GREEK *LAUSIAC HISTORY*

It would not be right to pass over in silence the famous deacon Evagrius, a man who lived in truly apostolic fashion. One should put these things in writing for the spiritual edification of those who happen to come across this account and for the glory of the goodness of our Savior. I believe it worth while to set forth from the beginning, to tell how he arrived at his goal and how he practiced asceticism in the right way and then died in the desert at the age of fifty-four. As Scripture has it, "in a short time he fulfilled many years" (Wis. 4:13). (Palladius, *Historia Lausiaca* 38.1)

INTRODUCTION TO EVAGRIUS IN THE COPTIC *LIFE OF EVAGRIUS*

I will now also begin to speak about Apa Evagrius, the deacon from Constantinople, upon whom the bishop Gregory laid hands. Indeed, it is right that we relate the virtues of him whom everyone praises: he lived the apostolic way of life. For it would not be just if we were silent about his progress and [works] acceptable to God, but it is especially right that we put them into writing for the edification and profit of those who read about them so they may glorify God our Savior who empowers human beings to do these things. Indeed, it

was also he who taught me the way of life in Christ and he who
helped me understand holy scripture spiritually and told me what
old wives' tales are, as it is written, in order that sin might be revealed as a sinner, for the whole time I was in that monastic community I was with him, each of us living enclosed and apart. I was
by his side Saturday night and during the day on Sunday. In order
that someone not think that I am praising him or showing favorit-
ism towards him, as Christ is my witness I saw the majority of his
virtues with my own eyes as well as the wonders that he performed.
These I will write down for you for the profit of those who will read
about them and for those who will hear them read so that they will
glorify Christ who gives power to his poor to do what is pleasing to
him. I myself have been deemed worthy to inform you how he lived,
from the beginning of his life until he arrived at these measures and
these great ascetic practices until he completed sixty years, and in
this way went to his rest, as it is written "In a short period of time
he completed a multitude of years" (Wis. 4:13). (Coptic *Life of Evagrius* 1–3)

In reading the first text, it is not obvious that Palladius himself was a disciple
of Evagrius—though Palladius mentions that explicitly elsewhere in the *Lausiac History* (namely, in 23.1, where he speaks of "my teacher Evagrius," and
in 35.3, where he says "I and those who were in the company of the blessed
Evagrius"). But in the second text, Palladius explains the full depth of his debt
to Evagrius. Such abbreviating appears again and again. The question is
whether the abbreviating comes directly from Palladius as he reworked his
earlier *Lives* and incorporated them into the *Lausiac History*. In some cases,
and perhaps here, it is possible that a later monastic editor, embarrassed by
Palladius's debt to Evagrius (who was later condemned as an Origenist),
pruned the Origenist material away.

   While one cannot presume that everything found in these Coptic *Lives*
goes back to Palladius, there are some interesting passages. Next is an account
describing a miracle not found in the Greek *Lausiac History*.

MACARIUS OF ALEXANDRIA AND THE MIMES

They also said about Saint Abba Macarius the Alexandrian that
when he was a young man living in Alexandria he was a mime by
trade and was world-famous. When he had become a monk, exalted
in virtue in the desert places, his fellow mimes heard that he had
become exalted in God's work. They came to see him in the desert,
seven in number, and when they had greeted him they sat beside
him. They were full of admiration for him and his way of life. When
it came time for them to eat, he put water in the pot and carried it
to the oven, wanting to cook some cereal for them. While he heated
the water to bring it a boil, before he poured the meal into the pot
he sat and chatted with them as he had when he had been a mime

living in the world. When they saw how he was behaving, they said to one another, "Weren't we told that he had become a man of God? Now look—he's the same as he was when he was in the world with us. We don't see any change from the way he behaved when he was with us in Alexandria." When Abba Macarius saw them speaking with one another about the great freedom of speech he used with them, he brought in an empty dish, gave it to the greatest among them, and said to him, "Fill this dish with sand and pour it into the pot so we can cook the cereal and eat." When they heard "sand," they joked among themselves, saying, "Truly Macarius has become more of a mime now than when he was with us in the world!" Once again he said to them, "Do what I told him." They obeyed him: they filled the plate with sand and poured it into the pot. He made the cereal and it turned out like a cereal made from tasty wheat. When the seven mimes saw the miracle that had taken place through the holy old man Abba Macarius, they did not return to Egypt but renounced the world. They became monks and adopted the practices of the holy old man Abba Macarius. (Coptic *Life of Macarius of Alexandria* 22)

For the analysis of the Coptic *Lives* (together with a French translation), see Adalbert de Vogüé and Gabriel Bunge, *Quatre érmites égyptiens: d'après les fragments coptes de l'Histoire Lausiaque*, SO 60 (Bégrolles-en-Mauges: Abbaye de Bellefontaine, 1994). The translations used here are from a series of articles by Tim Vivian; for the *Life of Pambo*, see *Coptic Church Review* 20, no. 3 (1999): 66–95; for the *Life of Evagrius*, see *Coptic Church Review* 21, no. 1 (2000): 8–23; for the *Life of Macarius of Egypt*, see *Coptic Church Review* 21, no. 3 (2000): 82–109; and for the *Life of Macarius of Alexandria*, see *Coptic Church Review* 22, no. 1 (2001): 2–22.

PART IV

Monastic Theologians

10

Evagrius Ponticus:
Ascetical Theory

In the 360s and 370s, intellectuals from around the empire began to take notice of Egypt. Athanasius's *Life of Antony* had sparked their attention, but word of mouth also played a part. Pilgrims to the Holy Land made side trips to the desert, as Rufinus and Melania the Elder had, and broadcast what they saw. A steady stream of works—the letters of Jerome, the translations of Rufinus, travelogues such as the *History of the Monks of Egypt* and Egeria's *Pilgrimage*—would help spread the word among the educated across the empire.

Some intellectuals came and stayed. Gruff, cantankerous Abba Arsenius was one of those. He had once moved in the most cultured circles in the empire and had even served for a time as tutor of the emperor's sons. Yet he placed himself at the feet of Coptic peasants. Someone once asked him, "Abba Arsenius, how is it that you with such a good Latin and Greek education, ask this peasant about your thoughts?" He answered, "I have indeed been taught Latin and Greek, but I do not even know the alphabet of this peasant."[1] Intellectuals like Arsenius realized that these often illiterate Egyptian peasants had discovered a new alphabet, the subtle inner lettering of the human heart. In the desert, the monks had made the human heart their text. Intellectuals among the monks would begin to take things a step further. They would devote their skills in Greek and Latin letters and begin recording, distilling, systematizing, and popularizing these new discoveries of the human heart.

One day, another brother came to Arsenius. He, like Arsenius, was a foreigner and, like Arsenius, had come to question the worth of his fine learning: "How is it that we, with all our education and our wide knowledge get nowhere, while these Egyptian peasants acquire so many virtues?" It was a question that the elite around the empire found themselves asking. Augustine, moments before his dramatic conversion in the garden in Milan, had asked himself the exact same question. Arsenius's answer was telling: "We indeed get nothing from our secular education, but these Egyptian peasants acquire the virtues by hard work." In the Alphabetical Collection, Arsenius's interrogator is unnamed. But in the Systematic Collection, his name is given: Evagrius Ponticus.[2]

Until the 1950s, Evagrius was a name little known, even in scholarly circles. Those familiar with the condemnation of Origen by the Council of Constantinople II in 553 would have recognized Evagrius's name as one of those it condemned as an Origenist. Early in the twentieth century, a quiet but remarkable reclamation of his writings began to occur. Some were rediscovered, buried in little-known Syriac and Armenian manuscripts. Other texts were discovered to have been disguised and passed on under the name of such venerable figures as Nilus of Ancyra. Meanwhile, scholars realized that John Cassian, whose writings profoundly shaped medieval Benedictine spirituality, had drawn heavily from Evagrius. Cassian never acknowledged his borrowings or even mentioned Evagrius's name, but the ideas are everywhere. Even church fathers who condemned Evagrius, such as Maximus the Confessor in the seventh century, were discovered to be deeply in his debt. Scholars began to realize that Evagrius was "one of the most important names in the history of spirituality, one of those that not only marked a decisive turning-point, but called forth a real spiritual mutation"[3] "he is the almost absolute ruler of the entire Syriac and Byzantine mystical theology, and . . . has influenced in a decisive manner Western ascetical and mystical teaching as well."[4]

Even ordinary Christians unfamiliar with Evagrius's name are familiar with his famous catalogue of human vices: the so-called seven deadly sins—though he calls them "thoughts," not sins, and has eight, not seven. Evagrius had learned from the great Egyptian masters how to read this new alphabet of the human heart. With his Greek literary and philosophical training, he was able to translate and transform Coptic spirituality for the Greek-speaking world, systematizing its insights into a gemlike brilliance. He would become the first great theoretician of the spiritual life.

The Desert Calligrapher

Much of what we know about the life of Evagrius comes from Palladius's *Lausiac History*. Palladius was a devoted disciple and extolled Evagrius as fearlessly as he did his other persecuted friend, John Chrysostom. While Palladius's account provides the basic framework, it can be confirmed and filled out from details in Evagrius's own writings as well from notices in the ancient historians Socrates, Sozomen, and Gennadius.[5]

Evagrius was born in Ibora in the province of Pontus, near the Black Sea, in what is today northern Turkey (for a map, see figure 10.1; for a chronological outline, see table 10.1). His father was a country bishop (*chorepiscopos*). In his teens, Evagrius was ordained lector by one of the pioneers of the monastic

FIGURE 10.1. Key locales in the career of Evagrius Ponticus.

movement, Basil of Caesarea. In the 370s, he followed Basil's friend, Gregory of Nazianzus, to Constantinople.[6] Evagrius always felt great affection for Gregory and in later years spoke of him as "Gregory the Just, the one who planted me," and as "a deep wellspring . . . the mouthpiece of Christ."[7] In Constantinople, Evagrius served as Gregory's archdeacon and helped man the front lines of the debate on the Trinity before and at the Council of Constantinople in 381. He was an important voice in the Nicene cause, "one most skillful in confuting all the heresies," as Palladius puts it.[8] The accuracy of this assessment has become clear with the discovery that a famous letter probing subtle aspects of Trinitarian doctrine, a letter long attributed to Basil, was in fact composed by Evagrius.[9]

Evagrius stayed on in Constantinople after Gregory's abrupt resignation and served his successor, Nectarius. Not long after this, Evagrius fell in love with an upper-class woman, the wife of a high imperial official. Apparently the risk of scandal was great, and, as Palladius notes, a sexual scandal would have risked the fragile hegemony of the Nicene cause in the capital city. Evagrius decided to break off the affair, but the woman was "by now eager and frantic."[10] One night he had an ominous dream. He imagined himself under military arrest, standing in chains and an iron collar. Suddenly an angel appeared and compelled him to swear on the book of the Gospels that he would leave town. When he awoke, he decided to fulfill the oath he swore in the dream vision and caught the first available ship to Jerusalem.

TABLE 10.1. Evagrius Ponticus and His Circle

c. 345	Birth of Evagrius
c. late 350s	Ordained lector by Basil of Caesarea
c. late 370s	Ordained deacon by Gregory of Nazianzus
381	Council of Constantinople
381	Gregory resigns as bishop of Constantinople
c. 382	Evagrius flees to Jerusalem, befriended by Melania the Elder
383	Settles in Nitria
385	Settles in Kellia
390s	Palladius in Nitria and Kellia
390s	John Cassian in Scetis
394	Epiphanius of Salamis lobbies John of Jerusalem to condemn Origenism
399	Death of Evagrius
399	Theophilus's *Festal Letter* against the Anthropomorphites
399	Theophilus begins persecution of the Origenists
c. 399 or 400	Palladius and John Cassian leave Egypt
403	Synod of the Oak deposes John Chrysostom
406–412	Palladius in exile in Syene
420s	Palladius publishes *Lausiac History* (includes account of life of Evagrius)
553	Second Council of Constantinople condemns Origen, Didymus, and Evagrius

There in Jerusalem, he met Melania the Elder and Rufinus and their circle. As we saw, their monastic community at the Mount of Olives was a remarkable intellectual center, one that introduced the Latin-speaking world to Eastern currents in both monasticism (e.g., Pachomius) and theology (e.g., Origen). There Evagrius's health took a bad turn. He reportedly suffered a six-month-long fever that left him emaciated. Various doctors were unable to diagnose his problem. So Melania took him in and challenged him: "Son, I am not pleased with your long sickness. Tell me what is in your mind, for your sickness is not beyond God's aid." Evagrius apparently confessed what had happened to him in Constantinople. She got him to promise to adopt the monastic life, and she promised to pray for his healing. He recovered quickly. According to Palladius, he "received a change of clothing at her hands."[11] This sounds like Melania formally invested Evagrius in monastic garb in the manner of a monastic superior.[12] She then sent him on to her contacts in Egypt.

Around 383, Evagrius arrived at Nitria. There he joined that remarkable circle of intellectual monks led by Ammonius the Earless and the Tall Brothers. They had been disciples of Abba Pambo and, in the later controversy, became the leaders of the Origenists. It did not take long for Evagrius's learning to attract attention and for his leadership skills to emerge. The group soon became known as the "entourage of Ammonius and Evagrius," or even as "the community of Evagrius."[13]

After a two-year stay at Nitria, Evagrius moved on to the more solitary lifestyle of Kellia. He would spend the remaining fourteen years of his life there.[14] Evagrius worked hard to learn and absorb the new alphabet of the Coptic monks he lived with. He apprenticed under two of the greatest of the desert fathers, Macarius the Egyptian and Macarius the Alexandrian. Socrates remarks that "Evagrius became a disciple of these men and acquired from them the philosophy of deeds, whereas before he knew only a philosophy of words."[15] In the *Praktikos*, Evagrius speaks of Macarius the Egyptian in glowing terms as "our holy and most ascetic master" and as "the vessel of election."[16] He also quotes Macarius on the need for a balanced asceticism: "the monk should always live as if he were to die on the morrow but at the same time he should treat his body as if he were to live on with it for many years to come."[17] Macarius, it seems, contributed to Evagrius's teaching on a whole variety of issues: combating anger, discernment and prayer, the naturalness of virtue, "remembering" God. To seek out Macarius's advice, Evagrius had to make the dangerous desert trek from Kellia to Scetis.

Evagrius's links to the other Macarius are less surprising, since the Alexandrian served as priest of Kellia until his death in 393. Evagrius records an interesting anecdote that highlights both Macarius's sense of quiet joy and his fierce asceticism. Once Evagrius went over to visit him at the hottest part of the day. Evagrius was thirsty and asked Macarius for some water. But Macarius advised him to count his blessings: "Be content with the shade, for many there are who are making a journey on land or on sea who are deprived of this." Evagrius found himself unable to bask in gratitude and struggled with his thoughts. So Macarius told him about his own ascetic regimen: "Take courage, my son. For twenty full years I have not taken my fill of bread or water or sleep. I have eaten my bread by scant weight, and drunk my water by measure, and snatched a few winks of sleep while leaning against a wall."[18]

Unlike most Egyptian monks, who earned their living by weaving rope, Evagrius worked as a calligrapher. Palladius mentions that Evagrius had graceful penmanship and wrote in the Oxyrhynchus style.[19] In the Middle Ages, copying manuscripts would become a routine monastic labor, but at this early date it was the exception. The contrast between the literate Evagrius and illiterate Coptic monks should not be overdrawn. It is ironic, for instance, that the learned Evagrius passes on two of the apophthegms most critical of book learning and book collecting. In the *Praktikos*, Evagrius tells of an encounter Antony had with some philosophers. One asked Antony, "How do you ever manage to carry on, Father, deprived as you are of the consolation of books?" Antony's reply: "My book, sir philosopher, is the nature of created things, and it is always at hand when I wish to read the words of God."[20] This seems to fit nicely with Athanasius's portrait of the unlearned Antony lecturing learned philosophers on the proper pursuit of wisdom. But it also exemplifies one of Evagrius's favorite ideas: creation as the handwriting of God.[21] Evagrius also passes on a quaint apophthegm about a monk who once owned a copy of the Gospels. Books were very valuable commodities. So the monk decided to sell his Bible and give the proceeds to the poor. When asked about it, he said he was simply fulfilling the Gospel's own command: "I have sold the very word that speaks to me saying, 'Sell your possessions and give to the poor.' "[22]

Evagrius emerged as a respected spiritual director. When the author of the *Historia monachorum* visited Kellia, he met Evagrius and described him as "a wise and learned man who was skilled in the discernment of thoughts, an ability he had acquired by experience."[23] This was also how his disciple Palladius remembered him. In the Coptic version of the *Lausiac History*, Palladius says that Evagrius "taught me the way of life in Christ and helped me understand Holy Scripture spiritually." Palladius goes on to describe the pedagogical routine practiced in Evagrius's circle at Kellia:

> This was his practice: The brothers would gather around him on Saturday and Sunday, discussing their thoughts with him throughout the night, listening to his words of encouragement until sunrise. And in this way they would leave, rejoicing and glorifying God, for Evagrius' teaching was very sweet. When they came to see him, he encouraged them, saying to them, "My brothers, if one of you has either a profound or a troubled thought, let him be silent until the brothers depart and let him reflect on it alone with me. Let us not make him speak in front of the brothers lest a little one perish in his thoughts and grief swallow him at a gulp." Furthermore, he was so hospitable that his cell never lacked five or six visitors a day who had come from foreign lands to listen to his teaching, his intellect, and his ascetic practice.[24]

One striking anecdote about Evagrius appears in the *Apophthegmata*. At an assembly at Kellia, Evagrius put forth his views on some issue. But one of the priests chided him: "Abba, we know that if you were living in your own country, you would probably be a bishop and a great leader; but at present you sit here as a stranger." It was a stern rebuke. Evagrius accepted it, quoting Job 40:5: "I have spoken once. But I will not do so a second time."[25] One can read this tense episode several ways. At one level, it lays bare what Evagrius's choice of the desert had cost him: home, ecclesiastical honors, even the right to the public voice normally accorded the educated. In this sense, it is a telling demonstration of Evagrius's humility—likely the reason it appears in the *Apophthegmata*.

But it can also be read as a foreshadowing of what was to come: while Evagrius accepted Egypt, Egypt did not accept Evagrius. In 399, on the feast of Epiphany, Evagrius was near death. He had to be carried to church to receive the Eucharist and died soon after. He was fifty-five—comparatively young, given the long lives that desert literature normally accords its leaders. That year, the patriarch of Alexandria, Theophilus, embarked on a ruthless persecution against Evagrius's friends and disciples. They were accused of the heresy of Origenism and forced to flee Egypt. Death spared Evagrius the bitter experience of exile and condemnation.

The Art of the Chapter

Evagrius deeply admired his old teacher, Gregory of Nazianzus, who, as patriarch of Constantinople, had eloquently defended the Nicene cause. No one embodied the rhetorical fashion of his day better than Gregory. He favored a mannered style, with intricate, flowing sentences, peppered with archaic vocabulary, daring wordplay, and subtle literary allusions. This style, known as Second Sophistic, was all the rage. Think in musical terms: what Bach is to classical music, Gregory is to Greek rhetoric. In lesser hands, this ornamented style could be all fluff and artifice—like bad baroque music—but with Gregory, it flowed forth with an effortless, natural spontaneity.

Evagrius shared his teacher's Nicene theology, but in style the two could not have been more different. Where Gregory is prolix, Evagrius is gnomic. Evagrius cultivated an artful brevity. All his best-known and most influential writings are collections of terse, proverblike sentences, clustered in brief, seemingly disconnected paragraphs called *kephalaia* ("chapters") One of the best descriptions of reading Evagrius is also one of the earliest. It comes from the seventh-century Nestorian Babai the Great:

> [Evagrius] does not write in a discursive or rhetorical manner, but he cites each chapter in itself and for itself, condensing it, gathering it together, enclosing it, delimiting it in itself and for itself, with a profound and marvelous wisdom. Then he abandons the subject of this chapter, as though to rest himself in some other dwelling-place, and he begins another subject, composing another chapter in the same way. He then returns to the first [idea, but] under another form. Then he leaves it in order to begin another one of them, then to return to the preceding one, treating sometimes divinity, sometimes creation and creatures, all in order to return again to providence. He . . . then once more returns to the first, turns himself back toward the last, in order to return to the intermediate, briefly, in a manner never the same and always different.[26]

What struck Babai strikes the modern reader: Evagrius's writings are an elegant polyphony, a fuguelike weave of motifs, built from self-contained morsels.

He carefully numbered his chapters, and numbers shape the larger architecture of many of his treatises. His *Praktikos* has 100 chapters and is the first known example of the literary genre called the century. It would set off a fashion in Greek spiritual writing and find great imitators, such as Diodochus of Photice and Maximus the Confessor.

Many of Evagrius's chapters have the ring of a proverb. For example, in his *Chapters on Prayer*, he writes:

> If you are a theologian, you pray truly;
> if you pray truly, you are a theologian.[27]

Others read like dictionary definitions. The opening chapter of the *Praktikos* sounds like something lifted from an old-fashioned catechism:

> Christianity is the dogma of Christ our Savior.
> It is composed of practice and physics and theology.[28]

The density of these sayings can make translation difficult. Partly this is because Evagrius developed his own systematic vocabulary. What I have translated here (rather crudely) as "physics" refers not to science. In Evagrius's
vocabulary, "physics" (*physikē*) means "contemplating the natural world," or,
more precisely, "contemplating the natural world so that one sees through it
to its divine order." The two other terms in the same sentence, "practice" and
"theology," have their own rich and somewhat idiosyncratic meanings in Evagrius's system.

Evagrius was quite a prolific author.[29] He grouped three of his most important treatises into a sort of theological trilogy.

Praktikos (The Practical Treatise)

The 100-chapter *Practical Treatise* focuses on the first phase of monastic life,
which he calls "practice" (*praktikē*), the practical acquisition of virtue. It contains an account of the eight evil "thoughts" (*logismoi*) and offers suggestions
for combating them. The last ten chapters are a mini-collection of *Apophthegmata*. The *Praktikos* was his most popular work and has been preserved in
numerous Greek manuscripts, as well as in Syriac and Armenian translations
(for an outline, see table 10.2).

Gnostikos (The Gnostic)

The *Gnostikos*, a brief fifty-chapter work, offers advice for advanced monks,
whom he calls "knowers" (*gnōstikoi*), and who now serve as teachers and have
a circle of disciples around them. The treatise offers perspectives on spiritual
pedagogy and principles of biblical exegesis. Toward the end, Evagrius quotes
excerpts from five theologians he admires: Gregory of Nazianzus, Basil of
Caesarea, Athanasius, Serapion of Thmuis, and Didymus the Blind.[30] Only
fragments of it remain in Greek, but the complete work is preserved in Syriac
(for an outline, see table 10.3).

Kephalaia gnostica (The Gnostic Chapters)

The *Kephalia gnostica* has 540 chapters, grouped in six centuries of 90. It is a
complex, often esoteric work and contains Evagrius's bold cosmological vision.
The original Greek text (except for a few fragments) has been lost. A Syriac
version had been published early in the twentieth century. But this was found
to have been a carefully sanitized text when, in 1952, Antoine Guillaumont
discovered an unexpurgated version in a Syriac manuscript in the British Museum. Before Guillaumont's discovery, scholars had wondered whether Evagrius had been unjustly accused of Origenism; after the discovery, they realized
that the *Kephalaia gnostica* contains all the bold Origenist theories for which
Evagrius had been anathematized by the Council of Constantinople in 553. It
describes, for instance, the preexistence of minds as well as a cosmic restoration and reintegration of all things into God (*apokatastasis*). A supplement of

TABLE 10.2. Outline of Evagrius's *Praktikos*

Preface: Letter to Anatolius on the symbolic meaning of monastic clothing
Chapters 1–5: Introduction
    #1: Christianity as *praktikē, physikē, theologikē*
    #2–3: Kingdom of God and knowledge of the Trinity
    #4: Desire, feeling, passion
    #5: The monastic combat against demons
Chapters 6–14: On the Eight Thoughts (*logismoi*)
    #6: List of the eight
    #7: Gluttony
    #8: Fornication
    #9: Love of money
    #10: Sadness
    #11: Anger
    #12: *Acēdia*
    #13: Vainglory
    #14: Pride
Chapters 15–33: Against the Eight Thoughts
Chapters 34–39: On the Passions
Chapters 40–53: Instructions
Chapters 54–56: On What Takes Place During Sleep
Chapters 57–62: On the State Close to Passionlessness (*apatheia*)
Chapters 63–70: On the Signs of Passionlessness
Chapters 71–90: Practical Considerations
Chapters 91–100: Sayings of Holy Monks
    #91: Fasting joined to charity leads to purity of heart
    #92: Antony and the philosophers
    #93: Macarius the Egyptian
    #94: Macarius [the Alexandrian]
    #95–99: Anonymous apophthegms
    #100: Loving the brethren
Epilogue: Prayer to Christ; rejoicing for the intercession of Gregory of Nazianzus

TABLE 10.3. Outline of Evagrius's *Gnostikos*

Chapters 1–3: Introduction
    #1: Knowledge of the ascetic vs. gnostic
    #2: Ascetic as passionless
    #3: Gnostic as teacher
Chapters 4–11: Virtues of the gnostic teacher
Chapters 12–15: Need for gnostic to adapt self to disciples
Chapters 16–21: Content of teaching: Exegesis
Chapters 21–36: The comportment of the gnostic when teaching
Chapters 37–43: Temptations and sins of the gnostic
Chapters 44–48: Quotes from theologians
    #44: Gregory of Nazianzus
    #45: Basil of Caesarea
    #46: Athanasius
    #47: Serapion of Thmuis
    #48: Didymus the Blind
Chapters 49–50: Conclusion

60 chapters was later attached to the original 540, making it an even 600 and thereby completing the incomplete centuries. This supplement—which is not part of the original *Kephalaia gnostica*—contains genuine sayings of Evagrius, drawn especially from a short treatise called *Reflections* (*Skemmata*).

Evagrius composed other important works. These include the following.

De Oratione (Chapters on Prayer)

The *Chapters on Prayer*, like Evagrius's great trilogy, is written in the style of terse gnomic sayings.[31] This treatise contains 153 chapters—a play on the number of fish netted in the miraculous catch described in the resurrection narrative of John 21 (for the text and an analysis, see appendix 10.1). It was preserved in Greek, disguised under the name of Nilus of Ancyra. Only in the 1930s did Irénée Hausherr finally demonstrate that Evagrius was its true author. It spells out Evagrius's vision of the mind's mystical ascent to the Trinity and describes his theory of "pure prayer," a mode of prayer that is both wordless and imageless.

Antirrhetikos (Counter-Arguments)

One might call the *Antirrhetikos* a scriptural battle manual. It is a listing of 487 temptations, grouped together under the eight evil "thoughts." After describing each temptation, Evagrius lists an apt text from scripture with which the monk can counter the temptation. The model here, as Evagrius notes in the preface, is Jesus's own behavior when he faced demonic temptation in the desert. The book was written at the request of Abba Loukios, who was one of the leaders of the famous Enaton monastery, located nine miles outside of Alexandria. This is the only work Palladius mentions in his account of the life of Evagrius—an indication of its high regard among Evagrius's disciples. The work survives only in Syriac and Armenian.

Scholia

A little-known side of Evagrius is his biblical commentaries. Two have been edited thus far, one on the book of Proverbs, a second on Ecclesiastes; a third, on the book of Psalms, is forthcoming. Evagrius did not compose verse-by-verse commentaries, nor are they detailed. They are *scholia*, brief comments on selected verses.

Letters

Evagrius authored some sixty-four letters. The most famous is his *Letter to Melania*, which offers a bold and straightforward account of his theological vision (including ideas on preexistence, the primordial fall into bodies, and the final bodiless reunion in God). Another, mentioned earlier, is a letter about aspects of the doctrine of the Trinity, attributed for centuries to Basil but now recognized as the work of Evagrius. The others are preserved only in Syriac. These show his wide-ranging friendships with notables around the empire, including Melania, Rufinus, and Gregory of Nazianzus. They also show his personal warmth and sensitivity and his devotion to the person of Christ. These counterbalance the impression sometimes given by his works in the chapter style that he was an intellectual overly prone to abstraction and system.

Other Works

Evagrius wrote other treatises as well. Two works, *On the Eight Spirits of Evil* and *On Thoughts*, explore further dimensions of his theory of the eight evil "thoughts." His *Foundations of Monastic Life* offers advice for beginners on basic issues: celibacy, renunciation, poverty, solitude, and manual labor. Two other works on monastic spirituality use metric sentences and are modeled on the biblical book of Proverbs: *To the Monks* and *To a Virgin* (for excerpts, see appendix 10.2).

While Evagrius's preference for proverbs and terse sentences had precedents in Greek literature, his choice seems to have flowed out of his experience in the desert. At the heart of desert spirituality were those momentous encounters when a monk begged an abba for a "word of salvation." Those encounters became enshrined in the literary form of the apophthegm and were brought together in the great collections of the *Apophthegmata Patrum*. The collections record stories from Evagrius's generation—about the two Macarii, John the Little, Moses, and Poemen. But these were only written down and assembled much later, in the late fifth or early sixth century. In fact, the *earliest* collection of *written* apophthegms are those that close Evagrius's *Praktikos*. There he tells anecdotes about Antony, Macarius the Egyptian, Macarius the Alexandrian, and others. Evagrius saw himself articulating an ancient and venerable tradition: "It is a very necessary thing also to examine carefully the ways of the monks who have traveled, in an earlier age, straight along the road and to direct oneself along the same paths."[32] And he thought of his monastic predecessors as heroes and healers: "Our old men are to be honored like the angels for it is they who have anointed us for the battles and who treat the wounds we suffer from the bites of wild beasts."[33]

Unlike most literature of the desert, Evagrius's works are not easy reading. His sentences are dense wisdom-sayings that need to be mulled over and, sometimes, deciphered. We know that he consciously cultivated a certain obscurity, at least on some matters. In the preface to the *Praktikos*, he quotes Jesus's saying that one should not "give what is holy to the dogs or cast our pearls before swine" (Matt. 7:6) and then adds: "Some of these matters will be kept in concealment and others alluded to only obscurely, but yet so as to keep them quite clear to those who walk along in the same path."[34] This studied obscurity poses a real challenge for contemporary commentators. One has to decode Evagrius. The approach pioneered by Irénée Hausherr and Antoine Guillaumont has been to use Evagrius to interpret Evagrius, to find parallels and doublets to decode key ideas. That resolves many but not all problems.

There is a great paradox in Evagrius's art of the chapter. One would imagine that his style would reflect his thought. In other words, one would presume that a writing style that broke thoughts into small, disconnected snippets would leave the thought itself piecemeal. In fact, the opposite is the case. The snippets, like the bright-colored tesserae used in ancient mosaics, come together and create a vast coherent landscape. His thinking about the spiritual life is startlingly consistent and complete.

The Eight Evil Thoughts

Evagrius is best known for his catalog of the human propensity for evil, what he called the eight evil thoughts (*logismoi*). He lists and explains them in the opening half of the *Praktikos*:

1. Gluttony (*gastrimargia*)
2. Fornication (*porneia*)
3. Love of money (*philarguria*)
4. Sadness (*lupē*)
5. Anger (*orgē*)
6. Listlessness (*acēdia*)
7. Vainglory (*kenodoxia*)
8. Pride (*huperēphania*)[35]

This list should look familiar. It would become, with slight modification, the seven deadly sins and enjoy a venerable place in the spirituality of the Middle Ages. And, eventually, in Dante's hands, it would come to define the very geography of the afterlife, both the Inferno and the Purgatorio. The one who brought Evagrius's scheme to the Latin West was his disciple, John Cassian, who discussed them at length in two works, *The Institutes* and *The Conferences* (for more on this, see chapter 12).[36]

Ancient commentators recognized the originality of Evagrius's scheme. Gennadius of Marseilles, in his fifth-century compendium of "illustrious" Christians, remarked, "Evagrius the monk, the intimate disciple of Macarius, ... wrote ... *Suggestions against the Eight Principal Vices*. He was the first to mention them, or at least, among the first to teach about these."[37] Evagrius's originality comes not from the list itself. One finds similar ones in Origen, and behind him in the New Testament. Rather, it stems from the classic descriptions he provides and from his insights into the psychology of their interplay.

Note that Evagrius calls them "thoughts," not sins. Sin implies consent and responsibility, as Evagrius notes: "It is not in our power to determine whether we are disturbed by these thoughts, but it is up to us to decide if they are to linger within us or not and whether or not they are to stir up our passions."[38] To see something of his insight, let us examine how he discusses three of them.

Vainglory

Vainglory is that all-too-human thirst for fame. The form Evagrius describes in the *Praktikos* is the vainglory not of a politician or athlete or actor, but of a monk:

> The thought of vainglory is a very subtle thought which masks itself easily among the virtuous. It prompts them to desire to publicize their fights, to chase after a man-made glory. It makes [the monk] imagine healing women, the demons uttering cries [as they flee the possessed], a crowd which comes to touch his cloak. It even predicts that he will be made a priest, that people stream to his door, coming to seek him out, that if he tries to fend them off, they tie him up and lead him off [to ordination]. Having exalted himself by these vain hopes, [the thought] takes flight and abandons him to the temptations either of the demon of pride or of that of sadness, which introduce in him other thoughts, contrary to his hopes. Sometimes it even delivers him to the demon of fornication—he who, just a moment earlier, was tied up and being carried off to be a holy priest.[39]

Evagrius here ruthlessly unmasks the secret hypocrisies of the holy men of his day: the desire to be acclaimed for one's healing touch, to send demons squealing, to have clients knocking at the door seeking tidbits of wisdom, to be forcibly enlisted into the ranks of the clergy. The image of a monk tied up and forcibly taken to town for ordination is not as far-fetched as it sounds. Forced ordination was a fairly common practice in the early church. Some of the leading church fathers—Gregory of Nazianzus, John Chrysostom, Ambrose, and Augustine—were ordained against their will.[40] The monk in Evagrius's description feigns humility so that the crowd has to tie him up. But as Evagrius's description makes clear, all this humility is false pretense. The monk loves nothing better than playing the act of refusing the honor. It is interesting to note that, according to the historian Socrates, Evagrius himself fled when Theophilus of Alexandria tried to ordain him bishop of Thmuis.[41]

Note how Evagrius shifts from the language of "thoughts" to the language of "demons." If one surveys his works, one finds that he refers almost indifferently to the "thought of vainglory" and the "demon of vainglory." The same flip-flopping between "thoughts" and "demons" appears when he speaks of the other vices. Note also that when the demon of vainglory runs its course, others take its place. Evagrius's demons are all specialists, each specializing in a given vice. In this case, pride, sadness, or fornication picks up where vainglory leaves off. Evagrius especially links vainglory with pride. As he says in *The Eight Spirits of Evil*: "The flash of lightning comes before the rumble of thunder; the presence of vainglory announces the arrival of pride."[42]

Fornication

Evagrius does not offer a generic portrait of the "demon of fornication." He limits his description to the form a monk might face: "The demon of forni-cation forces one to desire various bodies; it attacks violently those who live in abstinence, in order to get them to stop, persuading them that they achieve nothing by it; and it gets [the monk] to lower himself to shameful acts, dirtying the soul; it makes him say certain words and to listen, all as if the object [of his desire] were visible and present."[43] This description from the *Praktikos* is unusually terse. In the *Antirrhetikos*, Evagrius details more clearly each of the points he makes here. He notes, for example, the visual quality of this "desire for bodies": the "demon of fornication" appears as a sultry temptress (much as it does in the *Life of Antony*), "taking on the likeness of a naked woman, with languishing walk, her whole body indicating sensual delight."[44] Evagrius also notes the discouragement with and disgust for celibacy: this is "the demon who puts into my mind that I should marry a wife and become a father of sons, and not spend my time here starving and battling with foul thoughts."[45] Finally, Evagrius explains the rather vague reference about words spoken and heard. This refers to the monk imagining himself offering spiritual direction to women, using these occasions as a ruse for a hidden sexual agenda. Here the demon prompts "thoughts of spending long periods of time with a married woman, with frequent visits at close quarters, as if she were deriving great spiritual benefit from us"; or again, it suggests "the thought which takes the form of a beautiful woman engaging us in serious conversation, while we wish to do evil and shameful things with her."[46]

Acēdia

The *Apophthegmata*, in the very first of its 1000 stories, says that "the holy Abba Antony, when he lived in the desert, fell prey to *acēdia* and a great gloom of thoughts."[47] The Greek word *acēdia* has no easy equivalent in English. The medievals often translated it as "sloth," but that is not what the desert tradition means. For Evagrius, *acēdia* is a sort of restless boredom, a listlessness, and beneath that, discouragement. For centuries, Evagrius's translators have groped to find a single term that captures the rich meaning he gives the word *acēdia*. Early Syrian scholars, for instance, translated it as "despondency of spirit" or "ennui," while John Cassian translated it into Latin as *taedium cordis*, "weariness of heart."[48] But the solution taken by most translators, ancient and modern, has been simply to leave the Greek term untranslated and to let Ev-agrius's evocative descriptions suffice.

In the *Praktikos*, Evagrius gives a famous description of this most deadly of "thoughts":

> The demon of *acēdia*—also called the noonday demon—is the one that causes the most trouble of all. He presses his attack upon the monk about the fourth hour and besieges the soul until the eighth

hour. First of all he makes it seem that the sun barely moves, if at all, and that the day is fifty hours long. Then he constrains the monk to look constantly out the windows, to walk outside the cell, to gaze carefully at the sun to determine how far it stands from the ninth hour, to look now this way, that way to see if one of the brothers might . . . might . . . Then too he instills in the heart of the monk a hatred for the place, a hatred for his very life itself, a hatred for manual labor. He leads him to reflect that charity has departed from among the brethren, that there is no one to give encouragement. Should there be someone at this period who happens to offend him in some way or other, this too the demon uses to contribute further to his hatred. This demon drives him along to desire other sites where he can more easily procure life's necessities, more readily find work and make a real success of himself. He goes on to suggest that, after all, it is not the place that is the basis of pleasing the Lord. God is to be adored everywhere. He joins to these reflections the memory of his dear ones and of his former way of life. He depicts life stretching out for a long period of time, and brings before the mind's eye the toil of the ascetic struggle and, as the saying has it, leaves no leaf unturned to induce the monk to forsake his cell and drop out of the fight. No other demon follows close upon the heels of this one (when he is defeated) but only a state of deep peace and inexpressible joy arise out of this struggle.[49]

Here Evagrius masterfully sketches the face of boredom. We all know the feeling: when time moves at a crawl, when "the day is fifty hours long." Notice how he describes the monk repeatedly looking out the window to see how far it was from the "ninth hour" (three o'clock in the afternoon). That, of course, was when the monk ate his one meal of the day. Evagrius describes *acēdia* as the "noonday demon," a phrase he lifts from Psalm 60:6. This demon attacks not under the cover of darkness, but in broad daylight, from the "fourth" to the "eighth" hour (ten in the morning to two in the afternoon), when the sun is at its peak and the midday heat saps one's energy and robs one's concentration. Other demons—vainglory, fornication—work at night and conjure up dreams and fantasies. But this one induces the monk to stare at the hard, drab sameness of his life. Evagrius captures here the ebb and flow of feeling. On the one hand, the monk feels hatred: hatred for the narrow confines of his cell, hatred for the tedium of manual labor, hatred for monastic life itself. On the other hand, there are wistful desires: desire for family, for his old life, for a life elsewhere. Evagrius has an eye for the way religious people can invoke platitudes to mask the real issue. Here the monk complains about how community life is going downhill, how it has lost its Christian charity; the monk also invokes the truism that God can be worshipped anywhere to justify his plans to go somewhere else, anywhere else. Evagrius's portrait here illustrates a dynamic he describes in one of his letters: *acēdia* wages a two-pronged attack, "an entangled struggle of hate and desire. For the listless one hates whatever is in front of him and desires what is not there. And the more desire drags the monk down, the more hate chases him out of his cell."⁵⁰

The monk plagued by *acēdia* yearns for escape, for distraction of some sort, of any sort. That is why he keeps looking out the window, hoping for a visitor to drop by. Note the incomplete sentence in the middle of Evagrius's description, where he says that *acēdia* "constrains the monk to look . . . now this way, that way, to see if one of the brothers might . . . might. . . ."⁵¹ Evagrius uses this literary device, known as an ellipsis, to evoke the monk's desperate pining for companionship. In the treatise *On the Eight Spirits of Evil*, he describes this behavior more specifically:

> The eyes of the listless monk gaze out the windows again and again, and his mind imagines visitors. A sound at the door, and he jumps up. He has heard a voice, and from the window he reconnoiters the scene and won't leave it until he has to sit down from stiffness. When he reads, the listless monk yawns plenty and easily falls into sleep. He rubs his eyes and stretches his arms. His eyes wander from the book. He stares at the wall and then goes back to his reading for a little. He then wastes his time hanging on to the end of words, counts the pages, ascertains how the book is made, finds fault with the writing and the design. Finally he just shuts it and uses it as a pillow. Then he falls into a sleep not too deep, because hunger wakes his soul up and he begins to concern himself with that.⁵²

Here Evagrius teases out other features of this restless boredom: the yawning, the wandering eyes, the petty faultfinding, the inability to concentrate on anything—even sleep.

The heart of the temptation is, as Evagrius notes, "to induce the monk to forsake his cell and drop out of the fight." To leave the cell is to abandon his solitude. *Acēdia* is such a great temptation for the solitary precisely because it is an attack on his very identity as a solitary.⁵³ The only solution is to stay put, for "endurance cures *acēdia*."⁵⁴ In his poetic work *To the Monks*, Evagrius puts it this way: "If the spirit of *acēdia* grabs you, do not leave your house; and do not turn aside in that hour of profitable wrestling."⁵⁵ The language Evagrius uses here and elsewhere is the language of sports, of boxing and wrestling. To leave one's cell is to climb out of the boxing ring or get up from the wrestling mat in the middle of a bout. Thus, in the *Praktikos*, Evagrius counsels:

> One must not quit the cell at the hour of temptation, no matter how sensible seem the excuses. Rather one should stay seated inside and be patient and receive nobly the attackers, every one, but especially the demon of listlessness [*acēdia*] who, because he is the heaviest of all, brings the soul to its most proven point. For to flee such struggles and to avoid them teaches the mind to be unskilled and lazy and fugitive.⁵⁶

Note Evagrius's terminology: *acēdia* is the "heaviest" of the monk's wrestling opponents. He notes that where the other "thoughts" latch "on only one part of the soul," this "noonday demon is in the habit of enveloping the whole soul and suffocating the mind."[57] That is why when one defeats it, the monk does not have to turn and face new opponents. No other demons follow in its wake, and the monk enjoys "deep peace and inexpressible joy." In conquering *acēdia*, he recovers his very identity as a solitary.

According to Plutarch, the ancient biographer's task was "to capture the gesture which laid bare the soul."[58] Evagrius had an eye for such gestures and knew which ones could lay bare the soul. He also had a knack for word painting and invested his painterly gifts especially in these descriptions of the eight evil "thoughts." Some, like those in the *Praktikos* and in *On the Eight Spirits*, are finely wrought miniatures; others, like those in the *Antirrhetikos*, are thumbnail sketches that, in a few quick lines, capture a scene or a face and give the monk a window into the soul. Nor is it an accident that Evagrius focused his word painting on the pathologies of the soul. He speaks of the monastic teacher as a physician and describes the pedagogical task in medicinal metaphors.[59] Evagrius's word paintings are like plates in a medical textbook: they illustrate the symptomology of disease. Evagrius the word painter was at the same time Evagrius the doctor of souls who sought to cure the cataract on the soul's eye and make it ready to glimpse the light of the Trinity.

Combat with Demons

Demons figure prominently in the works of Evagrius, as they do in all desert literature. More than two-thirds of the *Praktikos* (67 out of 100 chapters) discusses demons, and his theory of the eight "thoughts" is simultaneously a demonology. There are two sides to Evagrius's reflections. One is more experiential, an analysis of the psychology of temptation. His approach here is entirely consistent with the desert tradition, but he brings to it both an astute eye for the vagaries of the human heart and a talent for synthesizing insights into a coherent whole. The other side is speculative, with daring hypotheses on the cosmological origins, nature, and destiny of demons. I will take up this second side in the next chapter.

Evagrius, as we saw, speaks of "thoughts" and "demons" as though they were synonyms. That does not mean he thought of demons as merely metaphorical, as a symbol for psychological dynamics. He believed that there really were demons. "Thoughts" were simply the most common mechanism by which desert solitaries encountered demons. Evagrius suggests that demons attack different people in different ways: they attack "men of the world chiefly through their deeds"; they attack cenobitic monks through the irritating habits of their brothers in community; but they attack the desert solitaries "by means of thoughts."[60] Combat at the level of "thoughts" is unusually fearsome: "Just as it is easier to sin by thought than by deed, so also is the war fought on the field of thought more severe than that which is conducted in the area of things and events. For the mind is easily moved indeed, and hard to control in the presence of sinful fantasies."[61] Evagrius would even say that the combat solitaries face is so fearsome because it is hand-to-hand combat.[62]

Evagrius's disciple Palladius says his teacher had repeated personal experiences with demons.[63] Likewise, the author of the *History of the Monks*—who apparently had met Evagrius—remarks that Evagrius's skill in the discernment of spirits was "acquired by experience."[64] Evagrius encouraged his disciples to reflect on their personal experience with demons.

> If there is any monk who wishes to take the measure of some of the
> more fierce demons so as to gain experience in his monastic art,
> then let him keep watch over his thoughts. Let him observe their in-
> tensity, their periods of decline, and follow them as they rise and
> fall. Let him note well the complexity of his thoughts, their periodic-
> ity, the demons which cause them, with the order of their succes-
> sion and the nature of their associations. Then let him ask from
> Christ the explanation of these data he has observed.[65]

Evagrius's recommendation is somewhere between a military commander's and a psychologist's: one needs to study the enemy to defeat him. But insight comes from what Christ himself tells the monk. Christ provides the *gnosis*, the knowledge.

Evagrius rejects a long-standing strain in ancient Christian demonology: that each person had a demon assigned to tempt him, a sort of demonic counterpart to one's guardian angel.[66] Demons, according to Evagrius, were specialists, and the monk had to face a gauntlet of them. Evagrius denied that demons can force us to do anything. Nor can they read our mind or hearts; "It is God alone, who has created us, who knows our spirits" and who can "discover the secrets in our hearts." Demons are more like animals with very acute senses: by observing our speech or even the slightest bodily gestures, they see signs "whether we have conceived their thought within us and bring it forth."[67]

Evagrius distinguishes between three parts or dimensions within the human soul: the rational (*logistikon*), the concupiscible (*epithymētikon*), and the irascible (*thymikon*). This threefold division derives ultimately from Plato, but Evagrius says that he learned this from "our wise teacher," Gregory of Nazianzus.[68] Evagrius uses this division to discuss the acquisition of virtue, but he also applies it to the workings of the demons. The concupiscible is the realm of the bodily and of desire. According to Evagrius, when demons attack this part of us, they produce fantasies of desire: "They employ for this combat phantasms (and we run to see them) which show conversations with our friends, banquets with our relatives, whole choruses and all kinds of other things calculated to produce delight." The irascible is the realm of psychic energy, which, when disordered, comes out as violence, anger, and fear. When the demons attack this part of the soul, they produce nightmarish hallucinations: "They constrain us to walk along precipitous paths where they have us encounter armed men, poisonous snakes and man-eating beasts."[69]

When facing demonic temptation, Evagrius advised "praying to Christ in our nightly vigils" and making use of "short and intense prayer."[70] So when the monk hears "crashing sounds and roars and voices and beatings—all of these coming from the devils . . . he does not lose courage nor his presence of mind. He calls out to God: 'I shall fear no evils for you are with me' (Ps.22: 4)."[71] His remarkable handbook, the *Antirrhetikos* (*Counter-Arguments*), catalogs some 487 temptations, listed under the headings of the eight "thoughts." After describing each temptation, he suggests a scriptural phrase. For instance, he cites the nightmarish fear of "human thoughts that are terrified by the sight of demons in the form of entwining snakes at one's back and to one's side in the confusion of the night." Against this he recommends that the monk recite Deuteronomy 20:3: "Let not the heart be faint; do not fear, or tremble, or shrink from facing them, for the Lord your God is he that goes with you, to fight for you against your evil enemies."[72] Evagrius's model here is Jesus, who recited words from scripture in his combat with Satan in the desert. As he says in the preface to the *Antirrhetikos*:

> Our Lord, Jesus Christ, who surrendered everything for our salvation, gave us authority "to tread upon snakes and scorpions, and over all the powers of the enemies" (Luke 10:19). In what remains of all his teaching he passed on to us what he did when he was tempted by Satan. . . . [Often] the words required to confute the enemies, who are the cruel demons, cannot be found quickly enough in the hour of conflict, because they are scattered throughout the Scriptures, and thus it is [more] difficult to make a stand against [the demons]. Therefore we have carefully chosen [certain] words from the Holy Scriptures, so that equipped with them, we can drive the Philistines out forcefully as we stand to the battle, as strong, valiant men and soldiers of our victorious king, Jesus Christ.[73]

Early in one's monastic life, one fights as though "in the darkness of night"; one is so immersed in the fight itself that one does not see "the basic meaning of the war."[74] And in this battle, one does not always win: "Wrestlers are not the only ones whose occupation it is to throw others down and to be thrown in turn; the demons too wrestle—with us. Sometimes they throw us and at other times it is we who throw them."[75] That is why he advises hard work: "Train yourself like a skilled athlete."[76] In time, one becomes a battle-hardened veteran. For Evagrius, there are no shortcuts to sanctity: "Wisdom is not won except by a battle, nor is the battle well fought except with prudence."[77] With wisdom and purity of heart, one learns to "make out the designs of the enemy."[78]

Evagrius's intricate ascetical theory is only one side of his thought. The other side is a mystical theology that tries to chart the soul's journey to God. To that, we can now turn.

NOTES

1. *AP* Arsenius 6 (PG 65:89; trans. Ward, CS 59:10).

2. *AP* Arsenius 5 (PG 65:88–89; trans. Ward, CS 59:10); *Verba Seniorum* 10.5 (PL 73:912–913).

3. Louis Bouyer, *History of Spirituality*, vol. 1, *The Spirituality of the New Testament and the Fathers* (reprint: New York: Seabury Press, 1982), 381.

4. Hans Urs von Balthasar, "The Metaphysics and Mystical Theology of Evagrius," *Monastic Studies* 3 (1965): 183.

5. Palladius's account is in *Historia Lausiaca* 38. Ancient accounts of Evagrius's life and work appear also in Socrates, *HE* 4.23; Sozomen, *HE* 6.30; and Gennadius, *De viris illustribus* 11. For an overview of Evagrius's life and works, see Antoine Guillaumont and Claire Guillaumont, *Évagre le Pontique: Traité pratique ou le Moine*, SC 170:21–112. For other studies, see the bibliography for chapter 10.

6. Palladius, *Historia Lausiaca* 38.2 (Butler, 117; ACW 34:111). Sozomen, *HE* VI.30 (PG 67:1384; NPNF 3:368), describes him as "archdeacon," that is, the right-hand man of the bishop, who often was chosen as the bishop's successor.

7. Evagrius, *Praktikos*, epilogue (SC 171:712; trans. my own). In *Gnostikos* 44 (SC 356:172), he again refers to Gregory as "the Just" and traces out what he learned from Gregory about the virtues necessary for contemplation. Michael O'Laughlin, "Origenism in the Desert: Anthropology and Integration in Evagrius Ponticus" (Th.D. diss., Harvard University, 1987), 13, has argued that Gregory served as Evagrius's teacher soon after the former's return from his studies in Athens. Among Gregory's writings is a letter that seems to have been written to Evagrius's father about his son's education.

8. Palladius, *Historia Lausiaca* 38.1–2 (Butler, 117; trans. Meyer, ACW 34:110–111).

9. Evagrius's *Epistula Fidei* is listed as *Ep.* 8 in Basil's writings.

10. Palladius, *Historia Lausiaca* 38.3 (Butler, 117; trans. Meyer, ACW 34:111). The Greek version of the *Historia Lausiaca* does not mention that the woman was married, but the Coptic does; so does Sozomen, *HE* 6.30 (PG 67:1384–1385; NPNF 3:368).

11. Palladius, *Historia Lausiaca* 38.9 (Butler, 119–120; trans. Meyer, ACW 34:113).

12. Cf. Evagrius, *Ep.* 22 (Frankenberg, 500), which is written to a "true father," speaks of receiving the monastic habit on Easter Sunday: "I praise the Lord and to the day of his resurrection on which you gave me the holy habit and admitted me to the 'number' of the monks. I ask that you pray for me so I might be worthy of your prayers. . . . Greetings to her who has suffered much in our Lord." Scholars are divided on whom Evagrius is addressing here. Wilhelm Bousset and Irénée Hausherr argued for Basil. Antoine Guillaumont and Gabriel Bunge believe that Rufinus is the one addressed and that the greetings are sent to Melania; if so, Palladius would be incorrect on attributing the investiture to Melania. O'Laughlin, "Origenism in the Desert," 47, rather implausibly argues that it is addressed to Macarius the Great after Evagrius's "two-year novitiate at Nitria."

13. Palladius, *Historia Lausiaca* 24 and 35 (Butler, 77–78 and 102; trans. my own).

14. Palladius, *Historia Lausiaca* 38.10 (Butler, 120; ACW 34:113).

15. Socrates, *HE* 4.23 (PG 67:516; trans. NPNF 3:107, modified).

16. Evagrius, *Praktikos* 29 and 93 (SC 170:566, 696; trans. Bamberger, CS 4:24, 39). Evagrius takes the latter the title from Acts 9:15, where it is applied to Saint Paul. Evagrius cites Macarius the Egyptian in *Antirrhetikos* IV.45 and in the *De oratione*, prologue. Evagrius's relationship with the two has been traced out in great detail in Ga-

briel Bunge, "Évagre le Pontique et les deux Macaires," *Irenikon* 56 (1983): 215–227, 323–360.

17. Evagrius, *Praktikos* 29 (SC 171:566–568; trans. Bamberger, CS 4:24).

18. Evagrius, *Praktikos* 94 (SC 171:698; trans. Bamberger, CS 4:40). According to Bunge, five other citations in Evagrius refer to Macarius the Alexandrian: *Antirrhetikos* IV.23, IV.58, and VIII.26, and *De malignis* 33 and 37.

19. Palladius, *Historia Lausiaca* 38.10 (Butler, 120; ACW 34:113).

20. Evagrius, *Praktikos* 92 (SC 171:694; trans. Bamberger, CS 4:39). This appears also in Socrates, *HE* 4.23 (PG 67:517; NPNF 2.2:107).

21. Evagrius, *Kephalaia Gnostica* 3.57 (PO 28:121; Parmentier, 22): "As those who teach letters to children trace them on tablets, thus also Christ, teaching his wisdom to the rational beings, has traced it in corporeal nature"; cf. *Ep. ad Melaniam* 2:35–48 (Parmentier, 8–9): "But God, out of his love, has provided creation as a mediator: it is like letters. . . . Just as someone who reads letters, by their beauty sense the power and ability of the hand and the finger which wrote them together with the intention of the writer, thus he looks upon creation with understanding, perceives the hand [= the Son] and the finger [= the Holy Spirit] of its Creator as well as his intention, that is, his love."

22. Evagrius, *Praktikos* 97 (SC 171:704; trans. Bamberger, CS 4:40). This would make its way into the collections of the *Apophthegmata*: *Verba Seniorum* 6.5 (PL 73: 889; LCC 12:78) = *AP* N 392 (ROC 18:144) = *AP* Ps-Rufinus 70 (PL 73:772–773).

23. *Historia monachorum in Aegypto* XX.15 (SH 53:123; trans. Russell, CS 34:107).

24. Palladius, *Historia Lausiaca* (Coptic): *Life of Evagrius*, E–F. The Coptic text is found in E. Amélineau, *De Historia Lausiaca* (Paris: 1887), 114–115; trans. Tim Vivian, "Coptic Palladiana II: The Life of Evagrius (Lausiac History 38)," *Coptic Church Review* 21, no.1 (2000): 17.

25. *AP* Evagrius 7 (PG 65:176; trans. Ward, CS 59:64). Socrates, *HE* 4.23 (PG 67: 521; NPNF 2.2:109), mentions that Theophilus of Alexandria had tried to make Evagrius bishop of Thmuis (i.e., Serapion's old see), but Evagrius resisted ordination.

26. Babai the Great, *Commentary* (Frankenberg, 46; trans. my own).

27. Evagrius, *De oratione* 60 (PG 79:1180; trans. my own).

28. Evagrius, *Praktikos* 1 (SC 171:498; trans. my own).

29. An ancient listing of his works is found in Socrates, *HE* IV.23 and in Gennadius, *De viris illustribus* 11. Socrates knew the *Praktikos, Gnostikos, Kephalaia gnostica, Antirrhetikos, Ad monachos,* and *Ad virginem,* and gives excerpts from the first two. Gennadius mentions making translations of several such as the *Antirrhetikos* into Latin.

30. Evagrius, *Gnostikos* 44–48 (SC 356:172–186).

31. There is as yet no critical edition of *De oratione*. Between the two best-known versions, that in PG 79 and that in the *Philokalia*, there are discrepancies in wording and numbering at key spots. Simon Tugwell has been working on a critical edition and circulated among his students at Oxford a preliminary version, together with a translation. I have consulted this text and found it very valuable but will cite currently available ones—despite their limitations.

32. Evagrius, *Praktikos* 91 (SC 171:692; trans. Bamberger, CS 4:39). Some scholars so emphasize the originality of Evagrius that they miss how much he stressed his own continuity with earlier generations. On this issue, see especially Bunge, "Évagre le Pontique et les deux Macaires," 215–227, 323–360; and Jeremy Driscoll, "Evagrius, Paphnutius, and the Reasons for Abandonment by God," *Studia Monastica* 40 (1998): 259–286.

33. Evagrius, *Praktikos* 100 (SC 171:710; trans. Bamberger, CS 4:41).

34. Evagrius, *Praktikos*, prologue 9 (SC 171:492–494; trans. Bamberger, CS 4:15). Cf. *Gnostikos* 44 (SC 356:174).

35. Evagrius, *Praktikos* 6 (SC 171:506–508; trans. my own).

36. Cassian devotes Books 5–12 of the *Institutes* to the eight "thoughts" (SC 109: 186–500). He also puts the discussion of them in the mouth of Abba Serapion in *Collationes* 5 (SC 42:188–217).

37. Gennadius, *De viris illustribus* 11 (TU 14.1:65; trans. my own).

38. Evagrius, *Praktikos* 6 (SC 171:508; trans. Bamberger, CS 4:17).

39. Evagrius, *Praktikos* 13 (SC 171:528–530; trans. my own). Similar themes and imagery appear in *Antirrhetikos* 7.8, 26, 34, 35, and 42.

40. On this, see Yves Congar, "Ordinations *invictus, coactus,* de l'église antique au canon 214," *Revue des sciences philosophiques et théologiques* 50 (1966): 169–197; reprinted in *Droit ancien et structures ecclésiales* (London: Variorum Reprints, 1982). See *AP* Isaac of the Cells 1 (PG 65:224; CS 59:99).

41. Socrates, *HE* 4.23 (PG 67:521; NPNF 2.3:109).

42. Evagrius, *De octo spiritibus malitiae* 17 (PG 79:1161; trans. my own).

43. Evagrius, *Praktikos* 8 (SC 171:510–512; trans. my own).

44. Evagrius, *Antirrhetikos* 2.32, quoted in Brown, *The Body and Society*, 374. This visual element appears also in *Peri logismon* 16 (SC 438:206; trans. my own), in which the "demon" presents images of "men and women playing together" and "makes the anchorite a spectator of shameful acts and attitudes."

45. Evagrius, *Antirrhetikos* 2.49, quoted in Brown, *The Body and Society*, 374.

46. Evagrius, *Antirrhetikos* 2.35 and 2.36, quoted in Brown, *The Body and Society*, 374.

47. *AP* Antony 1 (PG 65:76; trans. my own).

48. Cassian, *Institutes* 5.1 (SC 109:90; trans. Ramsey, ACW 58:117); 10.1 (SC 109: 384; ACW 58:219). On other oriental languages, see Antoine Guillaumont, *Évagre le Pontique: Traité pratique*, SC 170:85–86.

49. Evagrius, *Praktikos* 12 (SC 171:520–526; trans. Bamberger, CS 4:18–19). I have slightly altered the translation to try to give an English equivalent of the ellipsis in Evagrius's Greek.

50. Evagrius, *Ep.* 27.6. This is from a Greek fragment published by Claire Guillaumont, "Fragments grec inédits d'Évagre le Pontique," in *Texte und Textkritik: Eine Aufsatzsammlung* (Berlin: Akademie Verlag, 1987); the translation is by Jeremy Driscoll, "Listlessness in *The Mirror for Monks* of Evagrius Ponticus," *Cistercian Studies* 24 (1989): 211.

51. See the analysis of Guillaumont, *Évagre le Pontique: Traité pratique*, SC 170: 440–441.

52. Evagrius, *De octo spiritibus malitiae* 14 (PG 79:1160), quoted in Driscoll, "Listlessness," 208–209. Note the way the monk critiques both the style of writing and the bookbinding—interesting comments from someone who is himself a writer and copyist. This is one indication of the experiential roots of many of Evagrius's comments.

53. Guillaumont, *Évagre le Pontique: Traité pratique*, SC 170:89.

54. Evagrius, *De octo spiritibus malitiae* 14 (PG 79:1160; trans. my own).

55. Evagrius, *Ad monachos* 55 (Gressmann, 157; trans. my own).

56. Evagrius, *Praktikos* 28 (SC 171:364), quoted in Driscoll, "Listlessness," 211.

57. Evagrius, *Praktikos* 36 (SC 171:582), quoted in Driscoll, "Listlessness," 213.

58. Cox, *Biography in Late Antiquity*, xiv. The reference is to Plutarch's *Alexander* 1.1–2.

59. Evagrius, *Gnostikos* 25 (SC 356:128–129); cf. *De oratione* 25; *Teachers and Disciples* 13.

60. Evagrius, *Praktikos* 5 and 48 (SC 171:504 and 608; trans. Bamberger, CS 4: 16 and 29).

61. Evagrius, *Praktikos* 48 (SC 171:608; trans. Bamberger, CS 4:29).

62. Evagrius, *Praktikos* 5 (SC 171:504; CS 4:16).

63. Palladius, *Historia Lausiaca* 37 (Butler, 122; ACW 34:114).

64. *Historia monachorum in Aegypto* XX.15 (SH 53:123; trans. Russell, CS 34:107).

65. Evagrius, *Praktikos* 50 (SC 171:614–616; trans. Bamberger, CS 4:29–30).

66. Evagrius, *Praktikos* 59 (SC 171:638–640; CS 4:33). The idea of a "guardian demon" appears in the works of the second-century Christian prophet Hermas and in Origen; see R. Joly, *Hermas le Pasteur*, SC 53:172.

67. Evagrius, *Praktikos* 47 (SC 171:606; trans. Bamberger, CS 4:29).

68. Evagrius, *Praktikos* 89 (SC 171:680–688; trans. Bamberger, CS 4:38). On Gregory's role, see the commentary of Guillaumont, *Évagre le Pontique: Traité pratique*, SC 171:683–684. Gregory discusses the tripartite human soul in *Poems* II, I, 47 (PG 37:1381–1384).

69. Evagrius, *Praktikos* 54 (SC 171:624–626; trans. Bamberger, CS 4:31). Cf. *Kephalaia gnostica* 1.53 (PO 28:43).

70. Evagrius, *Praktikos* 54 (SC 171:626; trans. Bamberger, CS 4:31); and *De oratione* 98 (PG 79:1189; trans. Bamberger, CS 4:71).

71. Evagrius, *De oratione* 97 (PG 79:1188–1189; trans. Bamberger, CS 4:71).

72. Evagrius, *Antirrhetikos* IV.18 (Frankenberg, 504; trans. Michael O'Laughlin, in *Ascetic Behavior in Greco-Roman Antiquity*, ed. Vincent L. Wimbush [Minneapolis: Fortress Press, 1990], 253).

73. Evagrius, *Antirrhetikos* praef. (Frankenberg, 472; O'Laughlin, in *Ascetic Behavior*, 245–247).

74. Evagrius, *Praktikos* 83 (SC 171:672; trans. Bamberger, CS 4:37).

75. Evagrius, *Praktikos* 72 (SC 171:660; trans. Bamberger, CS 4:35).

76. Evagrius, *De oratione* 92 (PG 79:1187; trans. Bamberger, CS 4:92).

77. Evagrius, *Praktikos* 73 (SC 171:660; trans. Bamberger, CS 4:35).

78. Evagrius, *Praktikos* 83 (SC 171:672; trans. Bamberger, CS 4:37).

BIBLIOGRAPHY

The Writings of Evagrius Ponticus: Texts and Translations

Scholars have published critical editions of certain key works by Evagrius, but the editing remains an ongoing project. Some have been translated, at least partially, into English, though until recently, finding them has not been easy. Because of the density of Evagrius's style, it is best to move back and forth between the texts and the fine commentaries on them. At last, a fairly complete translation has been published: Robert E. Sinkewicz, *Evagrius of Pontus: The Greek Ascetic Corpus*, Oxford Early Christian Studies (New York: Oxford University Press, 2003).

Praktikos (The Practical Treatise)

For a critical edition of the Greek text, with a French translation, see Antoine Guillaumont & Claire Guillaumont, *Évagre le Pontique, traité pratique ou le Moine*, SC 170–171 (Paris: Éditions du Cerf, 1971). An older English translation with commentary has been done by John Eudes Bamberger, *Evagrius Ponticus: The Praktikos; Chapters on Prayer*, CS 4 (Kalamazoo, Mich.: Cistercian Publications, 1981), 13–42. See also Robert E. Sinkewicz, *Evagrius of Pontus: The Greek Ascetic Corpus*, Oxford Early Christian Studies (New York: Oxford University Press, 2003), 91–114.

Gnostikos (*The Gnostic*)

For a critical edition of the text, with a French translation, see Antoine Guillaumont, *Évagre Le Pontique: "Le gnostique" ou, À celui qui est devenu digne de la science*, SC 356 (Paris: Éditions du Cerf, 1989). There is as yet no English translation.

Kephalaia gnostica (*The Gnostic Chapters*)

For a critical edition of the Syriac text, with a French translation, see Antoine Guillaumont, *Les six centuries des "Kephalaia Gnostica": édition critique de la version syriaque commune et édition d'une nouvelle version syriaque*, PO 28, fasc. 1 (Paris: Firmin–Didot, 1958). An English translation of the first of the six "centuries" has been done by David Bundy and is found in *Ascetic Behavior in Greco-Roman Antiquity*, ed. Vincent L. Wimbush (Minneapolis: Fortress Press, 1990), 175–186.

De oratione (*Chapters on Prayer*)

The Greek text is found under the name of Nilus of Ancyra in PG 79:1165–1200. For an older English translation, see John Eudes Bamberger, *Evagrius Ponticus: The Praktikos; Chapters on Prayer*, CS 4:52–80. See also the valuable commentary by Irénée Hausherr, *Les Leçons d'un Contemplative: Le* Traité de l'Oraison *d'Evagre le Pontique* (Paris: Beauchesne, 1960). The *Chapters on Prayer* was also included in the eighteenth-century anthology put together by Nicodimus of the Holy Mountain and Macarius of Corinth, *The Philokalia*; this has been translated into English; see G. E. H. Palmer, Philip Sherrard, and Kallistos Ware, ed., *Philokalia: The Complete Text* (London: Faber and Faber, 1979), vol. 1:55–71. Robert E. Sinkewicz, *Evagrius of Pontus: The Greek Ascetic Corpus*, Oxford Early Christian Studies (New York: Oxford University Press, 2003), 183–209.

Skemmata (*Reflections*)

The Greek text is found in J. Muyldermans, "Evagriana," *Le Muséon* 44 (1931): 37–68 and 369–383. For a translation and commentary, see William Harmless and Raymond R. Fitzgerald, " 'The Sapphire Light of the Mind': The *Skemmata* of Evagrius Ponticus," *Theological Studies* 62 (2001): 498–529. See also Robert E. Sinkewicz, *Evagrius of Pontus: The Greek Ascetic Corpus*, Oxford Early Christian Studies (New York: Oxford University Press, 2003), 210–216.

Antirrhetikos (*Counter-Arguments*)

For the Syriac text, see Wilhelm Frankenberg, *Euagrios Ponticus*, Abhandlungen der königlichen Gesellschaft der Wissenschaften zu Göttingen; Philol. His. Klasse, Neue Folge, 13,2 (Berlin, 1912), 472–545. The fifth treatise, "Against the Demon of Anger," has been translated by Columba Stewart, "Evagrius on Prayer and Anger," in *Religions of Late Antiquity in Practice*, ed. Richard Valantasis (Princeton: Princeton University Press, 2000), 71–80. There is also a partial English translation done by Michael O'Laughlin, in *Ascetic Behavior in Greco-Roman Antiquity: A Sourcebook*, ed. Vincent L. Wimbush (Minneapolis: Fortress Press, 1990), 243–262.

De octo spiritibus (On the Eight Spirits of Evil)

Several works on the eight "thoughts," once attributed to Nilus of Ancyra, are recognized to be the work of Evagrius. One is *On the Eight Spirits of Evil* (*De octo spiritibus malitiae*), found in PG 79:1145–1164. A helpful edition of the Greek, with an Italian translation on facing pages is available: Francesca Moscatelli, *Evagrio Pontico: Gli Otto Spiriti della Malvagità* (Milan: Edizioni San Paolo, 1996). The first English translation is by Robert E. Sinkewicz, *Evagrius of Pontus: The Greek Ascetic Corpus*, Oxford Early Christian Studies (New York: Oxford University Press, 2003), 66–90, and uses the title *On the Eight Thoughts*.

Peri logismōn (On Thoughts)

Another work, similar in concern, is the treatise *On Thoughts* (*Peri logismōn*). The treatise has an unusually complex textual history and until quite recently has been known under the title *On the Various Kinds of Evil Thoughts* (*De malignis cogitationibus*). One version was published by Suarès in 1673 and appears in PG 79:1200–1233. A related recension is found in the *Philokalia* of Nicodimus of the Holy Mountain and Macarius of Corinth under the title "Texts on Discrimination in respect of Passions and Thoughts"; for an English translation, see *Philokalia: The Complete Text*, G. E. H. Palmer, Philip Sherrard, and Kallistos Ware, eds., (London: Faber and Faber, 1979), 1:38–52. A longer recension was published by J. Muyldermans, *À travers la tradition manuscrite d'Évagre le Pontique: essais sur les manuscrits grecs conservés à la Bibliothèque nationale de Paris*, Bibliotheque du Muséon 3 (Louvain: Bureau du Muséon, 1932), 47–55. A critical edition has recently been published by Paul Géhin, Claire Guillaumont, and Antoine Guillaumont, eds., *Évagre le Pontique: sur les pensées*, SC 438 (Paris: Éditions du Cerf, 1998). The first English translation is by Robert E. Sinkewicz, *Evagrius of Pontus: The Greek Ascetic Corpus*, Oxford Early Christian Studies (New York: Oxford University Press, 2003), 136–182.

Ad monachos (Sentences for Monks)

For a critical edition of the Greek text, see Hugo Gressmann, ed., *Nonnenspiegel und Mönchsspiegel des Euagrios Pontikos*, TU 39,4 (Leipzig: 1913), 152–165. For an English translation with a thorough commentary, see Evagrius Ponticus, *Ad Monachos*, trans. and commentary by Jeremy Driscoll, ACW 59 (New York: Paulist Press, 2003).

Biblical Commentaries

Two sets of Evagrius's biblical commentaries are now available. For his commentary on Proverbs, see Paul Géhin, *Évagre le Pontique: scholies aux Proverbes*, SC 340 (Paris: Éditions du Cerf, 1987); for his commentary on Ecclesiastes, see Paul Géhin, *Évagre le Pontique: scholies à l'Ecclésiaste*, SC 397 (Paris: Éditions du Cerf, 1993). Both have the Greek text with a facing French translation. Neither work has been translated into English. Evagrius's *Scholia on the Psalms* remains interspersed among the works of Origen; the Greek text has yet to be edited, and no translation has yet been attempted. For a key to it, see M.-J. Rondeau, "Le commentaire sur les Psaumes d'Évagre le Pontique," *Orientalia Christiana Periodica* 26 (1960): 307–348.

Epistula fidei (Letter on the Faith)

This document, usually referred as the "Letter on the Faith" or "Letter on the Holy Trinity," was for a long time attributed to Basil of Caesarea and has been preserved in collections of his writings as *Letter* 8. Evagrius is now recognized as the author. For the Greek text with an English translation, see Roy J. Deferrari, trans., *Saint Basil: The Letters*, LCL (Cambridge, Mass.: Harvard University Press, 1950), 1:46–93.

Ad Melaniam (Letter to Melania)

This has been preserved only in Syriac; Wilhelm Frankenberg knew only the first half and published it in his *Euagrios Pontikos*, 610–619; the remainder is found in Gösta Vitestam, *Seconde partie du traité, qui passe sous le nom de "La grande lettre d'Évagre le Pontique à Mélanie l'Ancienne," publiée et traduite d'après le manuscrit du British Museum Add. 17192*, Scripta minora 31 (Lund: Regiae Societatis Humaniorum Litterarum Lundensis, 1964). This important letter has been translated into English by Martin Parmentier, "Evagrius of Pontus and the 'Letter to Melania,' " *Bijdragen, tijdschrift voor filosofie en theologie* 46 (1985): 2–38, reprinted in *Forms of Devotion: Conversion, Worship, Spirituality, and Asceticism*, ed. Everett Ferguson (New York: Garland, 1999), 272–309.

Letters

Besides the *Letter to Melania* and the *Letter on the Faith*, sixty-two letters by Evagrius have been preserved in Syriac. For the text, see Wilhelm Frankenberg, *Euagrios Ponticus*, Abhandlungen der königlichen Gesellschaft der Wissenschaften zu Göttingen; Philol. His. Klasse, Neue Folge, 13,2 (Berlin, 1912), 564–611. There is no English translation, but a German one, together with a valuable commentary, has been done by Gabriel Bunge, *Evagrios Pontikos: Briefe aus der Wüste*, Sophia Bd. 24 (Trier: Paulinus-Verlag, 1985).

Theology and Spirituality of Evagrius: Studies

For a fine overview of Evagrius's life and thought, see Antoine Guillaumont and Claire Guillaumont, "Introduction" to *Évagre le Pontique: traité pratique ou le Moine*, SC 170 (Paris: Éditions du Cerf, 1971), 1:21–125; for a brief survey, see their article, "Évagre le Pontique," in *Dictionnaire de Spiritualité, ascetique et mystique: doctrine et histoire* (Paris: G. Beauchesne et ses fils, 1932–1995), 4:1731–1744. The Guillaumonts tend to emphasize Evagrius's theological system. Recent studies—especially those by Gabriel Bunge, Jeremy Driscoll, and Columba Stewart—have both filled out and challenged certain aspects of their interpretation. An older but still useful overview is the ninety-page introduction of John Eudes Bamberger, trans. *Evagrius Ponticus: The Praktikos; Chapters on Prayer*, CS 4 (Kalamazoo, Mich.: Cistercian Publications, 1971). For further studies, see the following:

Balthasar, Hans Urs von. "Metaphysik und Mystik des Evagrius Ponticus." *Zeitschrift für Aszeze und Mystik* 14 (1939): 31–47. [For an English translation, see "The Metaphysics and Mystical Theology of Evagrius," *Monastic Studies* 3 (1965): 183–195. Von Balthasar's sharp criticisms of Evagrius are often quoted and have influenced older textbook discussions of Evagrius. While intriguing, von Balthasar's summary judgments have met severe criticism.]

Bunge, Gabriel. *Akedia: Die geistliche Lehre des Evagrios Pontikos vom Überdruß*. Cologne: Luthe-Druck, 1989.

———. "Evagre le Pontique et les deux Macaire." *Irénikon* 56 (1983): 215–227, 323–360.

————. *Geistliche Vatershaft. Christliche Gnosis bei Evagrios Pontikos.* Studia Patristica et Liturgica 23. Regensburg: Friedrich Pustet, 1988.

————. " 'Priez sans cesse': aux origines de la prière hésychaste." *Studia Monastica* 30 (1988): 7–16.

————. "The 'Spiritual Prayer': On the Trinitarian Mysticism of Evagrius of Pontus." *Monastic Studies* 17 (1987): 191–208.

Driscoll, Jeremy. *The "Ad Monachos" of Evagrius Ponticus: Its Structure and A Select Commentary.* Studia Anselmiana 104, Rome: Benedictina Edizioni Abbazia S. Paolo, 1991.

————. "*Apatheia* and Purity of Heart in Evagrius Ponticus." In *Purity of Heart in Early Ascetic and Monastic Literature: Essays in Honor of Juana Rausch, O.S.B.*, ed. Harriet Luckman and Linda Kulzer, 141–159. Collegeville, Minn.: Liturgical Press, 1999.

————. "Evagrius, Paphnutius, and the Reasons for Abandonment by God." *Studia Monastica* 40 (1998): 259–286.

————. "Listlessness in *The Mirror for Monks* of Evagrius Ponticus." *Cistercian Studies* 24 (1989): 206–214.

————. "*Penthos* and Tears in Evagrius Ponticus." *Studia Monastica* 36 (1994): 147–163.

————. "Spiritual Progress in the Works of Evagrius Ponticus." In *Spiritual Progress: Studies in the Spirituality of Late Antiquity and Early Monasticism*, ed. Jeremy Driscoll and Mark Sheridan, 48–84. Rome: Pontificio Ateneo S. Anselmo, 1994.

Dysinger, Luke. "The *Logoi* of Providence and Judgment in the Exegetical Writings of Evagrius Ponticus." *Studia Patristica* 37 (2001): 462–471.

————. "The Significance of Psalmody in the Mystical Theology of Evagrius of Pontus." *Studia Patristica* 30 (1997): 176–182.

Elm, Susanna. "Evagrius Ponticus' *Sententiae ad Virginem.*" *Dumbarton Oaks Papers* 45 (1991): 97–120.

Gendle, Nicholas. "Cappadocian Elements in the Mystical Theology of Evagrius Ponticus." *Studia Patristica* 16 (1985): 373–384.

Guillaumont, Antoine. "Le gnostique chez Clément d'Alexandrie et chez Évagre le Pontique." In *Études sur la spiritualité de l'Orient chrétien*, 151–160. SO 66. Bégrolles-en-Mauges: Abbaye de Bellefontaine, 1996.

————. *Les "Kephalaia gnostica" d'Évagre le Pontique et l'histoire de l'origénisme chez les grecs et chez les syriens.* Patristica Sorbonensia 5. Paris: Éditions du Seuil, 1962.

————. "Un philosophe au désert: Évagre le Pontique." *Revue de l'histoire des religions* 181 (1972): 29–57. Reprinted in *Aux origines du monachisme chrétien: pour une phénoménologie du monachisme*, 185–212. SO 30. Bégrolles-en-Mauges: Abbaye de Bellefontaine, 1979.

————, "La vision de l'intellect par lui-même dans la mystique évagrienne." In *Études sur la spiritualité de l'Orient chrétien*, 143–150. SO 66. Bégrolles-en-Mauges: Abbaye de Bellefontaine, 1996.

Harmless, William. " 'Salt for the Impure, Light for the Pure': Reflections on the Pedagogy of Evagrius Ponticus." *Studia Patristica* 37 (2001): 514–526.

Harmless, William and Raymond R. Fitzgerald. " 'The Sapphire Light of the Mind': The *Skemmata* of Evagrius Ponticus." *Theological Studies* 62 (2001): 498–529.

Hausherr, Irénée. *Les leçons d'un contemplative: le traité de l'oraison d'Évagre le Pontique.* Paris: Beauchesne, 1960.

————. "L'origine de la théorie orientale des huit péchés capitaux." *Orientalia Christiana Analecta* 30 (1933): 164–175.

Kline, Francis. "The Christology of Evagrius and the Parent System of Origen." *Cistercian Studies* 20 (1985): 155–183.

McGinn, Bernard. *The Foundations of Mysticism: Origins to the Fifth Century*. New York: Crossroad, 1991.

O'Laughlin, Michael. "The Bible, the Demons, and the Desert: Evaluating the *Antirrheticus* of Evagrius Ponticus." *Studia Monastica* 34 (1992): 201–215.

———. "Elements of Fourth-Century Origenism: The Anthropology of Evagrius Ponticus and Its Sources." In *Origen of Alexandria: His World and His Legacy*, ed. Charles Kannengiesser and William L. Petersen, 355–373. Notre Dame: Notre Dame University, 1988.

———. "Origenism in the Desert: Anthropology and Integration in Evagrius Ponticus." Th.D. diss., Harvard University, 1987.

Refoulé, François. "La christologie d'Evagre et l'origénisme." *Orientalia Christiana Periodica* 27 (1961): 221–266.

———. "Evagre, fut-il origéniste?" *Revue des sciences philosophiques et théologiques* 47 (1963): 398–402.

———. "La mystique d'Évagre et l'Origénisme," *Vie spirituelle supplemente* 64 (1963): 453–472.

———. "Rêves et vie spirituelle d'après Évagre le Pontique," *Vie spirituelle supplemente* 56 (1961): 470–516.

Spidlik, Tomás. *The Spirituality of the Christian East: A Systematic Handbook*. Trans. Anthony P. Gythiel. CS 79. Kalamazoo, Mich.: Cistercian Publications, 1986.

Stewart, Columba. "Evagrius on Prayer and Anger." In *Religions of Late Antiquity in Practice*, ed. Richard Valantasis, 65–81. Princeton: Princeton University Press, 2000.

———. "Imageless Prayer and the Theological Vision of Evagrius Ponticus." *Journal of Early Christian Studies* 9 (2001): 173–204.

Young, Robin Darling. "Evagrius the Iconographer: Monastic Pedagogy in the *Gnostikos*." *Journal of Early Christian Studies* 9 (2001): 53–72.

APPENDIX 10.1

Evagrius's Number Symbolism

Evagrius was fascinated with numbers. One sees this in the design of his works. The *Praktikos* is consciously composed of 100 chapters, a so-called century. His treatise *Chapters on Prayer* (*De oratione*) is composed of 153 chapters and plays upon an elaborate symbolism. In the prologue, he first notes the biblical basis for the number and then teases out an elaborate combination of symbolic numbers. Charts are given to explain Evagrius's rather complicated description. Here is the text:

> I worked all night and caught nothing, but at your command, I let my nets down (one more time) and caught a large number of fish, not big ones, but 153 of them (cf. Luke 5:5). And so I'm sending them to you in a basket of love. . . . I have divided my book on prayer into 153 chapters—sending you a Gospel feast—to let you enjoy the pleasure of [this] symbolic number. It combines a *triangular* and a *hexagonal* figure. The *triangle* symbolizes spiritual knowledge of the Trinity; the *hexagon* symbolizes the order of a world created in 6 days. The number 100 is *square*, while the number 53 is both *triangular* and *spherical*, since 28 is *triangular* and 25 is *spherical* (5×5 being 25). So you have a *square* figure to express the 4-fold nature of the virtues, and also a *spherical* number, which represents the time's circular movement and so represents true knowledge of this age and world. For week follows week, month follows month, and year to year time turns, season to season, as we see in the movements of sun and moon, of spring and summer, etc. The *triangle* symbolizes knowledge of the holy Trinity. Or you can consider the sum total 153 as *triangular*, and so it symbolizes ascetic practice, physics, and theology; or faith, hope, and love; or gold, silver, and precious stones. Enough then about this number. (Evagrius, *De oratione*, Prologue)

To understand why the ancient Greek mathematicians referred to certain numbers as triangular, or square, or hexagonal, see the figures in the next section.

TRIANGULAR NUMBERS

A triangular number is the sum total of a continuous series of integers, starting with the number 1. The following are triangular numbers: 3 (= 1 + 2), 6 (= 1 + 2 + 3), 10 (= 1 + 2 + 3 + 4), etc.

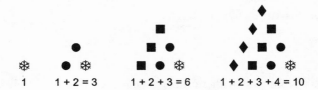

SQUARE NUMBERS

A square number is the sum of odd numbers, starting with the number 1. The following are square numbers: 4 (= 1 + 3), 9 (= 1 + 3 + 5), 16 (= 1 + 3 + 5 + 7), etc. See figures.

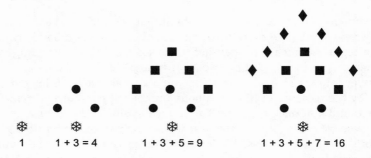

HEXAGONAL NUMBERS

A hexagonal number is the sum of every other odd number, starting with the number 1. The following are hexagonal numbers: 6 (= 1 + 5), 15 (= 1 + 5 + 9), 28 (= 1 + 5 + 9 + 13), etc. See the figures.

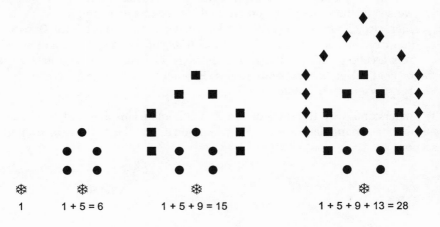

Spherical Numbers

A spherical number is one that, when multiplied by itself, appears as the last digit or digits of the new number. For example: $1 \times 1 = 1$; $5 \times 5 = 25$; $6 \times 6 = 36$; $25 \times 25 = 625$.

Therefore, in this passage, Evagrius is saying:

153 is triangular, since it is the sum of all integers from 1 to 17. That is, $1 + 2 + 3 + 4 + 5 \ldots + 17 = 153$.

153 is hexagonal, since it is the sum of every other odd number from 1 to 33. That is, $1 + 5 + 9 + 13 + 17 + 21 + 25 + 29 + 33 = 153$.

153 is the sum of 100 and 53:

100 is also a square number ($1 + 3 + 5 + 7 + 9 + 11 + 13 + 15 + 17 + 19 = 100$).

53 is the sum of 28 and 25:

28 is a triangular number ($1 + 2 + 3 + 4 + 5 + 6 + 7 = 28$).

25 is a spherical number ($25 \times 25 = 625$).

Note that Evagrius seems confused about why 25 is a spherical number. It is spherical not because $5 \times 5 = 25$, but because $25 \times 25 = 625$.

APPENDIX 10.2

Evagrius Ponticus, *Sententiae ad Virginem*

A remarkable and little-known work by Evagrius is the work excerpted here, *Sententiae ad virginem* ("Sentences to a Virgin"). Like so many of his works, it is a collection of brief proverblike sentences. In this case, there are fifty-five, which he addresses to a "woman of noble birth." This woman may have been Melania the Elder, or perhaps one of the members of her community, such as a deaconess named Severa, with whom Evagrius was known to have corresponded. This treatise, like his *Sententiae ad monachos* ("Sentences to a Monk"), uses balanced parallelisms, similar to the biblical Book of Proverbs. Here one finds stock Evagrian themes: advice on virtues (generosity, gentleness) and vices (anger, lust), and the need for unceasing prayer. It closes echoing the rich poetry of the Song of Songs.

INCESSANT PRAYER

Pray unceasingly and remember and recall Christ who engendered you. (Evagrius, *Sententiae ad virginem* 5)

ANGER AND GRUDGES

Anger and rage keep far from you, and do not bear grudges. (Evagrius, *Sententiae ad virginem* 8)

ALMSGIVING

Do not abandon the poor in their time of need, and the oil in your lamp shall not fail. (Evagrius, *Sententiae ad virginem* 17)

PSALM SINGING AND THE HEART

Sing from your heart, and do not just move your tongue in your mouth. (Evagrius, *Sententiae ad virginem* 35)

THOUGHTS AND PURE PRAYER

Do not give your soul to wicked thoughts, so that they will not defile your heart and distance you from prayer pure and clear. (Evagrius, *Sententiae ad virginem* 38)

LANGUAGE OF THE SONG OF SONGS

Virgin eyes will see the Lord, / And with their ears will virgins hear his words. / Lips of virgins will kiss their bridegroom, / and the virgin sense of smell will be filled with the scent of his perfume. / With their hands will virgins caress the Lord, / And purity of flesh will be received with honor. / The virgin soul will be garlanded, / And will live with her bridegroom forever. / She will be given a spiritual [baptismal] habit, / And will dance with angels in heaven. / The lamp she lights will never be extinguished, / And the oil in her vessel will not run out. / She will receive eternal riches, / And will inherit the kingdom of God. (Evagrius, *Sententiae ad virginem* 55)

For the Greek text, see Hugo Gressmann, *Nonnenspiegel und Mönchsspiegel des Euagrios Pontikos*, TU 39.4 (Leipzig, 1913), 152–165. Special thanks to Susanna Elm for use of excerpts from her unpublished translation. For a valuable study, see especially her essay "Evagrius Ponticus' *Sententiae ad virginem*," *Dumbarton Oaks Papers* 45 (1991): 97–120.

II

Evagrius Ponticus: Mystical Theology

A good pedagogue defines his terms. Evagrius knew this. As he remarks in the *Gnostikos*, "It is necessary to know the definition of things."[1] His writings are full of definitions, and over the course of his career he ended up creating a whole lexicon for the spiritual life (see appendix 11.1 for the key terms). Some of his definitions would be repeated for centuries—for example, his definition of prayer: "Prayer is the ascent of the mind to God."[2] As Evagrius saw it, prayer is more than words, more than voice or bodily gesture. It is ultimately a journey, an ascent at once inward to the highest part of the self and upward beyond the self to God. Journeys require itineraries, and Evagrius the pedagogue knew that the circle of monks under his direction needed some sort of map, some way of charting the mystical journey to God, both its stages and its pitfalls. Evagrius also knew that matters of spirit do not easily pass into speech, but that Christianity, at its core, is a theology, a "speaking of God." Yet Christian theology remains a paradox, for it both reveals and hides: that is, it reveals a path to a God who remains hidden, a God who defies definition. In this chapter, I will trace out both Evagrius's map of the mystical journey to God and the controversy that it provoked after his death, the so-called Origenist Controversy.

Mapping the Journey to God

Evagrius divides the spiritual life into two large stages: the life of ascetic practice (*praktikē*) and the life of mystical knowing (*gnostikē*) (for what follows, see also figure 11.1, Evagrius' Map of Spiritual Progress).

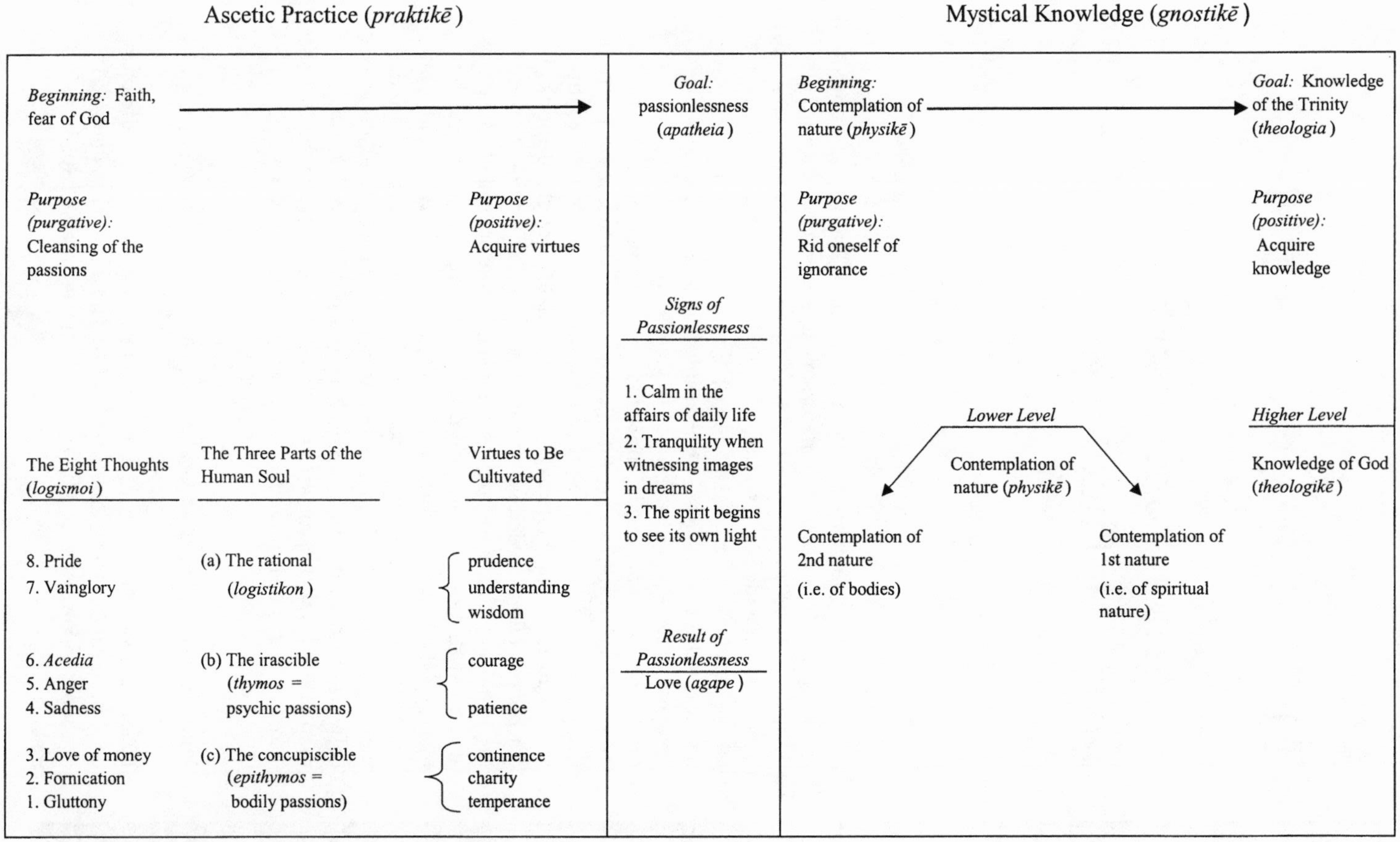

Ascetic Practice (praktikē)

Mystical Knowledge (gnostikē)

Beginning: Faith, fear of God

Purpose (purgative): Cleansing of the passions

Purpose (positive): Acquire virtues

Goal: passionlessness (apatheia)

Beginning: Contemplation of nature (physikē)

Purpose (positive): Acquire virtues

Purpose (purgative): Rid oneself of ignorance

Goal: Knowledge of the Trinity (theologia)

Purpose (positive): Acquire knowledge

Higher Level

Knowledge of God (theologikē)

Signs of Passionlessness

1. Calm in the affairs of daily life
2. Tranquility when witnessing images in dreams
3. The spirit begins to see its own light

Result of Passionlessness
Love (agape)

Lower Level

Contemplation of nature (physikē)

Contemplation of 1st nature (i.e. of spiritual nature)

Contemplation of 2nd nature (i.e. of bodies)

Virtues to Be Cultivated

The Three Parts of the Human Soul

(a) The rational (logistikon) — prudence, understanding, wisdom

(b) The irascible (thymos = psychic passions) — courage, patience

(c) The concupiscible (epithymos = bodily passions) — continence, charity, temperance

The Eight Thoughts (logismoi)

8. Pride
7. Vainglory

6. Acedia
5. Anger
4. Sadness

3. Love of money
2. Fornication
1. Gluttony

FIGURE II.I. Evagrius's map of spiritual progress.

First Stage: Praktikē

The beginning of the ascetic life, of *praktikē,* is the same as the beginning of Christian life: faith. And, as Evagrius notes, the "offspring of true faith" is "the fear of God." Evagrius uses the biblical term "fear of God" for that sense of awe and gratitude for the wonders of what God has done. This awe, serves as a "custodian" that leads one "in keeping the commandments."[3] None of this is very startling, but such basics should not be overlooked.

Evagrius goes on to define the first stage quite precisely: "The ascetic life is the spiritual method of cleansing the passionate part of the soul."[4] We saw earlier that Evagrius taught that the human soul had three parts: the rational, the concupiscible, and the irascible. The two lower ones—the concupiscible and the irascible—together form "the passionate part of the soul." And so the ascetic life requires purifying these two. Purifying the concupiscible means coming to grips with hungers, with sexual urges and fantasies, with our relentless acquisitiveness—the whole panoply of yearnings that can erupt to sully purity of heart. Purifying the irascible means coming to grips with anger, with fears that surface with difficulty, with unspoken resentments—the whole panoply of violence that lurks in the depths of the human heart. And this purification is to take place at the deepest levels of one's psyche. All that we have seen thus far of Evagrius's work—his analyses of the eight thoughts, his demonology—falls under the rubric of *praktikē.* He formulated these theories as a way to analyze this initial stage of the spiritual life.

To speak of cleansing, of purification, frames the task negatively. But Evagrius also describes the ascetic life positively: as acquiring virtue. In a key chapter in the *Praktikos,* Evagrius says that as one progresses, different parts of the soul give birth to different virtues. From the rational part emerge (1) prudence, (2) understanding, and (3) wisdom; from the irascible part, (4) courage and (5) patience; and from the concupiscible part, (6) continence, (7) charity, and (8) temperance. Finally, there is the virtue of justice, which "is located in the whole of the soul"; it "produces a certain harmony and symphony among the various parts of the soul."[5] As one progresses, the three parts of the soul begin to work right, to reintegrate, working the way God originally made them to work.

Transition: Apatheia *and* Agape

The quest during this first stage is freedom, freedom from the dominance of the passions. Evagrius says that "the practiced ascetic is one who has acquired passionlessness in the passionate part of his soul."[6] Evagrius's term here is *apatheia,* usually translated as "impassibility" or "passionlessness." *Apatheia* has nothing to do with "apathy," nor does it mean a lack of passion in the sense of a lack of emotion. Evagrius defines his understanding quite precisely in the *Skemmata:* "Passionlessness is a quiet state of the rational soul; it results from gentleness and self-control."[7] The term *apatheia* had been originally used by the Stoics, but Christian theologians soon adopted it. As we have seen, Athanasius speaks of Christ as "passionless," and in the *Life of Antony*, Athanasius describes his hero arriving at a state of dispassionate tranquility.[8] Evagrius's concern is prayer, and in his view passions interfere with true prayer:

> A man in chains cannot run. Nor can the mind
> that is enslaved to passion see the place of spiritual prayer.
> It is dragged along and tossed by these passion-filled thoughts
> and cannot stand firm and tranquil.[9]

Passionlessness, as Evagrius describes it, is not an all-or-nothing state; there are degrees. Think of health. One can be healthy in the sense of not being sick. Still, one can have certain nagging aches and pains. One can have good days and bad days and still be healthy. And then there is the robust health and fitness of an elite athlete. For Evagrius, *apatheia* is the state of the healthy soul.[10] Just because one has arrived at "passionlessness" does not mean the endless ebbs and flows of thoughts cease. Rather, they lose their ability to subvert self-control. The ascetic enjoys a measured calm during waking consciousness. But it also extends to the unconscious, to dreams: "The test of *apatheia* is that the mind . . . remains calm before visions [that occur] during sleep."[11] Here he intuits an insight developed in twentieth-century psychology: that dreams offer telltale signs about our psychic health.

Evagrius's *apatheia* is not some Stoic ideal of imperturbability. It is a relative calm on the far side of the storm—and a realistic calm that still must face the daily upsets of life. To be passionless was a sign of advance, but it was no guarantee of holiness. Evagrius knew that even advanced monks could fall, and fall badly.[12] Still, he believed that after long years of practice, the monk could, and should, arrive at a measure of genuine tranquility. When the monk's soul arrives at *apatheia*, it begins to enjoy a healthy inner harmony. Virtue becomes natural—or, better, the soul's God-given nature produces virtue naturally.

Evagrius calls *apatheia* "the flower of the ascetic life." *Apatheia*, in turn, produces its own offspring: love (*agape*).[13] As Evagrius says, "The goal of the ascetic life is charity."[14] This is important and easy to overlook. The ascetic life is about learning to love. Ultimately, the ascetic life makes one free to love others free of subtle compulsions and hidden agenda. It also means loving others as they really are. Evagrius stresses this in the concluding chapter of the *Praktikos*: "Love has the task of revealing itself to every image of God as being as nearly like its prototype as possible no matter how the demons ply their arts to defile them."[15] This takes a little decoding. When Evagrius speaks "every image of God," he means "every human being"; when he speaks of the "prototype" of that image, he means Christ. Evagrius is saying that love teaches us to see other human beings as sacred, as fragile glimpses of Christ, who is the true image of God and the prototype of what it means to be human. Seeing Christ in others is not easy because of "defilements." Some people hurt us, some annoy us, some may even have deep-seated evil habits or propensities. Evagrius argues that the gaze of love must pierce through the "defilements" and see the God-given dignity that lies beneath. But Evagrius was also realistic:

"It is not possible to love all the brethren to the same degree. But it is possible to associate with all in a manner that is above passion, that is to say, free of resentment and hatred."[16] Love, in turn, becomes "the doorway" to the next stage: mystical knowledge.[17]

Second Stage: Gnostikē

The second stage is the life of mystical knowledge, what Evagrius called *gnostikē*, from the Greek word *gnōsis* ("knowledge"). Here the monk embarks on a life of genuine contemplation. This does not mean that he leaves behind the ascetic life. Rather, ascetic disciplines—both physical and psychological—continue and provide the foundation for progress.

Whereas the starting point for the first stage, *praktikē*, is faith, the starting point for this second stage is examining creation. The term Evagrius uses is *physikē*, literally "physics." But he does not mean the scientific study of nature. Instead, this is the gift of seeing the divine presence in creation, of "revealing the truth hidden within all beings."[18] Evagrius calls this "natural knowledge" (*gnōsis physikē*) or "contemplation" (*theōria*). This form of contemplation has two sub-stages: "contemplation of the second nature," where the monk contemplates the visible beauty and order of created beings and of nature as a whole—whatever can be taken in by his senses—and "contemplation of the first nature," where the monk's contemplation pierces through the visible magnificence to grasp invisible created beings and the whole invisible order of creation. This sort of contemplation is natural to angels, but for those who enter into *apatheia* it becomes available to human beings. In other words, contemplation of nature starts with seeing God's presence in the visible creation, but goes beyond it.

For Evagrius, the visible world was created by Christ, the Logos of God. And Christ the Logos instilled in the visible world certain invisible "principles" (*logoi*) that form a hidden architecture and ecology beneath the world's visible surface. Andrew Louth has noted that for Evagrius, the problem comes from the fact that

> In the fallen world [these invisible principles] are no longer clear to us: we tend not to see *God's* meaning in the world and all its parts; rather we tend to see the world in relation to ourselves and read into it *our* meaning. As a result the world becomes an arena for human conflict, for we all see it differently, in a way that is focused on separated selves. To see the *logoi* of the natural order is to see it as it is and to be freed from private prejudices, which are rooted in the disorder created in our hearts by the passions. It is also to understand the providence and judgment of God, as Evagrius puts it, that is to understand how God has constituted the cosmos as a kind of arena in which fallen souls learn how to turn back their attention to God.[19]

The end point of the first stage of ascetic practice is passionlessness, which blossoms into love; the end point of this second stage is a mystical knowledge of God. The term Evagrius uses is "theology" (*theologia*).[20] We tend to think of theology as something one studies, something read in a book or examined in a classroom. Theology today is an academic enterprise, scholastic in the literal sense of the term. That is not what Evagrius envisions. For him, theology is a knowledge of God that comes not from books, but from prayer. Evagrius did not doubt the value of reading, of study, or of reason; nor did he doubt the profound value of dogma, of liturgy, and of ecclesiastical authority. But for him, theology in the strict sense is the encounter of the praying mind with God. That is the point underlying Evagrius's famous aphorism:

> If you are a theologian, you pray truly;
> if you pray truly, you are a theologian.[21]

And what this praying mind encounters is the Trinity: Father, Son, and Spirit. To know—experientially—the Holy Trinity is, according to Evagrius, the very definition of the "kingdom of God."[22]

Few have placed contemplation at the center of Christian living as single-mindedly as Evagrius. But the "gnostic"—Evagrius's term for an advanced monk—was not simply a contemplative, one who had achieved a measured calm of soul and a measured mastery over personal demons. The gnostic was also an elder, an *abba*; he had disciples around him and had weighty responsibilities as a teacher and spiritual guide. In the *Gnostikos*, Evagrius defines the gnostic as "one who plays the role of salt for the impure and that of light for the pure."[23] This division between "impure" and "pure," between beginners and advanced, mirrors Evagrius's division between the life of ascetic practice and the life of mystical knowledge. The task for beginners, the "impure," is to purify the passions; thus, pedagogically, the gnostic needs to act as salt, preserving them, helping them endure the hard battles against the demons. The task for the advanced, the "pure," is to move to a deeper knowledge; thus, pedagogically, the gnostic needs to act as light, enlightening disciples as they pass into an unfolding contemplation of creation, its principles, and ultimately the Trinity. Evagrius thus wanted the teacher to be salt and light, a preservative and an illumination.

Pure Prayer

Evagrius's views on mystical contemplation were as significant and influential as his views on the ascetical life. These appear especially in his influential *Chapters on Prayer* and his less well known *Skemmata* (for excerpts of the latter, see appendix 11.2).

Unceasing Prayer

First, Evagrius stressed that prayer be unceasing: "We have no command [from God] to work and to pass the night in vigils and to fast constantly. However, we do have the obligation to 'pray without ceasing.' "[24] The command Evagrius quotes here is Paul's exhortation in 1 Thessalonians 5:17. He echoes the traditional desert interpretation, found both in the *Life of Antony* and in the *Apophthegmata*.[25] In fifth-century Palestine, a concrete way of carrying out this command would emerge: the Jesus Prayer, the unceasing repetition of a short phrase such as "Lord Jesus Christ, Son of God, have mercy on me." This method of prayer would become one of the most beloved devotions in Byzantine and Russian Orthodox spirituality. We have no evidence that a prayer formula centered on the name of Jesus was used in fourth-century Egypt. But in recent excavations at Kellia—exactly where Evagrius lived for many years— archeologists have discovered inscriptions on the wall of a cell from the sixth-century that show that the Jesus prayer was part of the devotional pattern.[26] How did Evagrius expect this unceasing prayer to be carried out? He does not say. However, his disciple, John Cassian, advocated the constant repetition of a psalm verse: "God, come to my aid; Lord, make haste to help me" (Ps. 70:1).[27]

Imageless Prayer

Second, Evagrius stressed that true prayer be imageless:

> When you pray, do not try to represent the divine in yourself,
> do not let any specific form be imprinted on your mind.
> Instead approach the Immaterial immaterially,
> and then you will understand.[28]

For Evagrius, God is utterly beyond material confines, beyond shape, color, or time. To pray before any image, even a mental image, is idolatrous. Thus the one praying must seek complete transcendence:

> If the mind has not risen above the contemplation of the created world,
>   it has not yet seen the place of God perfectly.[29]

> Blessed the mind which in time of prayer has attained perfect formlessness.

> Blessed the mind which in undistracted prayer receives an ever-growing desire for God.

> Blessed the mind which in time of prayer becomes immaterial and stripped of everything.

> Blessed the mind which in time of prayer possesses perfect insensibility.[30]

At the very time Evagrius was writing these words, Egyptian Christians—including gangs of monks—were carrying out a violent iconoclastic campaign against pagan temples, ripping down and destroying statuary up and down the Nile River. One way of reading Evagrius is to see him as the "quintessential iconoclast, radicalizing and internalizing the historical anti-idolatry campaign waged by Theophilus in the last decade of the fourth century."[31] Applying iconoclasm to the mind did not sit well with some of Evagrius's monastic colleagues. Soon after the death of Evagrius, this issue would spark a bitter clash among the monks. Some of Evagrius's friends and disciples—the so-called Origenists—were be opposed by the less educated majority and eventually driven out of Egypt.

Wordless Prayer

Third, Evagrius suggests that prayer is, in the end, wordless. It is true that Evagrius speaks of prayer as "the conversation of the mind with God."[32] The term "conversation" (*homilia*) does seem to imply that he thought of prayer as words—interior words, perhaps, but words nonetheless. And he certainly allowed that one might use words in prayer, especially in prayers of petition or prayers for help against demonic attack. But this conversation, as Evagrius conceived it, is to move beyond words into wordless contemplation. Prayer in its higher form meant not simply moving beyond words; it meant "the stripping-away of thoughts."[33]

Evagrius refers to this wordless, imageless contemplation as "pure prayer" (or sometimes "true prayer" or "spiritual prayer"). Evagrius saw such prayer as a journey: "Prayer is the ascent of the mind to God."[34] Notice that here and elsewhere Evagrius uses the word "mind" (*nous*) to describe what in us prays. For most people today, the word "mind" implies the faculty of logic, of thinking, of rational deduction. But in the Greek tradition, the mind, the *nous*, is our intuitive side. It enables us to know and recognize the truth of things instantly, whether a friend's face or a mathematical proof. For Evagrius, the way the mind knows God is not a matter of logic, of thinking; it is a direct intuition. As he once put it, "for knowledge of God, one needs not a debater's soul, but a seer's soul."[35] In the Eastern theological tradition, the mind, the *nous*, is the highest dimension of the human person. It is the image of God within us, that which is most like its creator. And since it is the most Godlike part of us, it is the faculty most capable of knowing God. Evagrius would say that there is nothing more natural to us as human beings than praying: "The mind, by its very nature, is made to pray"[36]; "prayer is the activity best suited to the dignity of the mind"[37]; "undistracted prayer is the highest mindfulness of the mind."[38]

At a deeper level, Evagrius implies that prayer is not just an activity of mind; it is a state of mind, a *katastasis*. That means that prayer is not so much something one *does* as something one *is*.[39] And the mind wrapped in contemplation is utterly free of self-awareness: "Just as when we are asleep we do not know that we sleep, so neither when we are contemplating do we know that we have passed into contemplation."[40] Evagrius does not think of this higher form of prayer as ecstatic—at least, not in the strict sense. Ecstasy (*ekstasis*) literally means to "stand outside" oneself. For Evagrius, prayer is not *ekstasis*, not leaving oneself; it is a *katastasis*, a coming to one's true state.

The Sapphire Light of the Mind

Entering into "pure prayer" was signaled by a vision of formless light.⁴¹ Such an experience was only accessible to the advanced, to one who had arrived at passionlessness (*apatheia*).⁴² In fact, Evagrius cites this experience of "light" as one of three signs that one has crossed the frontier from the life of ascetic practice (*praktikē*) to the life of mystical knowledge (*gnostikē*).⁴³

Where does this formless light come from? Is this a direct vision of God? Or is this the light of the mind itself? It was an urgent question for Evagrius, so urgent that he and his friend Ammonius journeyed to consult John of Lycopolis, the great "Seer of the Thebaid." It would have been a demanding pilgrimage. When Palladius made the same journey some years later, it took him eighteen days, partly on foot through the desert, partly by boat down the Nile.⁴⁴ When Evagrius and Ammonius got to Lycopolis, they asked John about this experience of prayer: Did the light come out of the purified mind itself (implying that the mind's primordial nature is luminous)? Or did the light come directly from God, whose light then illuminated the mind (much as the sun illuminates the moon)? John's answer was a bit coy: "It is not in the power of human beings to explain it. Besides, the mind cannot be illuminated during prayer without the grace of God."⁴⁵

Evagrius himself answered the question a bit ambiguously. Sometimes he said that the light seen during the time of prayer is the "light of the holy Trinity"⁴⁶; other times he said that the mind "sees its own light."⁴⁷ In one key passage, he gave a more precise explanation: "When the mind—after having stripped off the old man—has been reclothed in the [new] one who comes from grace, then it will see its state, at the moment of prayer, similar to sapphire or to the color of the sky. This is what Scripture describes as the 'place of God'—what was seen by the ancients on Mount Sinai."⁴⁸ It sounds like Evagrius is describing a sensory experience: seeing a sapphire or sky-blue light.⁴⁹ But was this really a visual experience—at least, an interior one?

In this passage, Evagrius alludes to the great theophany described in the Book of Exodus. The biblical account says that Moses, Aaron, and the seventy elders climbed up Mount Sinai, and that there "they saw the God of Israel. Under his feet there was something like a pavement of sapphire stone, like the very heaven for clearness" (Ex. 24:9–10). In other words, the experience of pure prayer marked a return to Mount Sinai. The monk was to enjoy the same awe-inspiring experience of God's presence that Moses and the elders of ancient Israel enjoyed. The Hebrew text says bluntly that Moses and the elders "saw" God. But the Greek version of the Old Testament that Evagrius and other Greek-speaking Christians used—the Septuagint—says that the elders "saw" not God himself, but "the place of God."

What then was this "place of God"? Evagrius defines it in the *Skemmata*: "From holy David we have clearly learned what the 'place of God' is: 'His place is established in peace and his dwelling in Zion' (Ps. 75:3). The 'place of God' therefore is the rational soul, and his dwelling [is] the illuminated mind, which has renounced the pleasures of the world and has learned to contemplate from afar the [underlying] principles of the earth."[50] Here Evagrius reads the biblical text allegorically. First, he transposes outer realities into inner ones. Thus Mount Sinai, the "place of God," is not simply a place on a map of the Holy Land; it is an inner landmark, a center in the geography of the soul. The encounter with God is not limited to some past theophany. Rather the encounter is always possible because the place of encounter is within the "rational soul."[51] Second, he uses the Bible to interpret the Bible. Here he plays on the fact that the phrase "place of God" found in Exodus 24 appears also in Psalm 75. Thus Psalm 75 is read as a commentary on Exodus 24. This reading leads him to insist that the interior Mount Sinai is also an interior Mount Zion. The true "temple" is not in Jerusalem; it is in the mind.[52] In other words, the eternal dwelling-place of God is the human person; the human person is a place of divine presence, of illumination.

From these passages, we can piece together Evagrius's basic view. During pure prayer, the purified mind sees itself, its truest self, its true state. And the self that it sees is luminous. But that luminosity which permits it to see itself is the divine light. In seeing itself as luminosity, as light like sapphire or sky blue, the mind discovers its Godlikeness. At the same time, it sees and knows by seeing—indirectly, as in a mirror—the uncreated, immaterial light that God is.[53] That is why for Evagrius prayer is at once a moment of self-discovery and an encounter with ultimate mystery: "Prayer is the state of the mind that comes to be from the single-light of the Holy Trinity."[54]

Here we see the core of Evagrius's theology—and theology in his sense of the term: the encounter of the praying mind with God. Antoine Guillaumont has suggested that "in this description of pure prayer, Evagrius is certainly referring to an experience, both real and personal."[55] While Evagrius draws on intellectual tools—allegorical interpretation of the Old Testament, psychological analysis of the workings of the mind—he seems to be trying to make sense of his own most intense, most epiphanic experiences of prayer.

Cosmology

Evagrius was a bold, speculative thinker. His radicalism lies beneath the surface of his writings on practical asceticism and on mystical prayer. But it surfaces dramatically in his treatise *Kephalaia gnostica*, or *Gnostic Chapters*. This lengthy text, rediscovered in its unexpurgated form by Antoine Guillaumont only in 1952, offers Evagrius's speculations of the origin and destiny of the universe. Evagrius is often difficult to decipher, but this treatise on cosmology is unusually obscure, even esoteric. To help decode it, scholars generally turn to another of Evagrius's speculative works, his *Letter to Melania*.

Creation, Fall, and Second Creation

Evagrius drew on and even sharpened Origen's boldest hypotheses about cosmology. According to Evagrius, the visible universe we know now was not

God's first creation. Instead, God first created a vast assembly of disembodied spirits, what Evagrius called "rational beings" (*logikoi*) or "minds" (*noes*). These pure intellects were created equal to one another and were united to God and to one another in a loving communion of knowledge. This assembly formed what Evagrius called "the Unity" (*henad*). At some point, they began, one by one, to lapse from this primordial communion with God. Negligence was the first great sin. This sin brought an immediate effect: a great pre-cosmic Fall that Evagrius calls "the Movement" (*kenesis*). In this Fall, "minds" became "souls."[56] But God, because of his goodness and mercy, rescued these fallen beings by a second creation. The visible universe we know now is this second creation. In this creation, the fallen souls were given bodies. These bodies served as a sort of safety net that prevented the souls' lapsing into nothingness. As Evagrius puts it, "Before the Movement, God was good, powerful, wise, creator of the incorporeal beings, Father of the rational beings and almighty. After the Movement, he became creator of bodies, judge, governor, physician, shepherd, teacher, merciful and long-suffering, and especially a door, a way, high priest."[57]

In this second creation, each of the fallen minds received a body appropriate to the degree of its guilt in the great pre-cosmic Fall. Some were made angels, some human, and some demons. Each had a different chemistry, so to speak: "In angels there is a predominance of mind [*nous*] and fire; in human beings, there is a predominance of desire [*epithymia*] and earth; and in demons, there is a predominance of anger [*thymos*] and air."[58] Evagrius stressed the goodness of the body and sharply attacked any who denied the goodness of visible creation. To hate the body is to hate one's Creator. For Evagrius, the body is like a house for the soul, while its senses are windows that make it possible for it to see visible creation.[59] Still, the body is not really "us" in the fullest sense. Our truest self is the mind, the *nous*, our first identity. The body is secondary, a life raft and a ladder, something we dwell in for a time but will eventually shuck off.

Christology

According to Evagrius, there was one mind that did not neglect its loving communion with God at the time of the great pre-cosmic Fall. That one mind was Christ.[60] Because Christ remained united to God, Christ was appointed to preside over the second creation, the creation of the whole visible world. As a result, creation as we now know it is charged with the presence and wisdom of Christ: "Just as those who teach the alphabet to children trace the letters on wax tablets, so too Christ, in order to teach his wisdom to the rational beings, has inscribed it into corporeal nature."[61] The world, in fact, is a sort of book by which Christ teaches us the return to God:

> God, out of his love, has provided creatures as a mediator: they are
> like letters. He did this through his power and wisdom, that is, by
> the Son and the Spirit, in order that men might come to know the

love of God the Father through creation, but also his power and his wisdom. Just as someone who reads letters senses by their beauty the power and ability of the hand and the finger which wrote them together with the intention of the writer, thus he looks upon creation with understanding, perceives the hand [= the Son] and the finger [= the Holy Spirit] of its Creator as well as his intention, that is, his love.[62]

Christ did not only preside over creation and instill his wisdom into it. In the fullness of time, he became human. In a crucial passage in his *Letter to Melania*, Evagrius summarizes his account of the miracle of the incarnation:

His very nature is so good that . . . He created us in his image, without any persuasion, and made us heirs of all that is his naturally and essentially. Now what is both unnatural and natural to Him is that He came down and bore everything which happens to us from conception till death. . . . What was unnatural was that God was born of a woman. But God, because of his love for us, and because his nature is not bound by, or subjected to any law, was born of a woman because He wanted it so, without bringing to naught what He was, in order to deliver from conception and birth us that are subject to the curse and to sin, that He might give us second birth with a birth to which blessing and righteousness belong. For since we have ruined our nature by free will, we have come down to our present conception and birth which are subject to the curse. But [Christ], while remaining what He is, in his grace took upon Him, at birth, all the things which follow after birth until death, things which are not only unnatural to Him but also, I would say, unnatural to us. For we have fallen into these things because of the sin we have committed of our own free will. He delivers us from them, in that He voluntarily, without having sinned, loaded them upon Himself, for we are unable to rise above them by ourselves; because we have committed this sin we have fallen into them. Not only did He not remain in them, but He also pulled us out of them, because, as we have said, He had descended into them out of his love, not as a consequence of sin. What was supernatural, was that a man was born of a woman without intercourse: the virginity of his mother stayed intact. And what was also supernatural to men, was that a man died of his own free will and after his death rose of his own free will, without corruption and the help of others. Thus God who loves man, because man was born of his own free will, without intercourse, and He also died in the way He wanted, and rose again without corruption according to his will . . . this God who became man, while still being God.[63]

This is unexceptional in many ways—at least for a late-fourth-century Nicene. One finds Evagrius's teacher Gregory of Nazianzus and Evagrius's contemporary Augustine of Hippo making similar points about the miracle of the virgin birth.

Evagrius was adamantly opposed to Arians or Eunomians who denied the full divinity of the Son. While Evagrius shared with Gregory of Nazianzus the insistence on the full divinity of the Son, he also shared with many Nicenes of his time a certain awkwardness in expressing how divinity and humanity come together in the one Person of Christ. Note the way Evagrius distinguishes the Son or Word (Logos) from Christ. It strikes us as odd. For Evagrius, Christ is not the Logos; rather, Christ has the Logos within him. This language of "indwelling" would be associated with the Christology of Antioch. Yet one finds Evagrius insisting that Christ is one, not two:

> Our Lord has appeared as a man in our time, in our world, and in our measure. But in his own time, in his world, and in his kingdom, this man does not only appear to be God, but he truly is. And as in this world, there are not two beings, God and man, but one, God for himself and man for us; thus in this world too, there are not two beings, God and man, but one God who for himself is God and God who is man because God has become man.[64]

Eschatology

Evagrius agreed with Origen's bold vision of the "restoration" (*apokatastasis*)— the view that in the end, God will restore all things to himself and all will become one in him. Like Origen, he speculated that eventually fallen souls, in their return to God, would pass through different bodies and different worlds. All rational beings—presumably including demons—would recover their spiritual nature and recover their oneness with Christ. On the "seventh day," Christ would reign over all rational beings. Finally, on the "eighth day," Christ's kingdom will end. All rational spirits will recover their original unity and equality, becoming again Christ's equal, co-inheritors with him. All that was tied up with the second creation—bodies, matter, time—will disappear, and God will become all in all. In the *Letter to Melania*, Evagrius invokes a poignant analogy to explain his vision:

> And do not wonder at my saying that in the unification of the rational beings with God the Father, they will be one nature in three persons, without addition or subtraction. For take the case of the visible sea, which is one in nature, color and taste. Many rivers of different tastes mix into it. But not only does it not get changed into their variations; on the contrary, without difficulty, it changes them completely into its own nature, color and taste. How much more then is this the case with the intelligible sea, which is infinite and unchangeable, namely God the Father? When minds flow back to him like torrents into the sea, he changes them all completely into his own nature, color, and taste. They will no longer be many but

one in his unending and inseparable unity, because they are united and joined with him.[65]

This is an extraordinary vision: a return of the cosmos to its primordial origin, a flowing back of the many tributaries of being into the infinite Ocean that is God. For Evagrius, the inseparable unity of the persons of the Trinity becomes the icon for the final unity of creation with God. For Evagrius, salvation was, quite literally, deification.

In this same *Letter to Melania*, Evagrius not only sets out this cosmic vision. He also speaks touchingly of his own long and yet incomplete journey:

> I tell you, dear Sir, that as the prophet was struck with amazement when he saw all these things and cried "wonderful," thus I am struck by the wondrous aspect in all these things I come across on this path which I have chosen. But I have been prevented from reaching the goal for which I set out, as I am bound in the powerful chain of the love for those things which I have met with in an uncertainable way; I fail to bring to an end what I have begun. Yet it seems to me that this particular beginning has necessarily been made with a view to that particular end, for as the man who wants to stand at the end of all torrents, finds that his journey ends at the sea, thus he who wants to stand at the driving force of any of the creatures, finds that he arrives at the "wisdom full of distinctions" of Him who has fashioned him. And as the man who stands at the seashore is struck with amazement by its immensity, its taste, its color, by all that is possesses, by the fact that the rivers, torrents and streams which pour into it become themselves boundless and unlimited, possessing every quality which the sea has, thus also he who observes the making perfect of all intellects, is amazed greatly and marvels because he sees all these various distinct knowledges as they merge into one essential and unique knowledge, and that all those become this one, forever.[66]

Here we see Evagrius as he understood himself: a man driven by wonder, by awe. And this wonder, this awe, caused him to thirst for the origin of things, for the "driving force" of creation. Yet he found himself incomplete, bound by a "chain of love" for the beauty around him and for the magnificence he had met along the way. His analogy here parallels the one above: rivers coursing down to the ocean. This sea image is intriguing, coming from a man who began his life near the grandeur of the Black Sea and who ended his days settled far away, in an ocean of sand. He knew the incompleteness of being human—that for all his efforts, he had failed "to bring an end what I have begun." He would at least be spared from witnessing the Origenist Controversy.

The Origenist Controversy

The Origenist Controversy was one of the great crises of Egyptian monasticism.[67] It resulted in the purge and exile of leading intellectuals from the major centers of Nitria, Kellia, and Scetis. Ancient documents on the Origenist Controversy are abundant; they are also deeply biased and come from either participants or partisans. They detail not just theological argument, but ugly charges and countercharges of political shenanigans and gross immoralities; they also have glaring silences that distort matters. At certain junctures, it is hard to know what happened or whom to believe, but it is especially hard to sort out the real issues and motives behind what happened. While politics, personalities, and clash of cultures often fuel theological conflicts, that is especially the case here, where there is ample evidence of the bitterest personal vendettas.

In Egypt, the controversy exploded in 399. Theophilus, following the venerable custom of the bishops of Alexandria, sent out his annual festal letter announcing the date of Easter and used the occasion, as was customary, to single out for reflection a key issue touching the life and faith of the Egyptian church. In 399, he attacked the "heresy" of "anthropomorphism," that is, conceiving God in crudely human or materialist terms. He insisted, much as Origen had, that though Genesis 1:26 says that Adam was made in the "image and likeness of God," that did not mean God had human form. All biblical mention of God's face, hands, feet, and so on must be read allegorically; the true God is incorporeal, beyond body or matter. This letter, as was customary, was sent out and read in all the churches and monasteries of Egypt.

We know how it was received in Scetis, because John Cassian was there and provides an eyewitness account. He says that the monastic leaders who presided over three of the four congregations refused to promulgate Theophilus's festal letter. But in the fourth, led by Abba Paphnutius, it was read and provoked bitter opposition from leading monks. Abba Serapion, an elder renowned for his holiness, opposed it vigorously. To help calm things, Paphnutius invited a visiting deacon from Cappadocia named Photinus to discuss his experience of churches throughout the Greek East and how they viewed such matters. Photinus spoke at length, weaving biblical citations and theological argument, confirming that the ecumenical faith insisted on the utter incorporeality of God. The old monk Serapion granted the force of the arguments and reluctantly gave his assent. The congregation then began its prayer. Serapion, who for so many years had pictured God in his mind whenever he prayed, suddenly burst into tears, and threw himself on the ground, sobbing: "They have taken my God from me, and I have no one to lay hold of, nor do I know whom I should adore or address."[68]

This anguishing story brings the issue into high relief. The Origenist (and Evagrian) doctrine of divine incorporeality had practical consequences: it profoundly affected how ordinary Christians prayed. Cassian saw it as a matter of "naïve, rustic" monks, who had subconsciously remained pagans at heart—

who no longer worshipped physical images but still clung to inner ones.[69] Cassian's diagnosis may unwittingly point to the underlying theological politics. One can read Theophilus's attack on anthropomorphism as part and parcel of a wider campaign against paganism.[70] Theophilus recently had overseen the destruction of major temples, including the famous Serapeum in Alexandria— and monks had helped dismantle these great monuments; Theophilus's letter now turned the iconoclasm from outer to inner. Cassian leaves off his narrative there, using it as a morality tale about the follies of image-centered prayer and as a jumping-off point for a treatise on unceasing imageless prayer. His account seems disingenuous, because he leaves readers with the impression that that was the end of the story, that the Origenist view prevailed. In fact, the opposite was the case.

Monks outraged by Theophilus's festal letter marched to Alexandria and began violent demonstrations. They eventually confronted Theophilus face to face and even threatened his life. To placate them, he reportedly claimed, "In seeing you, I see the face of God."[71] When asked to anathematize the works of Origen, he readily assented. Over the next few years, Theophilus embarked on a wide-ranging campaign against Origenism: he gathered local synods of bishops to issue formal condemnations; he wrote letters to church leaders around the world, encouraging them to second his condemnations; he even led a violent attack on the monasteries of Lower Egypt. The fifth-century historians Socrates and Sozomen, from whom the account of these things comes, were not neutral reporters but had Origenist sympathies and portray Theophilus in the worst light. Socrates makes the unlikely claim that Theophilus, to win over simpleminded monks, denounced Origenism in a laughably crude theology, saying that "whereas according to the sacred Scripture God has eyes, ears, hands, and feet, as men have . . . the followers of Origen introduce the blasphemous dogma that God has neither eyes, ears, feet, nor hands."[72] Both historians treat the affair not as a conflict with real theological substance, but as a cynical exercise in ecclesiastical power politics. They point out, for instance, that Theophilus himself had read and used Origen for years before the crisis; that the Origenists he attacked had once been some of his closest associates; and that by 405, Theophilus himself was back reading Origen the way he always had. When challenged, he compared Origen's books to a flowered meadow: he plucked the beautiful flowers and stepped over the prickly ones.[73]

Both Socrates and Sozomen describe Theophilus as a man without scruple. They report that the first object of his attack was Isidore the Hosteller. The epithet comes from his function as official guestmaster for the Alexandrian church.[74] He had once hosted Melania the Elder when she came to visit the monasteries of Egypt and later hosted Palladius. He had also served Theophilus on sensitive diplomatic missions and had even been nominated by Theophilus to become the bishop of Constantinople, a post eventually won by John Chrysostom. Several incidents turned Theophilus against his subordinate. For example, a wealthy widow once donated 1000 gold pieces to the Alexandrian church to help clothe the poor of the city but made Isidore swear that he would conceal the donation from his boss lest the money be diverted to serve Theo-

philus's "lithomania" (his contemporaries say his thirst for monument building rivaled the pharaohs of old).[75] Theophilus, who had a whole network of
spies, was angered when he got word of the matter. Because of this and other
acts of insubordination, he excommunicated Isidore.

Palladius, another Origenist hostile to Theophilus, repeats this story in his
Dialogue on the Life of John Chrysostom and adds that Theophilus plotted against
Isidore and looked to ruin his good name. At a public ecclesiastical hearing,
he unearthed a deposition from eighteen years earlier that accused of Isidore
of a homosexual affair with a young sailor. Theophilus claimed that he had not
acted on it at the time because it had simply slipped his mind—he had been
too busy. Neither the sailor nor any other evidence could be brought forward
to substantiate the charge. So Theophilus bribed a young man to claim that
Isidore had had sex with him. The man initially agreed to carry out the perjury
but then turned over the bribe money to his mother, who reported things to
Isidore. The young man, fearing for his life, ran to a local church and claimed
sanctuary.[76] Despite the setback, Theophilus got what he wanted, and Isidore
was excommunicated.

Isidore fled to Nitria, where he had once lived and still had a cell. There
he was taken in by the Tall Brothers: Dioscorus, Ammonius the Earless, Euthymius, and Eusebius. We saw earlier that they were renowned not only for
their height, but also for their holiness and learning, and that Evagrius had
been a leading figure in their circle. They, like Isidore, had once enjoyed Theophilus's favor: Dioscorus had been made bishop of the delta town of Hermopolis, while Euthymius and Eusebius worked in Theophilus's diocesan administration. The latter two, disgusted by Theophilus's greed, resigned their posts,
claiming (diplomatically) that they yearned for the tranquility of desert life.[77]

Outraged that the Tall Brothers had given Isidore sanctuary, Theophilus
sent letters to nearby bishops ordering their expulsion and giving no reason.
When Ammonius came down to Alexandria to ask for an explanation, Theophilus reportedly choked him, then bloodied his nose and began yelling,
"Anathematize Origen, you heretic!"[78] Soon after, Theophilus had Dioscorus
removed as bishop and had the other brothers excommunicated by a local
synod. He also applied for and received an arrest warrant from the prefect of
Egypt and then personally led a military escort and rowdy entourage out to
Nitria. The brothers escaped detection by hiding in a cistern, but their cells
were ransacked and burned.[79]

The Tall Brothers and Isidore fled Egypt for the Holy Land, and some 300
monks went with them.[80] Some of these settled in Scythopolis, but Theophilus
was relentless and sent letters and agents ahead to local officials to ensure that
the monks received neither hospitality nor sympathy. Eventually, some forty,
including Isidore and the Tall Brothers, sailed to Constantinople and appealed
to John Chrysostom, who took them in. Though he handled the exiles with
great discretion—refusing, for instance, to admit them to communion—it still
proved a tragic miscalculation, for Theophilus soon turned his formidable political skills against John himself. In 403, Theophilus convoked a synod at "the
Oak," just across from Constantinople, where he heard testimony from John's

local enemies and successfully (if temporarily) had him deposed. It would prove the beginning of the end for John, who would be definitively exiled in 404 and die in custody in 407.

Theophilus's violent campaign was the Egyptian front in a wider international wrangle over Origen. The other major battlefield was the Holy Land, where Rufinus faced off against his onetime-friend-turned-bitter-enemy, Jerome. Jerome was known at the time as an outspoken promoter of the ascetical life, of its moral superiority, and his violent exaggerations won him both fame and infamy in elite circles in Rome. He had moved to the Holy Land in 386 and, with the aid of his wealthy patron Paula, had established a monastic complex in Bethlehem, much as Rufinus, with his patron, Melania the Elder, had established one in Jerusalem. As Henry Chadwick has noted,

> Jerome was a prickly, donnish figure of a familiar type: his immense scholarship could at times be put to the service of passionate resentments and petty jealousies. He could not endure criticism, and the nearer anyone stood to him, the more likely it was that the relationship would turn sour. Yet he exuded malice in so brilliant a manner and wrote biblical commentaries of such scholarly distinction that everyone wanted to read him.[81]

The clash in the Holy Land had been sparked by Epiphanius, bishop of Salamis in Cyprus (c. 315–403). Epiphanius had been denouncing Origen's theology for some time, notably in his massive catalog of heresies, the *Panarion* (*Medicine Chest*), written in 376. But in 394, he began traveling around Palestine and lobbying for an official condemnation. He visited John, the bishop of Jerusalem, who rebuffed him and embarrassed him in public. But Epiphanius won over Jerome to his cause. Jerome, earlier in his career, had translated sermons of Origen into Latin (as had Rufinus), drawn heavily on Origen for his learned biblical commentaries, and warmly sung his praises, acclaiming Origen "the greatest teacher in the Church since the Apostles."[82] Confronted by Epiphanius, he suddenly reversed himself and declared his opposition. Over the next few years, Jerome would turn his formidable literary energies and brilliance into ferocious polemic, beginning with his tract *Against John of Jerusalem*.

Initial squabbles over Origen damaged the already frayed relationship between Jerome and Rufinus. The two managed to patch up their differences in 397, just as Rufinus was leaving the Holy Land. But the truce did not hold. In 399, Rufinus, back in Rome, translated into Latin Origen's controversial *On First Principles*. Alerted by his friends there, Jerome launched a counterattack, publishing a counter-translation of controversial passages from *On First Principles* that, according to Jerome, Rufinus had conveniently deleted or smoothed over. Bitter polemical treatises began criss-crossing the Mediterranean: in 400, Rufinus wrote his *Apology against Jerome*, and Jerome answered with his multivolume *Apology against Rufinus*, beginning it even before he had Rufinus's work in hand and completing it after getting a copy. Once Theophilus weighed in on the anti-Origenist side, Jerome publicized it to his Latin-speaking readers, translating Theophilus's synodal letter of 400 and his festal letters of 401, 402, and 404; he also translated Epiphanius's correspondence and popularized his earlier attacks.[83]

Jerome's compendia of Origenist errors evolved gradually over the years. His clearest epitome appears late, in his letter to Avitus, written around 410. It lists the following errors: (1) that Father, Son, and Holy Spirit are unequal in majesty and power; (2) that rational creatures, originally incorporeal, lapsed into bodies because of a primordial negligence; (3) that there is a fluidity among rational creatures such that devils can become human or angelic while humans and angels can become demons; (4) that bodies rarefy as creatures ascend until they pass away altogether (a notion that denies any real resurrection of the body); (5) that there are a plurality of worlds, some preceding this one, others to follow; (6) that hellfire is not physical, but psychological, the burning stings of conscience; (7) that there will be a transmigration of souls; and (8) that Christ "will once more suffer in the sky for the salvation of demons."[84] Jerome continued his ad hominem attacks even after Rufinus's death, nicknaming him "grunting piggy" or "the scorpion."[85] One cannot overlook that behind each man were intricate and rival networks of friends, allies, and patrons, who contributed to and exacerbated conflicts by broadcasting gossip, copying letters and distributing tracts (sometimes in faulty or incomplete versions), and generally heightening the emotional pitch and all-round bad feelings.[86]

The name that never seems to show up in all this is that of Evagrius Ponticus. He had died in 399, of course, just before it all exploded. But given what we now know about his thought, especially his *Kephalaia gnostica* and his *Letter to Melania*, there is ample reason to see his as the real theology under fire. He had, as we have seen, reworked and perhaps even sharpened Origen's boldest hypotheses about the preexistence and primordial fall of "minds," about Christ as the one unfallen "mind" that remained united to Logos, and about the eventual "restoration" where in the end God becomes "all in all." The real theological target, in other words, was not so much Origen per se, but rather desert Origenism, the bold speculative Origenism of Evagrius and his friends. Some of Evagrius's closest friends were targets of polemic and persecution: Rufinus and Melania in Jerusalem and the Tall Brothers in Nitria. We know that Evagrius's disciple Palladius was driven out of Egypt and suspect that his disciple John Cassian was as well.[87] We also know that Evagrius, in his treatise *On Prayer*, had directly attacked the issue of praying with images—precisely the issue that so roused the monks' opposition to Theophilus's letter.[88] Jerome seems to have been slow to recognize Evagrius's importance but finally did so in a letter written in 414, years after the real storm of controversy had passed.[89]

One irony, little noted, is that efforts to suppress Origenism actually widened its influence. "Origenist" monks settled down elsewhere, put pen to parchment, and composed a host of influential histories and spiritual treatises. In the process, they impressed Evagrian ideas in locales ranging from Palestine to the Latin West. One of those Origenist monks was John Cassian, who ended up in southern France and became a potent force in Western monasticism. To him we can now turn.

NOTES

1. Evagrius, *Gnostikos* 17 (SC 356:114–115; trans. my own).
2. Evagrius, *De oratione* 35 (PG 40:1173; trans. my own).
3. Evagrius, *Praktikos* 81 (SC 171:670; trans. Bamberger, CS 4:36).
4. Evagrius, *Praktikos* 78 (SC 171:666; trans. Bamberger, CS 4:36).
5. Evagrius, *Praktikos* 89 (SC 171:688; trans. Bamberger, CS 4:38).
6. Evagrius, *Gnostikos* 2 (SC 356:90; trans. my own).
7. Evagrius, *Skemmata* 3 (Muyldermans, 374; trans. my own).
8. Athanasius, *Orationes contra Arianos* 3.34 (PG 396–397); *VA* 67 (SC 400: 312–314).
9. Evagrius, *De oratione* 71 (PG 79:1181; trans. Bamberger, SC 4:66).
10. Evagrius, *Praktikos* 56 (SC 171:630; CS 4:31).
11. Evagrius, *Praktikos* 64 (SC 171:648; trans. my own).
12. See Jeremy Driscoll, "Evagrius, Paphnutius, and the Reasons for Abandonment by God," *Studia Monastica* 40 (1998): 259–286.
13. Evagrius, *Praktikos* 81 (SC 171:670; trans. my own).
14. Evagrius, *Praktikos* 84 (SC 171:674; trans. Bamberger, CS 4:37).
15. Evagrius, *Praktikos* 89 (SC 171:680–688; trans. my own).
16. Evagrius, *Praktikos* 100 (SC 171:710; trans. Bamberger, CS 4:41).
17. Evagrius, *Praktikos* prologue (SC 171:492; trans. my own).
18. Evagrius, *Gnostikos* 49 (SC 356:190–191; trans. my own).
19. Andrew Louth, *Maximus the Confessor*, Early Christian Fathers (London: Routledge, 1996), 37. Louth shows how Maximus drew on some of Evagrius's ideas, rejected some, and transformed others.
20. Evagrius, *Praktikos* 87 (SC 171:678; CS 4:37); *Gnostikos* 49 (SC 356:190–191).
21. Evagrius, *De oratione* 60 (PG 79:1180; trans. my own).
22. Evagrius, *Praktikos* 3 (SC 171:500; CS 4:16).
23. Evagrius, *Gnostikos* 3 (SC 356:90; trans. my own).
24. Evagrius, *Praktikos* 49 (SC 171:610–612; trans. Bamberger, CS 4:29). Evagrius repeats this point in *Ad virginem* 5 (Gressmann, 146) and *Ep.* 19 (Frankenberg, 578).
25. *VA* 3 and 55 (SC 400:138, 282); *AP* Benjamin 4 (PG 65:145; CS 59:44), Epiphanius 3 (PG 65:164; CS 59:57); Lucius 1 (PG 65:253; CS 59:120–121), Nau 85, 123. See Kallistos Ware, "The Origins of the Jesus Prayer: Diadochus, Gaza, Sinai," in *The Study of Spirituality*, ed. Cheslyn Jones, Geoffrey Wainwright, and Edward Yarnold (New York: Oxford University Press, 1986), 175–184; and Gabriel Bunge, " 'Priez sans cesse': aux origines de la prière hésychaste," *Studia Monastica* 30 (1988): 7–16.
26. Antoine Guillaumont, "The Jesus Prayer among the Monks of Egypt," *Eastern Churches Review* 6 (1974): 66–71.
27. Cassian, *Conferences* 10.10 (SC 54:85–90; ACW 57:379–383).
28. Evagrius, *De oratione* 66 (PG 79:1181; trans. my own); cf. *De oratione* 114 (PG 79:1192; CS 4:74).
29. Evagrius, *De oratione* 57 (PG 79:1180; trans. my own).
30. Evagrius, *De oratione* 117–120 (PG 79:1193; trans. Andrew Louth, *Origins of the Christian Mystical Tradition* [Oxford: Clarendon Press, 1981], 112).
31. Elizabeth Clark, *The Origenist Controversy: The Cultural Construction of an Early Christian Debate* (Princeton: Princeton University Press, 1992), 84.
32. Evagrius, *De oratione* 3 (PG 79:1168; trans. my own).
33. Evagrius, *De oratione* 70 (PG 79:1181; trans. my own).

34. Evagrius, *De oratione* 35 (PG 79:1173; trans. my own). Note that there is a discrepancy in the recensions at this exact point: the version found in the *Philokalia* lists this as no. 36.
35. Evagrius, *Kephalaia gnostica* 4.90 (PO 28:175; trans. my own).
36. Evagrius, *Praktikos* 49 (SC 171:612; trans. my own).
37. Evagrius, *De oratione* 84 (PG 79:1185; trans. my own).
38. Evagrius, *De oratione* 34a (trans. my own). The Greek text is not found in PG but is in the *Philokalia;* see Hausherr, *Les leçons d'un contemplatif* (Paris Beaucheshe, 1960), 52–53.
39. Evagrius, *Skemmata* 27 (Muyldermans, 41); cf. *Kephalaia gnostica*, supplement 39 (Frankenberg, 454).
40. Evagrius, *Scholia in Ps* 126.2 (PG 12.1644A; trans. Stewart, *Cassian the Monk* [New York: Oxford University Press, 1998], 114).
41. On Evagrian mysticism, see Antoine Guillaumont, "La vision de l'intellect par lui–même dans la mystique évagrienne," 143–150; Harmless and Fitzgerald, "The Sapphire Light of the Mind," 498–529.
42. Evagrius, *Gnostikos* 45 (SC 356:178); cf. *Skemmata* 2 (Muyldermans, 38).
43. Evagrius, *Praktikos* 64 (SC 171:648).
44. Palladius, *Historia Lausiaca* 35 (Butler, 101; ACW 35:99–100).
45. Evagrius, *Antirrhetikos* VI.16 (Frankenberg, 524; trans. my own).
46. Evagrius, *Antirrhetikos*, prologue (Frankenberg, 474; O'Laughlin, *Ascetic Behavior*, 248).
47. Evagrius, *Praktikos* 64 (SC 171:648; trans. my own); cf. *Gnostikos* 45 (SC 356:178).
48. Evagrius, *Peri logismon* 39 (SC 438:286–288; trans. my own). Note that this passage appears also in the Syriac version of the *Skemmata* (but not in the Greek): *Kephalaia gnostica*, supplement 25 (Frankenberg, 450).
49. This imagery also appears in: *Skemmata* 2 (Muyldermans, 38) = *Kephalaia gnostica*, supplement 2 (Frankenberg, 424); *Skemmata* 4 (Muyldermans, 38) = *Kephalaia gnostica*, supplement 4 (Frankenberg, 426); *Ep.* 39 (Frankenberg, 592).
50. Evagrius, *Skemmata* 25 (Muyldermans, 41; trans. my own).
51. Cf. Evagrius, *Ep.* 39 (Frankenberg, 592), for a similar linking of Mount Sinai, sapphire light, and the "place of God."
52. Evagrius, *Skemmata* 23 (Muyldermans, 41; trans. my own).
53. Evagrius, *Kephalaia gnostica* 1.35 (PO 28:33; trans. my own): "God, in his essence, is light."
54. Evagrius, *Skemmata* 27 (Muyldermans, 41; trans. my own).
55. Guillaumont, "La vision de l'intellect," 148–149.
56. Evagrius, *Kephalaia gnostica* 3.28 (PO 28:109; trans. my own).
57. Evagrius, *Kephalaia gnostica* 6.20 (PO 28:225; trans. my own).
58. Evagrius, *Kephalaia gnostica* 1.68 (PO 28:49; trans. my own).
59. Evagrius, *Kephalaia gnostica* 4.68 (PO 28:167).
60. Evagrius, *Kephalaia gnostica* 3.2 (PO 28:100; trans. my own): "Christ is the one who alone has the Unity within himself and who has received the judgment of the reasons [*logikoi*]"; cf. *Ep. ad Melaniam* 6 (Parmentier, 12).
61. Evagrius, *Kephalaia gnostica* 3.57 (PO 28:121; trans. my own).
62. Evagrius, *Ep. ad Melaniam* 2. This translation is by Martin Parmentier, "Evagrius of Pontus and the 'Letter to Melania,' " *Bijdragen, tijdschrift voor filosofie en theologie* 46 (1985): 8–9; when it was reprinted in *Forms of Devotion: Conversion, Worship, Spirituality, and Asceticism*, ed. Everett Ferguson (New York: Garland, 1999), 272–309,

Parmentier made a number of small corrections; see the list of *errata* on p. 309. These corrections have been incorporated into the passages I have quoted.

63. Evagrius, *Ep. ad Melaniam* 11–12 (Parmentier, 18–19).

64. Evagrius, *Ep. ad Melaniam* 12 (Parmentier, 19).

65. Evagrius, *Ep. ad Melaniam* 6 (Parmentier, 13).

66. Evagrius, *Ep. ad Melaniam* 12 (Vitesam, 27–28; Parmentier, 20).

67. For studies of the Origenist controversy, see the bibliography for chapter 11.

68. Cassian, *Collationes* 10.3.1–4 (SC 54:76–78; ACW 57:372–373). For an analysis of Cassian's theology embedded in this narrative, see Stewart, *Cassian the Monk*, 86–90.

69. Cassian, *Collationes* 10.5.1–3 (SC 54:78–79: ACW 57:373–374).

70. This is the thesis of Elizabeth A. Clark, *The Origenist Controversy: The Cultural Construction of an Early Christian Debate* (Princeton: Princeton University Press, 1992), 52–58.

71. Socrates, *HE* 6.7 (PG 67:684; trans. NPNF 2.2:142); Sozomen, *HE* 8.11 (PG 67:1545; NPNF 2.2:406).

72. Socrates, *HE* 6.7 (PG 67:688; trans. NPNF 2.2:143).

73. Socrates, *HE* 6.17 (PG 67:716; NPNF 2.2:150).

74. Palladius, *Historia Lausiaca* 1.1 and 46.2–3 (Butler, 15–16, 134–135; ACW 34: 31, 123–124).

75. Sozomen, *HE* 8.12 (PG 67:1545, 1547; NPNF 2.2:406); also reported in Palladius, *Dialogus de vita s. Joannis Chrysostomi* 6 (SC 341:132; ACW 45:42). Theophilus's "Pharaonic lithomania" is confirmed by Isidore of Pelusium, *Ep.* 152 (PG 68: 285). Another incident was Isidore's support of Peter, the archpresbyter of Alexandria, against Theophilus's accusations of impropriety concerning a convert from Manichaeism; see Socrates, *HE* 6.9; repeated in Sozomen, *HE* 8.12.

76. Palladius, *Dialogus de vita s. Joannis Chrysostomi* 6 (SC 341:136; ACW 45: 42–43).

77. Socrates, *HE* 6.7 (PG 67:685; NPNF 2.2:143).

78. Palladius, *Dialogus de vita s. Joannis Chrysostomi* 6 (SC 341:138; trans. Meyer, ACW 45:44).

79. Palladius, *Dialogus de vita s. Joannis Chrysostomi* 7 (SC 341:140–146; ACW 45: 44–46).

80. Palladius, *Dialogus de vita s. Joannis Chrysostomi* 7 (SC 341:147; ACW 45: 44–46).

81. Chadwick, *Early Church*, 185.

82. Jerome, *Preface to the Book on Hebrew Names*, quoted by Rufinus, *Apologia contra Hieronymum* 2.19 (CCL 20:97). See Henry Chadwick, *The Church in Ancient Society: From Galilee to Gregory the Great*, Oxford History of the Christian Church (New York: Oxford University Press, 2001), 433–445.

83. Theophilus, *Synodica ep.* (A.D. 400) = Jerome, *Ep.* 92; Theophilus, *Ep. paschalis* 16 (A.D. 401) = Jerome, *Ep.* 96; *Ep. pashalis* 17 (A.D. 402) = Jerome, *Ep.* 98; and Theophilus, *Ep. paschalis* 21 (A.D. 404) = Jerome, *Ep.* 100.11–13.

84. Jerome, *Ep.* 124.1–15 (to Avitus) (PL 22:1059–1072; NPNF 2.6:238–244). For a study of Jerome's evolving polemic, see Clark, *The Origenist Controversy*, esp. 121–151.

85. Jerome speaks of Rufinus as "the grunter" (*grunnius*) or "the grunting piggy" (*grunnius corocotta porcellus*) in *In Esaiam*, pref. (CCL 73A:465), *Ep.* 125.18 (CSEL 56: 137), and *In Hieremiam*, prol. 4 (CCL 74:2). He calls him "scorpion" in *In Esiasam* X, prol. (CCL 73:396) and *In Hiezechielem*, prol. (CCL 75:3).

86. See Clark, *The Origenist Controversy*, esp. 11–42.

87. Evagrius's circle of disciples composed an identifiable group: John of Lycopolis, with his prophetic insight, had recognized immediately that Palladius was part of Evagrius's circle.

88. Guillaumont, *Les "Kephalaia gnostica,"* 61, argues that it was precisely Evagrius's teaching on pure prayer that provoked the dispute.

89. Jerome, *Ep.* 133.3 to Ctesiphon (CSEL 56:244–247). See Clark, *The Origenist Controversy*, 7, 14, 122, 146–147.

BIBLIOGRAPHY

The Origenist Controversy

The best starting point is the study by Elizabeth A. Clark, *The Origenist Controversy: The Cultural Construction of an Early Christian Debate* (Princeton: Princeton University Press, 1992). Two major players in the controversy were Jerome and John Chrysostom. On their place in the clash, see the biographies by J. N. D. Kelly: *Jerome: His Life, Writings, and Controversies* (Peabody, Mass.: Hendrickson, 1998) and *Golden Mouth: The Story of John Chrysostom, Ascetic, Preacher, Bishop* (Ithaca, N.Y.: Cornell University Press, 1995). See also:

Daley, Brian E. "What Did 'Origenism' Mean in the Sixth Century." In *Origeniana Sexta: Origen and the Bible*, ed. Giles Dorival and Alain le Boulleuc, 627–638. Leuven: Leuven University Press, 1995.

Gould, Graham E. "The Image of God and the Anthropomorphite Controversy in Fourth Century Monasticism." In *Origeniana Quinta: Historica, Text and Method, Biblica, Philosophica, Theologica, Origenism and Later Developments*, ed. R. J. Daly, 549–557. Leuven: University Press, 1992.

Guillaumont, Antoine. *Les "Kephalaia gnostica" d'Évagre le Pontique et l'histoire de l'origénisme chez les grecs et chez les syriens*. Patristica Sorbonensia 5. Paris: Editions du Seuil, 1962.

Vogüé, Adalbert de. *Histoire littéraire du mouvement monastique dans l'antiquité. Pt. 1, Le monachisme latin.* Vol. 3: *Jérôme, Augustin, et Rufin au tournant du siècle (391–405)*, esp. 15–90. Paris: Éditions du Cerf, 1996.

APPENDIX II.I

A Glossary of Evagrian Spirituality

Evagrius Ponticus developed a precise and consistent terminology to describe the stages of spiritual progress. Some of his key terms are given here.

Acēdia (ἀκηδία)): Often but inaccurately translated as "sloth"; more accurately translated as "listlessness" or "discouragement." One of the eight evil "thoughts" (*logismoi*).

Apatheia (ἀπάθεια): Passionlessness; impassibility; freedom from destructive passions. Not like the English word "apathy"; rather, a state of profound calm that reaches into the depths of the unconscious, a poised equanimity in the face of daily adversity. According to Evagrius, arrival at this state marks the transition from the life of ascetical practice (*praktikē*) to the life of mystical knowing (*gnostikē*).

Epithymia (ἐπιθυμία), or *epithymētikon* (ἐπιθυμητικόν): The concupiscible part of the soul; i.e., the source of desire, especially bodily desires (food, sex, wealth). Together with the irascible part (*thymos*), it makes up the passionate side of the soul. The virtues of the concupiscible part are temperance, charity, and continence.

Gnōstikē (γνωστική): The life of knowledge (*gnōsis*). Evagrius uses this term to refer the higher phase of monastic living, the life of mystical knowledge. He sometimes contrasts it with the earlier phase of ascetic practice (*praktikē*). For Evagrius, a "gnostic" is a mature monk, an *abba* who carefully passes on his insights to his circle of disciples.

Henad (ἑναδ): "Unity," Evagrius's term for the primordial assembly of pure intellects united to God in contemplative knowledge. According to Evagrius, that primordial unity will be restored at the end, what he calls the "eighth day."

Kenēsis (κενήσις): Literally, "movement"; Evagrius's term for the pre-cosmic fall of the pure intellects (*logika*).

Kephalaia (κεφάλαια): Chapters. Most of Evagrius's works are made up of numbered "chapters," actually brief paragraphs, generally one to four sentences in length. One hundred of these chapters is called a century.

Logika (λογικά): Reasonable beings. According to Evagrius, these were God's first, original creation, before a pre-cosmic fall into bodies. These beings were pure intellects (*noes*). With the pre-cosmic fall, these intellects became souls. In a second creation, God enclosed these fallen souls in bodies, either as angels, humans, or demons.

Logismoi (λογισμοί): Thoughts. For Evagrius, as for the desert tradition as a whole, the word generally has a negative connotation, e.g., "bad thoughts." In Evagrius's system, there are eight evil thoughts: (1) gluttony, (2) fornication, (3) greed, (4) sadness, (5) anger, (6) *acēdia*, (7) vainglory, and (8) pride. For each *logismos*, there is a corresponding demon.

Logistikon (λογιστικόν): The rational part of the human soul, the highest of the three parts. Evagrius sometimes contrasts this with the soul's two passionate parts, the *thymos* and the *epithymia*. The virtues of the rational part are prudence, understanding, and wisdom.

Nous (νοῦς): Mind, intellect. The highest part of the human person, the image of God within us. It is the contemplative part of us, the part whose nature it is to pray. According to Evagrius, the first creation—before the creation of this visible universe—God created a unity of pure intellects (νόες).

Physikē (φυσική): Literally, "physics." For Evagrius, this refers *not* to the scientific study of nature; rather, it is the mystical contemplation of nature—the gift of seeing the divine presence in creation. This is the first of the two degrees in the life of knowledge (*gnostikē*).

Praktikē (πρακτική): Practice, or specifically, the life of ascetic practice. Evagrius uses this term to refer the earlier phase of monastic living. It involves the acquisition of virtue. It also involves purification, learning to combat "thoughts." The goal is freedom from the passions, *apatheia*.

Theologia (θεολογία): Theology. For Evagrius, this does not mean the academic study of doctrine. Rather it refers to possessing a mystical knowledge of God as Trinity. This is the second and highest degree in the life of knowledge.

Theōria (θεωρία): Contemplation. For Evagrius, contemplation is the natural activity of the mind. Evagrius distinguishes two forms of contemplation: of nature and of God.

Thymos (θυμός), or *thymikon* (θυμικόν): The irascible part of the soul; negatively, the source of violent passions, such as anger and fear; positively, the energy of the soul. Together with the concupiscible part (*epithymia*), it makes up the passionate side of the soul. The virtues of the irascible part are courage and patience.

APPENDIX II.2

Evagrius Ponticus, *Skemmata*

Some of Evagrius's most important mystical views appear in a little-known treatise, the *Skemmata* (*Reflections*), a collection of sixty-two brief, proverblike chapters. At an early date, this work was attached as a supplement to his boldly speculative *Kephalaia gnostica* (to complete its deliberately incomplete six centuries). And along with the *Kephalaia*, it was translated into Syriac and came to influence Syriac spirituality. The *Skemmata*, excerpted here, takes up favorite Evagrian themes: the interplay among the eight deadly "thoughts" (*logismoi*), the distinction between the life of ascetic practice and the life of mystical knowledge, the nature of pure prayer, the purified mind as the "place of God"—a sort of interior Mount Sinai where one encounters the "sapphire light" of the Trinity.

THE SAPPHIRE LIGHT OF THE MIND

If one wishes to see the state of the mind, let him deprive himself of all representations, and then he will see the mind appear similar to sapphire or to the color of the sky. But to do that without being passionless is impossible, for one must have the assistance of God who breathes into him the kindred light. (Evagrius, *Skemmata* 2)

The state of the mind is an intellectual peak, comparable in color to the sky. Onto it, there comes, at the time of prayer, the light of the holy Trinity. (Evagrius, *Skemmata* 4)

ASCENT OF THE MIND TO GOD

The mind would not see the "place of God" in itself unless it has been raised higher than all the representations of objects. And it will not be raised higher unless it has stripped off all the passions that bind it to sensory matters via representations. And it will put away passions through virtues and (will put away) petty thoughts through spiritual contemplation. And this contemplation will happen when the light has been manifested to it. (Evagrius *Skemmata* 23)

THE MIND AS MOUNT ZION

From holy David we have clearly learned what the "place of God" is: "His place is established in peace and his dwelling in Zion" (Ps. 75:

3). The "place of God" therefore is the rational soul, and his dwelling (is) the illuminated mind, which has renounced the pleasures of the world and has learned to contemplate from afar the (underlying) principles of the soul. (Evagrius, *Skemmata* 25)

PRAYER AND THE TRINITY

Prayer is the state of the mind that comes into being from the single-light of the Holy Trinity (Evagrius, *Skemmata* 27). The mind is the temple of the Holy Trinity." (Evagrius, *Skemmata* 34)

For the Greek text, see J. Muyldermans, "Evagriana," *Le Muséon* 44 (1931): 37–68, 369–383. For a complete translation and commentary, see William Harmless and Raymond R. Fitzgerald, "The Sapphire Light of the Mind: The *Skemmata* of Evagrius Ponticus," *Theological Studies* 62 (2001): 498–529.

12

John Cassian

In the mid-sixth century, just as Rome and the West were falling to
pieces, a little-known Italian abbot, Benedict of Nursia, put together
a compendium of monastic practices and principles, the so-called
Regula, or *Rule*. It proved to be a work of legislative genius. In time
it came to define Western monasticism, its institutional contours
and its spiritual temper; and it remains, to this day, a vital constitu-
tion for monastic communities around the world. Near the end of
the *Rule*, Benedict appended a brief reading list, a bibliography of
sorts. He listed the Bible, of course, and then cited a few other titles:
the *Rules* of Basil of Caesarea, the "Lives of the Fathers" (presumably, Athanasius's *Life of Antony* and collections such as *History of
the Monks in Egypt*). He also included two other titles, both by John
Cassian: the *Institutes* and the *Conferences*.[1] John Cassian thus became required reading for Western monks. If Benedict created the
institutional frame of Latin monasticism, then Cassian helped define its inner life, its mystical aspirations. At the same time, Cassian's quite distinctive interpretation of Egypt became normative—
the definition of desert spirituality. Cassian, more than anyone else,
brought Egypt to the West.

Cassian the Silent

Cassian loved Egypt's silences and admired its monks' self-effacing
humility. His own silences and self-effacement make reconstructing
his biography a formidable task (for an outline of his career, see table 12.1, for a map, see figure 12.1).[2] There are a few autobiographical wisps here and there in his voluminous writings. Gennadius,

TABLE 12.1. Chronology: The Life of John Cassian*

c. 360	Birth of John Cassian
c. 380	Cassian settles in Bethlehem with Germanus
c. 385	Cassian and Germanus go to Egypt (Nile Delta first, then Scetis)
c. 392	Cassian and Germanus return briefly to Bethlehem
399	Theophilus drives the Origenists out of Egypt
c. 399 or 400	Cassian and Germanus leave Egypt
early 400s	Cassian and Germanus in Constantinople; Cassian ordained deacon by Chrysostom
404	Cassian and Germanus in Rome
c. 415	Cassian in Massilia (present-day Marseilles)
c. 415–425	Cassian writes *Institutes* and initial set of *Conferences*
c. 430	Cassian writes *On the Incarnation, Against Nestorius*
431	Council of Ephesus deposes Nestorius
432	Prosper of Aquitaine attacks Cassian in his *Against the Conferencer*
c. 435	Death of Cassian

*Dating the key events in the life of Cassian is unusually difficult; see the discussion in the section "Cassian the Silent."

writing *On Illustrious Men* a few generations later, gives a brief notice on his life and works, but the earliest mention of Cassian in the historical record—earlier than Cassian's own writings—are passing remarks in a letter by Pope Innocent I and in Palladius's *Dialogue on the Life of John Chrysostom*.[3] One could read Cassian's monastic texts without ever realizing that he had moved as a player on the world stage in controversies that convulsed the church for over three decades. While one can chart the main lines of his career, exact dates are often hard to come by, and long years remain about which we know almost nothing. And for all of Cassian's interest in the interior life, he remained an intensely private man and gave only the rarest glimpses of his own interior motives. In this, he is utterly unlike his contemporary, Augustine of Hippo. Cassian was both a victim and survivor of the Origenist controversy and saw at close range how it ruined friends' lives and blackened their reputations. One suspects that he learned the value of silence both for covering his tracks and for covering his anguish.

Even the most basic facts about Cassian are unclear. His name, for instance: contemporaries called him "Cassianus," while he twice refers to himself as "John"—perhaps his monastic name.[4] Most scholars date his birth to 360, but that is only a guess. Gennadius says that Cassian was a Scythian, which would mean he grew up in the Dobrudja, in modern Romania. But some scholars discount this and argue that he came from where he ended up: southern France.[5] He mentions his family's property, "how graciously and agreeably it stretched out to the reaches of the wilderness," with rich "forest recesses."[6] This sounds as though he came from a well-to-do family, as does the fact that he received a fine education in classical literature.[7]

Latin seems to have been his native language. He writes in a long-lined, sinewy Latin, and his literary style was much admired by later generations.[8]

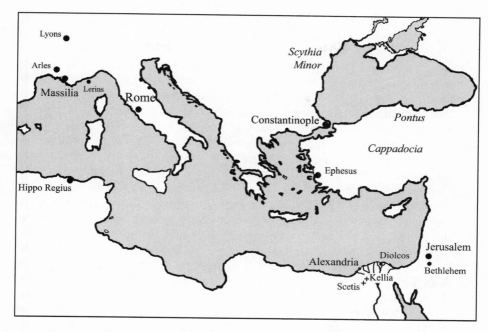

FIGURE 12.1. Key locales in the career of John Cassian.

He also knew Greek and spent much of his career in the Greek East. He certainly knew the Bible in Greek and displays familiarity with Greek theologians.[9] Few things are as clear about him as his bilingual skills. They defined his career, enabling him to serve an ambassadorial role in varied ways by bridging the growing divides between Greek East and Latin West. This bilingualism lends support to those who argue for Cassian's Balkan origins, for that area of the empire stood at a crossroads where Greek culture met Latin and their respective spheres of influence overlapped.

Around 380 (another guess), he went to Palestine with a friend named Germanus. Germanus was the elder, and the two remained companions for at least the next twenty-five years. They settled in Bethlehem and became monks. We know nothing of what moved them to take such a dramatic step, and to do so far from home. Cassian reports one life-defining event from this early period: meeting an old monk named Pinufius.[10] Abba Pinufius was, at the time, on the run and in disguise. He had been the abbot of an Egyptian monastery but found the responsibility overwhelming and fled first to Tabennesi and later to the Holy Land, where he ended up sharing a cell with Cassian and Germanus. Eventually, Pinufius's old disciples discovered his whereabouts and escorted him back to Egypt. But Pinufius's tales had so caught the imagination of the two young monks that they became determined to leave Bethlehem and see Egypt with their own eyes. Their colleagues at Bethlehem were reluctant to let them go and made them swear a solemn oath that they would return shortly. To add weight to its solemnity, they were made to take the oath at the shrine of the Nativity. This oath would haunt them and was left unfulfilled for some seven years.[11]

Cassian and Germanus found a home in Egypt. Scholars' best guess is that they lived there from 385 to 400, a stint interrupted by a return to Bethlehem around 392 (another estimate), in which they received forgiveness for their unfulfilled oath and a blessing to return to Egypt. The two first explored sites in the delta—Thenneaus, Thmuis, Panephysis, Diolcos—and met up with their old cellmate Pinufius. They eventually made their way to Scetis, where they settled down as permanent residents. Scetis, as we saw, was the great settlement in Wādī al-Natrūn founded in the 330s by Macarius the Great. Macarius may still have been alive when the two arrived, but Cassian only knows legends about him.[12] But Cassian did know and deeply admire other prominent figures of Scetis, ones who appear also in the *Apophthegmata*, such as Moses the Ethiopian.[13] By Cassian's time, there were four "congregations" at Scetis, and as we saw, he and Germanus were members of the one led by Abba Paphnutius.[14] When he later wrote his great work, *Conferences*, he chose figures from Scetis as his first and most important spokesmen and portrayed them as the pinnacle of monastic achievement, as men "who have established themselves in the vastest solitude and are separated from the companionship of all mortal beings, thereby possessing spiritual enlightenment, [and so] contemplate and proclaim things that will perhaps seem impossible."[15]

Cassian does not seem to have traveled further south, though he spoke at length about monastic customs of the Pachomian monasteries.[16] But his picture does not square well with what we know directly from Pachomian sources.

Cassian did make the dangerous cross-desert trek up to the other great anchoritic site, Kellia, and may have done so frequently. He names certain monks of Kellia, notably Theodore.[17] He fails to mention, however, that he knew and studied with one of Kellia's most famous monks: Evagrius Ponticus. Silences—self-protective and otherwise—lace Cassian's account, but this one is striking since Cassian's debt to Evagrius is so profound.[18] Evagrius's ideas, both great and small, both ascetical and mystical, reappear in Cassian, either without any acknowledgment or with attribution to other figures. While Cassian was undoubtedly a disciple of Evagrius, he was not an uncritical one. He often remolded his mentor's ideas, shifting emphases, altering terminology, truncating some matters, expanding others in new directions. We will see something of how he does so later. But Cassian's silence about so central an influence—especially when he names and praises so many other monastic forefathers—gives clues to the abiding scars left by the Origenist Controversy.

As we saw, Cassian was still in Egypt in 399 when Theophilus issued his festal letter against the Anthropomorphites. At some point not long after, Cassian and his friend Germanus left Egypt. He never says why or when or how. Scholars note this as another of Cassian's self-protective silences and presume that the two friends fled in 399 or 400, after Theophilus reversed course and unleashed his persecution against the Origenists.

We find the two friends a few years later in Constantinople, already part of John Chrysostom's inner circle. Germanus had been ordained a presbyter, while Cassian had been made a deacon. Only at the end of his life, in the closing words of his final treatise, did Cassian choose to speak openly of Chrysostom and offer him an eloquent and heartfelt homage:

> For I was admitted into the sacred ministry by the Bishop John, of blessed memory and offered to God, and even though I am absent in body yet I am still there (in Constantinople) in heart. . . . Remember him, I say. Follow him. Think of his purity, his faith, his doctrine, and holiness. Remember him ever, . . . a teacher in common both of you and of me, whose disciples and pupils we are. Read his writings. Hold fast to his instruction. Embrace his faith and merits, for though to attain this is a hard and magnificent thing; yet even to follow is beautiful and sublime.[19]

Cassian never mentions John's downfall in print, but we have two reports, one from Palladius and another from Innocent I, that Germanus and Cassian were part of the delegation sent to Rome on John's behalf in the wake of the final exile in 404. They carried letters to the pope detailing John's mistreatment and defending him against trumped-up charges of financial mismanagement. Cassian was a natural choice for such an ambassadorial role: he was thoroughly bilingual and had been an eyewitness of affairs both in Egypt and in Constantinople.

From this date until around 415, we know nothing certain of Cassian's movements—whether he stayed in Rome, returned to the Holy Land, moved up to Gaul, or went back, as Palladius had, to Constantinople. There is a tantalizing mention in two letters of Pope Innocent I of a presbyter named "Cassianus" who undertook an ambassadorial task from the church of Antioch. Is it the same Cassian? Perhaps. This would imply that Cassian was being used in sensitive papal diplomatic missions. Neither Cassian nor his contemporaries mention Germanus after 405, and scholars presume that Cassian's friend died not long after.

Cassian resurfaces in 415, having settled down in southern Gaul, in the port city of Massilia (present-day Marseilles). Gennadius records that Cassian, now a presbyter, founded two monasteries there, one for men, another for women. In Gaul, Cassian found his voice, so to speak, and wrote the two works for which he is still remembered, the *Institutes* and the *Conferences*. I will examine these influential works in a moment. My interest here is what they tell us about Cassian's biography. Most revealing is the list of powerful Gallic notables to whom they are dedicated, bishops such as Castor of Apta Julia and abbots like Honoratus of Lérins. There in Gaul, Cassian would forge a network of alliances among an aristocratic elite, men and women who shared his commitment to asceticism and who sought him out as a leading authority on worldwide monasticism. The role of monastic expert was one Cassian would carefully cultivate.

Cassian had already gotten caught in the crossfire of two ecumenical battles, the Origenist Controversy and the downfall of Chrysostom. Later in his career, he let himself be drawn into two others: the Pelagian and the Nestorian. In the mid-420s, Cassian composed *Conference* 13, which some contemporaries read as an attack on the foremost Latin theologian of the day, Augustine of Hippo. Whether Augustine was Cassian's real target has been recently reevaluated by scholars, and I will touch upon the question at the chapter's end. Here it is important simply to note that one of Augustine's most zealous disciples, Prosper of Aquitaine, lived in Marseilles at the time, and in 432 would write a stinging attack on Cassian, *Against the Conferencer* (*Contra collatorem*), accusing him (unfairly) of Pelagian leanings. Augustine himself would dedicate to Prosper two of his final and most radical treatises, *The Predestination of the Saints* and *The Gift of Perseverance*. This clash, the so-called Semi-Pelagian Controversy, damaged Cassian's later reputation and is the reason he was not widely recognized as a saint in the Latin West—though he is celebrated as one in Orthodox churches in the East, as well as locally in Marseilles.

In 430, Cassian moved onto the world stage one last time. Leo, who at the time was archdeacon of Rome and would go on to become one of the great popes of the early church, commissioned Cassian to write a treatise on Christ's humanity. This question had provoked the great clash between Nestorius and Cyril of Alexandria in the late 420s and led to the tumultuous and divisive Council of Ephesus in 431. Cassian responded to Leo's commission with a treatise of seven long and less-than-inspired books, entitled *On the Incarnation of the Lord, against Nestorius*. Leo must have presumed that Cassian, with his learning, his command of Greek, and his familiarity with Constantinople, was well equipped to address the question. But Cassian seems out of his element in doctrinal controversy. His work was mostly ignored by his contemporaries and has been dismissed as muddled and tiresome by recent scholars.[20]

This high-level commission is the last we hear from Cassian. His date of death is usually given as 435, but as with his date of birth, it is only an educated guess. He was buried in Marseilles in a tomb that was preserved for centuries but finally destroyed in the anticlerical rages of the French Revolution.

The *Institutes*

The first of Cassian's works is *The Institutes*, or more precisely *The Institutes of the Cenobites, and the Remedies for the Eight Principal Vices* (*De institutis coenobiorum et de octo principalium vitiorum remediis*) (for an outline, see table 12.2). As the title indicates, the text has a double focus. The first four books survey the basics of life in monastic community: how monks dress, how they pray, how they treat and instruct newcomers. The remaining eight books survey the eight "thoughts," and here Cassian passes on, adapts, and expands on what he had learned from Evagrius.

The preface lays out Cassian's program. He dedicates the work to Castor of Apta Julia, a bishop who aspired to found monasteries for his diocese and sought out Cassian's considerable expertise. Cassian compares himself to the foreigner Hiram, sent to help Solomon build the Temple in Jerusalem, noting,

TABLE 12.2. Outline of Cassian's *Institutes*

Book	Title	Topics
1	*De habitu monachorum*	The monastic habit and its allegorical meaning
2	*De canonico nocturnarum orationum et psalmorum modo*	Method of praying the psalms: night prayers
3	*De canonico diurnarum orationum et psalmorum modo*	Method of praying the psalms: day prayers
4	*De institutis renuntiantium*	Rules and instructions for new monks
5	*De spiritu gastrimargiae*	First Vice: Gluttony
6	*De spiritu fornicationis*	Second Vice: Fornication
7	*De spiritu filargyriae*	Third Vice: Love of money
8	*De spiritu irae*	Fourth Vice: Anger
9	*De spiritu tristitiae*	Fifth Vice: Sadness
10	*De spiritu acediae*	Sixth Vice: Listlessness (*acēdia*)
11	*De spiritu cenodoxiae*	Seventh Vice: Vainglory
12	*De spiritu superbiae*	Eighth Vice: Pride

"You are setting out to construct a true and spiritual temple not out of unfeeling stones but out of a community of holy men."[21] Cassian's advice is simple: follow the example of the East, above all the example of Egypt. He recognizes that the fit is not perfect, "that what I discern in the rule of the Egyptians to be impossible or hard or arduous for this country, because of either a harsh climate or difficulty and diversity of behavior, I shall temper somewhat by recourse to the customs of the monasteries in Palestine and Mesopotamia."[22] He knows local Gallic monastic customs and frequently derides them. It becomes a stock motif to contrast the slack or chaotic habits of Gaul with the rigorous and pristine customaries of Egypt.

Cassian also says that he does not plan to be a "tale weaver" of "God's marvels and signs." He certainly knows of such things and claims to have witnessed some with his own eyes. But he is equally convinced that "reading such things produces nothing more than wide-eyed wonder and instills nothing toward instruction in perfect living."[23] Cassian's sobriety should not be mistaken for modern skepticism. His concern is spiritual progress, and gaping at miracles, he believed, was a distracting irrelevancy. One suspects a jab here at popular texts such as the *History of the Monks*, which circulated in Rufinus's Latin version. He may have had a local target in mind, namely Sulpicius Severus's *Life of Martin of Tours*, which extols the wonders wrought by the reputed founder of Gallic monasticism (for excerpts, see appendix 12.1).

Instead of miracles, Cassian sets out "institutes" (*instituta*). He chose his vocabulary with care. The word means "rules," but, more broadly, the sense is closer to "foundational principles." The word *instituta* connotes both constructing and instructing. Cassian, like a good architect, wanted to institute this new monastic edifice by surveying the terrain and laying out a firm foundation. And, just as we speak of certain schools as "institutes," so Cassian, like a good pedagogue, wanted to institute monasticism by instructing the monks of the West in the ways of the East: "I consider it necessary to lay out the most ancient constitutions of the fathers, which is being observed by the servants of God even until now throughout Egypt, so that the uninstructed infancy in Christ of your new monastery may be initiated in the most time-tried customs of the most ancient fathers."[24]

The Institutes is concerned with externals, with "the institutes of the outer person."[25] Book 1 focuses on the monastic habit. Cassian describes its various articles: hood, tunic, belt, scapular, cape, goatskin, and staff. In each case, he turns from description to allegory and traces out the mystical meaning of each article. The hood, for instance, resembled a child's, and so symbolized a return to a childlike innocence in Christ, while the sleeveless tunic "suggests that [the monks] have cut off the deeds and works of this world."[26] Cassian, like other educated Christians, thought it natural and necessary to probe beneath the literal text of the Bible to uncover deeper allegorical truths. It is not surprising, therefore, that he brought an allegorical eye to monastic garb. His account parallels one found in Evagrius's prologue to the *Praktikos* (for a comparison, see table 12.3).

Books 2 and 3 survey externals of a different sort, namely the daily order for praying the psalms. We saw in chapter 6 the practice of psalmody at Scetis and drew there on Cassian's descriptions: the monks daily recited twelve psalms at vespers and again in the middle of the night, privately on weekdays, communally on weekends; they sat and did manual labor even in communal liturgies, only occasionally interrupting their handiwork with gestures of standing and prostration; and unlike Gallic monks, Egyptians did not punctuate the hours with the offices of psalms, but recited the psalms "continuously and spontaneously throughout the course of the whole day, in tandem with their work . . . taking up the whole day in offices that we celebrate at fixed times."[27]

Book 4 takes up the public instruction of novices, or "renunciants" (*renuntiantes*), as Cassian calls them. This is, in many ways, the heart of the work, for Cassian plots out a foundational theology of monastic life. He puts this theology in the mouth of a man he greatly admired, Abba Pinufius, his old cellmate in Bethlehem. Cassian claims to quote what Pinufius once said to a novice wishing to enter the monastery at Panephysis. Pinufius stressed that monastic life is Christian life, that it means following Christ crucified: "Renunciation is nothing else than a manifestation of the cross and of a dying. Therefore you should know that on this day you have died to the world and its deeds and desires and that, according to the Apostle, you have been crucified to this world and this world to you."[28] He noted Jesus's saying in Matthew 10:38 ("Whoever does not take up his cross and follow me is not worthy of me") and explored how this seemingly impossible saying can be lived out:

> Our cross is the fear of the Lord. Just as someone who has been
> crucified, then, no longer has the ability to move or to turn his
> limbs in any direction by an act of his mind, neither must we exer-
> cise our desires and yearnings in accordance with what is easy for
> us and gives us pleasure at the moment but in accordance with the
> law of the Lord and where it constrains us. And just as he who is

TABLE 12.3. The Monastic Habit of Egypt. John Cassian in Book I of the *Institutes* and Evagrius in the prologue of the *Praktikos* both describe the monastic habit of Egypt, and both pass on allegorical interpretations of the various articles. Some interpretations are similar, others differ. Here are the texts given side by side.

Item	Cassian's Interpretation	Evagrius's Interpretation
The hood/cowl	*De institutis* 1.3: "Thus, day and night they always wear small hoods that extend to the neck and the shoulders and that only cover the head. In this way they are reminded to hold constantly to the innocence and simplicity of small children even by imitating their dress itself. Those who have returned to their infancy repeat to Christ at every moment with warmth and vigor: 'Lord, my heart is not exalted, nor are my eyes lifted up. Neither have I walked in great things nor in marvels beyond me. If I thought not humbly but exalted my soul, like a weaned child upon its mother' (Ps. 131:1–2)"	*Praktikos*, prol. 2: "The cowl is a symbol of the charity of God our Savior. It protects the most important part of the body and keeps us, who are children in Christ, warm. Thus it can afford protection against those who attempt to strike and wound us. Consequently, all who wear this cowl on their heads sing these words aloud: 'If the Lord does not build the house and keep the city, unavailingly does the builder labor and the watchman stand his guard' (Ps. 126:1). Such words as these instill humility and root out that long-standing evil which is pride and which caused Lucifer, who rose like the day-star in the morning to be cast down to the earth."
The tunic (*colobia*)	*De institutis* 1.4: "They also wear colobia that barely reach the elbows and, for the rest, leave the hands free. The cutting off of their sleeves is to suggest that they have cut off the deeds and works of this world, and the wearing of linen clothing is to teach them that they have utterly died to a worldly way of life, that thus they may hear the Apostle addressing them daily: 'Put to death your members that are on earth.' Their very dress proclaims this as well: 'You have died, and your life is hidden with Christ in God.' And: 'I no longer live, but Christ lives in me.' And: 'the world has been crucified to me and I to the world.'"	

(continued)

TABLE 12.3. (continued)

Item	Cassian's Interpretation	Evagrius's Interpretation
The belt		*Praktikos*, prol. 5: "The belt which they wear about their loins signifies their rejection of all impurity and proclaims that 'it is a good thing for man not to touch a woman' (1 Cor. 7:1)."
The scapular	*De institutis* 1.5: "They wear thin ropes, too, which are braided with a double thickness of wool. These the Greeks refer to as αναλαβου, but we may call them cinctures or strings or, to be correct, cords. They descend from the top of the neck, separate on either side of the neck, go around the folds of the armpits, and are tucked up on both sides, so that when they are tightened the garment's fullness may be gathered close to the body. Thus their arms are freed, and they are unimpeded and ready for any activity as they strive wholeheartedly to fulfill the Apostle's precept: 'These hands have labored not only for me but also for those who are with me.' 'Nor did we eat anyone's bread for free, but we worked night and day in labor and weariness, lest we burden any of you.' And 'if anyone does not wish to work, neither should he eat.'"	*Praktikos*, prol. 4: "The scapular which has the form of a cross and which covers the shoulders of the monks is a symbol of faith in Christ which raises up the meek, removes obstacles and provides for free, untrammeled activity."
The Cape	*De institutis* 1.6: "After this they cover their necks and also their shoulders with a short cape, striving after both modest style and cheapness and economy. In this way they avoid the cost of coats and cloaks as well as any showiness. These are called *mafortes* in both our language and theirs."	
The Sheepskin (*Melote*)	*De institutis* 1.7: "The last pieces of their outfit are a goatskin, which is called a *melotis* or a *pera*, and a staff. These they carry in imitation of those who already in the Old Testament prefigured the thrust of this profession. Of them the Apostle says: 'They went about in *melotis* and goatskin, needy, in distress, afflicted, the world unworthy of them, wandering in deserts and mountains and caves and caverns of the earth.' This garment of goat-	*Praktikos*, prol. 6: "These men, to signify that they continually bear in their bodies the mortification of Jesus and check all the irrational passions, wear also a sheep-skin garment (*melote*)."

skin signifies that, once all the turbulence of their carnal passions has been put to death, they must abide in the most elevated virtue and no willfulness or wantonness of their youth and of former fickleness must remain in their bodies."

The Staff

De institutis 1.8: "That the same men also carried a staff is taught by Elisha himself, who was one of them, when he spoke to his servant Gehazi and sent him to raise up the woman's son: 'Take my staff; run and go and place it on the boy's face and he shall live.' The prophet would certainly not have given this to him to take if he were not accustomed to carry it about constantly in his hand. The carrying of it is, in a spiritual sense, a warning that they must never go out unarmed in the midst of numerous barking dogs of the vices and the invisible beasts of the evil spirits, from which blessed David begs to be freed when he says: 'Lord do not deliver over to the beasts the souls of one who trusts in you.' Rather, when they rush upon them they must beat them back by the sign of the cross and drive them far away, and when they rage against them they must destroy them by constantly recalling the Lord's suffering and by imitating his dying."

Praktikos, prol. 7: "They carry a staff which is the tree of life that affords secure footing to those who hold on to it. It allows them to support themselves upon it as upon the Lord."

fixed to the gibbet of the cross no longer contemplates present realities or reflects on his own afflictions; is not distracted by worry or
care for the morrow; is not stirred up by the desire for possessions;
is not inflamed by pride or wrangling or envy; does not sorrow over
present slights and no longer remembers those of the past; and, although he may still be breathing in his body, believes himself dead
in every respect and directs on ahead the gaze of his heart to the
place where he is sure that he will go; so also it is necessary for us
who have been crucified by the fear of the Lord . . . to have the eyes
of our soul set upon the place where we must hope that we shall go
any moment.[29]

We see here Cassian's vision: the true monk is the single-hearted, one whose
focus comes from staring death in the face—and beyond that, life with God.
That focus shapes everything else. Death's stark imminence gives life unexpected intensity, one otherwise lost sight of in the fretting over possessions or
reputation, past wounds or present yearnings. Cassian recognized how life,
even monastic life, fragments people, distracts them. He wanted his readers
to keep an unswerving gaze on heaven as the horizon for everything in life.
To shortchange his eschatological perspective, to write it off as mere spiritu-
alizing, is to miss Cassian's whole project.[30]

Books 5 through 12 treat the eight "principal vices," one vice per book. He
repeats the list he received from Evagrius: gluttony, fornication, avarice, anger,
sadness, acēdia, vainglory, and pride. His bilingualism comes through here,
for he lists some with their Greek names, which he quite precisely translates.
He notes, for instance, "filargyria, which means 'avarice,' or better expressed,
the 'love of money.' "[31] Cassian's exposition, when compared to Evagrius's
dense and elliptical proverbs, seems spacious and lucid. Cassian has a knack
for teasing out metaphors and illustrating abstract principles with common-
sense examples that use the secular to illuminate the monastic. He is also fond
of digressions that both nuance and entertain.

Take, for example, his discussion of gluttony. Like Evagrius, he insists that
"extinguishing of the belly's desire to gormandize" is "our first fight."[32] He
recognizes that the gluttony of the monk differs from the gluttony of the secular. Good pedagogue that he is, he catalogs the three principal manifestations
of monastic gluttony: eating before the canonical hour (three o'clock in the
afternoon); delighting in stuffing one's stomach; and getting special joy from
delicate and expensive taste treats. His ascetical principle is agere contra, "act
against." Against the first temptation, the monk needs to wait till "the lawful
moment" for breaking his fast; against the second, the monk needs to be
satisfied with eating less; against the third, the monk needs to be content with
cheaper fare.[33] Cassian avoids hard-and-fast rules and admits latitude and plu-
ralism: "A uniform rule concerning the manner of fasting cannot easily be
kept because not all bodies have the same strength. . . . There are different
times, manners, and qualities with respect to eating that are in accordance with
the varied conditions, ages, and sexes of bodies. . . . For each individual must

calculate for himself the degree of frugality that his bodily struggle and combat require."[34] More important, he refuses to isolate these monastic struggles from the larger goal: "For we shall never be able to spurn the pleasures of eating here and now if our mind is not fixed on divine contemplation and if it does not take delight, instead, in the love of virtue and the beauty of heavenly things."[35] He also insists that fasting is not an end in itself, but remains subject to love. He tells of visiting an old Egyptian monk who routinely dispensed his own fasting for the sake of hospitality. As he told Cassian, "Fasting, as beneficial and necessary as it may be, is nonetheless a gift that is voluntarily offered, whereas the requirements of the commandment demand that the work of love be carried out. And so I welcome Christ in you and must refresh him."[36] The old man added that on the day Cassian visited, he had had six visitors and had therefore eaten six times.

But Cassian offers more than prescription and nuance. He interlaces this whole discussion with a controlling metaphor: the monk as Olympic athlete. This ties together his larger perspective and gives it both emotional and ethical force. Just as Olympic athletes train and subject their bodies to fierce discipline to achieve mastery and freedom of action, so monks discipline their bodies to cease being "slaves of fleshly desires." Just as young athletes must move up the ladder of competition to qualify for the Olympics, so the young monk progresses from bodily disciplines to more interior ones: "Victory in the contests is never wanting to the athlete of Christ as he dwells in the flesh, but the stronger he grows through successive triumphs, the more demanding the series of struggles that awaits him."[37] And just as Olympic athletes keep their gaze fixed on their ultimate goal, the laurel crown (the ancient equivalent of the gold medal), so the monk keeps his gaze fixed and "does not run in uncertainty because, in looking upon the heavenly Jerusalem, he is clear as to where his swift and undeviating heart should be directed."[38]

Cassian draws this athletic motif from Saint Paul. He quotes 1 Corinthians 9:26–27 ("I do not fight as one beating against the air. But I chastise my body and subject it to servitude") as a biblical verse that joins athletics, physical self-mastery, and freedom. He goes on to draw on other Pauline texts to link the struggle of discipline with images of Olympic victory: Philippians 3:13–14 ("Forget what is behind, and stretching forward to what is before, on to the goal, to the prize of the heavenly calling of God in Christ Jesus") and 2 Timothy 4:7–8 ("I have fought the good fight, I have won the race, I have kept the faith. Now a crown of righteousness has been set aside for me, which the Lord, the just judge, will bestow on me on that day").[39] In other words, Cassian grounds his asceticism and his goal orientation in the teaching and person of Saint Paul. For Cassian, monasticism is, quite literally, apostolic.[40]

Cassian, early in Book 5, interrupts his discussion of gluttony with a digression on "blessed Antony," passing on a saying not found in other sources. According to Cassian, Antony asserted that the seeker cannot expect any one individual to possess all the virtues. Rather, on this side of the Second Coming, holy people specialize in different virtues. Some excel at humility, others at generosity, still others at mercy, and so on. So the young monk should be like "a most prudent bee" and collect "spiritual honey" from the many virtuous flowers and "lay it up carefully in the vessel of his heart." Antony then gave this portrait of holy diversity a Christological spin. Since Christ is not yet "all in all," one finds the virtues of Christ "now divided among each of the holy ones"; at the end of time, however, "when all are assembled together in the unity of faith and virtue, he appears as 'the perfect man,' completing the fullness of his body in the joining together and in the characteristics of the individual members."[41] This digression serves Cassian's overall program. His discussion of the eight vices, like Evagrius's, is focused not just on uprooting vice, but also cultivating virtue. And so by this digression, Cassian invokes Antony as an archetype and unquestioned authority for his larger ascetical program.

The *Conferences*

The *Conferences* (*Collationes*) is Cassian's magnum opus, a massive work, nearly 900 pages in a modern printed edition. It purports to record twenty-four conversations with leading Egyptian spiritual masters. Individual conferences focus, for the most part, on a single theme: renunciation, discernment, prayer, chastity, biblical interpretation, and so on. Each of the twenty-four dialogues has three cast members: Cassian, his friend Germanus, and the *abba* they are visiting. And each follows the same basic literary structure: Cassian sets the scene, giving background tidbits about the locale and the *abba*; Germanus plays the role of questioner, posing the initial spiritual query and adding follow-up questions as the discussion proceeds; and the *abba* acts as the voice of wisdom, answering Germanus's probings, usually at length and with considerable homiletic skill. Frequently, Cassian portrays a single *abba* conducting two or even three consecutive sessions. In terms of literary style, the *Conferences* draw on (and Christianize) the classical genre known as *erotapokriseis*, or question-and-answer session.[42]

It is important to remember that Cassian did not begin writing this account until at least two decades after leaving Egypt. The *Conferences*, therefore, cannot be read as though they were transcriptions (or even translated transcriptions). As Stewart has noted:

> The elders to whom he attributes the *Conferences* doubtless provided the basic elements of his doctrine, and memory of them and their teaching nourished Cassian's own reflection. The synthesis, however, is Cassian's. By ascribing his *Conferences* to them, he is placing his acknowledgments in his titles rather than in footnotes as a modern writer would. Furthermore, in the service of humility (and perhaps credibility) he does not shirk from inventive use of quotation marks as he places in the mouths of great elders the monastic teaching which has become his own.[43]

Cassian published the *Conferences* in three phases (for an outline, see table 12.4). The first set, *Conferences* 1–10, was intended to complement and complete

TABLE 12.4. Outline of Cassian's *Conferences*

First Set

Conference	Title	Topic	Speaker
1	*De monachi destinatione vel fine*	The goal and end of the monk	Moses (of Scetis)
2	*De discretione*	Discernment	Moses
3	*De tribus abrenunitationibus*	The three renunciations	Paphnutius (of Scetis)
4	*De concupiscentia carnis ac spiritus*	Desires of the flesh	Daniel (of Scetis)
5	*De octo vitiis principalibus*	The eight principle vices	Sarapion (of Scetis)
6	*De nece sanctorum*	The murder of saintly people	Theodore (of Kellia)
7	*De animae mobilitate et spiritalibus nequitiis*	Evil spirits and the soul's changeability	Serenus (of Scetis)
8	*De principatibus*	The principalities	Serenus
9	*De oratione*	Prayer (disposition, types)	Isaac (of Scetis)
10	*De oratione*	Prayer (unceasing, method)	Isaac

Second Set

Conference	Title	Topics	Speaker
11	*De perfectione*	Perfection	Chaeremon (an anchorite near Panephysis)
12	*De castitate*	Chastity	Charemon
13	*De protectione Dei*	Grace and free will	Charemon
14	*De spiritali scientia*	Spiritual knowledge, biblical interpretation	Nestoros (an anchorite near Panephysis
15	*De charismatibus diuinis*	Charisms	Nesteros
16	*De amicitia*	Friendship	Joseph (an anchorite near Panephysis)
17	*De definiendo*	Oaths and promises	Joseph

Third Set

Conference	Title	Topics	Speaker
18	*De tribus generibus monachorum*	Three types of monks	Piamun (of Diolcos, a cenobite turned anchorite)
19	*De fine coenobiotae et heremitae*	Cenobites and anchorites	John (of Diolcos, an anchorite turned cenobite)
20	*De paenitentiae fine et satisfactionis indicio*	Penitence and reparation	Pinufius (of Panephysis, cenobite)
21	*De remissione quinquagensimae*	Relaxing during Pentecost	Pinufius
22	*De nocturnis inlusionibus*	Dreams and nocturnal emissions	Pinufius
23	*De anamarteto*	Sinlessness	Theonas (of Scetis, an anchorite)
24	*De mortificatione*	Mortification, renunciation	Abraham (of Diolcos, an anchorite)

the literary project begun in the *Institutes*. As he notes in the preface, the *Institutes* had dealt with "the external and visible life of the monks," while the *Conferences* move from outer to inner, to the "invisible character of the inner man."[44] And whereas the *Institutes* were geared especially to cenobites, the *Conferences* portray the life and spirituality of anchorites—which, he admits, means moving into "deeper waters."[45] In this first set, Cassian's spokesmen are all anchorites and are from Scetis (except *Conference* 6, which uses Theodore of Kellia).

The first edition of the *Conferences* received a warm reception from friends in Gaul, and Cassian realized that he wanted to address other topics.[46] So he composed a second set, *Conferences* 11–17, which uses monks from the delta as spokesmen. This set forms not a sequel, but a prequel, since, chronologically speaking, Cassian had met these spokesmen *before* he met those from Scetis.[47] The third and final set, *Conferences* 18–24, seems more scattered, using spokesmen from two locales—both Scetis and the delta—and from two monastic lifestyles—both anchorites and cenobites. Although he had originally intended to write only the first ten, by the time he finished the full twenty-four, he came to see a mystical significance in the final number: just as the twenty-four elders in the book of Revelation sat with crowns before the Lamb, so "these twenty-four elders of ours have received crowns of glory because of the worthiness of their teaching."[48]

Although the *Conferences* speak of Egypt, the intended audience lived in southern Gaul. Cassian dedicated the first set to Leontius, bishop of Fréjus (c. 400–c. 432) and a monk named Helladius (later a bishop). Cassian positioned himself carefully with such a dedication, since under Leontius's jurisdiction was Gaul's greatest monastic center, the island of Lérins. Concern with Lérins also underlies the second set, which Cassian dedicates to Honoratus, then a superior at Lérins and later bishop of Arles, and to Eucherius, at the time a monk at Lérins, later bishop of Lyons and author of *In Praise of the Desert* (for excerpts, see appendix 12.2). The third set was dedicated to four monks who lived on islands near Marseilles. Three are unknown to us, but the fourth, Theodore, was credited with establishing Eastern-style cenobitic life in Gaul and later succeeded Leontius as bishop of Fréjus. These prefaces give a glimpse of Cassian's ascetical politics. He clearly wanted to disseminate his message to those who had the authority to bring it to fruition.

Cassian admitted that the immensity of his writing project overwhelmed him: "Having settled in a harbor of silence, this vast sea opens before my eyes: the institutes and teachings of such great men that I venture to hand down to the ages."[49] The "vast sea" of the *Conferences* can be equally daunting to the reader. Let me focus on three of the most famous of the *Conferences* to provide a few compass points for navigating this immensity: *Conference* 1, which focuses on purity of heart, and *Conferences* 9 and 10, which focus on unceasing prayer.

Purity of Heart

Conference 1 focuses on the goal of monastic life and is led by Abba Moses of Scetis, presumably the same Moses who appears in the pages of the *Apophthegmata* and the *Lausiac History*.[50] He begins with a comparison: farmers work hard, laboring in "the torrid rays of the sun one time and the frost and ice another, tirelessly tilling the soil and subduing the unyielding clumps of earth"; their immediate "goal" is to clear untilled fields, while their long-term "end" is a good harvest.[51] In a similar way, merchants set sail on hazardous seas in hopes of commercial success, while soldiers risk life and limb for honors and power.[52] Every profession demands risk, hardship, discipline. And that is no less true of the monastic profession. The monk faces hunger from fasts, exhaustion from vigils, bleak poverty, the unremitting heat of the desert, the anguish of solitude and the homesickness that comes from leaving behind family and friends. He endures these hardships—just as farmers, soldiers, and merchants do theirs—because of certain hoped-for goals and ends. Here Moses introduces a distinction between a goal (*skopos*, *destinatio*) and an end (*telos*, *finis*). The goal is the proximate target, the means to the greater and more remote end. The monk's end is the same end sought by all Christians: the kingdom of Heaven. But to find his way to the kingdom, the monk pursues a closer, more immediate goal: purity of heart.[53]

Purity of heart is the linchpin of *Conference* 1—indeed, of Cassian's monastic theology. The phrase has rich resonances, both biblical and philosophical, and Cassian exploits these as he maps the monastic journey.[54] Most obvious and most important is Jesus's promise in the Beatitudes: "Blessed are the pure in heart, for they shall see God" (Matt. 5:8).[55] Jesus's saying links goal to end, the goal of purity of heart with the end of a contemplative vision of God. When Abba Moses quotes this Beatitude, he tells Cassian and Germanus: "Those whose concern it is to press on to knowledge and to the purification of their minds have chosen, even while living in the present world, to give themselves this objective with all their power and strength."[56] Note the key phrase, "even while living in the present world." For Cassian, the monk's vocation is not to defer beatitude to the afterlife; it is to "see God" here and now—to get a glimpse, however brief, however tentative, of heaven on earth.

What then is purity of heart? Cassian does not give a single succinct definition but teases out its many strains in this and subsequent conferences. To modern ears, "heart" implies feeling, so purifying the heart implies cleansing affections and motives. That, for Cassian, is only one dimension, but an important one. He stresses turning our gaze inward, that "all the recesses of our heart be scrutinized" to sniff out whether "some psychic beast, whether lion or dragon, has secretly left footprints" amid the debris of our affections or, "in passing through," marked its territory with "pernicious traces" that other creatures may follow.[57] Cassian's theory of the eight vices—presented first in the *Institutes* and explored further in *Conference* 5—allows him to explore subtle undercurrents of human motivation. Like Evagrius, he is acutely conscious of the twists and turns of the human heart and our knack for self-deception. He cites, for instance, people who grandly give away vast wealth and properties in response to the call of Christ and then in their desert poverty become upset about a missing pen or a borrowed book.[58] He also tells cautionary tales, as Palladius had, of holiness gone mad: a monk named Heron who, after fifty years of rigorous asceticism, committed suicide by diving into a well after a vision of an angel of light; a deluded old monk who thought that he, like the patriarch Abraham, was called to execute his son as a human sacrifice to God.[59] So Abba Moses, in *Conference* 1, stresses that monks need to learn the fine art of discernment, to sort through the inner stream of thoughts and discern their origin, whether they arise from God, from the devil, or from themselves.[60] He compares the wise monk to a sharp-eyed money changer who can discern coins of pure gold from those alloyed with brass, or distinguish coins stamped with the image of the true emperor from those stamped with a usurper's image.[61]

Cassian also ties purity of heart to purity of body. The monastic regimen was intensely physical, both its initial renunciations (of homeland, wealth, pleasures, and marriage) and its daily disciplines (fasting, vigils, and manual labor).[62] Every human art has its tools, and these renunciations and disciplines were part of the monastic "art," the "tools of perfection."[63] At the same time, Cassian knew how monks in Egypt got caught up in ascetic one-upmanship and pursued physical disciplines as though they were ends in themselves. It is necessary "then to carry out the things that are secondary—namely, fasts, vigils, the solitary life, and meditation on Scripture—for the sake of the principal *skopos*, which is purity of heart or love, rather than for their sake to neglect this principal virtue"; "what is gained by fasting is less than what is spent on anger."[64] As Cassian saw it, the hard work of asceticism clears the ground: just as the farmer cuts through the gnarled undergrowth and breaks up the rock-hard dirt, so the monk uproots vices and "at every moment . . . cultivates the earth of our heart with the gospel plow."[65] Emblematic of the quest for purity is the quest for "perfect chastity," which Cassian distinguishes from mere continence. He discusses monastic sexuality bluntly, even clinically, in *Conference* 12. (His frankness proved too much for his nineteenth-century English translator, who simply skipped this conference in his otherwise complete translation.) In it Cassian charts the physiology and psychology of wet dreams, tracing out what they betoken about the last covert reservoirs of sexual impurity.[66]

For Cassian, purity of heart touched not just the heart (in the modern sense) or the body (in an extended sense), but also the mind. He routinely links purity of heart with tranquility of mind. The connection is not obvious to us. We tend to distinguish heart from mind, emotion from thinking. But Cassian, like many early Christian theologians, treats the biblical term "heart" (*cor* in Latin) as a synonym for "mind" (*mens*). In the ancient view, mind is much more than the locus of thinking; it is the conscious center of our experience as human beings, what we tend to call the self. And Cassian saw the mind—at least, the mind as it is now enfleshed in the physical world—as singularly unstable. In *Conference* 1, Abba Moses puts it this way: "It is inevitable that the mind which does not have a place to turn to or any stable base will undergo change from hour to hour and from minute to minute due to the variety of its distractions, and by the things that come to it from outside it will be continually transformed into whatever occurs to it at any given moment."[67] He goes on to compare the world to a rushing river that spins the mind round and round like a mill's whirling grindstone: "The mind cannot be free from agitating thoughts during the trials of the present life, since it is spinning around in the torrents of the trials that overwhelm it from all sides."[68] In other words, the world dis-integrates us, sends us spinning dizzily. Left to ourselves, we lack integrity, any genuine center. The quest is thus for peace of mind, for what the Greek tradition called *hesychia*, a deep interior stillness. Again and again, Cassian pairs the phrase "purity of heart" or "purity of mind" with words such as "stability" (*stabilitas*), "steadiness" (*immobilitas*), "integrity" (*integras*), and, most often, "tranquility" (*tranquillitas*).[69] Thus in *Conference* 19, Abba John insists that "nothing is more precious than tranquility of soul and perpetual purity of heart"[70] and in *Conference* 18, Abba Piamun claims that "the kingdom of God is attained in tranquility of mind."[71]

Scholars note that what Cassian calls "purity of heart," Evagrius had called "passionlessness" (*apatheia*).[72] Cassian, it seems, consciously sidestepped his mentor's controversial terminology.[73] Jerome, writing in 414 in his *Letter to Ctesiphon*, had attacked Evagrius by name and mocked Evagrian *apatheia* as a state in which the "soul is disturbed neither by any thought nor any vice, and— to put it simply—[this] means the soul is either a stone or God."[74] For Jerome, this goal was either stupid (to make oneself as imperturbable as a rock) or blasphemous (to claim to achieve a Godlike sinlessness and immutability). This is, of course, Jerome's usual ploy of caricature and is far removed from what Evagrius meant.

Evagrius, as we saw, described *apatheia* as a state of psychic integrity and deep calm achieved after long years of ascetic practice, a state that both makes possible selfless love (*agape*) and opens the door to mystical knowledge (*gnosis*). Cassian agreed, in the main. In the *Institutes*, he says that purity of heart comes only after one uproots vices and lets virtues blossom; this purity, in turn, makes "the perfection of apostolic charity" possible.[75] The deep interior tranquility wrought by purity of heart always remains (in this life) a less-than-perfect state, ever capable of lapse and certainly unsustainable without God's grace. Writing twenty-five years after the Origenist Controversy, in a different language and in a different milieu, Cassian chose not to use Evagrius's loaded and controversial Greek philosophical terminology. Cassian was not opposed, in principle, to importing Greek terminology; in fact, he did so repeatedly. But "purity of heart" better named the radiating core of the monastic goal as he saw it, and it had the obvious boon of phrasing it in unimpeachable biblical language, and specifically in the language of the Beatitudes, where Jesus links purity with seeing God.

Unceasing Prayer

Early monks were haunted by Saint Paul's terse admonition "Pray without ceasing" (1 Thess 5:17). They were convinced that Paul had meant it not as a pious exaggeration, but as a commandment to be carried out literally, absolutely. The issue of unceasing prayer preoccupies Cassian in *Conferences* 9 and 10.[76] His spokesman for these is the otherwise unknown Abba Isaac of Scetis.

That these two conferences now appear in the middle of the twenty-four blurs their real significance. When Cassian first conceived his project, he intended to write only ten conferences, and intended these two as the original close and climax. This cannot be stressed strongly enough: Cassian saw these conferences as the climax of his literary endeavor and the pinnacle of his spiritual theology. Years earlier, when writing the *Institutes*, he anticipated the topic, noting that while he first needed to discuss liturgical prayer, he eventually wanted to probe "how we can, in the words of the Apostle, pray 'without ceasing'. . . . when we have, with the Lord's help, begun to set out the conferences of the elders."[77] Again in the preface to the first set of *Conferences*, he says that he wants to proceed from outer to inner, from liturgical prayer to "the unceasing nature of that perpetual prayer which the Apostle commands."[78] And, when he opens *Conference* 9, he says that he has at last arrived at a point when he "will fulfill the promise made in the second book of the *Institutes* about the perpetual and unceasing continuity of prayer."[79]

For Cassian, the monk is a contemplative and is most truly himself when he prays. Abba Isaac, Cassian's spokesman here, makes this point in his opening words: "The end of every monk and the perfection of his heart incline him to constant and uninterrupted perseverance in prayer; and, as much as human frailty allows, it strives after an unchanging and continual tranquility of mind and perpetual purity."[80] Here Cassian comes full circle. *Conference* 1 had described the monastic quest for purity of heart as the goal and seeing God as the end; in *Conferences* 9 and 10, both goal and end come together in contemplative prayer. Cassian is a realist and always tempers his mystical ideals by what "human frailty allows." But that does not prevent him from insisting that tasting heaven here and now is possible:

> This, then, is the goal of the solitary, and this must be his whole intention—to deserve to possess the image of future blessedness *in this body* and as it were to begin to taste the pledge of that heavenly way of life and glory *in this vessel*. This, I say, is the end of the perfection—that the mind purged of every carnal desire may daily be elevated to spiritual things, until one's whole way of life and all the yearnings of one's heart become a single and continuous prayer.[81]

Cassian sees the monk as manning a frontier outpost between present and future, moving back and forth between them, tasting here and now "in this body, . . . in this vessel" some piece of heaven, a foretaste, "a pledge." He also insists that prayer cannot be severed from one's whole way of life and that "perfect prayer," the culmination of the long spiritual journey, is impossible without moral purification. Early in *Conference* 9, Abba Isaac gives a construction analogy: first, we dig up and clear out the "dead rubbish of the passions"; next, we lay "the firm foundation of simplicity and humility" on the "gospel rock"; then, we build "towers of spiritual virtues," which ascend into the heights of heaven; perfect prayer comes only at the end, as "the capstone."[82]

Conference 9 owes much of its agenda to Origen's famous treatise *On Prayer*. Like Origen, Cassian first discusses disposition: "We must prepare ourselves before the time of prayer to be the prayerful persons that we wish to be."[83] Also like Origen, Cassian focuses on the Pauline admonition: "I urge, first of all, that supplications, prayers, intercessions, and thanksgivings be made" (1 Tim. 2:1). He takes each of these four terms and distinguishes between them: "supplications" (*obsecrationes*) are prayers of compunction in which one seeks pardon for sin; "prayers" (*orationes*) are vows of renunciation of worldly honors and riches and commitments to chastity and to purgation of vices; "intercessions" (*postulationes*) are "fervent" prayers in which one prays for loved ones and for the peace of the world; and "thanksgivings" (*gratiarum actiones*) are contemplative prayers in which the monk gazes out onto God's providential action in the past, present, and future. Whereas Origen had used these four terms to create a taxonomy of prayer forms, Cassian sees them as deeper attitudes that mark the monk's progress from prayer focused on self to prayer focused on others.[84] Finally, like Origen, Cassian cites the Lord's Prayer as *the* model of Christian prayer and offers a phrase-by-phrase analysis.

Conference 10 articulates a spirituality at once mystical and practical. Cassian had inherited from Evagrius the view that "pure prayer" is unceasing, imageless, and wordless. Evagrius never says precisely how, practically speaking, such prayer might be done, but Cassian (in the voice of Abba Isaac) does. The *Conference* opens with the dramatic story we saw earlier: Abba Serapion's anguish over Theophilus's letter against anthropomorphism and his tragic cry, "They have taken my God from me." This anecdote poses the initial problem: how does one pray without images, even inner images? The second problem is the one raised throughout *Conference* 9: how does one fulfill the Pauline command to "pray without ceasing"? This second problem leads to a third, raised by Germanus, first in *Conference* 9 and again in *Conference* 10: how can the mind—given its instability and its vulnerability to distraction—possibly stay focused enough to pray unceasingly? Germanus situates the question in terms of the ancient monastic practice of *meditatio*, the recitation of and rumination on biblical texts:

> Our minds think of some passage of a psalm. But it is taken away
> from us without our noticing it, and stupidly, unknowingly, the
> spirit slips on to some other text of Scripture. It begins to think
> about it, but before it gets to fully grasp it another text slides into
> the memory and drives out the earlier one. Meanwhile another one
> arrives and there is a further turnabout. The spirit rolls from psalm
> to psalm, leaps from the gospel to Saint Paul, from Paul to the

prophets, from there to incidents of spirituality. Ever on the move, forever wandering, it is tossed along through all the body of Scripture, unable to settle on anything, unable to reject anything or to hold on to anything, powerless to arrive at any full and judicious study, a dilettante and speedy taster of spiritual ideas rather than their creator and possessor. And so the mind is always on the move, and at the time of assembly it is pulled, like a drunk, in every direction and it performs no task competently. . . . It seems to be a victim of chance.[85]

This description comes from one who has memorized the biblical text. It also comes from one schooled in ancient allegorical exegesis, which used the Bible to interpret the Bible. Monks such as Cassian and Germanus were used to leaping from passage to passage, book to book, to decipher meanings, much as people today leap from Web page to Web page. The problem was not memorization, nor exegetical leaps from text to text; rather, it was manic superficiality. The mind, as Germanus sees it, needs an anchor, a center, something to give it stability.

Abba Isaac answers these problems with a method of prayer, at once simple and practical: take a single text from Scripture and repeat it without cease, with every breath. The formula he recommends is Psalm 70:1: "Come to my help, O God; Lord, hurry to my rescue" (*Deus in adiutorium meum intende: domine ad adiuuandum mihi festina*). This way of praying allows the monk "who longs for the continual awareness of God" to pray "without ceasing in his heart," to pray without images, and to pray in a way that "drives out every other thought."[86] Abba Isaac adds that this discipline is of the greatest antiquity: "Just as this was handed down to us by a few of the oldest fathers who were left, so also we pass it on to none but the most exceptional, who truly desire it."[87] Isaac then defends this formula as a sort of "prayer for all seasons." Let me quote the passage at length, for it gives a taste of Cassian at his most eloquent:

To keep the thought of God always in your mind you must cling totally to this formula for piety: "Come to my help, O God; Lord, hurry to my rescue." It is not without good reason that this verse has been chosen from the whole of Scripture as a device. It carries within it all the feelings of which human nature is capable. It can be adapted to every condition and can be usefully deployed against every temptation. It carries within it a cry of help to God in the face of every danger. It expresses the humility of a pious confession. It conveys the watchfulness born of unending worry and fear. It conveys a sense of our frailty, the assurance of being heard, the confidence in help that is always and everywhere present. Someone forever calling out to his protector is indeed very sure of having him close by. This is the voice of the ardor of love and of charity. This is the terrified cry of someone who sees the snares of the enemy, the cry of someone besieged day and night and exclaiming that he cannot escape unless his protector comes to the rescue. This short verse is an indomitable wall for all those struggling against the onslaught of demons. It is an impenetrable breastplate and the sturdiest of shields. . . .

I am assailed by the passion of gluttony. I am on the watch for food of which the desert has nothing. Into the drabness of my solitary life come the fragrances of royal dishes and I feel myself dragged unwillingly along by my longing for them. And so I must say "Come to my help, O God; Lord, hurry to my rescue." . . .

Here I am, still fighting against my sins. The temptation of the flesh suddenly stirs me and with its smooth delight it tries as I sleep to drag me into giving my consent. And so if an alien raging fire is not to burn the sweetly fragrant flowers of chastity I must cry "Come to my help, O God; Lord, hurry to my rescue." . . .

I am troubled by the pangs of anger, of greed, of sadness. I am drawn to scatter that gentleness which I had embraced as my own. And so if I am not to be carried off by turbulent rage into bitterness I must groan mightily and call out "Come to my help, O God; Lord, hurry to my rescue."

I am tempted by *acēdia*, by vainglory, by pride. My mind takes subtle pleasure in the negligence or the easy-going attitude of others. And so if this devilish prompting of the enemy is not to overcome me I must pray in all contrition of heart "Come to my help, O God; Lord, hurry to my rescue."

I feel that my spirit has once more found a sense of direction, that my thinking has grown purposeful, that because of a visit of the Holy Spirit my heart is unspeakably glad and my mind ecstatic. Here is a great overflow of spiritual thoughts, thanks to a sudden illumination and to the coming of the Savior. The holiest ideas, hitherto concealed from me, have been revealed to me. And so if I am to deserve to remain thus for much longer, I must anxiously and regularly cry "Come to my help, O God; Lord, hurry to my rescue." . . .

The thought of this verse should be turning unceasingly in your heart. Never cease to recite it in whatever task or service or journey you find yourself. . . . This verse should be the first thing to occur you when you wake up. It should precede all your thoughts as you keep vigil. It should take you over as you rise from your bed and go to kneel. . . . You will write it upon the threshold and gateway of your mouth, you will place it on the walls of your house and in the inner sanctum of your heart. It will be a continuous prayer, an endless refrain when you bow down in prostration and when you rise up to do all the necessary things of life.[88]

This text is both intricate rhetoric and profound spirituality. Psalm 70:1 serves as a steady refrain, a drumbeat that punctuates the passage. And form mirrors content: Abba Isaac repeats the verse as he advocates the value of repeating the verse. Note also the way Cassian interlaces his praise of the psalm verse with his theory of the eight vices. He treats two singly (gluttony and lust) and groups the others in two threesomes (anger-greed-sadness and *acēdia*-vainglory-pride). While Abba Isaac extols the verse as a prayer for all seasons, the accent is on its power against temptation; it is "an indomitable wall" and "impenetrable breastplate" against demonic attack. Scholars speak of this type of prayer as "antirrhetic," that is, a brief prayer against temptation. As we saw, Evagrius wrote a work called *Antirrhetikos*, or "Counter-Arguments," in which he listed 487 temptations and paired each with an apt biblical text as a "counter-argument" against the devil; and Evagrius prefaced his work by noting that he drew his inspiration from what Jesus himself had done when tempted in the desert. But Cassian is not Evagrius. Where Evagrius gives 487 scripture verses to combat 487 temptations, Cassian gives one scripture verse to combat all. The deeper issue is the way this one verse encapsulates Cassian's most basic theology. He believes that we are deeply, radically dependent on God for help, for peace, for survival, for absolutely everything; that we need to acknowledge this with every breath and to seek God's grace no less often. At his core, Cassian is deeply anti-Pelagian in temperament and worldview.

In terms of method, Cassian is recommending monologistic prayer (literally, "one-word prayer"), a sort of Christian mantra. The classic form of Christian monologistic prayer would appear later, in fifth-century Palestine, in the so-called Jesus Prayer—the unceasing repetition of the name of Jesus, sometimes accompanied with a petition for mercy. The version best known today comes from an anonymous nineteenth-century Russian work, *The Way of the Pilgrim*, which counsels praying incessantly, first with one's lips, then with one's heart, the phrase "Lord Jesus Christ, have mercy on me, a sinner." Cassian's favored phrase became deeply influential, but not in the way the *Conferences* recommend. It did not become, as he hoped, a widely used monologistic prayer formula. Rather, his favorite psalm verse made its way into Western liturgy, and since at least the time of Benedict, it has served as the responsory that opens every Liturgy of the Hours.

Cassian, like Evagrius, believed that the highest prayer was not just imageless and unceasing, but also wordless. Thus Cassian presents this monologistic prayer formula not as an end point, but as a "basecamp" for higher ascent.[89] Here and there in *Conferences* 9 and 10, Cassian (in the voice of Abba Isaac) describes such wordless prayer. He notes that it is "known and experienced by very few," and that it is "ineffable, transcending all human thought, marked not by any sound of the voice, nor movement of the tongue, nor speaking of words."[90] This prayer is not only ineffable; it transports the one praying into an altered consciousness:

> And so our mind arrives at a prayer beyond corruption. . . . It not
> only ponders no image; it uses no words nor voice to follow along.
> Rather with the mind's aim ignited, on fire, this prayer thrusts up,
> through an ecstasy of heart that is ineffable, by a joy of spirit that is
> indescribable. The mind, lifted up beyond all sensation and visible

matters, pours itself out to God with speech-defying groans and sighs.[91]

Here Cassian, in trying to describe the indescribable, uses the language of ecstasy. "Ecstasy," from the Greek *ekstasis*, means to "stand outside" oneself. Greek Christian writers were sometimes wary of a term associated with the frenzy of pagan prophets. Evagrius, as we saw, avoided it and spoke of "pure prayer" not as an *ekstasis*, a leaving oneself, but as a *katastasis*, a coming to one's true state. Cassian, a disciple of Evagrius in so many ways, seems markedly un-Evagrian here. He speaks here and throughout his works of an "ecstasy of heart" (*excessus cordis*) or an "ecstasy of mind" (*excessus mentis*).[92] He says such moments are brief, passing[93]; they are graced, not earned, given as "the secret and hidden dispensations of God"[94]; they feel like out-of-body experiences[95], or like awakening from a deep sleep[96]; one sees "earthly realities as mere smoke and an empty shadow" and glimpses the future[97]; one's mind tastes enlightenment, "an infusion of heavenly light," while one's heart brims and "gushes forth as from a most abundant fountain."[98]

Cassian often links ecstasy and fire. He speaks of "fiery ecstasies of heart," of the "mind's intention on fire," of prayer "inflamed with spiritual ardor," of "a higher stage of that fiery . . . wordless prayer."[99] In such moments, the mind is seized by the Holy Spirit who does the actual praying, while the mind becomes "like a kind of ungraspable and devouring flame," and "pours out to God wordless prayers of the purest vigor."[100] Where did Cassian get this Pentecostalism? Neither this language of fire nor the language of ecstasy comes from Evagrius. One finds descriptions of fiery prayer and of ecstasy in the *Apophthegmata*—and so Cassian may have drawn from the same oral stream that later emerged in the sayings. There are some extraordinary parallels in literature associated with Syrian spirituality, the Pseudo-Macarian *Homilies* and the *Book of Steps*. Obviously, Syria is far from Egypt. Could Cassian have encountered Syrian literature through John Chrysostom, who had been a monk in Syria, and during his stay in Constantinople? It is possible, but as Stewart has noted, "Such questions, as intriguing as they are, elude historical or literary solution. The answer may not lie with history or texts at all, for Cassian's own experience could have been his source."[101] One of Cassian's younger Greek-speaking contemporaries, Diadochus of Photike (c. 400–c. 486), joins together what Cassian joins: Evagrian terminology with the language of ecstasy, heart, and fire.

Ultimately Cassian's spirituality is Christ-centered. In *Conference* 10, Abba Isaac stresses that contemplative prayer leads to a vision of Christ, albeit an imageless vision. The monk is not to see a mental figment, as the Anthropomorphite Abba Serapion had. Rather, the monk who has reached a graced purity of heart gains access to Christ in his divinity. The monk experiences what the apostles experienced on the mountain of Transfiguration, which, according to Cassian, lay in the desert: the monk goes off "with Christ to the lofty mountain of the desert" and there "sees Christ's Godhead with purest eyes"; there Christ "reveals the glory of his face and the image of his brightness to those who deserve to look upon him with the clean gaze of the soul."[102] Cassian goes on to speak of a union that fulfills Christ's prayer to the Father at the Last Supper: "That the love with which you have loved me may be in them and they in us"; "That all may be one, as you Father are in me and I in you, that they also may be one in us" (John 17:26, 21). Cassian then, in one of the most extraordinary passages in desert literature, speaks about what this union involves:

> This [union] will be the case when every love, every desire, every ef-
> fort, every undertaking, every thought of ours, everything that we
> live, that we speak, that we breathe, will be God, and when that
> unity which the Father now has with the Son and which the Son has
> with the Father will be carried over into our understanding and our
> mind, so that, just as he loves us with a sincere and pure and indis-
> soluble love, we too may be joined to him with a perpetual and in-
> separable love and so united with him that whatever we breath,
> whatever we understand, whatever we speak, may be God.[103]

Cassian here sets out the peak: one does not just say prayers; nor does one simply pray interiorly, purely, undistractedly; nor is prayer a matter of those occasional dazzling graced moments of fiery ecstasy; in the end, one becomes prayer, one's very existence is a prayer and a praying. This is deification: when all that we are may "be God."

Map Making

After *Conference* 10, Cassian moves down from the mystical peak of un-ceasing and ecstatic prayer to a broader monastic terrain. While I cannot, in this brief introduction, give his later *Conferences* the attention they deserve, several require at least a brief notice.

Conference 13

This conference, entitled "On Divine Protection," grapples with grace and free will. The issue may seem a little abstract at first sight, but it touches monastic life deeply and directly. Early monks, like all Christians, were committed to avoiding vice and cultivating virtue; but they did so with great intensity and at enormous cost, sacrificing the comforts of normal human living—family, mar-riage, food, sleep, companionship—and embracing a fierce ascetical regimen. The question was this: was a monk's progress in virtue the result of his own hard work, or was it the result of God's good grace? Monks, like Cassian, knew acutely how fragile virtue really is, how easily vice reasserts itself. They also knew that their victories over demons and temptation were, despite the felt-sense of wrestling and hard labor, ultimately an experience of God's grace.

This question of grace and free will had been a burning theological question in the Latin West for over a decade, the subject of a fierce debate between Augustine, bishop of Hippo in North Africa, and Pelagius, an ascetic who worked as a spiritual director among the Roman aristocracy. Augustine, the consummate born-again Christian, had recounted the journey of his conversion in the *Confessions*, seeing the promptings of God's grace permeating every corner of his life. In his long and voluminous debate with Pelagius, Augustine attributed all things to grace. To highlight grace's grandeur and Christ's saving work, Augustine portrayed the human condition in the bleakest terms: that while Adam might have had free will, Adam's choice for evil had damaged everyone else's free will every after; that the human will, left to its own devices, inevitably chooses badly; and that human beings need grace to do the good, to will the good. As Augustine saw it, the grace of God has to anticipate every good action, permeate it, and bring it to completion. The good character and good works of good people can be attributed only to gifts of grace. That grace is gratis, utterly unearned; it is not the reward for the hard work of virtuous behavior. Even faith itself is a gift. This perspective would lead Augustine to an uncompromising doctrine of predestination. By 418, Augustine and the North Africans had won the day, but the debate had not quieted. In monastic circles, both in North Africa and in Gaul, people wondered out loud whether Augustine's view of grace rendered the hard work of asceticism unintelligible.

Thus when Cassian wrote *Conference* 13, he was writing in a highly charged environment. Cassian's spokesman here is Abba Chaeremon, who led two previous sessions on perfection (*Conference* 11) and on perfect chastity (*Conference* 12). This context shapes the point of entry. Germanus opens with a challenge to Chaeremon: that the "labor's reward"—perfect charity—comes from the "laborer's toil."[104] Chaeremon turns Germanus's language against him, noting that farmers for all their toil are deeply dependent on God's gift of good weather, that "the laborer's toil can accomplish nothing without the help of God."[105] This agricultural analogy hints at Cassian's basic view that virtue comes from a subtle and inextricable mix of human effort and God's grace: "These things are mixed together and fused so indistinguishably that which is dependent on which is a great question as far as many people are concerned— that is, whether God has mercy on us because we manifest the beginning of a good will, or we acquire the beginnings of a good will because God is merciful."[106]

Cassian, in the guise of Abba Chaeremon, admits that "these two things— that is, the grace of God and free will—certainly seem mutually opposed to one another" but insists that the integrity of both be maintained.[107] He lines up biblical text after biblical text, some illustrating good will, some, the grace of God. For instance, he notes that Jesus calls "us in the gospel to hasten to him by our free will: 'Come to me, all you who labor and are burdened, and I will give you rest' " and yet "the same Lord testifies to its weakness when he says, 'No one can come to me unless the Father who sent me draws him.' "[108] Cassian knows that at times, grace overwhelms the unwilling, as in the case of Saint Paul, the ex-persecutor, and Saint Matthew, the ex–tax collector. Like Augustine, Cassian insists that grace anticipates our good deeds[109]; but unlike

Augustine, he insists that human will can in some instances initiate the good: "When [God's] kindness sees shining in us the slightest glimmer of good will, which he himself has in fact sparked from the hard flint of our heart, he fosters it, stirs it up, and strengthens it with his inspiration, 'desiring all to be saved and to come to the knowledge of the truth" (1 Tim. 2:4).' "[110]

Cassian does not underestimate "the hard flint" of the human heart, but insists that even that hardness contains "glimmers." Here and there, one senses subtle jabs at other Augustinian positions: "We must be on the watch lest we attribute all the good works of holy persons to the Lord in such a way that we ascribe nothing but what is bad and perverse to human nature."[111] In the end, Cassian insists on grace, but a grace that does not eradicate human freedom: "The God of the universe must be believed to work all things in all, so that he stirs up, protects, and strengthens, but not so that he removes the freedom of will that he himself once granted."[112]

Since the seventeenth century, this conference has been seen as the open-ing salvo of the so-called Semi-Pelagian Controversy.[113] This term is a serious misnomer. There is nothing Pelagian or even semi-Pelagian about Cassian. He insists on the complete necessity and centrality of grace. *Conference* 13 can even be read as Cassian's answer not to Augustine, but to Pelagius. But was it a backhanded attack on Augustine? One of Cassian's contemporaries there in Marseilles, Prosper, thought it was. He wrote letters to Augustine complaining that holy men, even bishops, challenged his views.[114] Augustine responded with two of his most uncompromising treatises, the *Gift of Perseverance* and the *Predestination of the Saints*, but even he recognized his opponents were "brothers," not heretics.[115] Some have seen Cassian's tactic here—that is, put-ting his own position into the mouth of one of the desert fathers—as disin-genuous. But that is to misunderstand Cassian's project and underestimate his genuine debt to Eastern views. Nonetheless Cassian does seem aware of Augustinian positions, and if at times he disagrees, he does so politely and without polemic. Over the next few years, Prosper tried to stir things up, writ-ing a treatise against "the Conferencer" and going to Rome to win papal sup-port. But by the early 430s, the main body of Gallic monks and bishops stood closer to Cassian, for all their genuine respect for Augustine, and Prosper had to back off from his campaign. Over the next century, the Gallic church sought to reconcile its dual theological inheritance from Cassian and Augustine. In the long run, Cassian's reputation would suffer a serious setback precisely because of this conference. The Council of Orange in 529 sided with Augustine against Cassian, insisting that the fallen human will is incapable of choosing the good without prior grace.

Conference 14

Conference 14, led by Abba Nesteros, has often been treated as a treatise on biblical interpretation. Cassian, following Origen, does explore how biblical texts can possess four levels of meaning. The first is the literal historical mean-ing, "the knowledge of past and visible things." Beyond this are three possible "spiritual" meanings: the allegorical, that is, prefigurations (usually in the Old Testament) of Christ and the church; the anagogical, that is, foreshadowings of the "future and invisible" mysteries of heaven; and the tropological, that is, deeper moral meanings.[116] Not every text has all four levels, but some do, and the Bible as a whole does. This fourfold scheme would influence later medieval exegesis. But Cassian's real concern is much broader: the monastic quest for insight into God's Word, for what he calls *spiritalis scientia*, "spiritual knowledge." This is quite different from book-learning or professional exegetical expertise; it is contemplative insight into "the secrets of invisible mysteries." It is possible only by God's grace—though it builds on and presumes a life of disciplined virtue and regular prayer.[117] The obscurity of the Bible is the fault not of the text, but of our vice-blinded hearts; however, "as our mind is increasingly renewed by this study, the face of Scripture will also begin to be renewed, and the beauty of a more sacred understanding will somehow grow with the person who is making progress."[118]

Conference 19

Conference 19 explores the two classic forms of monasticism: the anchoritic and cenobitic. Cassian attributes it to Abba John of Diolcos, a one-time anchorite who left his solitude to lead a cenobitic monastery in the Delta. John contrasts the end of the two monastic ways: "The end of the cenobite is to put to death and to crucify all his desires and . . . to have no thought for the next day," while "the perfection of the hermit is to have a mind bare of all earthly things and, as much as human frailty permits, to unite it thus with Christ."[119] What unites them is the quest for perfection. Abba John speaks romantically of bygone days when monks enjoyed buoyant freedom in the "expansive vastness of the desert" and "were frequently seized by heavenly ecstasies"; but the explosive popularity of monasticism "cramped" desert freedom and "chilled" ecstatic fires.[120] Despite the nostalgia, he does note the hazard of desert life: the singleminded pursuit of solitude often created men who "become so savage due to the unbroken silence of the desert" and become despisers of all human society.[121] He admitted that life in community freed him from the besetting sin of the anchorite, spiritual pride, and that while he himself suffered "some loss of purity of heart," he was "compensated by the gospel precept alone": namely, a life of humble obedience that modeled itself on Jesus's submission to the Father.[122]

The theme of the two monastic lifestyles is a thread that runs through Cassian's whole project. He dedicates the *Institutes* to issues of cenobitic life, while the first ten *Conferences* use anchorites as spokesmen and seem geared to anchoritic spirituality. This tidy division should not be overdrawn—as though the two works were intended for different audiences. That is clearly not the case. Cassian, in dedicating the second set of *Conferences*, speaks of Honoratus, a superior of cenobites, who was "so on fire with the praise of those sublime men from whom we received the *first* institutes of the *anchoritic* life" and "desires his *community* . . . to be instructed as well in the precepts of these fathers."[123] In other words, a cenobitic superior was enthusiastic about the anchoritic spirituality of the first *Conferences* and saw them as germane to the monks he directed. Cassian, in the preface to the third set of *Conferences*, notes their dual audience: "These conferences of the greatest fathers were so carefully composed and are so balanced in all respects that they are appropriate to both professions."[124] Recently it has been argued that "cenobite" and "anchorite" are better read allegorically—which is, of course, how Cassian and his contemporaries read the Bible and much else. This would mean that the *Institutes* and the cenobitic life they describe symbolize the externals of monastic living, while the *Conferences* and the anchoritic life they describe symbolize the interior journey of monastic living. Both works speak to both types of monks, since all monks must deal with both external patterns and interior states.[125]

But was one lifestyle superior to the other? It is true that the anchoritic was Cassian's first love and his stated ideal. He treasured his years at Scetis, and in the preface to the first set of *Conferences*, he insists that "the solitary life is greater and more sublime than that of the cenobia."[126] But the future of monasticism in the Latin West lay with the cenobitic, as Cassian probably began to realize. R. A. Markus has argued that as Cassian composed the *Conferences* his views gradually shifted, such that the superiority of the anchoritic life is "subtly but radically undermined" and by the final set "seems to vanish altogether."[127] While some shift is detectable, Cassian was deeply tolerant of variety and appreciated that roads to God varied. In a digression in *Conference* 14, he notes that there are "many professions and paths" and then sets out three lifestyles: the anchoritic, the cenobitic, and the active. The model anchorite was Antony, who like Elijah and Elisha in biblical times dedicated himself to pursuing purity of heart in the remote desert. The model cenobite was a certain John of Thmuis, whose community "shone forth with apostolic signs"—mirroring the extraordinary community of love described in the Acts of the Apostles.[128] The model of the active life was Macarius, guestmaster of Alexandria, who, like Abraham and Lot in biblical times, exercised a profound holiness in the way he welcomed strangers. Cassian then pointedly adds that the active life offers noble paths to holiness: "Some choose the care of the sick, others carry out the intercession that is owed to the downtrodden and the oppressed, some are intent upon teaching, and others give alms to the poor, and among great and noble men they have flourished by reason of their love and their goodness." For Cassian, it is not a matter of inherent superiority of this or that life; rather, "the journey to God follows many routes. So let each person take to the end and with no turning back the way he first chose so that he may be perfect, no matter what his profession may be."[129]

Columba Stewart, in his seminal study *Cassian the Monk*, has described the *Conferences* as "maps":

> Speaking through each abba, Cassian shuttles between present experience and future ideal, tracing and retracing the paths that connect them. Indeed the *Conferences* are perhaps best seen as maps of the

spiritual life. . . . They are not a scientific atlas, but a collection of pilgrim's maps: everything on them is oriented to a destination. In these maps one sees Cassian, that great traveler, charting the various ways to travel across the temporal and spiritual vastness between earth and heaven.[130]

Stewart also notes that Cassian is a man of many guises:

A young monk dazzled by monastic Egypt and an old man relating youthful experiences; an advisor of church leaders in Gaul and an apologist scarred by battle; a monastic founder concerned that new monasteries learn the right kind of monasticism; a spiritual writer integrating earlier traditions into a theology of the monastic life. These authorial personae coexist in the texts, generating an array of purposes and meaning. [131]

Sorting out Cassian's memories of Egypt from local Gallic politics or disentangling inherited traditions of Egyptian spirituality from Cassian's own spiritual agenda is nearly impossible. One cannot take Cassian's pose as neutral expert at face value. Cassian was not neutral. He transformed the legacy he received and in the process instituted—in a new language—a monasticism made for the harsher climate of the West. Cassian ended up sowing tough and hardy seeds that would endure, even prosper, in the harsh winter of barbarian invasion and Roman collapse. He exerted a profound influence first on fifth-century Gallic monasticism, then on Benedict and his *Rule*, and finally, through Benedict, on the whole medieval West. Cassian earned equal respect in the Greek East. He is the only Latin-speaking author whose sayings appear in the *Apophthegmata Patrum*, a singular honor. Whereas the West would begrudge him the title of "saint" and a place in its liturgical calendar, the Greek East felt no such inhibition.

NOTES

1. Benedict, *Regula* 73.5; cf. 42.3–5. See Adalbert de Vogüé, "Les mentions des oeuvres de Cassien chez saint Benoit et ses contemporains," *Studia Monastica* 20 (1978): 275–285. See the bibliography for chapter 12 for the text and translations of Cassian's *Institutes* and *Conferences*.

2. Cassian's elusiveness is noted in the major studies; e.g., Columba Stewart, *Cassian the Monk* (New York: Oxford University Press, 1998), 3, and Owen Chadwick, *John Cassian* (Cambridge: Cambridge University Press, 1950), 6. See the bibliography for chapter 12 for studies of Cassian.

3. Gennadius, *De viris illustribus* 62 (TU 14.1:82; NPNF 23:395); Palladius, *Dialogus de vita Chrysostomi* 3 (SC 341:76–68; ACW 45:27); Innocent, *Ep.* 7, quoted in Sozomen, *HE* 8.26 (PG 67:1585; NPNF 2.2:416).

4. Cassian, *De institutis* 5.35 (SC 109:246; ACW 58:137), *Collationes* 14.9.4 (SC 54: 193; ACW 57:512).

5. See, for example, K. Suso Frank, "John Cassian on John Cassian," *Studia Patristica* 30 (1997): 422–423, who argues that it is unlikely Cassian's sister, who lived in Marseilles with him, would have made the long voyage from Scythia.

6. Cassian, *Collationes* 24.1.3 (SC 64:172; trans. Ramsey, ACW 57:825).

7. Cassian, *Collationes* 14.12.1 (SC 54:199; ACW 57:516–517).

8. Cassiodorus, *Institutiones divinarum litterarum*, praef. (PL 70:1108), describes Cassian as *eloquentissimus*.

9. While Cassian knew both Old Latin translations of the Bible as well as Jerome's Vulgate, he quotes the Septuagint and Greek New Testament and sometimes ventures his own translations. See Stewart, *Cassian the Monk*, 35.

10. Cassian, *De institutis* 4.30.2–5 (SC 109:164–168; ACW 57:94–96); *Collationes* 20.1.1–2.3 (SC 64:57–59; ACW 58:693–695).

11. Cassian, *Collationes* 17.30.1–3 (SC 54:282–283; ACW 57:612–613).

12. Cassian, *Collationes* 15.3.1–5 (SC 54:212–215; ACW 57:539–540).

13. Moses appears as the inaugural spokesman in *Collationes* 1–2. See Stewart, "Appendix: Cassian on Monastic Egypt," in *Cassian the Monk*, 133–140, for a study of the links between the figures Cassian mentions and their appearances in other desert literature.

14. Cassian, *Collationes* 3.1.1, 10.2.3 (SC 42:139, 54:76; ACW 57:119, 372).

15. Cassian, *Collationes*, pref. 1.7 (SC 42:76; trans. Ramsey, ACW 57:30–31).

16. Cassian, *De institutis* 4.1 ff. (SC 109:122 ff.; ACW 58:79 ff.). See Chadwick, *John Cassian*, 55–60, for a summary of the differences.

17. *Collationes* 6 is given by Theodore of Kellia, perhaps the same Abba Theodore mentioned in *De institutis* 5.33–35.

18. See Salvatore Marsili, *Giovanni Cassiano ed Evagrio Pontico*, Studia Anselmiana 5 (Rome: Editrice Anselmiana, 1936), which, though dated, proves the essential connection.

19. Cassian, *De incarnatione* 7.31 (CSEL 17:389–390; trans. NPNF 2.11:620–621—modified).

20. See Stewart, *Cassian the Monk*, 22–24; Victor Codina, *El aspecto cristológico en la espiritualidad de Juan Casiano*, Orientalia Christiana Analecta 175 (Rome: 1966).

21. Cassian, *De institutis*, prol. 2 (SC 109:23; trans. Ramsey, ACW 58:11).

22. Cassian, *De institutis*, prol. 9 (SC 109:30–32; trans. Ramsey, ACW 58:14).

23. Cassian, *De institutis*, prol. 7 (SC 109:28; trans. my own).

24. Cassian, *De institutis* 2.2.2 (SC 109:60; trans. Ramsey, ACW 58:37).

25. Cassian, *De institutis* 2.9.3 (SC 109:74; trans. Ramsey, ACW 58:42–43).

26. Cassian, *De institutis* 1.3 and 4 (SC 109:42–44; trans. Ramsey, ACW 58:23–24).

27. Cassian, *De institutis* 3.2 (SC 109:92; trans. Ramsey, ACW 58:59).

28. Cassian, *De institutis* 4.34 (SC 109:172; trans. Ramsey, ACW 58:97).

29. Cassian, *De institutis* 4.35 (SC 109:174; trans. Ramsey, ACW 58:97–98).

30. On this, see Stewart, *Cassian the Monk*, 40.

31. Cassian, *De institutis* 5.1 (SC 109:190; trans. Ramsey, ACW 58:117).

32. Cassian, *De institutis* 5.14.3 (SC 109:212; trans. Ramsey, ACW 58:125).

33. Cassian, *De institutis* 5.23.1–2 (SC 109:230–232: ACW 58:131–132); cf. *Collationes* 5.11.1–2 (SC 42:199–200; ACW 57:190).

34. Cassian, *De institutis* 5.5.1, 9.1 (SC 109:196, 202; trans. Ramsey, ACW 58:119, 121).

35. Cassian, *De institutis* 5.14.4 (SC 109:214; trans. Ramsey, ACW 58:125).

36. Cassian, *De institutis* 5.24–25 (SC 109:232–234; trans. Ramsey, ACW 58:132–133).

37. Cassian, *De institutis* 5.19.1 (SC 109:222; trans. Ramsey, ACW 58:129).

38. Cassian, *De institutis* 5.17.2 (SC 109:218; trans. Ramsey, ACW 58:127).

39. Cassian, *De institutis* 5.12.1–19.1 (SC 109:208–222; trans. Ramsey, ACW 58: 123–129); cf. *Collationes* 1.5.3 (SC 42:82; ACW 57:44).

40. Cassian, *Collationes* 18, sees monasticism as apostolic living and sketches a sort of history of monasticism from the primitive church to his own day. That opinion appears in passing in *De institutis* 2.5.3–4 (SC 109:66–68; ACW 58:40). See Chadwick, *John Cassian*, 51–52.

41. Cassian, *De institutis* 5.4.1–3 (SC 109:194–196; trans. Ramsey, ACW 58: 118–119).

42. Stewart, *Cassian the Monk*, 30.

43. Stewart, "The Monastic Journey according to John Cassian," *Word and Spirit* 19 (1993): 31.

44. Cassian, *Collationes*, Pref. 1.5 (SC 42:75; trans. Ramsey, ACW 57:30).

45. Cassian, *Collationes*, Pref. 1.4 (SC 42:75; trans. Ramsey, ACW 57:30).

46. Cassian, *Collationes*, Pref. 2.2 (SC 54:99; trans. Ramsey, ACW 57:400).

47. Cassian himself admits this: *Collationes*, Pref. 2.2 (SC 54:99; ACW 58:399–400).

48. Cassian, *Collationes* 24.1.1 (SC 64:171; trans. Ramsey, ACW 57:825). Of course, Cassian has ignored the fact that he often has a single *abba* lead more than one conference—so that there are really only fifteen abbas for twenty-four conferences.

49. Cassian, *Collationes*, Pref. 1.3 (SC 42:75; trans. my own).

50. On Abba Moses, see Stewart, *Cassian the Monk*, 138–140; Ramsey, Cassian's most recent translator, seems unaware of this and presumes the Moses of *Conferences* 1 and 2 is different from Moses the robber mentioned in *Collationes* 3.5.2 (the figure mentioned in the *Apophthegmata* and *Lausiac History*).

51. Cassian, *Collationes* 1.2.1 (SC 42:79; trans. Ramsey, ACW 57:41–42).

52. Cassian, *Collationes* 1.2.2, 1.4.2 (SC 42:79–81; ACW 57:42, 43)

53. Cassian, *Collationes* 1.4.1–4, 1.5.2 (SC 42:80–82; ACW 57:42–44). Cassian's bilingualism comes through here, for he gives both words not only in Latin, but also in Greek. Note that Cassian does not distinguish between the "kingdom of Heaven" and the "kingdom of God" as Evagrius does; cf. *Praktikos* 1–2.

54. See the recent studies in Harriet A. Luckman and Linda Kulzer, eds., *Purity of Heart in Early Ascetic and Monastic Literature: Essays in Honor of Juana Raasch, O.S.B.* (Collegeville, Minn.: Liturgical Press, 1999).

55. Cassian, *Collationes* 1.10.4 (SC 42:89; ACW 57:49). Cassian cites this text only two other times: *De institutis* 8.20 (SC 109:362; ACW 58:202); *Collationes* 14.9.1 (SC 54:192; ACW 57:511). As Stewart, *Cassian the Monk*, 43, notes: "Cassian's infrequent quotation of this particular text reminds us that his understanding of purity of heart does not depend on one biblical text alone but is rooted in a rich biblical and post-biblical tradition."

56. Cassian, *Collationes* 1.10.4 (SC 42:89; trans. Ramsey, ACW 57:49).

57. Cassian, *Collationes* 1.22.2 (SC 42:106–107; trans. my own).

58. Cassian, *Collationes* 1.6.2 (SC 42:83; ACW 57:45).

59. Cassian, *Collationes* 2.5.1–4 and 2.7.1–2 (SC 42:116–117, 118–119; ACW 57: 87–90).

60. Cassian, *Collationes* 1.19.1 (SC 42:99–100; ACW 57:57).

61. Cassian, *Collationes* 1.20.1 (SC 42:101–102; ACW 57:59).

62. Cf. Cassian, *Collationes* 3.7.5 and 5.4.3 (SC 42:148, 191; ACW 57:126, 184).

63. Cassian, *Collationes* 1.7.3 (SC 42:85; trans. Ramsey, ACW 57:46).

64. Cassian, *Collationes* 1.7.2 (SC 42:85; trans. Ramsey, ACW 57:46).

65. Cassian, *Collationes* 1.22.2 (SC 42:107; trans. Ramsey, ACW 57:63).

66. See Brown, *The Body and Society*, 420–422; Stewart, *Cassian the Monk*, 62–84; David Brakke, "The Problematization of Nocturnal Emissions in Early Christian Syria, Egypt, and Gaul," *Journal of Early Christian Studies* 3 (1995): 419–460.

67. Cassian, *Collationes* 1.5.4 (SC 42:83; trans. Ramsey, ACW 57:44).

68. Cassian, *Collationes* 1.18.1 (SC 42:99; trans. Ramsey, ACW 57:57).

69. *Stabilitas*: e.g., "stability of mind" (*Collationes* 7.6.3, 19.6.5); "stability of heart" (*Collationes* 10.10.8); "stable" (*Collationes* 7.23.1, 9.2.1). *Immobilitas*, or, more often, its adjectival and adverbial forms: *Collationes* 1.8.1, 6.14.2, 18.13.1, 18.16.1. *Integras*: e.g., "integrity of mind" (*De intitutis* 4.24.2, 5.9, 5.10, 6.4.1, *Collationes* 12.2.5, 21.23.2); "integrity of heart" (*De institutis* 6.19, *Collationes* 4.15.2, 11.14, 19.16.3). *Tranquillitas* e.g., "tranquility of mind" (*Collationes* 1.7.4, 9.2.1, 9.6.5, 18.16.4); "tranquility of heart" (*Collationes* 11.9.2, 12.11.3, 15.10.3, 16.22.3, 19.6.5). Other key terms are *firmitas* ("firmness," "durability") and *constantia* ("constancy"). See Stewart, *Cassian the Monk*, 45–47, 168–169.

70. Cassian, *Collationes* 19.14.7 (SC 64:53; trans. my own).

71. Cassian, *Collationes* 18.16.4 (SC 64:32; trans. Ramsey, ACW 57:651).

72. Evagrius himself had connected the two. See Driscoll, "*Apatheia* and Purity of Heart in Evagrius Ponticus," in Luckman and Kulzer, *Purity of Heart*, 141–159.

73. This has been the standard interpretation for a number of years. See Marsili, *Giovanni Cassiano*, 115; Guillaumont, SC 170:103; Stewart, "Monastic Journey," 33–34. This has been recently challenged by Mark Sheridan, "The Controversy over ΑΠΑΘΕΙΑ: Cassian's Sources and His Use of Them," *Studia Monastica* 40 (1998): 287–310.

74. Jerome, *Ep.* 133.3 (CSEL 56:246; trans. my own).

75. See Pinafius's "ladder" of virtues in *De institutis* 4.43 (SC 109:184; ACW 58:102).

76. The Pauline verse appears repeatedly in these two conferences: see Cassian, *Collationes* 9.3.4, 9.6.5, 9.7.3, 10.14.2 (SC 54:42, 47, 48, 95; ACW 57:331, 334, 335, 386).

77. Cassian, *De institutis* 2.1.1 (SC 109:58; trans. Ramsey, ACW 58:37).

78. Cassian, *Collationes*, Pref. 1.5 (SC 54:75; trans. Ramsey, ACW 57:30).

79. Cassian, *Collationes* 9.1 (SC 54:40; trans. Ramsey, ACW 57:329).

80. Cassian, *Collationes* 9.2.1 (SC 54:40; trans. Ramsey, ACW 57:329).

81. Cassian, *Collationes* 10.7.3 (SC 54:82; trans. Ramsey, ACW 57:376).

82. Cassian, *Collationes* 9.2.1–2 (SC 54:40–41; trans. Ramsey, ACW 57:329).

83. Cassian, *Collationes* 9.3.3 (SC 54:42; trans. Ramsey, ACW 57:330–331).

84. Cassian, *Collationes* 9.9.1–17.3 (SC 54:49–55; ACW 57:336–340); see Stewart, *Cassian the Monk*, 107–109.

85. Cassian, *Collationes* 10.13.1–2 (SC 54:94; trans. Luibheid, CWS, 138–139).

86. Cassian, *Collationes* 10.10.2 (SC 54:85; trans. my own).

87. Cassian, *Collationes* 10.10.2 (SC 54:85; trans. Ramsey, ACW 57:379).

88. Cassian, *Collationes* 10.10.2–14 (SC 54:85–90; trans. Luibhéid, CWS, 132–136). Luibhéid's translation here better captures the rhetorical rhythm and energy of the original. I have altered it slightly, restoring the precise Evagrian terminology for the eight vices (e.g., "vainglory" for Luibhéid's "vanity").

89. Stewart, "Monastic Journey," 36.

90. Cassian, *Collationes* 9.25.1 (SC 54:61; trans. Stewart, *Cassian the Monk*, 114).

91. Cassian, *Collationes* 10.11.6 (SC 54:93; my own trans).

92. On the language of ecstasy, Cassian, *De institutis* 2.10.1, 3.3.4; *Collationes*

3.7.3; 4.5; 6.10.2; 9.14–15; 9.25; 10.10.12; 10.11.6; 12.12.6; 19.4.1; 19.5.1. See Stewart, *Cassian the Monk*, 116–122.

93. Cassian, *Collationes* 9.25.1 (SC 54:62; ACW 57:346).

94. Cassian, *Collationes* 12.12.6 (SC 54:142; trans. Ramsey, ACW 57:451); cf. *Collationes* 10.10.12 (SC 54:89; ACW 57:382).

95. Cassian, *Collationes* 6.10.2 (SC 42:229; ACW 57:225); cf. 3.7.3 (SC 42:147; ACW 57:125); 4.5 (SC 42:170; ACW 57:157); 19.4.1 (SC 64:41; ACW 57:671).

96. Cassian, *Collationes* 12.12.6 (SC 54:142; ACW 57:451).

97. Cassian, *Collationes* 6.10.2 (SC 42:229; trans. Ramsey, ACW 57:224–225).

98. Cassian, *Collationes* 9.25.1 (SC 54:62; trans. Ramsey, ACW 57:346).

99. Cassian, *Collationes* 12.12.2; 10.11.6; 6.10.2; 9.25.1 (SC 54:140, 54:93, 42:229, 54:62; trans. Ramsey, ACW 57:450, 385, 225, 345).

100. Cassian, *Collationes* 9.15.2 (SC 54:52; trans. Ramsey, ACW 57:339).

101. Stewart, *Cassian the Monk*, 115; see also his discussion on pp. 119–122.

102. Cassian, *Collationes* 10.6 (SC 54:80; trans. Ramsey, ACW 57:375).

103. Cassian, *Collationes* 10.7.2 (SC 54:81; trans. Ramsey, ACW 57:375–376).

104. Cassian, *Collationes* 13.2 (SC 54:148–149; trans. Ramsey, ACW 57:467).

105. Cassian, *Collationes* 13.3.1 (SC 54:149; trans. Ramsey, ACW 57:467).

106. Cassian, *Collationes* 13.11.1 (SC 54:162; trans. Ramsey, ACW 57:476).

107. Cassian, *Collationes* 13.11.4 (SC 54:163; trans. Ramsey, ACW 57:477–478).

108. Cassian, *Collationes* 13.10.3 (SC 54:161; trans. Ramsey, ACW 57:476).

109. Cassian, *Collationes* 13.12.10 (SC 54:167; trans. Ramsey, ACW 57:480).

110. Cassian, *Collationes* 13.7.1 (SC 54:155–156; trans. Ramsey, ACW 57:472).

111. Cassian, *Collationes* 13.12.5 (SC 54:165–166; trans. Ramsey, ACW 57:479).

112. Cassian, *Collationes* 13.18.4–5 (SC 54:181; trans. Ramsey, ACW 57:490).

113. For studies of the Semi-Pelagian Controversy, see the bibliography for chapter 12.

114. Prosper of Aquitaine, in the corpus of Augustine's *Letters* as *Ep.* 225.2 (PL 33:1002–1003; FC 32:120–121).

115. Augustine, *De praedestinatione sanctorum* 2 (PL 44:959; FC 86:219).

116. Cassian, *Collationes* 14.8.1–7 (SC 52:189–192; ACW 57:509–511).

117. Cassian, *Collationes* 14.1.2–2.1 (SC 54:184; ACW 57:505). Note that he cites Evagrius's terminology—even using the Greek words—of πρακτική ("practical knowledge which reaches its fulfillment in correction of behavior and in cleansing form vice") and θεωρητική ("which consists in the contemplation of divine things and in the understanding of most sacred meanings"). See Cassian's discussion of the mystical exegetical abilities of Abba Theodore in *De institutis* 5.33–34 (SC 109:242–244; ACW 58:136–137).

118. Cassian, *Collationes* 14.11.1 (SC 54:197; trans. Ramsey, ACW 57:515).

119. Cassian, *Collationes* 19.8.3–4 (SC 64:46; trans. Ramsey, ACW 57:675).

120. Cassian, *Collationes* 19.5.1–2 (SC 64:42; trans. Ramsey, ACW 57:672).

121. Cassian, *Collationes* 19.10.1 (SC 64:47–48; trans. Ramsey, ACW 57:676).

122. Cassian, *Collationes* 19.6.6 (SC 64:44–45; trans. Ramsey, ACW 674).

123. Cassian, *Collationes*, pref. 2.2 (SC 54:98; trans. Ramsey, ACW 57:399).

124. Cassian, *Collationes*, pref. 3.2 (SC 64:8–9; trans. Ramsey, ACW 57:625).

125. Stewart, *Cassian the Monk*, 30–31.

126. Cassian, *Collationes*, pref. 1.4 (SC 42:75; trans. Ramsey, ACW 57:29–30).

127. Markus, *End of Ancient Christianity*, 182.

128. It is not clear whether this Abba John of Thmuis is the same as John of Diolcos, the spokesman of *Conference* 19.

129. Cassian, *Collationes* 14.6 (SC 54:187; trans. Luibheid, CWS, 158).
130. Stewart, *Cassian the Monk*, 40–41.
131. Stewart, *Cassian the Monk*, 27.

BIBLIOGRAPHY

The *Institutes* (*De institutis cenobiorum*): Text and Translations

For an edition of the Latin text, together with French translation, see Jean-Claude Guy, ed., *Jean Cassien: institutions cénobitiques*, SC 109 (Paris: Éditions du Cerf, 1965). An English translation has been done recently by Boniface Ramsey, *John Cassian: The Institutes*, ACW 58 (New York: Paulist Press, 2000). A nineteenth-century translation by Edgar Gibson is found in the NPNF, 2nd ser., vol. 11:199–290.

The *Conferences* (*Collationes*): Text and Translations

For an edition of the Latin text, together with a French translation, see E. Pichery, *Jean Cassien: Conférences*, SC 42, 54, 64 (Paris: Éditions du Cerf, 1955, 1958, 1959). A complete English translation has been done by Boniface Ramsey, *John Cassian: The Conferences*, ACW 57 (New York: Paulist Press, 1997). Selections can be found in Colm Luibhéid, *John Cassian: The Conferences*, CWS (New York: Paulist Press, 1985), which translates *Conferences* 1–3, 9–11, 14–15, and 18. See also Gibson's translation in the NPNF, 2nd ser. 11:291–545.

John Cassian: Biography and Theology

The best place to start is the masterful study of Columba Stewart, *Cassian the Monk* (New York: Oxford University Press, 1998). An older and still valuable study is that of Owen Chadwick, *John Cassian*, 2nd ed. (Cambridge: Cambridge University Press, 1968). More specialized studies include:

Frank, K. Suso. "John Cassian on John Cassian." *Studia Patristica* 30 (1997): 418–433.
Kardong, Terrence. "Aiming at the Mark: Cassian's Metaphor for the Monastic
    Quest." *Cistercian Studies Quarterly* 22 (1987): 213–220.
_____. "John Cassian's Evaluation of Monastic Practices." *American Benedictine Review* 43 (1992): 82–105.
Levko, John J. *Cassian's Prayer for the Twenty-First Century*. Scranton: University of
    Scranton Press, 2000.
Leyser, Conrad. *Authority and Asceticism from Augustine to Gregory the Great*, 33–61.
    Oxford Historical Monographs. New York: Oxford University Press, 2001.
Rousseau, Philip. *Ascetics, Authority, and the Church in the Age of Jerome and Cassian*,
    167–234. New York: Oxford University Press, 1978.
Sheridan, Mark. "The Controversy over ΑΠΑΘΕΙΑ: Cassian's Sources and His Use of
    Them." *Studia Monastica* 40 (1998): 287–310.
_____. "Models and Images of Spiritual Progress in the Works of John Cassian." In
    Spiritual Progress: Studies in the Spirituality of Late Antiquity and Early Monasticism, ed. Jeremy Driscoll and Mark Sheridan, 101–126. Rome: Pontificio Ateneo
    S. Anselmo, 1994.
Stewart, Columba. "John Cassian on Unceasing Prayer." *Monastic Studies* 15 (1984):
    159–177.
_____. "The Monastic Journey According to John Cassian." *Word and Spirit* 19 (1993):

29–40. Reprinted in *Forms of Devotion: Conversion, Worship, Spirituality, and Asceticism*, ed. Everett Ferguson, 311–322. New York: Garland, 1999.

Vogüé, Adalbert de. "Les mentions des oeuvres de Cassien chez saint Benoit et ses contemporains." *Studia Monastica* 20 (1978): 275–285.

————. "Les sources de quatre premiers livres des *Institutions* de Jean Cassien: Introduction aux recherches sur les anciennes régles monastiques latines." *Studia Monastica* 27 (1985): 241–311.

————. "Understanding Cassian: A Survey of the *Conferences*." *Cistercian Studies Quarterly* 19 (1984): 101–121.

The Semi-Pelagian Controversy

For a brief overview, see Conrad Leyser, "Semi-Pelagianism," in *Augustine through the Ages: An Encyclopedia*, ed. Allan D. Fitzgerald (Grand Rapids, Mich.: Wm. B. Eerdmans, 1999), 761–766. For a detailed study, see Rebecca Harden Weaver, *Divine Grace and Human Agency: A Study of the Semi-Pelagian Controversy*, Patristic Monograph Series 15 (Macon, Ga.: Mercer University Press, 1996). See also:

MacQueen, D. J. "John Cassian on Grace and Free Will with Particular Reference to *Institutio* XIII and *Collatio* XII." *Recherches de théologie ancienne et médiévale* 44 (1977): 5–28.

Markus, R. A. *The End of Ancient Christianity*. Cambridge: Cambridge University Press, 1990.

————. "The Legacy of Pelagius: Orthodoxy, Heresy, and Conciliation." In *The Making of Orthodoxy: Essays in Honour of Henry Chadwick*, ed. Rowan Williams, 214–234. Cambridge: Cambridge University Press, 1989.

Smith, Thomas A. *"De Gratia": Faustus of Riez's Treatise on Grace and Its Place in the History of Theology*. Notre Dame: University of Notre Dame Press, 1990.

APPENDIX 12.1

Sulpicius Severus, *Life of Martins of Tours*

Sulpicius Severus's *Life of Martin* (*Vita Martini*) is one of the earliest works of Latin hagiography, written in 397. The account is unusual in several ways. First, it was written before Martin had died. Second, Martin combines the roles of monk and bishop. The combination hardly seems unusual to us, but it was at this time. Sulpicius portrays him as a miracle worker whose miracles served to dismantle local paganism. Here are a few excerpts.

SHARING A CLOAK WITH CHRIST

[Martin] was in the army for about three years before his baptism but he remained free from the vices in which men of this kind usually become entangled. . . . Although he had not yet been born again in Christ, in performing good works he behaved like a candidate for baptism: he supported those in trouble, he brought help to the wretched, he fed the poor, he clothed the naked and kept nothing of his military salary for himself apart from what he needed for food each day. . . . One day, then, in the middle of a winter more bitterly cold than usual . . . , when Martin had nothing with him apart from his weapons and a simple military cloak, he came across a naked beggar at the gate of the city of Amiens. The man begged the people who were passing to have pity on him but they all walked past him. Then Martin, who was filled with God's grace, understood that this man had been reserved for him, since the others were not showing him any mercy. But what was he to do? He had nothing apart from the cloak he was wearing. . . . So he seized the sword which he wore at his side, divided the cloak in two, gave half to the beggar and then put the remaining piece on again. . . . The following night, therefore, when Martin had fallen asleep, he saw Christ clothed in the part of his cloak which he had used to cover the beggar. He was told to look carefully at the Lord and to recognize the cloth which he had given. Then he heard Jesus saying in a clear voice to the host of angels standing all around, "Martin who is still a catechumen covered me with this cloak." (Sulpicius Severus, *Vita Martini* II.6–III.3)

MARTIN AS MONK-BISHOP

After he had succeeded to the episcopate . . . there was the same humility of heart, the same poverty of clothing. Full of authority and grace, he fulfilled the high office of bishop without abandoning his monastic commitment and virtue. For a time, therefore, he used a little cell adjoining the church; then when he could no longer bear the disturbance caused by those who flocked to see him, he built himself a cell some two miles outside the city. This place was so remote and secluded that it was equal to the solitude of the desert. For on one side it was bounded by the sheer rock of a high mountain, while on the level side, it was enclosed by a gentle bend in the river Loire. It could be approached by only one path and that a very narrow one. Martin lived in a small cell made of wood and a number of the brothers lived in a similar manner, but most of them had shelters for themselves by hollowing out the rock of the mountain which overlooked the place. There were about eighty disciples who had chosen to lead a life in accordance with their blessed master's example. (Sulpicius Severus, *Vita Martini* X.1–5)

MONASTERY AS SEMINARY

No one there possessed anything of his own, everything was shared. They were not allowed to buy or sell anything (as is the practice with most monks). No craft was practiced there, apart from that of the scribes; the young were set to this task, while the older ones spent their time in prayer. It was rare for anyone to leave his own cell except when they gathered at the place of prayer. They all received their food together after the period of fasting. . . . Most of them were dressed in camel-skin garments: they considered wearing of any softer material to be reprehensible. This is all the more remarkable since many of them were said to be noblemen who had been brought up in a very different way but had voluntarily adopted this life of humility and endurance. Later we saw several of them become bishops. For what city or church did not long to have a priest from Martin's monastery? (Sulpicius Severus, *Vita Martini* X.6–9)

For the Latin text, see J. Fontaine, *Sulpice Sévère: Vie de Saint Martin*, SC 133 (Paris: Éditions du Cerf, 1967). The translation is by Carolinne White and appears in *Early Christian Lives* (London: Penguin Books, 1998), 131–159.

APPENDIX 12.2

Eucherius of Lyons, *In Praise of the Desert*

Cassian dedicated his second set of *Conferences* to Honoratus, then superior of the monastic community at Lérins, and to Eucherius, an ascetic who lived on his family estates with his wife and family and who later became a monk of Lérins. Cassian reports that Eucherius desired to make a pilgrimage to Egypt to see it firsthand. To dissuade him and to spare him the dangers of travel, Cassian offered his *Conferences* as a substitute pilgrimage. Eucherius was eventually ordained bishop of Lyons and returned the favor by editing an epitome of Cassian's *Institutes*. He also composed two notable ascetical works of his own: *On Contempt of the World* and *In Praise of the Desert* (*De laude eremi*). In the latter, we see Eucherius's romanticism for the desert. Here are a few excerpts.

GOD'S PREFERENCE FOR THE DESERT AND ITS SILENCE

I would say that the desert deserves to be called a temple of our God without walls. Since it is clear that God dwells in silence, we must believe that he loves the solitary expanses of the desert. . . . Although God is present everywhere, and regards the whole world as his domain, we may believe that his preferred place is the solitudes of heaven and of the desert. (Eucherius of Lyons, *De laude eremi* 3)

DESERT AS WAY STATION FOR THE JOURNEY HOME

From the dwelling places in the desert, the road lies always open to our true homeland. Let those who desire "to see the good things of the Lord in the land of the living" (Ps. 27:13) take up their residence in an uninhabitable wasteland. Let those who strive to become citizens of Heaven be guests first of the desert. (Eucherius of Lyons, *De laude eremi* 16)

JOHN THE BAPTIST AND THE GOSPEL OF THE DESERT

Did not he also live in the desert who was greater than any man born of woman, he who was a voice crying in the desert? In the desert he instituted baptism, and in the desert he preached repentance. In the desert the Kingdom of Heaven was first heard of. In the desert he first commanded those mysteries to his listeners, because by going into the desert they could sooner merit them. It was highly fitting that this desert dweller, this angel sent before the face of the Lord, should open the way to the heavenly kingdom. He was both a precursor of Christ and a witness worthy to hear the Father speaking from heaven, to touch the Son as he baptized him, and to see the Holy Spirit descending. (Eucherius of Lyons, *De laude eremi* 21)

The Latin text is found in CSEL 31:178–194. The translation is by Charles Cummings; it has been revised by Jeffrey Burton Russell and appears in *The Lives of the Jura Fathers*, ed. Tim Vivian, Kim Vivian, and Jeffrey Burton Russell, CS 178 (Kalamazoo, Mich.: Cistercian Publications, 1999), 197–215.

PART V

Reflections

13

Monastic Origins: Perspectives, Discoveries, and Disputed Questions

Where did monasticism come from? John Cassian had no doubt: it came from the Apostles. In *Conference* 18, he asserts that the beginnings of Christianity and the beginnings of monasticism were one and the same. Cassian reminds his readers of the stories in Acts 4. There it says that the first Christian community in Jerusalem sprang up because of the preaching of the apostles. In this first fervor, they bound themselves together by mutual love and the love of God, and they agreed to hold all things in common. But after this, according to Cassian, once the apostles went out to evangelize the Gentiles, things began to go downhill. The apostles had to be lenient and allow private property. As the church expanded, fervor became more and more lukewarm. Still, the memory of those pure early days was kept alive by a small minority who left the towns and retired into remote locales. They avoided marriage and cut themselves off from family and from the seductive lures of this world. These renunciants, according to Cassian, "were called 'monks' or μοναζοντες because of the strictness of their individual and solitary lives." These "most ancient kind of monks" were "called cenobites from their common fellowship, and their cells and dwelling places are called *cenobia*." From these "roots" of holiness, "the flowers and fruit of the anchorites sprouted forth afterward."[1] In other words, Cassian claims that cenobites preceded anchorites. Even more striking: Antony was not the first monk, but rather monasticism's finest flower, a late bloom in the autumn of salvation history. Like most ancients, Cassian was uneasy about novelty; he, like them, believed that new was bad and old was good. And he was concerned to show that monasticism, far from being some newfangled fourth-century invention, was Christianity's oldest and most faithful remnant. Monks were living the apostolic life par excellence.

Cassian's fanciful theory brings us to this final chapter's focus: the origins of monasticism. It is a question I have sidestepped until now. It may seem odd to leave these beginnings to the very end. It certainly defies good chronology, but I believe it makes sense pedagogically. To follow current discussions among scholars, we first needed to know key figures and key texts, so as to be able to move rapidly between them, highlighting overlooked details and passing comments. Exploring origins also means exploring origins not just in Egypt, but elsewhere. So I will briefly survey monastic movements in Syria, Cappadocia, and Palestine. This will help draw out both Egypt's influence and its uniqueness, and let us see Egyptian monasticism as one thread—albeit a deeply influential thread—within the worldwide movement.

Throughout the chapter, I will map the figures and texts we have studied against a wider ascetical landscape. Scholars are aware that the classic texts have both biases and silences. These texts often downplay or ignore the numbers and the extent of alternative forms of asceticism—a host of ascetical roads-less-traveled and roads-less-publicized. In venturing into these alternative asceticisms, we step into what has been an intense focus of studies since the 1980s. One too long neglected is the place of women in the monastic movement. And then there are the varied organized groups outside what would become orthodoxy: for example, Manichees and Melitians. Finally, there are the leaders of Coptic monasticism, such as Shenoute of Atripe, whose presence and importance were ignored by the classic texts.

This chapter will be a little messy as it ranges around these diverse matters. It will be, as I say in the subtitle, an exploration of "perspectives, discoveries, and disputed questions." It is meant to be a first glimpse, suggestive, not exhaustive. It is an attempt both to wrap up unfinished business and at the same time to listen in on current discussions by scholars, who have been charting the subtle and variegated landscape that gave rise to monasticism.

Antony and the *Apotaktikoi*

Where did monasticism come from? The stock answer, still found in textbooks and encyclopedias, has been: (1) the founder of monasticism was Antony; (2) the founder of cenobitic monasticism was Pachomius; and (3) the birthplace of monasticism was Egypt.[2] Let me be blunt: these standard textbook claims are wrong. Do they hold some grain of truth? Yes. But put together, they give the impression that monasticism has well-known origins, traceable to one or two individuals and to a single region. This "big bang" theory of monastic origins simply does not stand up to critical scrutiny. It cannot even be sustained once one looks carefully at the classic texts we have studied. These claims are further undermined once one looks at the wide range of ancient Christian literature—not just Greek and Latin sources, but also texts in Syriac and Coptic—and at the full range of archeological and papyriological discoveries.

Certainly, Antony, Pachomius, and Egypt remain very important, but the origins of monasticism are a good deal messier and more ambiguous. The evidence we have is partial and fragmentary; this must be acknowledged. But partial and fragmentary as it is, it still shows that monasticism emerged and evolved in a very complex way, with lots of different local forces at work, and that the monasticism that surfaced in the early fourth century had a variety whose richness should not be underestimated.

Let us start with sources we have studied. Textbooks that describe Antony as the founder of monasticism point to Athanasius's *Life*. But as we have seen, the *Life* is deeply colored by Athanasius's wide-ranging political and theological concerns. It is naive to read it as a straightforward historical narrative. That is not to say that it has no or almost no historical value. But as James Goehring, a leading researcher on monastic origins, has argued: "To base a theory of monastic origins and development on the *Life of Antony* is . . . to base it on a literary model. The image of Antony as the father of Christian monasticism is dependent less on the historical understanding of Antony than on the literary success of the *Life of Antony*."[3] And if one looks at the full range of desert literature, one finds many Antonies. There is the demon-wrestling anti-Arian Antony of the *Life*, the wise Abba Antony of the *Apophthegmata*, the hospitable Antony of the *Lausiac History*, and the Origenist Antony of the *Letters*—to name a few.

Furthermore, not even Athanasius claimed Antony was the first monk. He portrays Antony, early in his career, selling all he has and apprenticing himself to a holy man at the edge of the village, and—Athanasius adds—this "old man" had practiced "the solitary life . . . from his youth."[4] Who was Antony's unnamed teacher? More to the point, how unique was a figure of this sort? Athanasius speaks of Antony's teacher in a matter-of-fact way, saying that ascetics of this sort were a routine part of the landscape of rural Christianity: "There were not yet many monasteries in Egypt . . . but each of those wishing to give attention to his life disciplined himself in isolation, not far from his own village."[5]

Mention of village holy men appears elsewhere. Macarius the Egyptian, according to the *Apophthegmata*, began his monastic career in the 330s following the exact same pattern: living as a celibate ascetic on the edge of a village. He only moved to the desert, to Scetis, after he had been cleared of the charge of getting a village girl pregnant.[6] Where did he get his inspiration for this lifestyle? There is no hint that Antony influenced him at an early date, either in his decision to become an edge-of-the-village ascetic or to leave for the "great desert." Their paths did cross later, after Macarius had already established a reputation for himself.[7] Similarly, in the 310s Pachomius began his career apprenticing under a local holy man, Palamon, "who had settled a little way from the village and had become a model and a father for many in his vicinity."[8] When later travelers such as Palladius and Cassian trooped around Egypt, they found ascetics not only in the desert, but up and down the Nile Valley and throughout the delta. The author of the *History of the Monks in Egypt* reports the same: he found that while some ascetics "live in desert caves [and] others in more remote places," "there is no town or village in Egypt and the Thebaid which is not surrounded by hermitages as if by walls."[9]

Was there an older and widespread tradition of edge-of-the-village ascetics? It seems possible, even likely. But when? If Athanasius's dates are trustworthy—and that is a big "if"—then Antony began his apprenticeship in the 270s, given Athanasius's claim that Antony was born in 251 and died in 356 at the age of 105. If these dates have any credibility, that would mean Antony's teacher would have embarked on his own ascetic career sometime around the mid-third century. This brings us back to the question: how unique was he? Could there have been other ascetics like him in Christian villages along the Nile already active in the third century?

In 1977, a recently discovered papyrus shed new light on these village-based ascetics (for the text, see appendix 13.1). The papyrus contains a legal petition, filed by a man named Aurelius Isidorus, from the town of Karanis, and is dated June 324 CE. Isidorus complains that a rival's cow had been damaging plantings in his fields. One day, as he was leading the wayward cow out of his fields, his rival assaulted him, beating him with a club. Isidorus adds that he would have been killed if it had not been for the intervention of "the deacon Antoninus and the monk Isaac."[10] This mundane legal document is extraordinary because it is the oldest surviving text to use the word "monk" (μοναχός). Remember that the text of Athanasius's *Life of Antony* was published some years later, around 358—even if Antony himself had been active in the late third and early fourth century (and his unnamed teacher, well before that).

Edwin Judge, in a pathbreaking study of monastic origins, has argued that this papyrus demonstrates that by 324 the monk was a "recognised figure in society" and that monasticism was a "public institution."[11] One would not put religious titles in a secular legal document if monks were not both recognized *and* respected—Isidorus, after all, would have wanted to help, not hurt, his case in court. But what kind of monk was this Isaac of Karanis? Judge believes that he is one example of a figure who appears more routinely in other fourth-century papyri, where they are called *apotaktikoi* (ἀποτακτικοί, "renouncers").[12] Judge argues these *apotaktikoi* were ascetics who "at last followed the pattern long set for virgins and widows, and set up houses of their own in town, in which the life of personal renunciation and service in the church would be practised."[13] Judge points to Jerome's famous *Letter 22 to Eustochium*. In it, Jerome says that there were three types of monks in Egypt: anchorites, cenobites, and *remnuoth*.[14] He adds that whereas anchorites live alone and cenobites live in ordered communities, these *remnuoth* live in small clusters in cities; they are quarrelsome, they snipe at the clergy, they freely visit women, and they dress in a flamboyant way. Jerome admits that they outnumber other kinds of monks and tells Eustochium to avoid them at all costs. Judge argues that Jerome's *remnuoth* are the same as the papyri's *apotaktikoi*: ascetics who "broke visibly with their ordinary domestic ties" but "retained a place in society" and "ranked as an order in the church."[15] In this they differed from Antonian desert anchorites and Pachomian cenobites. Judge also points to the numbers reported in the *History of the Monks*: there were 10,000 monks and 20,000 virgins at Oxyrhynchus.[16] According to Judge, this "apotactic movement" got lost in the ideological shuffle—either attacked by churchmen such as Jerome or largely ignored in a literature that celebrated desert virtuosi. This has, as a result, imbalanced the historical record.

Judge knew that his interpretations were bold, that the monk Isaac of Karanis was "the first landfall in a sea of speculation."[17] But his study has, for the most part, received a favorable reception. Goehring, in fact, has even pressed the interpretation a step further, reading the gap in the historical record in sharp, conspiratorial terms:

> The apotactic monk who resided in the village and participated in its social and ecclesiastical affairs was forgotten, or rather repudiated by a later Christianity that had embraced less politically active forms of asceticism. Desert hermits or "imprisoned" coenobites offered a less direct challenge to ecclesiastical and political authority and therefore flourish in the literature that survives, a literature that survives precisely because it represents that ecclesiastical and political authority. The motive behind the silence with respect to the apotactic movement is thus political and a history of monastic development must take this into account.[18]

Yet Goehring has challenged other aspects of Judge's interpretations. He is critical of Judge's reliance on Jerome's threefold division of anchorites, cenobites, and *remnuoth* (or *apotaktikoi*). He argues that if one surveys the full range of sources, one finds not a neat threefold scheme, but a "complex continuum from the fully solitary monk to the fully communal monk."[19] Goehring also notes that if one traces out the term *apotaktikoi* in the papyri and the literary sources—not just the Greek but also the Coptic—one finds subtle shifts in its meaning and application over time, and that one must distinguish whether it is used by Egyptians themselves or by non-Egyptians speaking about Egypt. The Pachomians—those communal monks par excellence—spoke of themselves as *apotaktikoi*, though only when they wrote about themselves in Coptic, not in Greek. But the issue is not simply terminology, which was often fluid, but the historical reality. And there is plenty of evidence of an apotactic movement, or whatever it should be called. As Goehring notes:

> The evidence of the apotactic movement certainly expands our understanding of ascetic practice in Egypt before the appearance of Antony and Pachomius. But it would be wrong to conclude that we are now closer to the "origins" of monasticism. The apotactic movement should not serve simply as the "missing link" between early ascetic practices within the home and the later institutionalized forms. Rather it underscores the complexity of the situation.[20]

These village-based and town-based *apotaktikoi* put Antony in a new perspective. He now appears not as founder, but as innovator. Athanasius said that earlier ascetics lived in close proximity to their villages, but that "no monk knew at all the great desert."[21] In other words, Antony's innovation was not the ascetic lifestyle, but his move to the desert. The *anachoresis*, the withdrawal, of edge-of-the-village ascetics had been more social than physical, a withdrawal from the social obligations of family and marriage and village politics. Goehring believes that Antony's physical withdrawal disrupted an older spiritual ecology between a village and its local holy man. He notes that villagers followed Antony out to his desert retreats; this "might be interpreted to mean not that they wished to emulate him but that they felt cheated by his departure. In seeking solitude in the desert away from the village, he was taking with him the power of God made available to the village through his presence. The ascetic had a function in the village, and Antony's innovative departure called this function into question."[22]

Yet how original was Antony? If Athanasius's dates can be accepted—and, I repeat, that is a big "if"—then Antony is the earliest *named* desert monk. Admittedly, Jerome claimed that a monk named Paul of Thebes had embraced the desert life even earlier than Antony. But Jerome's credibility is not good; even his fourth-century contemporaries accused him of making up the whole thing, saying that Jerome's *Life of Paul* was simply a work of fiction. Did Antony's withdrawal really set off a fashion in asceticism? We saw two other monastic pioneers make gestures similar to Antony's: Amoun, after eighteen years of living in a celibate marriage, established a cell in Nitria on the edge of the Libyan desert; and Macarius the Egyptian, after living as an ascetic on the fringe of the village, moved to the remote desert of Scetis. The sources give no hint that Antony inspired either move, and their monastic lifestyles and communities were quite different from Antony's—and from each other's. It is hard to see Antony as a progenitor of either man—however much both might have respected Antony. We also have papyri dating from the 330s that report Melitian monks living in a desert monastery. Can one reasonably trace Melitian monasticism to Antony?[23]

Or take the case of John of Lycopolis, for whom we have a number of eyewitness accounts. Although he began his monastic career much later, in the 350s, his lifestyle scarcely resembles the Antonian model—or that of Macarius or Amoun or Pachomius. Like those who embraced the desert, he withdrew to a somewhat remote and rugged site, but like the *apotaktikoi*, he remained close enough to the settled land to be an object of pilgrimage from nearby towns and villages. He was not a monastic founder, though he did have disciples, or at least attendants. Rather, he was a prophet, a living oracle. While the literature is replete with stories of monks who can read hearts—Macarius and Pachomius were both known for this—it rarely defines their careers in the way it did with John. He did not wander around the desert, as did Antony or Macarius, but was walled up in a small three-room cell, a lifestyle that would become a not uncommon pattern in sixth-century Palestinian monasticism. Is one to argue that John of Lycopolis looked on Antony as the inspiration for his monastic career? It seems hard to make such a case.

Was Antony then an innovator? To call him one seems more accurate than calling him the founder of monasticism. But do we know that he *alone* launched the innovative turn to the desert, that all later figures took their cues from him? It seems unlikely. The movement looks too widespread geographically and too varied in its styles. It might be better to speak of Antony not as an innovator, but as a symbol of an innovation. He symbolized a wide-ranging set of experiments of certain ascetics who were gradually moving their bases to the desert. This does not deny that Antony himself embarked on such a career, or that he was widely esteemed as a pioneer. But his withdrawal to the desert was indicative of a much wider trend, albeit one whose exact roots are inchoate.

Pachomius and the Melitians

What about Pachomius? Was he really the founder of cenobitic monasticism? Not even the various *Lives* written by his fourth-century disciples make this claim about him. In fact, they give evidence that undercuts it. Pachomius was clearly a charismatic leader who brought together monks—hundreds, perhaps thousands of them—into his *Koinonia*. Although he did found the monastery at Tabennesi, two of the earliest Pachomian monasteries, Šeneset and Thmoušons, were not his foundations, but had existed from "of old."[24] A third monastery in the *Koinonia*, the one at Tbewe, had been founded by Petronius, who went on to become Pachomius's very short-lived successor. Petronius had been a wealthy Christian who had turned a family estate into a monastery. In other words, however successful Pachomius was as a founder and organizer of monasteries, he was not alone in this effort. He may simply have been more successful or more charismatic than others in the region—which may have been one reason they decided to ally their monasteries with his.

It has been suggested that his originality may lie not in founding coenobitic monasticism per se, but in creating the alliance of monasteries he called the *Koinonia*.[25] However, even that suggestion has been challenged. The challenge comes from examination of Melitian monasticism. As we saw, the Egyptian church, because of the Great Persecution, was wracked by a schism that divided followers of Melitius of Lycopolis from those of Peter of Alexandria. The Council of Nicaea tried mandating a solution that met with partial success. And after the death of Alexander in 328, Athanasius and his followers began clashing, sometimes violently, with the Melitians, and the Melitians played a key role in getting Athanasius deposed by the Synod of Tyre in 335. We also saw that the Antony of Athanasius's *Life* denounces Melitians in no uncertain terms—including in his dying words.

The traditional sources give no real indication that the Melitians had monks, let alone organized monastic communities.[26] In 1924, H. Idris Bell published two archives of Melitian letters, the first dating from the 330s, the second, from the 340s.[27] This second archive is a set of seven letters addressed to a monk named Paphnutius. Most are touching requests for prayer. One writer tells Apa Paphnutius: "I always know that by your holy prayers I shall be saved from every temptation of the Devil and from every contrivance of men, and now I beg you to remember me in your holy prayers; for after God you are my salvation."[28] Another correspondent, a woman, writes complaining of a "grievous shortness of breath" and then insists, "I trust in your prayers to obtain healing, for by ascetics and devotees revelations are manifested."[29] These remind one of the language and sentiments found in the *Apophthegmata*. Paphnutius is called "Apa"; he is seen to possess unusual powers of prayer and intercession; he has revelations that enable him to discern the demonic and to foresee healings; and he dispenses oil for healing.

The discovery of a third archive, that of Nepheros, was announced in 1987. This archive's documents date from the 350s, and offer a vivid picture of a Melitian monastery in Hathor.[30] These letters tell us more about the monastery's dealings with the outside world than about its inner workings. As Roger Bagnall has noted, the "letters and contracts show an endless flow of goods in and out of the monastery, journeys by monks, prayers and requests for prayers of lay supporters, the borrowing of commodities, the buying and selling of real property, and the involvement of the clergy in the affairs of the neighboring villages."[31]

But it is Bell's first archive, dating from the 330s, that is most striking. It first attracted attention because of the light it shed on Athanasius's career. But our interest here is the glimpse it offers into Melitian monasteries and their structure. The papyri mention several Melitian monasteries: one in Hathor (in the Kynopolite nome), one on the island of Memphis, and a third somewhere in the "Upper Country" (presumably the Thebaid). There was also some sort of monastery or guest-house that Melitian monks used in Alexandria itself.[32] Especially intriguing is the papyrus known as *P. Lond.* 1913 (for the text, see appendix 13.2). It is dated March 19, 334, and concerns the leadership of "the monks of our monastery" in village of Hipponon. The superior, Pageus son of Horus, had been summoned by imperial order to appear at the Synod of Caesarea later in 334 "to come a decision concerning the purgation of the holy Christian body." (We know, from other sources, that at this synod Athanasius was scheduled to be tried on charges of murder.) With Pageus away at the synod, the community needed to have a temporary superior appointed. So the community met in the presence of local dignitaries, and the assembly chose Pageus's brother, Gerontios, as his replacement. The letter is a formal contract testifying to this temporary change of leadership and is signed by all present and addressed to "the Priors of the monastery of the monks called Hathor situated in the eastern desert of the Upper Kynopolite."[33]

This, like so many other papyri, looks quite mundane at first sight. Yet it gives important hints about Melitian monastic structure. It appears that one Melitian monastery believed it necessary to report in some official way to another Melitian monastery—as though to higher-ups or at least to a corporate partner. In other words, it gives evidence of some formal affiliation between the two Melitian monasteries, something like Pachomius's *Koinonia*. Consider the question of dates. Pachomius founded the monastery of Tabennesi around 323 and then established his second monastery at Pbow in 329; by 340, he had brought together nine monasteries into a formal alliance. This affiliation of two Melitian monasteries dates from 334. One could argue that the Pachomians were first, by four years, and even that the Melitians had imitated the Pach-omian model. But this document may well witness to an older, well-established Melitian practice. One must even consider the possibility that Pachomius drew his innovations from the Melitians. There is a passing reference in the *Letter of Ammon* that the Melitians tried to recruit Pachomius when they heard he had decided to be a monk.[34] If they had tried to recruit him, they must have known him, and he, them. But alliances between monasteries, whether Meli-tian or Pachomian, could just as easily be explained in terms of market forces. As the monastic movement prospered and monasteries expanded, it was nat-ural that individual monasteries come together to form alliances—a sort of corporate merger.

This document also illustrates one important difference between the Mel-itians and the Pachomians. Remember that the Pachomians experienced a terrible leadership crisis after the death of Pachomius. So much had revolved around Pachomius's charismatic leadership that when Pachomius died, so did the bond that knit together the various monasteries. In other words, the Pach-omians may have lacked the more businesslike contractual apparatus that the Melitians used to regulate changes of leadership.

Where does this leave Pachomius's originality? Just as I suggested that it might be better to speak of Antony as a symbol of the innovation of desert monasticism, so it might be better to speak of Pachomius as a symbol of the innovation of cenobitic monasticism. This is not to deny either Pachomius's status as a pioneer or his organizational brilliance. It simply means acknowl-edging that his was one of a wide-ranging set of fourth-century experiments in monastic living. The rediscovery of Melitian monasticism alerts us that some fascinating early achievements have fallen through the cracks of the historical record.

Monasticism outside Egypt: Syria, Cappadocia, and Palestine

The question of Antony's and Pachomius's originality is clearly more compli-cated than textbooks let on. What about the other stock claim—that Egypt was the birthplace of monasticism? We have looked at a number of the earliest and best-known works of early Christian monasticism, and clearly they give Egypt the lion's share of attention. Taken together, these texts can give the unintended impression that monasticism was an Egyptian invention. That impression is not accurate. It might be better to say that Egypt got the best "press," and that Egypt proved the most influential in the long run. But that does not mean that it alone was the birthplace of monasticism. To get a sense of Egypt's place in the wider scheme of things, I would like to do a quick tour of three other regions, highlighting their monastic achievements and local heroes.

Symeon the Stylite and Syrian Asceticism

Just as Greek was the common language of the eastern Roman Empire and Latin was that of the western, so Syriac was the common language of the ancient Near East—Syria, Palestine, and Mesopotamia. Syriac was a dialect of Aramaic, the language Jesus spoke, and the roots of Syriac Christianity were in those early Jewish Christian communities.

The best-known account of Syriac monasticism is the *Religious History* of Theodoret of Cyrrhus (c. 393–458).[35] (For excerpts, see appendix 13.3.) Theodoret was a leading Antiochene theologian who opposed Cyril of Alexandria at the Council of Ephesus and opposed Dioscorus at the Council of Chalcedon. (He once satirized Cyril's Christology in a treatise called *Eranistes*, "The Garbage Collector.") Theodoret had grown up in a well-to-do family in Antioch, had a fine Greek education, and could write in good literary Greek. But Antioch was a Greek-speaking enclave in a wider Syriac-speaking region. Theodoret himself knew Syriac, and his family had close links with Syriac-speaking holy men from the nearby mountains. One of them, Macedonius the Barley Eater, had even prophesied his birth. Theodoret's *Religious History*, like Palladius's *Lausiac History*, offers snapshot portraits of local holy men. Theodoret presents a procession of ascetic extremists, wild men in a wild landscape. Many rejected the barest accoutrements of civilization: clothing, fire, housing. Some grazed on grass like cattle, chained themselves to rocks, wore metal yokes, or imprisoned themselves in caves.

Theodoret's great hero was Symeon the Stylite (c. 390–459), one of the best-known and most eccentric figures in early Christian monasticism. His forty-year career standing atop a pillar has tantalized Christian imaginations, both ancient and modern. Symeon was born to a Christian family in a village near Nicopolis. He reportedly entered a monastery at Teleda but after about ten years was asked to leave. He then spent three years in the open air atop a hill. He first began to perch himself atop a pillar to escape the throngs who came to him for healing. In time, he moved to higher and higher pillars, from six cubits, to twelve, to twenty-four, to thirty-six. In time he became the object of international pilgrimage. Visitors from as far away as Britain and Spain sought him out for healing and intercession. His pillar was a stark, evocative symbol. From ground level, he seemed perched halfway between earth and heaven, arms raised in prayer, day and night. Pilgrims stood at the base counting his daily prostrations; one counted over 1400 prostrations—before he finally lost count. Symeon not only positioned himself as a mediator between humankind and God, but also served as an arbiter of lawsuits and political squabbles. He made the poor and oppressed his special charge, a task reportedly given him by the prophet Elijah.[36]

Symeon and other such holy men, however extreme their behavior and however remote their base of operation, served a special role in regional Syrian politics. Their outsider status, celebrated in their extravagant ascetic rituals, enabled them to stand free of the gnarled web of vested interests. They were beyond local politics—and thus singularly equipped to play the political role of arbiter. Thus the paradox: those who had withdrawn from society and its webs of patronage became the ultimate patrons, mediating between God and the human race.

Theodoret not only treats fifth-century figures such as Symeon, whom he knew personally, but also passes on stories of earlier figures, some dating from the mid-fourth century. This might give the impression that Syrian monasticism is a late phenomenon, or that its rise may even owe something to Egypt. That impression is not accurate. Scholars believe that later Syrian monasticism flows out of older ascetical traditions, older even than those known from Egypt, and that its fourth-century spirituality and monastic organization is very much its own and owes nothing, at its formative stages, to Egypt.

Syria had long been and would long be a stronghold of ascetical radicalism. In the late second century, the early Christian writer Tatian left Rome and returned to his native Syria, where he not only denounced Greco-Roman culture, but also condemned marriage and procreation. He became a leading spokesman of the encratite movement (from *enkrateia*, "continence"). His harsh views were not unusual in Syria. Until sometime in the third century, celibacy may have been a requirement for baptism in the Syrian church.[37] We have reports of small celibate communities—not unlike the Shakers of nineteenth-century America. Some individuals lived alone, while others lived together as couples in "spiritual marriages" (much as Amoun and his wife had). These celibates were known as the "sons/daughters of the Covenant" (*bnay/bnāt qyāmâ*). They did not retreat to the mountains, but remained within the larger Christian communities, embracing an asceticism far removed from the fierce gestures celebrated by Theodoret.

This type of ascetic was also called an *îhîdāyâ*, the Syriac equivalent of the Greek *monachos*. The Syriac term had a rich cluster of associations. It meant "single" in the sense of "unmarried," or "celibate"; it also meant "single-minded," undivided in heart. But in the Syriac version of the New Testament, Christ is called the *Îhîdāyâ*, the "only-begotten." So becoming "single" meant becoming Christlike. This terminology encapsulates a distinctive spirituality—that the singlehearted ascetic images the singularity of Christ. It also indicates that the origins of Syriac monasticism lay not in desert dwelling, but in consecrated celibacy.[38]

The best-known ancient writer on Syriac asceticism was Ephrem the Syrian (306–373). He has been called "the greatest poet of the patristic age and, perhaps, the only theologian-poet to rank beside Dante."[39] His surviving writings are mostly hymns (*madrāšâ*) and metrical homilies (*mêmrâ*). Ephrem spent much of his career in Nisibis (modern-day Nusaybin in Syria), a prosperous garrison town on the border between the Roman and Persian Empires. In 363 he was forced to move to Edessa (modern-day Urfa in Turkey) after Nisibis was ceded to the Persians in the wake of the Emperor Julian's disastrous military excursion. Later tradition portrayed Ephrem as a monk, but that is not accurate. He was an ascetic, one of those "sons of the Covenant," and worked as a composer, musician, and chorus leader.

Ephrem's poetry gives voice to a key element of Syriac ascetic spirituality:

428 PART V. REFLECTIONS

that the *îhîdāyê* lived the "angelic life." It was not just their sexual continence that imbued them with angelic freedom. They, like the angels, did not sleep, but kept vigil, praying always before the face of God. Ephrem's preferred term for angels was "watchers" or "wakers"—those who were always awake, who did not suffer the little daily death of sleep, who were fed by contemplating God, and who were the singers of the heavenly court. Ephrem uses the term both for the angels and for their earthly counterparts, the ascetic *îhîdāyê*. Ephrem also applied the term "watcher" or "waker" to Christ: "Because Adam introduced into the world the sleep of death in sins, (Christ) the Wakeful One came down to wake us up from being submerged in sin."[40] The ascetics, in their watchful all-night prayer vigils, were iconic both of Christ the Awakener, who awakens us from the sleep of death, and of the church vigilant, which waits wide-eyed like the wise virgins in Jesus's parable, ever ready for the bridegroom's sudden arrival.[41]

Syria would, in time, draw on currents from Egyptian monastic spirituality. The writings of Evagrius Ponticus clearly struck a chord, and were quickly translated into Syriac. In fact, several key works—*Gnostikos, Kephalaia gnostica,* and *Antirrhetikos*—have been completely preserved only in Syriac. The *Apophthegmata* was also translated into Syriac, by 'Ânân Îshô' in the seventh century. One intriguing intersection of Syria and Egypt is a set of fifty homilies, wrongly attributed to Macarius the Egyptian. But these so-called *Macarian Homilies* are of Syrian, not Egyptian, provenance. They date from the fourth century and may stem from the Messalians, a radical ascetical group. This text deeply touched not only Byzantine monasticism, but also the spirituality of John Wesley, founder of Methodism. The *Macarian Homilies* have been treasured for their rich Spirit-centered theology, their evocative poetic images, and their exploration on the heart as the spiritual locus.[42]

Ironically, the Syrians forgot their own ancient ascetical roots and began attributing the origins of Syrian monasticism to Egypt. A late legend—attested no earlier than the ninth century—began circulating that a onetime disciple of Pachomius named Mar Augen imported monasticism to Syria from Egypt.

Basil of Caesarea and Cappadocian Monasticism

Cappadocia (now in central Turkey) had been a vital Christian center from New Testament times. Three of the greatest theologians of the early church were from the region: Basil of Caesarea (330–370), his brother Gregory of Nyssa (334–c. 395), and their friend Gregory of Nazianzus (329–389).[43] The three were the leading Nicenes in the generation after Athanasius and put together both the classic defense of the divinity of the Holy Spirit and the classic exposition of the doctrine of the Trinity. The three have made passing appearances in earlier chapters. As we saw, Evagrius Ponticus had been ordained a lector by Basil and had served as Gregory of Nazianzus's archdeacon in Constantinople.

Basil and his brother came from a well-to-do and pious Christian family in Caesarea. In his mid-twenties, Basil completed advanced studies in rhetoric in Athens and returned home, where, after a brief teaching career, he decided to seek baptism. At the same time, he converted to the "philosophic life"—that is, to asceticism—and embarked on a far-flung tour, visiting monastic sites in Mesopotamia, Syria, Palestine, and Egypt.[44] He both admired and was critical of what he saw. In 357, on a family estate in Pontus near the Black Sea, he began his first monastic experiments and invited his good friend and study partner, Gregory of Nazianzus, to join him.[45] Together, they studied Origen and put together an ascetic anthology of texts from him, the *Philokalia*. Basil eventually formulated his own unique vision of monasticism, articulated in a collection of treatises entitled the *Asceticon*. The major section of this collection is called the *Long Rules*. The title is a bit deceptive, because these "rules" are not practical dos and don'ts. Rather, they are guiding principles, rooted in scripture, that articulate a coherent monastic spirituality. While Basil was deeply supportive of the monastic quest for contemplation and a measured solitude, he could be sharply critical of the anchoritic life, seeing it as a distortion of human nature and of the Christian message:

> Who does not know that man is a tame and sociable animal, and not a solitary and fierce one? For nothing is so characteristic of our nature as to associate with one another, to need one another and to love our kind. So the Lord himself first gave us the seeds of these things, and accordingly demands their fruits, saying, "A new commandment I give to you, that you love one another" (John 13:34). And wishing to stir up our souls to keep this commandment, he demanded as a proof that we are his disciples, not signs and miracles— and yet he granted the working of these too in the Holy Spirit— What does he say? "By this all will know that you are my disciples, if you have love for one another" (John 13:35).[46]

In one of his most famous passages in the *Long Rules*, Basil protested against the self-absorbed hermits. He noted that Christ had served humankind, symbolizing his life of humble service by washing the feet of his disciples. Basil then chided the hermits: "Whose feet then will you wash?"[47]

Basil was no mere theorist. He had great skills as an administrator, and once he was ordained a priest and, later, was made bishop of Caesarea, he brought his monastic vision to the city. Basil took care to harness the energies of ascetic communities and fit them better into the structure of the larger church.[48] His monks combined a life of prayer and a life of service to the poor. His close friend, Gregory of Nazianzus, highlighted this in a famous funeral oration commemorating Basil's life:

> Basil . . . reconciled most excellently and united the solitary and the community life. . . . He founded cells for ascetics, but at no great distance from his cenobitic communities, and, instead of distinguishing and separating the one from the other, as if by some intervening wall, he brought them together and united them, in order that the contemplative spirit might not be cut off from society, nor the active life be uninfluenced by the contemplative, but that, like

sea and land, by an interchange of their several gifts, they might
unite in promoting the one object, the glory of God.[49]

Basil established not only monasteries in the city, but also hospitals for the
poor and hospices for Christian pilgrims. This complex, later known as the
Basileidos, was at the heart of Basil's effort to institutionalize Christian charity
on a citywide scale. He was widely admired in his own time for his achievements, and his influence on Greek Orthodox monasticism has been profound—comparable to Benedict's influence on the Latin West. Basil also influenced Western monasticism. Benedict knew Basil's *Asceticon* (via a Latin
translation done by Rufinus) and specifically recommends Basil by name in
the *Rule*.[50]

Basil's achievement has been recently reassessed. He is no longer seen as
the founder of Cappadocian monasticism, nor is Egypt seen as a decisive influence on his monastic vision. Recent research has stressed that he owed
much to two sources, both local. One was Eustathius of Sebaste (c. 300–c. 377).
According to Sozomen, Eustathius had been the real founder of monasticism
in the region.[51] Eustathius, the son of a Christian bishop, began organizing
ascetic communities in and around his native Armenia in the 330s—about the
same time Pachomius, Amoun, and Macarius were doing so in Egypt. A synod
of bishops met in Gangra in 340 and issued ecclesiastical censures against
Eustathius and his followers. The synod's canons give us a glimpse—even if
hostile and exaggerated—of what Eustathius and his followers taught and practiced. The bishops accused the Eustathians of condemning marriage and over-
praising virginity; of encouraging slaves to rebel against their masters; of wearing "strange dress to the downfall of the common mode of dress"; of allowing
women to dress as men, shave their heads, and abandon their children; of
refusing to receive communion from married priests; and of celebrating liturgies without priests.[52] It is hard to be sure, but it sounds as though Eustathius
and his followers were arguing for and living out some radical form of Christian equality that broke down barriers between slave and free and between
male and female. It was a volatile mix of asceticism and social protest. In 356,
Eustathius became bishop of Sebaste. He and two other ascetic bishops in the
region were noted for founding both monasteries and hospices for the poor.

It was just about this time that Basil returned from his studies in Athens
and was baptized. A close study of Basil's letters shows how he came under
the influence of Eustathius, whom he admired as a "philosopher," a true lover
of wisdom. It is now clear that Eustathius helped shape elements of Basil's
monastic vision—that unique mix of ascetical commitment and service to the
poor. In the early 370s, the bond between disciple and mentor broke down
irreparably. The cause was, in large measure, theological. Eustathius clung to
an older theology. He was not a Nicene, but a Homoiousian, and refused to
call the Holy Spirit "God." Basil, by this time, was a committed Nicene and
had worked out his theology of the Holy Spirit and the Trinity. Basil's theology,
of course, would become the foundation of Christian orthodoxy. As a result,
one scholar has noted, "Eustathius was thus pushed into the heretical twilight

and official history came to regard Basil as the founder of monasticism in Asia Minor."[53]

Eustathius was not Basil's only monastic mentor. He was deeply influenced by someone closer to home, his sister Macrina (c. 327–380). She had embarked on a very successful experiment in monastic community-building years before Basil. What we know of Macrina comes from another member of the family, Gregory of Nyssa. Gregory's *Life of Saint Macrina* is an eloquent homage to his sister.[54] Susanna Elm, in her study *Virgins of God*, has reconstructed the slow evolution of Macrina's experiments in household asceticism.[55] Macrina seems to have enjoyed a fine education at home, not unlike other well-to-do women of the age. At age twelve, she was engaged to be married, but when her fiancé died, she declared herself a widow and refused all further suitors. After her father's death, the family moved to Annisi in Pontus. Macrina embraced an ascetic regimen: prayer, a frugal diet, and humble housework. The last was quite striking, for it symbolized her embrace of the lot of a household slave. Eventually Macrina persuaded her mother to give up all the privileges of being the "great lady" of the house and to embrace a radical community of equals, putting all, even house slaves, on equal footing. Gregory describes it this way:

> Then . . . the virgin's life became her mother's guide to this philosophical non-materialistic life-style. Macrina, who had already renounced all the conventionalities, brought her mother on an equal footing with the whole group of virgins, so that she shared with them in equality the same table, the same kind of bed and all the same necessities of life. All differences of rank were removed from their way of life.[56]

Macrina, not her mother, emerged as superior. Eventually other widows, some of aristocratic background, joined the expanding ascetic household. Finally, in 368, Macrina's community adopted a number of girls orphaned during a local famine. What began in the 350s as family asceticism became by 380 a burgeoning monastic community.

Macrina's efforts were not the only ascetic experiment on the family property. Her younger brother Naucratis embarked on a five-year experiment in anchoritic living. In 352, he and a servant set up a hermitage in one of the wild and remote areas on the property, supporting some elderly locals with their hunting and fishing. When Basil returned from his tour of the monastic Middle East, he found two quite different family experiments in asceticism underway: Macrina's ascetical household and Naucratis's anchoritic experiment. In 357 Naucratis and his companion both drowned in a tragic fishing accident. Basil, it seems, began his own monastic career by taking over his brother's hermitage project—but he would take it in a cenobitic direction as time went on.

This new appreciation of Eustathius, Macrina, and Naucratis upsets older readings of monastic history. Basil was not the founder of monasticism in Cappadocia; he was not even the earliest monastic founder in his own family.

Given what we now of Eustathius's efforts and those of Basil and his family, it is clear that various ascetic experiments, some communal, some anchoritic, were underway in Cappadocia at a relatively early date—and with minimal Egyptian influence.[57]

Sabas and Palestinian Monasticism

Palestinian monasticism was, from the beginning, international. In the fourth century, the Holy Land became a magnet for pilgrims from around the empire and beyond. Some pilgrims stayed on and either joined or established monastic communities. As we saw, the young John Cassian and his friend Germanus entered a monastery in Bethlehem in the early 380s. Around the same time, a Spanish nun named Egeria toured Egypt and Palestine. She left a fascinating eyewitness report of shrines and holy places she visited in which she describes routine encounters with monks who resided near these sites and conducted tours for pilgrims.

Some pilgrims from the West established Latin-speaking monasteries. The most famous of these, the foundation established by Melania the Elder and Rufinus on the Mount of Olives in 373, has appeared repeatedly in this book. Their community welded a life of asceticism with a life of scholarship and earned them a worldwide reputation for their work of translating Greek monastic and theological works for the Latin West. The community also served as a conduit for monastic pilgrims going to Egypt. Evagrius Ponticus and Palladius both lived there for a time before moving on to Egypt. So did the anonymous author of the *History of the Monks in Egypt*. And, as we saw, Rufinus and Melania's community became a lightning rod of controversy during the Origenist Controversy. The other Latin-speaking enclave was established by Jerome and Paula (347–404) in Bethlehem. It was here that Jerome worked on his massive project of translating the Bible from the original Hebrew and Greek into Latin. And Jerome, of course, was a bitter rival of Rufinus and Melania and carried on acerbic battles against both during the Origenist Controversy.

Jerome authored various brief monastic biographies. In one, he claims that the origins of Palestinian monasticism go back to the early fourth century, to a figure named Hilarion (c. 293–after 356). Hilarion reportedly grew up in a village near Gaza and went to school in Alexandria. There, at the age of fifteen, he fell under the spell of Antony. He returned home not long after, and when his parents died, he gave away his inheritance and took up the anchoritic life in a seaside cell a few miles from the port of Gaza. After twenty years, he attracted a number of followers who set up hermitages in the area, but after the death of Antony, he disappeared. Scholars are suspicious of the veracity of Jerome's *Life of Hilarion*. Even if there was an early Palestinian monk named Hilarion, Jerome's work simply sounds too much like a melodramatic recasting of the *Life of Antony*.

There are other scattered and hard-to-assess reports of monastic origins in Palestine. Eusebius of Caesarea, in his *Church History*, mentions that sometime between 180 and 212, Narcissus, then bishop of Jerusalem, became frustrated by local church politics and retired to the nearby desert for some years.[58] This is sometimes cited as though it marked the beginnings of Palestinian monasticism—but it is hard to see it as such, even if it is accurate.

More intriguing are reports of a figure named Chariton (d. c. 350). He was reportedly from Iconium (modern-day Konya in Turkey) and suffered torture in a persecution (in the 270s? the 300s?). In the early fourth century, he made his way to Jerusalem to visit the holy places, and after this he founded three monasteries in the surrounding region: Pharan (northeast of Jerusalem), Douka (near Jericho), and Souka (northeast of Tekoa). The problem is that the source for this, the anonymous *Life of Chariton*, was written several centuries later, no earlier than the mid-sixth century, and its chronology is muddled.[59] But if the traditions it cites have any credibility, they would imply monastic beginnings in Palestine as early as those in Egypt, and without any clear connection to it.

Chariton is credited with founding the distinctive form of Palestinian monasticism: the *laura*.[60] The *laura* was a unique amalgam of the anchoritic and cenobitic. It was a colony of hermits subject to the authority of an abbot (*hegumenos*) who was assisted by a steward (*oikonomos*). Most *lauras* revolved architecturally around several core buildings, that usually included a church and a bakery. The monks lived alone in cells scattered around this communal core, and the cells were linked by a paved footpath (the Greek word *laura* can mean "path"). Monday through Friday, the monks remained in their cells working and praying, while on Saturday and Sunday, they came together for liturgy and a common meal. This organization resembles in intriguing ways the organization found in Scetis.

These *lauras* sprang up in the Judean desert east and south of Jerusalem, a region with profound scriptural resonances for the monks who came there. It had been home to great biblical figures: Elijah, Elisha, and John the Baptist. And not far from there the Qumran community had produced the Dead Sea scrolls. It is harsh terrain, with steep cliffs and deep ravines. Some early *lauras* were built along cliff faces, with cells and chapels hewn out from caves. While the monasteries themselves were in austere desert locales, desert and city were not that far apart. Most were only about a day's walk from Jerusalem. *Lauras* were not the only monastic establishments in the desert: there were certainly hermitages, but also large cenobia, which were seen as necessary proving grounds before one could enter the *lauras*.

The best-known account of Palestinian monasticism comes from Cyril of Scythopolis (c. 525–after 559). His *Lives of the Monks of Palestine* is not actually a single work, but seven separate biographies tracing the adventures of monastic leaders active in the Judean desert from 400 to 550. The first of Cyril's portraits is of Euthymius the Great (377–473). Euthymius was an Armenian from Melitene. In his late twenties, he made a pilgrimage to the Holy Land and decided to stay on as a monk. He was already a priest and had worked with monks back in Armenia. In 405, he settled in Chariton's *laura* of Pharan. In time, he founded other *lauras* and cenobia. Euthymius was a strong supporter of Chalcedon, at a time and in a place where its famous *Definition* was considered heretical by many Palestinian monks.

The second of Cyril's portraits is of Sabas (439–532). Sabas was, like so many others, a foreigner, growing up near Caesarea in Cappadocia. He came to Palestine at the age of eighteen and apprenticed in the monastic life under disciples of Euthymius. In 478, he took up residence in a cliff cave in the Kidron Valley and began attracting disciples. There he established the Great Laura, one of the most important monasteries of Palestine. Sabas is best known as a monastery builder: he established ten monasteries, most in the Kidron Valley. Cyril knew Sabas personally and records a few reminiscences. Once, when Cyril was only a small boy, Sabas happened to visit Scythopolis. Sabas, seeing the young Cyril with his father, picked him up, embraced him, and announced: "From now on this boy is my disciple and a son of the fathers of the desert."[61] Cyril looked back on the incident as the origin of his monastic vocation. Sabas was a forceful personality, and some of his own monks rebelled against him and established the New Laura in 507. This breakaway monastery would become a center of the Origenist Controversy of the sixth century. For two decades, there was fierce rivalry between the monks of the Great Laura and those of the New Laura. This ended in 553 with the formal condemnation of Origenism by the Emperor Justinian and the Second Council of Constantinople.

The other center of Palestinian monasticism was Gaza. Some monks in this area were immigrants from Egypt. In the fourth century, Silvanus—who figures prominently in the *Apophthegmata*—left Egypt and spent time in Sinai before settling in Gaza with his disciples. A century later, Isaiah of Scetis made a pilgrimage to the Holy Land and ended up in Gaza. There he shut himself up in a cell and handled all consultation through his disciple Peter. Despite this strict enclosure, he governed a local cenobium. This style—a monastery led by a permanently enclosed abbot—reappears in the same region in the sixth century. Two solitaries, Barsanuphius (nicknamed "the Great Old Man") and John of Gaza (nicknamed "the Other Old Man"), led a community through intermediaries and dictated hundreds of answers to inquiries from their monks and from lay visitors. Their remarkable correspondence is still being edited and published.[62] Barsanuphius and John carried on such regular correspondence that even with this partial publication, scholars can trace the ups and downs of the spiritual journeys of various correspondents. These letters allow us to see at close range how ancients practiced the delicate art of spiritual direction.

At the beginning of this section, I raised the question: did monasticism come from Egypt? The answer should now be clear: no, Egypt was not *the* birthplace, but *a* birthplace. Syria has at least an equal claim, and Palestine and Cappadocia may as well. True, the best-known texts about Egyptian monasticism are earlier than the best-known texts from other regions, but that says nothing about the age of their respective monasticisms. Scholars now believe that varied ascetical undercurrents were at work in various locales in the third century. Once Christianity was legalized in the early fourth century, various independent monasticisms surfaced simultaneously. There was diversity not just between regions. Each locale, as we saw, forged its own local diversity. The diversity witnessed in Egypt was matched, even surpassed, by the diversity in international asceticism.

Here we have surveyed only the Greek and Syriac East. If we were to look at the Latin West, we would see a similar diversity both within and between regions. The emerging monasticisms of North Africa, Italy, and Gaul differed from one another and from movements in the East. While western monasticism might not match the antiquity of its eastern counterparts, the Latins quickly developed their own local contours. There were already fiercely held local traditions that did not go away quietly when John Cassian tried to import his Egyptian brand into southern Gaul. It is also true that Egyptian monasticism influenced everyone in varied ways eventually. But that influence took hold only because local experiments were already under way and prospering. There is the old saying that "all politics is local"; the same might be said about asceticism.

Monasticism outside Christianity: The Manichees

Was Christian monasticism inspired by contact with some other religion? Did Christianity import either the concept of monasticism or its monastic practices from some other religious tradition? Occasionally one comes across baseless speculation that the roots of Christian monasticism lie in Buddhism. It is true that Buddhism had had a centuries-long and venerable monastic tradition. It is also true that during this period Buddhist missionaries were active in the various parts of the Asia and soon enjoyed great successes in China and Tibet. Could Buddhist missionaries have made their way into the Roman Empire, establishing themselves in Alexandria or some other Egyptian port? While not impossible, there is simply no evidence for it at all.

What about Judaism? It is true that first-century Judaism did have a movement that vaguely resembled desert monasticism: the community at Qumran that created the Dead Sea Scrolls. But it would be quite a jump chronologically and geographically to link a Jewish sect decimated by the Romans in the mid first century with Egyptian monastic settlements of the fourth century. It would be even more of a jump if one compares theological views and the nitty-gritty specifics of their ascetical practices. Closer at hand are reports by the Jewish philosopher Philo of a first-century Jewish philosophical community known as the Therapeutae.[63] This somewhat obscure group was active just outside Alexandria, near Lake Mareotis. The case of the Therapeutae avoids the geographical objection, but formidable chronological, theological, and ascetical gaps remain. It must be granted that when the fourth-century church historian Eusebius of Caesarea read Philo, he mistakenly presumed that Philo was describing not a Jewish community, but a Christian one.[64] But Eusebius does not report this as the origins of monasticism. In fact, monasticism plays no role in his *Church History*. The misidentification says more about Eusebius than about monasticism. Eusebius, like Cassian, presumed that Christian communities had been ascetical from the days of the apostles, and Philo's Therapeutae seemed confirmation of his own bias.[65]

As strange as it may sound, we do know of one group active in Egypt indebted both to Jewish sectarians and to Buddhist monks: the Manichees. Their founder, Mani (216–277), was born in southern Babylonia, then part of the Persian (Sassanian) Empire. His family belonged to the Elkasaites, a Jewish-Christian baptismal sect. At age twelve and again at age twenty-four, he experienced a series of visions, revelations he ascribed to his heavenly twin, the Syzygos. These convinced him that he was called to complete what previous religious founders—Buddha, Zoroaster, and Jesus—had left incomplete. Mani believed himself called to found the first truly world religion. He began proclaiming his "Religion of Life" and described himself as the "apostle of Jesus Christ." (His followers went further, calling him "the Paraclete," the "spirit of truth" prophesied by Jesus.) In 242 Mani journeyed as far as India and gained some familiarity with Buddhist monastic practices.[66] After returning, he converted members of the Persian court and even won support of the Persian king, Shapur I, who permitted him to carry on wide-ranging missionary work for thirty years. After Shapur's death in 273, Mani fell from favor and, in 277, was arrested, tortured, and executed.

From the beginning, Mani had universal aspirations for his doctrine. He claims that the Syzygos instructed him, "You were not sent into this sect [of the Elkasaites] alone, but into every nation and teaching and every city and place. . . . A great many people will [accept] your word. Therefore, go forth and go round about."[67] Mani sent missionaries out in all directions. Two early missionaries, Addā and Patīk (or Patteg), brought Manichaeism to Egypt sometime before the end of the third century, perhaps as early as the 270s—just when Christian monasticism seems to have been getting underway. Over the next few centuries, Mani's religion spread rapidly via merchants and missionaries, east to China and west to North Africa, Rome, and Spain. In the early twentieth century, archaeologists discovered remnants of Manichaean monasteries and manuscripts in the oasis of Turfan in central Asia, where the eighth-century Uighur Turks had adopted Manichaeism as the state religion.

The religion of Mani owed much to Gnosticism. Like Christian Gnostics before him, Mani claimed to reveal knowledge both of God and of the universe's origin and destiny. As one of the Manichaean psalms proclaims: "Let us bless our Lord Jesus who sent us (Mani), the Spirit of Truth. He came; he separated us from the error of the world. He brought us a mirror. We looked; (we) saw this universe in it."[68] The universe revealed in Mani's "mirror" was a universe at war, a vast cosmic battleground between the Kingdom of Light and the Kingdom of Darkness: "When the Holy Spirit came, he revealed to us the way of truth. He taught us that there are two natures, that of the Light and that of the Darkness, (separate) from one another from the beginning."[69]

At its core, Manichaean theology proclaimed a cosmic dualism. The present world, in Mani's view, is a war-torn frontier land, a temporary buffer state, created from the great cosmic clash between the Kingdoms of Light and Darkness. Like earlier Gnostic theorists, Mani preached an intricate mythology, a cosmogonic drama of divine emanations and cosmic powers: Primal Man, the Great Builder, the Third Messenger, the Maid of Light, the Prince of Darkness, and the Instinct of Death. The tale of their upperworldly battles and deceptions explains the wretched state of the present universe, its corruption and heartache.

Every person, according to Mani, carries this cosmic battle within himself or herself: we are souls trapped in material bodies. Our souls are, in reality, precious fragments of divine light, but most of us have forgotten this, forgotten who we really are, forgotten because we have become drunk from long years trapped in the darkness of matter. Manichaean teaching opens us to the truth: "I have known my soul and the body that lies upon it, / That they are enemies to each other before the creations."[70] Manichees saw the task of redemption as a slow, painstaking recovery of the tiny bits and scraps of light that lie scattered about, embedded in matter: "All life, the remnant of the Light which is in every place, [the redeemer will] gather to himself."[71] They viewed the present universe as a vast light-processing factory, a place where the dross of matter and darkness are steadily distilled away and shirked off, while tiny fragments of divine light are recovered like precious diamonds from a dark subterranean mine. The sun and moon are two key celestial refineries in this cosmic purification process: "The sun and (the) moon were established; they were placed on high (to) purify (the) soul. Daily they take up the purified part to the height; this sediment, however, they scrape (off and cast it below; and the) mixed (portion) they rotate, now above and now below."[72] Manichees could look up at the night sky and see the Milky Way—what they called "the Pillar of Glory"—as evidence of distilled light-souls gathering together and making their way back to the Kingdom of Light. Each person was called to shirk off the flesh and seek the way to this Paradise of Light, and along the way free the imprisoned particles of Light within himself and within the world.

Manichees did not form loose study circles, as earlier Gnostics had. Rather, they had well-organized churches noted for their beautiful liturgies and hymn singing. They also had a canon of scripture, writings by Mani and his disciples, preserved in manuscripts famed for their calligraphic elegance. Local Manichaean congregations had two levels of membership: elect and catechumens (or "hearers"). The Manichaean elect resembled monks in certain respects. They were a celibate elite, ascetics who followed strict dietary regulations, including abstention from meat and wine. They renounced all material goods and were expected to be lifelong travelers and evangelists. Catechumens formed the majority of local congregations. They could be married and were expected to house itinerant elect and support them financially. Scholars have noted certain parallels between this organization and patterns found in Buddhism.

We tend to look back and see Manichaeism as an independent religion. But in practice, it tended to blend in with whatever religious surroundings it found itself in. So Manichees in China looked like Buddhists and spoke of Mani as "the Buddha of Light." In Egypt, they presented themselves as "authentic" Christians and berated orthodox Christianity for its "judaizing." "Jesus of the Splendor" figures prominently in the myth and devotions of western Manichees, but he is far removed from the Christ of orthodox Christianity.

Authorities in the Roman Empire opposed Manichaeism from an early date. The Emperor Diocletian, who had begun the Great Persecution against the Christians, also persecuted Manichees, seeing them as a sort of fifth-column intrusion from Rome's Persian enemies. Later, under the Christian emperors, Manichees were persecuted as Christian heretics. Despite such efforts, Manichees survived and even thrived underground, winning numerous converts in Egypt, Rome, and North Africa. The most famous, of course, was Augustine of Hippo, who spent ten years as a Manichaean hearer before abandoning them and converting to orthodox Christianity in the mid-380s.

There have been extraordinary discoveries of Manichaean documents in Egypt. In 1929, workmen stumbled upon a cache of papyri in Medimet Madi in the Fayyum. The discovery, published in 1933, included the remarkable Manichaean *Psalm Book* and a lengthy theological tract, entitled the *Kephalaia of the Teacher*. Even more remarkable was the discovery of the *Cologne Mani Codex*, first discovered in 1969 and published in 1979. This pocket-sized codex probably came from Lycopolis in Upper Egypt and dates from the fourth or early fifth century. Its real title is *Concerning the Origin of His Body*. It purports to be Mani's autobiography and includes an anthology of his words and deeds compiled by his students. The most recent discoveries have come from the ancient village of Kellis in Middle Egypt (for a sample, see appendix 13.4). Archaeologists have begun uncovering not only Manichaean documents, but also are beginning to reconstruct something of the ordinary life of a thriving Manichaean community.[73]

Manichaean incursions were an urgent concern to Egyptian monks. According to Athanasius, Antony refused to have "friendly conversations with Manichaeans . . . except to admonish them to convert to piety, for he thought and affirmed that friendship and conversation with such persons was harmful and destructive to the soul."[74] The earliest Egyptian treatise against the Manichees was authored by Antony's disciple and Athanasius's friend, Serapion of Thmuis. The *Apophthegmata* reports that one of the desert mothers, Amma Theodora, advised her disciples that Manichees and Christians held very different estimates of the body, however similar their apparent ascetical practices might look: "Give the body discipline and you will see the body is for him who made it."[75] In the *History of the Monks in Egypt*, the author reports a confrontation between a Manichaean teacher and Abba Copres. After unsuccessfully debating the Manichee, Copres challenges his opponent to a duel by ordeal. Copres walks through a fire unhurt, while the Manichee is badly burned. While typical of the *History*'s stress on the miraculous, it does indicate public confrontations between Manichees and monks—not just with words, but displays of power.[76]

Could Christian monasticism owe its beginnings to the Manichees? One sometimes hears people who dismiss all Christian asceticism as "Manichaean." But such people rarely know anything of real Manichaeism, its theology, practices, or history. For them, it is simply a term of abuse. But there is a real question here: could the Manichees have actually inspired the birth of Christian monasticism? Could the Manichaean elect have actually influenced monastic lifestyles or organizations?

One contemporary expert on Manichaeism, Gedaliahu Strousma, has actually made that precise claim: "It is . . . unlikely . . . that the Manichaean ascetical movement, which preceded the emergence of Christian cenobitic monasticism by about half a century, did not influence the latter in some way."[77] This claim—phrased with a confusing double negative—suggests "some" influence. But in what way? In asceticism? Theology? Organization? He never points to specific parallels. Strousma goes on to claim that "at least some Manichaean elect, who had the most to fear from delation to the authorities, must have looked for a hiding place in the ascetical communities in the desert, i.e., in the Pachomian monasteries."[78] This too is an interesting claim. But is there any proof for either assertion? Even those sympathetic to Strousma's explorations admit that it is, at best, speculation.[79] It is true that Manichaean elect may have looked a lot like wandering Christian monks and that they would certainly have claimed to be Christians. But there is no evidence to suggest that Manichaean methods of prayer or ascetical practices—to say nothing about Manichaean theology—had any known influence on Christian monasticism. At most, one might argue that the Manichees may have provided some competition. Even if, as Strousma claims, a member of the Manichaean elect had decided to hide himself in a Pachomian monastery—possible in principle, but something for which there is no evidence—it is hard to imagine that he could have so successfully infiltrated Pachomian monasticism that he could have decisively shaped its asceticism, theology, or organization.

Hypotheses about Buddhist, Jewish, or Manichaean influence rely on an unspoken assumption: that Christianity could not have developed monasticism on its own, that monasticism must surely be an external accretion, something unnatural to Christianity. But is that assumption justified? Christianity grew up in an ascetical world, to be sure. But it also had ascetical strains at its foundational core, in the person of Jesus and in the person of Paul. Praying in deserts, fasting, celibacy, renunciation of family and wealth—these occupy a large place in the narratives and the ethical teaching of the New Testament. The challenge for historians is to account for the ways these things began to take institutional form in the fourth century and to account for their institutionalization not just in Egypt, but across the early Christian world. Vague similarities, such as the celibacy and the voluntary poverty of the Manichaean elect, do not take into account the very real differences in ascetical practice, in monastic organization, and in theological outlook. One must ask: is the Manichaean hypothesis attractive because there is a solid historical basis for it? Or is it because Manichaeism still has that old heresiological ring of being a body-hating heresy—and thus, Christian monasticism can be dismissed as un-Christian at its roots? (For classic attacks on monasticism, see appendices 13.5 and 13.6.)

Monasticism Underreported: Virgins, Widows, and Ammas

One day, a disciple of Abba Sisoes said to him, "Abba, you're getting old. Let us go back closer to the settled land." The old man agreed, but insisted, "Let us go where there are no women." His disciple was baffled: "Where else is there that has no women except the desert?" And so Sisoes said, "Well then, take me to the desert."[80]

It is fashionable nowadays to speak of "desert mothers," pairing the term with the more traditional "desert fathers." But is it accurate? Is it true that women were equally prominent and active in the desert? This important question is part of a wide-ranging reassessment of early Christian asceticism. Some quite creative contemporary scholarship has focused on putting together a better picture of the social world of women in late antiquity and on reassessing women's contributions to early Christianity. And the study of women's asceticism has been part of that.[81] Here I will simply touch on a few aspects of that investigation by going back through the key sources, highlighting what they say about women, what they don't, and what their biases seem to be.

Let us begin with the *Apophthegmata*. Its stories and sayings are told from the point of view of a male celibate. Women often are cast in a negative light— as temptresses, sometimes human, sometimes demonic, who come at night to haunt monks, rousing their lust or luring them to abandon their monastic commitments and return to the settled land for the amenities of family life. But here and there, one finds scattered reports of women who took up residence in the desert. For example, there is the story told of Abba Bessarion and his disciple Doulas, who, on a journey to Lycopolis, encountered an old man living in a cave. The old man never paused from his rope plaiting, never once looked up or said a word to his visitors. When the two monks returned from their trip to the city, they stopped by again but found the monk dead. It was then that they discovered the old man had in fact been an old woman. Bessarion exclaimed—and this is clearly the moral to the story—"See how women triumph over Satan, while we still behave badly in the towns."[82]

Listed among the 120 *abbas* in the *Apophthegmata* are 3 *ammas* (mothers): Theodora, Sarah, and Syncletica. As is the case with most figures in the *Apophthegmata*, biographical details are scant, and the trustworthiness of any ascription is difficult to prove. The sayings attributed to Amma Theodora are striking. Earlier I cited her assertion that the contrast between Christian and Manichaean asceticisms lay in their contrasting views on the Creator.[83] In another saying, she touches on Christian claims about the resurrection. It was a much-disputed topic. Platonist philosophers such as the second-century Celsus had mocked the Christian view of the Resurrection as "the hope of worms"; and at least one prominent Egyptian ascetic thinker, Hieracas of Leontopolis, was known for his denials of resurrection of the body.[84] It is against such a background that Theodora insisted on the reality of the Resurrection, by pointing to "Christ our God" whom we have "as pledge, example, and prototype."[85] Other sayings address asceticism, and her advice was traditional. She, like

Evagrius, stressed the hazards of *acēdia* and urged perpetual prayer.[86] She also emphasized that neither fasting nor vigils nor separation from the world could defeat demons, since they neither ate nor slept and since they made deserts their home; only humility could defeat them.[87] For Theodora, the ascetical life was "the narrow gate" to the kingdom. She offered an analogy: "Just as the trees, if they have not stood before the winter's storms cannot bear fruit, so it is with us"; we need to endure the winter "storm of the present age," for by its harsh struggles one bears the fruit for the coming kingdom.[88] One saying describes Theodora making a formal inquiry to Theophilus of Alexandria. From this scholars presume that she was active in the 390s or 400s, probably near Alexandria. Did she actually live in the desert? There is no way to be sure. She could just as easily have lived in the city itself or in one of the ascetic enclaves that lined the roads leading into the city.

Nine sayings are attributed to Amma Sarah. Several refer to her struggles with lust. In one instance, she prayed not that the battle stop, but that she be given the strength to overcome it.[89] Like other desert figures, she stressed the need always to "place death before my eyes"—only in this way could one begin up the rungs of the spiritual ladder.[90] Two of her sayings touch on gender. Once two venerable elders challenged her humility, suggesting that she may have experienced pride because they had sought advice from "a mere woman." She did not flinch: "According to nature I am a woman, but not according to my thoughts."[91] Another saying reports her challenge to visiting monks: "It is I who am a man, you who are women."[92] These two sayings raise interesting perspectives. They certainly play on and move against ancient stereotypes of the "weak woman." But there may be more at work here, something about the way asceticism can transfigure gender. These sayings seem reminiscent of Gregory of Nyssa's remarks about his sister Macrina: "A woman was the starting-point for our story, if indeed one may call her a woman, for I do not know whether it is appropriate to call someone a woman who was by nature a woman, but who, in fact, was far above nature."[93] A similar paradox is voiced in Palladius's description of Melania the Elder as "that 'female man of God.' " Susanna Elm, in her study, has argued that such gender reversals point to a unique and overlooked spirituality: "For the perfect ascetic the question of male or female no longer exists, because he or she has risen above the limits determined by the body; asceticism means annihilation of sexual distinction."[94]

Was Amma Sarah really a desert anchorite? Recent commentators have presumed that she was.[95] I am not sure it is clear. She is reported to have lived "sixty years . . . beside a river" and to have been visited by anchorites in the "area of Pelusium." That would imply that she, like anchorites visited by Cassian, lived not in the desert, but somewhere in the delta. Pelusium is at the mouth on the easternmost branch of the Nile, and it seems quite possible that she lived there. According to another saying, she was visited by monks of Scetis—which would be quite a distance from the delta town of Pelusium. It is also possible that the "Pelusium" mentioned here was upriver, in the Fayum, in the Arsinoite nome (though that is still quite a distance from Scetis).

The third great desert mother is Amma Syncletica. Twenty-six of her sayings have been preserved in various versions of the *Apophthegmata*. In several cases, she uses images of sailing to explain the vagaries of the spiritual life. She notes that the spiritual journey begins with favorable winds and full sails, but eventually one must face changing weather, sometimes tempests, sometimes dead calm. While the ascetic sets the course heading by the "sun of justice," there are times when the ascetic must sail in darkness, always alert to perils of rocks. "So it is with us, when we are driven by the spirits who are against us; we hold to the cross as our sail and so we can set a safe course."[96] She was critical of monks and nuns who wandered perpetually. She compared them to mother birds who laid eggs, but abandoned them before their offspring hatched.[97] She also noted that the geography of where one lived did not necessarily match one's interior geography: "There are many who live in the mountains and behave as if they were in the town, and they are wasting their time. It is possible to be a solitary in one's mind while living in a crowd, and it is possible for one who is a solitary to live in the crowd of his own thoughts."[98] The source for these sayings is a fifth-century work entitled *The Life and Regimen of the Holy and Blessed Teacher Syncletica*.[99] The text has been wrongly attributed to Athanasius (who, of course, had long been dead). The work opens with a brief biography. Syncletica was born in Alexandria, but her family was originally from Macedonia. Her parents tried to persuade her to get married, but at a young age she chose a life of asceticism and celibacy. After her parents died, she gave the family's holdings to the poor. She then cut off her hair and moved into a family tomb outside of Alexandria. In time, she attracted a number of disciples who supposedly recorded her sayings. She died in her eighties, apparently of cancer. The bulk of the text is her ascetical teaching, and it owes much to the spirituality of Evagrius.

The *Apophthegmata*'s accounts of desert mothers, while intriguing, are sparse. It raises the question whether it is even accurate to speak of "desert mothers." The editors of the *Apophthegmata*, of course, were not trying to write a balanced history of desert monasticism, but to gather wise sayings and stories that could inform the spiritual journey of their readers. It may well be that there were many more women in the desert than the text reports. But this category of "desert" can distract us from where the real evidence lies. In fact, there are frequent reports of women ascetics, and some of these women were active at a very early date. Athanasius reports that after Antony had sold his family property but before he apprenticed himself to the local ascetic, he sent his younger sister to "respected and faithful virgins" to be raised "in virginity."[100]

Who were these "respected and faithful virgins"? A collection of Egyptian church laws, the so-called *Canons of Hippolytus*, dating from the 330s, legislates certain duties and procedures for such designated virgins (*parthenoi*). One canon mentions that "virgins and widows fast frequently and pray for the Church"; another says that virgins are to wear a veil to church.[101] Other canons focus on widows. Widows were formally enrolled, but "not ordained; . . . prayers are not said over them; since ordination is for men."[102] Other texts speak of a "vow of virginity."[103] Some of these women would have lived alone, some with their parents, some in community with other virgins; some even cohabited with a monk in a "spiritual marriage"—though this option received sharp criticism from commentators such as Athanasius. Virgins could be a political force in the Alexandrian church. We know that at the beginning of the Arian Controversy, some of Arius's strongest political support came from the virgins in his church. Not surprisingly, Athanasius with his shrewd political sense sought to enlist the support of virgins. Two letters of his addressed to virgins, one preserved only in Coptic, the other preserved only in Syriac, were rediscovered in 1955 and have recently been translated into English.

Earlier we saw that the papyri contain reports of *apotaktikoi* ("renouncers"); they also mention *apotaktikai*, "women renouncers." I cited in chapter 1 a papyrus from Oxyrhynchus, dating from the year 400, that contains a rental contract between two sisters, Theodora and Tauris, who agreed to lease a downstairs apartment to a Jewish man. The two women are referred to as *monachai apotaktikai* ("female-monk renouncers").[104] This shows ascetic women active not in the desert, but in a bustling town, owning property and doing business across religious boundaries. How numerous were they? It is hard to say. The author of the *History of the Monks in Egypt*, who came through this area in 393, says Oxyrhynchus had 20,000 nuns. But, as we have seen, the work displays a fondness for uncritical exaggeration. However scholars suspect that the women mentioned in this and similar papyri were close to the norm: they practiced asceticism, prayer, and celibacy, and at the same time they remained active in their local church and local community.

But there are also reports of organized communities, notably double monasteries. We have seen two instances from outside Egypt: the community led by Melania the Elder in Jerusalem and the community led by Macrina in Pontus. Egypt too had its double monasteries. In 329, Pachomius's sister Mary came to visit him—just about the same time Athanasius was making his first journey to the region. Although Pachomius had not seen his sister in fifteen years, he refused to meet with her face to face. Instead, he sent out the porter with an invitation "to share in this holy life so that you may find mercy before God." She was initially upset but accepted, and the monks built "a monastery for her in that village, a short distance from his own monastery; it included a small oratory." In time, other women joined her. Pachomius appointed an old man, Apa Peter, to oversee the community and to serve as its preacher and spiritual guide. According the *Bohairic Life*, the women "practised *ascesis* eagerly with her, and she was their mother and their worthy elder until her death."[105] Pachomius's arrangement here had a significant effect. It meant that women could enjoy and share in the security and economic benefits of the emerging *koinonia*. And in a world in which the bonds of family are paramount, it addressed a deeply felt need. As Susanna Elm has noted:

> It addressed a dilemma faced by virtually every ascetic: like Antony
> before him and Basil several decades later, Pachomius and most of
> his followers had a family. But unlike Antony, who gave his sister to
> "pious virgins" and thus freed himself of all responsibility, Pachom-

ius expanded his original concept to include his sister. In so doing, he created an ideal way in which two seemingly contradictory demands of an ascetic's life could be combined: the ascetic, like Pachomius himself, could completely sever all ties with his family without having to relinquish all responsibilities towards it—and the weight and extent of those responsibilities upon the individual cannot be overestimated.[106]

The coming of Pachomius's sister may have also spurred his decision to write down his rules. According to the *Bohairic Life*, Pachomius "wrote down in a book the rules of the brothers and sent them to them through [Apa Peter] so that they might learn them."[107] Pachomius was not the only Egyptian monastic organizer to have communities of women paired with communities for men. As we will see, Shenoute developed a similar arrangement for the White Monastery.

In the classic texts, women are rarely the narrative focus. One exception is Palladius's *Lausiac History*. Describing women's quest for holiness was part of his stated purpose. As he told Lausus, he wanted his narrative to celebrate "the manly women to whom God granted the capacity struggles equal to those of men."[108] Note the paradoxical term here: "manly women" (*gunaikōn andreiōn*). The athletic strengths that his culture associated only with men were now, through asceticism, open to women. Palladius insisted that the pursuit of holiness crossed all sorts of borders: between nations, between classes, and between genders. And so, scattered through his account, Palladius offers portraits that display a wide range of women's ascetical lifestyles. There is the unnamed virgin who risked her life to hide Athanasius during his years on the run from imperial authorities.[109] There is Piamoun, whose life of home-based asceticism seemed quite ordinary on the surface (she made her living spinning flax), but who at a key juncture "was deemed worthy of the gift of prophecy." Once she alerted village elders to a coming violent attack; thanks to her prayers, the attackers' feet became immobilized, and they were unable to carry out their raid.[110] There is the story of Elias, a wealthy citizen of Athribis, who built a large monastery for some 300 women—perhaps homeless refugees or perhaps ascetic wanderers. Palladius also mentions that Ammonius the Earless went to the desert "with his three brothers *and two sisters*" and that each "created a hermitage" (*monē*) at some distance from the others.[111] This implies a fascinating amalgam: a family in which both men *and* women have become anchorites in the desert.

This survey, admittedly far too brief, is meant mainly to highlight the limits and biases of our sources. They do indicate that there were women ascetics and that, at least in certain locales, the numbers may have been large. These same sources devote relatively little narrative space to women, their organizations, their spiritual development, and their monastic theology. There is no Egyptian equivalent to Gregory of Nyssa's *Life of Macrina* that might allow us to see the progress of women's asceticism at closer range. Palladius's *History* helps, but the ascetic woman whose life he most celebrates is Melania the

Elder, a Latin active in Palestine, not Egypt. Overall, one might say women's asceticism in Egypt is underreported. The evidence, while both faint and fragmentary, does imply that women's asceticism had sizable numbers, varied lifestyles, and considerable vigor.

Monasticism Overlooked: Shenoute of Atripe

This chapter has mapped out various ascetical roads-less-traveled and roads-less-publicized: Melitians and Manichees, *apotaktikoi* and ascetic virgins. It is clear that the classic sources only hint at the full range of ancient experiments in ascetical Christianity. Who gets remembered and who gets forgotten depends much on which texts get preserved and which texts are deemed classics. The classic texts for reconstructing the history of early monasticism are in Greek and Latin. This linguistic bias has meant that other pioneers have been forgotten.

The most obvious example is Shenoute of Atripe (c. 348–c. 464).[112] Shenoute, utterly ignored by Greek or Latin sources, was a brilliant stylist and pioneer of Coptic literature and remains one of the most venerated figures of the Coptic Orthodox Church. Our knowledge of Shenoute comes from two principal sources: his own rather extensive writings and a biography by his disciple, Besa. Shenoute's own writings have come down to us in two clusters: the *Canons*, a set of nine collections of letters written to monks under his charge; and the *Discourses* (*Logoi*), a set of public sermons. Unfortunately, these have been poorly preserved. Much survives only in damaged or hard-to-decipher manuscripts; many texts have been preserved out of sequence, and only recently has their original order begun to be sorted out. No critical edition has yet been produced, and little has been translated.

Nonetheless, the basics of Shenoute's life and work are known. He grew up in the Thebaid and entered a monastery begun by his uncle Pcol. It was located outside Akhmim in Upper Egypt, near the modern village of Sohag, 250 miles south of Cairo. It became known as the White Monastery because of the color of its walls. In 385, Shenoute was chosen as abbot, apparently the monastery's third.[113] Under his leadership, numbers expanded rapidly. An Arabic version of Besa's *Life* reports huge numbers—2200 monks and 1800 nuns—but given this version's propensity for exaggeration, scholars are uncertain about its accuracy. If accurate, it would mean that Shenoute's monastery rivaled the nearby Pachomian foundations in size.

In some ways, life in Shenoute's monastery resembled one in the Pachomian system.[114] Monks lived in individual houses governed by a housemaster (or housemistress) who was assisted by a "second." Work duties, such as harvesting reeds, baking bread, or making clothes, were assigned to individual houses. There were central buildings: a church, a refectory, and an infirmary. There was a morning service of psalms and scripture readings held before work each day, and there were communal meals. Unlike the Pachomians, but like the monks of Scetis, Shenoute's monks ate only once a day, around three o'clock in the afternoon.

Scholars have noted that at the White Monastery, corporal punishment was a commonly used discipline. Shenoute himself administered some beatings and floggings. He even admits in one letter that a monk died during a beating that he had given.[115] All this clearly shocks modern sensibilities. It is important to remember that civil society in the ancient world routinely used corporal punishment and judicial torture. Corporal punishment also played some part in monastic culture. Palladius, for instance, mentions a place for public whippings in the monastery of Nitria.[116] What makes Shenoute unique here is not the practice, but a first-person defense of its use.[117]

A recent study by Rebecca Krawiec has focused on Shenoute's complex relationship with the women of the White Monastery. Drawing on Shenoute's letters, she has pieced together vivid, if fragmentary, snapshots of practical crises he faced. Some monks refused to accept superiors he appointed or sought transfers to escape a superior they despised. Some women had "menfolk" or "sons" in the male community and, contrary to the rules, paid them visits. He had to cope with monks who were gossipmongers or who stole food. Before his tenure as abbot, the women's monastery had enjoyed greater autonomy. So when he first asserted more direct authority, he faced an uphill battle. And even when his authority was accepted in principle, he still faced resistance, from quiet disobedience to overt confrontation. His personal visits were not always welcome, and his behavior could be criticized. Once, to express his outrage, he tore his cloak, a gesture he meant as prophetic. But superiors in the women's monastery promptly criticized the gesture as improper and sexually charged, an accusation he felt forced to rebut.

Shenoute not only served as abbot of the White Monastery. He also worked as a passionate and eloquent evangelist for Christianity. He sometimes targeted pagan survivals within ordinary Christian piety:

> Those fallen into poverty or in sickness or indeed some other trial abandon God and run after enchanters or diviners or indeed seek other acts of deception, just as I myself have seen: the snake's head tied on someone's hand, another one with the crocodile's tooth tied to his arm, and another with fox claws tied to his legs. . . . Listen to this impiety! Fox claws! Snakes' heads! Crocodiles' teeth! . . . It is about them that the Prophet Elijah blamed Israel in that time, saying, "How long will you limp on two legs? If the Lord is God, follow him, but if Baal, then follow him" . . . If the oracle sanctuary of demons is useful to you—and enchanters and drug-makers and all the other things that thus work for lawlessness—then go to them, so that you will receive their curse on earth and eternal punishment on the day of judgment! But if it is the house of God, the Church, that is useful to you, go to it.[118]

Shenoute did more than preach against paganism. He and his monks moved about the countryside as a sort of mobile wrecking crew, dismantling old pagan temples. Other times, he and his monks would "purify" temples, stripping them of their hieroglyphs and reconsecrating them for Christian worship. In a sermon delivered outside an old temple, he pointed to the ancient hieroglyphs—"the likenesses of the snakes and scorpions, the dogs and cats, the crocodiles and frogs"—and speaks of them as "prescriptions for murdering man's soul." His sermon celebrated the temple's reconsecration for Christian use: "At the site of a shrine to an unclean spirit, it will henceforth be a shrine to the Holy Spirit. And at the site of sacrificing to Satan and worshipping and fearing him, Christ will henceforth be served there, and He will be worshipped, bowed down to and feared. And where there are blasphemings, it is blessings and hymns that will henceforth be there."[119]

Shenoute also opposed various schisms and heresies. His own writings speak against various groups we have seen: Manichees, Melitians, Arians, and Origenists. Scholars are not sure whether all of these were still vital groups in his era or whether his verbal onslaughts may have targeted some who had already faded from the scene. There were still Origenists, apparently. We have a letter ascribed to Dioscorus of Alexandria warning Shenoute to expel some Origenist monk who sought shelter in Upper Egypt. Shenoute also accompanied Cyril to the Council of Ephesus. Besa even claims that Shenoute attacked Nestorius physically, slapping him. In his own writings, Shenoute seems to display little mastery of the intricacies of the Christological debate.

Shenoute is a difficult figure to assess. Armand Veilleux, an expert on Pachomian literature, reads Shenoute in the darkest terms: as "authoritarian, harsh, and violent"; as one "whose spirituality, lacking any mystical dimension, his best specialist (J. Leipoldt) describes as 'Christ-less' "; as "a volcano in perpetual eruption."[120] This assessment seems imbalanced, if not unfair, in light of recent research. John McGuckin has suggested that Shenoute was seen by Besa, his biographer, as a prophet like Elijah. In Old Testament narratives, Elijah is portrayed not only as a prophet and wonder worker, but also as a violent opponent of the cult of Baal. According to McGuckin, "This biblical archetype of the wonder-working prophet who was jealous for the honor of his God and thus attacked the priests of Baal undoubtedly is behind much of Shenoute's hagiography and likely behind most of his own understanding of the monastic state and his own place within it."[121] Recent research indicates that Besa's view reflects Shenoute's self-understanding. Shenoute saw himself as a divinely appointed prophet, a "suffering servant," and a medium both of God's message and of God's judgment.[122] Any assessment of Shenoute must consider the way he defended the rights of the poor against the powerful, the way he welcomed refugees, the way he and his monks worked to feed the hungry. A balanced assessment will only be possible once his works have been reedited, published, translated, and studied by a wider range of students.

But the case of Shenoute is an important reminder of the limits of the classic sources. Important figures have sometimes been forgotten for no other reason than language. They dropped off the radar screen of history because either they or their disciples wrote in a language unknown to the Greco-Roman culture that created the standard history.

This exploration of monastic origins has been, in part, a negative enterprise, a matter of debunking old truisms. We have seen that old claims about Antony, Pachomius, and Egypt simply do not stand up to critical scrutiny. We have also seen that early monasticism was a messy, diverse phenomenon. Only a small part of the story has been given much "airtime" in the classic texts. Antony and Pachomius and the Macarii were simply the best-publicized figures in a much larger and much more diverse movement. And the monastic mainstream had lots of competition, some friendly, some not. Various ascetics were either undercounted or undervalued, either marginalized by or deleted from the later historical record. Sometimes it was because of language (as in the case of Shenoute), sometimes because of definitions of orthodoxy (e.g., the Manichees) or because of ecclesiastical politics (e.g., the Melitians). Some historians read silences in the historical record in conspiratorial terms, following the old truism that history is the story of the victors. I do not think it is so simple. Some religious groups simply lacked scribes to broadcast their achievements. That is how I would read much of the neglect of the *apotaktikoi*, the virgins and the widows. If a group has sufficient scribes, its message can survive even fierce persecution. We saw that four leading early monastic writers were Origenists: Evagrius, Cassian, Palladius, and Rufinus. They certainly suffered, but their message was preserved because they had the wherewithal to write books—and because they had important things to say.

Any exploration of origins has real limits. Columba Stewart recently opened a short introduction to early monasticism saying: "Most early monastic Christians are inaccessible to us."[123] This is masterful understatement—and a truth important to savor. When studying history in general and ancient history in particular, we have to be very conscious of what we know and what we do not. While we do know interesting things about certain monks and certain monasteries, we do not know what happened to the overwhelming majority. Most early monks voiced their spiritual experience, if at all, orally, to their *abbas* or *ammas* in private conversations. They never wrote it down. Reconstructing early Christian monasticism, its origins and contours, from surviving documents and surviving archaeological sites is inescapably difficult and necessarily tentative. It is all right to admit that we do not know much about where certain important things come from.

NOTES

1. Cassian, *Collationes* 18.5.1–4 (SC 64:14–16; trans. Ramsey, ACW 57:637–638). Cf. *De institutis* 2.5.3–4.

2. Versions of this appear even in writings of some experts. For example, Hugh Evelyn-White writes in his *Monasteries of Wadi 'n Natrûn*, 281: "Monasticism as a Christian institution came to birth in Egypt; and of the two forms in which it manifested itself from the first, that which was initiated by Saint Antony is equal in importance to—and perhaps more characteristically Egyptian than—the system established by Pachomius."

3. Goehring, "The Origins of Monasticism," in *Ascetics, Society, and the Desert*, 19.

4. *VA* 3 (SC 400:136–138; trans. Gregg, CWS, 32).

5. *VA* 3 (SC 400:136; trans. Gregg, CWS, 32).

6. *AP* Macarius 1 (PG 65:257–260; CS 59:124–125).

7. *AP* Macarius 4 and 26 (PG 65:263 and 273; CS 59:127–128 and 153).

8. *Bohairic Life* 10 (CSCO 89:7–8; trans. Veilleux, CS 45:30); cf. *First Greek Life* 6 (SH 19:4–5; CS 45:301).

9. *Historia monachorum in Aegypto*, prol. 10 (SH 53:8; CS 34:50).

10. For the text and for an analysis, see Edwin A. Judge, "The Earliest Use of Monachos for 'Monk' (*P. Coll. Youtie* 77) and the Origins of Monasticism," *Jahrbuch für Antike und Christentum* 20 (1977): 72–89.

11. Judge, "Earliest Use," 72 and 75.

12. Judge, "Earliest Use," 80–82.

13. Judge, "Earliest Use," 85.

14. Jerome, *Ep.* 22.34 (Labourt, 1:149–150); Cassian, *Collationes* 18.4 (SC 64:14; ACW 57:637), has a similar threesome: *coenobiotae, anchoretae,* and *sarabaitae*; cf. Egeria, *Itinerarium* 23.3 (SC 296:228; ACW 38:87), who also has a threesome that includes *aputactitae* ("renouncers").

15. Judge, "Earliest Use," 85–86.

16. Judge, "Earliest Use," 80; *Historia monachorum in Aegypto* 5.2–6 (SH 53:42–53; CS 34:67).

17. Judge, "Earliest Use," 88.

18. Goehring, "The Origins of Monasticism," in *Ascetics, Society, and the Desert,* 31–32.

19. Goehring, "Through a Glass Darkly: Images of the Ἀποτακτικοί (αἱ) in Early Egyptian Monasticism," in *Ascetics, Society, and the Desert,* 54. As we have seen, Jerome may have been influential, but was rarely fair-minded about things ascetic nor particularly well informed about Egypt.

20. Goehring, "The Origins of Monasticism," in *Ascetics, Society, and the Desert,* 31.

21. *VA* 3 (SC 400:136; trans. Gregg, CWS, 32).

22. Goehring, "The Origins of Monasticism," in *Ascetics, Society, and the Desert,* 21.

23. Chitty, *The Desert a City,* 9, recognizes the problem and considers it a possible, but not likely, hypothesis that the "Melitians [found in Bell's papyri] may well have been Antony's disciples in the days before the schism crystallized."

24. *First Greek Life* 54 (SH 19:37; CS 45:334–335) = *Bohairic Life* 49–51 (CSCO 89:51–52; CS 45:71–72).

25. Goehring, "The Origins of Monasticism," in *Ascetics, Society, and the Desert,* 28, but he has modified that view in light of his research on the Melitians.

26. One exception is the mention of Melitian monastic presence in a saying about Abba Sisoes: *AP* Sisoes 48 (PG 65:405; CS 59:185).

27. H. Idris Bell, ed., *Jews and Christians in Egypt: The Jewish Troubles in Alexandria and the Athanasian Controversy, Illustrated by Texts from Greek Papyri in the British Museum* (London: British Museum, 1924), 38–99, for the first set; 100–120 for the second set. Bell was not certain whether or not the second set was indeed Melitian. The consensus is now that it is indeed Melitian, in light of the discoveries of the archive of Nepheros. See Goehring, "Monastic Diversity and Ideological Boundaries in Fourth-Century Christian Egypt," in *Ascetics, Society, and the Desert,* 200–203.

28. *P. Lond.* 1923 (Bell, 103–104).

29. *P. Lond.* 1926 (Bell, 109).

30. Bärbel Kramer and John C. Shelton, *Das Archiv des Nepheros und verwandte Texte* (Mainz: Philipp von Zabern, 1987).

31. Roger S. Bagnall, *Egypt in Late Antiquity* (Princeton: Princeton University Press, 1993), 203.

32. *P. Lond.* 1913.3, 1920.2, 1917.9, 1917.18, and 1914.6 (Bell, 49–50, 92–93, 81–83, 58–62).

33. *P. Lond.* 1913 (Bell, 49–50).

34. *Ep. Ammon.* 12 (Goehring, 132, 165).

35. On Syrian monasticism, see the bibliography for chapter 13. For a translation of Theodoret's text, see R. M. Power, *A History of the Monks of Syria by Theodoret of Cyrrhus*, CS 88 (Kalamazoo, Mich.: Cistercian Publications, 1985). See also Robert Doran, *The Lives of Symeon Stylites*, CS 112 (Kalamazoo, Mich.: Cistercian Publications, 1992), which has Theodoret's version as well as an anonymous *Life* composed in Syriac and a *Life* composed in Greek by a disciple named Antonius.

36. Syriac *Life of Symeon* 43 (CS 112:127); cf. Theodoret of Cyrrhus, *Historia religiosa* 26.2 and 26.12 (SC 257:160–162, 186; CS 88:161, 165–166).

37. Robert Murray, "The Exhortation to Candidates for Ascetical Vows at Baptism in the Ancient Syrian Church," *New Testament Studies* 21 (1974–75): 58–79.

38. Robert Murray, *Symbols of Church and Kingdom: A Study in Early Syriac Tradition* (Cambridge: Cambridge University Press, 1975), 13–14; Sebastian Brock, *The Luminous Eye: The Spiritual World Vision of Saint Ephrem*, CS 124 (Kalamazoo, Mich.: Cistercian Publications, 1992), 136–137.

39. Murray, *Symbols of Church and Kingdom*, 131. For a fuller discussion, see Sidney H. Griffith, "Asceticism in the Church of Syria: the Hermeneutics of Early Syrian Monasticism," in Wimbush and Valantasis, *Asceticism*, 223–229.

40. Ephrem, *Hymns on the Nativity* 1.62 (CS 124:141).

41. Kathleen McVey, *Ephrem the Syrian: Hymns*, CWS (New York: Paulist Press, 1989), 229n36.

42. For a translation, see George A. Maloney, *Pseudo-Macarius: The Fifty Spiritual Homilies and the Great Letter*, CWS (New York: Paulist Press, 1992). See the study by Columba Stewart, *"Working the Earth of the Heart": The Messalian Controversy in History, Texts, and Language to AD 431* (New York: Oxford University Press, 1991).

43. See the bibliography for chapter 13.

44. Basil of Caesarea, *Ep.* 223 (to Eustathius of Sebaste) (LCL 3:292–294; FC 28:128).

45. Basil of Caesarea, *Ep.* 14 (to Gregory of Nazianzus) (LCL 1:106–110; FC 13:46–48).

46. Basil of Caesarea, *Regulae fusius tractatae* 3 (PG 31:917); trans. Augustine Holmes, *A Life Pleasing to God: The Spirituality of the Rules of St. Basil*, CS 189 (Kalamazoo, Mich.: Cistercian Publications, 2000), 89.

47. Basil of Caesarea, *Regulae fusius tractatae* 7 (PG 31:933; trans. Holmes, CS 189:142).

48. Sozomen, *HE* 6.34 (PG 67:1397; NPNF 2.2:371); cf. Basil of Caesarea, *Ep.* 31 and 94.

49. Gregory of Nazianzus, *Oratio* 43.62 (SC 384:260; trans. NPNF 7:415–416).

50. Benedict, *Regula* 73 (RB 1980:296). See Joseph T. Lienhard, "St. Basil's *Asceticon Parvum* and the *Regula Benedicti*," *Studia Monastica* 22 (1980): 231–242.

51. Sozomen, *HE* 3.14.31–36 (SC 418:132–134; NPNF 2.2:293–294).

52. For a translation of these canons, see O. Larry Yarbrough, "Canons from the Council of Gangra," in Wimbush, *Ascetic Behavior in Greco-Roman Antiquity*, 448–455.

53. Holmes, *A Life Pleasing to God*, CS 189:42.

54. For the Greek text, see Pierre Maraval, ed., *Grégoire de Nysse: Vie de Sainte*

Macaire, SC 178 (Paris: Éditions du Cerf, 1971). For a translation, see Joan M. Petersen, *Handmaids of the Lord: Contemporary Descriptions of Feminine Asceticism in the First Six Christian Centuries*, CS 143 (Kalamazoo, Mich.: Cistercian Publications, 1996), 41–86.

55. Susanna Elm, *Virgins of God: The Making of Asceticism in Late Antiquity*, Oxford Classical Monographs (New York: Oxford University Press, 1994), 60–136.

56. Gregory of Nyssa, *Vita s. Macrinae* 11 (SC 178:174–176; CS 143:59).

57. Holmes, *A Life Pleasing to God*, CS 189:26–27; compare this to the old-fashioned, Egypt-centered presentation in W. K. L. Clarke, *The Ascetic Works of Saint Basil* (London: SPCK, 1925), 44.

58. Eusebius, *HE* 6.9.8 (SC 41:98).

59. *Vita Charitonis.* The Greek text has been edited by G. Garitte, "La vie prémetaphrastique de S. Chariton," *Bulletin de l'Institut historique Belge de Rome* 21 (1941): 16–46. For a translation, see Leah di Segni, "The Life of Chariton," in Wimbush, *Ascetic Behavior in Greco-Roman Antiquity*, 393–421.

60. For a valuable study of the archaeology and architecture of Palestinian *lauras*, see Yizhar Hirschfeld, *Judean Monasteries in the Byzantine Period* (New Haven: Yale University Press, 1992).

61. Cyril of Scythopolis, *V. Sabas* 180 (TU 49.2:180; CS 114:189).

62. The preliminary study of the correspondence of Barsanuphius and John of Gaza had been begun by Derwas Chitty. For an overview, see Chitty, *The Desert a City*, 132–140.

63. Philo, *On the Contemplative Life* IV (LCL, 9:113–169). For a translation, see Gail Peterson Carrington, "Philo: On the Contemplative Life," in Wimbush, *Ascetic Behavior in Greco-Roman Antiquity*, 134–155. For a study, see Antoine Guillaumont, "Philon et le origines du monachisme" and "Perspectives actuelles sur les origines du monachisme," in *Aux origines du monachisme chrétien*, SO 30:25–37 and 216–227.

64. Eusebius of Caesarea, *HE* 2.16 (LCL, 1:145).

65. Goehring, "The Origins of Monasticism," in *Ascetics, Society, and the Desert*, 14–18.

66. Samuel N.C. Lieu, "Precept and Practice in Manichaean Monasticism," *Journal of Theological Studies* n.s. 32 (1981): 158.

67. *Cologne Mani Codex* 104.1 (trans. Valantasis, *Religions of Late Antiquity*, 169).

68. *Coptic Manichaean Psalm-Book*, Psalm 223.2. For the Coptic text, with an English translation, see C. R. C. Allberry, *A Manichaean Psalm-Book*, part 2 (Stuttgart: W. Kohlhammer, 1938). I have used here the recent translation by Jason D. BeDuhn, "Manichaean Theology," in Valantasis, *Religions of Late Antiquity*, 482.

69. *Coptic Manichaean Psalm-Book*, Psalm 223.3 (BeDuhn, 482).

70. *Coptic Manichaean Psalm-Book*, Psalm 248.26–27 (Allberry, 56).

71. *Coptic Manichaean Psalm-Book*, Psalm 223.16 (BeDuhn, 483).

72. *Coptic Manichaean Psalm-Book*, Psalm 223.14 (BeDuhn, 483).

73. Iain Gardiner, "The Manichaeans Community at Kellis: A Progress Report," in Paul Mirecki and Jason BeDuhn, *Emerging from Darkness: Studies in the Recovery of Manichaean Sources*, Nag Hammadi and Manichaean Studies 43 (Leiden: Brill, 1997), 161–176.

74. *VA* 68 (SC 400:314; trans. Brakke, *Athanasius and the Politics of Asceticism*, 23).

75. *AP* Theodora 4 (PG 65:202–204; trans. Ward, CS 59:83). Cf. *Verba Seniorum* 5.13.2 (PL 73:945).

76. *Historia monachorum in Aegypto* 10.30–32 (SH 53:87–88; CS 34:86–87). Man-

ichaean texts report similar contests with Christians, but with the Manichees achieving victories over the Christians. See the Sogdian fragment quoted in Samuel N. C. Lieu, *Manchaeism in Mesopotamia and the Roman East* (Leiden: E. J. Brill, 1994), 31.

77. Gedaliahu G. Strousma, "The Manichaean Challenge to Egyptian Christianity," in Pearson and Goehring, *Roots of Egyptian Christianity*, 308.

78. Strousma, "Manichaean Challenge," 309.

79. Goehring, "The Origins of Monasticism," in *Ascetics, Society, and the Desert*, 28–30, and "Monastic Diversity," in *Ascetics, Society, and the Desert*, 197–198, seems sympathetic to the idea, though he argues, "Even if Pachomius had been directly influenced by the Manichaean movement organizationally, it does not establish a single Manichaean origin of cenobitic monasticism" (29).

80. *AP* Sisoes 3 (PG 65:392; trans. my own).

81. For women and asceticism, see the bibliography for chapter 13.

82. *AP* Bessarion 4 (PG 65:140–141; trans. Ward, CS 59:41).

83. *AP* Theodora 4 (PG 65:201–204; CS 59:83).

84. Celsus, quoted in Origen, *Contra Celsum* 5.14 (Chadwick, 274–275). On Hieracas of Leontopolis, see Brakke, *Athanasius and the Politics of Asceticism*, 44–57; and Goehring, "Hieracas of Leontopolis: The Making of a Desert Ascetic," in *Ascetics, Society, and the Desert*, 110–133.

85. *AP* Theodora 10 (= Suppl. 1) (Guy, 23; trans. Ward, CS 59:84).

86. *AP* Theodora 3 (PG 65:201; CS 59:83).

87. *AP* Theodora 6 (PG 65:204; CS 59:84).

88. *AP* Theodora 2 (PG 65:201; trans. Ward, CS 59:83).

89. *AP* Sarah 1 and 2 (PG 65:420; CS 59:229–230).

90. *AP* Sarah 6 (PG 65:421; trans. Ward, CS 59:230).

91. *AP* Sarah 4 (PG 65:420; trans. Ward, CS 59:230).

92. *AP* Sarah 9 (= Suppl. 1) (Guy, 34; trans. Ward, CS 59:230).

93. Gregory, *Vita s. Macrinae* 1.14–18 (SC 178:140; trans. Petersen, CS 143:51).

94. Elm, *Virgins of God*, 267.

95. This is mentioned both by Elm, *Virgins of God*, 265–266, and by Ward, "Apophthegmata Matrum," *Studia Patristica* 16 (1985): 65.

96. *AP* Syncletica 9 (PG 65:424–425; trans. CS 59:232–233) and 25 (= Suppl. 8) (Guy, 35; CS 59:235); cf. *AP* Syncletica 26 (= Suppl. 9) (Guy, 35; CS 59:235), in which she compares humility to the nails that hold together a ship.

97. *AP* Syncletica 6 (PG 65:421–424; CS 59:231).

98. *AP* Syncletica 19 (= Suppl. 1) (Guy, 34; trans. Ward, CS 59:234).

99. For a translation, see Elizabeth Bryson Bongie, *The Life of Blessed Syncletica, by Pseudo-Athanasius* (Toronto: Peregrina, 1996).

100. *VA* 3 (SC 400:136; trans. my own).

101. Canon 32 (PO 31.2:402–404). See the discussion in Elm, *Virgins of God*, 229 ff.

102. Canon 9 (PO 31.2:362).

103. Athanasius, *Ep. virg.* 1.33 (trans. Brakke, *Athanasius and the Politics of Asceticism*, 285).

104. *P. Oxy.* 3203.

105. *Bohairic Life* 27 (CSCO 89:26–28; trans. Veilleux, CS 45:49–50).

106. Elm, *Virgins of God*, 291.

107. *Bohairic Life* 27 (CSCO 89:27; trans. Veilleux, CS 45:50).

108. Palladius, *Historia Lausiaca* 41 (Butler, 128; trans. Meyer, ACW 34:117).

109. Palladius, *Historia Lausiaca* 63 (ACW 34:144–145).

110. Palladius, *Historia Lausiaca* 31 (Butler, 86; ACW 34:90–91).

111. Palladius, *Historia Lausiaca* 11 (Butler, 32; trans. my own).

112. These dates, which imply that Shenoute lived about 116 years, seem to strain credibility, but they accurately reflect the results of careful analysis of the sources. On this, see Stephen L. Emmel, "Shenoute's Literary Corpus" (Ph.D. diss., Yale University, 1993), 3–11. For studies of Shenoute, see the bibliography for chapter 13.

113. Emmel, "Shenoute's Literary Corpus," 7. Emmel's research has reversed the traditional description of Shenoute as his uncle's immediate successor and as the monastery's second abbot. Between Pcol and Shenoute was the monastery's second abbot, a man named Ebonh.

114. For a reconstruction of daily life in Shenoute's monastery, see Rebecca Krawiec, *Shenoute and the Women of the White Monastery* (New York: Oxford University Press, 2002).

115. Krawiec, *Shenoute and the Women*, 43–46.

116. Palladius, *Historia Lausiaca* 7.3 (Butler, 26; ACW 34:40).

117. See the judicious remarks of Krawiec, *Shenoute and the Women*, 28–29.

118. Shenoute of Atripe, *Against the Origenists*, 255–262; quoted in Frankfurter, "Popular Religious Practices in Fifth-Century Egypt," in *Religions of Late Antiquity in Practice*, ed. Richard Valantasis (Princeton: Princeton University Press, 2000), 474.

119. Shenoute of Atripe, from an unedited sermon preserved in Michigan ms. 158, quoted in Frankfurter, *Religion in Roman Egypt*, 265.

120. Veilleux, preface to David N. Bell, *Besa: The Life of Shenoute*, CS 73 (Kalamazoo, Mich.: Cistercian Publications, 1983), v and xi.

121. John McGuckin, "Shenoute of Atripe," in *Encyclopedia of Monasticism*, ed. William W. Johnston (Chicago: Fitzroy Dearborn, 2000) 2:1161.

122. Krawiec, *Shenoute and the Women*, 55–72.

123. Stewart, "Monasticism," in *The Early Christian World*, ed. Philip E. Esler (New York: Routledge, 2000), 1:344.

BIBLIOGRAPHY

Origins of Monasticism

A valuable overview is James E. Goehring, "The Origins of Monasticism," reprinted in *Ascetics, Society, and the Desert: Studies in Egyptian Monasticism* (Harrisburg, Pa.: Trinity Press International, 1999), 13–35. Other essays by Goehring in the same volume expand on aspects of this; see especially "Monastic Diversity and Ideological Boundaries in Fourth-Century Christian Egypt" (196–218); "Through a Glass Darkly: Diverse Images of the Ἀποτακτικοί (αἱ) in Early Egyptian Monasticism" (53–72); and "Melitian Monastic Organization: A Challenge to Pachomian Originality" (187–195). Current evaluations draw heavily (but not uncritically) on the pathbreaking and rather technical study of Edwin A. Judge, "The Earliest Use of Monachos for 'Monk' (*P. Coll. Youtie* 77) and the Origins of Monasticism," *Jahrbuch für Antike und Christentum* 20 (1977): 72–89. See also:

Guillaumont, Antoine, "Perspectives actuelles sur les origines du monachisme," in *Aux origines du monachisme chrétien*, 216–227. SO 30. Bégrolles-en-Mauges: Abbaye de Bellefontaine, 1979.

Gould, Graham. "Early Egyptian Monasticism and the Church." In *Monastic Studies:*

The Continuity of Tradition, ed. J. Loades, 1–10. Bangor, Gwynedd: Headstart History, 1990.

Gribomont, Jean. "Monasticism and Asceticism: Eastern Christianity." In *Christian Spirituality: Origins to the Twelfth Century*, ed., Bernard McGinn and John Meyendorff, 89–112. New York: Crossroad, 1985.

Rousseau, Philip. "Christian Asceticism and the Early Monks." In *Early Christianity: Origins and Evolution to A.D. 600*, ed. Ian Hazlett. Nashville: Abingdon Press, 1991.

Rubenson, Samuel. "Christian Asceticism and the Emergence of the Monastic Tradition." In *Asceticism*, ed. Vincent L. Wimbush and Richard Valantasis, 49–57. New York: Oxford University Press, 1991.

Stewart, Columba. "Monasticism." In *The Early Christian World*, ed. Philip E. Esler, 1: 344–366. New York: Routledge, 2000.

Syrian Asceticism

A good starting point is the introduction by R. M. Power, *A History of the Monks of Syria*, *by Theodoret of Cyrrhus*, CS 88 (Kalamazoo, Mich.: Cistercian Publications, 1985). The classic scholarly study, now challenged on various issues, is Arthur Vööbus, *A History of Asceticism in the Syrian Orient: A Contribution to the History of Culture in the Near East*, 3 vols., CSCO 184, 197, and 500 (Louvain: Secrétariat du Corpus SCO, 1958–1988). One of the best known and most influential articles on early Christian asceticism focuses especially on Syria: Peter Brown, "The Rise and Function of the Holy Man in Late Antiquity," *Journal of Roman Studies* 61 (1971): 80–101, reprinted in *Society and the Holy in Late Antiquity* (Berkeley: University of California Press, 1982). See also:

Brock, Sebastian. *The Luminous Eye: The Spiritual World Vision of Saint Ephrem*. CS 124. Kalamazoo, Mich.: Cistercian Publications, 1992.

Brock, Sebastian, trans. *Syriac Fathers on Prayer and the Spiritual Life*. CS 101. Kalamazoo, Mich.: Cistercian Publications, 1987.

Brock, Sebastian, and Susan Ashbrook Harvey, trans. *Holy Women of the Syrian Orient*. Transformation of the Classical Heritage 13. Berkeley: University of California Press, 1987.

Griffith, Sidney H. "Asceticism in the Church of Syria: the Hermeneutics of Early Syrian Monasticism." In *Asceticism*, ed. Vincent L. Wimbush and Richard Valantasis, 220–245. New York: Oxford University Press, 1995.

———. "Ephraem, the Deacon of Edessa, and the Church of the Empire." In *Diakonia: Studies in Honor of Robert T. Meyer*, ed. Thomas Halton and Joseph P. Williman, 22–52. Washington, D.C.: Catholic University of America Press, 1986.

Harvey, Susan Ashbrook. "The Sense of a Stylite: Perspectives on Simeon the Elder." *Vigiliae Christianae* 42 (1988): 376–394.

———. "The Stylite's Liturgy: Ritual and Religious Identity in Late Antiquity." *Journal of Early Christian Studies* 6 (1998): 523–539.

Murray, Robert. *Symbols of Church and Kingdom: A Study in Early Syriac Tradition*. Cambridge: Cambridge University Press, 1975.

Palestinian Monasticism

A good starting point is Yizhar Hirschfeld, *The Judean Desert Monasteries in the Byzantine Period* (New Haven: Yale University Press, 1992). On Cyril of Scythopolis, see John Binns, *Ascetics and Ambassadors of Christ: The Monasteries of Palestine, 314–631*, Oxford

Early Christian Studies (New York: Oxford University Press, 1994). Also valuable is the classic study of Derwas Chitty, *The Desert a City: An Introduction to the Study of Egyptian and Palestinian Monasticism under the Christian Empire* (London: Basil Blackwell, 1966; reprint: Crestwood, N.Y.: St. Vladimir's Seminary Press). See also:

Segni, Leah di. "The Life of Chariton." In *Ascetic Behavior in Greco-Roman Antiquity: A Sourcebook*, ed. Vincent L. Wimbush, 393–421. Studies in Antiquity and Christianity. Minneapolis: Fortress Press, 1990.

Hirschfeld, Yizhar. "The Founding of the New Laura." In *Asceticism*, ed. Vincent L. Wimbush and Richard Valantasis, 267–289. New York: Oxford University Press, 1995.

——. "Life of Chariton in Light of Archeological Research." In *Ascetic Behavior in Greco-Roman Antiquity: A Sourcebook*, ed. Vincent L. Wimbush, 425–447. Studies in Antiquity and Christianity. Minneapolis: Fortress Press, 1990.

Patrich, Joseph. *Sabas, Leader of Palestinian Monasticism: A Comparative Study in Eastern Monasticism, Fourth to Seventh Centuries*. Dumbarton Oaks Studies 32. Washington, D.C.: Dumbarton Oaks, 1995.

Price, R. M., trans. *Lives of the Monks of Palestine, by Cyril of Scythopolis*. CS 114. Kalamazoo, Mich.: Cistercian Publications, 1991.

Wheeler, Eric P., trans. *Discourses and Sayings: Dorotheos of Gaza*. CS 33. Kalamazoo, Mich.: Cistercian Publications, 1987.

Wortley, John. *The Spiritual Meadow, by John Moschos*. CS 139. Kalamazoo, Mich.: Cistercian Publications, 1992.

Cappadocian Monasticism

A good starting point is Augustine Holmes, *A Life Pleasing to God: The Spirituality of the Rules of St. Basil*, CS 189 (Kalamazoo, Mich.: Cistercian Publications, 2000). This has a commentary on Basil's monastic rules, prefaced with a fifty-page introductory survey of Basil's career and spirituality. See also:

Elm, Susanna. *Virgins of God: The Making of Asceticism in Late Antiquity*, 60–136. Oxford Classical Monographs. New York: Oxford University Press, 1994.

Fedwick, Paul Jonathan, ed. *Basil of Caesarea: Christian, Humanist, Ascetic*. 2 vols. Toronto: Pontifical Institute of Medieval Studies, 1981.

Gribomont, Jean. *Saint Basile: évangile et église*. 2 vols. SO 36–37. Bégrolles-en Mauges: Abbaye de Bellefontaine, 1984.

McGuckin, John. *Saint Gregory of Nazianzus: An Intellectual Biography*. Crestwood, N.Y.: St. Vladimir's Seminary Press, 2001.

Rousseau, Philip. *Basil of Caesarea*. Transformation of the Classical Heritage 20. Berkeley: University of California Press, 1994.

Monasticism in the Latin West

See Conrad Leyser, *Authority and Asceticism from Augustine to Gregory the Great*, Oxford Historical Monographs (New York: Oxford University Press, 2001). For early Latin monastic biographies, including Sulpicius Severus's *Life of Martin of Tours*, Gregory the Great's *Life of Benedict*, and the various lives by Jerome, see Carolinne White, trans., *Early Christian Lives*, Penguin Classics (New York: Penguin Books, 1998). For Benedict, see Timothy Fry, ed., *RB 1980: The Rule of St. Benedict: In Latin and English with Notes* (Collegeville, Minn.: Liturgical Press, 1980), Here are a few other recent studies:

Kardong, Terrence G. *Benedict's Rule: A Translation and Commentary*. Collegeville,
    Minn.: Liturgical Press, 1998.
Lawless, George. *Augustine of Hippo and His Monastic Rule*. New York: Oxford Univer-
    sity Press, 1987.
Lawrence, C. H. *Medieval Monasticism: Forms of Religious Life in Western Europe in the
    Middle Ages*. 3rd ed. New York: Longman, 2001.
Rousseau, Philip. *Ascetics, Authority, and the Church in the Age of Jerome and Cassian*.
    New York: Oxford University Press, 1978.
Stewart, Columba. *Prayer and Community: The Benedictine Tradition*. Traditions of
    Christian Spirituality Series. Maryknoll, N.Y.: Orbis Books, 1998.
Vogüé, Adalbert de. *Histoire littéraire du mouvement monastique dans l'antiquité*. Paris:
    Éditions du Cerf, 1991–.
———. *The Rule of Saint Benedict: A Doctrinal and Spiritual Commentary*. Trans. John
    Baptist Hasbrouck. CS 54. Kalamazoo, Mich.: Cistercian Publications, 1983.

Women's Asceticism

A number of remarkable studies have come out in the last fifteen years, revolutionizing
our understanding of women's contributions to ascetical movements in early Christianity. The best place to start is Susanna Elm's *Virgins of God: The Making of Asceticism
in Late Antiquity*, Oxford Classical Monographs (New York: Oxford University Press,
1994). The first half focuses on Cappadocia, especially the contributions of Macrina,
while the latter half focuses on Egypt. All this needs to be understood within the social
world that women moved in. A good place to begin is Gillian Clark, *Women in Late
Antiquity: Pagan and Christian Life-Styles* (New York: Oxford University Press, 1993. See
also:

Bongie, Elizabeth Bryson, trans. *The Life and Regimen of the Blessed and Holy Teacher,
    Syncletica by Pseudo-Athanasius*. Toronto: Peregrina, 1996.
Brakke, David. "Female Virginity and Ecclesiastical Politics in Alexandria." In *Athana-
    sius and the Politics of Asceticism*, 17–79. New York: Oxford University Press, 1995.
    [See also the appendix of this work for a translation of Athanasius's two *Letters to
    Virgins* (274–302).]
Brown, Peter. *The Body and Society: Men, Women, and Sexual Renunciation in Early
    Christianity*, 241–284. New York: Columbia University Press, 1988.
Clark, Elizabeth A. *Ascetic Piety and Women's Faith: Essays on Late Ancient Christianity*.
    Studies in Women and Religion 20. Lewiston, N.Y.: Edwin Mellen Press, 1986.
    [See especially "Ascetic Renunciation and Feminine Advancement: A Paradox of
    Late Ancient Christianity."]
———. "Holy Women, Holy Words: Early Christian Women, Social History, and the
    'Linguistic Turn.' " *Journal of Early Christian Studies* 6(1998): 413–430.
Clark, Gillian. "Women and Asceticism in Late Antiquity." In *Asceticism*, ed. Vincent
    L. Wimbush and Richard Valantasis, 33–48. New York: Oxford University Press,
    1995.
Cloke, Gillian. *This Female Man of God: Women and Spiritual Power in the Patristic
    Age, AD 350–450*. New York: Routledge, 1995.
Coon, Lynda L. *Sacred Fictions: Holy Women and Hagiography in Late Antiquity*. Phila-
    delphia: University of Pennsylvania Press, 1997.
Forman, Mary. "Purity of Heart in the Life and Words of Amma Syncletica." In *Purity
    of Heart in Early Ascetic and Monastic Literature: Essays in Honor of Juana Raasch*,

O.S.B., ed. Harriet A. Luckman and Linda Kulzer, 161–174. Collegeville, Minn.: Liturgical Press, 1999.

Parker, A. S. E. "The *Vita Syncleticae*: Its Manuscripts, Ascetical Teachings and Its Use in Monastic Sources." *Studia Patristica* 30 (1997): 231–234.

Petersen, Joan M. *Handmaids of the Lord: Contemporary Descriptions of Feminine Asceticism in the First Six Christian Centuries.* CS 143. Kalamazoo, Mich.: Cistercian Publications, 1996.

Scholer, David M., ed. *Women in Early Christianity.* Studies in Early Christianity 14 New York: Garland, 1993.

Stewart, Columba. "The Desert Mothers: The Portrayal of Women in the Sayings and Stories of the Desert." *Vox Benedictina* 2 (1985): 5–23.

Ward, Benedicta. "Apophthegmata Matrum." *Studia Patristica* 16 (1985): 63–66. Reprinted in *Signs and Wonders: Saints, Miracles, and Prayer from the Fourth Century to the Fourteenth.* London: Variorum Reprints, 1992.

————. *Harlots of the Desert: A Study of Repentance in Early Monastic Sources.* CS 106. Kalamazoo, Mich.: Cistercian Publications, 1987.

Mani and Manicheism

For a survey, see Samuel N. C. Lieu, *Manichaeism in the Later Roman Empire and Medieval China: A Historical Survey* (Manchester: Manchester University Press, 1985). Two recent anthologies include excerpts from Manichaean texts from Egypt. Richard Valantasis's *Religions of Late Antiquity in Practice* (Princeton: Princeton University Press, 2000) contains excerpts from the *Cologne Mani Codex* (trans. Ellen Bradshaw Aitken) and the *Coptic Manichaean Psalm-Book* (trans. Jason David BeDuhn). Vincent L. Wimbush's *Ascetic Behavior in Graeco-Roman Antiquity: A Sourcebook*, Studies in Antiquity and Christianity (Minneapolis: Fortress Press, 1990), has selections from the *Kephalaia of the Teacher* (trans. Michael H. Browder, 187–212). See also:

BeDuhn, Jason David. *The Manichaean Body: In Discipline and Ritual.* Baltimore: Johns Hopkins University Press, 2000.

Brown, Peter. "The Diffusion of Manichaeism in the Roman Empire." *Journal of Roman Studies* 59 (1969): 92–103. Reprinted in *Religion and Society in the Age of Saint Augustine*, 94–118. New York: Harper & Row, 1972.

Gardiner, Iain. "The Manichaeans Community at Kellis: A Progress Report." In *Emerging from Darkness: Studies in the Recovery of Manichaean Sources*, ed. Paul Mirecki and Jason BeDuhn, 161–176. Nag Hammadi and Manichaean Studies 43. Leiden: Brill, 1997.

Gardiner, Iain, ed. *Kellis Literary Texts.* Dakhleh Oasis Project, Monograph 4. Oxford: Oxbow, 1996.

————. *The Kephalaia of the Teacher: The Edited Coptic Manichaean Texts in Translation with Commentary.* Nag Hammadi and Manichaean Studies 37. Leiden: E. J. Brill, 1995.

Johnson, David. "Coptic Reactions to Gnosticism and Manichaeism." *Le Muséon* 100 (1987): 199–209.

Klimkeit, Hans-Joachim, trans. *Gnosis on the Silk Road: Gnostic Texts from Central Asia.* San Francisco: Harper San Francisco, 1993.

Lieu, Samuel N. C. *Manichaeism in Mesopotamia and the Roman East.* Religions in the Graeco-Roman World 118. Leiden: E. J. Brill, 1994.

————. "Precept and Practice in Manichaean Monasticism." *Journal of Theological Studies* n.s. 32 (1981): 153–173.

Stroumsa, Gedaliahu G. "The Manichaean Challenge to Egyptian Christianity." In *The Roots of the Egyptian Christianity*, ed. Birger A. Pearson and James E. Goehring, 307–319. Studies in Antiquity and Christianity. Philadelphia: Fortress Press, 1986.

Shenoute of Atripe

The study of Shenoute has largely been limited to specialists in Coptic literature, due to the disarray of the manuscripts and the lack of a critical edition of his writings. For a helpful introduction to the issues and the scholarship, see Rebecca Krawiec, *Shenoute and the Women of the White Monastery: Egyptian Monasticism in Late Antiquity* (New York: Oxford University Press, 2002). While focused on women's experience, Krawiec's study provides a detailed and up-to-date overview for English-speaking readers and corrects certain misconceptions about Shenoute's career and personality. For a translation of a fifth-century biography of Shenoute, see David N. Bell, trans., *The Life of Shenoute, by Besa*, CS 73 (Kalamazoo, Mich.: Cistercian Publications, 1983). See also:

Emmel, Stephen L. "Shenoute's Literary Corpus." Ph.D. diss., Yale University, 1993.
Kuhn, Karl H. "A Fifth-Century Abbot." *Journal of Theological Studies* n.s. 5 (1954): 36–38, 174–187; 6 (1955): 34–48.
———. "Shenute, Saint." In *The Coptic Encyclopedia*, ed. Aziz S. Atiya, 7:2131–2133. New York: Macmillan, 1991,
Liepolt, Johannes, *Schenute von Atripe und die Entstehung des national äegyptischen Christentums*. TU 25. Leipzig: J. C. Hinrichs, 1903.
Liepolt, Johannes, and W. E. Crum, eds. *Sinuthii Archimandritae: Vita et Opera Omnia*. CSCO 41, 42, 73. Paris: Imprimérie nationale, 1906–1913.
Orlandi, Tito. "A Catechesis against Apocryphal Texts by Shenute and the Gnostic Texts of Nag Hammadi." *Harvard Theological Review* 75 (1982): 85–95.
———. "Coptic Literature." In *The Roots of Egyptian Christianity*, ed. Birger A. Pearson and James E. Goehring, 51–81. Studies in Antiquity and Christianity. Philadelphia: Fortress Press, 1986.
Timbie, Janet. "The State of Research on the Career of Shenoute of Atripe." In *The Roots of Egyptian Christianity*, ed. Birger A. Pearson and James E. Goehring, 258–270. Studies in Antiquity and Christianity. Philadelphia: Fortress Press, 1986.

APPENDIX 13.1

Papyrus: Earliest Use of the Word "Monk"

The following is the earliest known text to use the word "monk" (μοναχός). This papyrus was first brought to the attention of scholars by Edwin A. Judge, in his famous article, "The Earliest Use of *Monachos* for 'Monk' and the Origins of Monasticism," *Jahrbuch für Antike und Christentum* 20 (1977): 72–89.

> To Dioscorus Caeso, Praepositus of the 5th pagus, from Isidorus son of Ptolemaeus of the village of Karanis in your pagus. The cattle of Pamounis and Harpalus damaged the planting which I have and what is more [their cow] grazed in the same place so thoroughly that my husbandry has become useless. I caught the cow and was leading it up to the village when they met me in the fields with a big club, threw me to the ground, rained blows upon me, and took away the cow—as indeed (the marks of) the blows all over me show— and if I had not chanced to obtain help from the deacon Antonius and the monk Isaac, who happened by, they would quickly have finished me off completely. Therefore I submit this document, asking that they be brought before you to preserve my claim (to be heard) in the prefectural court both in the matter of the planting and in the matter of the assault. The consuls-to-be for the fourth time, Payni 12. (*P. Coll. Youtie* 77)

APPENDIX 13.2

Papyrus: Melitian Monasticism

In 1924, H. Idris Bell published a small archive of papyri that shed new light on the career of Athanasius and on the existence of Melitian monasticism. Given here is the text of one of those papyri, a formal contract outlining a change of leadership while the abbot is away attending the Synod of Caesarea, which took place in 334 (and at which Athanasius was to have been put on trial). Ellipses signify gaps in the papyrus.

> In the consulship of Flavius Optatus, Patrician, and Anicius Pauli-
> nus the most illustrious, Phamenoth 23. Aurelius Pageus son of Ho-
> rus, of the village of Hipponon in the Heracleopolite nome, priest,
> to the Priors of the monastery of the monks called Hathor situated
> in the eastern desert of the Upper Cynopolite nome. Whereas sacred
> Imperial letters have been sent up by the most pious Emperor Con-
> stantine ordering certain persons from Egypt, both Bishops and
> priests and many others and myself among them . . . to proceed to
> Caesarea in Palestinian Syria to come to a decision concerning the
> purgation of the holy Christian body and I am desirous to make a
> journey of this kind to the aforewritten Caesarea to fulfill the orders
> given, it is necessary for me to appoint a deputy in my place until
> my return, [wherefore] I gathered together the monks of our monas-
> tery in the presence of Patabaesis, priest of Hipponon, and Papnu-
> tius the deacon of Paminpesla and Prôous, former monk, and many
> others; and they . . . and approved with unanimity, voluntarily and
> spontaneously and with irrevocable decision, Aurelius Gerontius my
> full brother as a person fitted to occupy my place until my return
> temporarily (?) [and] to supervise and administer and control all the
> affairs of the monastery, both as regards . . . and to choose the stew-
> ards of the monastery in the same way as myself, and that no inno-
> vations shall be made without the consent of (?) the priors of the
> monastery in the matter of the . . . monks and of those who desire
> to depart. . . . The deed of appointment is valid wheresoever it is pro-
> duced, and in reply to the formal question I have given my consent.
> I Aurelius Pageus the aforesaid have signed the deed. We the afore-
> said . . . and . . . and Colluthus and Dioscorides . . . I Colluthus have
> written on behalf of the others, as they are illiterate. We . . . and

Prôous . . . are present (?) [and approve?]. I Papnuthius . . . have given my approval. (*P. Lond.* 1913)

For the Greek text, with a translation and commentary, see H. Idris Bell, ed., *Jews and Christians in Egypt: The Jewish Troubles in Alexandria and the Athanasian Controversy, Illustrated by Texts from Greek Papyri in the British Museum* (London: British Museum, 1924), 45–53.

APPENDIX 13.3

Theodoret of Cyrrhus, *The Religious History*

Theodoret of Cyrrhus was both a leading theologian and a chronicler of Syrian monasticism. In his *Religious History*, he gives eyewitness accounts of seeing one of the remarkable radicals of early Christian monasticism, Symeon the Stylite. Here are a few excerpts:

Symeon Atop the Column

More than all this I myself admire [Symeon's] endurance. Night and day he is standing within the view of all; for having removed the doors and demolished a sizeable part of the enclosing wall, he is exposed to all as a new and extraordinary spectacle—now standing for a long time, and now bending down repeatedly and offering worship to God. Many of those standing by count the number of these acts of worship. Once one of those with me counted one thousand two hundred and forty-four of them, before slackening and giving up count. In bending down he always makes his forehead touch his toes—for his stomach's receiving food once a week, and little of it, enables his back to bend easily. . . . During the public festivals he displays another form of endurance: after the setting of the sun until it comes again to the eastern horizon, stretching out his hands to heaven he stands all night, neither beguiled by sleep nor overcome by exertion. (Theodoret of Cyrrhus, *Historia religiosa* 26.22–24)

Pilgrim Attraction

As his fame circulated everywhere, everyone hastened to him, not only the people of the neighborhood but also people many days' journey distant, some bringing the paralyzed in body, others requesting health for the sick, others asking to become fathers; and they begged to receive from him what they could not receive from nature. On receiving it and obtaining their requests, they returned with joy; and by proclaiming the benefits they had gained, they sent out many times more, asking for the same things. So with everyone arriving from every side and every road resembling a river, one can behold a sea of men standing together in that place, receiving rivers from every side. Not only do the inhabitants of our part of the world flock together, but also Ishmaelites, Persians, Armenians subject to them, Iberians, Homerites, and men even more distant than these; and there came many inhabitants of the extreme west, Spaniards, Britons, and the Gauls who live between them. (Theodoret of Cyrrhus, *Historia religiosa* 26.11)

EVANGELIZING BEDOUINS

Theodoret tells a remarkable anecdote of Symeon's evangelizing desert Bedouins. Note his eyewitness description of the way he was attacked by a mob, the way that some modern celebrities and rock stars are:

> For the Ishmaelites, who were enslaved in their many tens of thousands to the darkness of impiety, have been illuminated by his standing on the pillar. For this dazzling lamp, as if placed on a lampstand, has sent out rays in all directions, like the sun. . . . The Ishmaelites, arriving in companies, two or three hundred at the same time, sometimes even a thousand, disown with shouts their ancestral imposture; and smashing in front of this great luminary the idols they had venerated and renouncing the orgies of Aphrodite— it was this demon whose worship they had adopted originally—they receive the benefit of the divine mysteries, accepting laws from this sacred tongue and bidding farewell to their ancestral customs, as they disown the eating of wild asses and camels. I myself was an eyewitness of this, and I have heard them disowning their ancestral impiety and assenting to the teaching of the Gospel. And I once underwent great danger: he told them to come up and receive from me the priestly blessing, saying they would reap the greatest profit therefrom. But they rushed up in a somewhat barbarous manner, and some pulled at me from in front, some from behind, others from the sides, while those further back trod on the others and stretched out their hands, and some pulled at my beard and others grabbed at my clothing. I would have been suffocated by their too ardent approach, if he had not used a shout to disperse them. (Theodoret of Cyrrhus, *Historia religiosa* 26.13–14)

For the Greek text, see Pierre Canivet and Alice Leroy-Molinghen, *Théodoret de Cyr: Histoire des moines de Syrie*, SC 234 and 257 (Paris: Éditions du Cerf, 1977–1979). The translation here is by R. M. Price, *A History of the Monks of Syria by Theodoret of Cyrrhus*, CS 88 (Kalamazoo, Mich.: Cistercian Publications, 1985).

APPENDIX 13.4

Manichees in Egypt: New Discoveries

Archeologists have been excavating the ancient village of Kellis (modern Ismant el-Kharab) and have uncovered a variety of Manichaean texts, the remains of what seems to have been a thriving Manichaean community. Many papyri are fragmentary and difficult to decipher, but a few are in fairly good condition. One of these, excerpted here, contains Manichean hymns.

> [I will] pray to the Third / Ambassador. He sent / unto me Jesus the Splendour, the / apostle of light, the / redeemer of souls. He [bore?] me / to the Light Mind, / the Virgin of Light. / The spirit of truth, our lord / Manichaios, he gave to me / his knowledge. He made me strong in his / faith. He has fulfilled me in his / commandments. The image of my / counterpart came unto me, with her three / angels. She gave to me the garment and / the crown and the palm and the victory. / He took me to the judge without / any shame; for what he / entrusted to me I have perfected. / I washed in the Pillar. I was perfected / in the Perfect Man. They gave / me my first mind in the living / atmosphere. I rose up to the ship of / living water; unto the father, the First / Man. He gave me his image, / his blessing, and his love. I / rose up to the ship of living fire; / unto the Third Ambassador, / the apostle of light, the good / father. They ferried me / up to the land of light, to / the first righteous one and the / Beloved of the Lights. I came to rest / in the kingdom of the household.

Note the emphasis on salvation as a journey to the Kingdom of Light. Mani promises "knowledge," esoteric knowledge, that enables one to be saved and to escape this lower world of darkness. This hymn is dotted with Manichaean mythological figures:

- The Third Ambassador: A cosmic divinity who has the sun as his throne.
- Jesus the Splendour: A god in Manichaean mythology, described here as an "apostle of light" (i.e., a messenger from the celestial kingdom of light) and as the "redeemer of souls."
- The Light Mind: An emanation of Jesus who becomes incarnated in the Apostles.
- The Virgin of Light: The female counterpart of the Third Ambassador. Manichaean mythology is full of such male-female pairings.

- Manichaios: Mani, the Paraclete foretold by Jesus. Where as Jesus is the "redeemer of souls," Mani possesses the "spirit of truth."
- The First Man: The god who first descended to combat the lower darkness. He sacrificed himself and became entangled in the darkness. Redeemed souls descend from him (who is thus their "father," and they are his "image") and will return to him.

One also sees hints here of the astronomical vision of salvation. Redeemed souls are ferried back to the Kingdom of Light. "The Pillar" is the Milky Way, the visible manifestation of the flow of ascending light-souls returning back to heaven. "The ship of living water" is the moon, while the "ship of living fire" is the sun. Both sun and moon are intermediate stops on the cosmic journey back.

The Coptic text, *T. Kell. Copt.*, Text A5, and its translation are found in *Kellis Literary Texts*, vol. 1, ed. Iain Gardner (Oxford: Oxbow, 1996). For studies of Manichaeism, see the bibliography for chapter 13.

APPENDIX 13.5

Monks Despised: Ancient Views

In the bleakest days of the Middle Ages, Christian monks became the great curators of Western civilization, preserving classics of literature, pagan and Christian alike. We cannot imagine how startling, indeed abhorrent, the monks were to many of their early contemporaries. The following passages are from three pagan orators and politicians who were appalled by Christian monasticism and who saw monks as uncivilized and destructive.

MONKS AS MADMEN

A filthy island filled by men who flee the light. / They call themselves "monks"—a Greek name—/ Because they will to live alone, unseen by any. / The gifts of fortune they fear . . . / Mad folly of a demented brain. (Rutilius Namatianus, *De Reditu Suo*, ll. 440–448)

MONKS AS BLACK-ROBED PIGS

At the time they brought into holy places so-called monks: men by all appearances, though they lived like pigs; and they openly tolerated and indeed executed, evil deeds past number or description. Yet it was seen as a work of piety to despise the divine: for any man at that time dressed in black, and ready to demean himself in public, possessed a tyrannical power. Such was the depth to which human virtue had declined. (Eunapius of Sardis, *Vita Sophistarum* vi; Trans. Philip Rousseau, *Ascetics*, 1)

MONKS AS TEMPLE DESTROYERS

You [Theodosius] did not order the temples to be closed or forbid them to be frequented, nor did you remove from temples and altars the fire, the offering of frankincense, or the honors arising from the other incense offerings, but the men in black—these eat more than elephants and by the amount they drink make a real task for those who with singing pass the liquor along to them—and all this they conceal under a pallor artificially induced!—anyhow, with the law still in force they rush on the temples carrying poles, stones, and iron instruments, and any without these bring hands and feet to bear. Then the roofs are knocked in, walls leveled to the ground, images overturned, and altars uprooted—they are a prey to all—while the priest must suffer in silence or die. . . . The monks make merry out of the misfortunes of others, yet they serve their god by going hungry, as they say! (Libanius, *Pro Templis* 8.9)

APPENDIX 13.6

Monks Despised: Edward Gibbon

The eighteenth-century historian Edward Gibbon (1737–1794) was a brilliant and eloquent writer, a scholar who enjoyed a masterful command of the ancient sources. His masterpiece, the massive *History of the Decline and Fall of the Roman Empire*, did much to shape how whole generations viewed the ancient world. Gibbon despised monasticism and saved some of his most eloquent venom for his account of ancient monks. The following passages are from volume 3, chapter 37.

MAN AS CRIMINAL, GOD AS TYRANT

Prosperity and peace introduced the destruction of the vulgar and the Ascetic Christian. The loose and imperfect practice of the religion satisfied the conscience of the multitude . . . but the Ascetics who obeyed and abused the rigid precepts of the gospel, were inspired by the savage enthusiasm, which represents man as a criminal, and God as a tyrant.

MONKS AS FANATICS WHO DESTROY FREEDOM OF MIND

The freedom of the mind, the source of every generous and rational sentiment, was destroyed by the habits of credulity and submission; and the monk, contracting the vices of a slave, devoutly followed the faith and passions of an ecclesiastical tyrant. The peace of the Eastern Church was invaded by a swarm of fanatics, incapable of fear, or reason, or humanity; and the imperial troops acknowledged, without shame, that they were much less apprehensive of an encounter with the fiercest barbarians.

CRUEL UNFEELING TEMPER

A prince, who should capriciously inflict such tortures, would be deemed a tyrant; but it would surpass the power of a tyrant, to impose a long and miserable existence on the reluctant victims of his cruelty. This voluntary martyrdom must have gradually destroyed the sensibility both of the mind and body; nor can it be presumed that the fanatics, who torment themselves, are susceptible of any lively affection for the rest of mankind. A cruel unfeeling temper has distinguished the monks of every age and country: their stern indifference, which is seldom modified by personal friendship, is inflamed by religious hatred, and their merciless zeal has strenuously administered the holy office of the Inquisition.

MONKS' CREDULITY RUINED CHRISTIANITY

But the golden legend of their lives was embellished by the artful credulity of their interested brethren; and a believing age was easily persuaded, that the slightest caprice of an Egyptian or a Syrian monk had been sufficient to interrupt the eternal laws of the universe. The favorites of Heaven were accustomed to cure inveterate disease with a touch, a word, or a distant message; and to expel the most obstinate daemons from the souls, or bodies, which they possessed. They familiarly accosted, or imperiously commanded, the lions and serpents of the desert; infused vegetation into a sapless trunk; suspended iron on the surface of the water; passed the Nile on the back of a crocodile, and refreshed themselves in a fiery furnace. These extravagant tales, which display the fiction, without the genius, of poetry, have seriously affected the reason, the faith, and the morals, of the Christians. Their credulity debased and vitiated the faculties of the mind: they corrupted the evidence of history; and superstition gradually extinguished the hostile light of philosophy and science. Every mode of worship which had been practised by the saints, every mysterious doctrine which they believed, was fortified by the sanction of divine revelation, and all the manly virtues were oppressed by the sterile and pusillanimous reign of the monks.

Afterword

In 1980, Henri Nouwen taught a class at Yale Divinity School called "Desert Spirituality & Contemporary Ministry." One of his graduate students was a Japanese artist named Yushi Nomura. When Nomura read the *Apophthegmata*, he was deeply touched by the poignancy of the stories and sayings. They reminded him of the terse, enigmatic encounters between monks and masters he knew from the literature of Zen Buddhism. He was also familiar with the way that Zen artists had created delightful cartoonish sketches of leading Zen masters, accompanied by poems in elegant calligraphic script. So Nomura, an accomplished painter, decided to apply the fine art of Japanese caricature to the desert fathers and put together a book entitled *Desert Wisdom* (figure 1).

Nomura's encounter with the literature of early Christian monasticism is not an uncommon one. There is something entrancing about these early tales. Beneath their spare narrative lies a strange density of wisdom and unexpected insight into the subtle art of being human. While these stories come from a foreign and somewhat exotic past, they seem peculiarly equipped to leap across barriers—of time, geography, language, and culture—and touch something universal. Their message is not always comfortable or reassuring. At the outset, I cited a story from the Anonymous Collection of the *Apophthegmata*, a story of the three friends who yearned to live out the rigors of the Gospel. Two of them, a peacemaker and a healer, had gone and visited their friend who had gone to the desert to become a monk. The monk had them stare into a bowl of water. He reminded them—and us—that we need to take a hard look at ourselves, we need to get past the agitation and turmoil if we want to have any hope of seeing our true face. There is something about

One day Abba Arsenius was asking an old Egyptian man for advice about what he was thinking. There was someone who saw this and said to him: Abba Arsenius, why is a person like you, who has such a great knowledge of Greek and Latin, asking a peasant like this about your thoughts? He replied: Indeed, I have learned the knowledge of Latin and Greek, yet I have not learned even the alphabet of this peasant.

Abba Poemen said about Abba Pior that every single day he made a fresh beginning.

FIGURE I. The desert fathers and Zen. Yushi Nomura was deeply struck with the fascinating similarities between Zen masters and the desert fathers and decided to wed desert aphorisms from the *Apophthegmata* with Zen traditions of cariacature. These are two examples from his *Desert Wisdom* (Maryknoll, N.Y.: Orbis Books, 2001), plates 1 and 23. Used with permission.

these monks and their odd stories that makes us peer into the agitated water of our busy lives and catch an occasional glimpse of our true faces in the still water.

Almost every ancient author we examined encouraged his readers to imitate the people they were going to read about. The guiding concern was mimetic and moral. I do not know how many of us would ever seriously consider making a life of desert living. And—more to the point—I doubt that many of us would see these desert Christians as people whose lifestyles we would want to imitate. They seem like extremists or eccentrics. They remind me of people who climb Mount Everest. Climbing Everest is an extraordinarily dangerous enterprise. It requires extraordinary physical fitness and athletic discipline. It requires extraordinary commitment and long years of practice. It also requires the expert guidance of more experienced climbers. Yet even the best sometimes fail, and fail badly. Elite mountain climbers must be alert to the simplest, most basic things: breathing, walking, seeing. It demands extraordinary focus. Climbing Mount Everest is not something most of us would want to do. But we can appreciate—even applaud—the effort. We admire elite climbers because they probe and push the limits of human endurance. These desert Christians, in a similar way, probed and pushed the limits of being human. They took on everything we are most afraid of: darkness, starvation, loneliness, madness, death. They faced the deepest human fears and emerged the confrontation from—at least, most of the time—remarkably sane and sober. And their mountain climbing of the spirit gives us something to shoot for, or at least to ponder.

One extraordinary story appears only in that little-known Ethiopic text I cited in chapter 8, the *Collectio Monastica*. It seems especially apt for those of us today who live in large cities. A disciple of Poemen, Abba Agueras, complains that he can find no peace, that, in the all-too-famous words of Athanasius, the desert had become a city. For Athanasius, the desert-becoming-a-city was a miracle of God's grace. But for some desert dwellers, desert cities seemed a nuisance. The monks did not leave one city to go found a new one. They wanted peace and quiet. But as Poemen recognized, the issue was not the desert, but the desert heart. Here is the way Abba Agueras recounts the encounter:

> I went one day to Abba Poemen and said to him: "I have gone everywhere to [find somewhere to] live, but I have not found any peace. Where do you wish me to live?" The old man had responded to him: "There is no longer hardly any desert in our days. Go, look for a good-sized crowd. Go live among them and conduct yourself like someone who does not exist. Say to yourself: 'I've got no worries.' Then you will taste a royal peace."[1]

We city dwellers of the twenty-first century may yearn for the peace and silence of the desert. But the desert fathers remind us that the desert can have its own bustle. It also has its demons, though often enough we bring our own demons with us from the city. If we are to know "a royal peace," we need to etch out a desert heart.

NOTE

1. Ethiopic *Collectio Monastica* 14.66 (CSCO 238:126; trans. my own).

Index